Lecture Notes in Computer Science

Lecture Notes in Artificial Intelligence   14115

Founding Editor

Jörg Siekmann

Series Editors

Randy Goebel, *University of Alberta, Edmonton, Canada*
Wolfgang Wahlster, *DFKI, Berlin, Germany*
Zhi-Hua Zhou, *Nanjing University, Nanjing, China*

The series Lecture Notes in Artificial Intelligence (LNAI) was established in 1988 as a topical subseries of LNCS devoted to artificial intelligence.

The series publishes state-of-the-art research results at a high level. As with the LNCS mother series, the mission of the series is to serve the international R & D community by providing an invaluable service, mainly focused on the publication of conference and workshop proceedings and postproceedings.

Nuno Moniz · Zita Vale · José Cascalho ·
Catarina Silva · Raquel Sebastião
Editors

Progress in Artificial Intelligence

22nd EPIA Conference on
Artificial Intelligence, EPIA 2023
Faial Island, Azores, September 5–8, 2023
Proceedings, Part I

Springer

Editors
Nuno Moniz (iD)
Lucy Family Institute for Data and Society
Notre Dame, IN, USA

INESC TEC
Porto, Portugal

José Cascalho (iD)
GRIA—LIACC
University of Azores
Ponta Delgada, Portugal

Raquel Sebastião (iD)
IEETA
University of Aveiro
Aveiro, Portugal

Zita Vale (iD)
GECAD
Polytechnic of Porto
Porto, Portugal

Catarina Silva (iD)
CISUC
University of Coimbra
Coimbra, Portugal

ISSN 0302-9743 ISSN 1611-3349 (electronic)
Lecture Notes in Artificial Intelligence
ISBN 978-3-031-49007-1 ISBN 978-3-031-49008-8 (eBook)
https://doi.org/10.1007/978-3-031-49008-8

LNCS Sublibrary: SL7 – Artificial Intelligence

This Springer imprint is published by the registered company Springer Nature Switzerland AG
The registered company address is: Gewerbestrasse 11, 6330 Cham, Switzerland

Paper in this product is recyclable.

Preface

The 22nd EPIA Conference on Artificial Intelligence was held in Faial, Azores, from the 5th to the 8th of September 2023.

EPIA is a well-established conference that aims to promote research in all Artificial Intelligence (AI) areas, covering theoretical and fundamental questions and applications, allowing scientific exchange between researchers, engineers and professionals in related disciplines. As with previous editions, this conference received support from the Portuguese Artificial Intelligence Association (APPIA).

The EPIA program, similarly to previous years, included thematic tracks dedicated to specific areas in AI. This year's conference featured the following 17 tracks:

- AI, Generation and Creativity (AIGC);
- Ambient Intelligence and Affective Environments (AmIA);
- Artificial Intelligence and IoT in Agriculture (AIoTA);
- Artificial Intelligence and Law (AIL);
- Artificial Intelligence for Industry and Societies (AI4IS);
- Artificial Intelligence in Medicine (AIM);
- Artificial Intelligence in Power and Energy Systems (AIPES);
- Artificial Intelligence in Smart Computing (AISC);
- Artificial Intelligence in Transportation Systems (AITS);
- Ethics and Responsibility in AI (ERAI);
- General AI (GAI);
- Intelligent Robotics (IROBOT);
- Knowledge Discovery and Business Intelligence (KDBI);
- MultiAgent Systems: Theory and Applications (MASTA);
- Natural Language Processing, Text Mining and Applications (TeMA);
- Planning, Scheduling and Decision-Making in AI (PSDM);
- Social Simulation and Modelling (SSM).

EPIA received 165 submissions from 29 different countries this year. Out of these submissions, 108 had a student as the first author. Each submission was double–blind reviewed by at least three Program Committee (PC) members of each thematic track. These two volumes contain all the accepted papers from the thematic tracks, totalling 85 papers.

The conference also received four keynote speakers: Pétia Georgieva (University of Aveiro, Portugal) with a talk on "Machine Learning Algorithms for Brain-Machine Interfaces"; Martin Visbeck (University of Kiel, Germany) with a talk on "Digital Twins of the Ocean"; Josep Domingo-Ferrer (Universitat Rovira i Virgli, Spain) with a talk on "On the Use (and Misuse) of Differential Privacy in Machine Learning"; and Nitesh Chawla (University of Notre Dame, USA) with a talk on "Learning on Graphs". The invited talks' abstracts are included in these proceedings front matter.

The Program Chairs thank the Award Committee, composed of Bernardete Ribeiro, Juan Pavon and Nathalie Japkowicz, for selecting the Best Paper and the Best Student

Paper, and Springer for the financial support for the awards. This year, the Best Paper Award was given to Tânia Carvalho, Nuno Moniz and Luís Filipe Antunes for the paper "A Three-Way Knot: Privacy, Fairness, and Predictive Performance Dynamics". The Best Student Paper Award was given to Luís Filipe Cunha for the paper "Event Extraction for Portuguese: A QA-driven Approach using ACE-2005", co-authored with Alípio Jorge and Ricardo Campos.

Reinforcing the focus on young researchers and following last year's edition, the conference included a student symposium, where students in the early stages of their study programmes presented their main research ideas and discussed them with other students and researchers, and a mentoring session with senior researchers from related fields was provided. The organization thanks the AI Journal and APPIA for the scholarships for student support.

This year's edition included a panel on Interdisciplinary Challenges and a Discussion on AI and Society open to the general public.

The EPIA organizers are thankful to the student symposium chairs and mentors, the thematic track organizing chairs, their respective Program Committee members, and the student volunteers Bruno Ribeiro, Daniel Ramos, Daniela Pais, Louis Carrette and Teresa Pereira. All did amazing work, contributing to a very successful conference. Finally, the organization would also like to express their gratitude to all the EPIA International Steering Committee members for their guidance regarding the scientific organization of EPIA 2023.

September 2023

Nuno Moniz
Zita Vale
José Cascalho
Catarina Silva
Raquel Sebastião

Organization

General/Program Chairs

Nuno Moniz   Lucy Family Institute for Data and Society, USA/INESC TEC, Portugal
Zita Vale   Polytechnic of Porto/GECAD, Portugal
José Cascalho   University of Azores/GRIA—LIACC, Portugal
Catarina Silva   University of Coimbra/CISUC, Portugal
Raquel Sebastião   University of Aveiro/IEETA, Portugal

Organization Chairs

Gui Menezes   University of Azores/OKEANOS, Portugal
Rita P. Ribeiro   University of Porto/INESC TEC, Portugal
Armando B. Mendes   University of Azores/GRIA—LIACC, Portugal
João Vinagre   Joint Research Centre—European Commission, Spain

Steering Committee

Ana Bazzan   Universidade Federal do Rio Grande do Sul, Brazil
Bernardete Ribeiro   Universidade de Coimbra, Portugal
Ernesto Costa   Universidade de Coimbra, Portugal
Eugénio Oliveira   Universidade do Porto, Portugal
Helder Coelho   Universidade de Lisboa, Portugal
José Júlio Alferes   Universidade Nova de Lisboa, Portugal
Juan Pavón   Universidad Complutense Madrid, Spain
Luís Paulo Reis   Universidade do Porto, Portugal
Paulo Novais   Universidade do Minho, Portugal
Pavel Brazdil   Universidade do Porto, Portugal
Virginia Dignum   Umeå University, Sweden

Track Chairs

Ambient Intelligence and Affective Environments

Paulo Novais	University of Minho, Portugal
Goreti Marreiros	Polytechnic of Porto, Portugal
João Carneiro	Devoteam Portugal, Portugal
Peter Mikulecky	University of Hradec Kralove, Czechia
Sara Rodriguez	University of Salamanca, Spain

Ethics and Responsibility in Artificial Intelligence

Catarina Silva	University of Coimbra, Portugal
Nuno Moniz	Lucy Family Institute for Data and Society, University of Notre Dame, USA
Branka Hadji Misheva	Bern University of Applied Sciences, Switzerland

General Artificial Intelligence

Nuno Moniz	Lucy Family Institute for Data and Society, University of Notre Dame, USA
Zita Vale	GECAD/ISEP—IPP, Portugal
José Cascalho	GRIA—LIACC/Universidade dos Açores, Portugal
Catarina Silva	CISUC, Universidade de Coimbra, Portugal
Raquel Sebastião	IEETA/Universidade de Aveiro, Portugal

Intelligent Robotics

Luís Paulo Reis	Universidade do Porto/LIACC, Portugal
Nuno Lau	Universidade de Aveiro/IEETA, Portugal
João Alberto Fabro	Universidade Tecnológica Federal do Paraná, Brazil

Knowledge Discovery and Business Intelligence

Paulo Cortez	University of Minho, Portugal
Alfred Bifet	Télécom ParisTech/Université Paris-Saclay, France
Luís Cavique	Universidade Aberta, Portugal
João Gama	University of Porto/INESC TEC, Portugal
Nuno Marques	FCT Universidade Nova de Lisboa, Portugal
Manuel Filipe Santos	University of Minho, Portugal

MultiAgent Systems: Theory and Applications

João Balsa	Universidade de Lisboa, Portugal
João Fabro	Universidade Tecnológica Federal do Paraná, Brazil
Henrique Lopes Cardoso	Universidade do Porto, Portugal
José Cascalho	Universidade dos Açores, Portugal

Natural Language Processing, Text Mining and Applications

Joaquim Silva	Universidade Nova de Lisboa, Portugal
Pablo Gamallo	Universidade de Santiago de Compostela, Spain
Paulo Quaresma	Universidade de Évora, Portugal
Irene Rodrigues	Universidade de Évora, Portugal
Hugo Oliveira	Universidade de Coimbra, Portugal

Planning, Scheduling and Decision-Making in Artificial Intelligence

Adriano Lino	Universidade Federal do Oeste do Pará, Brazil
Luís Paulo Reis	Universidade do Porto, Portugal
Jorge Barbosa	Universidade do Porto, Portugal
Alexandra Oliveira	Retail Consult, Portugal
Vítor Rodrigues	Retail Consult, Portugal

Social Simulation and Modelling

Pedro Campos	Universidade do Porto/INESC TEC, Portugal
Luis Antunes	Universidade de Lisboa/LabMAg, Portugal
Fernando Oliveira	University of Bradford, UK

Artificial Intelligence, Generation and Creativity

Pedro Martins	University of Coimbra, Portugal
João Miguel Cunha	University of Coimbra, Portugal
Helena Sofia Pinto	University of Lisbon, Portugal
María Navarro	Univesidad de Salamanca, Spain
Juan Romero	University of A Coruña, Spain
Maria Hedblom	Jönköping University, Sweden

Artificial Intelligence and Law

Pedro Miguel Freitas	Universidade Católica Portuguesa, Portugal
Ugo Pagallo	University of Torino, Italy
Massimo Durante	University of Torino, Italy
Paulo Novais	Universidade do Minho

Artificial Intelligence in Power and Energy Systems

Zita Vale	Polytechnic of Porto, Portugal
Tiago Pinto	UTAD/INESC TEC, Portugal
Pedro Faria	Polytechnic of Porto, Portugal
Elena Mocanu	University of Twente, The Netherlands
Decebal Constantin Mocanu	Technical University of Eindhoven, The Netherlands

Artificial Intelligence in Medicine

Manuel Filipe Santos	University of Minho, Portugal
Carlos Filipe Portela	University of Minho, Portugal
Allan Tucker	Brunel University London, UK
Manuel Fernandez Delgado	Universidade de Santiago de Compostela, Spain

Artificial Intelligence and IoT in Agriculture

Filipe Neves dos Santos	INESC TEC, Portugal
José Boaventura Cunha	University of Trás-os-Montes and Alto Douro, Portugal
Josenalde Barbosa	Federal University of Rio Grande do Norte, Brazil
Paulo Moura Oliveira	University of Trás-os-Montes and Alto Douro, Portugal
Raul Morais	University of Trás-os-Montes and Alto Douro, Portugal

Artificial Intelligence in Transportation Systems

Tânia Fontes	INESC TEC, Portugal
Alberto Fernandez	Universidad Rey Juan Carlos, Spain
Rosaldo Rossetti	University of Porto, Portugal

Artificial Intelligence in Smart Computing

Sherin M. Moussa	Université Française d'Égypte, Egypt
Dagmawi Lemma	Addis Ababa University (Ethiopia)/African Center of Excellence in IoT (Rwanda)

Artificial Intelligence for Industry and Societies

Filipe Portela	University of Minho, Portugal
Sherin M. Moussa	Université Française d'Égypte, Egypt
Teresa Guarda	Universidad Estatal de la Península de Santa Elena, Equador
Ioan M. Ciumasu	University of Paris-Saclay/University of Versailles, France

Program Committee

Ambient Intelligence and Affective Environments

Hector Alaiz Moreton
Patrícia Alves
Zoltan Balogh
Francisco Bellas
Orlando Belo
F. Amílcar Cardoso
João Carneiro
Luís Conceição
Fernando De La Prieta
Dalila Alves Durães
Florentino Fdez-Riverola
Antonio Fernández-Caballero
Lino Figueiredo
Marco Gomes
Miguel J. Hornos
Eva Hudlicka
Javier Jaen
Vicente Julian
Shinichi Konomi
Luis Macedo
José Machado
Peter Mikulecky
Karel Mls
Jose M. Molina
Paulo Moura Oliveira
Tatsuo Nakajima
Tereza Otcenaskova
Martín Pérez-Pérez
Abraham Prieto García
Joao Ramos
Sara Rodríguez
Ricardo Santos
Ichiro Satoh

Ethics and Responsibility in Artificial Intelligence

Tiago Araújo
Marcelo Augusto Vieira Graglia
Joana Costa
Oleg Deev
Karla Figueiredo
Petia Georgieva
Joe Germino
Paolo Giudici
Nuno Lourenço
Marcos Machado
Ana Madureira
Ana Nogueira
Paolo Pagnottoni
Emanuela Raffinetti
Rita P. Ribeiro
Jennifer Schnur
Luís Teixeira

General Artificial Intelligence

Jose Julio Alferes
Amparo Alonso-Betanzos
Pedro Barahona
Luís Camarinha-Matos
F. Amílcar Cardoso
Davide Carneiro
Jose Cascalho
Paulo Cortez
Arlindo Oliveira
Andrea Omicini
Juan Pavón
Tiago Pinto
Paulo Quaresma
Luís Paulo Reis
Ana Paula Rocha
Alvaro Costa Neto
Petia Georgieva
Joe Germino
Vicente Julian
Grigorii Khvatskii
Joao Leite

José Machado
Jose M. Molina
Gabriel Santos
Jennifer Schnur
Luís Seabra Lopes
Raquel Sebastião
Catarina Silva
Zita Vale

Intelligent Robotics

João Fabro
Eurico Pedrosa
Brígida Mónica Faria
Armando Sousa

Knowledge Discovery and Business Intelligence

Fernando Bacao
Orlando Belo
Agnès Braud
Luís Camacho
Rui Camacho
Margarida Cardoso
Nielsen Castelo
Pedro Castillo
Luís Cavique
Paulo Cortez
Jose Alfredo Ferreira Costa
Andre de Carvalho
Marcos Aurélio Domingues
Elaine Faria
Manuel Fernandez Delgado
Carlos Ferreira
Roberto Henriques
Alipio M. Jorge
Philippe Lenca
Nuno Marques
Armando Mendes
Sorin Moga
Sérgio Moro
João Moura-Pires
Amilcar Oliveira

Rita P. Ribeiro
Fátima Rodrigues
Murat Caner Testik

MultiAgent Systems: Theory and Applications

Cristina Baroglio
Juan Carlos Burguillo
Rafael C. Cardoso
Cristiano Castelfranchi
Daniel Castro Silva
Alberto Fernandez
Adriana Giret
Marin Lujak
Luis Macedo
Luís Nunes
Gauthier Picard
Alessandro Ricci
David Sarne
Onn Shehory
Takao Terano
Viviane Torres da Silva
Paulo Urbano
Giovanni Varricchione
Rosa Vicari

Natural Language Processing, Text Mining and Applications

Manex Agirrezabal
Miguel A. Alonso
Sophia Ananiadou
Fernando Batista
Pavel Brazdil
Luisa Coheur
Béatrice Daille
Victor Darriba
Gaël Dias
Antoine Doucet
Pablo Gamallo
Marcos Garcia
Hugo Gonçalo Oliveira
Marcio Inácio
Adam Jatowt

Nuno Marques
Bruno Martins
Shamsuddeen Muhammad
Sérgio Nunes
Paulo Quaresma
Alexandre Rademaker
Francisco J. Ribadas-Pena
Irene Rodrigues
João Rodrigues
Roney L. S. Santos
Altigran Silva
Joaquim Silva
João Silva
Mário Silva
Alberto Simões
Luís Trigo
Jesús Vilares

Planning, Scheduling and Decision-Making in Artificial Intelligence

Filipe Alvelos
Jorge Barbosa
Breno Willian Carvalho
Guilherme Conde
Brígida Mónica Faria
Paulo Leitao
Adriano Lino
Luis Macedo
José Machado
Paulo Novais
Antonio Pereira
Viviane Torres da Silva

Social Simulation and Modelling

Luis Antunes
Pedro Campos

Artificial Intelligence, Generation and Creativity

F. Amílcar Cardoso
Tania Carvalho
Nuno Correia
Joe Germino
João Gonçalves
Maria Hedblom
Carlos León
Carlos António Roque Martinho
Pedro Martins
Tiago Martins
Piotr Mirowski
Caterina Moruzzi
María Navarro
Senja Pollak
Prashanth Thattai Ravikumar
Sérgio Rebelo
Ana Rodrigues
Anna Sokol
Brad Spendlove
Thomas Winters

Artificial Intelligence and Law

Francisco Andrade
Teresa Coelho Moreira
Massimo Durante
Pedro Miguel Freitas
Carlisle George
Luis Gomes
Vicente Julian
Jose Machado
Eduardo Magrani
Clara Martins Pereira
Manuel Masseno
Paulo Novais
Arlindo Oliveira
Ugo Pagallo
Tito Rendas
Ana Rodríguez Álvarez
Cristina Salgado
Giovanni Sartor

Artificial Intelligence in Power and Energy Systems

Hugo Algarvio
Alfonso Briones
João Catalão
Ana Estanqueiro
Nuno Fidalgo
Luis Gomes
Nouredine Hadjsaid
Nikos Hatziargyriou
Bo Jorgensen
Germano Lambert-Torres
Fernando Lopes
Zheng Ma
Gonçalo Marques
Goreti Marreiros
Hugo Morais
Dagmar Niebur
João Peças Lopes
Gabriel Santos
Tiago Soares
Brígida Teixeira

Artificial Intelligence in Medicine

António Abelha
João Almeida
Susana Brás
Rui Camacho
Beatriz De La Iglesia
Manuel Fernandez Delgado
Júlio Duarte
Göran Falkman
Brígida Mónica Faria
Pedro Gago
Luis Gomes
Barna Iantovics
Giorgio Leonardi
José Machado
Goreti Marreiros
Ricardo Martinho
Hugo Peixoto
Cinzia Pizzi

Inna Skarga-Bandurova
Shabbir Syed-Abdul
Allan Tucker
Henrique Vicente

Artificial Intelligence and IoT in Agriculture

Jos Balendonck
Jayme Barbedo
Josenalde Barbosa
João-Paulo Coelho
Pedro Couto
Vítor Filipe
Grigorii Khvatskii
Andres Muñoz
Emanuel Peres
Veronica Saiz-Rubio
Javier Sanchis Saez
José Boaventura Cunha
Tania Carvalho
Aneesh Chauhan
Laura Santana
José Antonio Sanz Delgado
Carlos Serodio
Eduardo Solteiro-Pires
Joaquim João Sousa
Antonio Valente
Joao Valente
Fedro Zazueta

Artificial Intelligence in Transportation Systems

António Pedro Aguiar
Mobyen Uddin Ahmed
Elisabete Arsenio
Carlos Bento
Holger Billhardt
Abderrahmane Boubezoul
Eduardo Camponogara
Hilmi Berk Celikoglu
Gonçalo Correia
António Costa
Daniel G. Costa

Gianluca Di Flumeri
Juergen Dunkel
Qiaochu Fan
Sara Ferreira
Rui Gomes
Carlos A. Iglesias
João Jacob
Zafeiris Kokkinogenis
Pedro M. D'Orey
Eftihia Nathanail
Luís Nunes
Sascha Ossowski
Sara Paiva
Joel Ribeiro
Javier J. Sanchez Medina
Thiago Sobral
Marco Veloso
Giuseppe Vizzari
Fenghua Zhu

Artificial Intelligence in Smart Computing

Nouran Abdalazim
Abdelaziz Abdelhamid
Waleed Adel
Yasmine Afify
Marco Alfonse
Ayalew Belay
Faten Chaieb
Roaa Elghondakly
Anna Fabijanska
Dina Fawzy
Fekade Getahun
Safwat Hamad
Christine Lahoud
Dagmawi Lemma
Mahmoud Mounir

Artificial Intelligence for Industry and Societies

Mohamed Abdelaziz
Waleed Adel
Yasmeen Adel
Yasmine Afify
Ioan Ciumasu
Roaa Elghondakly
Dina Fawzy
Panos Fitsilis
Felix J. Garcia Clemente
Mariam Gawich
Alfonso González Briones
Sergio Ilarri
Hanmin Jung
Anna Kobusinska
Juan-Ignacio Latorre-Biel
Vicente Ferreira De Lucena Jr
José Machado
Fabrizio Messina
Antonio Moreira
Marco Alfonse
Ana Azevedo
Jorge Bernardino
Chiara Braghin
Mahmoud Mounir
Hatem Mrad
Sara Paiva
Spyros Panagiotakis
Michela Piccarozzi
Carlos Filipe Portela
Nelson Rodrigues
Henrique Santos
Inna Skarga-Bandurova
George Stalidis
Cihan Tunc
Daniel Urda
Johannes Winter
Muhammad Younas

Additional Reviewers

João Almeida
Tiago Araújo
Luís Camacho
Breno Willian Carvalho
Tânia Carvalho
Nielsen Castelo
Álvaro Costa Neto
Victor Darriba
Qiaochu Fan
Joe Germino
Safwat Hamad
Marcio Inácio
João Jacob
Grigorii Khvatskii
Sorin Moga
Shamsuddeen Muhammad
Dagmar Niebur
Tiago Pinto
Francisco J. Ribadas-Pena
João Rodrigues
Nelson Rodrigues
Gabriel Santos
Jennifer Schnur
João Silva
Anna Sokol
Brígida Teixeira
Luís Trigo
Giovanni Varricchione

Sponsors

Organization

Keynotes

Machine Learning Algorithms for Brain-Machine Interfaces

Pétia Georgieva

University of Aveiro, Portugal

Abstract Brain–machine interfaces (BMIs) create alternative communication channels between the human brain and the external world. Neural activity is recorded, for example through an Electroencephalogram (EEG), and the BCI systems aim to transform these electrophysiological signals into control commands or use them to restore lost function, most commonly motor function in paralyzed patients. This talk will give an overview of the past, the present and the future of BMIs, focusing on machine learning algorithms such as Convolutional Neural Networks and Neural Autoencoders as promising approaches to build noninvasive BMIs.

Digital Twins of the Ocean

Martin Visbeck

University of Kiel, Germany

Abstract Thanks to recent advances in digitalization and improvements in ocean system model performance, the marine community is envisioning the development of Digital Twins of the Ocean (DTO) as a method to monitor and protect the world's oceans. Digital Twins (DT) are digital replicas of real-world objects. They depend critically on effective data model fusion and the compression, exploitation and presentation of data. AI and ML techniques are central to making those processes effective and as such essential to advancing DT frameworks and technology. The value of DTs comes from the ability to make informed decisions that are guided by interactions with data. And due to their easy accessibility, DTs can be used by a variety of stakeholders: by scientists to understand the ocean, by policymakers to make well-informed decisions, and by citizens to improve ocean literacy. As such, DTs present a valuable opportunity to future-proof sustainable development. Creating a DTO requires a multidisciplinary approach: data scientists to identify the gaps in ocean data and decide upon interoperable data standards, ocean modelers to improve model accuracy and resolution, IT experts to advance HPC, ML and AI infrastructures and scientific visualization experts to deliver the data in a comprehensive, user-friendly manner.

On the Use (and Misuse) of Differential Privacy in Machine Learning

Josep Domingo-Ferrer

Universitat Rovira i Virgili, Spain

Abstract Machine learning (ML) is vulnerable to security and privacy attacks. Whereas security attacks aim at preventing model convergence or forcing convergence to wrong models, privacy attacks attempt to disclose the data used to train the model. This talk will focus on privacy attacks. After reviewing them, I will examine the use of differential privacy (DP) as a methodology to protect against them, both in centralized and decentralized ML (federated learning). I will show that DP-based ML implementations do not deliver the "ex ante" privacy guarantees of DP. What they deliver is basically noise addition similar to the traditional statistical disclosure control approach. The actual level of privacy offered must be assessed "ex post", which is seldom done. I will present empirical results that show that standard anti-overfitting techniques in ML can achieve a better utility/privacy/efficiency trade-off than DP.

Learning on Graphs

Nitesh Chawla

University of Notre Dame, USA

Abstract Graphs are ubiquitous across a variety of use-cases, and have emerged as a powerful means of representing complex systems. Graph Neural Networks have demonstrated exceptional effectiveness in handling graph data; however, there are numerous challenges, from multiple data modalities to lack of labeled data. In this talk, I'll introduce our work on learning from multiple data, and also the ideas of learning from limited data, including few-shot and self-supervised learning. I'll also discuss applications of these methods.

Contents – Part I

General Artificial Intelligence

Intelligent Robotics

Knowledge Discovery and Business Intelligence

MultiAgent Systems: Theory and Applications

Natural Language Processing, Text Mining and Applications

Planning, Scheduling and Decision-Making in AI

Social Simulation and Modelling

Contents – Part II

Artificial Intelligence in Power and Energy Systems

Artificial Intelligence in Medicine

Artificial Intelligence and IoT in Agriculture

Artificial Intelligence in Transportation Systems

Artificial Intelligence in Smart Computing

Artificial Intelligence for Industry and Societies

Ambient Intelligence and Affective Environments

Simulation-Based Adaptive Interface for Personalized Learning of AI Fundamentals in Secondary School

Sara Guerreiro-Santalla[1], Dalila Duraes[2], Helen Crompton[3], Paulo Novais[2], and Francisco Bellas[1]([✉])

[1] CITIC Research Center, Universidade da Coruña, A Coruña, Spain
{sara.guerreiro, francisco.bellas}@udc.es
[2] LASI/Algoritmi Centre, University of Minho, Braga, Portugal
{dad,pjon}@di.uminho.pt
[3] Old Dominion University, Norfolk, VA, USA
crompton@odu.edu

Abstract. This paper presents the first results on the validation of a new Adaptive E-learning System, focused on providing personalized learning to secondary school students in the field of education about AI by means of an adaptive interface based on a 3D robotic simulator. The prototype tool presented here has been tested at schools in USA, Spain, and Portugal, obtaining very valuable insights regarding the high engagement level of students in programming tasks when dealing with the simulated interface. In addition, it has been shown the system reliability in terms of adjusting the students' learning paths according to their skills and competences in an autonomous fashion.

Keywords: Adaptive e-learning · Intelligent tutoring system · Personalized learning · Adaptive interfaces · AI education · Robot simulation

1 Introduction

Personalized learning is a key goal in education [1], trying to adapt the contents and methodologies to each particular student in order to maximize his/her understanding and development in a given subject. Traditionally, personalized learning has been responsibility of the teachers, relying on their own experience and empathy. But nowadays, digital technologies allow to achieve certain levels of personalized learning through specific software tools, which analyse the student's profile to provide an adapted experience in an autonomous way [2].

Within this challenging scope, Adaptive E-learning Systems (AES) refers to the "set of techniques and approaches that are combined together to offer online training to the learners with the aim of providing customized resources and interfaces" [3]. There are different aspects of AES that can be personalized, like the contents, the learning path, the learning style, or the graphical user interface. In any case, it is necessary to define the

N. Moniz et al. (Eds.): EPIA 2023, LNAI 14115, pp. 3–15, 2023.
https://doi.org/10.1007/978-3-031-49008-8_1

relevant data to be captured from the learner (understanding and engagement), classify it into categories, and then provide an adapted response [4]. One of the most relevant and promising approaches in this realm are Intelligent Tutoring Systems (ITS), which apply artificial intelligence techniques like machine learning, rule-based logic, or fuzzy logic to model such data and achieve the desired adaptation in an autonomous fashion [5, 6]. This is the scope of the current work.

The relevance of developing new ITS is supported by 2015–2030 Sustainable Development Goals (SDGs), namely, 4C's, to increase the supply of qualified tutors. Access and interactions with a tutor have a direct connection to student engagement, grades, and school attendance [7]. Nonetheless, it appears that the tutor shortage is on a negative trend as it is anticipated that there are going to be fewer teachers in the future [8]. ITS could be a tool to ameliorate this lack of tutors. It can also offer teachers an opportunity to further personalize education for their students beyond what they can accomplish individually as a single teacher with multiple students.

The challenge of developing education that adapts to the learners' needs has been the specialized domain of ITS that has a long history from Computer-Assisted Instruction [9]. The past development of ITS is costly and with specialized authoring tools and learning platforms [10]. Current research and open architecture allow for more rapid development with flexible student modelling [11]. The most successful cases have been applied to "traditional" subjects, like mathematics, science, or history, where literacy, evaluation metrics, and methodologies are well established [12]. The last years have seen several breakthroughs in ITS produced for students and tutors to use as expressive and exploratory tools that assist in exploring scientific ideas and developing scientific ways of thinking [13, 14]. Companies like Carnegie Learning and Math-Whizz provide various degrees of provision for intelligent support, interactivity, and personalization, being these the trending topics in this scope.

This paper presents the first results on the validation of a new ITS, focused on providing personalized learning to secondary school students in the field of education about AI by means of an adaptive interface based on a 3D simulator. Thus, the rest of the document is structured in the subsequent manner. The succeeding section provides a rationale for the significance of our objective and expounds on our distinct contribution to the domain of Adaptive E-learning Systems. Section 3 showcases the Robobo initiative, its framework, and the way it functions. Section 4 introduces two activities that were implemented as lessons. Section 5 displays the validation conducted in a secondary school setting. Lastly, Sect. 6 concludes the paper.

2 Education About AI

The impact of AI in education can be observed from two different angles. On one side, we have AI-based tools to support students, teachers, and institutions in different aspects, like automatic assessment, creation of materials and plans, and, of course, providing personalized learning as commented above [15]. In this approach, education is just an application field for AI technologies. On the other side, we have training about AI topics. Not only there is a chronic shortage of trained AI professionals, but an entire generation of young people are also growing up in a world increasingly impacted by

AI. Consequently, developing an AI literacy for pre-university students is a key goal for most of the education administrations around the world [16, 17].

Since 2019, the authors of the current paper have been developing the AI + Erasmus + project, aimed at creating an AI curriculum tailored for high school students in Europe [18]. Within it, a set of formal teaching units were developed and tested with teachers and students of six different schools belonging to five countries. These teaching units followed a hands-on approach to AI, where students had to face small projects by programming real-world devices to learn about fundamental topics like perception, representation, reasoning, or machine learning. From this experience, we realized that, to implement an AI curriculum at pre-university level in the short-term, two main issues must be faced: (1) The students' proficiency in programming: the practical approach to AI followed in the project, which is also recommended by other initiatives [19], requires a minimum and homogeneous programming level in the group. Otherwise, the learning results are not successful. (2) The teachers' confidence in teaching AI: since it is an emerging discipline at the pre-university level, it will take many years to have a fully trained group of teachers capable of teaching AI confidently.

With the aim of providing a path towards solving them, this work proposes the development of an ITS which, by means of providing personalized learning to students, allows to leverage their programming skills while supports teachers in those AI topics where they have less experience. This ITS does not pretend to substitute the teachers' role but to help in the transition towards a more stable situation in terms of education about AI at pre-university levels.

The proposed ITS has been named *RoboboITS*. To cope with the hands-on approach to AI learning, *RoboboITS* is based on solving robotic challenges with the Robobo educational robot [20] by means of a 3D simulator called RoboboSim [21], which makes up the interface with the student. From a methodological perspective, using robots in classes promotes learning by doing, interdisciplinary training, cooperative learning, and project-based learning [22]. From a literacy point of view, they allow learning about the main AI topics for this age range [18].

As commented in the previous section, the number of existing ITS is increasing and improving but, up to the authors' knowledge, there is no other tutoring system specifically focused on education about AI, neither based on 3D robotic simulator as interface. We can find several approaches using robots as tutors in education, in a sub-field that is called Intelligent Tutoring Robots (ITR) [23]. But the main feature of ITRs, is that they use a real robot as interface with the students, which implies a set of considerations that are out of the scope of this research. Regarding applying robotic simulation environments for educational purposes, some remarkable initiatives can be highlighted. In this sense, the Constructsim [24] provides course material and exercises with online simulations. It is aimed at experienced robotics developers and bachelor or master students. The focus is more on technical aspects of robotics programming using the ROS/ROS2 system. Blockly Games [25] provides a very simple graphical programming environment aimed at teaching programming to young students, with the possibility of using robots. Coderz [26] and OpenRoberta [27] provide a very simple graphical programming environment to program the behaviour of real and simulated robots in 2D or 3D. Robotbenchmark [28] provides a series of interactive realistic 3D robot simulation challenges which students have to address by programming the behaviour of robots in the Python language. Although these initiatives combine programming and robotic simulations, none of them include an ITS to support autonomous learning.

Summarizing, the RoboboITS is a novel contribution to the Adaptive E-learning Systems, first because it faces the two main issues of short-term education about AI, and second because it provides personalization by means of an adaptive interface based on 3D robotic simulations. The following sections are devoted on presenting the details of its prototype version, and the validation results obtained with students in three schools at USA, Spain, and Portugal. The goal in this paper is to analyze them from a functional perspective based on subjective and objective measures.

3 The RoboboITS

Robobo [20] is an educational robot composed of a mobile base coupled to a smartphone, wirelessly connected to each other (see Fig. 1 left). Robobo has been chosen for this development due to the high technological level it provides, appropriate for AI teaching. The use of the smartphone allows to have a camera, microphone, speaker, touch screen, WIFI and a powerful CPU. Furthermore, it can be programmed through Scratch and Python, which allows facing different educational levels with the platform. The RoboboITS presented here is based on the RoboboSim 3D simulator [21], which was developed using the Unity3D technology, leading to a computationally light application, suitable for pre-university schools, and with a usability and aesthetics like video games, appropriate for most of students at this age (see Fig. 1 right).

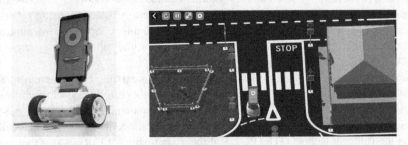

Fig. 1. Left: Robobo real robot. Right: RoboboSim interface.

3.1 RoboboITS Architecture

The RoboboITS internal architecture is represented in Fig. 2, and it is based on four main modules [5]: domain, tutor, student, and interface. The *Domain* Module is endowed with the specific knowledge about AI, obtained from the teaching units developed within the AI + project commented above. Specifically, it contains the goals of the activities proposed to students, the learning objectives, and the code with the solutions. The *Tutor* Module encompasses the teacher's experience in aspects like student's feedback, guidance to problem solving, assessment, and activity adaptation. Here, it contains the division of activities into sub-activities, as explained later, so personalized guidance can be provided at the level of problem solving. This module also performs automatic activity assessment by comparing student's solution with the correct one obtained from the *Domain* Module.

For the *Student* Module, it contains the initial and acquired knowledge, different interactions with the GUI, the code of the programs, the number of trials, the time required to solve the activity, and the *level* of each student, which makes up an *estimation of his/her required guidance in the project completion*. Finally, the *Interface* Module connects students with the tutoring system in a bidirectional way. Its main element is the RoboboSim 3D simulation interface, created with Unity3D, which is basic not only for program testing but also for student engagement. In this sense, the RoboboITS aims to take advantage of the computer game-like interface of the simulator, together with the Robobo aspect, to increase student's motivation. As it will be explained later, the simulator allows to include visual clues and other gamification strategies to improve the personalization of learning.

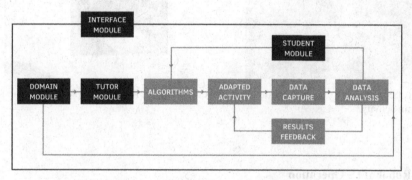

Fig. 2. Schematic representation of the RoboboITS architecture.

It should be pointed out that the students program their solutions using Python or Scratch, the languages supported by RoboboSim [21]. But these programming interfaces are independent of the RoboboITS interface. This is a very relevant feature, because this ITS does not provide feedback about the student's code, just about the result obtained after running it on the simulation. Code feedback could be interesting too, but the goal of the RoboboITS is not on teaching programming, but AI through robotics, so what is relevant here is the final result of the code application and not the code itself.

The diagram of Fig. 2 is a sort of flowchart of the architecture. Starting with the grey blocks, the *Algorithms* one is devoted with the adaptation of the activity and the explanation to the student's profile. The current version of RoboboITS uses a rule-based approach for this adaptation. Once an activity is selected, the *Adapted Activity* block is executed, which represents a period in which the activity is carried out by the student. In this stage, the *Data* block runs, capturing relevant information to assess the student's performance and activity completion. The student solution is evaluated by running it on the simulator. From such execution, the following data is captured: (*d1*) time required to solve the activity, (*d2*) number of attempts, (*d3*) student's level at the beginning and end of the activity, (*d4*) time required to read the statements, (*d5*) number of times the student opens the documentation, and (*d6*) number of times the student reads the statements.

Next, the *Data Analysis* block is executed and personalized *Feedback* is provided to the student through the simulator interface, of two main types:

1. *Sub-activity*: if the number of attempts (*d2*) is higher than a predefined threshold, the student's level is decreased. This implies that the global activity is divided into smaller ones, so student can face a simpler problem.
2. *Visual clues*: the time required to solve the activity (*d1*) and the number of attempts (*d2*) trigger the arousal of visual clues through the simulator interface, with the aim of providing support to the student before downgrading the level.

Fig. 3. Left: Example of question from the initial questionnaire. Right: Example of statement for the main activity.

3.2 RoboboITS Operation

RoboboITS aims to train pre-university students on AI fundamentals, so no previous knowledge on these topics is required. But as it is based on the curriculum developed for the AI + project, this first version is suitable for students between 15 and 18 years old, because it is assumed a minimum background in mathematics and technology. In terms of programming, previous experience is required, but RoboboITS has been designed to leverage different profiles, so it adapts to students with low skills who require more guidance, as well as those with a higher level who are more autonomous. The RoboboITS operation can be summarized in the following consecutive steps:

1. *The system assesses the student's initial level:* the first time the ITS is used, the student must complete a questionnaire that allows knowing his/her skills in programming and the previous knowledge about AI. The former is very important, because it establishes the competence level in which the ITS starts. To this end, it includes questions about programming experience, in which language, for how long, and specific ones to evaluate their knowledge, such as the one shown in Fig. 3 left. Regarding AI knowledge, this data is captured to evaluate the progress of the student at the end of the session in the core topics to be trained.

2. *The statement of the challenge is displayed:* it is adapted to the level (Fig. 3 right) and it must be carefully read by students. The learning goal of the ITS is that all leaners reach the same final level by solving the AI challenge. So, depending on the initial level, it proposes the activities with different guidance levels (sub-activities described in the previous section). In the highest level, the system will propose the student just to complete the global activity, being the division into small sub-activities part of his/her work.

3. *The student implements the program to solve the challenge*: to this end, the interface is organized in *practice* stage and a *trial* stage. In the first one, the student' executions are not evaluated, while in the second one the system checks if the solution is correct. If it is, the next activity or sub-activity is presented, and if it is not, the student will receive feedback and return to the practice stage. The visual clues introduced above are provided at all levels when the student fails in trial stage or when the time elapsed in practice stage is too long. They can be graphics, text, or recommendations to read the documentation.

4. *Continuous working*: the system allows to continue the activity at any time. When RoboboITS is executed for the first time, a unique code is assigned to the user. This code can be used if the application is closed, so when the user returns, he/she starts at the same point where it was. In addition, the student can access to all necessary documentation at any time from the interface. It contains one button to open the activity statement, and a second one that opens the Robobo programming manual.

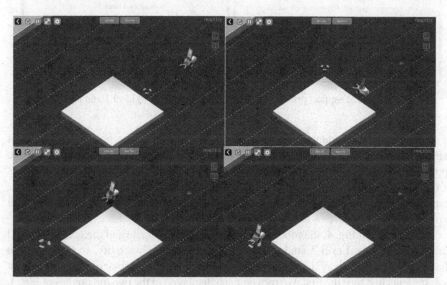

Fig. 4. Four snapshots of the video that shows students the final response to achieve.

4 AI Lesson Implemented

For a first test of the RoboboITS, a lesson related with the AI topic of *perception and actuation* for autonomous robotics has been developed, which corresponds to two specific teaching units on the AI+ project. Regarding perception, the lesson focuses on distance and orientation sensors, and regarding actuation it relies on basic motors. These are fundamental topics in autonomous robotics, from which latter lessons can be focused on more complex sensors and actuators (cameras, tactile screens, speech production, and others). The learning objective in terms of AI is that students learn what autonomy is in this scope, so the robot must be programmed relying on sensor measures and avoiding predefined thresholds. In addition, for this first test, only 3 competence levels are considered in the ITS. Finally, the programming must be performed using the Scratch blocks of the Robobo robot [20]. The version of the RoboboITS that implements this topic is accessible to download and test.[1]

Once the initial questionnaire is completed, and the student is therefore already assigned to a level, the final challenge for this lesson is presented: *programming Robobo so it can autonomously avoid an obstacle, regardless of its position and size.* The expected robot response is presented through a video (see four snapshots in Fig. 4) that students can play every time they need. This challenge was organized in two activities.

Fig. 5. Visual support provided in activity 1 for students in level 1 and level 2.

In the first one, students must program Robobo to avoid the obstacle but without using any sensor, just adjusting speed and time of the Robobo wheel motors using the appropriate Scratch blocks. The obstacle is always in the same position and its always of the same size. Hence, by solving this activity students get familiar with the motor response and, as main goal, they understand that adjusting specific values for this case is possible, but it requires a trial-and-error stage which is highly time consuming.

As observed in Fig. 4, the robot starts in front of the obstacle and the goal is to avoid it for its right side. Level 3 students do not receive any sub-activity, so they face the challenge in an open way. For level 2, the ITS proposes two sub-activities. In the first one, students just face the first two movements, displayed in the two top images of Fig. 4. Until they complete them, the second sub-activity is not presented. On it, their goal is to finish the remaining movements as shown in the bottom images of Fig. 4. Moreover, some visual support regarding the motor programming is provided, as displayed in Fig. 5 left. Lastly, level 1 students must solve five independent sub-activities, one for

---

[1] https://cutt.ly/I20RYDQ.

each movement shown in Fig. 4, which are evaluated independently. In addition, the specific Scratch blocks they must use are provided on the interface, as shown in Fig. 5 right. Therefore, level 2 and level 1 students receive a personalized challenge, with higher guidance level according to their programming skills.

In activity 2, the final challenge is the same, but now the position and size of the obstacle changes randomly every time the students run their solution. Consequently, they realize that their previous program does not work in this setup, as it was adjusted for a particular environment. This is the key concept to understand in this lesson. So, to solve now the challenge, they must rely of Robobo sensors, specifically, on the infrared sensor to detect distance to the obstacle, and the orientation sensor to turn.

The division into sub-activities depending on the level is the same as in Activity 1, but now students receive more information related to the sensor they must use. For level 3, they only receive information about the Robobo sensors they should use, which must be checked at the documentation (see Fig. 6 right). In the case of the level 2, the programming pseudocode is provided (see Fig. 6 middle). Level 1 receive the full program on the interface, and students must copy it and adjust the sensor values to make it work properly (see Fig. 6 left).

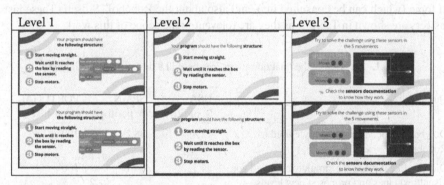

Fig. 6. Statement for the 3 different levels in activity 2, with adapted guidance information.

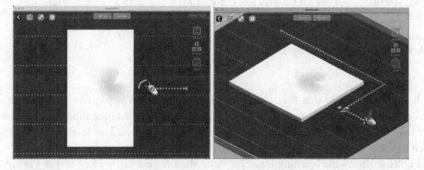

Fig. 7. Left: visual clue for students in level 1. Right: visual clue for level 2.

For all levels, and in both activities, students receive visual clues if measures $d1$ and $d2$ are above a threshold, as explained in the two previous sections. In this activity, the clues show the path to follow, the degrees to turn, and the point where the robot should stop, as displayed in Fig. 7. Again, these clues are adaptive, and they arise just if the ITS detects that the student requires them, so some of them could never see them.

5   Secondary School Validation

The validation of this first version of the RoboboITS was carried out in 2022 in three secondary schools of three different countries. The first was held at Virginia (USA), with a group of 17 students. The second one was held at Fene (Spain), and 17 students attended to the workshop. Finally, a last validation was carried out at Caldas das Taipas (Portugal), with 24 students. In all cases, the students' age ranged between 14 and 17 years, and their programming background was heterogeneous.

The validation was organized in two workshops, performed in different days. In the first one, an introduction to the Robobo programming with RoboboSim was carried out, but no AI topics were trained. In the second one, students used the RoboboITS to solve the challenge explained in the previous section. At the end of this second session, all students filled a questionnaire containing comprehension questions about the specific AI topic (which can be consulted in[2]), and also about the RoboboITS itself. These last answers are shown in Table 1, as they are relevant in the scope of this work.

Table 1. Answers to the final questionnaire about ITS design and functioning.

Question	USA % positive	SPAIN % positive	PORTUGAL % positive
Do you like the video game style used in RoboboSim?	82,4	88,2	100
Did you like it when the simulator showed you visual/text clues and proposed new levels (sub-activities) to advance?	94,1	94,1	100
Would you like to use more intelligent tools, like RoboboITS, as you study at school?	100	88,2	91,7
Would you like to use more intelligent tools, like RoboboITS, as you study at home?	76,5	70,6	66,7

It can be observed that the simulation-based interface was positive for students in all countries (question 1), as well as the visual clues it included (question 2). Moreover, they felt motivated and engaged to learn with the tool (question 3) at school, but not that much to use it as homework (question 4).

Figure 8 shows the learning trace for three students during the last test in Portugal, just to give a clear example of how they interact with the ITS. The first student on the top started on level 3, and it took 90 min to finish the challenge, with no clues. The

---

[2] https://drive.google.com/drive/u/1/folders/1LzFew5mF9sHEj9h83BKU31d_n9JOI4IW.

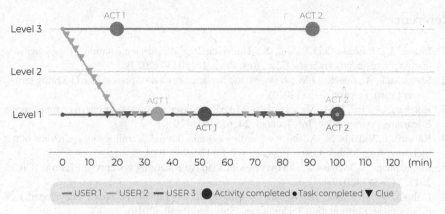

Fig. 8. Progress of three students on the RoboboITS in the Portugal workshop.

second one also started on level 3, but he/she was downgraded twice, because he/she required a lot of clues to solve the activity in the original setup. In fact, this student did not reach the final goal, although he/she was able for finish activity 1 quickly once in level 1. The third one (bottom line) was always in level 1, and he/she required 5 clues to solve the challenge, which was achieved in 100 min. What is relevant here is that the RoboboITS showed a reliable and stable functioning in all sessions, profiling students in an autonomous way, and allowing all of them to properly learn with adapted materials and interface. Some students did not reach the final goal in the session duration, but all of them improved autonomously.

6 Conclusions

Our study focusses on the importance of personalized learning in education and how Adaptive E-learning Systems can achieve this through analysing students' profiles and providing customized resources and interfaces. The development and validation of the RoboboITS is presented, an Intelligent Tutoring System that uses a 3D simulator called RoboboSim and a hands-on approach to learning AI with the Robobo robot. The system is a novel contribution to the field, addressing the issues of short-term AI education and providing personalization through adaptive 3D robotic simulations. Details of its prototype version and validation results obtained with students in three schools in the USA, Spain, and Portugal was also presented. Overall, the results suggest that the RoboboITS is a valuable support to teachers in teaching AI concepts to students.

Acknowledgments. The work of D. Durães and P. Novais has been supported by FCT–Fundação para a Ciência e Tecnologia within the R&D Units Project Scope: UIDB/00319/2020. The work of F. Bellas was supported by Grant TED2021-131172B-I00 funded by MCIN/AEI/ https://doi.org/10.13039/501100011033 and by the "European Union NextGenerationEU/PRTR". The "Programa de ayudas a la etapa predoctoral" from Xunta de Galicia supported this work through Sara Guerreiro's grant. Finally, F. Bellas and S. Guerreiro-Santalla wish to acknowledge the CITIC research center, funded by Xunta de Galicia and European Regional Development Fund (grant ED431G 2019/01).

References

1. Zhang, L., Basham, J.D., Yang, S.: Understanding the implementation of personalized learning: a research synthesis. Educ. Res. Rev. **31**, 100339 (2020)
2. Shemshack, A., Spector, J.M.: A systematic literature review of personalized learning terms. Smart Learn. Environ. **7**, 33 (2020)
3. Kolekar, S.V., Pai, R.M., Manohara Pai, M.P.: Rule based adaptive user interface for adaptive E-learning system. Educ. Inf. Technol. **24**, 613–641 (2019)
4. Katsaris, I., Vidakis, N.: Adaptive e-learning systems through learning styles: a review of the literature. Adv. Mobile Learn. Educ. Res. **1**(2), 124–145 2021
5. Ennouamani, S., Mahani, Z.: An overview of adaptive e-learning systems. IEEE Proc. ICICIS **2017**, 342–347 (2017)
6. Holmes, W.: Artificial Intelligence in Education. In: Tatnall, A. (eds.) Encyclopedia of Education and Information Technologies. Springer, Berlin (2019)
7. Quin, D.: Longitudinal and contextual associations between teacher-student relationships and student engagement: a systematic review. Rev. Educ. Res. **87**(2), 345–387 (2017). https://doi.org/10.3102/0034654316669434
8. Wiggan, G., Smith, D., Watson-Vandiver, M.J.: The national teacher shortage, urban education and the cognitive sociology of labor. Urban Rev. **53**, 43–75 (2021). https://doi.org/10.1007/s11256-020-00565-z
9. du Boulay, B.: Recent meta-reviews and meta–analyses of AIED systems. Int. J. Artif. Intell. Educ. **26**(1), 536–537 (2016)
10. Aleven, V., et al.: Example-tracing tutors: intelligent tutor development for non-programmers. IJAIED **26**, 224–269 (2016)
11. Holstein, K., Yu, Z., Sewall, J., Popescu, O., McLaren, B.M., Aleven, V.: Opening up an intelligent tutoring system development environment for extensible student modeling. In: International Conference on Artificial Intelligence in Education, pp. 169–183. Springer, Cham (2018)
12. E. Mousavinasab, N., Zarifsanaiey, S.R., Niakan Kalhori, M., Rakhshan, L., Keikha, M.: Ghazi Saeedi: intelligent tutoring systems: a systematic review of characteristics, applications, and evaluation methods. Interact. Learn. Environ. **29**(1), 142–163 (2021)
13. Crompton, H., Jones, M., Burke, D.: Affordances and challenges of artificial intelligence in K-12 education: a systematic review. J. Res. Technol. Educ. (2022). https://doi.org/10.1080/15391523.2022.2121344
14. Crompton, H., Burke, D.: Artificial intelligence in higher education: the state of the field. Int. J. Educ. Technol. High. Educ. **20**(22) (in press). https://doi.org/10.1186/s41239-023-00392-8
15. Holmes, W., Tuomi, I.: State of the art and practice in AI in education. Eur. J. Educ. **57**(4), 542–570 (2022)
16. Miao, F., Holmes, W.: AI and education: guidance for policy-makers, UNESCO (2021). https://unesdoc.unesco.org/ark:/48223/pf0000376709. Accessed 13 Jan 2023
17. European Commission: Digital Education Plan 2021–2017 (2020). https://ec.europa.eu/education/education-in-the-eu/digital-education-action-plan_en. Accessed 13 Jan 2023
18. Bellas, F., Guerreiro-Santalla, S., Naya, M., Duro, R.J.: AI curriculum for European high schools: an embedded intelligence approach. Int. J. Artif. Intell. Educ. (2022).https://doi.org/10.1007/s40593-022-00315-0
19. UNESCO: K-12 AI curricula: a mapping of government-endorsed AI curricula (2022). https://unesdoc.unesco.org/ark:/48223/pf0000380602.locale=en. Accessed 13 Jan 2023
20. Bellas, F., et al.: The Robobo project: bringing educational robotics closer to real-world applications. In: Advances in Intelligent Systems and Computing, vol. 630. Springer, Berlin (2018)

21. RoboboSim simulator. https://github.com/mintforpeople/robobo-programming/wiki/Unity. Accessed 13 Jan 2023
22. Anwar, S., Bascou, N.A., Menekse, M., Kardgar, A.: A systematic review of studies on educational robotics. J. Pre-Coll.E Eng. Educ. Res. (J-PEER) **9**(2), Article 2 (2019)
23. Yang, J., Zhang, B.: Artificial intelligence in intelligent tutoring robots: a systematic review and design guidelines. Appl. Sci. **9**, 2078 (2019)
24. The Construct!, https://www.theconstructsim.com. Accessed 13 Jan 2023
25. Blockly Games. https://blockly.games. Accessed 13 Jan 2023
26. CoderZ. https://gocoderz.com. Accessed 13 Jan 2023
27. OpenRoberta. https://lab.open-roberta.org. Accessed 13 Jan 2023
28. Robotbenchmark. https://robotbenchmark.net. Accessed 13 Jan 2023

Gamified CollectiveEyes: A Gamified Distributed Infrastructure for Collectively Sharing People's Eyes

Risa Kimura[1]([✉]), Tatsuo Nakajima[1], and Ichiro Satoh[2]

[1] Department of Computer Science and Engineering, Waseda University, Tokyo, Japan
{risa.kimura,tatsuo}@dcl.cs.waseda.ac.jp
[2] National Institute of Informatics, Tokyo, Japan
ichiro@nii.ac.jp

Abstract. This paper presents the design and evaluation of *Gamified CollectiveEyes* that is a digital infrastructure to collectively share human eyes. Gamified CollectiveEyes collects people's viewpoints in the world anywhere at all times, and a user sees several collected viewpoints simultaneously in a 3D virtual space. For navigating human viewpoints collected by Gamified CollectiveEyes, we propose a novel abstraction named *topic channel* in the paper, where a user can choose appropriate viewpoints and hearings that he/she wants to see. After presenting an overview of Gamified CollectiveEyes, we show two user studies to investigate potential opportunities and pitfalls of Gamified CollectiveEyes: the first user study is to investigate the human motivation mechanism to offer their viewpoints and the second user study is to investigate the configuration to present multiple viewpoints. We also show the limitation and future work of the current development of Gamified CollectiveEys.

Keywords: Collectively sharing human eyes · Gamification · Topic channel · Human motivation · Serendipity

1 Introduction

Distributed digital infrastructures that allow multiple participants to connect to them, interact with them, and create and exchange value are rapidly transforming our daily lives. In particular, digital sharing infrastructures are gaining popularity as they enable a variety of attractive and innovative services [3, 9, 10]. Such digital infrastructures allow individuals to offer their personal belongings and free time for the purposes of others. In this study, we examine the lending of parts of the human body, especially human vision, to others. Motivational design in conventional digital sharing infrastructures has been well studied [12, 13], but digital infrastructures that share human eyes with a group of people are very different from conventional shared objects in terms of human viewpoints, so a new approaches are needed.

In recent years, our lives have been transformed by the widespread use of smartphones. Current mobile have strong computing power and provide easy access to a wide

N. Moniz et al. (Eds.): EPIA 2023, LNAI 14115, pp. 16–28, 2023.
https://doi.org/10.1007/978-3-031-49008-8_2

variety of information. In the near future, wearable smart gadgets like smart glasses [21] and smart earphones [6] will be developed. These wearable appliances should be able to more easily collect diverse information about the world around us. Images and sounds collected from these wearable appliances can be used by others to hone their own visual and auditory abilities. Exposure to the visual and auditory senses of others allows people to think more flexibly and more deeply. For example, an earable device such as eSense provides the ability to analyze a person's behavior with earphones [6], and the ambient sounds captured can be used to develop a variety of digital services.

A distributed digital infrastructure for collectively sharing human eyes becomes a core infrastructure to help people to enhance their abilities through diverse viewpoints of others. *Gamified CollectiveEyes* is an infrastructure to capture and store viewpoints of people in the world. In this paper, for navigating human viewpoints collected by Gamified CollectiveEyes, we propose a novel abstraction named *topic channel* in the paper, where a user can choose viewpoints and hearings that he/she wants to see by changing like a TV channel. After presenting an overview of Gamified CollectiveEyes, we show two user studies to demonstrate the potential opportunities and pitfalls of Gamified CollectiveEyes: the first user study is to investigate the human motivation mechanism to offer their viewpoints and the second user study is to investigate the configuration to present multiple human viewpoints for finding serendipitous viewpoints.

The remainder of this paper is organized as follows. In Sect. 2 shows an overview of Gamified CollectiveEyes. In Sect. 3, we show several insights extracted from a user study how the current topic channel design influences human motivation. In Sect. 4, we show some insights extracted from a user study how the topic channel triggers human serendipity. Section 5 presents several related concepts to the approaches introduced in the paper. Section 6 shows the limitation of the current study. Finally, Sect. 7 concludes the paper.

2 Gamified CollectiveEyes

Gamified CollectiveEyes is a distributed infrastructure to collect and share human eyes; the infrastructure enables us to build novel services that would allow us to adopt someone else's seeing capabilities. The infrastructure uses a user's gaze-focused gestures to choose which viewpoint the user wants to access. The infrastructure assumes that each user is equipped with a wearable appliance that embeds a camera and microphone. In [8], we presented the opportunities and pitfalls of the earlier version of Gamified CollectiveEyes. The current version presented in the paper is enhanced from the earlier version to implement a topic channel abstraction that is essential extension to adopt gamification strategies proposed in the paper. The design presented in Sect. 2.1 and Sect. 2.2 is the almost same as the original version and the details are explained in [8].

2.1 Seeing Several Viewpoints Simultaneously

When presenting several eye views, the viewpoints are shown in a virtual space as shown in Fig. 1. Gamified CollectiveEyes provides the following two viewpoint presentation modes with which to present the several viewpoints. One viewpoint presentation mode is the spatial view mode as shown in the left picture of Fig. 1. Another viewpoint presentation mode is the temporal view mode as shown in the right picture of Fig. 1. When using the spatial view mode, the four views to present respective viewpoints are selected automatically and shown in a 3D virtual space. When using the temporal mode, one viewpoint is selected and shown. Then, the viewpoint can be replaced to another viewpoint successively until the most preferable viewpoint can be found.

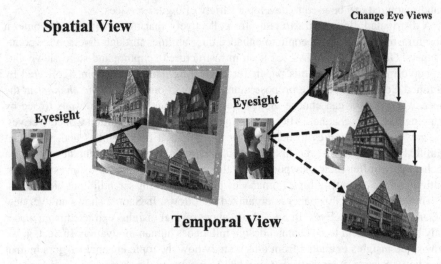

Fig. 1. Watching multiple viewpoints

2.2 Navigating Views with Gaze-Focused Gesture

One of the most striking features of Gamified CollectiveEyes is to adopt gaze-focused gestures for every control. Gamified CollectiveEyes offers the following four basic commands. The first is the *SELECT* command, which is employed by a user to select a target person by moving his/her viewpoint from top to bottom. The second is the *DESELECT* command, which is used to return to the previous view by a user moving his/her viewpoint from bottom to top. The third is the *CHANGE* command, which is used to change a user's current view to the view of another randomly selected person near him/her by moving his/her viewpoint top to bottom in the current view. The fourth and last is the *REPLACE* command, which is used to remove a view that a user wants to replace by moving his/her viewpoint from bottom to top on the view.

2.3 Topic Channels

A user specifies a topic channel to select presenting viewpoints that are shown around the user, much like a TV channel selector, from stored captured viewpoints in the database. While each person's viewpoint is captured by his/her wearable appliance through the camera embedded to the appliance, the person registers appropriate topic labels corresponding to respective topic channels that can be seen in his/her current viewpoint as hashtags for Gamified CollectiveEyes. In the current prototype infrastructure, the person whose viewpoints are captured registers the topic labels into the infrastructure manually.

The viewpoints captured from a person who wears a wearable appliance are clustered through topic labels and some of viewpoints are shown as icons in a 3D virtual space. The icons are clustered according to topic labels as respective icon clouds and displayed as shown in the top left screenshot of Fig. 2. A user chooses one of the icon clouds through his/her wearable appliance. The lower right screenshot of Fig. 2 shows a view after selecting one topic channel. Several viewpoints are displayed in a 3D virtual space, and the user navigates these viewpoints. If the user chooses one of them, he/she can see the viewpoint immersively as if it is his/her own viewpoint.

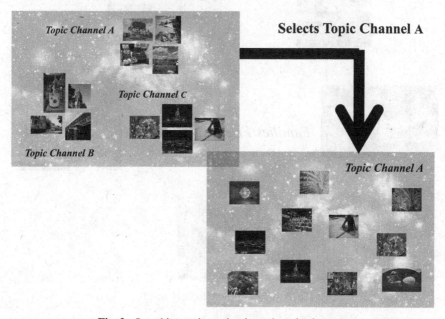

Fig. 2. Searching a viewpoint through topic channels

2.4 Thing-Focused and Value-Focused Topic Channel

For managing a large amount of viewpoints through topic channel, we investigate to use world models for categorizing diverse viewpoints in the real world into respective topic channels. In the current design of topic channels, we consider two approaches to model diverse viewpoints. These approaches are extracted from the sociomateriality perspective, and respective approaches treats the world from different attitudes and perspectives to materialize the world [7].

One approach is to categorize viewpoints-focused on *things* appeared in the viewpoints. The second approach is to categorize the viewpoints-focused on *values* appeared in the viewpoints. In the first approach, we model the world according to classifying concrete things appeared in the real world. The classification contains the following categories: the first is *Personal Belonging*, the second is *Curiosity*, the third is *Food*, the fourth is *Friends/Families*, and the fifth is *Landscape*, as shown in Fig. 3. Gamified CollectiveEyes chooses viewpoints that a user likes to see according to the topic channel. The classification used for the topic channel is named as *thing-focused topic channel*, and each viewpoint's category is identified as a different topic in the thing-focused topic channel.

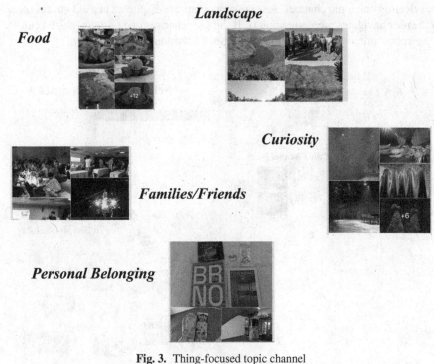

Fig. 3. Thing-focused topic channel

Another approach is to model the world according to abstract values on respective viewpoints in the world. We consider that people usually like to see somethings based on their perceived values. The classification contains the following categories: the first is *Aesthetic*, the second is *Enjoyable*, the third is *Cute*, the fourth is *Historical*, and the fifth is *Frightening*, as shown in Fig. 4. The classification used for the topic channel is named as *value-focused topic channel*.

2.5   Gamification Strategies in Gamified CollectiveEyes

The topic channel abstraction is a significant extension from the previous CollectiveEyes to identify what a user likes to see and how to assign topic labels to viewpoints to use gamification strategies in CollectiveEyes. While each person's viewpoint is collected

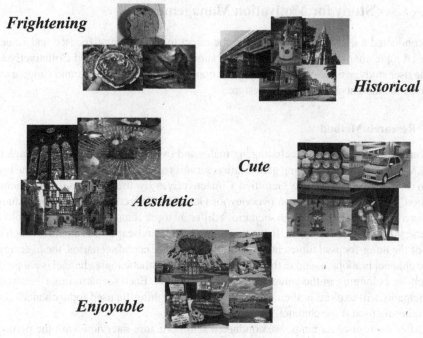

Frightening

Historical

Cute

Aesthetic

Enjoyable

Fig. 4. Value-focused topic channel

by his/her wearable appliance through the camera attached to the appliance, the person submits an appropriate topic label that is identified a belonging topic channel and that can be seen in his/her view as hashtags. The person whose viewpoints are collected registers the topic label of the current viewpoint into the infrastructure manually as shown below.

Gamified CollectiveEyes assumes that each captured and stored viewpoint assigns a topic label for selecting viewpoints under the topic channel that a user specifies. Gamified CollectiveEyes needs to consider the two aspects to exploit crowd power similar to traditional digital sharing infrastructures [12, 13, 18]. The first aspect is to explicitly assign different topic labels to respective viewpoints by users. The second aspect is to collect a large amount of viewpoints in the world.

The current Gamified CollectiveEyes infrastructure adopted two gamification-focused strategies to investigate the above aspects. The first gamification-focused strategy is to incorporate a gauge representing abilities to watch others' viewpoints. The gauge is increased when offering his/her viewpoints to Gamified CollectiveEyes. Also, the amount to increase the gauge depends on the assigned topic labels of the viewpoints. The amount of the gauge of each label is changed according to the current situation. Thus, a user needs to consider which viewpoints are appropriate to more increase his/her gauges so he/she needs to be aware of what he/she will be watching next. The second gamification-focused strategy is to assign a topic label to each viewpoint by each user. It is hard to recognize the topic of an viewpoint automatically through the current image recognition techniques. Thus, we adopted the human computation method like shown in [20] for manually assigning topic labels to respective viewpoints by a user.

3   A User Study for Motivation Management

We conducted a user study to investigate the effect to use the thing-focused and value-focused topic channel for designing gamification strategies in Gamified ColletiveEyes. In the user study, we collect and analyze the opinions from participants, and summarize them as the insights of the current design.

3.1   Research Method

We hired eight participants including six males and two females, whose average age is 27.8, where they are developing gamification services as their research topics, and asked them to act scenarios to use Gamified CollectiveEyes by using the user enactments method [16] after explaining an overview of Gamified CollectiveEyes. The user study prepared three scenarios. In each scenario, a different topic channel is selected to explore diverse viewpoints in the world. In the first scenario, the landscape topic channel which is one of the thing-focused topic channel is adopted, in the second scenarios, the historical topic channel is adopted, and in the third scenario, the aesthetic topic channel is adopted, which are belonging in the value-focused topic channel. Each scenario describes what participants will explore in their viewpoints under the thing-focused topic channel and the value-focused topic channel.

After the user enactments, we conducted semi-structure interview with the participants for understanding their motivation to register their viewpoints to Gamified CollectiveEyes. We summarize the participants' opinions acquired from the interviews into a document in accordance with the thematic analysis method [15]. We also adopted the affinity diagram method [11] to help our analysis process in reviewing codes and searching appropriate topics. Finally, we identified the following three themes.

3.2   Effects of Topic Channels

Many people use thing-focused topic channels when they want to see something specific, and use value-focused topic channels when they want to discover something new. For example, using a value-focused topic channel makes it more likely that different people will label viewpoints according to their own value judgments, and that the ambiguity arising from these value judgments will provide viewpoints that they have not imagined. Therefore, more abstract topic channels increase the likelihood of discovering serendipity. Specifically, "seeing something you don't know or an image that is not currently in your mind can lead to unexpected ideas," "ideas and desires that were not in your mind will be recalled, leading to new experiences," and "rather than using a thing-centric topic channel, you have the opportunity to get many different things in the same label."

3.3   Effects of Gamification

Opinions were divided on whether a different gauge for each label would be an incentive to provide viewpoints. Some said, "If you put different gauges on labels, the number of viewpoints for a particular label will increase, and the reliability of Gamified CollectiveEyes will decrease because you will be providing gauges in *point collection* for the viewpoints of labels with higher gauges." On the other hand, some said, "If Gamified CollectiveEyes is really useful to me, I would like to use Gamified CollectiveEyes to provide viewpoints for higher gauges."

Some of the specific comments are interesting, such as the following:

(1) I would like to provide viewpoints when I find a scene that I think is worth providing, so I don't think the viewpoints that Gamified CollectiveEyes provides would change much with a higher gauge.
(2) I thought I would not look at the labeled viewpoints because I feel that offering popular viewpoints to earn points is a very selfish motive and that viewpoints with high gauge labels are offered to collect points.
(3) If the distribution of points is unequal for each label, a variety of viewpoints will not be offered, and the Gamified CollectiveEyes.
(4) If the distribution of points is uneven for each label, it may not provide a variety of viewpoints, and the motivation to use Gamified CollectiveEyes may be inhibited. Another commented.
(5) Because Gamified CollectiveEyes allows for differences in sensitivity between myself and others, I am more motivated to use Gamified CollectiveEyes not only when they provide viewpoints that I do not expect.

3.4 Effects of Consciousness

There were various comments that labeling increases the opportunity to be aware of "what I am watching now" and "my feelings about what I am watching." Other comments included, (1) "I think I will actively try to find meaning in my viewpoint", (2) "The more viewpoints I provide, the more opportunities I have to be aware of what I am watching and how I feel about what I am doing", (3) "Gamified CollectiveEyes gives me an opportunity to think about what is reflected in this viewpoint and what value it has.", (4) "Even if we automate the recognition of viewpoints, the manual label registration increases awareness of what we are looking at, so the policy does not necessarily make sense in terms of the significance of Gamified CollectiveEyes."

On the other hand, another commented, "I am not aware of it when I am looking at it now, but I will be aware of it later when I look back at that viewpoint."

4 A User Study for Serendipity Management

We also conducted an additional user study to investigate the effect to use the thing-focused and value-focused topic channel for investigating how a user navigates diverse viewpoints in Gamified CollectiveEyes.

4.1 Research Method

We recruited twelve participants including ten males and two females, and their average age is 27.0. We asked them to perform scenarios to use Gamified CollectiveEyes based on the user enactments method as same as the first user study after explaining an overview of Gamified CollectiveEyes. The user study prepared the following scenarios. Each scenario adopts a different topic channel to explore diverse viewpoints in the world. One scenario adopts the landscape topic channel which is one of the thing-focused topic channel, and another scenario adopts the aesthetic topic channel, which are belonging in the value-focused topic channel. Each scenario describes what participants will explore their viewpoints under the thing-focused topic channel and the value-focused topic channel.

In the user study, viewpoints selected by a topic channel specified by a participant are shown in Fig. 2, and several viewpoints shown in each topic channel are configured in several ways. For the first scenario named Scenario A and the second scenario named Scenario B, we setup these respective four configuration as shown in Table 1.

After the user enactments, we asked participants to answer the following question-naires.

A-(Q1): *Can you find favorite viewpoints in Scenario A: Configuration (i)?*
A-(Q2): *Can you find serendipitous viewpoints in Scenario A: Configuration (i)?*
A-(Q3): *Can you find serendipitous viewpoints in Scenario A: Configuration (ii)?*
A-(Q4): *Can you find serendipitous viewpoints in Scenario A: Configuration (iii)?*
A-(Q5): *Can you find serendipitous viewpoints in Scenario A: Configuration (iv)?*
B-(Q1): *Can you find favorite viewpoints in Scenario B: Configuration (i)?*
B-(Q2): *Can you find serendipitous viewpoints in Scenario B: Configuration (i)?*
B-(Q3): *Can you find serendipitous viewpoints in Scenario B: Configuration (ii)?*
B-(Q4): *Can you find serendipitous viewpoints in Scenario B: Configuration (iii)?*
B-(Q5): *Can you find serendipitous viewpoints in Scenario B: Configuration (iv)?*

We investigated participants' scores on the points using a five-point Likert scale (4: induced, 3: to some extent, 2: cannot say either, 1: sometimes induced, 0: not induced) on each question. After the answering the questionnaires, we conducted semi-structure interview with the participants to understand their experiences with seeing serendipitous viewpoints.

Table 1. Configurations for Scenario A and Scenario B

Scenario A	Configuration (i)	Landscape 100%	Configuration (ii)	Landscape 70%, Food 30%
	Configuration (iii)	Landscape 70%, Friends/Families 30%	Configuration (iv)	Landscape 40%, Food 30%, Friends/Families 30%
Scenario B	Configuration (i)	Aesthetic 100%	Configuration (ii)	Aesthetic 70%, Enjoyable 30%
	Configuration (iii)	Aesthetic 70%, Historical 30%	Configuration (iv)	Aesthetic 40%, Enjoyable 30%, Historical 30%

4.2 Effects of Serendipity

As shown in Fig. 5, what is interesting about the tendency of many participants' opinions is that the focus of the viewpoint to be displayed becomes blurred and serendipity decreases as the number of topic channels increases when using the thing-focused topic channel, but the discovery of serendipity does not decrease even if the number of topic channels increases when using the value-focused topic channel. The argument is supported from the opinion that the viewpoints provided by the value-focused topic channel are collected by abstract categories, so even when displaying viewpoints in multiple topic channels, it is possible to discover attractive or serendipitous viewpoints.

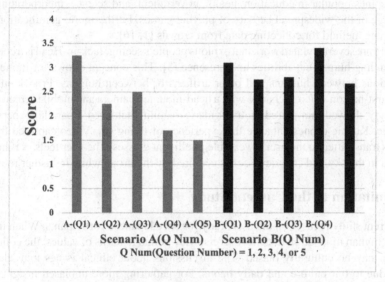

Fig. 5. Results of questionnaires

Offering an viewpoint that is different from a participant's current viewpoint is effective in discovering serendipity for him/her. In particular, presenting the current viewpoint of a user from different angles or presenting his/her current viewpoint at different distances is effective for discovering serendipity. A large number of participants answered that the displaying diverse viewpoints was effective in offering attractive viewpoints. On the other hand, when using the thing-focused topic channel, the participants felt that it would be annoying if they were not interested in the viewpoints in the current topic channel.

5 Related Work

Digital sharing infrastructures include Airbnb, a P2P lodging service, and Uber, a P2P transportation network for sharing goods and services, among a growing number of multifaceted digital infrastructures and offline activities. These infrastructures use information technology to provide information to individuals, businesses, non-profit organizations, and governments to optimize resources through the redistribution, sharing, and reuse of surplus goods and services [3]. Crowdsourcing is also a type of digital sharing infrastructure that shares human skills by dividing tasks into various micro-tasks and asking the crowd to complete them. Crowdsourcing in general uses monetary rewards to motivate crowds like Amazon Mechanical Turk [10]. The use of gamification in crowd-sourcing infrastructures to encourage the execution of more microtasks is one of the current hot topics in gamification research [12, 13].

` Gamification is the process of making a task more game-like by incorporating game elements [2, 14]. For example, visualizing the achievement of a task as a score or compar-ing the achievement with others can motivate users to accomplish a task. Gamification has become common in the private sector like operating social media. Now gamification also becomes popular in education, health, government, and science, incorporating the advantage of the widespread activity of playing games. Furthermore, gamification is a appropriate method for collecting data from crowds [1, 16].

There are several related work that exploits people's seeing. Jack-in-Head is a concept for extending human capabilities and presence [5]. This concept allows for immersive connections between humans and other artifacts or between humans. Procyk studied paired first-person video exchange with a head-mounted camera and mobile screen [17]. This study showed that paired mutual video streaming achieved a parallel experience in public. Kinetic drones enhance the experience of flying [4]. Video captured by the drone is transmitted to the user's wearable intelligent glasses. The user feels as if he/she is flying in the sky and can view scenes acquired by the drone while in his/her room.

6 Limitation of the Current Study

The current study focuses on the user study for only Japanese participants. When inves-tigating human motivation to collect diverse viewpoints in terms of values, the collected insights may be culturally biased. The discussions about ethical issues may also be biased due to our culture and daily habits. For gathering more unbiased insights, we need to conduct the user study for participants belonging to other cultures for under-standing how seeing and hearing in the world is different in respective cultures. Also, as shown in [19], people's answers about their attitude about ethics may be different from their actual behavior. Thus, we will need to observe their real behavior to use Gamified CollectiveEyes not only the survey of their attitude.

The current research method focused on a qualitative method for designing gamification-based strategies of Gamified CollectiveEyes so we need to adopt more quantitative approaches to optimize the strategies. We also need to investigate the effect of the manual registration of a topic label of each viewpoint: whether the con-scious registration of a topic label is essential to increase the significance of Gamified CollectiveEyes.

7 Conclusion and Future Work

The paper presented the design of Gamified CollectiveEyes to motivate people for encouraging collectively sharing human eyes and ears. We conducted a series of user studies and investigated some findings in the current design. The most important find-ing in terms of the gamification aspect is that modelling the world meaningfully offers additional information to users, and the information increase human motivation to act them more consciously.

Our approach suggests that digital technology can give us great power. The dreams and fictions in past novels and movies will become reality in the near future. Cerebro, for example, is a fictional scientific device that appears in Marvel Comics' X-Men. As society becomes increasingly complex, we need new sophisticated tools that amplify our ability to think and make decisions in order for society to thrive. Because of the simplicity of our approach in providing diverse human viewpoints, it is possible that the diverse viewpoints could help enhance decision making as a tool to improve the ability to think about the various human biases found in the behavioral economics research. As a future direction, we would like to investigate how Gamified CollectiveEyes can reframe our abilities of seeing and hearing activities and expand our ability to think by presenting multiple people's viewpoints. By enhancing these abilities, we may be able to transform our daily lives into something more enjoyable and enriching through more diverse and introspective thoughts and lifestyles.

References

1. Crowley, D.N., Breslin, J.G., Corcoran, P., Young, K.: Gamification of citizen sensing through mobile social reporting. In: Proceedings of the 2012 IEEE International Games Innovation Conference. Rochester (2012)
2. Deterding, S., Dixon, D., Khaled, R., Nacke, L.: From game design elements to gamefulness: defining "gamification". In: Proceedings of the 15th International Academic MindTrek Conference (2011)
3. Hamari, J., Sjöklint, M., Ukkonen, A.: The sharing economy: why people participate in collaborative consumption. J. Assoc. Inf. Sci. Technol. **67**(9) (2015)
4. Ikeuchi, K., Otsuka, K., Yoshii, A., Sakamoto, M., Nakajima, T.: KinecDrone: enhancing somatic sensation to fly in the sky with Kinect and AR.Drone. In: Proceedings of the 5th Augmented Human International Conference (AH '14) (2014)
5. Kasahara, S., Rekimoto, J.: JackIn: integrating first-person view with out-of-body vision generation for human-human augmentation. In: Proceedings of the 5th Augmented Human International Conference (AH '14) (2014)
6. Kawsar, F., Min, C., Mathur, A., Montanari, A.: Earables for personal-scale behavior analytics. IEEE Pervasive Comput. **17**(3) (2018)
7. Kimura, R., Nakajima, T.: Digitally enhancing society through structuralism: virtualizing collective human viewpoint and hearing capabilities as a case study. Lecture Notes in Computer Science, vol. 12203. Springer, Cham (2020)
8. Kimura, R., Nakajima., T.: Collectively sharing people's visual and auditory capabilities: exploring opportunities and pitfalls. SN Comput. Sci. **1**(5), 298:1–24, Springer Nature (2020)
9. Kimura, R., Nakajima, T.: Gathering people's happy moments from collective human eyes and ears for a wellbeing and mindful society. Lecture Notes in Computer Science, vol 12197. Springer, Berlin (2020)
10. Kittur, A., Chi, E.H., Suh, B.: Crowdsourcing user studies with mechanical turk. In: Proceedings of the 2008 SIGCHI Conference on Human Factors in Computing Systems (2008)
11. Lucero, A.: Using affinity diagrams to evaluate interactive prototypes. In: Human–Computer Interaction—INTERACT 2015. Lecture Notes in Computer Science, vol. 9297. Springer, Cham (2015)

12. Morschheuser, B., Hamari, J., Koivisto, J.: Gamification in crowdsourcing: a review. In: Proceedings of the 49th Hawaii International Conference on System Sciences (2016)
13. Morschheuser, B., Hamari, J., Koivisto, J., Maedche, A.: Gamified crowdsourcing: conceptualization, literature review, and future agenda. Int. J. Hum.-Comput. Stud. **106** (2017)
14. Nicholson, S.: A user-centered theoretical framework for meaningful gamification. In: Proceedings of Game+Leaning+Socoety 8.0. (2012)
15. Nowell, L.S., Norris, J.M., White, D.E., Modules, N.J.: Thematic analysis: striving to meet the trustworthiness criteria. Int. J. Qual. Methods **16**, 1– 13 (2017)
16. Odom, W., Zimmerman, J., Davidoff, S., Forlizzi, J., Dey, A.K., Lee, M.K.: A fieldwork of the future with user enactments. In: Proceedings of the Designing Interactive Systems Conference (DIS '12), pp. 338–347 (2012)
17. Procyk, J., Neustaedter, C., Pang, C., Tang, A., Judge, T.K.: Exploring video streaming in public settings: shared geocaching over distance using mobile video chat. In: Proceedings of the SIGCHI Conference on Human Factors in Computing Systems (CHI '14) (2014)
18. Reddy, S., Estrin, D., Hansen, M., Srivastava, M.: Examining micro-payments for participatory sensing data collections. In: Proceedings of the 12th ACM International Conference on Ubiquitous Computing (2010)
19. Sundar, S.S., Kang, H., Wu, M., Go, E., Zhang, B.: Unlocking the privacy paradox: do cognitive heuristics hold the key? In: CHI '13 Extended Abstracts on Human Factors in Computing Systems (CHI EA '13) (2013)
20. von Ahn, L., Dabbish, L.: Designing games with a purpose. Commun. ACM **51**, 8 (2008)
21. Google Glass. https://www.google.com/glass/. Accessed 1 April 2023

Design and Development of Ontology for AI-Based Software Systems to Manage the Food Intake and Energy Consumption of Obesity, Diabetes and Tube Feeding Patients

Diogo Martinho[1]([✉])[iD], Vítor Crista[1][iD], Ziya Karakaya[2,3][iD], Zahra Gamechi[4],
Alberto Freitas[5][iD], José Neves[6,7][iD], Paulo Novais[6,7][iD], and Goreti Marreiros[1,7][iD]

[1] Institute of Engineering, GECAD, Polytechnic of Porto, Porto, Portugal
{diepm,vvrpc,mgt}@isep.ipp.pt
[2] Computer Engineering Department, Konya Food & Agriculture University, Konya, Turkey
ziya.karakaya@gidatarim.edu.tr
[3] ARD Grup Bilişim Tenolojileri A.Ş., Koç Kuleleri, A-Blok, Ankara, Turkey
[4] Almende BV, Rotterdam, The Netherlands
zahra@almende.org
[5] Faculty of Medicine, CINTESIS@RISE, MEDCIDS, University of Porto, Porto, Portugal
alberto@med.up.pt
[6] ALGORITMI Centre, University of Minho, Guimarães, Portugal
{jneves,pjon}@di.uminho.pt
[7] Intelligent Systems Associate Laboratory, Guimarães, Portugal

Abstract. Poor and sedentary lifestyles combined with bad dietary habits have an impact on our health. Nowadays, diet-related diseases have become a major public health issue, threatening the sustainability of healthcare systems, and new strategies to promote better food intake are now being explored. In this context, the use of ontologies has gained importance over the past decade and become more prevalent. By incorporating ontologies in the healthcare domain, artificial intelligence (AI) can be enhanced to better support healthcare systems dealing with chronic diseases, such as obesity and diabetes requiring long-term progress and frequent monitoring. This is especially challenging with current resource inefficiency; however, recent research suggests that incorporating ontology into AI-based technological solutions can improve their accuracy and capabilities. Additionally, recommendation and expert systems benefit from incorporating ontologies for a better knowledge representation and processing to increase success rates. This study outlines the development of an ontology in the context of food intake to manage and monitor patients with obesity, diabetes, and those using tube feeding. A standardized vocabulary for describing food and nutritional information was specified to enable the integration with different healthcare systems and provide personalized dietary recommendations to each user.

Keywords: Ontology · Semantic web · Food recommendation · Personalized healthcare

© The Author(s), under exclusive license to Springer Nature Switzerland AG 2023
N. Moniz et al. (Eds.): EPIA 2023, LNAI 14115, pp. 29–40, 2023.
https://doi.org/10.1007/978-3-031-49008-8_3

1 Introduction

Our dietary habits have a significant impact on our health, and diet-related diseases pose a major public health concern, threatening the sustainability of healthcare systems. Unbalanced food intake, in terms of both quantity and quality, can lead to various medical conditions, including metabolic disturbances, malnutrition, overweight, poor mental performance, and medical risk factors such as hypertension, osteoporosis, cardiovascular diseases, type 2 diabetes, hip fractures, liver pathologies, Alzheimer's disease, and even cancer [1]. These diet-related diseases continue to be a major public health concern and endanger the sustainability of healthcare systems [2, 3]. Therefore, it becomes necessary to study and develop effective tools to monitor and support users in either single or group contexts to make better decisions in their daily lives regarding the adoption of healthier behaviors [4–6] and to support achieving health related goals [7]. As a result, dietary habits will be improved to prevent and manage the aforementioned diseases. In this context the FoodFriend project[1] was established as a novel technology aimed at addressing these challenges in three different uses cases: prevention of malnutrition in nursing homes and patients using tube feeding (1); and nutritional transmural care of chronic diseases such as obesity (2) and type 2 diabetes (3). Traditional food intake monitoring methods can be labor-intensive and time-consuming [8], and feedback is not always absorbed correctly by the end-user. Therefore, the FoodFriend project focuses on developing a complete toolset that can automatically measure a person's food intake with minimal user-input and provide personalized, actionable feedback. The FoodFriend toolset consists of both hardware, such as sensors, and software, such as an application or web portal, that can automatically monitor a person's food intake, reducing the workload and problems associated with traditional food monitoring. Additionally, the FoodFriend toolset can benefit various groups of users, including dieticians, nutritionists, caterers, and individuals seeking to improve their dietary habits. For dieticians and nutritionists, the tool can provide insight into their clients' eating habits, while clients can benefit from a reduced workload during the monitoring process. Additionally, the comprehensive tool can lower the threshold for individuals not involved in dietary coaching to get involved in improving their nutritional habits. The FoodFriend project uses health behavior-change recommendation techniques, such as the transtheoretical model of health behavior change [9, 10] to provide personalized suggestions to end-users based on the collected data. The recommendation process is supported by visualization techniques, enabling dieticians to provide feedback and steer the recommendation process. Furthermore, FoodFriend platform also includes mobile device implementations to improve accessibility. Finally, the project delivers a research database and a nutrition-wise ontology for modeling nutritional behavior, providing semantic interoperability between heterogeneous data sources and enabling data integration between the three use cases of the project based on existing ontologies available in the literature that consider the same concepts and relationships shared with the proposed ontology for the Food-Friend project. In this work we present the methodological approach undertaken in the FoodFriend project to establish a common shared ontology between the three different

---

[1] https://itea4.org/project/food-friend.html.

use cases and we provide a representation of this ontology including the main concepts and relationships identified.

In the next section, all the related works presenting different ontologies in the context of food representation are described with a discussion of their application and relatedness to the FoodFriend project. In Sect. 3, the methodology undertaken for each use case is specified describing the associated concepts and relations in the context of each use case. In Sect. 4, the architecture of the common shared ontology for the FoodFriend project is presented. A discussion regarding the results achieved in this work is presented in Sect. 5 and the main conclusions are drawn in the last section of this work.

2 Related Works

This section summarizes the current State of the Art regarding existing ontologies in the context of Food representation. Each relevant ontology will be described in terms of structure and main concepts and relationships as well as associated limitations in the context of the FoodFriend project.

2.1 FoodOn Ontology

Perhaps the most well-known food ontology, FoodOn [11, 12] is an open-source, comprehensive ontology structured with several term hierarchy facets that cover basic raw food source ingredients, process terms for packaging, cooking and preservation, and an upper-level variety of product type schemes under which food products can be categorized. FoodOn has been initially designed with several terms retrieved from LanguaL, a library science and ontology friendly food classification system that is composed by 14 food product description facets including plant or animal food source, chemical additive, preservation or cooking process, packaging, and standard national and international upper-level product type schemes. Currently, at least 3400 terms are used in FoodOn to describe "the individual plant, animal, or chemical food source from which the food product or its major ingredient is derived". Furthermore, FoodOn describes the organism's food source terms using intermediate groups like "stem or spear vegetable" but separates chemicals (mainly additives) into a "food component class" to differentiate whole organism references (see Fig. 1).

Additionally, FoodOn works in partnership with other OBOFoundry related ontologies which together represent the Joint Food Ontology Workgroup (JFOW). JFOW is an informal group of ontology stakeholders and has the main goal of standardizing the content of food products and research related ontologies. As such, this group aims to simplify the annotation of datasets to meet interoperable FAIR data standards [13], as well as to enhance plug-and-play, queryable knowledge graph search and provide vocabularies for nutritional analysis, including chemical food components which are factors in diet, health and plant and animal agricultural rearing research.

Other members of JFOW include:

- Food-Biomarker Ontology (FOBI)—An ontology with two interconnected sub-ontologies: one to describe raw foods and multi-component foods terms and a Biomarker Ontology to describe chemical classes.

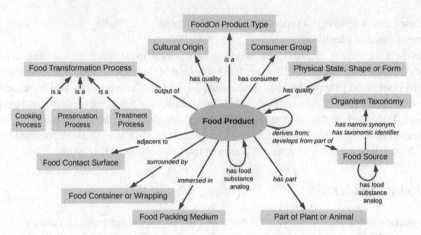

Fig. 1. FoodOn Ontology—adapted from [12].

- Ontology for Nutritional Studies (ONS)—Developed within the ENPADASI European project, has the main goal to represent a comprehensive resource for the description of concepts in the broader human nutrition domain covering classes necessary for describing and querying for nutritional studies.
- Animal Health Surveillance Ontology (AHSO)—An ontology to describe animal health data which can promote the secondary use of these data for surveillance (data-driven surveillance, or syndromic surveillance).
- Crop Nutritional Data Ontology (CDNO)—An ontology structured with terminologies to describe nutritional attributes of material entities that contribute to human diet.
- Ontology for Nutritional Epidemiology (ONE)—An ontology to describe nutritional epidemiologic studies accurately.
- Medical Actions Ontology (MAxO)—An ontology that provides a structured vocabulary for medical procedures, interventions, therapies, and treatments, including nutrition based medical interventions.
- Environmental Conditions, Treatments, and Exposures Ontology (ECTO)—An ontology to describe experimental treatments of plants and model organisms, exposures of humans or any other organisms to stressors through a variety of routes, stimuli, any kind of environmental condition or change in condition that can be experienced by an organism or population of organisms on earth.

Although FoodOn, and the associated ontologies part of the JFOW group already cover a wide spectrum of elements associated to the Food variable these are still lacking in terms of describing and modelling the human variable and associated characteristics which including dietary and health issues (such as diabetes and obesity) leading to the scope of FoodFriend project and the necessity to model this concept.

2.2 Quisper Ontology

Eftimov and colleagues proposed in 2018 [14] a food ontology named Quisper ontology that has been developed in a semi-automatic way and can be used for the harmonization and enable research in the domain of personalized dietary web services. Additionally, the proposed ontology combines aggregated data from different sources to provide new knowledge to contribute for healthier lifestyles. The defined ontology (see Fig. 2) has been initially designed to include 5 main groups (Component, Food, FoodGroup, Personal and SNP) and 7 main classes (Component, Food, FoodGroup, Personal, SNP, Unit, and WebService).

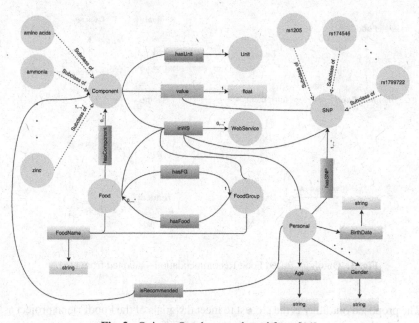

Fig. 2. Quisper Ontology—adapted from [14].

With this structure, the authors express the advantage of the ontology not being focused only on food-related data, but also to include information for everyone from his/her user profile, biomarker analysis, dietary reference intakes and recommendations.

This ontology goes in line with the goals of the FoodFriend project, however the current description of the person/human variable is still very limited in terms of understanding characteristics which include dietary and health issues as well to understand and describe the person's meal intake over the days.

2.3 Ontology Based Food Recommendation

More recently, in 2022 [15], Chivukula and colleagues proposed a new food ontology, named Ontology Based Food Recommendation to model in the food domain to help people in getting the right recommendation about the food, based on their health condition. Some of the key concepts that were considered are related to the food domain and include types of food, flavors and textures, and different kinds of food courses and meals (see Fig. 3). Additionally, information on recipes and corresponding ingredients together with their nutritional values is also described. Finally, the user variable with the details of physical attributes such as age, weight with health history is also maintained. The authors explain how the proposed ontology could be used in different food and dietary domains, for example, by people with culinary interests, nutritionists, restaurants, and chefs.

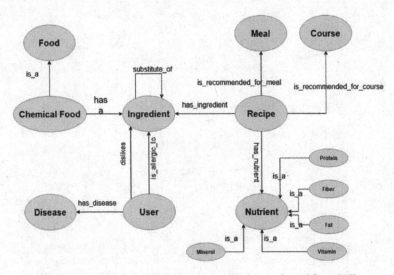

Fig. 3. Ontology Based Food Recommendation—adapted from [15].

The proposed ontology is the closest to meet the goals of the FoodFriend project as it considers both food, human and even meals variables. However, additional concepts must still be considered to correctly describe the user Meal Intake and additional components are also necessary. For example, the Food variable should also include information which is relevant to manage dietary and food issues such as Diabetes by considering information on the associated glycemic index of each food.

3 Methodology

This section describes the different concepts and corresponding relationships associated with each Use Case of the FoodFriend project. These concepts will be then combined into a common FoodFriend Ontology which is described in the following section of this document.

3.1 Diabetes Use Case

Diabetes use case focuses on the creation and validation of technologies for objective self-monitoring and management of patients with diabetes type 2. The major outcome will be a quantified self, evidence-based coaching solution for self-monitoring and management of diabetes type II disease based on food intake and lifestyle monitoring. The transparent integration of this type of technology in the daily routine of patients will improve self-monitoring of disease, increase treatment adherence and the promotion of healthy behaviors, having as consequence diminishing the acute complications of diabetes. By specifying an ontology in the context of the management of diabetes disease, it is possible to develop a recommendation system using a structured and standardized representation of knowledge, enabling efficient information retrieval and inference. In this context, ontologies can be used to organize and categorize food-related data, such as nutritional information and personal preferences to deliver personalized and accurate dietary suggestions based on individual needs and constraints. Currently, a recommendation system has been developed regarding the type 2 diabetes use case. The rules composing this system were generated based on the guidelines from the WHO (World Health Organization), related to the consumption of the main macronutrients. The application daily sends users' macronutrient intake, and recommendations are subsequently generated if the macronutrients exceed the specified levels or fall below the recommended levels [16].

In the context of Diabetes Use case the following concepts and corresponding relationships have been identified:

- *User—Food*—The person (user) has interests regarding each food available/inserted in the system. These interests can cover aspects such as preferences and allergies.
- *User—Meals Intake*—Each person keeps track of all the meals intake, which corresponds to any ingested food information provided to the system. These meals usually refer to breakfast, lunch, dinner, and snacks.
- *Meal—Food*—As mentioned previously, each meal taken by the person will include one or more foods. Additionally, each food (and its information) will also be related to the types of meal for which that food is most recommended. For example, a bowl of milk and cereal could be recommended for breakfast while a roast chicken could be recommended for either lunch or dinner.
- *Food—Nutritional Values*—Foods have nutrients and therefore, each food available in the system must also contain nutritional information regarding key nutrients to manage a healthy diet. These nutrients correspond to proteins, carbohydrates, fibers, fats, minerals (such as salt and sugar) and vitamins.

3.2 Obesity Use Case

Obesity use case focuses on people with desk jobs having a higher risk on obesity due to their limited physical activity in daily life. The major idea is to detect every food consumption of the user depending on the data collected via their mobile devices like location of the user, movement of the user, social media sharing, mail sending activity, incoming/outgoing calls, etc. In addition to concepts and corresponding relationship described in Diabetes Use Case, we have identified the followings valuable for Obesity Use Case:

- *User—Energy Consumption Activity*—While food intake behavior of the user has significant impact on weighing, the energy consumption during "Physical Activities", "Resting", and "Sleeping" has as much impact as the level of food intake. In addition to the duration of these activities, the energy consumption rate is also affected by the attributes of the user, such as basal metabolism.
- *User—Goal—Dietary Plan*—Users have goals to achieve. The goals can be assigned by the user itself or by professionals either as distinct goals or by combining with their dietary plan.
- *User—Disabilities*—Physical activities suitable for the user will naturally depend on their disabilities if they exist.
- *User—Allergenics*—Having allergies will affect the recommendation of food and ingredients. Users may be allergic to some foods or constituents. This information must be taken into account by professionals and AI based food recommendations.
- *User—Disease*—Users may have comorbidities which should be regarded in recommendation operation. Some foods may seem good for persons having obesity conditions but may also threaten other disease treatment. The FoodFriend system should not create any threat to patients.

3.3 Tube Feeding Use Case

Food intake of patients on tube feeding is performed by gathering data from the tube feeding pump and determine the energy expenditure of the patient with indirect calorimetry and accelerometers. Based on the obtained data and insights into the nutritional status of the patient, personalized feedback can be provided through an easy-to-use platform and incorporated into the treatment plans of dietitians. Also, by giving the patient more insight into his/her nutritional status, compliance with the therapy will increase. The concepts and relationships regarding the Tube Feeding use case are as follows:

- *User—Feeding Pack*—The user takes available/recommended feeding packages. The recommended feeding package can be based on the users medical and health status.
- *User—Food Intake*—The feeding pump tracks the food intake of the user. For any food intake (meals or beverages) the user utilizes the feeding pump. The food intake can be a feeding pack, water, or coffee.
- *Feeding Pack—Intake Status (Feeding Pump)*—For each user based on the medical status, a special intake status is recommended. The intake volume, flow rate, dose, as well as the intake duration can be adjusted to the user's demand. Each of these elements have an influence on the health status of the user. These elements can be adjusted and recorded automatically by the feeding pump.
- *Feeding Pack—Nutritional Values*—Each feeding package has nutrients and energy produced by that. This information can be accessed by scanning the barcode of each feeding package. The factsheet provided for each feeding package reveals the amount of energy, protein, carbohydrate, fat, fiber, water, minerals, Vitamins, and other trace elements.

4 Proposed Ontology

This section describes the FoodFriend Ontology according to the scope of each Use Case and how the knowledge representation is structured according to the different concepts and relationships previously identified. All ontological structures from each use case have been merged into a single ontology as is presented in Fig. 4. Furthermore, the proposed ontology has also been inspired by the literature reach made in the context of this Task and deliverable to consider essential concepts and relationships also like the scope of the FoodFriend project.

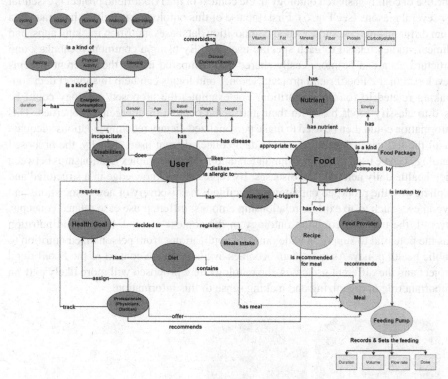

Fig. 4. FoodFriend ontology

The two main classes of the FoodFriend Ontology are the User and Food. A user will contain demographic information such as age, gender, weight and height, and other characteristics such as the recommended daily energetic consumption and food-related diseases and may also have disabilities which incapacitate daily energetic consumption. The user will be given different health goals that can be included in a diet (which is created by a health professional). The user will also register his/her meals intake for each meal taken throughout the day (breakfast, lunch, dinner, snacks, etc.). These meals are part of a diet which is necessary to correctly accomplish an established health goal. Additionally, certain meals have recommended recipes that can be provided by a food provider. The user will relate to food in terms of preferences and allergies to certain types of food. Each food has its own nutritional information associated in terms of total number of fats, vitamins, fibers, carbohydrates, etc. Certain foods can also be stored in the feeding packages with the means of a feeding pump. The intake status is a crucial element in tube feeding which is managed by the feeding pump. Foods are also part of recipes and relate to food diseases as appropriate/inappropriate and can be recommended by health professionals.

5 Discussion

The use of common shared ontology in the context of the FoodFriend project is essential for several reasons (see Fig. 5). First, the use of this ontology can help to integrate data from different sources, such as food composition databases, nutrition tracking apps, and clinical studies related to each specific use case. By using a common vocabulary and structure, data can be more easily shared and compared across the different systems developed in the FoodFriend project. Second, ontologies can help to support decision-making related to food and nutrition. For example, the proposed ontology could be used to classify foods based on their nutritional content or allergenic properties. This information could then be used to make personalized dietary recommendations adequate to all the use cases depending on the data collected from users. Finally, the proposed ontology can be used to advance our understanding of the complex relationships between diet, health, daily activity, and diseases. By representing knowledge in a structured and explicit way, the proposed ontology can facilitate the discovery of new associations and hypotheses such as to explore relationship amongst different use case related concepts. Overall, the use of a common ontology in the context of food, eating, and nutrition has the potential to support a wide range of applications, from personalized nutrition to public health policy. As more data becomes available in the context of the FoodFriend project and the different use cases, the ontology here proposed will more likely play an important role in organizing and making sense of this information.

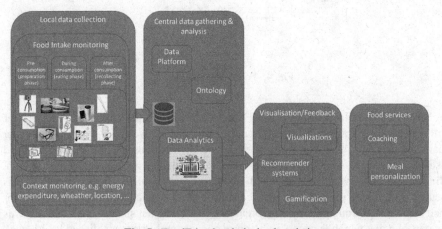

Fig. 5. FoodFriend technical value chain

6 Conclusions

Ontologies play a crucial role in many areas of knowledge representation and data management, including the domain of food intake and nutrition. An ontology is a formal representation of knowledge in a particular domain, defining a set of concepts and the relationships between them. In the context of food intake and nutrition, an ontology can provide a standardized vocabulary for describing food, nutrients, and dietary recommendations, allowing for more accurate and consistent data analysis and decision-making. The use of ontologies in the context of food intake and nutrition has become increasingly important in recent years, as more and more data is being generated by various sources such as wearable devices, mobile applications, and electronic health records. These data sources often use different terminologies and standards for representing food and nutritional information, making it difficult to compare and integrate data from different sources. By using an ontology, it becomes possible to reconcile these different terminologies and create a unified representation of food and nutritional data that can be easily shared and integrated with other systems. This can lead to improved decision-making in areas such as personalized nutrition, clinical research, and public health policy. The FoodFriend project is presented in this work leveraging the use of ontologies in the context of food intake and nutrition to develop a personalized nutrition platform that considers individual preferences, nutritional needs, and health goals. As such, the use of ontologies in this project is essential to create a standardized vocabulary for describing food and nutritional information, which will enable the integration of data from various sources such as food diaries, wearable devices, and clinical records. As a result, the FoodFriend platform will be able to provide personalized dietary recommendations that are tailored to the specific needs and preferences of each user. In this work we have presented the methodological approach undertaken to define a common shared ontology for food intake in the context of the FoodFriend project. By using ontologies to standardize the representation of food and nutritional data, the FoodFriend project is paving the way for a more personalized and effective approach to nutrition and health management.

Acknowledgements. This research work was developed under the project Food Friend—"Autonomous and easy-to-use tool for monitoring of personal food intake and personalised feedback" (ITEA 18032), co-financed by the North Regional Operational Program (NORTE 2020) under the Portugal 2020 and the European Regional Development Fund (ERDF), with the reference NORTE-01–0247-FEDER-047381 and by National Funds through FCT (Fundação para a Ciência e a Tecnologia) under the project UI/DB/00760/2020. The work of Paulo Novais has been supported by FCT–Fundação para a Ciência e Tecnologia within the R&D Units Project Scope: UIDB/0031/2020.

References

1. Bidlack, W.R.: Interrelationships of food, nutrition, diet and health: the National Association of State Universities and Land Grant Colleges White Paper. J. Am. Coll. Nutr. **15**, 422–433 (1996)
2. Seely, S., Freed, D.L., Silverstone, G.A., Rippere, V.: Diet-related diseases: the modern epidemic. Routledge (2022)

3. Jacobson, M.F., Krieger, J., Brownell, K.D.: Potential policy approaches to address diet-related diseases. JAMA **320**, 341–342 (2018)
4. Marreiros, M.G.C.: Agentes de Apoio à Argumentação e Decisão em Grupo. Universidade do Minho (2007)
5. Carneiro, J., Martinho, D., Marreiros, G., Novais, P.: Arguing with behavior influence: a model for web-based group decision support systems. Int. J. Inf. Technol. Decis. Mak. **18**, 517–553 (2019)
6. Carneiro, J., Martinho, D., Alves, P., Conceição, L., Marreiros, G., Novais, P.: A multiple criteria decision analysis framework for dispersed group decision-making contexts. Appl. Sci. **10**, 4614 (2020)
7. Martinho, D., Carneiro, J., Neves, J., Novais, P., Corchado, J., Marreiros, G.: A reinforcement learning approach to improve user achievement of health-related goals. In: EPIA Conference on Artificial Intelligence, pp. 266–277. Springer (2021)
8. Rutishauser, I.H.: Dietary intake measurements. Public Health Nutr. **8**, 1100–1107 (2005)
9. Prochaska, J.O., DiClemente, C.C.: Transtheoretical therapy: Toward a more integrative model of change. Psychotherapy: Theory, Res. Pract. **19**, 276 (1982)
10. Prochaska, J.O., Velicer, W.F.: The transtheoretical model of health behavior change. Am. J. Health Promot. **12**, 38–48 (1997)
11. Griffiths, E.J., Dooley, D.M., Buttigieg, P.L., Hoehndorf, R., Brinkman, F.S., Hsiao, W.W.: FoodON: A global farm-to-fork food ontology. In: ICBO/BioCreative, pp. 1–2 (2016)
12. Dooley, D.M., Griffiths, E.J., Gosal, G.S., Buttigieg, P.L., Hoehndorf, R., Lange, M.C., Schriml, L.M., Brinkman, F.S., Hsiao, W.W.: FoodOn: a harmonized food ontology to increase global food traceability, quality control and data integration. npj Sci. Food **2**, 1–10 (2018)
13. Bezuidenhout, L.: Being fair about the design of FAIR data standards. Digit. Govern.: Res. Pract. **1**, 1–7 (2020)
14. Eftimov, T., Ispirova, G., Finglas, P., Korosec, P., Korousic-Seljak, B.: Quisper ontology learning from personalized dietary web services. In: KEOD, pp. 277–284 (2018)
15. Chivukula, R., Lakshmi, T.J., Sumalatha, S., Reddy, K.L.R.: Ontology based food recommendation. In: IOT with Smart Systems: Proceedings of ICTIS 2021, vol. 2, pp. 751–759. Springer (2022)
16. Martinho, D., Crista, V., Pinto, A., Diniz, J., Freitas, A., Carneiro, J., Marreiros, G.: An architecture for a coaching system to support type 2 diabetic patients. In: International Symposium on Ambient Intelligence, pp. 167–178. Springer (2022)

A System for Animal Health Monitoring and Emotions Detection

David Sec[✉] and Peter Mikulecky

Faculty of Informatics and Management, University of Hradec Kralove,
Hradec Kralove, Czechia
{david.sec,peter.mikulecky}@uhk.cz

Abstract. We are used to seeing the manifestations of various emotions
in humans, but animals also show emotions. A better understanding of
animal emotions is closely related to creating animal welfare. Research in
this direction may impact other ways to improve the lives of domestic and
farm animals or animals in captivity. In addition, better recognition of
negative emotions in animals can help prevent unwanted behaviour and
health problems caused by long-term increased levels of stress or other
negative emotional states. Research projects focused on the emotional
needs of animals can benefit animals and contribute to a more ethical
and sustainable relationship between humans and animals. This article
is focused on the one hand on the description of the system that was
created in the previous related research for monitoring the vital functions
of animals, and on the other hand, especially on the investigation of the
possibilities of how the given system can be used to identify the emotional
states of animals.

Keyword: Animal health, Animal emotions, Monitoring, Detecting,
IoT

1 Introduction

Much research on the positive psychology of animals and pets has been proposed
as a reaction to increase animals' welfare and help detect abnormal behaviours in
their everyday life, which may indicate stress or illness. For these purposes, a data
collection and algorithms system was developed and proposed to detect these
abnormalities, which could indicate an underlying medical condition requiring
attention. This information could also be used to adjust an animal's living conditions, diet, or exercise routine to improve its overall well-being. In addition,
by monitoring the vital functions of animals, it is also possible to determine or
estimate the emotions that the monitored animal feels in a given state. Evaluation algorithms were discovered in the System for Detailed Monitoring of Dog's
Vital Functions [27]. This system was operated with the coordination of local Vet
stations, and more than 900 GB of data was collected from 35 animals, primarily dogs, 30, and 5 cats. Overall, the System for Detailed Monitoring of Dog's

N. Moniz et al. (Eds.): EPIA 2023, LNAI 14115, pp. 41–52, 2023.
https://doi.org/10.1007/978-3-031-49008-8_4

Vital Functions has been essential in advancing our understanding of animal behaviour and well-being. Further research and development can revolutionise how we care for and interact with animal companions. This work aims to show that the created system can, in addition to monitoring and evaluating the vital functions of animals (especially dogs), also be used to determine or estimate the emotions that the animal feels at a given moment, which can also help to understand its condition better and direct its care.

A better understanding of animal emotions can improve further research on animal welfare. It can also identify other ways to improve the lives of home and farm animals or captivity animals. Additionally, better recognition of negative emotions in animals can help prevent undesirable behaviour and health issues caused by long-term increased stress levels or other negative emotional states. A better understanding of animal emotion can also lead to improved quality of products produced by farm animals. One of the essential benefits of emotion recognition is that society increasingly recognises ethical aspects. Animal welfare regulations and laws have been developed in previous years due to unethical mass production in agriculture. More studies focused on the emotional needs of animals can benefit the animals and contribute to a more ethical and sustainable relationship between humans and animals.

2   Related Works

Detecting animals' emotions is a subject of ongoing research in animal behaviour and cognitive science. While animals cannot communicate their emotions as humans do, they display observable behaviours and physiological changes that suggest emotional states (see, e.g., [2,4,8,20,24,25] or [26]. For example, dogs wag their tails when happy, and their body language indicates whether they're confident or fearful. Cats may purr when content, and their pupils dilate in response to certain emotions. Similarly, primates may use facial expressions and vocalizations to convey their emotions.

According to [2], many animals experience in their lives quite often emotions such as joy, fear, love, despair, and grief. It means these emotions are not unique to humans and are considered universal across species. However, as [8] stressed, different species may express emotions differently, making it challenging to develop a universal approach. Paul and her colleagues [26] study the similarities and differences in emotional experiences between humans and animals and discuss the neural correlates and subjective aspects of emotion. The authors note that while there are many similarities in the primary dynamic systems of humans and animals, we cannot make confident comparisons between humans and animals in the critical domain of conscious affect.

According to [3], evidence suggests that many animals experience emotions similar to humans. Research has shown that animals have complex nervous systems and brain structures that are involved in processing emotions. Various studies have shown that animals can exhibit a range of emotions, such as joy, fear, anger, sadness, and even empathy. However, as [22] stressed, researchers should remember that if they translate from human emotional concepts, they risk missing out on emotional states that other species may have, but humans do not.

Various methods for studying the neural correlates of emotion in humans and animals are used, including neuroimaging techniques such as fMRI and PET scans and electrophysiological methods such as EEG and single-unit recordings. An overview of current methodologies for studying animal emotion, including those based on behaviour, cognition, and physiology, is presented by Kremer [20]. The authors emphasized that the study of animal emotion poses several challenges, such as difficulty directly assessing emotional experiences in non-verbal beings and the need to understand how different animal species experience emotions. Currently, technology for monitoring the health status of farm animals is developing considerably, and research into technologies for monitoring their emotions is gaining importance. A whole series of articles provides information on systems for automatic monitoring of the condition of farm animals, which gradually includes monitoring their vital functions and changes in their weight and other indicators of their overall well-being. Here are some examples of sophisticated systems built for this purpose.

According to [15], three main categories of smart technologies are used in animal welfare: wearable devices, environmental sensors, and video or image analysis [13]. Wearable devices are used in animal welfare to track and monitor animals' behaviour, health, and location. Environmental sensors are used in animal welfare to monitor and control the environment of animals, and video and image analysis is used for visual analysis of various expressions of emotions in animals to identify or distinguish these expressions.

The review [16], devoted to recent advancements in the architecture of systems for animal healthcare, states quite clearly that for the successful deployment of methods for monitoring the health status of animals, the technology of the Internet of Things (IoT) can currently be used well. Implementing IoT in animal healthcare systems can improve animal welfare, increase farming operations productivity, and reduce farmers' costs.

Another useful survey is [18] on various animal health monitoring and tracking techniques using ZigBee module. The ZigBee technology has a low power consumption range of 10–3000 m and can support up to 64000 devices having a distance of 50 m. This makes it an ideal choice for animal health monitoring and tracking. The sensors used in such a system include temperature, heart rate, pulse rate, and respiratory. Systems of this type are very useful in farming applications.

As an example of a pet location monitoring system based on a wireless sensor network, the system described in [1] can be mentioned. Of course, this is not about monitoring the monitored animal's vital functions, but tracking a pet's movement in a locked apartment can sometimes be extremely necessary and can prevent property damage or even the health of the observed animal (e.g. a dog).

We have given only a few examples of systems for monitoring the vital functions of animals and other functional parameters, such as the animal's movement, which are essential both in livestock breeding on farms and, for example, in homes when caring for pets. A couple of further related research results are described. e.g. in [5,7,11,17] and elsewhere. There are already many theoretical works proving the existence of emotions in animals, experimental connection to academic results is only a matter of time. None of them was used for recognizing emotions in monitored animals described in detail. However, it is reasonable to assume such usage, and an early publication in this area is anticipated in the future.

3   Methodology

Many existing pieces of research confirm the correlation between Heart Rate Variability (HRV) and emotions in animals with different approaches [2,8,24,26]. Still, they conclude with similar results that animal emotional changes can lead to measurable changes in HRV. In this research, all requirements for measurement and sensors will be defined to provide reliable and satisfactory results for further data processing.

HRV forms one of the physiological markers used in emotion detection because it's influenced and regulated by the autonomic nervous system (ANS). In ANS, two branches can be identified: the sympathetic nervous system (SNS) and the parasympathetic nervous system (PNS). While The SNS is responsible for the "fight or flight" responses, the second PNS branch is responsible for the "rest and digest" responses. When an animal experiences some vigorous activity like fear or excitement, this change leads to the corresponding action in ANS activity change, which also affects HRV. For example, fearful animals exhibit notably reduced HRV as a result of increased SNS activity. Articles [12,19] refer to those positive emotions usually leading to increased HRV, while negative emotions lead to their decline. Nowadays, many exciting studies have been provided to measure HRV to study emotions, including dogs, cats, and horses. For example, study [21] and many similar studies confirm that HRV can be a valuable indicator of a horse's response to therapy and reflects their emotional state. Conversely, calm and relaxed animals may have higher HRV due to increased PNS activity. Overall, HRV can provide a helpful tool for studying animal emotions and help determine the current state of mind. This technique offers a non-invasive and objective measure of ANS activity that can be beneficial for easy and fast identification of emotional states and evaluation of the effectiveness of interventions to reduce stress and promote animal well-being.

4   System Overview

The proposed solution is designed to monitor the health of animals in veterinary clinics and provides mechanisms for automatic data collection and evaluation based on a concept of edge computing where the system operates in three cooperating layers: a sensor layer, a middle edge layer, and a lower edge layer. The lowest sensor layer is responsible for acquiring the measured data, operating the individual measurement sensors, and sending the data to the higher layers of the system for evaluation and processing, The resulting measurement data is sent to the middle edge layer, where other metadata containing essential information about the type of monitored animal is added and, in some cases, data from different sensors and then processed. The result is a set of values that indicate the animal's current health status, and various responses can be triggered, such as displaying a warning on a monitor, sending a message to a veterinarian or animal owner, or executing another predefined action by sending a command to the lower edge layer.

The architecture assumes at least one computing node in each measurement point, like a clinic or farm animal shelter, to provide complete control and management of sensors connected to the local network and enable full communication even in a complete internet connection failure. The system's basic structure is shown in Fig. 1, which provides an overview of the individual system layers and the identification of basic functional units but does not provide specific implementation methods or technologies for system development. Therefore, this section presents only a brief overview of the individual system modules, their function, the data set each layer has, and any dependencies the module may have on other components in the system.

The system's sensor layer can include various sensors for detecting animals' breathing and heartbeat rates, monitoring their movements, and measuring their current weight. The estimated data from these sensors are sent to the higher layers of the system for evaluation and processing. The middle edge layer enriches the raw measured data with metadata containing essential information about the type of monitored animal and, in some cases, data from other sensors. This layer is responsible for processing the data and generating values indicating the animal's health status. The lower edge layer is accountable for executing predefined actions triggered by events, such as displaying a warning on a monitor or sending a message to a veterinarian or animal owner. This sensor layer is also responsible for acquiring the measured data, operating the individual measurement sensors, and sending the data to the higher layers of the system for evaluation and processing. This layer includes various sensors for detecting animals' breathing and heartbeat rates and monitoring their movements. The resulting measurement data is sent to the higher layers of the system, where it is enriched with metadata and processed to generate a set of values indicating the animal's current health status.

The middle edge layer is responsible for processing the data received from the sensor layer and generating a set of values that indicate the animal's current health status. This layer enriches the raw measured data with metadata containing essential information about the type of monitored animal and, in some cases, data from other sensors. The processing algorithms used in this layer are designed to detect and identify patterns and anomalies in the data to accurately assess the animal's health status. This layer's output is a set of values indicating the animal's current health status and potential health risks. The purpose of each computing unit in the second layer is to provide complete control and management of sensors connected to the local network and enable their full communication even without an internet connection. The sensor and middle edge layers form the system's edge, responsible for data acquisition and processing. The lower edge layer forms the system's core and executes predefined actions triggered by events.

The last higher cloud layer provides remote access to the system and allows for data storage, management, and analysis. The system can also operate offline without an internet connection when data are stored locally until a connection is restored. The cloud layer also includes data visualization, reporting, and extended analytics modules.

The system design is based on industry-standard practices. It is expected to provide accurate and reliable monitoring of the health of animals in veterinary clinics or farms or animal home care. This multi-layer modular system architecture is flexible to various sensors. It can also be extended to include additional modules and sensors based on the specific requirements of the veterinary clinic. The system is designed to be scalable, and different computation nodes can be added to handle the increased data load. The system can also be integrated with other healthcare systems to provide a complete view of the animal's health status.

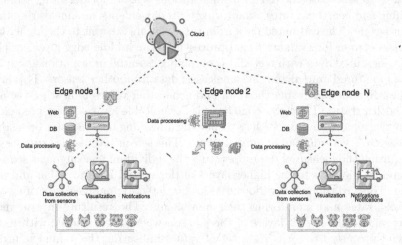

Fig. 1. System overview

5   Experiments

In summary, while methods such as the hollow ECG and chest strap can provide high-precision beat-to-beat heart monitoring and breathing measurement, they are not practical for long-term portable use in dogs. The ballistocardiography method, which measures the mechanical micro-movements induced by cardiac activity, can be measured using sensitive accelerometers or gyroscopes with a high signal-to-noise ratio. This method is especially effective during sleep and can examine the moments preceding seizures in epileptic dogs. To achieve the necessary precision in measurement, minimal sampling frequencies are required, as defined by the Nyquist-Shannon sampling theorem. For accurate beat-to-beat precision, a sampling frequency of at least 100 Hz is necessary to detect every heartbeat with sufficient accuracy (about ten milliseconds). A minimum sampling frequency of 5 Hz is required for heart rate monitoring.

For this purpose, we used the system previously used to detect epileptic seizures in dogs [27]. This system used three-dimensional accelerometers attached to the dog's collar and station with wireless data transfer to the evaluation server. The process for data evaluation will cover all steps from data collection using the custom system to result in interpretation utilizing a monitoring system.

The first part of the system is responsible for data collection. For this purpose, was used raw data collected from the sensor on dog's collar, which was evaluated in real-time into heart rate (HR) and breath rate (BR). For evaluation, ballistocardiography methods (BCG) were used, which detect mechanical movement induced by heartbeat. This method was proven as an effective non-invasive method for the measurement of heart activity of animals [6] and effectively eliminating animals' external movements. External factors like noise, ambient light, skin colour, and coat length cannot negatively affect results. This method requires no electrodes with a conductive gel or local hair removal, so it is suitable for most animals. However, other methods, such as electrocardiography (ECG) or photoplethysmography (PPG), can provide comparable results in some exceptional cases.

The second part of the system is the data processing unit responsible for processing HRV data. This additional procession will remove unexpected artefacts and extract relevant signals from the data. Various methods are available to extract HR/HRV from the measured signal. We decided to use algorithms based on [10,14], which provided an exact determination of heart rate variability, which was necessary for further construction of decision models. To extract variability from the measured signal, autocorrelation was used. Although this method may have some similarities with pattern recognition, it only focuses on the measured signal's time base. It neglects minor variations, providing an excellent solution for our use case. Calculating breathing information can use analogous methods; however, eliminating the cardiac-related part of the signal is crucial using appropriate frequency filters.

Based on the quick spectrogram distribution analysis shown in Fig. 2 that most of the measured frequencies are lower than 50 Hz, which indicates that sampling frequencies of about 100 Hz will be sufficient to detect most of the vital information about heartbeat and breath rate. However, patterns with signals above 100 Hz are also presented in the spectrogram, where they are repeated in regular intervals. These patterns could indicate the presence of noise from the external environment but can also be a result of muscle activity or other anomalies like pain or reaction to medical treatment. Therefore, further research

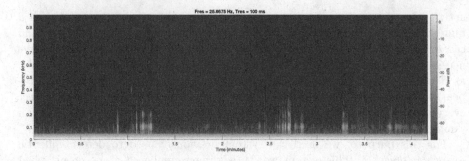

Fig. 2. Frequencies distribution chart

will be conducted to analyze better and interpret these higher-frequency signals to understand the underlying physiological processes. In addition, it will also be essential to consider the potential impact of noise on the accuracy and reliability of the recorded signals and to explore methods for minimizing or mitigating its effects.

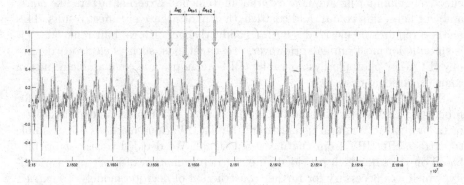

Fig. 3. Heart rate variability

To identify the heart rate in the ECG signal, the local maximum was calculated to detect the R wave in the signal, which is presented as the highest peak in the QRS complex. This R peak has a typical amplitude of about ten mV and can be used to calculate the variation in time intervals between successive heartbeats. These RR intervals are then used to compute various time-domain and frequency-domain measures of HRV, such as the standard deviation of NN intervals (SDNN), mean root square of successive RR interval differences (RMSSD), and power spectral density of HRV in different frequency bands (e.g., low frequency (LF), high frequency (HF), shallow frequency (VLF)). The extracted features should be analyzed to determine the most pertinent parts for emotion detection. This can be done using statistical methods like correlation analysis or feature selection algorithms. Figure 3 describes the R wave peak detection process. Red marks represent individual heart strokes. The measured sample number is described on the X-axis, and on the Y-axis, there is the rate of change of each accelerometer axes.

To train a machine learning model: A machine learning model, such as a support vector machine (SVM), neural network, or decision tree, can be trained using the selected features and corresponding emotion labels. To model training will be used calculated HR variations with notes from medics or pet owners, or dog breeders and, with their cooperation, tried to identify the actual emotions of animals or the scale of emotions. This self-report measurement can be a valuable source of information related to HRV. The second option which can help to detect animal emotions is a measurement of the physiological signs of animals. These measures can involve recording physiological signals associated with emotions like skin conductance and facial or vocal expressions. But these detection techniques are hard to achieve in the home environment and are more suitable for medical facilities or laboratories. The model should be trained on a labelled dataset that includes HRV data and corresponding emotional states. After the machine learning model is trained on a sufficient number of measurements, the function of this model can be tested on a separate dataset to evaluate its performance in detecting emotions. The model's performance can be assessed using various metrics, such as accuracy, sensitivity, specificity, and F1 score. The results of the emotion detection model can be interpreted to gain insights into the relationship between HRV and emotions. The model can also predict an individual's emotional state in real-time based on their HRV data.

6   Results Evaluation

This article has defined the requirements for an emotion monitoring system. We described a real-time data collection and evaluation system, which can calculate measured animals' heart rate, breath rate, and heart rate variability. In our previous research, we estimated 35 animals, primarily dogs and cats, in a medical environment and collected more than 900 GB of medical notes with factual information about animals like animal breeds, age, actual weight, and kind of disease or surgery was the reason for visiting the veterinary facility. On admission, heart rate was always measured using a calibrated medical device, which was recorded in the notes. All these values were later valid for data classification. In the experiments section, we described algorithms to identify heart and breath rates and methods for constructing a machine-learning model.

Unfortunately, because the data was mainly focused on veterinary medicine, creating a model for emotion detection was hard. Even if notes contain detailed information about the current state of health and administered medication, which was helpful for verification of the evaluation algorithm, due to the lack of knowledge about emotions was tough to construct and train a machine learning model that would provide satisfactory results.

Overall this article demonstrates the potential for using heart and breath rates to detect emotions in animals. With further development and adaptation of the existing model, we hope to advance to understand better and identify animals' emotions and their relation to physiological signs, even if we cannot successfully detect them. A couple of related articles confirm a demonstrable correlation between emotions and heart rate variability, and it is worth devoting further research to this topic.

7   Future Works

Since data collection and evaluation modules were tested adequately during this research, in our future work, we would like to focus more on the research on the emotion detection algorithm, which has not yet provided satisfactory results and will require further analysis. There is also an opportunity to investigate pain and muscle activity from measured signals. The system discovered in this article also has the potential for long-term collection of data in traditional human health-care for monitoring emotions and vital functions like heart and breath activity, including anomalies during hospitalization, post-treatment care or monitoring of long-term chronic diseases.

8   Conclusion

We are used to working with our emotions, experiencing them and trying to manage them. Likewise, we often encounter other people's emotions, and we are more or less able to handle them or react to them adequately or less adequately at other times. This area is pretty well covered in human emotion research but not in recognizing and responding to emotions in different types of animals. As Feighelstein [8] points out, research in automatic recognition of emotional states in animals is still considerably undersized. The few publications that touch on the given issue mainly focus on selecting a suitable methodology and then carefully approaching the creation of the application and its practical use. Research in this direction includes [9], where the authors, as perhaps the only ones so far, deal with recognizing the emotional states of dogs, or the work [23], focused on the detection of affective states in macaques, based on distinguishing their facial expressions.

In our research, we developed and described a system aiming to increase animals' welfare and help detect abnormal behaviours in their everyday life, which may indicate stress or illness. The developed system aims to collect data and apply suitable algorithms to detect these abnormalities, which could indicate an underlying medical condition that requires attention. This information could also be used to adjust an animal's living conditions, diet, or exercise routine to improve its overall well-being.

Our experience so far from the practical use of the system in measuring the vital functions of dogs and several cats shows that the approach to recognizing the emotional states of these animals based on evaluating their vital parameters is possible. Still, it requires further experiments in cooperation with veterinarians or breeders of these animals. All this will be the subject of our subsequent research.

Acknowledgments. The research has been partially supported by the Faculty of Informatics and Management UHK specific research project 2107 Integration of Departmental Research Activities and Students' Research Activities Support III. The authors also thank Patrik Urbanik, a doctoral student, for his help in preparing the manuscript.

References

1. Aguirre, E., Lopez-Iturri, P., Azpilicueta, L., Astrain, J.J., Villadangos, J., Santesteban, D., Falcone, F.: Implementation and analysis of a wireless sensor network-based pet location monitoring system for domestic scenarios. Sensors **16**(9), 1384 (2016)
2. Bekoff, M.: Animal emotions: exploring passionate natures. Bioscience **50**(10), 861–870 (2000)
3. Berridge, K.C.: Evolving concepts of emotion and motivation. Front. Psychol. 1647 (2018)
4. Bliss-Moreau, E., Rudebeck, P.H.: Animal models of human mood. Neurosci. Biobehav. Rev. **120**, 574–582 (2021)
5. Cheng, Y.H.: A development architecture for the intelligent animal care and management system based on the internet of things and artificial intelligence. In: 2019 International Conference on Artificial Intelligence in Information and Communication (ICAIIC), pp. 078–081. IEEE (2019)
6. Cimr, D., Studnička, F.: Automatic detection of breathing disorder from ballistocardiography signals. Knowl.-Based Syst. **188**, 104973 (2020)
7. Devi, N.R., Suganya, T., Vignesh, S., Rathish, R.J., Nguyen, T.A., Rajendran, S.: Animal health monitoring using nanosensor networks. In: Nanosensors for Smart Agriculture, pp. 573–608. Elsevier (2022)
8. Feighelstein, M.G.: Towards automatic recognition of emotional states of animals. In: Eight International Conference on Animal-Computer Interaction, pp. 1–4 (2021)
9. Franzoni, V., Milani, A., Biondi, G., Micheli, F.: A preliminary work on dog emotion recognition. In: IEEE/WIC/ACM International Conference on Web Intelligence-Companion Volume, pp. 91–96 (2019)
10. Fujii, T., Nakano, M., Yamashita, K., Konishi, T., Izumi, S., Kawaguchi, H., Yoshimoto, M.: Noise-tolerant instantaneous heart rate and r-peak detection using short-term autocorrelation for wearable healthcare systems. 2013 35th Annual International Conference of the IEEE Engineering in Medicine and Biology Society (EMBC) (2013)
11. Gameil, M., Gaber, T.: Wireless sensor networks-based solutions for cattle health monitoring: a survey. In: Proceedings of the international conference on advanced intelligent systems and informatics 2019, pp. 779–788. Springer (2020)
12. Hachenberger, J., Li, Y.M., Siniatchkin, M., Hermenau, K., Ludyga, S., Lemola, S.: Heart rate variability's association with positive and negative affect in daily life: an experience sampling study with continuous daytime electrocardiography over seven days. Sensors **23**(2), 966 (2023)
13. Hernández-Luquin, F., Escalante, H.J., Villaseñor-Pineda, L., Reyes-Meza, V., Villaseñor-Pineda, L., Pérez-Espinosa, H., Reyes-Meza, V., Escalante, H.J., Gutierrez-Serafín, B.: Dog emotion recognition from images in the wild: Debiw dataset and first results. In: Proceedings of the Ninth International Conference on Animal-Computer Interaction, pp. 1–13 (2022)

14. Holderith, M., Schanze, T.: Cross-correlation based comparison between the conventional 12-lead ECG and an EASI derived 12-lead ECG. Curr. Direct. Biomed. Eng. **4**(1), 621–624 (2018)

15. Jukan, A., Masip-Bruin, X., Amla, N.: Smart computing and sensing technologies for animal welfare: a systematic review. ACM Comput. Surv. (CSUR) **50**(1), 1–27 (2017)

16. Karthick, G., Sridhar, M., Pankajavalli, P.: Internet of things in animal healthcare (iotah): review of recent advancements in architecture, sensing technologies and real-time monitoring. SN Comput. Sci. **1**, 1–16 (2020)

17. Katemboh, E.M., Abdulla, R., Jayapal, V., Selvaperumal, S.K., Ratnadurai, D.: Integrated animal health care using IoT. Int. J. Adv. Sci. Technol. **29**(1), 42–56 (2020)

18. Keertana, P., Vanathi, B., Shanmugam, K.: A survey on various animal health monitoring and tracking techniques. Int. Res. J. Eng. Technol. **4**(2), 533–536 (2017)

19. Kok, B.E., Coffey, K.A., Cohn, M.A., Catalino, L.I., Vacharkulksemsuk, T., Algoe, S.B., Brantley, M., Fredrickson, B.L.: How positive emotions build physical health: perceived positive social connections account for the upward spiral between positive emotions and vagal tone. Psychol. Sci. **24**(7), 1123–1132 (2013)

20. Kremer, L., Holkenborg, S.K., Reimert, I., Bolhuis, J., Webb, L.: The nuts and bolts of animal emotion. Neurosci. Biobehav. Rev. **113**, 273–286 (2020)

21. Kwiatkowska-Stenzel, A., Sowińska, J., Witkowska, D.: The effect of different bedding materials used in stable on horses behavior. J. Equine Vet. **42**, 57–66 (2016)

22. Mendl, M., Neville, V., Paul, E.S.: Bridging the gap: human emotions and animal emotions. Affect. Sci. **3**(4), 703–712 (2022)

23. Morozov, A., Parr, L.A., Gothard, K., Paz, R., Pryluk, R.: Automatic recognition of macaque facial expressions for detection of affective states. Eneuro **8**(6) (2021)

24. Neethirajan, S.: Affective state recognition in livestock-artificial intelligence approaches. Animals **12**(6), 759 (2022)

25. Paul, E.S., Mendl, M.T.: Animal emotion: descriptive and prescriptive definitions and their implications for a comparative perspective. Appl. Anim. Behav. Sci. **205**, 202–209 (2018)

26. Paul, E.S., Sher, S., Tamietto, M., Winkielman, P., Mendl, M.T.: Towards a comparative science of emotion: affect and consciousness in humans and animals. Neurosci. Biobehav. Rev. **108**, 749–770 (2020)

27. Sec, D., Matyska, J., Klimova, B., Cimler, R., Kuhnova, J., Studnicka, F.: System for detailed monitoring of dog's vital functions. In: Computational Collective Intelligence: 10th International Conference, ICCCI 2018, Bristol, UK, September 5–7, 2018, Proceedings, Part I 10, pp. 426–435. Springer (2018)

Ethics and Responsibility in Artificial Intelligence

A Three-Way Knot: Privacy, Fairness, and Predictive Performance Dynamics

Tânia Carvalho[1]([✉])[iD], Nuno Moniz[2][iD], and Luís Antunes[1,3][iD]

[1] Faculty of Sciences, University of Porto, Porto, Portugal
tania.carvalho@fc.up.pt
[2] Lucy Family Institute for Data & Society, University of Notre Dame, Indiana, USA
[3] TekPrivacy, Porto, Portugal

Abstract. As the frontier of machine learning applications moves further into human interaction, multiple concerns arise regarding automated decision-making. Two of the most critical issues are fairness and data privacy. On the one hand, one must guarantee that automated decisions are not biased against certain groups, especially those unprotected or marginalized. On the other hand, one must ensure that the use of personal information fully abides by privacy regulations and that user identities are kept safe. The balance between privacy, fairness, and predictive performance is complex. However, despite their potential societal impact, we still demonstrate a poor understanding of the dynamics between these optimization vectors. In this paper, we study this three-way tension and how the optimization of each vector impacts others, aiming to inform the future development of safe applications. In light of claims that predictive performance and fairness can be jointly optimized, we find this is only possible at the expense of data privacy. Overall, experimental results show that one of the vectors will be penalized regardless of which of the three we optimize. Nonetheless, we find promising avenues for future work in joint optimization solutions, where smaller trade-offs are observed between the three vectors.

Keywords: Synthetic data · Privacy · Fairness · Predictive performance

1 Introduction

Growing privacy concerns have led to several approaches aiming to preserve the confidentiality of individuals' information. Among the most prevalent approaches to privacy preservation is the process of data synthesis, which mimics the original data while maintaining its global properties [8]. The creation of synthetic data offers a promising avenue, as it generates a protected version of the original data that can be publicly available. Usually, approaches for data synthetization include sampling methods or deep learning-based models [19]. However, despite

N. Moniz et al. (Eds.): EPIA 2023, LNAI 14115, pp. 55–66, 2023.
https://doi.org/10.1007/978-3-031-49008-8_5

significant progress in recent years, the challenge of synthetic data generation methods in preserving the confidentiality of personal data and generating unbiased and accurate machine learning models remains an ongoing area of research and development. The interplay between privacy, fairness, and predictive performance in synthetic data generation is a fundamental issue that requires attention to facilitate the responsible utilization of data in machine learning applications.

This paper explores the dynamics between preserving privacy and improving fairness and predictive performance in machine learning models. First, to address privacy concerns, we apply privacy-preserving techniques for secure data publication, particularly data synthetization methods, where each synthetic data variant is evaluated concerning its re-identification risk. Then, in the evaluation process for fairness and predictive performance, models are trained and optimized for each synthetic data variant using fairness-agnostic (standard machine learning algorithms) and fairness-aware algorithms. Our main goal is to discover the dynamics of optimizing each vector. The experiments conducted in this study use some of the most popular data sets in FAccT[1] research [11,23].

The main conclusions of this work indicate that *(1)* solutions that achieve a balance between predictive performance and fairness are only possible at the expense of data privacy, and *(2)* generally, optimizing any of the vectors will impact at least another one, but *(3)* three-way optimization demonstrates promise for future research.

The remainder of the paper is organized as follows. Section 2 includes some preliminaries on privacy and fairness in machine learning and overviews of related work on this topic. The experimental study is described in Sect. 3, including a description of data, methods, and results. Section 4 discusses such results. Conclusions are provided in Sect. 5.

2   Background

Existing literature outlines the key concepts of identifying and measuring privacy and algorithmic fairness in machine learning applications [10,24]. In the subsequent sections, we provide concise definitions of relevant background knowledge.

2.1   Privacy

Releasing or sharing data about individuals often implies de-identifying personal information for privacy preservation [8,30]. Conventional de-identification approaches involve applying privacy-preserving techniques such as generalization or suppression to reduce data granularity or introduce noise to the data causing distortion. These transformations are usually applied to a set of quasi-identifiers, i.e., attributes that, when combined, generate a unique signature that may lead to re-identification (e.g., date of birth, gender, profession, and ethnic group), as well as sensitive attributes like religion and sexual orientation which are highly

---

[1] Acronym for Fairness, Accountability, and Transparency.

critical. In the case of synthetic data generation, de-identification is generally performed for all attributes and instances to capture the overall characteristics, creating a new data set through generative models [19].

Even in a de-identified data set, it is crucial to evaluate the privacy risks as it is challenging to know who the intruder is or what information he may possess. The privacy measures depend on the types of disclosure [8]. Identity disclosure is one of the most critical for data privacy. k-anonymity [28] is the most popular measure indicating how many individuals share the same information concerning a set of quasi-identifiers, defined according to assumptions on an intruder's background knowledge. A record is unique when $k = 1$, meaning an intruder can single it out. Additionally, linking records between different data sets is an approach that allows measuring the probability of re-identification through different data sets. Record linkage [18] is also widely used but focuses on the ability to link records, usually between de-identified data and the original.

2.2   Fairness

Diverse approaches to handling fairness address different parts of the model life-cycle. Several methods to enhance fairness have been proposed in the literature, commonly classified into three categories: pre-processing, in-processing, and post-processing. We focus on in-processing methods which involve modifying the machine learning models during training to remove discrimination by incorporating changes into the objective function or imposing a constraint. Adversarial debiasing [17] and exponentiated gradient [1] are prevalent algorithms.

In classification tasks, the most commonly used measures of group fairness include demographic parity [16] and equalized odds [20]. Demographic parity, also known as statistical parity [16], compares the difference in predicted outcome $\hat{Y}$ between any two groups, $|P[\hat{Y} = 1|S = 1] - P[\hat{Y} = 1|S \neq 1]| \leq \epsilon$. Better fairness is achieved with a lower demographic parity value, indicating more similar acceptance rates. A limitation of this measure is that a highly accurate classifier may be unfair if the proportions of actual positive outcomes vary significantly between groups. Therefore, the equalized odds measure was proposed to overcome such limitation [20]. This measure computes the difference between the false positive rates $|P[\hat{Y} = 1|S = 1, Y = 0] - P[\hat{Y} = 1|S \neq 1, Y = 0]| \leq \epsilon$, and the difference between the true positive rates of two groups $|P[\hat{Y} = 1|S = 1, Y = 1] - P[\hat{Y} = 1|S \neq 1, Y = 1]| \leq \epsilon$, where smaller differences between groups indicate better fairness.

2.3   Related Work

The increasing interest in synthetic data generation has led to studies on how this type of data protects the individual's privacy and reflects the inherent bias and predictive performance in machine learning applications.

Bhanot et al. [5] proved the presence of unfairness in generated synthetic data sets and introduced two fairness metrics for time series, emphasizing the importance of evaluating fairness at each evaluation step in the synthetic data generation. Additionally, Chang and Shokri [12] have shown that fair algorithms tend to memorize data from the under-represented subgroups, increasing the model's information leakage about unprivileged groups. Their experiments evaluate how and why fair models leak information on synthetic train data.

Machine learning models' efficiency and fairness have also been investigated using synthetic data generated by differentially private GANs. The experiments conducted by Cheng et al. [14] show that integrating differential privacy does not give rise to discrimination during data generation in subsequent classification models. Still, it unfairly amplifies the influence of majority subgroups. Also, the authors demonstrate that differential privacy reduces the quality of the images generated from the GANs and, consequently, the utility in downstream tasks. Recently, Bullwinkel et al. [7] analyzed the interplay between loss of privacy and fairness in the context of models trained on differentially private synthetic data. The experiments focused on binary classification, showing that a notable proportion of the synthesizers studied deteriorated fairness.

The potential of synthetic data in providing privacy-preserving solutions for several data-related challenges and their important role in striving for fairness in machine learning applications prompted our experiments to center around synthetic data generation. Although there are exciting and promising approaches for synthetic data generation incorporating differential privacy, the current state of software is still in its early stages, and only DP-CGANS [29] is a viable option for our experiments. However, this tool is considerably time-consuming, and due to this limitation, we do not account for differentially private synthetic data.

Privacy-protected data sets have not yet been analyzed, considering the three vectors of privacy, fairness, and predictive performance. Especially, conclusions about the impact of maximizing each of the vectors remain unclear. Moreover, we focus on the risk of re-identification in privacy-protected data sets rather than membership attacks on predictive models (e.g. [12])—identity disclosure can cause severe consequences for individuals and organizations.

3   Experimental Study

In this section, we provide a thorough experimental study focused on the impact of optimization processes for privacy, fairness, and predictive performance in machine learning. We aim to answer the following research questions. What are the impacts associated with optimizing a specific vector (**RQ1**), what are the impacts in prioritizing the remaining vectors (optimization paths) (**RQ2**), and is there a solution capable of providing a balance between the three vectors (**RQ3**)? We describe our experimental methodology in the following sections, briefly describing the data used, methods, and evaluation procedures, followed by presenting experimental results.

3.1   Data

In this section, we provide an overview of the commonly used data sets for fairness-aware machine learning [11,23]. A general description of the main characteristics of these data sets is provided in Table 1. The number of attributes and instances were obtained after the cleaning, such as missing data removal. The selection for the protected attributes and quasi-identifiers adheres to previous literature. As fairness measures require protected attributes in a binary form, categorical attributes are grouped; for instance, race={caucasian, african-american, hispanic, other} is transformed to race={white, non-white}, and continuous attributes are discretized like age={< 25, >= 25}. Such discretization is also defined in the literature and is determined based on privileged and unprivileged groups.

Table 1. General description of the used data sets in the experimental study.

Dataset	# Instances	# Attributes	Domain	Quasi-identifiers	Protected attributes
Adult	48.842	15	Finance	Education, age, gender, race, occupation, native country	Gender, race, age
German Credit	1.000	22	Finance	Purpose, years of employment, age, years of residence, job, gender, foreign worker	Gender, age
Bank marketing	45.211	17	Finance	Age, job, marital, education, housing	Age, marital
Credit card clients	30.000	24	Finance	Gender, education, marriage, age	Gender, marriage, education
COMPAS	6.172	34	Criminology	Gender, age, race, recidivism	Gender, race
Heart disease	1.025	14	Healthcare	Gender, age, heart rate, chest pain	Gender
Ricci	118	6	Social	Position, race, combined score	Race

3.2 Methods

In this section, we describe the *(i)* methods used in generating privacy-preserving data variants; *(ii)* the learning algorithms and respective hyper-parametrization optimization details employed to generate models, which include standard machine learning (fairness-agnostic) and fairness-aware algorithms; followed by *(iii)* evaluation metrics used and *(iv)* the overall experimental methodology.

Synthetic Data Variants The synthetic data variants are obtained using two different approaches, PrivateSMOTE and deep learning-based solutions. PrivateSMOTE [9] generates synthetic cases for highest-risk instances (i.e., single-out) based on randomly weighted interpolation of nearest neighbors. We apply PrivateSMOTE with $ratio \in \{1, 2, 3\}$, $knn \in \{1, 3, 5\}$ and $\epsilon \in \{0.1, 0.3, 0.5\}$, where ϵ is the amount of added noise. On the other hand, deep learning-based solutions rely on generative models. For comparison purposes, we only synthesize the single-out instances using conditional sampling. Such instances and all attributes are replaced with new cases. We leverage the Python SDV package [25] to create different deep-learning variants for this aim. The experiments include Copula GAN, TVAE, and CTGAN with the following parameters: $epochs \in \{100, 200\}$, $batch\_size \in \{50, 100\}$ and $embedding\_dim \in \{12, 64\}$. Each set of parameters produces a different synthetic data variant.

Learning Algorithms There are two types of algorithms used in our experimental evaluation: standard machine learning algorithms (fairness-agnostic) and fairness-aware algorithms. Concerning the former, we leverage three classification algorithms through *Scikit-learn* [26] toolkit: Random Forest [21], XGBoost [13] and Logistic Regression [2]. Final models for each algorithm are chosen based on a 2*5-fold cross-validation estimation of evaluation scores for models based on a grid search method. For fairness mitigation, we use FairMask [27] and exponentiated gradient from Fairlearn [6]. Table 2 summarizes this information.

Table 2. Learning algorithms and respective hyper-parameter grid used in the experimental study.

Algorithm	Parameters
Random Forest	$n\_estimators \in \{100, 250, 500\}$ $max\_depth \in \{4, 7, 10\}$
Boosting	$n\_estimators \in \{100, 250, 500\}$ $max\_depth \in \{4, 7, 10\}$ $learning\_rate \in \{0.1, 0.01\}$
Logistic Regression	$C \in \{0.001, 1, 10000\}$ $max\_iter \in \{10e^5, 10e^6\}$

Evaluation All synthetic data variants are evaluated in terms of re-identification risk, fairness, and predictive performance.

To assess the potential of re-identification, we use the *Python Record Linkage Toolkit* [15] to compare each variant with the original considering a specified set of quasi-identifiers. In this study, we focus on exact matches, where all values for the quasi-identifiers match, resulting in a 100% likelihood of re-identification. Such comparisons are carried out in the sets of single-out instances. In the learning phase, we use equalized odds difference for fairness evaluation and Accuracy for predictive performance concerning the testing data.

Experimental Methodology For conciseness, our experimental methodology is illustrated in Fig. 1. The experimental study begins by splitting each original data into training and test sets corresponding to 80% and 20%, respectively. Then, we generate several synthetic data variants using the training data set for privacy constraints, in which re-identification risk is evaluated by comparing each synthetic data variant to the original data. Then, models are generated using both fairness-agnostic and fairness-aware algorithms. After the training phase, out-of-sample predictive performance and fairness of the models are measured.

3.3   Experimental Results

The following set of results refers to the probability of each optimized vector winning or losing when compared to the remaining vectors. We construct optimization paths, as demonstrated in Fig. 2, to analyze the relevance of prioritizing a specific vector. To calculate the probabilities, we select the best models estimated via cross-validation in out-of-sample. Each solution, i.e., privacy-protected data variant outcome, is compared to a baseline. For visual purposes, "A@", "FM@" and "FL@" refers to the fairness-agnostic and fairness-aware algorithms, namely, Agnostic, FairMask, and Fairlearn.

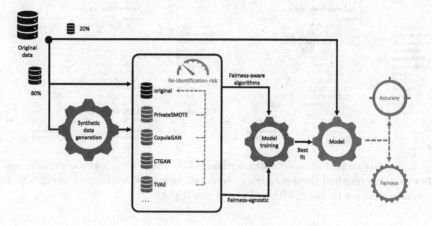

Fig. 1. Workflow of our experimental methodology

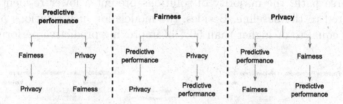

Fig. 2. Optimization paths for each vector

Predictive performance vector. The left image in Fig. 3 shows the probabilities of each solution's fairness winning and losing against the baseline as well as the probabilities of privacy winning and losing, while the right image shows the reverse path. Such a baseline corresponds to the best solution in terms of predictive performance for each data set. Note that the probabilities refer to the percentage of the cases in the total number of privacy-protected data variants for each fairness-agnostic and fairness-aware algorithms. Results show that models optimized towards predictive performance demonstrate a balanced probability of winning or losing w.r.t. fairness. Also, when the models outperform the baseline, the solutions tend to be more private, however, the opposite is not necessarily true: the reverse path shows that except for PrivateSMOTE, all synthetic approaches outperform the baseline in terms of privacy. Therefore, optimizing predictive performance results in losses for privacy but it is possible to attain fairer models to a certain extent. Additionally, we observe that Fairlearn leads to fairer and more private solutions.

Fairness vector. Concerning this vector, Fig. 4 illustrates the probabilities of each solution's predictive performance winning or losing compared to the baseline (best solution in terms of equalized odds) with the respective probabilities of privacy winning and vice-versa. A notable outcome is the outperformed solutions

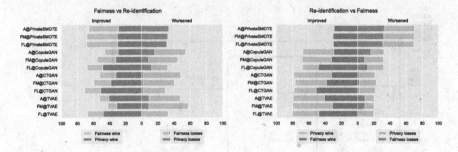

Fig. 3. Predictive performance optimization paths. Total wins/losses comparing each solution to the baseline (best solution in terms of Accuracy) for fairness along with the respective wins for privacy (left) and vice-versa (right)

in terms of predictive performance with the same probability of privacy wins. In the reverse path, the majority of solutions present a lower re-identification risk compared to the baseline. Besides, the models for such solutions present a probability equal to or higher than 50% of improving predictive performance.

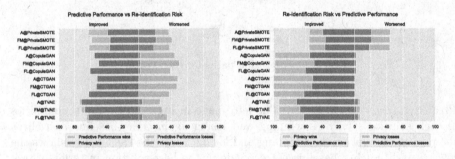

Fig. 4. Fairness optimization paths. Total wins/losses comparing each solution to the baseline (best solution in terms of equalized odds) for predictive performance along with the respective wins for privacy (left) and vice-versa (right)

Privacy vector. Lastly, Fig. 5 illustrates the total wins and losses of each solution's predictive performance compared to the baseline (best solution in terms of re-identification risk) along with the respective probabilities of fairness winning and vice-versa. In this scenario, the baseline has a probability greater than 50% of outperforming the remaining solutions in w.r.t. predictive performance. On the other hand, when we prioritize fairness, the baseline tends to lose.

All vectors optimized. In the previous set of results, we show the impacts of optimizing a single vector. However, an optimal solution should maintain a balance across all the vectors. Therefore, we aim to analyze to what extent is possible to obtain such a balance. Figure 6 provides a comparison reporting the statistical

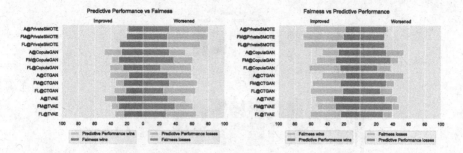

Fig. 5. Privacy optimization paths. Total wins/losses comparing each solution to the baseline (best solution in terms of re-identification risk) for predictive performance, and respective wins for fairness (left) and vice-versa (right)

tests using the Bayes Sign Test [3,4] with a ROPE interval of $[-1\%, 1\%]$ to evaluate the statistical significance concerning the percentage difference for each vector optimization. This percentage is defined as $\frac{R_a - R_b}{R_b} * 100$ where R_a is the solution under comparison and R_b is the baseline. ROPE (Region of Practical Equivalence) [22] is used to specify the probability of the difference of values being inside a specific interval as having practically no effect. If the percentage difference is within the specified range, they are of practical equivalence (draw), and if the percentage difference is less than -1%, b outperforms solution a (lose). Such a baseline corresponds to the best solutions for each vector while the solutions under comparison correspond to the ones with the best average rank across the three vectors for each data set.

Figure 6 shows the comparisons for each synthetic approach between the optimal solutions for each vector and the solutions with the best-averaged rank across all vectors. Concerning predictive performance, the average rank solutions' models are, for the most part, capable of providing practical equivalence to the optimal solutions of this vector with a probability higher than 50%. Although the privacy vector presents higher losses for some solutions, A@CopulaGAN and A@CTGAN stand out with a probability of drawing to the baseline greater than 80%. However, the models for these solutions are less fair. Additionally, such an outcome shows that it may be possible to obtain a balance between the three vectors, through TVAE-based solutions.

4 Discussion

Given the results of the experimental evaluation presented above, conclusions imply that developing safe machine learning applications—one that protects individual data privacy and prevents disparate treatment with a negative impact on protected groups, may face even greater challenges than currently construed. This leads to questions that require attention in future work:

- **(RQ1)** A notable finding for future work is the relationship between the different optimization vectors. Figures 3 and 4, show that many solutions

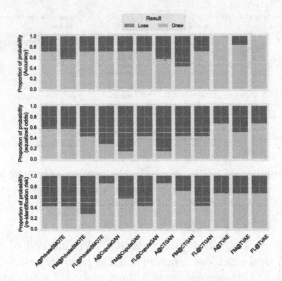

Fig. 6. Proportion of probability for each candidate solution drawing or losing significantly against the solution with the best-averaged rank between the three vectors, according to the Bayes Sign Test

tested and which do not improve their respective optimization vector exhibit a considerable ability to reduce re-identification risk when privacy is the priority in the optimization path. Also, we observe in Figs. 3 and 5 that optimizing predictive performance or privacy shows a similar impact on fairness.

- **(RQ2)** Although it is unlikely to obtain a solution with practically no losses, the optimization paths allow us to find which vector should be prioritized to prevent higher losses. When optimizing privacy (Fig. 5), and prioritizing predictive performance, we observe that the majority of the solutions maintain the ability to produce accurate models. Such an outcome shows that it is possible to obtain private solutions with minimal impact on predictive performance but this comes at the expense of fairness.
- **(RQ3)** Nevertheless, finding a solution that balances the three vectors is crucial. However, as shown in Fig. 6, it is, in general, very improbable to achieve a good balance between all vectors. Despite our experiments demonstrating that TVAE-based solutions are, to a certain degree, capable of obtaining such a balance, that does not happen for the remaining approaches.

5   Conclusion

This paper thoroughly analyzes the dynamics between privacy, fairness, and predictive performance by assessing the impact of optimizing a single vector on the remaining vectors. We generate multiple privacy-protected data variants from the original data using synthetization methods and evaluate each variant in terms of privacy w.r.t re-identification risk but also fairness and predictive performance for both fairness-agnostic and fairness-aware algorithms.

The main conclusions indicate that in single vector optimization, the remaining vectors will suffer from losses. Nevertheless, optimizing privacy and prioritizing predictive performance allows for obtaining private solutions while maintaining the predictive performance intact. However, it is difficult to navigate a balance between the three vectors. These results highlight the importance of further developments in discriminatory bias when the goal is to release or share personal information. For future work, we plan to analyze the effects of data preparation on fairness as the presence of inherent biases in a data set may pose challenges in achieving fairer models [31]. The Python code and data necessary to replicate the results shown in this paper are available at *https://tinyurl.com/yku3s7du*.

References

1. Agarwal, A., Beygelzimer, A., Dudík, M., Langford, J., Wallach, H.: A reductions approach to fair classification. In: International Conference on Machine Learning, pp. 60–69. PMLR (2018)
2. Agresti, A.: An Introduction To Categorical Data Analysis. Wiley (1996)
3. Benavoli, A., Mangili, F., Corani, G., Zaffalon, M., Ruggeri, F.: A bayesian wilcoxon signed-rank test based on the dirichlet process. In: Proceedings of the 31st International Conference on International Conference on Machine Learning - Volume 32, p. II-1026–II-1034. ICML'14, JMLR.org (2014)
4. Benavoli, A., Corani, G., Demšar, J., Zaffalon, M.: Time for a change: a tutorial for comparing multiple classifiers through bayesian analysis. J. Mach. Learn. Res. **18**(1), 2653–2688 (2017)
5. Bhanot, K., Qi, M., Erickson, J.S., Guyon, I., Bennett, K.P.: The problem of fairness in synthetic healthcare data. Entropy **23**(9), 1165 (2021)
6. Bird, S., Dudík, M., Edgar, R., Horn, B., Lutz, R., Milan, V., Sameki, M., Wallach, H., Walker, K.: Fairlearn: A toolkit for assessing and improving fairness in ai. Microsoft, Tech. Rep. MSR-TR-2020-32 (2020)
7. Bullwinkel, B., Grabarz, K., Ke, L., Gong, S., Tanner, C., Allen, J.: Evaluating the fairness impact of differentially private synthetic data (2022). arXiv:2205.04321
8. Carvalho, T., Moniz, N., Faria, P., Antunes, L.: Survey on privacy-preserving techniques for microdata publication. ACM Comput. Surv. (2023). https://doi.org/10.1145/3588765, just Accepted
9. Carvalho, T., Moniz, N., Faria, P., Antunes, L., Chawla, N.: Privacy-preserving data synthetisation for secure information sharing (2022). arXiv:2212.00484
10. Caton, S., Haas, C.: Fairness in machine learning: A survey (2020). arXiv:2010.04053
11. Chakraborty, J., Majumder, S., Menzies, T.: Bias in machine learning software: why? how? what to do? In: Proceedings of the 29th ACM Joint Meeting on European Software Engineering Conference and Symposium on the Foundations of Software Engineering, pp. 429–440 (2021)
12. Chang, H., Shokri, R.: On the privacy risks of algorithmic fairness. In: 2021 IEEE European Symposium on Security and Privacy (EuroS&P). IEEE (2021)
13. Chen, T., Guestrin, C.: Xgboost: A scalable tree boosting system. In: Krishnapuram, B., Shah, M., Smola, A.J., Aggarwal, C.C., Shen, D., Rastogi, R. (eds.)

Proceedings of the 22nd ACM SIGKDD International Conference on Knowledge Discovery and Data Mining, San Francisco, CA, USA, August 13–17, 2016, pp. 785–794. ACM (2016). https://doi.org/10.1145/2939672.2939785

14. Cheng, V., Suriyakumar, V.M., Dullerud, N., Joshi, S., Ghassemi, M.: Can you fake it until you make it? impacts of differentially private synthetic data on downstream classification fairness. In: Proceedings of the 2021 ACM Conference on Fairness, Accountability, and Transparency, pp. 149–160 (2021)

15. De Bruin, J.: Python Record Linkage Toolkit: A toolkit for record linkage and duplicate detection in Python. Zenodo (2019)

16. Dwork, C., Hardt, M., Pitassi, T., Reingold, O., Zemel, R.: Fairness through awareness. In: Proceedings of the 3rd Innovations in Theoretical Computer Science Conference, pp. 214–226 (2012)

17. Elazar, Y., Goldberg, Y.: Adversarial removal of demographic attributes from text data (2018). arXiv:1808.06640

18. Fellegi, I.P., Sunter, A.B.: A theory for record linkage. J. Am. Stat. Assoc. **64**(328), 1183–1210 (1969)

19. Figueira, A., Vaz, B.: Survey on synthetic data generation, evaluation methods and gans. Mathematics **10**(15), 2733 (2022)

20. Hardt, M., Price, E., Srebro, N.: Equality of opportunity in supervised learning. Advances in Neural Information Processing Systems 29 (2016)

21. Ho, T.K.: The random subspace method for constructing decision forests. IEEE Trans. Pattern Anal. Mach. Intell. **20**(8), 832–844 (1998)

22. Kruschke, J., Liddell, T.: The bayesian new statistics: Two historical trends converge. ssrn electron. j (2015)

23. Le Quy, T., Roy, A., Iosifidis, V., Zhang, W., Ntoutsi, E.: A survey on datasets for fairness-aware machine learning. Wiley Interdisciplinary Reviews: Data Mining and Knowledge Discovery, p. e1452 (2022)

24. Mehrabi, N., Morstatter, F., Saxena, N., Lerman, K., Galstyan, A.: A survey on bias and fairness in machine learning. ACM Comput. Surv. (CSUR) **54**(6), 1–35 (2021)

25. Patki, N., Wedge, R., Veeramachaneni, K.: The synthetic data vault. In: 2016 IEEE International Conference on Data Science and Advanced Analytics (DSAA), pp. 399–410 (2016). https://doi.org/10.1109/DSAA.2016.49

26. Pedregosa, F., Varoquaux, G., Gramfort, A., Michel, V., Thirion, B., Grisel, O., Blondel, M., Prettenhofer, P., Weiss, R., Dubourg, V., et al.: Scikit-learn: Machine learning in python. J. Mach. Learn. Res. **12**, 2825–2830 (2011)

27. Peng, K., Chakraborty, J., Menzies, T.: Fairmask: Better fairness via model-based rebalancing of protected attributes. IEEE Trans. Softw. Eng. (2022)

28. Samarati, P.: Protecting respondents identities in microdata release. IEEE Trans. Knowl. Data Eng. **13**(6), 1010–1027 (2001)

29. Sun, C., van Soest, J., Dumontier, M.: Improving correlation capture in generating imbalanced data using differentially private conditional gans (2022). arXiv:2206.13787

30. Torra, V.: Guide to Data Privacy: Models, Technologies. Solutions. Springer Nature (2022)

31. Valentim, I., Lourenço, N., Antunes, N.: The impact of data preparation on the fairness of software systems. In: 2019 IEEE 30th International Symposium on Software Reliability Engineering (ISSRE), pp. 391–401. IEEE (2019)

A Maturity Model for Industries and Organizations of All Types to Adopt Responsible AI—Preliminary Results

Rui Miguel Frazão Dias Ferreira[1](✉), António Grilo[2] (iD), and Maria João Maia[3] (iD)

[1] FCT NOVA School of Science and Technology, 2829-516 Caparica, Portugal
rmf.ferreira@campus.fct.unl.pt
[2] FCT NOVA School of Science and Technology, 2829-516 Caparica, Portugal
antonio.grilo@fct.unl.pt
[3] Karlsruhe Institute of Technology (KIT), Karlstrasse 11, 76133 Karlsruhe, Germany
maria.maia@kit.edu

Abstract. Competition in Artificial Intelligence (AI) technologies is at its fiercest, pushing companies to move fast and sometimes cut corners regarding the risks to human rights and other societal impacts. Without simple methodologies and widely accepted instruments is hard for an organization to adopt a safe pace on how to develop and deploy AI in a trustworthy way. This paper presents a Maturity Model for Responsible AI, inspired in the EU Ethics Guidelines for Trustworthy AI and other principles and codes of conduct. The core component is a self-assessment tool that generates a roadmap for organizations to improve their approach to AI related development, enabling a positive effect in their business value. It includes requirements to achieve Trustworthy AI, and the methods and key practices that will enable the principles outlined. The result is a consistent and horizontal approach to all industries and functions, taking into consideration that a simple and generic Maturity Model, specific for Responsible AI, is still not available. The model presented in this paper is purposed to fill that gap. The model was pre-tested in two organizations, improved and pre-tested again. Results are presented in this paper. The next phase is to apply the model in several other organizations, and conduct interviews at different hierarchical levels and promote case study discussions. Its final version is planned to be published at the end of 2023.

Keywords: Responsible artificial intelligence · Artificial intelligence regulation · Maturity model · Ethical · Legal and social issues · Responsible research and innovation

N. Moniz et al. (Eds.): EPIA 2023, LNAI 14115, pp. 67–78, 2023.
https://doi.org/10.1007/978-3-031-49008-8_6

1 Introduction

1.1 Context and Justification

The past several decades have seen information technology revolutionise many different sectors, bringing countless achievements for our life.

In particular, AI technologies have great potential to disrupt most of the human life experience, bringing huge benefits in areas such as climate action and sustainable infrastructure, health and well-being, and quality education and digital transformation. At the same time, AI may introduce significant risks to human rights and other societal impacts, such as illegal and unethical identification and tracking of individuals, enabled citizen scoring in violation of fundamental rights, and lethal autonomous weapon systems (European Commission, Ethics Guidelines for Trustworthy AI, 2019).

AI technologies refer to solutions, algorithms, platforms, frameworks and machine learning data and training services. In a simpler way, OECD defines an AI system as a machine-based system that can, for a given set of human defined objectives, make predictions, recommendations, or decisions influencing real or virtual environments (OECD, Digital Economy Papers No. 291, 2019).

It is therefore important to understand how organisations and stakeholders involved in the development of AI, especially in the Research and Innovation (R&I) phases, are considering and dealing with those threats and risks, especially the ethical, legal and social issues (ELSI). In fact, it is in the R&I process, at the earlier stage, that societal intervention can help to avoid technologies to fail, and that their positive and negative impacts are better governed and exploited (von Schomberg, 2011).

1.2 Why a Maturity Model for Responsible Artificial Intelligence (RAI)?

The objective of this paper is to understand how organisations involved in the design, development and deployment of AI technologies, are addressing the values, needs and expectations of society, and to identify ways to make those processes more responsible.

To pursue these objectives, several research questions were addressed, as identified in Table 1.

Researchers urge the discussion of ethical boundaries to guide research and development of the technologies mentioned above (Schwab, 2019), but the task is not simple, as ethical questions around technology or science are, on one hand, often complex and uncertain while increasingly influencing our everyday lives (Hahn et al., 2014). On another hand, de Woot (2016) states that economic creativity operates in an "ethical vacuum", as it serves a logic of means to maximise the creation and use of scarce resources and the benefits that result therefrom, not a logic of ends.

At the bottom line, moral and ethics are not easily standardised and can be highly contested; the weighing of different values and belief systems can vary substantially across society (Hahn et al., 2014).

Technology Assessment (TA) and Responsible Research and Innovation (RRI) are considered specific approaches to assess how research and innovation processes should deal with Ethical, Legal and Social Issues (ELSI). Nevertheless, there are several authors that point out several contradictions and problems that can limit the potential success of

Table 1 Research questions addressed in this research.

Research question	Objective
How are the Ethical, Legal and Social Issues (ELSI) protected by current AI development processes?	To understand the maturity of current AI development processes to manage ELSI values threads
How the size and type of the different organizations affect the way they deal with ELSI values threats in the AI development processes?	To understand if the solutions to mitigate ELSI values threats should be different depending on the organization's size and type
How the hierarchical level and functions of the people involved in the AI development processes affect the way they deal with ELSI values threats?	To understand if the approach to mitigate ELSI values threats should be different depending on the hierarchical level and functions of the people involved

RRI and TA. Stahl et al. (2017) mention the desire of RRI to broaden the conversation about R&I to include wider stakeholder groups, to justify the unsolvable difficulty to encompass that aspiration with the traditionally tightly focused definition of excellence in research. Regarding another challenge for RRI, those authors also state that much of the RRI discourse concerns publicly funded research. This is obviously problematic, especially for this present research, because a significant amount of research, and a large proportion of innovation activities in AI are conducted by privately funded organisations including companies.

Besides recent interesting attempts to foster the implementation of RRI in small and medium enterprises (SMEs) and to start-ups, such as the EU PRISMA and COMPASS projects, it is not immediately obvious whether the arguments in favour of RRI are relevant to companies, or whether the incentive structures that are being put in place resonate with companies' R&D processes.

Maturity Models (MM) is a widely accepted tool to assess the maturity (i.e. competency, capability, level of sophistication) of a selected domain based on a more or less comprehensive set of criteria (de Bruin et al., 2005).

Developing a Maturity Model for Responsible Artificial Intelligence seems to be a well-suited way to prepare AI practitioners for "the job" as van Merkerk and Smits R. (2007) suggests. According to the author, actors involved in the innovation process must be better prepared to change the actions and interactions for the actual shaping to be altered. Those actions and interactions are "the job", in this context.

In 2019 the European Commission presented the Trustworthy AI approach to enable "responsible competitiveness", by providing the foundation upon which all those affected by AI systems can trust that their design, development and use are lawful, ethical and robust, both from a technical and social perspective.

In sequence, the EU assembles the High-Level Expert Group on Artificial Intelligence (AI HLEG) that produces the Ethics Guidelines and the Assessment List for Trustworthy AI, a reference model to manage how values, needs and expectations of society should be addressed by organisations evolved in developing AI technologies, in Europe.

Another important development was made by the Responsible AI Institute (RAII), that issued a white paper, providing detailed maturity scores for several dimensions and sub-dimensions, which will determine the certification level that can be attributed for the AI system. (The Responsible AI Institute, The Responsible AI Certification - White Paper, 2022) The RAII approach constitutes an innovative and coherent approach, but eventually too complex for most of the organizations, with too many instruments, assessments, metrics and recommendations, different for each industry and function, demanding a significant effort and dedication of third-party consultancy to drive the work inside the organization. For most of them, at least in Europe, it makes sense to use a simpler approach, common to all industries and functions, that allows for self-assessment and identification of key improvement practices, capabilities, and competences.

This paper presents the development of a Maturity Model (MM) for Responsible AI inspired in the EU Ethics Guidelines for Trustworthy AI and other principles and codes of conducts published by UNESCO, OECD, NIST, IEEE, Google and others. The result is a consistent approach to find answers for the research questions posted, taking in consideration that it is still not available a simple and generic Maturity Model for Responsible AI.

2 Methodology

The methodology used to develop the RAI Maturity Model took as reference the framework developed by de Bruin et al. (2005), which is summarised in the sequence below:

Scope >Design >Populate >Test >Deploy >Maintain

Table 2 describes the main characteristics of each phase proposed by de Bruin et al. (2005) and the options adopted by this research.

3 The Maturity Model for Responsible AI

The proposed Maturity Model (MM) adopts a prescriptive model as the overall objective is the development of a roadmap for organizations to improve, enabling a positively affect in their business value.

Figure 1 represents the MM structure, inspired by the Capability Maturity Model (CMM) from the Software Engineering Institute (SEI). It shows that Maturity Levels are organized by Requirements for Trustworthy AI. Those are related with Methods to Ensure Trustworthy AI, which contain Key Practices.

Table 3 presents the main components of the MM for RAI.

The RAI Maturity Model adopts the following 4-level model (Table 4) based on the level definitions suggested by Ellefsen et al. (2019) and Stahl et al. (2017).

The proposed model includes the same seven requirements as the ones of the EU Ethics Guidelines for Trustworthy AI (European Commission, 2019) (Table 5).

Table 2 Phases of a Maturity Assessment Model and its relation to the present research.

Phase #	Phase name	Options adopted by this research
Phase 1	Scope/Focus of Model	The focus of this Maturity Model is Responsible Artificial Intelligence
	Development Stakeholders	The stakeholders involved in the development and test of the model are the industry (large companies, SMEs and startups), research centres and public institutions evolved in the development of AI in Portugal
Phase 2	Define the number of stages	This research uses a model of 4 levels, for reasons of simplicity and the relative novelty and complexity of the RAI subject
	How maturity stages can be reported to the audience	This research uses the EU Guidelines for Trustworthy AI seven requirements and its several sub-components
Phase 3	Populate	A self-assessment with several questions to each requirement and each sub-requirement was developed For each requirement, the RAI MM is presented in an intuitive, clear and convincing way, to help the organizations easily find their maturity level Methods to ensure Trustworthy AI and key-practices are generated to offer a roadmap for improvement
Phase 4	Pre-Test	This RAI MM was pre-tested in 2 organizations. Based on the results of this pre-test, the model was tuned, complemented, and sophisticated in terms of is comprehensiveness and readiness for application, regarding either the assessment and the tools for the improvement roadmap

(continued)

The model provides several technical and non-technical methods that can be employed to implement the requirements to ensure Trustworthy AI, once again inspired in the EU Ethics guidelines for trustworthy AI (2019).

Technical methods focus on developing and implementing specific technical mechanisms or algorithms to ensure trustworthy AI, such as Architectures for Trustworthy AI and Testing and validating.

Non-technical methods are broader in scope and encompass various organizational, legal, and societal measures such as:

Table 2 (*continued*)

Phase #	Phase name	Options adopted by this research
	Test	The model will be case studied in several organizations, different than the ones that participated in the pre-test. To identify possible differences of perspectives, the model will be tested in each organization at 3 hierarchical levels: C level (ex. CEO), managerial level and operational level (ex. AI developers) The case studies will include individual interviews to each respondent and a group discussion to evaluate the model, having the overall results for all organizations assessed in place, but maintain the results anonymous. This process will help to ensure a company isn't answering questions in an unfair or biased manner (intentionally or not) which could affect their performance
Phase 5	Deploy	Extract conclusions from the test phase, redefine the aspects of the model that needs improvement and then publish it
Phase 6	Maintain	The author plans to repeat the exercise regularly, each 12 to 24 months, in all or some of the organizations, to understand if there are or not progress and the reasons behind the evaluation

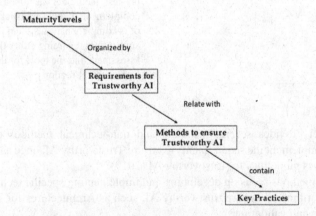

Fig. 1. The RAI MM structure, based on the CMM Structure (Paulk et al., 1993).

Table 3. Main components of the MM for RAI.

RAI MM component	Definition	CMM constituent equivalent
Maturity Levels	A maturity level is a well-defined evolutionary plateau toward achieving a mature process. Each maturity stage provides a layer for the continuous process improvement. Maturity implies a potential for growth in capability and indicates both the richness of an organization's process and the consistency with which it is applied in projects through cut the organization (Paulk et al., 1993)	Maturity Levels
Requirements for Trustworthy AI	Requirements are the concrete translation to achieve the principles outlined for Trustworthy AI. It includes systemic, individual and societal aspects. Each requirement encompasses several sub-requirements	Key Process Areas
Methods to ensure Trustworthy AI	To implement the requirements, both technical and non-technical methods can be employed. These methods encompass all stages of an AI system's life cycle	Common Features
Key Practices	For each sub-requirement, the model presents several actions and best practices that could be implemented and institutionalized to effectively minimize the risks while maximising the benefit of AI	Key Practices

- Regulation involve developing frameworks, regulations, and policies to govern the use and deployment of AI systems. These measures outline ethical guidelines, data protection regulations, and legal frameworks that AI systems should adhere to.
- Stakeholder participation and social dialogue Encouraging multi-stakeholder involvement, including users, developers, researchers, policymakers, and civil society organizations, to collectively shape the development and deployment of AI systems.

Table 4. Maturity Model stages adopted in this research.

Stage name	Level definition
Unaware	The organization is not aware of RAI or its components and does not incorporate it in its processes
Exploratory/reactive	The organization has a reactive response to external pressures concerning aspects of RAI
Proactive	The organization realizes the benefits of RAI and increasingly integrates these into its business processes
Strategic	The organization has adopted RAI as a component of its strategic framework and aims to ensure that all R&D activities consider the RAI components

Table 5. Requirements for Trustworthy AI, from the EU Ethics Guidelines for Trustworthy, European Commission, 2019.

Requirements	Definition
Human agency and oversight	AI systems should follow the principle of respect for human autonomy. This requires that AI systems should support user agency and decision-making and uphold fundamental rights
Technical robustness and safety	This requirement deals with AI system's dependability (the ability to deliver services that can justifiably be trusted) and resilience (robustness when facing changes). Includes resilience to attack and security, fall back plan and general safety, accuracy, reliability and Reproducibility
Privacy and data governance	. Prevention of harm to privacy necessitates adequate data governance that covers the quality and integrity of the data used, its access protocols and the capability to process data in a manner that protects privacy. Includes respect for privacy, quality and integrity of data, and access to data
Transparency	Transparency in AI systems refers to the ability to understand, interpret, and explain the decision-making processes and algorithms used by artificial intelligence systems. This includes the ability to identify and explain why certain outputs were generated and how inputs and variables influenced these results. Includes traceability, explainability and communication

(continued)

Table 5. (*continued*)

Requirements	Definition
Diversity, non-discrimination and fairness	AI systems should be user-centric and designed in a way that allows all people to use AI products or services, regardless of their age, gender, abilities or characteristics Including the avoidance of unfair bias, accessibility and universal design, and stakeholder participation
Societal and environmental wellbeing	Measures to secure the environmental friendliness of an AI system's entire supply chain should be encouraged. Includes sustainability and environmental friendliness, social impact, society and democracy
Accountability	Accountability addresses the way mechanisms are put in place to ensure responsibility for the development, deployment and/or use of AL systems. Including auditability, minimisation and reporting of negative impact, trade-offs and redress

As AI systems are continuously evolving, an evaluation should be made to choose the methods best suited to the level of maturity and to each particular AI system's life cycle stage.

For each sub-requirement, the model presents several key actions and best practices that could be implemented and institutionalized to effectively minimize the risks while maximising the benefit of AI.

For example, for the Human Agency and Autonomy sub-requirement, the following key-practices are suggested, depending on the maturity level:

- Prevent end-users over-relying on the AI system by actively made end-user aware that a decision, content, advice or outcome of the AI system is the result of an algorithmic decision.
- Detect if end-users or subjects in case they develop a disproportionate attachment to the AI System, like addictive behaviour or addiction. If so, take measures to deal with possible negative consequences.
- Take measures to avoid the AI system affect human autonomy by generating over-reliance by end-users.
- Take measures to avoid the AI system affect human autonomy by interfering with the end-user's decision-making process in any unintended and undesirable way.

4 Implementation, Results and Discussion

The implementation starts with a Responsible AI Self-Assessment composed by 58 statements, inspired by the Assessment List of Trustworthy AI (ALTAI) and by the Ethical OS toolkit checklist. The assessment uses a Likert scale with the following response options:

"strongly agree," "somewhat agree", "somewhat disagree," and "strongly disagree". Examples of the statements are:

- "My organisation made end-user aware that a decision, content, advice or outcome of the AI system is the result of an algorithmic decision" for the Human Agency and Autonomy sub-requirement".
- "My organisation plan fault tolerance via, e.g. a duplicated system or another parallel system (AI-based or 'conventional'), for the General Safety sub-requirement.
- "My organisation implemented any sort of recourse for people demanding explanation from your AI system, for example people who feel they have been incorrectly or unfairly assessed" for the Explainability sub-requirement.

To assess the maturity level for each subsection, the research uses the following formula:

$$MR = Psum/(Number\ of\ Valid\ Questions \times 4)$$

where **MR** refers to the Maturity Result expressed in a percentage, used to determine the Maturity Level in each requirement/ sub requirement, according to the key offered in the Table 7.

Where **Psum** refers to the accumulated points assigned accordingly the Table 6, for the valid questions, where 4 is the biggest score possible in each question, means the reference for 100%.

Table 6. Points assigned in each response.

Strongly agree	4
Somewhat agree	3
Somewhat disagree	2
Strongly disagree	0

Table 7 Maturity level assignment related to the percentage calculated in the formula above.

Strategic	>80%
Proactive	<= 80%> = 50%
Reactive	<50%> = 25%
Unaware	<25%

The model was first pre-tested in two organizations, one large research centre and an early-stage startup, both working in AI and both in Portugal. Then the model was improved and pre-tested again in the early-stage startup.

The following radar diagram presents the maturity level for each Trustworthy AI requirement for this start-up. The radar diagram presents maturity as far from the centre the better. The radar shows that the start-up is performing best in Human Agency and Oversight and, in the other extreme, is performing low regarding Accountability requirement (Fig. 2).

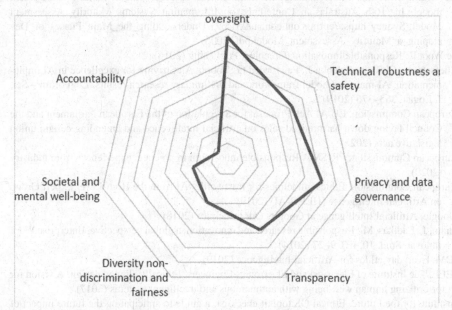

Fig. 2. Radar diagram for the start-up organization for each Trustworthy AI requirement assessed in the pre-test.

5 Conclusions

The development of a Maturity Model (MM) for Responsible AI was presented, including a self-assessment tool, requirements to achieve the principles outlined, the methods to ensure Trustworthy AI and the key practices that will enable Trustworthy AI. The result is a consistent and horizontal approach to all industries and functions, considering that it is not yet available a simple and generic MM for Responsible AI.

Considering the result of the pre-tests, the model was tuned, complemented, and sophisticated in terms of is comprehensiveness and readiness for application, mainly regarding the tools for the improvement roadmap: the Methods to Ensure Trustworthy AI and the Key Practices. The next phase is to apply the model in several other organizations, including interviews at different hierarchical levels and provide case study discussions. The author plans to repeat the exercise regularly, each 12 to 24 months, in all or some of the organizations, to understand if there are or not progress and the reasons behind the evaluation.

This way, the author hopes to have a simple, intuitive and improvement-oriented instrument to help large to small organizations involved in developing AI systems to adopt a set of responsible AI competences and processes, in order to better safeguard values and expectations of society.

References

De Bruin, T. et al.: Understanding the main phases of developing a maturity assessment model. In: 16th Australasian Conference on Information Systems Maturity Assessment Model. Sydney https://eprints.qut.edu.au/25152/1/Understanding_the_Main_Phases_of_Dev eloping_a_Maturity_Assessment_Model.pdf (2005)

de Woot P.: Responsible Innovation. Greenleaf Publishing (2016)

Ellefsen, A., Oleśków-Szłapka J., Pawłowski G., Toboła A.: Striving for excellence in AI implementation: AI maturity model framework and preliminary research results. LogForum – Sci. J. Logist. 363–376 (2019)

European Commission, EU AI Act, Proposal for a regulation of the European Parliament and the Council laying down harmonized rules on artificial intelligence and amending certain union legislative acts (2021)

European Commission, PRISMA Responsible innovation in practice: experiences from industry (2020)

European Commission. Ethics guidelines for trustworthy AI from the High-Level Expert Group on Artificial Intelligence (HLEG-AI) (2019)

Google, Artificial Intelligence at Google: Our principles (2018)

Hahn, J., Ladikas, M.: Responsible research and innovation: a global perspective. Enterprise Work Innovat. Stud. 10, IET 9–27 (2014)

IBM, Everyday ethics for Artificial Intelligence (2019)

IEEE, The Institute of Electrical and Electronics Engineers, Ethically aligned design: A vision for prioritizing human well-being with autonomous and intelligent systems (2017)

Institute for the Future, Ethical OS toolkit checklist, a guide to anticipating the future impact of today's technology, https://ethicalos.org/wp-content/uploads/2018/08/Ethical-OS-Toolkit.pdf (2018)

OECD, Scoping the OECD AI Principles, Deliberations of the Expert Group on Artificial Intelligence (AIGO). OECD Digital Economy Papers No. 291 (2019)

Paulk, M., Curtis, B., Chrissis, M., Weber, C.: Capability Maturity Model. Carnegie Mellon University, Software Engineering Institute (1993)

Stahl et al.: Responsible research and innovation (RRI) maturity model, Special issue responsible research and innovation (RRI) in industry (2017)

Schwab K.: Reshaping the 4th Industrial Revolution, WEF (2018)

The Responsible AI Institute, The Responsible AI Certification - White Paper (2022)

UNESCO, UNESCO Recommendation on the Ethics of Artificial Intelligence (2023)

Von Schomberg, R.: Towards responsible research and innovation in the information and communication technologies and security technologies fields. SSRN Electron. J. (2011). https://doi.org/10.2139/ssrn.2436399

Completeness of Datasets Documentation on ML/AI Repositories: An Empirical Investigation

Marco Rondina[(✉)] [iD], Antonio Vetrò [iD], and Juan Carlos De Martin [iD]

Politecnico di Torino, Torino, Italy
{marco.rondina,antonio.vetro,juancarlos.demartin}@polito.it

Abstract. ML/AI is the field of computer science and computer engineering that arguably received the most attention and funding over the last decade. Data is the key element of ML/AI, so it is becoming increasingly important to ensure that users are fully aware of the quality of the datasets that they use, and of the process generating them, so that possible negative impacts on downstream effects can be tracked, analysed, and, where possible, mitigated. One of the tools that can be useful in this perspective is dataset documentation. The aim of this work is to investigate the state of dataset documentation practices, measuring the completeness of the documentation of several popular datasets in ML/AI repositories. We created a dataset documentation schema-the Documentation Test Sheet (dts)-that identifies the information that should always be attached to a dataset (to ensure proper dataset choice and informed use), according to relevant studies in the literature. We verified 100 popular datasets from four different repositories with the dts to investigate which information were present. Overall, we observed a lack of relevant documentation, especially about the context of data collection and data processing, highlighting a paucity of transparency.

Keywords: Data documentation · AI transparency · AI accountability

1 Introduction and Motivation

Machine Learning/Artificial Intelligence (ML/AI) research made great strides in recent years, and its industrial applications became increasingly pervasive within society, automating organizational processes and decisions in several fields.

Datasets are fundamental in the ML/AI ecosystem and many issues related to fairness, transparency, and accountability in ML/AI systems are rooted in the data collection and in the data processing procedures [11]. Every decision made during the workflow may contain implicit values and beliefs [21], so tracking them can improve transparency [1]. The information accompanying them plays a very significant role in uncovering data issues [5], in fostering reproducibility and auditability [13], in ensuring accountability [10], users' trust [2], and in avoiding *data cascading* effects on the entire ML/AI pipeline [20]. With documentation,

N. Moniz et al. (Eds.): EPIA 2023, LNAI 14115, pp. 79–91, 2023.
https://doi.org/10.1007/978-3-031-49008-8_7

it is possible to better understand the characteristics of the training data to at least partially mitigate the risks of downstream negative effects [4]. This is particularly true for those technologies where the impact of biased results can be severe, such as Speech Language Technologies (SLT) [16]. Documentation production should be seen as an essential part of dataset production, as a place to disclose fundamental choices, in parallel with what is proposed to be documented in terms of models [15,19] or rankings [25,26].

This study focuses on the dataset documentation state of practice. The aim was to measure whether and how much relevant information about data collection and data processing procedures is present in the documentation of the most popular (and influential [12]) datasets. The research question which directed the design of the research is: **Which of the information, that should be transparent to dataset users, is present in the most popular datasets in ML/AI repositories?** In order to answer this research question, we developed a test schema to measure the completeness of dataset documentation: Sect. 2 will describe the construction of the DTS. Subsequently, Sect. 3 describes the selection of repositories and datasets. The results of the application of the DTS are presented in Sect. 4. Finally, limitations (Sect. 5), future work (Sect. 7) and the conclusions (Sect. 6) are presented. Furthermore, we provide additional materials in the online Appendices.[1]

2   Documentation Test Sheet from Related Works

We built a collection of recommended information that should be present in dataset documentation to ensure a proper choice of dataset and informed use. The aim was to recognize, with a study of relevant work in the literature of dataset documentation schemas, which information are important to be present in dataset documentation to achieve transparency, accountability, and reproducibility. The goal of this schema is to measure how complete a dataset documentation is: this property is the first necessary element to be scrutinized for enabling any further analysis on further quality dimensions of documentation (e.g., correctness). We called this schema the *Documentation Test Sheet* (DTS).

2.1   Fields of Information

The list of *Test Fields* is largely based on *Datasheets for Datasets* [7], with some further insights from relevant documentation standardization proposals in the literature [3,9]. We grouped the information into 6 sections, following the categorization presented in *Datasheets for Datasets* (DfD): 1 *Motivation,* 2 *Composition,* 3 *Collection processes,* 4 *Data processing procedures,* 5 *Uses,* 6 *Maintenance.* In addition to dataset metadata, some characteristics of the

---

[1] The appendices available at https://doi.org/10.5281/zenodo.8052683 contain: the DTS (A), the provenance of the field of information composing it (B), the metadata of the selected datasets (C), the reading principles that guided the documentation investigation (D), the raw results (E) and additional tables and figures (F).

data were tracked in section **c** *Characteristics*. We discarded the *Distribution* section because it proved inapplicable when testing documentation of datasets already published in public repositories. The full DTS can be found in Appendix A, but the list of *Test Fields* is also available in Table 2. Further details on the motivations behind this choice, and a description of the provenance of each information field, are reported in Appendix B. One of the novelties of this work is the design of the individual *Test Fields* as concepts expressed by few words to which it is easy to answer 'yes' or 'no', depending on the presence or absence of the related information in the documentation under analysis. Some fields from the related work were collapsed in a few *Test Fields* for the sake of brevity and ease of application. We designed the DTS to be generalizable as possible to any type of documentation, so that it can be used for datasets pertaining to different areas of ML/AI.

2.2 Measurement

The other core elements of the DTS are the *Presence Check Values* and the *Presence Averages*. During the analysis of the documentation, each *Test Field* is associated with a value indicating the presence or the absence of the represented information. Specifically, the *Presence Check Value* can take on one of the following three possible values:

- 1: it is possible to retrieve the information represented by the *Test Field*;
- 0: it is not possible to retrieve the information represented by the *Test Field*;
- NA: the information represented by the *Test Field* does not apply to dataset.

The *Presence Average* represents the completeness measure of the DTS. It is obtained by averaging the *Presence Check Values* of the group of *Test Fields* under analysis such as dataset (*Dataset Presence Average*), section (*Section Presence Average*), and field (among different datasets, *Field Presence Average*).

3 Study Design

One of the novel elements of this study concerns the analysis of the information found in the very same place where the data can be accessed, instead of selecting datasets from a corpus of academic papers [8,17]. The documentation in the public repository provides information about how the dataset is actually used in practice. Since the purpose of a scholarly article is different from that of a repository, some information may have no reason for inclusion in the article, and vice versa. For this reason, the documentation being analysed is the documentation web page where data can be downloaded. Given this design choice, we first selected the repositories under analysis, as described in Sect. 3.1. In the second step, we collected the metadata useful to perform the dataset selection, as described in Sect. 3.2. We focused on the most popular datasets, as seen in other work [6]. This is because these datasets are the most influential ones, and therefore studying their documentation is an important step in the path towards a deeper understanding of common documentation practices. We then collected data on the presence of information in the documentation.[2]

3.1 Repositories Under Analysis

The choice of repository is a relevant decision in this study, due to the design decision to analyse the online documentation present in the same place where the data are hosted. Indeed, different repositories have different documentation and metadata schemas. Therefore, we decided to select more than one repository to avoid obtaining too specific results. We selected four well-known and commonly used repositories to capture different practices in the ML/AI community. The criteria used for the choice were: free access; the presence of popularity proxies among the metadata; the presence of hundreds of datasets. We consulted the Wikipedia *List of portals suitable for multiple types of ML applications*[3] and, as a result, the following repositories have been selected: Hugging Face(HUG), Kaggle (KAG), OpenML (OML) and UC Irvine ML Repository (UCI).

3.2 Datasets Selection

To guarantee the feasibility of the research, it was also necessary to limit the number of datasets for each repository. For this reason, we selected 25 datasets from each repository, for a total of 100 datasets to be examined. We decided to focus on the concept of *popularity*, so that we could analyse some of the most used and influential datasets: where available, the number of *downloads* was identified as the best proxy; where not available, number of *views* was identified as a good alternative. The resulting metrics used are: HUG, number of downloads (APIs); KAG, platform upvotes and then the number of downloads (APIs)[4]; OML, number of downloads (web scraping); UCI, number of views (web scraping). We eliminated any duplicates within the same or different repositories (the comparison of information about the same dataset in different repositories was not a central aim of this research). As a selection criterion between duplicates, we used the highest 'popularity'. In the case of two datasets at the same ranking position, we eventually observed whether one of them was the primary source of the other. The full list of selected datasets, together with the date of data collection, can be found in Appendix C. The principles that guided the reading of the documentation are presented in the Online Appendix D.

4 Results and Discussion

In this section, we present the results and their discussion for each of the following levels: dataset (Sect. 4.1), DTS section (Sect. 4.2), *Test Fields* (Sect. 4.3).

---

[2] For reasons of space, summary tables with raw data are presented in Appendix E.

[3] https://en.wikipedia.org/wiki/List_of_datasets_for_machine-learning_research.

[4] Due to the unavailability of direct download count APIs, datasets were sorted by upvotes via APIs and then sorted by download count, as presented in the results.

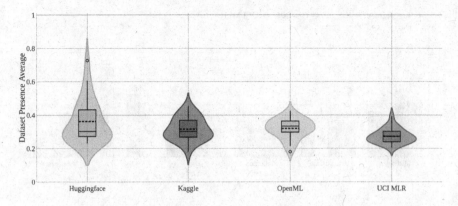

Fig. 1. Distribution of Dataset Presence Averages grouped by repository.

Table 1. Characteristics of the 100 selected datasets (25 for each repository).

Repository	Data is people related	Presence of explicit target variable	Dataset is a sample or a reduction of a larger set	Recently updated
Hugging Face	04	21	01	25
Kaggle	12	08	02	05
OpenML	11	25	07	00
UCI MLR	11	22	04	00
Total	38	76	14	30

Additional information on the distribution and dispersion of values is included in Appendix F.

4.1 Datasets Level

The dataset with the most comprehensive documentation was **hug16**, the *cnn dailymail* from Hugging Face (HUG). It contains over 300k unique news articles written by journalists. Its *Dataset Card* (i.e. its documentation) was comprehensive in all the different sections, and it can be considered a positive reference from the point of view of documentation practice. Figure 1 shows that overall very few datasets achieved more than 50% completeness, and variation between repositories is small. The selected datasets from HUG have the highest mean of the *Dataset Presence Average* distribution, while the ones from UCI have the lowest mean of the *Dataset Presence Average* distribution. One of the contributing factors to this result is that the three most complete documentations belong to HUG datasets.

In Table 1 it is possible to observe specific characteristics of the datasets: most datasets did not contain personal data, had an explicit target variable,

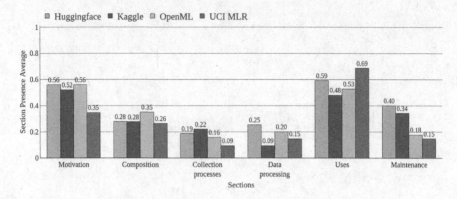

Fig. 2. *Section Presence Averages.*

and were not a sample or reduction of a larger set. All datasets updated after 1 January 2021 were considered 'Recently updated': all datasets from HUG and five datasets from KAG have been recently updated in terms of data or documentation, while all the OML and UCI datasets have not been updated in this timeframe. Additional statistics can be found in Appendix F.

4.2   Sections Level

As can be seen in Fig. 2, the *Uses* section was the most complete one, followed by the *Motivation* section. Sections *Collection processes* and *Data processing procedures* had the lowest values of *Section Presence Average*. Additionally, we observed that the results of the *Maintenance* section are very different between repositories. These results suggest that the documentation of public datasets is currently utilisation-oriented, with less attention to the previous stages of the dataset construction pipeline. This aspect is also correlated with the high *Section Presence Average* of the *Motivation* section: the purpose of the dataset often encapsulates the meaning of why the data within it should be used. The low completeness of the *Composition, Collection processes* and *Data processing procedures* sections suggests that either little effort is devoted to describing the early stages of the dataset construction phase. Frequently, there is no information at all about these delicate phases. The failure to take into account these contextual aspects can lead to various problems in the models trained on such undocumented data [20]. Recent work devoted to partially automating the documentation process could help users to easily complete the *Composition* section [18,22,23]. Finally, the *Maintenance* results, although very variable between repositories, confirmed recent studies in the literature about the opportunities to improve documentation in datasets repositories and the lack of attention paid to what happens after the dataset is published [14,24]. As for the other aggregation level, the distributions of measurements are provided in Appendix F.

4.3 Test Fields Level

Table 2 shows the *Presence Average* value of each information field, globally and by the repository. Results show that certain documentation fields are very commonly used, such as the **2.01** *Description of the instances* (0,92), **2.02** *Number of the instances* (0,90) and **5.01** *Description of the tasks in which the dataset has already been used and their results* (0,95). In many cases, the high level of completeness could be explained by the ability of the repository's metadata structure to promote the presence of a particular piece of information. Indeed, the information represented by these fields was very much present in repositories that structurally expose this information in the metadata schema of the repository. Conversely, it was almost completely absent in repositories that do not include such information in their metadata schema. Some examples are: **2.11** *Statistics* (HUG 0,00; KAG 1,00; OML 1,00; UCI 1,00), **5.04** *Repository that links to papers or system that use the datasets* (HUG 0,92; KAG 0,00; OML 0,00; UCI 1,00), **5.05** *Description of license and terms of use* (HUG 0,48; KAG 0,68; OML 1,00; UCI 1,00). This highlights the role played by repository hosts, who have the potential to trigger virtuous documentation practices.

In the *Motivation* section, on the one hand, it was very common to find information about the authors (the 'resource creators'), while on the other hand, it was rare to find details about who funded the creation of the dataset, important information for achieving accountability. Within the *Composition* section, basic information such as the description or number of instances was usually present. On the contrary, information about data confidentiality and dangerousness was usually absent. It is important to note that data protection laws may have been different before the datasets were made available (see Sect. 5 for more details). The analysis of information related to *Collection processes* pointed out, in a context of a general scarcity of details, the near total absence of specifics about ethical review processes and about analysis of potential impacts of dataset uses. With regard to the *Data processing procedures*, we observed that the 'Dataset Card' in HUG favoured the presence of (at least) some useful tags to obtain indications on the workers involved in these procedures. As already mentioned above, in terms of *Uses*, much attention on the part of dataset creators is paid to the description of the previous usage of the dataset and to the description of the recommended uses. The same cannot be said for non-recommended uses: only the documentation of a couple of HUG datasets contained this information. Surprisingly, although it was common to find details on the subject that supports or manages the dataset, the contact of the owner was rarely present. Furthermore, in terms of *Maintenance*, the DOI was quite rare and no information on the management of older dataset versions could be retrieved.

Table 2. *Field Presence Averages*: overall and for each repository.

ID	Field description	Tot	HUG	KAG	OML	UCI
1.01	*Purpose for the dataset creation*	0,57	0,64	0,52	0,68	0,44
1.02	*Dataset creators*	0,86	0,88	0,96	1,00	0,60
1.03	*Dataset funders*	0,06	0,16	0,08	0,00	0,00
2.01	*Description of the instances*	0,92	1,00	1,00	0,80	0,88
2.02	*Number of the instances*	0,90	0,92	0,72	1,00	0,96
2.03	*Information about missing values*	0,50	0,00	0,12	1,00	0,88
2.04	*Recommended data splits*	0,31	0,92	0,08	0,12	0,12
2.05	*Description of errors, noise or redundancies*	0,13	0,00	0,16	0,08	0,28
2.06	*Information about data confidentiality*	0,04	0,08	0,08	0,00	0,00
2.07	*Information about possible data dangerousness (offensive, insulting, threatening or cause anxiety) or biases*	0,03	0,12	0,00	0,00	0,00
2.08	*Information about people involved in data production and their compensation (if people related)*	0,43	0,25	0,42	0,64	0,31
2.09	*Description of identifiability for individuals or subpopulations (if people related)*	0,15	0,50	0,17	0,09	0,08
2.10	*Description of data sensitivity (if people related)*	0,03	0,25	0,00	0,00	0,00
2.11	*Statistics*	0,50	0,00	1,00	1,00	0,00
2.12	*Pair plots*	0,00	0,00	0,00	0,00	0,00
2.13	*Probabilistic model*	0,00	0,00	0,00	0,00	0,00
2.14	*Ground truth correlations*	0,00	0,00	0,00	0,00	0,00
3.01	*Description of instances acquisition and data collection processes*	0,53	0,52	0,60	0,64	0,36
3.02	*Information about people involved in the data collection process and their compensation*	0,08	0,16	0,12	0,00	0,04
3.03	*Time frame of data collection*	0,19	0,04	0,48	0,12	0,12
3.04	*Information about ethical review processes*	0,01	0,04	0,00	0,00	0,00
3.05	*Information on individuals' knowledge of data collection (if people related)*	0,05	0,25	0,00	0,09	0,00
3.06	*Information on individuals' consent for data collection (if people related)*	0,05	0,25	0,00	0,09	0,00
3.07	*Analysis of potential impacts of the dataset and its use on data subjects*	0,00	0,00	0,00	0,00	0,00
4.01	*Description of sampling, preprocessing, cleaning, labelling procedures*	0,39	0,32	0,24	0,56	0,44

Table 2. continued

ID	Field description	Tot	HUG	KAG	OML	UCI
4.02	*Information about people involved in the data sampling, preprocessing, cleaning, labelling procedures and their compensation*	0,11	0,44	0,00	0,00	0,00
4.03	*Description of others possible sampling, preprocessing, cleaning, labelling procedures*	0,02	0,00	0,04	0,04	0,00
5.01	*Description of the tasks in which the dataset has already been used and their results*	0,95	0,92	1,00	1,00	0,88
5.02	*Description of recommended uses or tasks*	0,62	0,56	0,72	0,64	0,56
5.03	*Description of not recommended uses*	0,02	0,08	0,00	0,00	0,00
5.04	*Repository that links to papers or system that use the datasets*	0,48	0,92	0,00	0,00	1,00
5.05	*Description of license and terms of use*	0,79	0,48	0,68	1,00	1,00
6.01	*Information about subject supporting, hosting, maintaining the dataset*	0,84	0,36	1,00	1,00	1,00
6.02	*Contact of the owner*	0,30	0,20	0,80	0,16	0,04
6.03	*DOI*	0,09	0,24	0,04	0,08	0,00
6.04	*Erratum*	0,00	0,00	0,00	0,00	0,00
6.05	*Information about dataset updates*	0,38	1,00	0,52	0,00	0,00
6.06	*Information about management of older dataset versions*	0,00	0,00	0,00	0,00	0,00
6.07	*Information about the mechanism to extend, augment, build on, contribute to the dataset*	0,26	1,00	0,04	0,00	0,00

5   Threats to Validity and Limitations

One of the main limitations of this research is the non-scalability of the proposed procedure, which was primarily based on manual inspection of dataset documentation: the alignment of repositories metadata with the documentation fields proposed in the literature, and included in the DTS, was very poor.

The choice of repositories may have influenced the final result. However, by focusing on some of the most prominent repositories and the most popular datasets in each repository, we analysed the documentation of influential datasets. The dataset selection criteria—*popularity*—was implemented slightly differently to the different repositories, due to differences in the metadata schemas: however, the number of downloads was present in three out of four repositories, and for the remaining one we selected the most reasonable and available proxy (visualizations). In addition, popularity tends to be a proxy for longevity: this criterion may have introduced a selection bias, favouring datasets from a time when documentation was less important or emphasized and with different data protection laws. On the contrary, the lack of documentation updates on such datasets reinforces the findings of this study, i.e. poor attention/availability on dataset documentation.

Despite the fact that considerable effort has been made to make the data collection as accurate and standardized as possible, the study design, strongly based on human reading and interpretation of documentation texts, is inherently prone to the risk of interpretation errors. We controlled this threat by providing the reading principles in Appendix D.

Finally, due to lack of resources, the DTS was not tested for consistency and validation with target users: however, the information fields were all derived from documentation schemes already available in the academic literature.

6   Conclusions

We empirically investigated the state of documentation practice in the most popular datasets in the ML/AI community. A set of information that should always be clear to the users of the datasets, in order to achieve transparency and accountability, was adapted into a *Documentation Test Sheet* (DTS) able to measure the completeness of documentation. The DTS was applied to 100 dataset documentations from Hugging Face, Kaggle, OpenML and UC Irvine MLR repositories.

This investigation brought out some relevant results about the state of practice of documentation of datasets manufacturing. First, it emerged that information related to how to use the dataset was the most present. On the contrary, maintenance over time or processes behind the data generation were very poorly documented. In general, a lack of relevant information was observed, highlighting a paucity of transparency. All these observations are even more relevant when considering that the analysis was restricted to some of the most popular and well-known datasets. Finally, the potential of repositories to help curators of datasets to produce better documentation emerged.

Altogether, these results let us hypothesize that efforts of the ML/AI community in devoting more attention to the dataset documentation process are necessary. These efforts might enable the reuse of datasets in a way that is more aware of the choices, assumptions, limitations and other aspects of their creation, and ultimately facilitating human-respectful ML/AI innovations. The proposed DTS can be an easy-to-use tool in the hands of dataset creators, maintainers, and hosts to move a further step in this direction.

7   Future Work

The first hypothesis of future work relates to increasing the number of datasets and repositories under investigation. Moreover, a complementary analysis of a

selection of recent datasets could tell us if the growing awareness of data cura-
tion is bringing some results in common practice. Quantitative expansions of
the research could be put investigating the feasibility of an automatic system
capable of controlling the presence of information. This possibility, however, is
fully dependent on the evolution of the repositories, and actions made possible
by dataset hosts to standardize documentation and make it machine-readable.

From the qualitative point of view, it might be possible to expand the DTS
to measure other aspects of documentation quality. For example, comparing
the information found in the repositories with the information retrieved from
academic articles using those datasets could reveal further insights to understand
documentation practices, reduce documentation debt and possibly integrate it
with additional aspects (e.g., 'sparsity' [6], dataset quality). Finally, a test with
target users that also explores the differences between different types of dataset
users could be useful for prioritizing DTS Test Fields according to possible users
and uses.

Acknowledgments. This study was carried out within the FAIR - Future Artificial Intelligence Research and received funding from the European Union Next-
GenerationEU (PIANO NAZIONALE DI RIPRESA E RESILIENZA (PNRR) -
MISSIONE 4 COMPONENTE 2, INVESTIMENTO 1.3 - D.D. 1555 11/10/2022,
PE00000013). This manuscript reflects only the authors' views and opinions, neither
the European Union nor the European Commission can be considered responsible for
them.

References

1. Afzal, S., Rajmohan, C., Kesarwani, M., Mehta, S., Patel, H.: Data readiness
report. In: 2021 IEEE International Conference on Smart Data Services (SMDS),
pp. 42–51 (2021). https://doi.org/10.1109/SMDS53860.2021.00016
2. Arnold, M., Bellamy, R.K.E., Hind, M., Houde, S., Mehta, S., Mojsilović, A., Nair,
R., Ramamurthy, K.N., Olteanu, A., Piorkowski, D., Reimer, D., Richards, J., Tsay,
J., Varshney, K.R.: FactSheets: increasing trust in AI services through supplier's
declarations of conformity. IBM J. Res. Dev. **63**(4/5), 6:1–6:13 (2019). https://
doi.org/10.1147/JRD.2019.2942288
3. Bender, E.M., Friedman, B.: Data Statements for Natural Language Processing:
Toward Mitigating System Bias and Enabling Better Science. Trans. Ass. Comp.
Ling. **6**, 587–604 (2018). https://doi.org/10.1162/tacl_a_00041
4. Bender, E.M., Gebru, T., McMillan-Major, A., Shmitchell, S.: On the Dangers of
stochastic parrots: can language models be too big? In: Proceedings of the 2021
ACM Conference on FAccT, pp. 610–623. FAccT '21. ACM (2021). https://doi.
org/10.1145/3442188.3445922
5. Boyd, K.L.: Datasheets for datasets help ML engineers notice and understand
ethical issues in training data. Proc. ACM Hum.-Comput. Interact. **5**(CSCW2),
438:1–438:27 (2021). https://doi.org/10.1145/3479582
6. Fabris, A., Messina, S., Silvello, G., Susto, G.A.: Algorithmic fairness datasets: the
story so far. Data Min. Knowl. Disc. **36**(6), 2074–2152 (2022). https://doi.org/10.
1007/s10618-022-00854-z

7. Gebru, T., Morgenstern, J., Vecchione, B., Vaughan, J.W., Wallach, H., III, H.D., Crawford, K.: Datasheets for datasets. Commun. ACM **64**(12), 86–92 (2021). https://doi.org/10.1145/3458723
8. Geiger, R.S., Yu, K., Yang, Y., Dai, M., Qiu, J., Tang, R., Huang, J.: Garbage in, garbage out? Do machine learning application papers in social computing report where human-labeled training data comes from? In: Proceedings of the 2020 Conference on FAccT, pp. 325–336 (2020). https://doi.org/10.1145/3351095.3372862
9. Holland, S., Hosny, A., Newman, S., Joseph, J., Chmielinski, K.: The Dataset Nutrition Label: A Framework To Drive Higher Data Quality Standards (2018). arXiv:1805.03677 [cs]
10. Hutchinson, B., Smart, A., Hanna, A., Denton, E., Greer, C., Kjartansson, O., Barnes, P., Mitchell, M.: Towards Accountability for machine learning datasets: practices from software engineering and infrastructure. In: Proceedings of the 2021 ACM Conference on FAccT, pp. 560–575. FAccT '21, ACM (2021). https://doi.org/10.1145/3442188.3445918
11. Jo, E.S., Gebru, T.: Lessons from archives: strategies for collecting sociocultural data in machine learning. In: Proceedings of the 2020 Conference on FAccT, pp. 306–316 (2020). https://doi.org/10.1145/3351095.3372829
12. Koch, B., Denton, E., Hanna, A., Foster, J.G.: Reduced, Reused and Recycled: The Life of a Dataset in Machine Learning Research (2021). https://doi.org/10.48550/arXiv.2112.01716
13. Königstorfer, F., Thalmann, S.: Software documentation is not enough! requirements for the documentation of AI. Digital Policy, Regul. Gov. **23**(5), 475–488 (2021). https://doi.org/10.1108/DPRG-03-2021-0047
14. Luccioni, A.S., Corry, F., Sridharan, H., Ananny, M., Schultz, J., Crawford, K.: A framework for deprecating datasets: standardizing documentation, identification, and communication. In: Proceedings of the 2022 ACM Conference on FAccT, pp. 199–212. FAccT '22, ACM (2022). https://doi.org/10.1145/3531146.3533086
15. Mitchell, M., Wu, S., Zaldivar, A., Barnes, P., Vasserman, L., Hutchinson, B., Spitzer, E., Raji, I.D., Gebru, T.: Model cards for model reporting. In: Proceedings of the Conference on FAccT, pp. 220–229. FAT* '19. ACM (2019). https://doi.org/10.1145/3287560.3287596
16. Papakyriakopoulos, O., Choi, A.S.G., Thong, W., Zhao, D., Andrews, J., Bourke, R., Xiang, A., Koenecke, A.: Augmented datasheets for speech datasets and ethical decision-making. In: Proceedings of the 2023 ACM Conference on FAccT, pp. 881–904. FAccT '23, ACM (2023). https://doi.org/10.1145/3593013.3594049
17. Peng, K., Mathur, A., Narayanan, A.: Mitigating Dataset Harms Requires Stewardship: Lessons from 1000 Papers (2021). arXiv:2108.02922 [cs]
18. Petersen, A.H., Ekstrøm, C.T.: dataMaid: Your assistant for documenting supervised data quality screening in R. J. Stat. Softw. **90**, 1–38 (2019). https://doi.org/10.18637/jss.v090.i06
19. Richards, J., Piorkowski, D., Hind, M., Houde, S., Mojsilović, A.: A Methodology for Creating AI FactSheets. arXiv:2006.13796 [cs] (2020). https://doi.org/10.48550/arXiv.2006.13796
20. Sambasivan, N., Kapania, S., Highfill, H., Akrong, D., Paritosh, P., Aroyo, L.M.: "Everyone wants to do the model work, not the data work": data cascades in high-stakes AI. In: Proceedings of the 2021 CHI Conference on Human Factors in Computer System, pp. 1–15. CHI '21. ACM (2021). https://doi.org/10.1145/3411764.3445518

21. Scheuerman, M.K., Denton, E., Hanna, A.: Do datasets have politics? Disciplinary values in computer vision dataset development. In: Proceedings of ACM Human-Computer Interaction **5**(CSCW2), 1–37 (2021). https://doi.org/10.1145/3476058

22. Schramowski, P., Tauchmann, C., Kersting, K.: Can machines help us answering question 16 in datasheets, and in turn reflecting on inappropriate content? In: Proceedings of 2022 ACM Conference on FAccT, pp. 1350–1361. FAccT '22. ACM (2022). https://doi.org/10.1145/3531146.3533192

23. Sun, C., Asudeh, A., Jagadish, H.V., Howe, B., Stoyanovich, J.: MithraLabel: flexible dataset nutritional labels for responsible data science. In: Proceedings of 28th ACM International Conference on Information and Knowledge Management, pp. 2893–2896. CIKM '19. ACM (2019). https://doi.org/10.1145/3357384.3357853

24. Thylstrup, N.B.: The ethics and politics of data sets in the age of machine learning: deleting traces and encountering remains. Media, Culture & Soc. **44**(4), 655–671 (2022). https://doi.org/10.1177/01634437211060226

25. Yang, K., Stoyanovich, J., Asudeh, A., Howe, B., Jagadish, H.V., Miklau, G.: A Nutritional label for rankings. In: Proceedings of 2018 International Conference on Management of Data, pp. 1773–1776 (2018). https://doi.org/10.1145/3183713.3193568

26. Zehlike, M., Yang, K., Stoyanovich, J.: Fairness in Ranking: A Survey (2021). https://doi.org/10.48550/arXiv.2103.14000

Navigating the Landscape of AI Ethics and Responsibility

Paulo Rupino Cunha⬛ and Jacinto Estima(⬛)⬛

Department of Informatics Engineering, University of Coimbra, Coimbra, Portugal
{rupino,estima}@dei.uc.pt

Abstract. Artificial intelligence (AI) has been widely used in many fields, from intelligent virtual assistants to medical diagnosis. However, there is no consensus on how to deal with ethical issues. Using a systematic literature review and an analysis of recent real-world news about AI-infused systems, we cluster existing and emerging AI ethics and responsibility issues into six groups - broken systems, hallucinations, intellectual property rights violations, privacy and regulation violations, enabling malicious actors and harmful actions, environmental and socioeconomic harms - discuss implications, and conclude that the problem needs to be reflected upon and addressed across five partially overlapping dimensions: Research, Education, Development, Operation, and Business Model. This reflection may be relevant to caution of potential dangers and frame further research at a time when products and services based on AI exhibit explosive growth. Moreover, exploring effective ways to involve users and civil society in discussions on the impact and role of AI systems could help increase trust and understanding of these technologies.

Keywords: Ethical AI · Responsible AI · Trustworthy AI · AI risks · AI regulation

1 Introduction

Research and use of artificial intelligence (AI) are enjoying great momentum. For example, ChatGPT, released only a few months ago, is already considered the fastest-growing consumer application in history [1]. Advances in software and hardware over the last few years have enabled many useful applications in widespread areas, from intelligent virtual assistants to autonomous vehicles or medical diagnosis tools.

However, those same impressive advances, specifically in large language models, such as the one underlying ChatGPT, have raised grave concerns for a group of figures in academia (namely in AI), technology, and business [2]. Citing extensive research, they caution of profound risks to society (specifically, democracy) and humanity. Sam Altman, the CEO of Open AI–the company behind ChatGPT–acknowledges these risks and admits that AI will reshape society and that the prospect scares him [3].

Compounding these concerns is an apparent trend to disregard ethical issues in big tech players, such as Microsoft, Twitter, Meta, or Google, who have recently fired or constrained their ethical and responsible innovation teams [4–7].

N. Moniz et al. (Eds.): EPIA 2023, LNAI 14115, pp. 92–105, 2023.
https://doi.org/10.1007/978-3-031-49008-8_8

Conversely, national and state governments, as well as national and international organizations have released ethical principles and legislation [8, 9]. However, these are often deemed abstract and difficult to implement and operationalize [10]. Even so, new efforts keep emerging, such as the first-ever global agreement on the Ethics of AI promoted by UNESCO a few months ago [11].

Most AI ethics and responsibility discussions seem to focus on algorithmic solutions, while the challenges are of a much broader nature. In this context, we decided to examine the literature to find out how it addresses the topic. Thus, our research question is:

RQ: What AI ethics and responsibility issues are currently being discussed?

The remainder of this paper is organized as follows: in Sect. 2 we present the process and protocol used in our systematic review of the literature, which we analyze in Sect. 3. In Sect. 4, we provide a clustering of AI ethics and responsibility issues and suggest that the topic traverses several overlapping dimensions. We close with some conclusions, limitations, and future work in Sect. 5.

2 Research Methodology

To answer our research question, we performed a systematic literature review using guidance from [12, 13]. Preliminary experiments to tune the search keywords led us to the final expression shown in Table 1.

Table 1. Final search expression.

TITLE-ABS-KEY ("ethical AI" OR "responsible AI") AND (LIMIT-TO (DOCTYPE, "cp") OR LIMIT-TO (DOCTYPE, "ar")) AND (LIMIT-TO (SUBJAREA, "COMP")) AND (LIMIT-TO (LANGUAGE, "English"))

We searched by title, abstract, and keywords on the Scopus database in April 2023, restricting the results to the computer science area. Our inclusion criteria were papers published in conferences and journals written in English with no date constraints.

We obtained 333 results, which we exported as a. RIS file and imported into Rayyan, a web-based collaborative tool to manage systematic literature reviews [14]. Rayyan automatically identified 10 possible duplicates, which we analyzed and resolved.

We have then screened the remaining papers to identify those relevant to our research. We used researcher triangulation to decrease biases and improve validity [15, 16]. Each author independently reviewed titles, abstracts, and keywords, classifying papers as "include," "maybe," or "exclude." Interrater reliability, indicating the level of agreement [17], was 85%. To conduct this study, we selected only the papers that both researchers marked as "include". As a result, 24 papers remained for full-text analysis. From those, we excluded three additional papers, one preprint and two papers that were not available. The steps of the SLR process are summarized in Fig. 1.

Of the resulting 21 papers, 13 are journal papers and 8 are conference papers. Chrono-logically, the number of studies has been evolving throughout the last 5 years, with 1 paper in 2018, 2 papers in 2021, 6 papers in 2022, and 12 papers in 2023 (up to now).

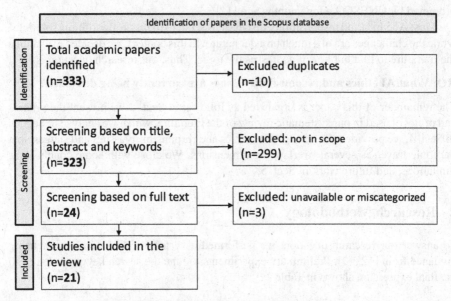

Fig. 1. PRISMA flowchart of the systematic literature review.

3   Analysis of the Literature

Most studies on ethical and responsible AI are recent, with the majority being published in the last five years. This probably contributes to the lack of consensus on what these concepts truly entail. Table 2 offers an overview of the terminology used in five of these studies, highlighting the diversity of terms used.

Transparency and fairness are the most consensual, appearing in five studies, followed by explainability and accountability, which are used in four, and privacy and security, employed in three. Ethics, data quality, and safety are mentioned in only two studies, while the remaining 39 terms are each used in only one study. Besides, all these papers refer to the terms in different ways, e.g., barriers, risks, aspects, or principles.

In most papers, three key terms are commonly used: Responsible AI, Ethical AI, and Trustworthy AI. While some may use more than one of these terms, two do not use any of them. The distribution of papers using these different terms is illustrated in Fig. 2.

Two papers have contributed to the classification of information. Yu et al. [23] proposed AI governance taxonomy that categorizes ethical concerns into four groups: exploring ethical dilemmas, individual ethical decision frameworks, collective ethical decision frameworks, and ethics in human-AI interactions. Weidinger et al. [24] focused on language models and classified risks into six areas, including discrimination, hate

Table 2. List of issues/risks/aspects/principles used as the basis of specific studies.

Issues/Risks/Aspects/Principles	[18]	[19]	[20]	[21]	[22]
Accessibility/digital divide reduction				x	
Accountability	x	x	x		x
Accuracy		x			
Bias		x			
Civil society interaction/inclusion				x	
Completeness		x			
Correction of existing inequalities in society				x	
Data Protection		x			
Data quality	x	x			
DEI regulation conformity				x	
Diluting Rights		x			
Diversity in learning datasets				x	
Diversity in the AI sector				x	
Equity				x	
Ethical issues/Ethics	x		x		
Explainability	x	x	x		x
Extintion		x			
Fairness	x	x	x	x	x
Human decisions made				x	
Human dignity				x	
Inclusion				x	
Interpretability		x			
Justice	x				
Legal	x				
Liability		x			
Manipulation		x			
Moral		x			
Nondiscrimination				x	
Opacity		x			
Organizational culture	x				
Perception	x				
Power		x			

(*continued*)

Table 2. (*continued*)

Issues/Risks/Aspects/Principles	[18]	[19]	[20]	[21]	[22]
Privacy	x	x	x		
Protection		x			
Reliability		x			
Remedies for discrimination				x	
Representativeness				x	
Resistance	x				
Responsibility	x				
Safety		x	x		
Security	x	x	x		
Semantic		x			
Skillful workers	x				
Social justice				x	
Systemic		x			
Transparency	x	x	x	x	x
Trust	x				

speech, and exclusion; information hazards; misinformation harms; malicious users; human-computer interaction harms; and environmental and socioeconomic harms.

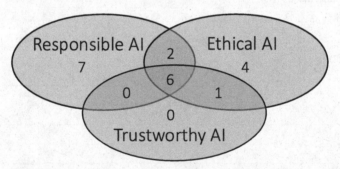

Fig. 2. Number of papers using the different key umbrella terms.

Sham et al. [25] stands out as one of the few papers delving into the technical aspects of ethical and responsible AI. The authors analyzed racial bias in facial expression recognition methods and found bias towards the races present in the training data. They further noted that an increase in performance can exacerbate bias, especially if the training dataset is imbalanced. Including more variance in the training data can partially mitigate bias but does not eliminate it. To improve the performance of these methods, they recommend adding missing races equally. In contrast, Papakyriakopoulos and Xiang [26] focused on best practices for ethical speech datasets for responsible AI. They highlighted the limitations of existing datasets and advocate for a human-centered approach and interdisciplinary research when developing AI applications. The proposed best practices aim to mitigate harm and ensure inclusivity.

Discussions about ethics and responsibility in AI often center on algorithmic solutions. Lu et al. [10] reinforce this idea, highlighting that recently issued high-level principles, guidelines, and regulations are difficult to implement in practice. The authors argue that a system-level approach is necessary for responsible AI, encompassing multiple components of the software engineering lifecycle. They also identify a gap in the literature concerning the design of responsible AI systems and propose a set of design patterns that can be integrated into AI systems to promote responsible AI by design.

Minkkinen et al. [27] interviewed 15 experts in responsible AI (RAI) to understand their work expectations and compared them with those identified in the European ecosystem's technological frame. The study found congruent and incongruent expectations, each with further sub-classes, and proposed ecosystems as a mediating level between regulation, ethical principles, and organizational AI implementation. In a similar vein, Gianni et al. [28] analyzed current national strategies and ethics guidelines to provide solutions to societal, ethical, and political issues posed by AI systems. However, based on their limitations, the authors proposed an alternative approach to enhance society's active involvement in discussing the impact and role of AI systems.

Abbu et al. and Treacy [29, 30] propose frameworks for ethical considerations in AI systems. Abbu et al. developed a conceptual model based on interviews with leaders of digitally mature organizations, identifying six key areas that organizations should consider: leadership, data, talent, visual analytics, standards, and governance. Meanwhile, Treacy developed a theoretical framework based on judgement studies with data science experts, which identifies six performance areas and includes constraints and mechanisms to ensure ethical expectations are met throughout the AI system's lifecycle. Implementation of these frameworks can improve trust between technology and people, with significant implications for research and practice in information systems.

Most papers discuss the issues themselves, regardless of the areas of application, while four papers specifically address health (two papers) and military (two papers) fields. Trocin et al. [31] provide a systematic analysis of Responsible AI in digital health, identifying ethical concerns that are both epistemic (i.e., quality of the evidence) and normative (i.e., fairness of the action and its effects) in nature. They suggest that these concerns are especially critical in healthcare, where lives are at risk and sensitive considerations may not be as pertinent in other domains beyond healthcare. Epistemic concerns include inconclusive, inscrutable, and misguided evidence, while normative concerns relate to unfair outcomes and transformative effects. Traceability is a concern that is related to both epistemic and normative concerns. El-Sappagh et al. [32] conducted a review of recent developments in the Trustworthy AI (TAI) domain, including standards and guidelines, with a specific focus on the diagnosis and progression of Alzheimer's Disease (AD). They proposed several requirements that need to be addressed in the design, development, and deployment of TAI systems.

In the military domain, the discussion has focused on the use of lethal autonomous weapon systems and the potential dangers of providing AI systems with too much autonomy. Meerveld et al. [33] address this topic, calling for solutions subject to meaningful human control and considering military effectiveness and the decision-making chain in military operations. One solution is to team human and AI systems to facilitate faster and more appropriate decision-making under pressure and uncertainty and use AI systems for adaptive training of military personnel, thus helping mitigate decision-making biases. Boulanin and Louis [34] propose the concept of "responsible reliance" as a means to ensure compliance with international humanitarian law and accountability when using AI tools in armed conflicts. They argue that states should establish a framework to enable natural persons involved in the use of AI tools to responsibly rely on the tool's technical aspects, the conduct of other people involved in its development and use, and the policies and processes implemented at the state level.

The analysis of the 21 papers reveals a lack of real-world examples that illustrate the importance of ethical considerations in AI. While five papers mention real cases, only three provide detailed descriptions of their relevance. Squadrone [35] discusses bias issues in multiple datasets used to train machine learning algorithms, such as the Correctional Offender Management Profiling for Alternative Sanctions (COMPAS) dataset, the German credit dataset, the adult dataset, the default credit card clients, and the law school dataset. Varsha [36] discusses the gender distortion in Amazon's AI recruiting tool, Airbnb's customer rejection issue, and concerns about bias, privacy, and data transparency in Google Ad personalized page. Belle [37] details the COMPAS dataset problem, the infamous trolley problem, and the Tesla Model S crash in 2016. Besides, the trolley problem is mentioned in the study by Yu et al. [23], while Teixeira et al. [19] refers to several real problems such as the Cambridge Analytica revealed, the Self-Driving Uber car that killed a pedestrian, the Tesla autopilot fatal car crash, the IBM Watson Recommending "unsafe and incorrect" cancer, the Amazon Facial recognition which wrongly identified 28 lawmakers, the Facebook security breach that exposed 50 million users, as well as the unfairness detected in the COMPAS system.

4 Discussion

Combining our findings from the literature with an increasing stream of real-word news about recent developments in AI-infused products, we clustered existing and emerging AI ethics and responsibility issues into the following categories. Weidinger et al. [24] have also identified some similar ones in the context of language models.

Broken systems: These are the most mentioned cases. They refer to situations where the algorithm or the training data lead to unreliable outputs [38]. These systems frequently assign disproportionate weight to some variables, like race or gender, but there is no transparency to this effect, making them impossible to challenge. These situations are typically only identified when regulators or the press examine the systems under freedom of information acts. Nevertheless, the damage they cause to people's lives can be dramatic, such as lost homes, divorces [39], prosecution, or incarceration [40]. Besides the inherent technical shortcomings, auditors have also pointed out "insufficient coordination" between the developers of the systems and their users as a cause for ethical considerations to be neglected [41]. This situation raises issues about the education of future creators of AI-infused systems, not only in terms of technical competence (e.g., requirements, algorithms, and training) but also ethics and responsibility. For example, as autonomous vehicles become more common, moral dilemmas regarding what to do in potential accident situations emerge, as evidenced in this MIT experiment [42]. The decisions regarding how the machines should act divides opinions and requires deep reflection and maybe regulation [43].

Hallucinations: The inclusion of erroneous information in the outputs from AI systems is not new. Some have cautioned against the introduction of false structures in X-ray or MRI images [44], and others have warned about made-up academic references [45]. However, as ChatGPT-type tools become available to the general population, the scale of the problem may increase dramatically. Furthermore, it is compounded by the fact that these conversational AIs present true and false information with the same apparent "confidence" instead of declining to answer when they cannot ensure correctness. With less knowledgeable people, this can lead to the heightening of misinformation and potentially dangerous situations. Some have already led to court cases [46].

Intellectual property rights violations: This is an emerging category, with more cases prone to appear as the use of generative AI tools–such as Stable Diffusion, Midjourney, or ChatGPT–becomes more widespread. Some content creators are already suing for the appropriation of their work to train AI algorithms without a request for permission or compensation [47–49]. Perhaps even more damaging cases will appear as developers increasingly ask chatbots or assistants like CoPilot for ready-to-use computer code. Even if these AI tools have learned only from open-source software (OSS) projects, which is not a given, there are still serious issues to consider, as not all OSS licenses are equal, and some are incompatible with others, meaning that it is illegal to mix them in the same product. Even worse, some licenses, such as GPL, are viral, meaning that any code that uses a GPL component must legally be made available under that same license. In the past, companies have suffered injunctions or been forced to make their proprietary source code available because of carelessly using a GPL library [50].

Privacy and regulation violations: Some of the broken systems discussed above are also very invasive of people's privacy, controlling, for instance, the length of someone's last romantic relationship [51]. More recently, ChatGPT was banned in Italy over privacy concerns and potential violation of the European Union's (EU) General Data Protection Regulation (GDPR) [52]. The Italian data-protection authority said, "the app had experienced a data breach involving user conversations and payment information." It also claimed that there was no legal basis to justify "the mass collection and storage of personal data for the purpose of 'training' the algorithms underlying the operation of the platform," among other concerns related to the age of the users [52]. Privacy regulators in France, Ireland, and Germany could follow in Italy's footsteps [53]. Coincidentally, it has recently become public that Samsung employees have inadvertently leaked trade secrets by using ChatGPT to assist in preparing notes for a presentation and checking and optimizing source code [54, 55]. Another example of testing the ethics and regulatory limits can be found in actions of the facial recognition company Clearview AI, which "scraped the public web—social media, employment sites, YouTube, Venmo—to create a database with three billion images of people, along with links to the webpages from which the photos had come" [56]. Trials of this unregulated database have been offered to individual law enforcement officers who often use it without their department's approval [57]. In Sweden, such illegal use by the police force led to a fine of €250,000 by the country's data watchdog [57].

Enabling malicious actors and harmful actions: Some uses of AI have been deeply concerning, namely voice cloning [58] and the generation of deep fake videos [59]. For example, in March 2022, in the early days of the Russian invasion of Ukraine, hackers broadcast via the Ukrainian news website Ukraine 24 a deep fake video of President Volodymyr Zelensky capitulating and calling on his soldiers to lay down their weapons [60]. The necessary software to create these fakes is readily available on the Internet, and the hardware requirements are modest by today's standards [61]. Other nefarious uses of AI include accelerating password cracking [62] or enabling otherwise unskilled people to create software exploits [63, 64], or effective phishing e-mails [65]. Although some believe that powerful AI models should be prevented from running on personal computers to retain some control, others demonstrate how inglorious that effort may be [66]. Furthermore, as ChatGPT-type systems evolve from conversational systems to agents, capable of acting autonomously and performing tasks with little human intervention, like Auto-GPT [67], new risks emerge.

Environmental and socioeconomic harms: At a time of increasing climate urgency, energy consumption and the carbon footprint of AI applications are also matters of ethics and responsibility [68]. As with other energy-intensive technologies like proof-of-work blockchain, the call is to research more environmentally sustainable algorithms to offset the increasing use scale.

These categories show that AI ethics and responsibility needs to be reflected upon and addressed across various partially overlapping dimensions, as shown in Fig. 3.

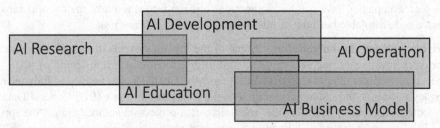

Fig. 3. Dimensions of AI ethics and responsibility in a social and political environment.

AI Research must be ethical and responsible, considering which avenues to follow, why, how, and when. AI Education of future professionals should emphasize ethical considerations alongside technical skills to prepare them for addressing ethical issues. Lessons from current broken systems should guide the AI Development of the next generation of tools. AI Operation and AI Business Models should align with ethical standards, avoiding the launch of products that provide erroneous information and violate intellectual property, privacy, and regulations. The military and healthcare fields exemplify the need for a cross-dimensional approach to addressing ethical and responsible AI applications.

Philosopher Karl Popper wrote, "One of the few things we can do is to try to keep alive, in all scientists, the consciousness of their responsibility" [69]. Some argue that, like medical doctors, computer scientists should also take a Hippocratic oath that their work does no harm to society [70].

5 Conclusion

We provided a reflection on AI ethics and responsibility. Departing from a systematic literature review [12, 13], we identified several key cases and issues that have led to the development of taxonomies, conceptual models, and official regulations, to better understand these issues and propose potential solutions to address them. In our discussion, we classified real-world cases of unethical or irresponsible uses of AI into six groups—broken systems, hallucinations, intellectual property rights violations, privacy and regulation violations, enabling malicious actors and harmful actions, environmental and socioeconomic harms—providing examples and discussing implications. We concluded that AI ethics and responsibility need to be reflected upon and addressed across five partially overlapping dimensions: Research, Education, Development, Operation, and Business Model.

We must acknowledge two main limitations of our work. First, our literature review was restricted to Scopus, potentially excluding relevant papers not indexed in this database. Second, our reflection on the AI ethics and responsibility across the five identified dimensions is brief and should be considered only as a seed for further work.

This literature review has identified several promising avenues for future research. First, more discussion and consensus-building are needed regarding the meaning of key umbrella terms used in the literature and shown in Fig. 2. Further study of the identified issues, risks, aspects, and principles would enhance understanding of these concepts. Second, exploring ways to involve users and civil society in discussions on the impact and role of AI systems could foster trust and comprehension. This could include investigating citizen perceptions of AI systems and ways to engage them in developing and implementing such systems. Third, research is needed to assess the effectiveness of ethical frameworks and government regulations on AI development and deployment. Finally, investigating how to align AI systems with diverse ethical values, cultural norms, and societal expectations also holds promise.

Acknowledgments. This work was partially funded by FCT-Foundation for Science and Technology, I.P./MCTES through national funds (PIDDAC), within the scope of CISUC R&D Unit-UIDB/00326/2020 or project code UIDP/00326/2020.

References

1. Hu, K.: ChatGPT sets record for fastest-growing user base - analyst note (2023). https://www.reuters.com/technology/chatgpt-sets-record-fastest-growing-user-base-analyst-note-2023-02-01/. Accessed 2023

2. Future of Life: Pause Giant AI Experiments: An Open Letter (2023). https://futureoflife.org/open-letter/pause-giant-ai-experiments/. Accessed 2023

3. Ordonez, V., Dunn, T., Noll, E.: OpenAI CEO Sam Altman says AI will reshape society, acknowledges risks: "A little bit scared of this" (2023). https://abcnews.go.com/Technology/openai-ceo-sam-altman-ai-reshape-society-acknowledges/story?id=97897122.   Accessed 2023

4. Schiffer, Z., Newton, C.: Microsoft just laid off one of its responsible AI teams (2023). https://www.platformer.news/p/microsoft-just-laid-off-one-of-its. Accessed 2023

5. DeGeurin, M.: Welp, There Goes Twitter's Ethical AI Team, Among Others as Employees Post Final Messages(2022). https://gizmodo.com/twitter-layoffs-elon-musk-ai-ethics-1849743051. Accessed 2022

6. Horwitz, J.: Facebook Parent Meta Platforms Cuts Responsible Innovation Team (2022). https://www.wsj.com/articles/facebook-parent-meta-platforms-cuts-responsible-innovation-team-11662658423. Accessed 2022

7. Hayden, F.: One year after promising to double AI ethics team, Google is light on details (2022). https://www.emergingtechbrew.com/stories/2022/06/07/one-year-after-promising-to-double-ai-ethics-team-google-is-light-on-details. Accessed 2022

8. European Commission: Artificial Intelligence for Europe (2018). https://eur-lex.europa.eu/legal-content/EN/TXT/?uri=COM%3A2018%3A237%3AFIN. Accessed 2018

9. European Commission: Coordinated Plan on Artificial Intelligence (2018). https://eur-lex.europa.eu/legal-content/EN/TXT/?uri=CELEX%3A52018DC0795&qid=1683368591075. Accessed 2018

10. Lu, Q., Zhu, L., Xu, X., Whittle, J.: Responsible-AI-by-design: a pattern collection for designing responsible AI systems. IEEE Softw. 1–7 (2023). https://doi.org/10.1109/MS.2022.3233582

11. UNESCO: Recomendation on the Ethics of Artificial Intelligence (2022). https://unesdoc.unesco.org/ark:/48223/pf0000381137. Accessed 2022

12. Webster, J., Watson, R.T.: Analyzing the past to prepare for the future: writing a literature review. MIS Q. **26**, xiii–xxiii (2002)

13. Kitchenham, B.: Procedures for Performing Systematic Reviews. (2004)

14. Ouzzani, M., Hammady, H., Fedorowicz, Z., Elmagarmid, A.: Rayyan—a web and mobile app for systematic reviews. Syst. Rev. **5**, 210 (2016). https://doi.org/10.1186/s13643-016-0384-4

15. Denzin, N.K.: The Research Act in Sociology: A Theoretical Introduction to Sociological Methods. Butterworths, London (1970)

16. Jick, T.D.: Mixing qualitative and quantitative methods: triangulation in action. Adm. Sci. Q. **24**, 602–611 (1979). https://doi.org/10.2307/2392366

17. Fink, A.: Survey Research Methods. In: Peterson, P., Baker, E., McGaw, B. (eds.) International Encyclopedia of Education, 3rd edn., pp. 152–160. Elsevier, Oxford (2010)

18. Merhi, M.I.: An assessment of the barriers impacting responsible artificial intelligence. Inf. Syst. Front. (2022). https://doi.org/10.1007/s10796-022-10276-3

19. Teixeira, S., Rodrigues, J., Veloso, B., Gama, J.: An exploratory diagnosis of artificial intelligence risks for a responsible governance. In: Proceedings of the 15th International Conference on Theory and Practice of Electronic Governance, pp. 25–31. Association for Computing Machinery, New York, NY, USA (2022)

20. Brumen, B., Göllner, S., Tropmann-Frick, M.: Aspects and views on responsible artificial intelligence. In: Nicosia, G., Ojha, V., La Malfa, E., La Malfa, G., Pardalos, P., Di Fatta, G., Giuffrida, G., and Umeton, R. (eds.) Machine Learning, Optimization, and Data Science, pp. 384–398. Springer Nature Switzerland, Cham (2023)

21. Cachat-Rosset, G., Klarsfeld, A.: Diversity, equity, and inclusion in artificial intelligence: an evaluation of guidelines. Appl. Artif. Intell. **37**, 2176618 (2023). https://doi.org/10.1080/088 39514.2023.2176618

22. Werder, K., Ramesh, B., Zhang, R. (Sophia): Establishing data provenance for responsible artificial intelligence systems. ACM Trans. Manag. Inf. Syst. **13**, 22:1–22:23 (2022). https://doi.org/10.1145/3503488

23. Yu, H., Shen, Z., Miao, C., Leung, C., Lesser, V.R., Yang, Q.: Building ethics into artificial intelligence. In: Proceedings of the Twenty-Seventh International Joint Conference on Artificial Intelligence, pp. 5527–5533. International Joint Conferences on Artificial Intelligence Organization, Stockholm, Sweden (2018)

24. Weidinger, L., Uesato, J., Rauh, M., Griffin, C., Huang, P.-S., Mellor, J., Glaese, A., Cheng, M., Balle, B., Kasirzadeh, A., Biles, C., Brown, S., Kenton, Z., Hawkins, W., Stepleton, T., Birhane, A., Hendricks, L.A., Rimell, L., Isaac, W., Haas, J., Legassick, S., Irving, G., Gabriel, I.: Taxonomy of risks posed by language models. In: 2022 ACM Conference on Fairness, Accountability, and Transparency, pp. 214–229. Association for Computing Machinery, New York, NY, USA (2022)

25. Sham, A.H., et al.: Ethical AI in facial expression analysis: racial bias. SIViP **17**, 399–406 (2023). https://doi.org/10.1007/s11760-022-02246-8

26. Papakyriakopoulos, O., Xiang, A.: Considerations for ethical speech recognition datasets. In: Proceedings of the Sixteenth ACM International Conference on Web Search and Data Mining, pp. 1287–1288. Association for Computing Machinery, New York, NY, USA (2023)

27. Minkkinen, M., Zimmer, M.P., Mäntymäki, M.: Co-shaping an ecosystem for responsible AI: five types of expectation work in response to a technological frame. Inf. Syst. Front. **25**, 103–121 (2023). https://doi.org/10.1007/s10796-022-10269-2

28. Gianni, R., Lehtinen, S., Nieminen, M.: Governance of responsible AI: from ethical guidelines to cooperative policies. Front. Comput. Sci. **4** (2022)

29. Abbu, H., Mugge, P., Gudergan, G.: Ethical considerations of artificial intelligence: ensuring fairness, transparency, and explainability. In: 2022 IEEE 28th International Conference on Engineering, Technology and Innovation (ICE/ITMC) & 31st International Association for Management of Technology (IAMOT) Joint Conference, pp. 1–7 (2022)

30. Treacy, S.: Mechanisms and constraints underpinning ethically aligned artificial intelligence systems: an exploration of key performance areas. In: Presented at the 3rd European Conference on the Impact of Artificial Intelligence and Robotics, ECIAIR 2021 (2021)

31. Trocin, C., Mikalef, P., Papamitsiou, Z., Conboy, K.: Responsible AI for digital health: a synthesis and a research agenda. Inf. Syst. Front. (2021). https://doi.org/10.1007/s10796-021-10146-4

32. El-Sappagh, S., Alonso-Moral, J.M., Abuhmed, T., Ali, F., Bugarín-Diz, A.: Trustworthy artificial intelligence in Alzheimer's disease: state of the art, opportunities, and challenges. Artif. Intell. Rev. (2023). https://doi.org/10.1007/s10462-023-10415-5

33. Meerveld, H.W., Lindelauf, R.H.A., Postma, E.O., Postma, M.: The irresponsibility of not using AI in the military. Ethics Inf. Technol. **25**, 14 (2023). https://doi.org/10.1007/s10676-023-09683-0

34. Boulanin, V., Lewis, D.A.: Responsible reliance concerning development and use of AI in the military domain. Ethics Inf. Technol. **25**, 8 (2023). https://doi.org/10.1007/s10676-023-09691-0

35. Squadrone, L., Croce, D., Basili, R.: Ethics by design for intelligent and sustainable adaptive systems. In: Dovier, A., Montanari, A., Orlandini, A. (eds.) AIxIA 2022–Advances in Artificial Intelligence, pp. 154–167. Springer International Publishing, Cham (2023)

36. Varsha P.S.: How can we manage biases in artificial intelligence systems–a systematic literature review. Int. J. Inf. Manag. Data Insights **3**, 100165 (2023). https://doi.org/10.1016/j.jjimei.2023.100165

37. Belle, V.: Knowledge representation and acquisition for ethical AI: challenges and opportunities. Ethics Inf. Technol. **25**, 22 (2023). https://doi.org/10.1007/s10676-023-09692-z

38. Geiger, G.: How Denmark's Welfare State Became a Surveillance Nightmare (2023). https://www.wired.com/story/algorithms-welfare-state-politics/. Accessed 2023

39. Meaker, M.: The Fraud-Detection Business Has a Dirty Secret (2023). https://www.wired.com/story/welfare-fraud-industry/. Accessed 2022

40. Harwell, D.: Federal study confirms racial bias of many facial-recognition systems, casts doubt on their expanding use (2019). https://www.washingtonpost.com/technology/2019/12/19/federal-study-confirms-racial-bias-many-facial-recognition-systems-casts-doubt-their-expanding-use/. Accessed 2019

41. Burgess, M., Schot, E., Geiger, G.: This Algorithm Could Ruin Your Life (2023). https://www.wired.com/story/welfare-algorithms-discrimination/. Accessed 2023

42. Awad, E., et al.: The moral machine experiment. Nature **563**, 59–64 (2018). https://doi.org/10.1038/s41586-018-0637-6

43. Taylor, M.: Self-Driving Mercedes-Benzes Will Prioritize Occupant Safety over Pedestrians (2016). https://www.caranddriver.com/news/a15344706/self-driving-mercedes-will-prioritize-occupant-safety-over-pedestrians/. Accessed 2016

44. Smith, S.G.: Hallucinations Could Blunt ChatGPT's Success (2023). https://spectrum.ieee.org/ai-hallucination#toggle-gdpr. Accessed 2023

45. Wilkinson, D.: Be Careful… ChatGPT Appears to be Making up Academic References (2023). https://oxford-review.com/chatgpt-making-up-references/. Accessed 2023

46. Petkauskas, V.: OpenAI ordered to delete ChatGPT over false death claims (2023). https://cybernews.com/news/openai-ordered-delete-chatgpt/. Accessed 2023

47. Vincent, J.: Getty images is suing the creators of AI art tool stable diffusion for scraping its content (2023). https://www.theverge.com/2023/1/17/23558516/ai-art-copyright-stable-diffusion-getty-images-lawsuit. Accessed 2023

48. Vincent, J.: AI art tools stable diffusion and midjourney targeted with copyright lawsuit (2023). https://www.theverge.com/2023/1/16/23557098/generative-ai-art-copyright-legal-lawsuit-stable-diffusion-midjourney-deviantart. Accessed 2023

49. Robinson, T.: The Wes Anderson artbot craze is a fun trend, but it clarifies AI art's ethical issues (2022). https://www.polygon.com/23494958/wes-anderson-midjourney-ai-art-generator-viral-trend

50. Welte, H.: The gpl-violations.org project. https://gpl-violations.org/

51. Constantaras, E., Geiger, G., Justin-Casimir, B., Dhruv, M., Aung, H.: Inside the Suspicion Machine (2023). https://www.wired.com/story/welfare-state-algorithms/. Accessed 2023

52. McCallum, S.: ChatGPT banned in Italy over privacy concerns (2023). https://www.bbc.com/news/technology-65139406. Accessed 2023

53. Mukherjee, S., Pollina, E., More, R.: Italy's ChatGPT ban attracts EU privacy regulators (2023). https://www.reuters.com/technology/germany-principle-could-block-chat-gpt-if-needed-data-protection-chief-2023-04-03/. Accessed 2023

54. Mauran, C.: Whoops, Samsung workers accidentally leaked trade secrets via ChatGPT (2023). https://mashable.com/article/samsung-chatgpt-leak-details

55. Cohen, M.: Workers are secretly using ChatGPT, AI and it will pose big risks for tech leaders (2023). https://www.cnbc.com/2023/04/30/the-big-cyber-risks-when-chatgpt-and-ai-are-secretly-used-by-employees.html. Accessed 2023

56. Hill, K.: What Happens When Our Faces Are Tracked Everywhere We Go? (2021). https://www.nytimes.com/interactive/2021/03/18/magazine/facial-recognition-clearview-ai.html. Accessed 2021

57. Heikkila, M.: Clearview scandal exposes limits of transatlantic AI collaboration (2021). https://www.politico.eu/article/clearview-scandal-exposes-limits-transatlantic-ai-facial-recognition-collaboration/. Accessed 2021

58. ElevenLabs: ElevenLabs-Prime AI Text to Speech|Voice Cloning. https://beta.elevenlabs.io/
59. O'Sullivan, D.: Inside the Pentagon's race against deepfake videos. CNN Business (2019)
60. Debunking a deepfake video of Zelensky telling Ukrainians to surrender (2022). https://www.france24.com/en/tv-shows/truth-or-fake/20220317-deepfake-video-of-zelensky-telling-ukrainians-to-surrender-debunked. Accessed 2022
61. iperov: DeepFaceLab (2023). https://github.com/iperov/DeepFaceLab
62. Home Security Heroes: 2023 Password Cracking: How Fast Can AI Crack Passwords? https://www.homesecurityheroes.com/ai-password-cracking/
63. McNeal, R.: A novice just used ChatGPT to create terrifyingly sophisticated malware (2023). https://www.androidauthority.com/chatgpt-malware-3310791/. Accessed 2023
64. Merian, D.: ChatGPT Hacking Prompts, SQLi, XSS, Vuln Analysis, Nuclei Templates, and more (2023). https://systemweakness.com/chatgpt-hacking-prompts-sqli-xss-vuln-analysis-nuclei-templates-and-more-dba6fa839a45. Accessed 2023
65. Roose, K., Newton, C., Land, D., Cohn, R., Poyant, J., Moxley, A., Powell, D., Lozano, M., Niemisto, R.: Google C.E.O. Sundar Pichai on Bard, A.I. 'Whiplash' and Competing With ChatGPT (2023). https://www.nytimes.com/2023/03/31/podcasts/hard-fork-sundar.html. Accessed 2023
66. Blain, L.: The genie escapes: Stanford copies the ChatGPT AI for less than $600 (2023). https://newatlas.com/technology/stanford-alpaca-cheap-gpt/. Accessed 2023
67. Gravitas, S.: Auto-GPT: An Autonomous GPT-4 Experiment (2023). https://github.com/Significant-Gravitas/Auto-GPT. Accessed 2023
68. Walsh, P., Bera, J., Sharma, V.S., Kaulgud, V., Rao, R.M., Ross, O.: Sustainable AI in the cloud: exploring machine learning energy use in the cloud. In: 2021 36th IEEE/ACM International Conference on Automated Software Engineering Workshops (ASEW), pp. 265–266 (2021)
69. Popper, K.R.: The moral responsibility of the scientist. Bull. Peace Propos. 2, 279–283 (1971). https://doi.org/10.1177/096701067100200311
70. Sample, I.: Maths and tech specialists need Hippocratic oath, says academic (2019). https://www.theguardian.com/science/2019/aug/16/mathematicians-need-doctor-style-hippocratic-oath-says-academic-hannah-fry. Accessed 2023

Towards Interpretability in Fintech Applications via Knowledge Augmentation

Catarina Silva, Tiago Faria, and Bernardete Ribeiro[⊠]

University of Coimbra, Coimbra, Portugal
{catarina,bribeiro}@dei.uc.pt

Abstract. The financial industry is a major player in the digital landscape and a key driver of digital transformation in the economy. In recent times, the financial sector has come under scrutiny due to emerging financial crises, particularly in high-risk areas like credit scoring models where standard AI models may not be fully reliable. This highlights the need for greater accountability and transparency in the use of digital technologies in Fintech. In this paper, we propose a novel approach to enhance the interpretability of AI models by knowledge augmentation using distillation methods. Our aim is to transfer the knowledge from black-box models to more transparent and interpretable models, e.g., decision-trees, enabling a deeper understanding of decision patterns. We apply our method to a credit score problem and demonstrate that it is feasible to use white-box techniques to gain insight into the decision patterns of black-box models. Our results show the potential for improving interpretability and transparency in AI decision-making processes in Fintech scenarios.

Keywords: Knowledge augmentation · Interpretability · Distillation

1 Introduction

Fair, Explainable, and Interpretable Artificial Intelligence (AI) refers to the development and deployment of AI systems that are fair, transparent, and easily understood by humans [12]. This type of AI is particularly relevant for the financial technology (Fintech) industry, which is heavily regulated and relies on data to make informed decisions [5]. It ultimately helps to address challenges such as ethical considerations, regulatory compliance, and consumer trust in Fintech by making AI systems more understandable and verifiable.

In this paper, we propose a new method for enhancing the interpretability of deep neural networks (DNNs) by distilling knowledge from them into decision trees. Our approach involves using the logits from the DNN as targets to train a decision tree for regression. The goal is to recreate the decision-making process of the DNN in a format that is both interpretable and actionable.

The main contributions include:

- A decision tree surrogate model to transfer knowledge from deep models to understand the decision patterns in different applications and provide actionability to support human decision.
- Demonstration of the potential in interpretability of such distilled models to case studies of credit scoring and loan prediction
- Generalization with no restriction on the type of application.

The rest of the paper is organized as follows. Next section presents some background on interpretability of AI focusing on Fintech. Section 3 details the knowledge augmentation strategy proposed in this work, while Sect. 5 describes the experimental setup, including datasets and evaluation metrics. Section 6 analysis the results and Sect. 7 delineates the conclusions and future work.

2   Interpretability in Fintech

Interpretability can be used to augment knowledge in Fintech in several ways [14]:

- **Improved decision-making**: By making the decision-making process of AI models more transparent and understandable, interpretability can help Fintech stakeholders to make better-informed decisions. This can improve the accuracy of predictions and reduce the risk of incorrect or unethical decisions.
- **Increased trust**: Interpretability can help to build trust in AI models by making the decision-making process more transparent and understandable. This can improve the adoption and implementation of AI technologies in Fintech, and increase the confidence of stakeholders in the decisions made by AI models [13].
- **Bias identification and mitigation**: Interpretability can help to identify potential sources of bias in AI models and make the decision-making process more transparent. This can help to reduce the risk of biased decisions and increase fairness in Fintech [10].
- **Regulatory compliance**: Interpretability can help Fintech organizations to meet regulatory requirements by making the decision-making process of AI models more transparent and understandable. This can help to reduce the risk of regulatory violations and improve compliance [11].
- **Improved model development**: Interpretability can provide insights into how AI models are making decisions, allowing Fintech organizations and researchers to improve the development of future models. This can improve the accuracy and effectiveness of AI models over time [18].

Regulatory bodies play a significant role in shaping the form of AI in Fintech by setting standards and guidelines for the development, deployment, and use of AI technologies. Through regulation, regulatory bodies can influence the ethical, transparent, and accountable use of AI in Fintech [3] as, for example, by setting out standards.

They can also help to address the potential for bias and unfair outcomes in by setting guidelines for the development and deployment of AI models. This can include guidelines for data collection and processing, as well as requirements for fairness and impartiality in the decision-making process of AI models.

Consumer rights are protected by setting standards and guidelines for the use of AI in consumer-facing Fintech products and services. One of the main activities of regulatory bodies includes monitoring the compliance of Fintech organizations with AI regulations and guidelines, and enforce penalties for non-compliance.

2.1 Interpretability Approaches

When it comes to classifying interpretability approaches, there are typically three categories that are commonly used [9]:

- **Scope**–is an important factor to consider when classifying interpretability approaches, as it refers to the extent or coverage of the model's predictions that we aim to explain. If the aim is to achieve global explanations in order to get an understanding of the holistic decision making process of a model as whole we are talking about **global scope** techniques. On the other hand, if we are trying to understand how a model came up with a prediction for a specific observation we are talking about local explanations and therefore **local scope**.
  There have been numerous works and two particularly notable contributions are Baehrens et al.'s method [2] for explaining local decisions made by arbitrary nonlinear classification algorithms, and Ribeiro et al.'s [15] LIME for Local Interpretable Model-Agnostic Explanation.
- **Methodology**—relates to the fundamental concept of the algorithm that enables it to generate explanations, i.e., which information and process is used to extract knowledge use. A traditional approach is to use **perturbation** of inputs to analyze the impact on output, as LIME does [15]. Another approach is to use **back-propagation** information, namely the error gradients to understand the impact that the different input neurons have on the output.
- **Relation to the model**—relates to whether the technique is dependent on the specific model being used. Methods dependent on the model they are being applied to are called **model-intrinsic**, as in [6]. Interpretability techniques that can be applied to any model are **model-agnostic**. The drawback of model-intrinsic techniques is that they are limited to a specific class of models, which is why there is a preference for model-agnostic methods like knowledge distillation. On the other hand, model-intrinsic approaches can sometimes leverage specific characteristics of a model that may not be captured by model-agnostic methods.

Several works in the field of interpretable machine learning have resulted in the development of toolboxes for generating explanations, such as ELI5 [1], which provides local explanations and is closely connected to LIME [15]. Another example is Shap, which leverages the concept of Shapley values from game theory to determine the impact of features on a model's outcome by assigning them corresponding weights across their entire range of values.

2.2 Surrogate Models

Surrogate models are simplified models that are used to approximate the behavior of complex AI models, such as deep neural networks. The goal of using surrogate models is to provide a more interpretable and manageable representation of the complex model, without sacrificing too much accuracy. Surrogate models can be classified in two types: global surrogate models and local surrogate models [9].

A global surrogate model is a model that is trained to mimic a black-box model giving a global overview of what the black-box model is trying to achieve. This model is usually interpretable and can be used to draw conclusions about the way the mimicked model is trying to make its predictions.

Local surrogate models on the other hand are interpretable models that are used to explain individual predictions of black-box machine learning models. LIME [15] makes use of linear models as surrogate models. Local surrogate models do not mind all the data and rather focus on a specific observation and how small perturbations on its features affect the outcome on the black-box model.

3   Knowledge Extraction and Augmentation

3.1   Knowledge Extraction Methods

One way of interpreting black-models would be making then interpretable (white-box) in the first place, but that is usually not feasible as most models already in-place or with the desired performance, usually deep nets, are black-box. This is often referred to as the trade-off between interpretability and performance: more interpretable models tend to be less accurate and vice-versa [16]. That would mean we would have to replace those models with completely new interpretable ones, structured to solve very specific problems that might not be as accurate as the previous one sand they could be expensive to run. Moreover, they would be limited to the specific problems they are designed to solve. Knowledge extraction techniques aim to provide explanations about the internal workings of complex models such as deep neural nets. One approach to this is through model distillation.

Knowledge distillation

Knowledge distillation transfers the "dark knowledge" from a complex deep neural network (referred to as the "teacher") to a more interpretable model, e.g., a decision tree (referred to as the "student"). Distillation is a process that enables the transfer of information from a complex model to a simplified one, preserving the essence of the original model while making it more accessible.

"Dark knowledge", also known as hidden or latent knowledge, refers to the information contained in the hidden layers of a neural network model. This information includes the weights and connections of each neuron, the inputs, and the way they activate in response to specific observations. In other words, it represents the hidden information that is not easily visible to the human eye.

By transferring this dark knowledge to a decision tree the goal is to provide a more interpretable representation of the complex neural network model, while preserving its predictive performance. The decision tree, with its simple structure and clear decision rules, offers a more accessible way to understand the model's decision-making process and provides insight into the key factors that influence the model's predictions.

In the context of model distillation for deep neural networks, the focus is often on the last layer of the model, which can be viewed as the layer where the decision or prediction is made.

Consider a model M for classification of 3 classes: "class 1", "class 2", "class 3", with a softmax layer l_s as the last layer, and, for a given input i we know that the model outputs

$$M(i) = \text{"class 2"}. \tag{1}$$

If we are interested in dark knowledge we need to look deeper into the model. We find that the result is given by

$$argmax(output(l_s)), \tag{2}$$

and

$$output(l_s) = [0.3, 0.6, 0.1]. \tag{3}$$

We can understand why the model output was "class 2", which is the class with the highest predicted probability. We can also see that for the specific input i, the model learned that it is 3 times more likely to be classified in "class 1" than in "class 3".

This type of information, dark knowledge, is the rationale on which model distillation operates. It can be particularly useful when classes are strongly related and it has been shown to enable the creation of smaller, yet still accurate models [4].

Model compression [4] is also referred many times in the literature as one of the first examples of model distillation originally proposed to reduce the computational cost of a model at run-time by reducing its complexity which was later explored for interpretability.

Tan et al. [17] proposed that model distillation can be used to distill complex models into transparent models like generalized additive models and Splines. Che et al. [7] introduced in their paper a knowledge-distillation approach called Interpretable Mimic Learning, to learn interpretable phenotype features for making robust prediction while mimicking the performance of deep learning models.

A recent work by Xu et al. [19] presented DarkSight, a visualization method for interpreting the predictions of a black-box classifier on a data set in a way inspired by the notion of dark knowledge. This method combines ideas from knowledge distillation, dimension reduction and visualization of deep neural nets. The premise in all of the methods mentioned above is to use the capabilities of deep neural nets and translate the processes they learned during training to another model. We are interested not only on the ability to make the same class of models more efficient [4], but also in the ability of possibly changing their class [7] to a more interpretable one.

3.2 Knowledge Augmentation Methods

Knowledge augmentation through information extraction from intelligent models refers to the process of extracting interpretable and actionable insights from AI models that can facilitate decision-making by humans.

The goal of knowledge augmentation is to offer stakeholders a transparent comprehension of how an AI model generated its conclusions and to simplify the application of insights produced by the model to practical scenarios. To achieve this goal, it is necessary to have a certain level of interpretability and explainability that goes beyond just providing raw predictions or classifications.

In a Fintech context, an AI model may predict the likelihood of loan default for a specific borrower. Actionable interpretation of this model would involve not only presenting the raw prediction, but also providing information such as the causes that influenced the prediction, the level of confidence in the prediction, and recommended actions to mitigate the risk of default.

Knowledge augmentation can help address this challenge by enabling stakeholders to make informed decisions based on the outputs of AI models.

4   Proposed Approach

In this work we propose to augment the available knowledge by distillation, paving the way to unlocking the interpretability of AI models, providing insights into how decisions are made. By examining the interactions between classes, we can gain a better understanding of a model's reasoning and make informed decisions based on its predictions.

Prior research has explored the use of knowledge distillation to transfer information from complex models to more interpretable ones. For example, Tan et al. utilized Generalized Additive Models (GAMs) and splines in their work [17]. However, these models are limited in their visual appeal, making it challenging to effectively interpret the decision-making process.

Figure 1 depicts the knowledge augmentation approach. With the aim of augmenting knowledge and improving interpretability, we propose a distillation approach to transfer the knowledge from a deep neural network to a decision-tree model. This is achieved by matching the logits, or the scores before the last softmax layer of the neural network, and using these logits as targets to train a decision-tree for regression. The outcome of this process is a surrogate model that accurately reflects the decision-making process of the deep neural

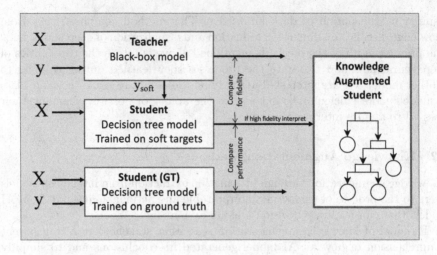

Fig. 1. Proposed knowledge augmentation approach

network, including both its strengths and weaknesses. The resulting decision-tree can be evaluated for its interpretability and actionability, providing a clear and intuitive representation of the underlying decision-making process. For each defined problem with input X and output y, we define a supervised training dataset:

$$D_{train} = \{X, y\}. \tag{4}$$

For each dataset we train a deep neural net model, which we will call "**Teacher**". We then extract the **logits** (values of the last layer before the softmax), y_{soft}, and use them as soft targets to train a decision-tree based model, which we call "**Student**" using XGBoost toolkit.[1]

We compare the performance of the deep neural network model and its surrogate, the decision-tree, by evaluating their results on the same observations. If the evaluation metrics are similar between the two models, it can be concluded that the decision-tree accurately mimics the decision-making process of the deep neural network.

To further validate the effectiveness of our approach, we train a third model, the "**Student (Ground-Truth)**" model, on the ground-truth labels. This model serves as a control group to assess the necessity of using a deep neural network in the first place. If the "**Student (Ground-Truth)**" model outperforms both the deep neural network and its surrogate, it implies that the problem is not complex enough to warrant the use of deep neural networks and thus the use of knowledge distillation is not necessary.

---

[1] https://xgboost.readthedocs.io/en/stable/.

5   Experimental Setup

5.1   Evaluation Metrics

The evaluation of the models was performed using standard metrics to assess their performance. The comparison was done between the "teacher" and "student" models to determine how closely the latter was mimicking the former. To gauge the decision task, a contingency matrix was used to visualize the outcomes of the classification.

In situations where false positives and false negatives carry different costs or in imbalanced datasets, it is more appropriate to use metrics that take these differences into consideration. For our problem, we prioritize the F1-score and Recall over accuracy as more meaningful evaluation metrics. If the F1-score/Recall of the student models are comparable to or better than the teacher model, it can be considered a reliable surrogate. In particular scenarios where the weight of false negatives is higher, such as credit risk classification, Recall score becomes of greater importance while still striving for a good F1-score.

5.2   Case Studies

To validate the proposed approach, we propose to use two different datasets:

- **German credit dataset** from the UCI ML Repository [8], a well-known dataset for credit scoring, was utilized. This dataset contains 1000 instances that classify individuals based on a set of attributes into either good or bad credit risks. This scenario can be easily adapted to other use cases, such as classifying good or bad values in a health prognosis system, or sensor readings in a predictive maintenance system.
  There are 20 explanatory variables with seven being numerical and 13 being categorical, with 30% observations accounting for the positive class.
- **Prosper Marketplace dataset**. The Prosper Marketplace, Inc. is a San Francisco-based peer-to-peer lending company. This dataset offers a more comprehensive and raw data compared to the German Credit dataset. This dataset was chosen to test the proposed approach, as it offers a real-world scenario that allows us to assess the performance of the method in the presence of noise and different dynamics. The aim was to translate the results obtained from the German Credit dataset to this more complete one, to evaluate the robustness and reliability of the method.
  The dataset is comprised of 113937 instances with each consisting of a group of 80 descriptive attributes that characterize the outcome of an individuals loan. After clearing up all null values and dropping some unnecessary columns, the set still consists 106290 instances and a total of 59 attribute columns. The considered target for classification was the loan status (Default, Problematic, and Good).

Two neural network architectures were used for the teacher model. A feed-forward neural network for the credit risk classification dataset with 2 layers of 256 and 128 hidden units respectively and a long short-term memory architecture for the stock movement prediction problem with 2 layers of 256 hidden units.

The selected interpretable model is a gradient boosted regression tree from XBGBoost's python library with the default parameters.

6   Analysis of Results

The models were evaluated based on their respective accuracy, precision, recall, and F1-score, with particular attention given to the F1-score and recall.

We have indications that the student model is closely capturing the decision-making of the teacher model, as evidenced by the similarity in scores across all four metrics. Of particular note is the recall metric, which is identical in both the student and teacher models (refer to Figs. 2 and 3).

In the context of credit scoring, accurately identifying individuals with bad credit is critical, and misclassifying them as having good credit (false negatives) can have far more significant consequences than the opposite (false positives). Therefore, a neural network's higher complexity is believed to be particularly helpful in classifying this minority class, making it an especially beneficial approach for credit scoring.

In this scenario, the minority class comprises only 30% of the total observations. Despite this, the F1-score results across all tree models suggest that

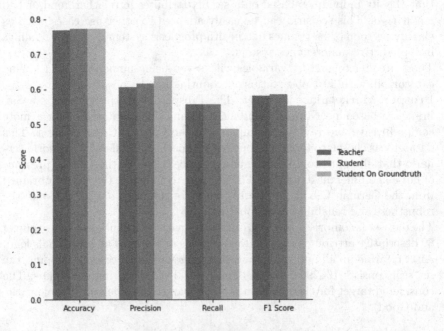

Fig. 2. Results on the German credit dataset

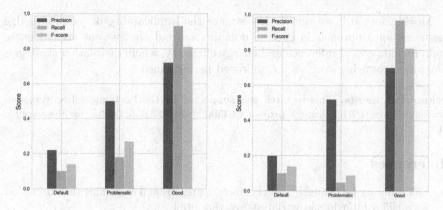

Fig. 3. Results on the Prosper loan dataset

```
Rules used to predict sample number 1694(True Outcome:Good||Predicted Outcome(Defaulted)):

decision node 0  : Employed_1 was less than [[0.5]] with a value of [[0.]]
decision node 1  : PublicRecordsLast10Years was less than [[0.9981714]] with a value of [[0.]]
decision node 2  : TotalProsperLoans was less than [[2.36902097]] with a value of [[0.]]
decision node 3  : InvestmentFromFriendsCount was less than [[0.50000001]] with a value of [[0.]]
decision node 4  : InquiriesLast6Months was less than [[29.44195014]] with a value of [[0.]]
decision node 5  : OpenRevolvingAccounts was less than [[15.5000006]] with a value of [[0.]]
decision node 6  : DelinquenciesLast7Years was less than [[27.01995751]] with a value of [[5.]]
decision node 7  : PublicRecordsLast10Years was less than [[0.99651877]] with a value of [[0.]]
decision node 8  : CurrentDelinquencies was less than [[9.5414045]] with a value of [[1.]]
decision node 9  : Investors was less than [[531.49999762]] with a value of [[25.]]
decision node 10 : Investors was less than [[447.50000101]] with a value of [[25.]]
decision node 11 : Reno_1 was less than [[0.5]] with a value of [[0.]]
decision node 12 : Investors was less than [[29.50000011]] with a value of [[25.]]
decision node 13 : BorrowerRate was less than [[0.31490613]] with a value of [[0.182]]
```

Fig. 4. Rules extracted from the white-box surrogate model for the German credit dataset

leveraging the "dark knowledge" from a neural network during model training could potentially enhance the performance of simpler models. The student model exhibited the best performance, suggesting that utilizing information from a neural network can enhance the classification of the minority class.

The potential of the proposed approach is demonstrated in Fig. 4, where an example of the extracted rules from the white-box surrogate model is presented.

7   Conclusions and Future Work

In this study, we proposed a methodology to distill knowledge from deep neural networks into decision-tree models, with the objective of obtaining understandable and practical insights into the decision-making mechanisms. Our results illustrate the potential of this method to produce transparent and easily interpretable models applicable to various domains.

We intend to extend this study and develop a comprehensive framework that can be utilized in any scenario, making the advantages of interpretability and actionability available to a broader range of domains.

Moving forward, we aim to investigate the applicability of our knowledge augmentation approach in diverse domains beyond the present study. These could include causal inference and energy efficiency, where distillation strategies may offer promising avenues for improved performance.

Acknowledgments. This research was supported by the Portuguese Recovery and Resilience Plan (PRR) through project C645008882-00000055, Center for Responsible AI.

References

1. Eli5, a library for debugging ml classifiers/regressors and explaining their decisions. www.eli5.readthedocs.io/en/latest/overview.html
2. Baehrens, D., Schroeter, T., Harmeling, S., Kawanabe, M., Hansen, K., Müller, K.R.: How to explain individual classification decisions. J. Mach. Learn. Res. **11**(61), 1803–1831 (2010). www.jmlr.org/papers/v11/baehrens10a.html
3. Ben-Israel, I., Cerdio, J., Ema, A., Friedman, L., Ienca, M., Mantelero, A., Matania, E., Muller, C., Shiiroyama, H., Vayena, E.: Towards regulation of AI systems-global perspectives on the development of a legal framework on artificial intelligence (AI) systems based on the council of Europe's standards on human rights, democracy and the rule of law (2020). www.rm.coe.int/prems-107320-gbr-2018-compli-cahai-couv-texte-a4-bat-web/1680a0c17a
4. Bucila, C., Caruana, R., Niculescu-Mizil, A.: Model compression. In: KDD'06 (2006)
5. Cao, L., Yang, Q., Yu, P.S.: Data science and ai in fintech: an overview. Int. J. Data Sci. Anal. 81–89 (2021)
6. Caruana, R., Lou, Y., Gehrke, J., Koch, P., Sturm, M., Elhadad, N.: Intelligible models for HealthCare. In: Proceedings of the 21th ACM SIGKDD International Conference on Knowledge Discovery and Data Mining. ACM (Aug 2015). 10.11452F2783258.2788613
7. Che, Z., Purushotham, S., Khemani, R., Liu, Y.: Distilling knowledge from deep networks with applications to healthcare domain (2015)
8. Dua, D., Graff, C.: UCI machine learning repository (2017). www.archive.ics.uci.edu/ml
9. Faria, T., Silva, C., Ribeiro, B.: Interpreting decision patterns in financial applications. In: Progress in Pattern Recognition, Image Analysis, Computer Vision, and Applications: 25th Iberoamerican Congress, CIARP (2021)
10. Ghai, B., Mueller, K.: D-bias: a causality-based human-in-the-loop system for tackling algorithmic bias. IEEE Trans. Visual Comput. Graphics **29**(1), 473–482 (2023)
11. Ghanta, S., Subramanian, S., Sundararaman, S., Khermosh, L., Sridhar, V., Arteaga, D., Luo, Q., Das, D., Talagala, N.: Interpretability and reproducability in production machine learning applications. In: 2018 17th IEEE International Conference on Machine Learning and Applications (ICMLA), pp. 658–664 (2018)
12. Huang, C., Zhang, Z., Mao, B., Yao, X.: An overview of artificial intelligence ethics. IEEE Trans. Artif. Intell. **1**(01), 1–21 (2022). https://doi.org/10.1109/TAI.2022.3194503
13. Lyu, D., Yang, F., Kwon, H., Dong, W., Yilmaz, L., Liu, B.: Tdm: trustworthy decision-making via interpretability enhancement. IEEE Trans. Emerg. Topics Comput. Intell. **6**(3), 450–461 (2022). https://doi.org/10.1109/TETCI.2021.3084290

14. Molnar, C.: Interpretable Machine Learning: A Guide For Making Black Box Models Explainable (2022). www.christophm.github.io/interpretable-ml-book/
15. Ribeiro, M.T., Singh, S., Guestrin, C.: Why Should I Trust You? : Explaining the Predictions of Any Classifier (2016)
16. Sarkar, S., Weyde, T., Garcez, A., Slabaugh, G., Dragicevic, S., Percy, C.: Accuracy and interpretability trade-offs in machine learning applied to safer gambling. In: CoCo@NIPS (2016)
17. Tan, S., Caruana, R., Hooker, G., Lou, Y.: Distill-and-compare. In: Proceedings of the 2018 AAAI/ACM Conference on AI, Ethics, and Society (Dec 2018). https://doi.org/10.1145/3278721.3278725
18. Valente, F., Henriques, J., Paredes, S., Rocha, T., de Carvalho, P., Morais, J.: Improving the compromise between accuracy, interpretability and personalization of rule-based machine learning in medical problems. In: 2021 43rd Annual International Conference of the IEEE Engineering in Medicine & Biology Society (EMBC), pp. 2132–2135 (2021)
19. Xu, K., Park, D.H., Yi, C., Sutton, C.: Interpreting deep classifier by visual distillation of dark knowledge (2018)

General Artificial Intelligence

Revisiting Deep Attention Recurrent Networks

Fernando Fradique Duarte[1]([✉]) [iD], Nuno Lau[2] [iD], Artur Pereira[2] [iD],
and Luís Paulo Reis[3] [iD]

[1] Institute of Electronics and Informatics Engineering of Aveiro, University of Aveiro, Aveiro,
Portugal
fjosefradique@ua.pt

[2] Department of Electronics, Telecommunications and Informatics, University of Aveiro,
Aveiro, Portugal
{nunolau,artur}@ua.pt

[3] Faculty of Engineering, Department of Informatics Engineering, University of Porto, Porto,
Portugal
lpreis@fe.up.pt

Abstract. Attention-based agents have had much success in many areas of Artificial Intelligence, such as Deep Reinforcement Learning. This work revisits two such architectures, namely, Deep Attention Recurrent Q-Networks (DARQNs) and Soft Top-Down Spatial Attention (STDA) and explores the similarities between them. More specifically, this work tries to improve the performance of the DARQN architecture by leveraging elements proposed by the STDA architecture, such as the formulation of its attention function which also includes the incorporation of a spatial basis into its computation. The implementation tested, denoted Deep Attention Recurrent Actor-Critic (DARAC), uses the A2C learning algorithm. The results obtained seem to suggest that the performance of DARAC can be improved by the incorporation of some of the techniques proposed in STDA. Overall, DARAC showed competitive results when compared to STDA and slightly better in some of the experiments performed. The Atari 2600 videogame benchmark was the testbed used to perform and validate all the experiments.

Keywords: Deep attention recurrent networks · Soft top-down attention · Deep reinforcement learning

1 Introduction

Attention-based agents have achieved much success in many areas of Artificial Intelligence (AI). Examples of this success include work in text translation [1], object tracking [2], question-answering [3], video classification [4], image classification [5] and Deep Reinforcement Learning (DRL) [6–8]. In the context of DRL more specifically, attention has sparked much interest due to its ability to afford potential performance gains, computational speedups, and better interpretability [7], all of which are desirable properties that most AI agents should exhibit, particularly when dealing with black-box agents that must process large amounts of information (e.g., 2D images) and/or in training scenarios where computational resources are scarce [6, 7].

© The Author(s), under exclusive license to Springer Nature Switzerland AG 2023
N. Moniz et al. (Eds.): EPIA 2023, LNAI 14115, pp. 121–132, 2023.
https://doi.org/10.1007/978-3-031-49008-8_10

Given this, the family of Deep Attention Recurrent Models is of particular interest, specifically two of its instantiations: Deep Attention Recurrent Q-Networks (DARQNs) [7] and Soft Top-Down Spatial Attention (STDA) [6]. While representing different architectural flavors, based on dissimilar attention functions, these models share some similarities which can potentially be exploited to improve the existing models or derive new ones. More specifically, this work seeks to leverage the techniques proposed in STDA to improve DARQN. The rationale for this is the following.

First, the similarities between the two models allow some of the techniques proposed in STDA, such as the use of a spatial basis in the computation of the attention function, to be readily incorporated in DARQN. Second, more recent DRL architectures, such as STDA, have begun to enrich their memory modules by incorporating additional information concerning the dynamics of the environment, such as the action performed, and the reward obtained. This may also help improve performance.

Finally, although the authors of DARQN report equal or improved results in comparison to the Deep Q-Network (DQN) [9] agent used as the baseline in their original work, they also report poor results on a particular game, Breakout. This fact raises some interesting questions. Was the instability observed due to the architectural implementation used or was it due to the formulation of the attention function? If so, can this instability be mitigated by incorporating techniques proposed in STDA?

The results obtained seem to suggest that the incorporation of some of the techniques proposed in STDA can improve the performance of DARQN. Overall, the implementation tested, denoted Deep Attention Recurrent Actor-Critic (DARAC), showed competitive results when compared to STDA and slightly better in some of the experiments performed. The Atari 2600 videogame benchmark was the testbed used to perform and validate all the experiments.

The remainder of the paper is structured as follows: Sect. 2 presents the related work, including a brief overview of the technical background, Sect. 3 discusses the experimental setup, which includes the presentation of the methods proposed and the training setup, Sect. 4 presents the experiments carried out and discusses the results obtained and finally Sect. 5 presents the conclusions.

2   Related Work

This section includes a high-level presentation of DARQN and STDA in terms of their overall architecture and attention function formulation. The similarities between the two models are explored at the end of the section.

2.1   Deep Attention Recurrent Q-Network

DARQN [7] is based on the Deep Recurrent Q-Network (DRQN) [10] algorithm, a variant of DQN that incorporates a Long-Short Term Memory (LSTM) [11] into the architecture of the agent. While DRQN leverages the ability of memory-based models to integrate information over longer sequences of agent-environment interactions[1],

---

[1] In the limit, at each timestep t this memory module could potentially integrate information from the $k \leq t-1$ past observations, effectively compressing the whole history.

DARQN focuses on the potential performance gains, computational speedups and added interpretability[2] afforded by attention-based models. DARQN proposes two attention mechanisms: 'soft' and 'hard' attention. This work explores soft attention.

At a high-level the soft attention architecture can be described as follows: at each time step t, a set of l convolutional layers processes the state of the environment s_t into a set of d feature maps $f = \{f_1,...,f_d\}, f_i \in \Re^{s \times n}$, which are transformed into a set of $m = s \times n$ location vectors $v = \{v_1,...,v_m\}, v_i \in \Re^d$. The attention network g computes the weights g_i for each vector v_i, denoting the vector's relative importance, according to Eq. 1, where $Linear(x) = Wx + b$ represents an affine transformation with weight matrix W and bias term b and h_{t-1} denotes the hidden state of the memory module at time step $t-1$. Next, the context vector $z_t \in \Re^d$ is computed as a weighted sum of the vectors v_i according to Eq. 2 and used to update the internal state h_t of the memory module. Finally, h_t is used to compute both the action a_t to take at the current time step t and the next context vector z_{t+1}. Figure 1 illustrates the computation of z_t.

$$g(v_i, h_{t-1}) = Softmax(Linear(Tanh(Linear(v_i) + Wh_{t-1}))) \tag{1}$$

$$z_t = \sum_{i=1}^{m} g(v_i, h_{t-1})v_i \tag{2}$$

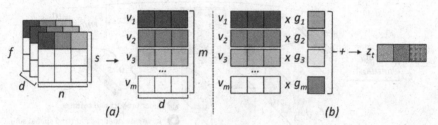

Fig. 1. (**a**) the set of feature maps f is converted into the set of vectors v. (**b**) the context vector z_t is computed as a weighted sum of the vectors v_i with their weights g_i.

In practice, the implementation[3] does not follow the formulation presented in Eq. 2. More specifically, instead of using linear layers, the implementation uses convolutional layers as follows: $g(v_i, h_{t-1}) = Softmax(Conv(Tanh(Conv(v_i) + Wh_{t-1})))$, where $Conv$ denotes a convolutional layer with kernel size 1 and stride 1.

2.2 Soft Top-Down Spatial Attention

STDA [6] focuses on the increased interpretability afforded by attention-based models. According to the authors, by incorporating attention as an explicit bottleneck into the architecture of the agent, the resulting attention maps can be used as a more direct form of interpretation of the decision process, therefore increasing the interpretability of the

---

[2] The 'where' and 'what' driving the decision process.

[3] https://github.com/5vision/DARQN.

agent's inner workings. Other capabilities explored by this attention method include the ability to plan ahead and the ability not only to focus attention on specific spatial locations ('where'), but also on specific entities or objects ('what').

At a high-level the STDA architecture can be summarized as follows: at each timestep t, the state of the environment s_t is processed by a vision encoder with output o_{vis}. This vision encoder is composed of a set of convolutional layers followed by a recurrent layer rnn_{down} (ConvLSTM [12]). O_{vis} is then split into a keys vector k_{vis} and a values vector v_{vis} and a spatial basis is concatenated to each of these vectors to encode spatial information. A set of j attention heads further processes these vectors.

More specifically, for each attention head j_i, a query network produces query q based on the previous hidden state h_{t-1} of a second recurrent network rnn_{top} (LSTM). The inner product between q and all spatial locations of k_{vis} (QK^T) is computed and passed through a softmax to produce the attention map Λ. Λ is then pointwise multiplied with v_{vis} and the result is spatially summed to derive the answer vector ans. Rnn_{top} uses q and ans to update its hidden state h_t. Figure 2 depicts this process. Finally, h_t is used to compute the action a_t to take at the current time step t and the next query. Noticeably, q is a function of h_t, not s_t. This allows for a top-down attention mechanism, where task relevant information can be actively queried from the input (easier) instead of being filtered from it (harder).

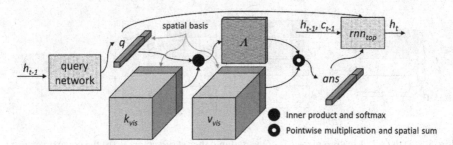

Fig. 2. Detail of an attention head (adapted from [6]).

2.3 Similarities Between DARQN and STDA

The formulation of the attention function used in STDA is based on the attention function proposed in [1], specifically, $Attention(Q, K, V) = Softmax(QK^T)V$. The formulation proposed in DARQN can be conceptually thought of as an approximation to this formulation. More concretely, in Eq. 1, $Linear(v_i)$ can be interpreted as a projection of each v_i into its corresponding key vector $k_i \in K$, whereas the expression Wh_{t-1} may be interpreted as the projection of the memory state into a query vector $q_i \in Q$. The values matrix V would be $v = \{v_1,...,v_m\}$.

Given this interpretation, $Linear(Tanh(Linear(v_i) + Wh_{t-1}))$ can be interpreted as an approximation to the computation QK^T performed in STDA. In other words, considering its matrix form, Eq. 1 can be rewritten as $Linear(Tanh(K + Q)) \approx QK^T$. The remaining computation, specifically, $Softmax(.)V$ is similar in both cases. This similarity allows for a straightforward integration of some of the techniques proposed in STDA into the formulation of the attention function used in DARQN.

3 Experimental Setup

This section presents all the agents implemented, including the different DARAC variants tested. The training setup is presented at the end of the section and includes the testing and training protocols used and the parameterization of the agents.

3.1 Extensions to the DARQN Architecture

As previously mentioned, this work aims to leverage the techniques proposed in STDA to try to improve DARQN. These improvement efforts included testing different architectural choices and variations of the formulation of the attention function, as proposed in DARQN. The agents implemented are presented below.

DARAC. This is the baseline agent. Its architecture consists of four modules: encoder, attention, memory and policy. The encoder consists of 4 convolutional layers configured with (1, 32, 64, 64) input and (32, 64, 64, 256) output channels, kernel sizes (8, 4, 4, 4), strides (4, 2, 2, 1) and no padding, respectively. Each layer is followed by batch normalization [13] and a Rectified Linear Unit (ReLU) nonlinearity. The attention module follows the original implementation already discussed in Sect. 2.1. The memory module is an LSTM of size 256. The output from the encoder is used as the input for this module. Finally, the policy module consists of a linear layer of size 128, followed by layer normalization [14] and a ReLU nonlinearity. This layer feeds two other linear layers: the actor, responsible for choosing the action at each timestep and the critic, in charge of computing the value of each state. This overall architecture is shared by all the (DARAC) agents.

DARAC (alr). This agent enriches the memory module by incorporating additional information (into its input) concerning the dynamics of the environment, namely: the action previously performed a_{t-1}, and the reward obtained r_{t-1}, similarly to more recent DRL models. This can also potentially improve performance. All the remaining agents use this formulation for their memory modules.

DARAC Cat (alr). This agent uses a slight variation of the attention function, where the summation operation in Eq. 1 is substituted by a concatenation operation (*cat*), specifically: $g(v_i, h_{t-1}) = Softmax(Conv(Tanh(cat(Conv(v_i), Wh_{t-1}))))$. On the one hand, this allows the tensors to have different sizes. On the other hand, this also injects less bias into the formulation of the attention function. The remaining DARAC variants also use concatenation. For convenience, $Conv(v_i)$ and Wh_{t-1} have similar size in the channels dimension $C = 256$.

DARAC (SB). This agent implements another variation of the attention function, namely it incorporates a spatial basis in its formulation, similarly to STDA. As already discussed in Sect. 2.3, the context vector z_t is derived via a spatial sum. However, this summation is invariant to permutations of the spatial positions. In STDA this issue is mitigated by incorporating a spatial basis into the computation of the attention function to encode spatial information. The objective is to assess to what extent this change can impact the performance of the agent. The spatial basis used is similar to the one used in STDA, with size 64.

Additionally, the architecture of the attention network g was reformulated. Batch normalization and a ReLU nonlinearity were added after the $Conv(v_i)$ operation, Wh_{t-1} was substituted by the query network presented in the next Sect. 3.2 and the last convolutional layer of g was substituted by two convolutional layers configured with $(448, 64)$ input and $(64, 1)$ output channels, kernel size 1, stride 1 and no padding, respectively. The first layer is followed by batch normalization and a ReLU nonlinearity. The *tanh* operation was also removed. The objective of this reformulation was to add capacity to g given that less bias is being injected and the network must 'learn' more about the attention function computation.

DARAC Dual (SB). This agent implements a combination of changes. Similarly to STDA, it incorporates the rnn_{down} and rnn_{top} memory modules in its architecture. The attention formulation is similar to DARAC (SB). Also, given that this agent uses rnn_{down} on top of the encoder, the size of the last layer of the encoder was changed to 64 (instead of 256). Overall, this agent is closer to STDA architecturally while still maintaining a more 'abstract' formulation of the attention function.

3.2 Top-Down Spatial Attention Agent

The Top-Down Spatial Attention agent (*TDA (4H)*) consists of five modules: vision encoder, query network, attention, memory and policy. Rnn_{down} was configured with 64 input/output channels, kernel size 3 and stride 1 with padding 1. Rnn_{top} has size 256. The query network is composed of three linear layers with sizes $(256, 128, 1280)$, respectively, each followed by layer normalization and a ReLU nonlinearity. The attention function was implemented according to [6]. Four attention heads were used in the experiments.

3.3 Training Setup

All agents were trained for a minimum of 16,800,000 frames, which can be extended until all current episodes (a set of l lives) are concluded, similarly to what is proposed in [15]. A total of 8 training environments were used in parallel to train the agents using a synchronous version of the Advantage Actor-Critic (A2C) algorithm [16]. Adam [17] was used as the optimizer. The learning rate is fixed and set to 1e-4. The loss was computed using Generalized Advantage Estimation with $\lambda = 1.0$ [18]. The training results were computed at every 240,000th frame over a window of size $w = 50$ and correspond to the return scores (averaged over all the agents) obtained during training in the last w fully completed episodes.

Each trained agent played 100 games and the scores obtained were used to derive the test results per episode. These results include the overall median values and the average result and standard deviation obtained by the best agent for each experiment. Two agents were used to perform each experiment. The Atari 2600 videogame platform, available via the OpenAI Gym [19] toolkit, was the benchmark used. More specifically the games used were Seaquest and Breakout (with frame skipping). The one-way ANOVA and the Kruskal-Wallis H-test were used for the statistical significance tests ($\alpha = 0.05$). The null hypothesis $H0$ considers that all the agents have the same return mean results.

In terms of pre-processing steps, the input image at each time step t is converted to grayscale and cropped to 206 by 158 pixels with no rescaling. Also, the internal state of the memory module is never reset to zero during the training procedure. It is only set to an empty state (i.e., all zeros), representing the state of no previous knowledge, at the beginning of training. The agents were parameterized according to Table 1.

Table 1. Hyperparameters. The term 'scale' denotes a scaling factor.

Entropy scale	Critic scale	Reward clipping	Discount factor (γ)
1e-2	0.5	$[-1, 1]$	.99

4 Experimental Results

This section presents the experimental results obtained. The preliminary results are first presented. The comparative results between *DARAC* and *TDA* are discussed next. The visualization of the attention maps derived by these agents is presented at the end of the section, along with an overall discussion of the results obtained.

4.1 Preliminary Results

To assess the most promising DARAC variants for further experimentation, some preliminary tests were first carried out. For these initial tests the agents were trained for 7,200,000 steps. The results of these tests are depicted in Fig. 3. Overall, *DARAC (SB)* seems to be the most promising variant for further experimentation. On the one hand enriching the memory module with additional information about the dynamics of the environment by itself does not seem to provide a clear improvement in performance. Also, simply substituting the summation operation by a concatenation operation seems to hinder performance. This seems intuitive since the concatenation operation is less explicit about the intended computation of the attention function. On the other hand, while *DARAC (SB)* and *DARAC Dual (SB)* provided a boost in performance in Breakout (they are also statistically indistinguishable), *DARAC Dual (SB)* performed poorly in Seaquest. It should also be noted that *DARAC (SB)* and *DARAC Dual (SB)* use concatenation and implement more complex architectures, thus may need more training time when compared to *DARAC*. Given this, both *DARAC* and *DARAC (SB)* were trained for an additional 4,800,000 frames (12 million in total).

Figure 4 depicts the training and test results obtained by the agents after additional training. As can be seen, *DARAC* continues to perform better although *DARAC (SB)* is not far behind. Looking at the training curve it seems plausible to assume that with more training *DARAC (SB)* could potentially be able to reach a similar level of performance to that of *DARAC*.

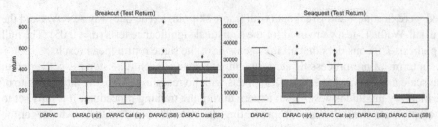

Fig. 3. Test return: (**Breakout**) DARAC 288 with best (270/120), DARAC (alr) 342 with best (315/83), DARAC Cat (alr) 232 with best (256/110), DARAC (SB) 400 with best (381/88) and DARAC Dual (SB) 399 with best (377/72), (**Seaquest**) DARAC 20245 with best (21302/7758), DARAC (alr) 9860 with best (14957/8244), DARAC Cat (alr) 11935 with best (14663/6748), DARAC (SB) 15900 with best (16792/8468) and DARAC Dual (SB) 7350 with best (7603/1164). H0 is rejected in all experiments except: (**Breakout**) DARAC vs DARAC Cat (alr) with p-value 0.47 and DARAC (SB) vs DARAC Dual (SB) with p-value 0.61, (**Seaquest**) DARAC (alr) vs DARAC Cat (alr) with p-value 0.74.

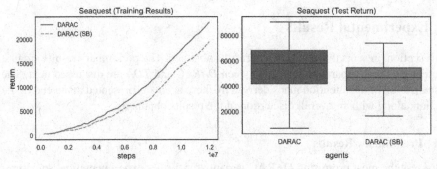

Fig. 4. Extended training and test results for Seaquest: DARAC 58245 with best (55671/15654) and DARAC (SB) 47150 with best (45723/13652). The results are statistically significant.

4.2 Comparative Results (DARAC vs. TDA)

This comparative experiment tested the performance of *DARAC (SB)* versus *TDA (4H)*. Overall, *DARAC (SB)* proved to be competitive with *TDA (4H)* and even slightly better in some cases, as depicted in Fig. 5. All the results are statistically significant except for the results obtained in Breakout (p-value 0.56).

4.3 Visualization of the Attention Maps

Visualizing the attention maps can bring further insight into the decision process of the agent. This can be achieved by projecting the attention maps to the original size of the image and overlaying both images using alpha blending, similarly to [6]. This section presents this analysis for *DARAC (SB)* and *TDA (4H)*.

Overall, both agents seem to focus their attention on the main elements of the games, namely: the agent itself, the enemies, and locations/objects of interest such as the oxygen

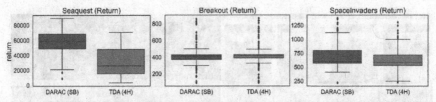

Fig. 5. Test return: (**Seaquest**) DARAC (SB) 58610 with best (59168/12851) and TDA (4H) 25810 with best (45687/14213), (**Breakout**) DARAC (SB) 413 with best (419/110) and TDA (4H) 417 with best (429/124) and (**SpaceInvaders**) DARAC (SB) 600 with best (708/183) and TDA (4H) 588 with best (624/189).

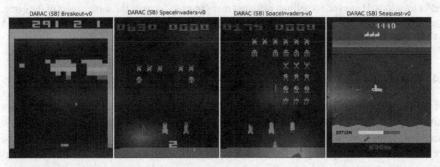

Fig. 6. Visualization for DARAC (SB). The attention map derived by DARAC (SB) focuses on several elements of the game and can be more diffuse at times.

level in Seaquest and the ball in Breakout. This is depicted in Figs. 6 and 7 for *DARAC (SB)* and *TDA (4H)*, respectively. The red blobs represent the attention maps.

The four attention maps derived by *TDA (4H)*, *TDA(i)*, with $i = 1,2,3,4$ seem to focus on different aspects of the game most of the time. Sometimes however, some of the maps focus on the same aspects and seem to complement each other. Several examples of this can be seen in Fig. 7. Also, some of the attention maps change their focus throughout the course of the game, whereas others remain unchanged. This can be seen in Fig. 7 for Seaquest, where initially *TDA (3)* is focused primarily on the top left corner of the screen, but changes focus entirely as the game progresses. *TDA (4)* on the other hand remains focused on the center bottom part of the screen (near the oxygen meter) throughout the entire game. This may be a hint that the agent needs further training to fully finetune its attention maps.

The attention map derived by *DARAC (SB)* on the other hand, focusses on several aspects of the game at the same time and can be more diffuse at times. *DARAC (SB)* is especially proficient in Seaquest, particularly at guiding its projectile to kill a nearby target while moving towards the next target. Figure 6 depicts an example of this maneuver. This may also hint to the fact that, at least for the games tested, a single attention map may be sufficient to perform reasonably well. Overall, both agents seem to be following the attentional clues provided by their attention maps to plan ahead.

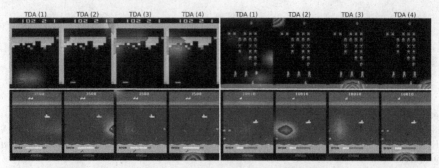

Fig. 7. Visualization for TDA (4H). Overall, the attention maps seem to focus on different objects and/or locations, However, sometimes different maps seem to focus on the same aspect of the game, complementing one another in a certain way. Examples of this can be seen in Breakout for TDA (3) and TDA (4) and Seaquest for TDA (2) and TDA (3).

4.4 Discussion

Of all the DARAC variants tested, *DARAC* (*SB*) seems to be the most promising for further research. One possible reason for this may be the fact that this agent strikes a more balanced tradeoff between the level of abstraction of the attention function and the architecture and/or capacity of the attention network used for its derivation. The results seem to suggest that simply enriching the memory module with additional information or changing the level of abstraction of the attention function without reformulating the underlying architecture accordingly, can be detrimental to the performance of the agent.

Nevertheless, *DARAC* (*SB*) can still be further finetuned. Although *DARAC* (*SB*) was able to improve the performance scores in Breakout, when compared to the baseline (*DARAC*), it was not able to do the same in Seaquest. Further experiments, using more games, may provide a clearer picture of the difference in performance between the two agents. *DARAC Dual* (*SB*) may also be an interesting option for further research, although its architecture still needs further improvements to be competitive, as hinted by the results obtained in Seaquest.

Also, incorporating the spatial basis into the computation of the attention function did not seem to make much difference, at least in Seaquest, although it seems more theoretically sound to incorporate it to mitigate the invariance issue discussed in Sect. 3.1. Interestingly the poor performance results observed in Breakout and reported in the original paper were not observed in this work. The reason for those original observations remains unclear, but it may have been due to the training rate used originally (4 steps). In this work the agents were trained every 5 steps.

Another interesting point to note is the fact that, provided a suitable architecture, more abstract formulations of the attention function are possible while retaining similar performance when compared to a more handcrafted attention function. This may be interesting in scenarios where it is not clear what and how the attention function should be derived. Overall, *DARAC* (*SB*) was able to achieve competitive results, and even slightly better in some cases, when compared to an agent based on a more recent architecture, namely *TDA* (*4H*), using a more abstract formulation of the attention function.

5 Conclusion

This paper revisited DARQN and explored its similarities with STDA. This provided an opportunity to experiment with some extensions inspired by STDA, namely: a formulation of the memory module more in line with more recent DRL models, a different architecture that allows information to be actively queried from the input as opposed to being filtered from it, a more complex attention network architecture and a revised formulation of the attention function, also at its abstraction level. The results obtained seem to suggest that the DARQN architecture can be further improved, even when using a more abstract formulation of the attention function, coupled with a suitable attention network architecture. In conclusion, DARQN variants such as *DARAC* (*SB*) seem to be an interesting topic for further research.

Acknowledgements. This research was funded by Fundação para a Ciência e a Tecnologia, grant number SFRH/BD/145723 /2019–UID/CEC/00127/2019.

References

1. Vaswani, A., et al.: Attention is all you need. In: Advances in Neural Information Processing Systems 30: Annual Conference on Neural Information Processing Systems 2017, pp. 5998–6008 (2017)
2. Kosiorek, A.R., Bewley, A., Posner, I.: Hierarchical attentive recurrent tracking. In: Advances in Neural Information Processing Systems 30: Annual Conference on Neural Information Processing Systems 2017, pp. 3053–3061 (2017)
3. Hermann, K.M., et al.: Teaching machines to read and comprehend. In: Advances in Neural Information Processing Systems 28: Annual Conference on Neural Information Processing Systems 2015, pp. 1693–1701 (2015)
4. Shan, M., Atanasov, N.: A spatiotemporal model with visual attention for video classification (2017). CoRR, abs/1707.02069
5. Mnih, V., Heess, N., Graves, A., Kavukcuoglu, K.: Recurrent models of visual attention. In: Advances in Neural Information Processing Systems 27: Annual Conference on Neural Information Processing Systems 2014, pp. 2204–2212 (2014)
6. Mott, A., Zoran, D., Chrzanowski, M., Wierstra, D., Rezende, D.J.: Towards interpretable reinforcement learning using attention augmented agents. In: Advances in Neural Information Processing Systems 32: Annual Conference on Neural Information Processing Systems 2019, NeurIPS 2019, pp. 12329–12338 (2019)
7. Sorokin, I., Seleznev, A., Pavlov, M., Fedorov, A., Ignateva, A.: Deep Attention Recurrent Q-Network (2015). CoRR, abs/1512.01693
8. Zambaldi, V.F., et al.: Deep reinforcement learning with relational inductive biases. In: 7th International Conference on Learning Representations, ICLR (2019)
9. Mnih, V., et al.: Human-level control through deep reinforcement learning. Nature **518**(7540), 529–533 (2015)
10. Hausknecht, M., Stone, P.: Deep recurrent Q-learning for partially observable MDPs. In: AAAI Fall Symposium-Technical Report, AI Access Foundation, pp. 29–37 (2015)
11. Hochreiter, S., Schmidhuber, J.: Long short-term memory. Neural Comput.Comput. **9**(8), 1735–1780 (1997)

12. Shi, X., Chen, Z., Wang, H., Yeung, D.-Y., Wong, W.-K., Woo, W.: Convolutional LSTM network: a machine learning approach for precipitation nowcasting. In: Advances in Neural Information Processing Systems 28: Annual Conference on Neural Information Processing Systems 2015, pp. 802–810 (2015)
13. Ioffe, S., Szegedy, C.: Batch normalization: accelerating deep network training by reducing internal covariate shift. In: Proceedings of the 32nd International Conference on Machine Learning, ICML 2015, pp. 448–456 (2015)
14. Ba, L.J., Kiros, J.R., Hinton, G.E.: Layer normalization (2016). CoRR, abs/1607.06450
15. Machado, M.C., Bellemare, M.G., Talvitie, E., Veness, J., Hausknecht, M.J., Bowling, M.: Revisiting the arcade learning environment: evaluation protocols and open problems for general agents. J. Artif. Intell. Res.Artif. Intell. Res. **61**, 523–562 (2018)
16. Mnih, V., et al.: Asynchronous methods for deep reinforcement learning. In: Proceedings of the 33nd International Conference on Machine Learning, ICML 2016, pp. 1928–1937 (2016)
17. Kingma, D.P., Ba, J.: Adam: a method for stochastic optimization. In: 3rd International Conference on Learning Representations, ICLR (2015)
18. Schulman, J., Moritz, P., Levine, S., Jordan, M.I., Abbeel, P.: High-dimensional continuous control using generalized advantage estimation. In: 4th International Conference on Learning Representations, ICLR (2016)
19. Brockman, G., et al.: OpenAI Gym (2016). CoRR, abs/1606.01540

Pre-training with Augmentations for Efficient Transfer in Model-Based Reinforcement Learning

Bernardo Esteves[1,2]([✉]), Miguel Vasco[1,2], and Francisco S. Melo[1,2]

[1] INESC-ID, Lisbon, Portugal
[2] Instituto Superior Técnico, University of Lisbon, Lisbon, Portugal
bernardo.esteves@tecnico.ulisboa.pt

Abstract. This work explores pre-training as a strategy to allow reinforcement learning (RL) algorithms to efficiently adapt to new (albeit similar) tasks. We argue for introducing variability during the pre-training phase, in the form of *augmentations* to the observations of the agent, to improve the sample efficiency of the fine-tuning stage. We categorize such variability in the form of perceptual, dynamic and semantic augmentations, which can be easily employed in standard pre-training methods. We perform extensive evaluations of our proposed augmentation scheme in model-based algorithms, across multiple scenarios of increasing complexity. The results consistently show that our augmentation scheme significantly improves the efficiency of the fine-tuning to novel tasks, outperforming other state-of-the-art pre-training approaches.

Keywords: Reinforcement learning · Transfer learning · Representation learning

1 Introduction

Reinforcement learning (RL) approaches have been successfully applied to complex scenarios like games [18,23], robotics [16] and control [17]. In spite of these sounding success stories, RL methods are known for being "data-hungry": they require millions of interaction steps between the learning agent and the environment, which makes the deployment of RL-based systems extremely expensive and difficult in real-world scenarios, where such intense levels of interaction are prohibitive. As an example, Rainbow [12] required over $34,000$ GPU hours (over $1,400$ days) to train, not considering hyper-parameter tuning [20]. Additionally, a RL system trained for a particular task often fails to generalize to other, similar tasks [11]. Such behavior stands in contrast to the human learning process:

This work was partially supported by national funds through Fundação para a Ciência e a Tecnologia (FCT) with ref. UIDB/50021/2020 and the project RELEvaNT, ref. PTDC/CCI-COM/5060/2021. MV acknowledges the FCT PhD grant SFRH/BD/139362/2018.

N. Moniz et al. (Eds.): EPIA 2023, LNAI 14115, pp. 133–145, 2023.
https://doi.org/10.1007/978-3-031-49008-8_11

humans efficiently reuse knowledge of similar tasks (such as motion primitives and environmental physics) to efficiently learn to perform novel tasks [13]. This stark difference motivates the need for knowledge transfer approaches that may help to address the sample-efficiency of RL algorithms.

According to Laskin et al. [15], two families of approaches have been proposed in literature to address sample complexity of RL methods: (i) introducing auxiliary tasks, usually relying on data augmentation approaches, that seek to build general-purpose representations for the perceptual observations of the agent that facilitate the learning of control policies [15,21]; and (ii) learning environment models that allow the generation of artificial samples that can be used for learning, thus requiring less interactions with the actual environment [9,22]. This paper builds on the benefits of these two lines of research and addresses the question: *"how does pre-training using different augmentations impact the data efficiency of fine-tuning model-based RL in novel downstream tasks?"*

We focus on the problem of pre-training model-based RL agents and contribute with an in-depth categorization of *transferable features* across similar tasks. In particular, we discuss transfer between tasks that share *perceptual, dynamic* and *semantic* features. Driven by our discussion, we contribute a novel pre-training scheme for model-based RL that exploits such transferable features, which we name *Multiple-Augmented Pre-training Scheme* (MAPS). During the pre-training phase, MAPS introduces multiple variations on the observations of the agents, obtained from the current task or similar tasks, forcing the learning of more general-purpose representations and thus improving the efficiency of a subsequent fine-tuning phase in novel downstream tasks. The introduction of such variability in data has already been explored in contexts such as computer vision [5,8] and natural language processing [4,7].

We evaluate MAPS against different pre-training approaches in scenarios of increasing complexity, considering a state-of-the-art model-based RL framework (namely, DreamerV2 [9]). We perform an ablation study on the Mini-Grid environment that highlights how changes in the perceptual and dynamical conditions affect the transfer of information in model-based RL to similar tasks. Furthermore, in a more complex Mini-Grid scenario, we highlight the role of further introducing semantic variability during the pre-training phase, showing that MAPS outperforms other standard pre-training schemes. Finally, in an Atari environment, we highlight the scalability of MAPS to more complex scenarios, and show how pre-training with MAPS significantly improves the fine-tuning performance. In summary, the contributions of this work are threefold.

- We contribute a categorization of *transferable features* for the pre-training of model-based RL agents;
- We introduce Multiple-Augmented Pre-training Scheme (MAPS) that exploits such features to introduce variability during the pre-training phase;
- We evaluate MAPS against different pre-training approaches in scenarios of increasing complexity, showing how our approach allows agents to efficiently fine-tune to novel downstream tasks.

2 Related Work

Transferring knowledge to new tasks is often related to the field of Transfer Learning, which seek to bring learning improvements by relaxing assumption that the data used for learning between old and new tasks must be independent and identically distributed [25]. *Pre-training* is considered the predominant approach to perform experience transfer: we train a model on an initial task, also known as *pre-training task*, and then adapt the model on a new *downstream task*, by using the previously learned weights, via *fine-tuning* [3]. Pre-training has been successfully applied to a variety of fields beyond RL. For example, in computer vision, self-supervised representation learning approaches have seen significant developments, both in contrastive [5,10] and predictive methods [8]. In this work, inspired by these pre-training approaches in computer vision, we explore self-supervised augmentations in the field of model-based RL.

During the pre-training phase, it is common to train the model on large amounts of general data, and is common to use other learning objectives that are only used for pre-training. For example, in SimCLR [5], the authors present a new contrastive method to pre-train a large model with a large unlabeled dataset with 1.2 million images, that can then be fine-tuned with a small labeled dataset. However, in our work we do not have access to a huge dataset with millions of highly diverse trajectories and millions of diverse games easily available, thus we try to focus the pre-training on a small set of more similar tasks to attempt to extract information from these to the desired downstream task. In RL settings, both CURL [15] and ATC [24] propose contrastive auxiliary objectives for learning general representations of the agent's environments. However, they consider only model-free agents and employ only perceptual augmentations. In this work, we consider how perceptual, dynamical and semantic augmentations improve the transfer of model-based RL agents. In SGI [21] the authors propose to employ multiple auxiliary tasks to pre-train and the fine-tune an agent on the same task, and shown negative results on transferring representations between Atari games on a small data regime. Contrary to our work, they focus only on model-free methods, and only use random crops and intense jittering (both perceptual augmentations). In RAD [14] the authors explore ten different types of data augmentations, and show how using augmentations while learning the same task it helps improve the data-efficiency and generalization of RL methods. Compared with our work, RAD uses only perceptual augmentations and focus on model-free single task learning.

3 Method

In this work, we address the problem of adapting RL agents to novel downstream tasks. In particular, we consider a two-stage transfer approach: we initially *pre-train* agents on a given task T_p and subsequently transfer the agents to a novel downstream task T_d, where we *fine-tune* the agents to the novel task.

One of the challenges of the transfer process resides in the difference between the information provided to the agent in T_p and in T_d. During the pre-training

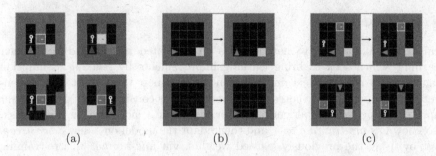

(a)   (b)   (c)

Fig. 1. Our proposed augmentation scheme for efficient adaptation: **a** *perceptual* augmentations exploit global transformations of the original observations (in red), such as color inversion, cropping and flipping; **b** *dynamical* augmentations exploit counterfactual transformations of original transitions in the environment (in red), such as randomly introducing "NoOp" actions; **c** *semantic* augmentations exploit conceptual transformations over the original observations (in red), such as changing the sprites of the player and objects

phase, the agent experiences a set of observations $O_p \in \mathcal{O}$, with $\mathcal{O}$ the set of all possible observations in the space of all possible tasks. From such observations, and auxiliary reward signals provided by the environment, the agent learns to perform the pre-training task T_p. However, during the adaptation phase, the agent reuses its experience to learn the downstream task T_d from a set of observations $O_d \in \mathcal{O}$, potentially disjoint from O_p, along with a new reward signal.

However, in many tasks there are intrinsic similarities that, if exploited, could improve the transfer procedure. For example, despite the differences in the observations in each scenario, the games "Space Invaders" and "Pepsi Invaders", depicted in Fig. 3c, d respectively, share some features between them; both share similar core semantics and dynamics of a shooting up game.

To exploit the potential intrinsic similarities between the pre-training and downstream tasks, we propose to introduce *augmentations* during the pre-training phase: we expand the set of pretraining observations $O_p^\star \supseteq O_p \in \mathcal{O}$ through augmentation functions $A(o)$ to allow the efficient adaptation to downstream tasks. In Sect. 3.1, we propose a categorization of augmentation functions to exploit *perceptual*, *dynamical* and *semantic* similarities between T_p and T_d. Additionally, in Sect. 3.2 we show how our augmentations can be easily introduced into standard pretraining schemes, with minimal computational overhead, an approach we denote by *Multiple Augmented Pre-training Scheme* (MAPS).

3.1 Augmentation Scheme

We now focus our attention on the nature of the augmentation functions $A(o)$ to improve the efficiency of the fine-tuning process on unknown, novel tasks T_d. As shown in Fig. 1, we propose three different categories of augmentations: *perceptual*, *dynamical* and *semantic*.

Perceptual Augmentations One of the significant ways observations can change from the T_p to T_d concerns features of the perceptions of the agents, such as color, orientation and size. We propose to expand the set of observations O_p to introduce such variability by considering *perceptual* augmentations.

As shown in Fig. 1a, perceptual augmentations correspond to global transformations on the observations of the agents. These augmentations introduce variability in general features of the observations, having no impact on the underlying task and dynamics of the environment. Moreover, perceptual augmentations are agnostic to the semantics in the perception itself (such as the players and enemies). Examples of such augmentations include color inversion for the whole observation, or random cropping and mirroring across different axes.

The use of augmentations has been explored by several self-supervision methods, such as SimClr [5] and CURL [15], that learn transferable representations by employing visual-based augmentations on image data. In this work, we introduce two more categories of augmentations to the observations of the agents.

Dynamical Augmentations Another potential change in the sequence of observations experienced by the agents from the T_p to T_d concerns the dynamics of the environment, i.e., how the environment changes as a function of the actions of the agent. We propose to expand the standard set of observations O_p in order to introduce such variability by considering *dynamical* augmentations.

As shown in Fig. 1b, dynamical augmentations correspond to changes on the observations of the agent, due to transformations on its actions. Contrary to perceptual augmentations, dynamical augmentations can only be perceived across multiple time-steps, having no impact in the general features nor in the semantics of the observation. Examples of such augmentations are operations of randomly employing "NoOp" actions or swapping the actions of the agent.

Semantic Augmentations Finally, observations from T_p and T_d can also differ regarding local, higher-level features of the observations, such as the sprites of the agent and the enemies. We propose to expand the set of observations O_p in order to introduce such variability by considering *semantic* augmentations.

Semantic augmentations correspond to local transformations on the observations of the agent. Much like dynamical augmentations, semantic augmentations often can only be perceived across multiple time-steps (see Fig. 1c) through specific visual modifications to game elements such as the player, or surrounding elements important to solve the task. Contrary to perceptual augmentations, these augmentations require prior knowledge over the semantics of the observations. As such knowledge is often difficult to obtain and manipulate in complex scenarios, we propose to use similar tasks to T_d, such as video games from the same type or genre, as a way to provide meaningful semantic augmentations.

3.2   Pre-training with Augmentations

Motivated by recent approaches in self-supervised visual learning [5,15], we argue that by pre-training an agent on the augmented set of observations O_p^*, we force it to learn features that are more general, and thus able to transfer to the downstream task T_d more efficiently, during the fine-tuning stage.

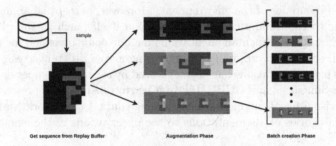

Fig. 2. The *Multiple-Augmented Pre-training Scheme* (MAPS) for efficient transfer of RL agents to novel similar tasks: initially, we obtain a sequence of observations that is used to train the agent; subsequently, we augment each specific sequence with a user-defined transformation; finally, we stack the multiple augmented sequences into a single training batch.

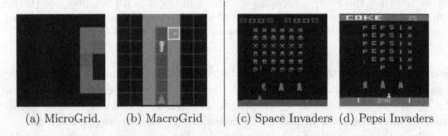

(a) MicroGrid.   (b) MacroGrid   (c) Space Invaders (d) Pepsi Invaders

Fig. 3. The environments employed in the evaluation of MAPS.

We denote our simple pre-training scheme with augmentations as *Multiple Augmented Pre-training Scheme* (MAPS). In MAPS, as shown in Fig. 2 each training sequence (either from the replay buffer or from the environment) is augmented with a random set of perceptual, dynamical and semantic augmentations. An augmentation can be applied per time-step or across multiple time-steps (such as throughout the episode). We then concatenate the diverse augmented sequences into a single batch, to be used in the training of the RL controller.

Despite the simplicity of the approach, we show in Sect. 4 that the joint pre-training approach of MAPS is able to outperform other transfer approaches in terms of sample-efficiency of the fine-tuning stage. By learning with the help of augmentations task, MAPS is able to generalize across a larger number of representations, thus being able to more easily adapt to new games.

4   Evaluation

We evaluate MAPS against other standard pre-training schemes in scenarios of increasing complexity, showing how our approach allows pre-trained model-based RL agents to efficiently transfer to novel, similar tasks.

4.1   Experimental Setup

To fully exploit the perceptual, dynamical and semantic variability within MAPS, we consider two different grid-based scenarios in our evaluation:

– *MicroGrid*: A smaller 5×5 grid world based on MiniGrid (Fig. 3a);
– *MacroGrid*: A larger 8×8 grid world based on MiniGrid, where the visual observations of the agents are upscaled to 64×64 pixels (Fig. 3b).

Both scenarios allow for fine control over the elements of the environment (such as colors, shapes and grid sizes), facilitating the creation of the necessary perceptual and dynamical augmentations for MAPS. In addition, the higher-resolution MacroGrid scenario allows to exploit semantic variability by changing the object sprites present in the environment. In both scenarios, we consider the *DoorKey* navigation task, which requires that the agent obtains a key to unlock the door that allows it to reach the goal. We instantiate the following classes of augmentations for MAPS in the grid-based scenarios:

– *Perceptual* (P): static color changes, color changes on every step, spatial visual changes;
– *Dynamical* (D): modifications that do not change optimal policy (random NoOp action), modifications that change the optimal policy (swap actions);
– *Semantic* (S): image occlusions (blinking), swap object sprites positions (only in MacroGrid), use different object sprites (only in MacroGrid).

We employ a subset of 5 different augmentations as modified tasks: two perceptual augmentations (exterior noisy color swap and horizontal image flip), one dynamic augmentation (random NoOp action) and two semantic tasks (random black flicker, MacroGrid with semantic data).

Furthermore, we also test the MAPS framework in the Atari game environment [2], as shown in Fig. 3c, d , with image-based augmentations as the previous case. We evaluate the sample-efficiency of MAPS by following the metrics presented in [26]: an algorithm is more sample efficient than another if it reaches a higher performance in the same training window. If the algorithms present similar asymptotic performances, then we compare the jump-start performance and area under the curve.

4.2   Pre-training of Model-Based RL Agents

We introduce MAPS in the pre-training phase for a successful transfer of model-based agents. We initially consider two transfer scenarios: we pre-train the agent in the MicroGrid or MacroGrid scenario for 225k or 250k time steps, respectively. Then we transfer the learned world model to learn the downstream task, that consists of the original task with an augmentation previously not seen during the pre-training, following the augmentations in Sect. 4.1. We compare the fine-tuning performance of the agents that were pre-trained with MAPS against agents pre-trained without MAPS and agents without pre-training (learning from scratch). Furthermore, we also compare the MAPS approach to a meta learning approach that uses the same data augmentations, as meta learning as been successfully employed for transfer learning. As such we employ Reptile [19], a state-of-the-art first-order algorithm, as a baseline.

For these environments, we attempt multiple augmentation settings to better ascertain how the increase of pre-training variability can help transfer: single augmentations in perceptual (P) and dynamical (D) categories, combinations of augmentations like perceptual-dynamical (P+D) and complete perceptual-dynamical-semantic augmentations (P+D+S). We present the evaluation results for the MicroGrid scenario in Fig. 4. Overall, the results show that MAPS has a significant contribution to a positive transfer to the downstream task. This improvement is clearly seen for the *Exterior noisy color swap* downstream tasks,

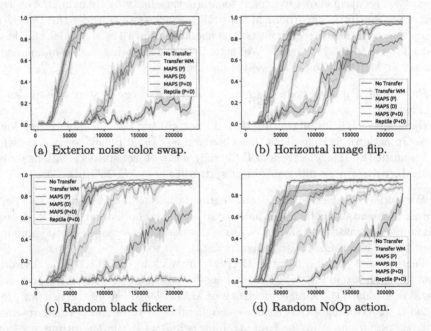

(a) Exterior noise color swap.   (b) Horizontal image flip.

(c) Random black flicker.   (d) Random NoOp action.

Fig. 4. Transfer performance of pretrained agents in MicroGrid to an augmentation task $(T_p \neq T_d)$. Results averaged over 10 randomly-seeded runs.

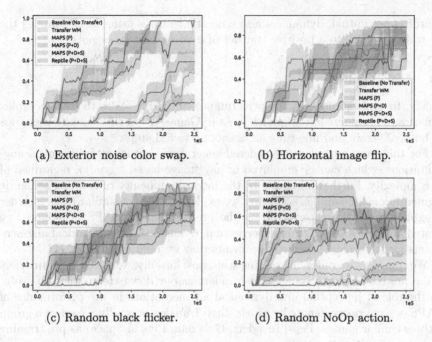

(a) Exterior noise color swap.   (b) Horizontal image flip.

(c) Random black flicker.   (d) Random NoOp action.

Fig. 5. Transfer performance of pretrained agents in MacroGrid to an augmentation task ($T_p \neq T_d$). Results averaged over 10 randomly-seeded runs.

where introducing perceptual augmentations with MAPS during pre-training allows the agent to efficiently adapt to the downstream task. The improvement can be extended to all other augmentations, where transferring the world model pre-trained with MAPS results either in a higher asymptotic performance or/and a better jump-start learning performance. The same results are valid when comparing MAPS with Reptile, where MAPS always has a higher asymptotic performance or/and a better jump-start learning performance.

We verify a similar trend in the results for the MacroGrid scenario, presented in Fig. 5. The results show, once again, that transferring the world model pre-trained with MAPS results overall in a higher asymptotic fine-tuning performance or/and a better jump-start fine-tuning performance. Moreover, in the MacroGrid scenario we can also evaluate the transfer to tasks with distinct semantic features (such as when changing the sprites of the objects in the environment). We present such results in Fig. 6: only the agent that pre-trains with MAPS, considering perceptual and semantic augmentations, is able to positively transfer to this challenging task, with a significant jump-start fine-tuning performance over the baselines. The results also show that MAPS outperforms or has similar performance to the meta-learning approach of Reptile, thus showing that joint-training of tasks can still be a strong alternative over meta-learning methods. Overall, the results attest to the importance of introducing variability regarding perceptual, dynamical and semantic features using MAPS during the pre-training phase to a positive transfer of model-based RL agents.

4.3 Atari Games

Finally, to understand how the performance of MAPS scales to more complex scenarios, we evaluate our approach in Atari Games [2]. In this complex scenarios we both pre-train and fine-tune all agents up to 5M steps.

For this environment we considered general perceptual and dynamical augmentations, which can be employed in any image-based scenario, regardless of its complexity. Furthermore, due to the intrinsic difficulty of creating semantic augmentations in complex scenarios, we explore the use of similar tasks in order to exploit semantic features during the pre-training of MAPS. Therefore, we created and use a set of general perceptual, dynamical and semantical augmentations for any image based environments that we refer only as *MAPS*.

We consider two different training scenarios: initially, we select Pepsi Invaders as the pre-training task and Space Invaders as our downstream task, to evaluate the role of perceptual and dynamical augmentations in the performance of MAPS, a scenario we denote by *Single Task Transfer*. Secondly, we select a group of three similar games (Pepsi Invaders, Galaxian, Pigs in Space) as pre-training

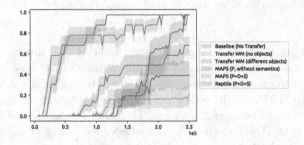

Fig. 6. Transfer performance of pretrained agents in MacroGrid to a semantically-augmented task $(T_p \neq T_d)$. Results averaged over 10 randomly-seeded runs.

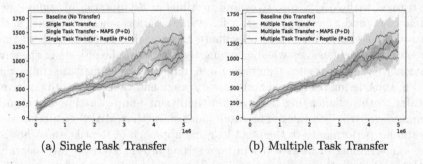

(a) Single Task Transfer   (b) Multiple Task Transfer

Fig. 7. Transfer performance of pretrained agents in **a** Pepsi and **b** 3 similar task to Space Invaders. Results averaged over 5 randomly-seeded runs

Table 1. Comparison of the final score at step 5M in Space Invaders.

Method	5M Avg. Score
DQN [18]	808 ± 38
C51 [1]	1035 ± 30
Rainbow [12]	1086 ± 81
IQN [6]	$\mathbf{1602 \pm 153}$
DreamerV2 [9]	1141 ± 295
Single Task Transfer	1393 ± 466
Single Task Transfer—MAPS (P+D)	$\mathbf{2032 \pm 774}$
Multiple Task Transfer	863 ± 335
Multiple Task Transfer—MAPS (P+D)	$\mathbf{1813 \pm 576}$
Single Task Transfer—Reptile (P+D)	1226 ± 458
Multiple Task Transfer—Reptile (P+D)	1719 ± 483

tasks, to exploit semantic variability, and transfer the agent to Space Invaders, a scenario we refer as *Multiple Task Transfer*. The selected pre-training tasks share the same grid-like structure of the enemies as the fine-tuning task.

We present our results in Fig. 7. In the Single Task Transfer we verify that pre-training on the similar Pepsi task yields a positive improvement, while pre-training jointly on Multiple Task Transfer has a negligible to negative performance over training from scratch. Using MAPS brings a significant improvement over the Single Task pre-training, making it the best performing method for training the Space Invaders tasks with 5M time-steps when compared with other publicly available results in Table 1. In the Multiple Task Transfer scenario (Fig. 7), the results show once again that employing MAPS allows for a significant positive transfer over the baseline and over the naive pre-training approach. Is worth mentioning that while both pre-training methods with MAPS have a high mean, both also have a big variance in the results, as seen in Table 1. This higher variance in the performance results also seems to be a characteristic of the DreamerV2 method. Thus, we can ascertain that our methods using MAPS are better with a 95% CI than DQN [18], C51 [1] and Rainbow [12], while being competitive with IQN [6] and baseline DreamerV2 [9]. On another hand, we can also conclude that learning using Multiple Task Transfer with MAPS is significantly better than without.

5 Conclusions

In this work, we investigated the introduction of perceptual, dynamical and semantic variability during the pre-training of model-based RL agents for an efficient transfer of the agents to novel tasks. We contributed with MAPS, a novel pre-training scheme that introduces augmentations over the observations of the agent to take advantage of such variability. Our results show that MAPS improves the fine-tuning efficiency of pre-trained agents to novel downstream tasks. In future work, we will explore how MAPS can be used to improve transfer in model-free RL, as well as accessing MAPS in other model-based agents, which might employ different auxiliary losses like contrastive learning methods.

References

1. Bellemare, M., Dabney, W., Munos, R.: A distributional perspective on reinforcement learning. In: Proceedings of the 34th International Conference on Machine Learning, pp. 449–458 (2017)
2. Bellemare, M., Naddaf, Y., Veness, J., Bowling, M.: The arcade learning environment: an evaluation platform for general agents. J. Artif. Intell. Res. **47**, 253–279 (2013)
3. Bommasani, R., Hudson, D., Adeli, E., Altman, R., Arora, S., von Arx, S., Bernstein, M., Bohg, J., Bosselut, A., Brunskill, E., et al.: On the opportunities and risks of foundation models. CoRR abs/2108.07258 (2021)
4. Brown, T., et al.: Language models are few-shot learners. CoRR abs/2005.14165 (2020)
5. Chen, T., Kornblith, S., Norouzi, M., Hinton, G.: A simple framework for contrastive learning of visual representations. In: Proceedings of the 37th International Conference on Machine Learning, pp. 1597–1607 (2020)
6. Dabney, W., Ostrovski, G., Silver, D., Munos, R.: Implicit quantile networks for distributional reinforcement learning. In: Proceedings of the 35th International Conference on Machine Learning, pp. 1096–1105 (2018)
7. Devlin, J., Chang, M., Lee, K., Toutanova, K.: BERT: Pre-training of deep bidirectional transformers for language understanding. CoRR abs/1810.04805 (2018)
8. Grill, J., et al.: Bootstrap your own latent: A new approach to self-supervised learning. In: Advances in Neural Information Processing Systems, vol. 33, pp. 21271–21284 (2020)
9. Hafner, D., Lillicrap, T., Norouzi, M., Ba, J.: Mastering Atari with discrete world models. CoRR abs/2010.02193 (2020)
10. He, K., Fan, H., Wu, Y., Xie, S., Girshick, R.: Momentum contrast for unsupervised visual representation learning. In: Proceedings of the IEEE/CVF Conference on Computer Vision and Pattern Recognition, pp. 9729–9738 (2020)
11. Henderson, P., et al.: Deep reinforcement learning that matters. In: Proceedings of the 32nd AAAI Conf. Artificial Intelligence, pp. 3207–3214 (2018)
12. Hessel, M., et al.: Rainbow: combining improvements in deep reinforcement learning. In: Proceedings of the 32nd AAAI Conference on Artificial Intelligence, pp. 3215–3222 (2018)
13. Lake, B., Ullman, T., Tenenbaum, J., Gershman, S.: Building machines that learn and think like people. Behav. Brain Sci. **40** (2017)
14. Laskin, M., Lee, K., Stooke, A., Pinto, L., Abbeel, P., Srinivas, A.: Reinforcement learning with augmented data. In: Advances in Neural Information Processing Systems, vol. 33, pp. 19884–19895 (2020)
15. Laskin, M., Srinivas, A., Abbeel, P.: CURL: contrastive unsupervised representations for reinforcement learning. In: Proceedings of the 37th International Conference on Machine Learning, pp. 5639–5650 (2020)
16. Levine, S., Finn, C., Darrell, T., Abbeel, P.: End-to-end training of deep visuomotor policies. CoRR abs/1504.00702 (2016)

17. Lillicrap, T., et al.: Continuous control with deep reinforcement learning. CoRR abs/1509.02971 (2015)
18. Mnih, V., et al.: Human-level control through deep reinforcement learning. Nature **518**(7540), 529–533 (2015)
19. Nichol, A., Achiam, J., Schulman, J.: On first-order meta-learning algorithms. CoRR abs/1803.02999 (2018)
20. Obando-Ceron, J., Castro, P.: Revisiting Rainbow: Promoting more insightful and inclusive deep reinforcement learning research. In: Proceedings of the 38th International Conference on Machine Learning, pp. 1373–1383 (2021)
21. Schwarzer, M., et al.: Pretraining representations for data-efficient reinforcement learning. In: Advances in Neural Information Processing Systems, vol. 34 (2021)
22. Sekar, R., Rybkin, O., Daniilidis, K., Abbeel, P., Hafner, D., Pathak, D.: Planning to explore via self-supervised world models. CoRR abs/2005.05960 (2020)
23. Silver, D., et al.: Mastering the game of Go with deep neural networks and tree search. Nature **529**(7587), 484–489 (2016)
24. Stooke, A., Lee, K., Abbeel, P., Laskin, M.: Decoupling representation learning from reinforcement learning. In: Proceedings of the 38th International Conference on Machine Learning, pp. 9870–9879 (2021)
25. Tan, C., Sun, F., Kong, T., Zhang, W., Yang, C., Liu, C.: A survey on deep transfer learning. In: Proceedings of the International Conference on Artificial Neural Networks, pp. 270–279 (2018)
26. Taylor, M., Stone, P.: Transfer learning for reinforcement learning domains: a survey. J. Mach. Learn.Res. **10**(7) (2009)

DyPrune: Dynamic Pruning Rates
for Neural Networks

Richard Adolph Aires Jonker[1]([✉]) [iD], Roshan Poudel[2] [iD], Olga Fajarda[1,3] [iD],
José Luís Oliveira[1,3] [iD], Rui Pedro Lopes[2,3] [iD], and Sérgio Matos[1,3] [iD]

[1] IEETA- Institute of Electronics and Informatics Engineering of Aveiro, University
of Aveiro, Aveiro, Portugal
{richard.jonker,olga.oliveira,jlo,aleixomatos}@ua.pt
[2] Research Centre in Digitalization and Intelligent Robotics, Polytechnic Institute of
Bragança, Bragança, Portugal
{roshan,rlopes}@ipb.pt
[3] LASI - Intelligent Systems Associate Laboratory, Guimarães, Portugal

Abstract. Neural networks have achieved remarkable success in various
applications such as image classification, speech recognition, and natural language processing. However, the growing size of neural networks
poses significant challenges in terms of memory usage, computational
cost, and deployment on resource-constrained devices. Pruning is a popular technique to reduce the complexity of neural networks by removing
unnecessary connections, neurons, or filters. In this paper, we present
novel pruning algorithms that can reduce the number of parameters in
neural networks by up to 98% without sacrificing accuracy. This is done
by scaling the pruning rate of the models to the size of the model and
scheduling the pruning to execute throughout the training of the model.
Code related to this work is openly available.

Keywords: Machine learning · Neural networks · Pruning

1 Introduction

Deep neural networks have shown tremendous success in various fields including computer vision, natural language processing, speech recognition, and reinforcement learning. These models, however, are characterized by their large size,
complexity, and computational requirements, which pose significant challenges in
terms of training time, memory utilization, and hardware constraints. In particular, the deployment of deep learning models on resource-limited devices requires
efficient resource utilization and reduced memory footprint.[1]

Neural network pruning has emerged as a promising technique to address
these challenges by reducing the size and complexity of deep neural networks
without compromising their performance. Pruning involves selectively removing

---

[1] https://github.com/richardjonker2000/DyPrune.

ⓒ The Author(s), under exclusive license to Springer Nature Switzerland AG 2023
N. Moniz et al. (Eds.): EPIA 2023, LNAI 14115, pp. 146–157, 2023.
https://doi.org/10.1007/978-3-031-49008-8_12

redundant or insignificant connections or neurons from the network while maintaining or even improving its accuracy. Pruning has been shown to significantly reduce the model size and computational requirements, making it more suitable for deployment on resource-limited devices or real-time applications [1] . The intuition behind removing weights is based on the output of a neuron, defined as:

$$h_i = \sigma(\sum_{j=1}^{N} W_{ij}x_j + B_i^{hid}) \tag{1}$$

where σ is the activation function, N is the number of inputs to neuron i, W_{ij} is the weight from neuron j to neuron i, x_j is the corresponding input to the neuron, and B_i^{hid} is a bias added to the neuron. As can be seen, there is no further manipulation of the input besides the multiplication of the weight. This shows that very small weights have little impact on the model. Furthermore, once a weight is zeroed out, the input is essentially zero.

In recent years, there has been a surge of research interest in pruning techniques, and numerous methods have been proposed to achieve high pruning efficiency with minimal accuracy loss [1,6]. Although it can be assumed that as the number of parameters in a model decreases, the accuracy also decreases, this is not true in many cases. Pruning also offers the added benefit of reducing overfitting in the model by reducing model complexity, allowing the model to generalize better.

There are various different types of unstructured pruning: pruning of weights, pruning of nodes, and pruning of layers. There are also different ways to select the parameters to prune.

- **Magnitude pruning:** Weights are selected based on the lowest absolute values in the network. This approach is intuitive and continues to achieve good results whilst being lightweight to implement [3,4,14].
- **Gradient magnitude pruning:** In addition to the magnitude of the weight, the value of the gradient is also considered. This allows the model to consider how much the weights are changing as well [1,10,12].
- **Random pruning:** Weights get randomly selected to be pruned.

In general, pruning techniques can be applied to a model as a whole (global) or layerwise. In the case of layerwise techniques, the pruning rate is equal across the layers, to ensure a balanced removal of items. Global pruning techniques have been shown to be more accurate than layerwise pruning techniques [1]. It is also important to note that different pruning techniques work better for different models and sizes.

Many pruning algorithms were derived from a study by Han et al. in 2015 [5]. In this work, the authors trained a network, pruned weights that are below a certain threshold, and then retrained the sparse network accordingly. They also mentioned that they reduced their dropout rate after pruning the network due to having fewer connections in the network. They reiterated the importance of retraining the model in order to compensate for the weights removed. They also suggested that this can be an iterative process in which the model is trained, pruned, trained, and then pruned again.

Although unstructured pruning is a good starting point to reduce a neural network (NN) size, the weight matrices become sparse and the complexity of the models may not be reduced. This is where the technique of structured pruning comes into play, and entire sections of a model are removed. A section can be anything from a neuron [8] to a convolution filter [11] in the case of Convolutional Neural Networks. Similarly, in this work, a combination of both structured and unstructured pruning techniques is used, where unstructured pruning is applied to a neural network, and various neurons are removed if sufficient weights in the neuron are pruned.

In literature there are various techniques to apply pruning to a neural network:

- **Train and Sparsify:** the model is trained fully and the pruning is applied, and often the model is fine tuned afterwards [7].
- **Sparsify during training:** pruning is applied iteratively during training, with a linear or non linear function. This approach is also called sparse scheduling [2].
- **Sparse training:** pruning is applied before the model is trained [13].

The most similar work to that proposed in this study is the work by Zhu et al. [17] in 2017. The pruning method proposed by the authors gradually applies pruning to models using a scheduler, which has achieved good results. In this work, we further build on this idea by scaling the pruning rate with the number of parameters in order to decay the pruning rate of models as they become smaller.

The remainder of the paper is organized as follows: Sect. 2 describes the framework and techniques used in the work. Section 3 presents the results of the work. Section 4 is a discussion of the results, which is finally followed by the conclusion of the work is Sect. 5.

2   Methodology

In this section, we provide a detailed description of the different pruning techniques, their advantages and disadvantages, and the experimental methodology used to evaluate their effectiveness. This work was conducted using the PyTorch framework. The model architecture is defined initially as a fully connected Neural Network (NN) with an input layer, an output layer, and an undefined number of hidden layers. By default, the standard categorical loss function, namely, cross entropy loss, is applied.

2.1   Dataset

The dataset selected for this study was the Fashion-MNIST [15]. This dataset was selected mainly for allowing fast training and inference times. The dataset was created in 2017 as a more complex replacement of the popular MNIST dataset [9]. The dataset contains 60,000 train images and 10,000 test images, of size 28 × 28 pixels. The training dataset is further split into 50,000 train images and 10,000 validation images. There are ten classes in this dataset, each representing a different item of clothing.

2.2 Pruning Weights

In order to prune the variables of a model, PyTorch has built in implementations for pruning. The implementation is a wrapper that allows for custom pruning on a network. The pruning in PyTorch works by multiplying a mask with the original weight during any forward step. In this study only weights were considered for pruning, and the magnitude pruning technique was used. For this technique, L1 weight selection was performed, selecting the weights with the lowest absolute values.

The main novelty introduced is the method of selecting the number of weights to be pruned, that is, the dynamic pruning rate. Generally, pruning is conducted based on a raw number of parameters to remove or a percentage of parameters to be removed. However, in this study, the goal is to prune the parameters and continue training, and then repeat the process, similar to a scheduler. This can lead to a situation where the model removes too many parameters to be able to successfully carry out its task, so an adaptive way to determine the number of parameters to be removed is needed. This is defined as

$$y = \frac{ln(|W|) - 6}{10},\tag{2}$$

where y is the percentage of the model that will be pruned and $|W|$ is the number of weights currently in the model. Subtracting 6 from the logarithm acts as a rescaling factor. This value is used to enforce a lower bound onto the pruning rate. The value was taken by approximating the logarithm of 1000 to 6, so if more parameters are required for more complex tasks, this value can be increased. The goal of the pruning rate is to have harsher pruning in models with higher number of parameters. The target goal when developing this formulation was for the model to have around 1000 parameters.

A model is not pruned if the pruning rate is ≤ 0, which will occur once the model has fewer than $e^6 \approx 403$ parameters. An upper limit of pruning is set to 90% of the model. This occurs when the model has more than $e^{15} \approx 3,269,017$ parameters.

A visualization of the number of parameters present during training can be seen in Fig. 1. When looking at a model with 5,000 parameters, we see that the model has less pruning than a fixed 30% pruning rate. As the number of parameters of the initial model increases, so does the pruning rate, which significantly increases the rate of pruning once there are 1,000,000 starting parameters in the model.

The other advantage of a dynamic pruning rate is that it ensures that a sufficient number of weights remain. This value can also be tuned by adjusting the constant in Eq. 2.

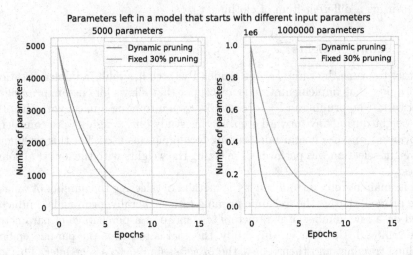

Fig. 1. Comparing the number of parameters against the epochs of a dynamic pruning algorithm versus a fixed 30% pruning algorithm.

Now that the pruning rate has been decided, it is important to discuss when pruning will occur. The ideal loss of a model can be seen as a hyperbolic function. Generally, a loss function starts at a fairly high arbitrary loss value, where it rapidly decays, until the model is sufficiently trained, where the loss plateaus. In practice, loss graphs seldom look like this, and there is usually more noise in the loss graph, be it from unforeseen variations in model training or additional training techniques. Further problems that occur during training will also affect the shape, for example, if the model is not complex enough, the graph will not stabilize and will start spiking, not converging to any specific value.

It is important to note that pruning is expected to have an effect on the loss of the model. On the first epoch immediately after pruning, it is expected to see an increase in the loss of the model and a decrease in accuracy due to the large change in the model. After the first epoch following pruning, it is expected that the loss and accuracy begin to recover. By pruning the model we also force the model to learn, because the weights that were lost from the pruning force a change in the model, where the rest of the model needs to be able to compensate for the loss of the model. After a few epochs, the model would have stabilized again, and if there are sufficient weights in the model, the model will perform similarly. If the model has lost too many weights, it loses stability, and is unable to recover the loss.

Following the above, pruning should not occur every epoch because this can interfere with the learning of the model by introducing too much variation in the model. This can cause weights to struggle to converge to the optimum. First, the model should have a warm up stage, where the model has time to train and converge before it gets pruned. Similarly, the model should have a significant number of epochs to train after the last pruning iteration to recover the loss from the last pruning attempt. Two approaches can be adopted when a model is pruned.

- **Static Pruning Iterations:** Using a fixed value for selecting how often pruning will occur. For example, after every n epoch, pruning will be executed on the model. The advantage of this approach is that there is a relatively high control over how the model will change its shape. The problem with this approach is that it cannot adapt to different recovery times of the model and can, hence, easily overprune the model.
- **Dynamic Pruning Iterations:** A different approach would be to base the pruning on the loss of the model. Analytically, pruning would happen during an elbow of the loss when the loss starts to flatten out. This is a good time to prune the model, as it has already learned many parameters. Mathematically, the gradient of the loss is normalized by dividing it by the smallest gradient the model saw up to that point of training. From this point, a range can be set in which pruning should occur. The main problem with this approach is the assumption that the loss of the model will behave in a predictable manner. In edge cases, where the model is too complex or not complex enough, the loss of the model might not behave in this predictable way, which will cause discrepancies in the loss. When a model is sufficiently large and the dataset is relatively simple, the initial loss will be very low, and there will be relatively high variation in the loss of the model, however, the model is actually stable and needs to be pruned.

2.3   Removing Neurons

To further reduce the complexity of the network, neurons can also be removed under some conditions. For a neuron to be safe to remove, it cannot have any weights connecting it to other neurons. We can further relax this condition by defining that if there are no weights connecting to the neuron, the input of the neuron will be zero, and hence, the output will just be the bias. Similarly, if there are no connections leaving the neuron, there is no benefit in having the neuron, as it does not contribute to anything further in the model besides its bias. This is done by examining the weight matrix of the model and identifying whether the columns or rows are zero.

3   Results

In this section, the results are presented for the various tests ran to investigate the performance of the proposed architecture. The tests were conducted on a docker container running on a server with an Intel Xeon CPU and a Nvidia

Tesla K80.[2] All tests were conducted 10 times to account for variations in the random initialization of the model. During training, model progress was monitored based on accuracy and loss. After the model was trained, it was evaluated using accuracy and macro F1 score.

Table 1. The baseline model is presented followed by the pruned model. The best performing model is shown in bold for each case.

ID	Avg # Neurons in HLs	Avg. # Eff. Weights	Sparsity (%)	Time to Prune(s)	F1 Score
1	5.0, 5.0, 5.0	4,020.0	–	–	0.7416
7	5.0, 4.9, 5.0	1,462.2	63.62	0.082	**0.7812**
2	15.0, 15.0, 15.0	12,360.0	–	–	**0.8514**
8	15.0, 15.0, 14.8	2,919.5	76.37	0.0852	0.849
3	25.0, 25.0, 25.0	21,100.0	–	- -	**0.8626**
9	24.8, 24.9, 24.3	3,895.8	81.36	0.0867	0.8587
4	100.0, 100.0, 100.0	99,400.0	–	- -	**0.8784**
10	94.8, 95.5, 86.2	9,131.4	90.12	0.0985	0.8747
5	100.0, 10.0, 10.0	79,600.0	–	–	**0.8698**
11	85.3, 8.9, 9.6	7,534.2	88.88	0.0915	0.8653
6	1000.0, 1000.0, 1000.0	2,794,000.0	–	–	0.8785
12	776.4, 820.1, 575.4	31,340.6	98.18	0.3903	**0.8799**

Dynamic pruning rates were applied statically to the model. The models were pruned after every 4 epochs, as shown in Table 1. The average number of effective weights refers to the average number of non zero weights in the model. All these models took 85.84 s to train. With static pruning, pruning occurs 5 times during training with 25 epochs. In almost all cases, static pruning occurs more times than in dynamic pruning. This allows much higher sparsity percentages in larger models and fewer parameters. For example, the last model that started with 1000 neurons per layer (6) ended with 31, 340 parameters, on average, and still outperformed the unpruned model. The time required to prune the model is negligible, as shown in the table. Results with static pruning show that models do not require a large number of parameters in order to be successful on this dataset, and that in many cases, it is beneficial for the model to be sparse. Looking at how models are pruned, we can see that generally the last layer has more neurons removed from it as opposed to the first. This again shows that the first layers are more important to the model and, by definition, would have higher weights as opposed to the rest of the model. When the number of non-zero parameters are compared, the true effects of pruning can be seen. For example, comparing the model at run 10 with a similar size model before pruning, model

---

[2] Due to the fact that the server is a shared resource for the research group, only one GPU core was used.

2, the pruned model with the same effective number of parameters outperforms the non pruned model by more than 2% points.

Table 2. Results with dynamic pruning rates with dynamic pruning iterations on the Fashion MNIST dataset. The baseline model is presented followed by the pruned model. The best performing model is shown in bold for each case.

ID	Avg # Neurons in HLs	Avg. # Eff. Weights	Sparsity (%)	# Times Pruned	F1 Score
1	5.0, 5.0, 5.0	4,020.0	–	–	0.7416
13	5.0, 4.9, 5.0	1,664.8	58.58	4.7	**0.7637**
2	15.0, 15.0, 15.0	12,360.0	–	–	**0.8514**
14	14.9, 14.9, 14.8	2,757.4	77.52	5.3	0.8430
3	25.0, 25.0, 25.0	21,100.0	–	–	**0.8626**
15	24.6, 24.5, 23.9	4,254.7	79.51	4.8	0.8568
4	100.0, 100.0, 100.0	99,400.0	–	–	0.8784
16	97.3, 98.6, 92.5	19,877.1	79.44	2.9	**0.8785**
5	100.0, 10.0, 10.0	79,600.0	–	–	**0.8698**
17	78.5, 8.5, 9.4	7,524.8	87.99	4.7	0.8580
6	1000.0, 1000.0, 1000.0	2,794,000.0	–	–	0.8785
18	921.5, 952.0, 737.3	742,188.7	71.76	1.2	**0.8870**

Dynamic pruning rate was applied to the models using dynamic pruning iterations (Table 2). In half of the tests, the F1 score of the model increased with pruning. Furthermore, in the cases where the F1 score did not increase, they were only minimally affected. When comparing static pruning iterations with dynamic pruning iterations on larger models, the number of times the models get pruned becomes inconsistent, leading to less pruning.

Next, static pruning rates was applied every 4 epochs to evaluate the performance versus dynamic pruning rates (Table 3). Using dynamic pruning on a model with 1000 neurons in three hidden layers (12), the model achieved an F1 score of 0.88 with 31340.6 parameters. Overall, we can see that static pruning on a large model requires a high pruning value to obtain the same level of pruning (22). In this case, the model performed slightly worse, with fewer parameters, which is to be expected. In run 20, we see the model with the best performance seen so far, however, this model still has a comparatively large number of parameters (169,280). In runs 23 and 24, static pruning does compare with dynamic pruning (runs 13 and 15 respectively), however, the two static pruning methods do prune too much in comparison to dynamic pruning. In 25 and 26, a similar conclusion can be drawn, with the reference being 22.

The thresholds for dynamic pruning were also tested (Table 4). The goal is to evaluate the threshold relative to the size of the models. Looking at the data as a whole, the results are expected, and the number of times the model is pruned generally increased by increasing the dynamic pruning range. For the

Table 3. Results with various static pruning rates with static pruning occurring every 4 epochs on the Fashion MNIST dataset.

ID	Avg # Neurons in HLs	Pruning Rate	Avg. # Eff. Weights	Sparsity (%)	F1 Score
6	1000.0, 1000.0, 1000.0	–	2,794,000.0	–	0.8785
19	917.3, 983.0, 903.6	0.3	538,737.2	78.60	**0.8908**
20	857.3, 920.5, 814.9	0.5	169,280.0	92.37	**0.8913**
21	1000.0, 1000.0, 998.5	0.1	1,513,518.0	45.80	0.8852
22	712.1, 831.8, 589.4	0.7	24,550.9	98.51	0.8707
3	25.0, 25.0, 25.0	–	21,100.0	–	**0.8626**
23	24.5, 23.9, 23.3	0.5	1,335.0	93.51	0.8259
24	25.0, 25.0, 24.6	0.3	4,381.8	79.22	0.859
2	15.0, 15.0, 15.0	–	12,360.0	–	**0.8514**
25	13.0, 13.5, 13.4	0.5	764.8	92.81	0.7938
26	14.9, 14.9, 14.9	0.3	2,583.6	78.94	0.8471

smaller model, this is also true, where the number of epochs pruned is 7. If more pruning is required on the model with dynamic pruning, the range for dynamic pruning should be increased, or static pruning should be used to ensure that pruning will occur.

Table 4. Results with dynamic pruning rates with dynamic pruning iterations, testing the dynamic pruning range on the Fashion MNIST dataset.

ID	Avg. # Neurons in HLs	Pruning Range	Avg. # Eff. Weights	Sparsity (%)	# Epochs Pruned	F1 Score
18	921.5, 952.0, 737.3	[0, 0.05]	742,188.7	71.76	1.2	0.8870
27	893.4, 930.5, 718.1	[-0.05, 0.15]	489,022.2	80.33	1.4	**0.8903**
28	889.2, 907.1, 739.2	[-0.05, 0.05]	714,477.9	72.71	1.8	0.8883
29	882.3, 901.1, 677.5	[-0.05, 0.25]	396,427.3	84.36	2.2	0.8872
15	24.6, 24.5, 23.9	[0, 0.05]	4,254.7	79.51	4.8	0.8568
30	24.3, 24.2, 23.7	[-0.05, 0.15]	2,701.2	86.78	7.0	0.8512
31	24.2, 24.8, 24.2	[-0.05, 0.05]	3,662.1	82.07	5.2	0.8544
32	24.4, 24.2, 22.6	[-0.05, 0.25]	2,762.7	86.51	7.0	0.8535

A summary of various tests with different configurations is presented in Fig. 2. It can be seen from the figure that in almost all cases, pruned models have fewer parameters and higher F1 scores than models that were not pruned. By pruning the models, the number of parameters was allowed to decrease significantly, whilst still achieving high F1 scores.

4   Discussion

It is clear that pruning is a very beneficial technique that can be applied to a model, as seen in the existing literature. Not only can the number of parameters

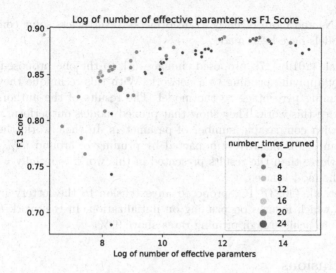

Fig. 2. Log of the number of effective parameters versus the F1 score on the Fashion MNIST dataset. The color and size of the markers refer to the number of times the models were pruned.

be reduced, but pruning also allows for some performance increases in certain models. In cases where no performance gains can be observed, most of the time the performance of the model does not significantly decrease. Discussing firstly the pruning rate, the dynamic pruning rate technique is the most novel work presented here with the best performance. By dynamically setting the pruning rate, one can ensure that the model is sufficiently pruned and prevent over-pruning in most cases. In most cases, this technique produces excellent results, because models with fewer parameters get pruned less harshly. In general, it is noticed that when pruning and removing neurons, more neurons are removed from the last layer of the models. Regarding the frequency of pruning, dynamic pruning iterations do not work consistently enough to be used. Static pruning allows for significantly more control over the model. In most cases, models with a larger number of parameters got pruned less frequently with dynamic pruning, because the initial loss of the model was much lower. Furthermore, extending the epochs the models were trained for, could increase the number of times pruning occurred, but not the frequency. Increasing the pruning range did not make this technique more consistent, which further indicates that a better metric should be used. On the other hand, static pruning consistently performed well.

Due to the nature of this work, it is hard to directly compare to other state of the art pruning models. The effects of pruning has already been studied and it has been established that pruning models is beneficial, however their lacks consistent ways to measure and compare such models [1]. It is important to compare this work to other state of the art methods, however this is difficult due to the fact that many approaches apply pruning to different architectures such as CNNs and more recently, transformers. Nevertheless some comparisons to other models have been made:

- Zhu et. al. (2019) [17], proposed similar work to the one proposed here, by gradually applying pruning to a network. With this technique they apply a fixed pruning percentage to the model. The results of the authors work is in line with this work. They show that pruned models outperform unpruned models with comparable number of parameters. In their work, the models' performance was negatively impacted by pruning of around 90%, which is slightly worse than the results presented in this work, especially when comparing the models size.
- Zhang et. al. (2023) [16], proposed an extension to the lottery hypothesis problem which focuses on pruning on initialization. In this work they were also able to achieve high pruning rates above 99%.

5 Conclusions

Many of the models in this work have shown that they are capable of being 90% sparse with little to no impact on the performance, with some cases in which pruned models with less than 2% of the original parameters were still able to perform relatively well. In this work, it is clear that there are often many parameters in a NN architecture that can be removed without a significant impact on the performance of the model. This work shows that there is an optimal point of number of parameters versus performance of the models, and this point is much lower when the use of pruning is involved.

In future work, it would be interesting to see the effects of applying similar techniques to more complex architectures, such as transformers and CNNs, which are currently producing state-of-the-art results for the tasks they perform. It is expected that the effects of pruning would be the same as seen in this work, which would lead to large time savings and a largely reduced number of parameters, should a sparse representation of weights be used. A limitation with these more complex models is that adding and removing neurons would not necessarily be possible due to their architecture implementations, and the only useful technique would be pruning of weights.

Acknowledgments. This work was supported by national funds through the Foundation for Science and Technology (FCT) in the context of the project DSAIPA/AI/0088/2020 and project UIDB/00127/2020.

References

1. Blalock, D., Gonzalez Ortiz, J.J., Frankle, J., Guttag, J.: What is the state of neural network pruning? Proc. Mach. Learn. Syst. **2**, 129–146 (2020)
2. Finnoff, W., Hergert, F., Zimmermann, H.G.: Improving model selection by non-convergent methods. Neural Netw. **6**(6), 771–783 (1993). https://doi.org/10.1016/S0893-6080(05)80122-4

3. Gale, T., Elsen, E., Hooker, S.: The State of Sparsity in Deep Neural Networks (2019). https://doi.org/10.48550/arXiv.1902.09574, arXiv:1902.09574 [cs, stat]

4. Hagiwara, M.: Removal of hidden units and weights for back propagation networks. In: Proceedings of 1993 International Conference on Neural Networks (IJCNN-93-Nagoya, Japan). vol. 1, pp. 351–354 vol 1 (1993). https://doi.org/10.1109/IJCNN.1993.713929

5. Han, S., Pool, J., Tran, J., Dally, W.: Learning both Weights and Connections for Efficient Neural Network. In: Advances in Neural Information Processing Systems. vol. 28. Curran Associates, Inc. (2015)

6. Hoefler, T., Alistarh, D., Ben-Nun, T., Dryden, N., Peste, A.: Sparsity in deep learning: pruning and growth for efficient inference and training in neural networks. J. Mach. Learn. Res. **22**(1), 241:10882–241:11005 (2021)

7. Janowsky, S.A.: Pruning versus clipping in neural networks. Phys. Rev. A **39**(12), 6600–6603 (1989). https://doi.org/10.1103/PhysRevA.39.6600,

8. Kruschke, J.K., Movellan, J.R.: Benefits of gain: speeded learning and minimal hidden layers in back-propagation networks. IEEE Trans. Syst. Man Cybern. **21**(1), 273–280 (1991)

9. Lecun, Y., Bottou, L., Bengio, Y., Haffner, P.: Gradient-based learning applied to document recognition. Proc. IEEE **86**(11), 2278–2324 (1998). https://doi.org/10.1109/5.726791

10. LeCun, Y., Denker, J., Solla, S.: Optimal brain damage. Advances in Neural Information Processing Systems, vol. 2 (1989)

11. Li, H., Kadav, A., Durdanovic, I., Samet, H., Graf, H.P.: Pruning filters for efficient convnets (2016). arXiv:1608.08710

12. Molchanov, P., Tyree, S., Karras, T., Aila, T., Kautz, J.: Pruning convolutional neural networks for resource efficient inference (2016). arXiv:1611.06440

13. Narasimha, P.L., Delashmit, W.H., Manry, M.T., Li, J., Maldonado, F.: An integrated growing-pruning method for feedforward network training. Neurocomputing **71**(13), 2831–2847 (2008). https://doi.org/10.1016/j.neucom.2007.08.026,

14. Thimm, G., Fiesler, E.: Evaluating pruning methods. In: Proceedings of the International Symposium on Artificial Neural Networks, pp. 20–25 (1995)

15. Xiao, H., Rasul, K., Vollgraf, R.: Fashion-MNIST: a Novel Image Dataset for Benchmarking Machine Learning Algorithms (2017). https://doi.org/10.48550/arXiv.1708.07747, arXiv:1708.07747 [cs, stat]

16. Zhang, Q., Zhang, R., Sun, J., Liu, Y.: How Sparse Can We Prune A Deep Network: A Geometric Viewpoint (2023). https://doi.org/10.48550/arXiv.2306.05857, arXiv:2306.05857 [cs, stat]

17. Zhu, M., Gupta, S.: To prune, or not to prune: exploring the efficacy of pruning for model compression (2017). https://doi.org/10.48550/arXiv.1710.01878,, arXiv:1710.01878 [cs, stat]

Robustness Analysis of Machine Learning Models Using Domain-Specific Test Data Perturbation

Marian Lambert[1]([✉]) [iD], Thomas Schuster[2] [iD], Marcus Kessel[3] [iD], and Colin Atkinson[3] [iD]

[1] XPACE GmbH, Blücherstr. 32, 75177 Pforzheim, Germany
marian.lambert@xpace.de
[2] Pforzheim University, Tiefenbronner Str. 65, 75177 Pforzheim, Germany
thomas.schuster@hs-pforzheim.de
[3] University of Mannheim, 68131 Mannheim, Germany
{marcus.kessel,colin.atkinson}@uni-mannheim.de

Abstract. This study examines how perturbations in image, audio, and text inputs affect the performance of different classification models. Various perturbators were applied to three seed datasets at different intensities to produce noisy test data. Then, the models' performance was evaluated on the generated test data. Our findings indicate that there is a consistent relationship between larger perturbations and lower model performance across perturbators, models, and domains. However, this relationship varies depending on the characteristics of the specific model, dataset, and perturbator.

Keywords: Domain-specific test input generation · Robustness testing · Machine learning testing · Sensitivity analysis

1 Introduction

The increasing use of machine learning (ML) systems in safety-critical fields (e.g., autonomous driving or medical diagnosis) has raised concerns about their behavior, particularly with regards to correctness, robustness, privacy, efficiency, and fairness. As a result, the field of *ML testing* has emerged as an important area of study, dedicated to identifying discrepancies between the expected and observed behavior [16].

Testing the *robustness* of ML models is essential for their real-world application, as only robust systems can be trusted to perform reliably. Robustness refers to a model's ability to function properly on noisy or otherwise perturbed data [16]. For instance, a speech recognition model trained on high-quality audio recordings might encounter background noise, dialects, artefacts, and echoes during actual operation. A model with low robustness would exhibit a significant drop in performance when faced with real-world data.

© The Author(s), under exclusive license to Springer Nature Switzerland AG 2023
N. Moniz et al. (Eds.): EPIA 2023, LNAI 14115, pp. 158–170, 2023.
https://doi.org/10.1007/978-3-031-49008-8_13

Evaluating a model's robustness typically involves assessing its accuracy when applied to noisy test data [16]. It is common practice to generate noisy test data using *domain-specific input generation* methods, which introduce perturbations to already-existing, high-quality seed data, to produce new test data [16]. These perturbations, which may involve image, audio, or text manipulations, mimic the noise present in real-world scenarios and allow for the production of vast volumes of test data in a highly controlled manner.

However, little is known about the relationship between the strength of domain-specific perturbations (i.e., the magnitude or intensity of changes made to input data) and the resulting penalty on model performance. This is important knowledge because perturbations that only affect performance at high intensities may not be relevant for robustness testing, as they are unlikely to occur in realistic scenarios. Additionally, the papers that have been written on this subject have typically only considered a limited range of perturbations.

To fill this gap, our research paper presents several key findings in the domain of machine learning robustness testing, specifically exploring the relationship between perturbation strength and model performance in image, text, and audio domains. Our work provides insights that can help researchers and practitioners develop more effective strategies for testing and improving the robustness of ML models.

Our research distinguishes itself from previous work as follows: (1) we conduct our experiments with a greater variety of perturbation types, particularly in the audio and text domains. This allows us to provide a more comprehensive understanding of how different types of perturbations impact the robustness of machine learning models in these domains. (2) we employ a higher sampling frequency than previous research, enabling us to conduct a more fine-grained analysis of how perturbation strength affects model performance. By collecting data at a higher frequency, we were able to identify patterns and trends that may have been missed in previous research.

The remainder of this paper is structured in the following ways: We first review existing literature and highlight gaps in Sect. 2. Section 3 outlines our experimental setup, including details about datasets, models, and perturbation techniques. In Sect. 4, we present our findings on the impact of domain-specific perturbations on model performance, including a wider range of perturbation types in the audio and text domains at a higher sampling frequency than previous research. Finally, we conclude by summarizing our research and discussing its implications in the last section.

2 Literature Review

The use of domain-specific input generation to evaluate the robustness of ML models is a well-established research area, with several systems proposed that successfully uncover robustness issues in ML models. This section provides an overview of the small number of publications that investigate the relationship between the perturbation strength and corresponding impact on model performance.

2.1 Image

Within the image domain, [4] investigated the impact of blur, noise, contrast, JPEG, and JPEG2000 distortions on the performance of five different state-of-the-art models for object detection. They report that higher distortion level naturally resulted in lower model performance across all distortion types. However, particularly the noise and blur distortions had a significant impact on model performance even at low intensities. The authors suggest that researchers prioritize improving their models' robustness to these types of distortions to achieve better real-world performance.

Similar results were found in [6] where they investigate how CNN-based face recognition models are impacted by different types of blur and noise, contrast changes, occlusion, color balances and color channel changes. The study found that the models were particularly sensitive to blur, noise, and occlusion changes, while demonstrating robustness to color distortions and changes in color balance.

Roy et al. focus their investigation on the impact of various types of noise and blur on image classification models and explore differences between CNN architectures [14]. Their findings suggest that, while all models were susceptible to image quality degradation, shallower models exhibited greater robustness.

Similarly, [17] investigate the effect of two types of blur and gaussian noise on the performance of image classification models. The study reveals that defocus had a greater impact on model performance than motion blur, and that the combination of all perturbations resulted in the highest performance degradation.

2.2 Audio

In the audio domain, [12] conduct a comprehensive analysis of different speech recognition models, focusing on their word error rate (WER) in the presence of additive white noise and restaurant background noise at varying intensities. Their findings show that the WER remains relatively constant until the signal-to-noise ratio drops to approximately 20 dB, after which there is a significant decrease in performance. Interestingly, their results suggest that the impact of both types of noise on WER is similar.

Another study in [5] investigates the effects of different audio codecs on speaker recognition models when combined with environmental noise and impulse responses. They observe that the codec used has a considerable impact on model performance, and while the added noise does increase the equal error rate (EER), the impact is not as significant as that of the codec.

Finally, [9] explore how different lossy MP3 compression techniques and additionally additive noise impacts speech recognition performance. They report that, generally, lower compression bit rates led to higher word error rates though a significant performance impact was only found at very high compression intensities. Also, they find that adding noise to these compressed recordings often improved performance—slightly in lower compression settings but quite significantly in higher compression settings. They attribute this to the fact that the added noise can mask gaps in the spectrum introduced by lossy compression thus increasing performance for highly compressed or spectrally distorted signals.

2.3 Text

In the text domain, a comprehensive analysis of the impact of various types of grammatical errors on several NLP systems is conducted in [10]. This includes tasks such as named entity recognition, neural machine translation, and morpho-syntactic analysis on multiple languages. The study reveals that the performance of these systems drops linearly with the number of token edits across tasks, languages, and profiles. However, the impact of specific types of grammatical errors depends heavily on the particular NLP task. For example, spelling and affix errors were found to have the most significant performance drop in named entity recognition, neural machine translation, and morpho-syntactic analysis. Meanwhile, casing errors were more crucial for named entity recognition.

Similarly, [15] compared the impact of eleven types of text corruptions on a range of deep learning models for four NLP tasks, namely question answering, natural language inference, named entity recognition, and sentiment analysis. Their findings suggest that the performance impact of individual perturbations is task-specific, but in general, higher perturbation strengths result in higher performance penalties. They also observed that more context-aware models such as BERT or ELMo did not exhibit significant improvements in robustness compared to more traditional neural networks that used embedding systems.

Finally, [2] explored the impact of natural and synthetic noise on character-based neural machine translation models. Their results indicate that performance drops roughly linearly with the percentage of tokens changed (in line with both [10,15]). Among the various types of noise introduced, randomly scrambling words had the most significant performance impact compared to only swapping individual characters, scrambling the middle of words, or introducing keyboard typos (swapping characters with neighboring characters on the keyboard).

This literature review reveals that the image domain has received the most extensive research attention within this area, with only a handful of publications exploring the audio and text domains. However, these studies were often limited in the number of perturbation types and sampling frequency, especially in the audio domain. Consequently, there is a gap in the literature that we aim to fill using our experimental setup, which is introduced in the next section.

3 Experimental Setup

To further explore how the strength of data perturbations affects model performance, we ran experiments on three distinct datasets and five deep learning models covering the three domains: image, audio, and text. In particular, we employed the `ImageNetV2` [13], `SpeakerRecognition` [7] and `AclImDB` [8] datasets for the image, audio and text domain respectively.

ImageNetV2. The `ImageNetV2` dataset is a scaled-down version of the original image classification dataset `ImageNet` introduced in [3]. It includes 10 images for each of the 1,000 original classes. For this dataset, we conduct robustness tests on three different models which are all trained on the original `ImageNet` dataset. Our goal is to analyze how different model architectures respond to noise in test data. The first model, XCeption, is a convolutional neural network designed for image recognition tasks with 23 million parameters. The second architecture, InceptionResnetV2 is significantly larger than XCeption with 56 million parameters. Finally, we also consider the MobileNetV2 model, which is the smallest of the three models, containing only 3.6 million parameters.

SpeakerRecognition. The SpeakerRecognition dataset comprises 7,501 one-second audio recordings of speeches delivered by five different political speakers. We use 6,751 files (90%) from this dataset to train a deep learning model for the task of identifying the speaker from a given one-second recording.

To accomplish this, we employ a specialized one-dimensional convolutional neural network architecture optimized for audio processing, as described in the official Keras documentation [1].

After training the model, we evaluate its performance on the remaining 750 files in the dataset, which are reserved for testing purposes. Our aim is to determine the effectiveness of our model at accurately recognizing the speaker from an audio recording.

AclImDB. The AclImDB dataset consists of 50,000 reviews from the ImDB platform, comprising both positive and negative feedback. We use 80% of these reviews to train a sentiment analysis model, while the remaining 20% is reserved for conducting our experiment.

For this task, we employ a text classification model architecture that is specifically designed for this purpose, as detailed in the Keras documentation [11]. Our aim is to evaluate the robustness of the model against noisy test data generated through various transformations.

The experiment is designed to evaluate each model's robustness against noisy test data generated by applying different perturbations to the seed dataset (see Table 1). To achieve this, we repeatedly apply each perturbator to samples taken from the seed dataset, gradually increasing the perturbation strength at each iteration.

We assess the effectiveness of each model on the perturbed dataset and compare it with that of the seed dataset and other datasets with varying degrees of perturbation. To accomplish this, we rely on the concept of metamorphic relationships between the seed and mutant inputs which originate from traditional software testing and describe the relationship between a change in input and the corresponding change in model output [16]. Put simply, we expect the perturbed data to have the same target variable as the pristine data.

To ensure a reliable assessment of the underlying relationship between perturbation strength and model performance, we sample perturbation intensities from the full spectrum of possible values. This approach enables us to evaluate the model's ability to generalize to a wide range of perturbation strengths and provides insights into its robustness against noise.

Table 1. Perturbators applied in the image, audio and text domains

Name	Description	Varied parameter
Image		
Noise	Adds salt-and-pepper noise (black and white speckles) with a ratio of 1 to 1	Percentage of pixels occupied by the noise ranging from 0% to 30%
Brightness'	Increases or decreases image brightness	Brightness enhancement factor ranging from 0% (black image) to 300% where 100% returns the original image
Contrast	Increases or decreases image contrast	Contrast enhancement factor ranging from 0% (gray image) to 300% where 100% returns the original image
Sharpness	Increases or decreases image sharpness	Sharpness enhancement factor ranging from 0% (blurred image) to 300% where 100% returns the original image
Occlusion	Adds black occlusion artefacts at random positions with a width and height sampled from a normal distribution ($\mu = 10$; $\sigma = 5$)	Percentage of occluded pixels ranging from 0% to 50%
Compression	Adds JPEG compression artefacts	Inverse JPEG image quality factor ranging from 0% (no compression) to 100%
Pixelation	Pixelates the image by scaling it down then scaling it up again	Scale-down factor ranging from 0% (no pixelation) to 90%
Audio		
White Noise	Adds white noise to the audio signal	Noise level ranging from 0% (no noise) to 100%
Compression	Applies MP3 compression to the audio signal	Compression factor ranging from 0% (no compression; 320bit/s) to 100% (8bit/s)
Pitch	Changes the pitch of the audio signal without changing its speed	Number of semitones to shift the pitch ranging from -12 (down) to $+12$ (up)
Clipping	Clips (i.e. removes) samples above and below a certain percentile from the audio signal	Percentage of samples to remove ranging from 0% (original audio) to 80%. where 80% removes samples below the 10th and above the 90th percentile
Volume	Changes the gain of the audio signal	Number of decibels to change the gain from -20 (quieter) to $+20$ (louder)
Echo	Overlays a delayed version of the original audio signal	Echo delay ranging from 0 s (no delay) to 1 s
Text		
Typo	Randomly switches words in the text with commonly occurring typos	Probability of changing a given word into a misspelled version ranging from 0% (original text) to 100%
Word Removal	Removes random words from the text	Percentage of words to remove ranging from 0% (original text) to 100%
Word Switch	Switches random neighboring words in the text	Percentage of words to switch ranging from 0% (original text) to 100%
Character Switch	Switches random neighboring characters in the text	Percentage of characters to switch ranging from 0% (original text) to 100%

4   Results

The results indicate that higher levels of perturbation significantly affect model performance. Figures 1 and 2 visualize the outcomes of our experiments. Figure 1 depicts the relationship between perturbation strength and model performance for each of the tested `ImageNet` models. Similarly, Fig. 2 illustrates speaker recognition (left) and sentiment analysis models (right). The figures depict perturbation impacts on the model performance (accuracy). Full experimental results can be found in our online repository.[1]

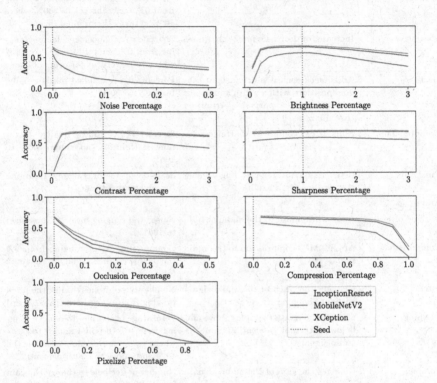

Fig. 1. Impacts of perturbation strength on model performance of `ImageNet` models

ImageNet. The analysis of Fig. 1 reveals a consistent trend in our experiment: higher perturbation strengths lead to lower model performance across all models and perturbation types. In other words, there is a negative correlation between perturbation strength and model performance, indicating that as perturbation strength increases, the model's ability to correctly classify images decreases.

This result was expected and is consistent with previous research (see [4,6,14]), as stronger perturbations lead to the generation of data less similar to the original training data. Furthermore, our results indicated that the

---

[1] Available under https://github.com/ecapx/ml-robustness-analysis-paper.

three assessed models exhibited a comparable pattern in terms of the correlation between perturbation strength and model performance, with `MobileNetV2` consistently demonstrating the lowest performance and being the least resilient to noise, which may be attributed to its smaller size. The former finding is consistent with previous studies [6,14] while the latter observation does not seem to align with [14].

Our experiment suggests that the relationship between perturbation strength and model performance is dependent on the type of perturbation applied. For instance, the model's performance for the *Noise* and *Occlusion* perturbators showed a rapid decline at the beginning, with low perturbation strength, and then plateaued. This finding is consistent with the results reported by [14]. In contrast, the tested models exhibited robust behavior on the *Compression* and *Pixelize* perturbators at low perturbation strengths, but the models' performance deteriorated as the perturbation strength increased. This relationship was also reported by [4,14] for the *Compression* perturbator. One explanation for this is that these perturbators are designed to introduce minimal changes to their input. The *Compression* perturbator aims to retain as much information from the original image as possible while reducing its size, and the *Pixelize* perturbator attempts to reconstruct the original image as accurately as possible during the upscaling phase. It appears that these strategies work well for lower parameter values, but begin to fail as perturbation strength increases.

For *Brightness*, *Contrast*, and *Sharpness* perturbators, it is important to consider two separate parameter ranges. Values in the range $0 < \sigma < 1$ decrease image brightness, contrast, or sharpness, while values in the range $\sigma > 1$ increase them. Consequently, the relationship between these parameter ranges and model performance needs to be explored separately. For the *Brightness* and *Contrast* perturbators, our experiment showed that model performance decreased exponentially when the parameter was reduced below 1 (i.e., making the image darker or grayer; consistent with [4]), but increased linearly when the parameter was increased. This is likely due to the fact that image brightness and contrast have an open upper range, but a hard lower limit of 0 as the resulting image is then entirely black or gray with no discernible contents. Images with higher parameter settings may become blown out or over-sharpened but still recognizable.

The *Sharpness* perturbator appeared to have little effect on model performance. Surprisingly, the highest model performance was achieved by slightly *increasing* sharpness, and even very high or very low parameter values did not have a significant impact though we did notice that the `PIL` library used for generating these perturbations only produced a slightly blurred image, even for sharpness values of 0. This contradicts the findings of [4], who reported that blur (sharpness values smaller than 1) had a significant impact on performance.

Speaker Recognition. It is evident that higher perturbation strength results in lower model performance (as shown in the left column of Fig. 2). This is consistent with previous studies [5,9,12], however, no clear and consistent trend could be identified across different types of perturbations. Impact of the *White Noise* perturbator was minimal at very low perturbation strengths, but quickly increased before settling into a linear relationship. This can possibly be attributed to the fact that some of the seed recordings already had a small amount of white noise, which could have helped the model perform reasonably well with low levels of noise but resulted in poor performance on higher-noise test cases. Nevertheless, this finding is consistent with previous studies such as [12].

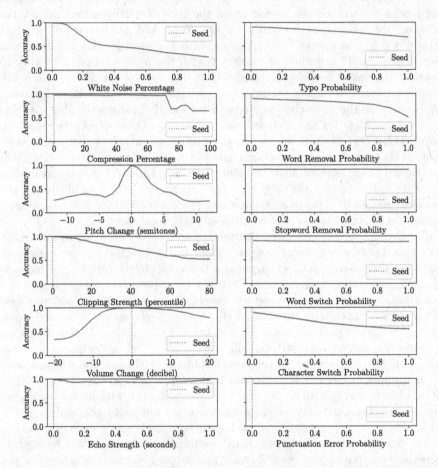

Fig. 2. Relation between perturbation strength and model performance per perturbator from the perturbation strength experiment for the sentiment analysis (left) and speaker recognition models (right)

Similarly, the *Compression* perturbator had no significant impact on model performance until a high perturbation strength was reached. This can probably be attributed to the fact that, just like in the image domain, compression algorithms are capable of retaining a large amount of information from the seed input at low strengths. Moreover, the dataset used for evaluating the speaker recognition model is already of fairly low audio quality, so the compression perturbator likely does not remove much valuable information in general.

Model performance on the *Pitch* perturbator showed a bell-shaped curve, dropping rapidly for parameter settings close to the seed and then flattening out for stronger perturbation strengths. This is expected as both higher and lower pitch recordings should equally affect model performance. However, the curve flattens out for very high and very low parameter values because the random guessing accuracy is around 20% (the dataset contains five classes), and the model's accuracy approaches this level.

The *Clipping* perturbator was found to create linear impact on model performance, which is consistent with the expectation that removing more information from the seed audio recordings would lead to a performance decrease. However, even at high levels of clipping, model performance remained relatively high, reaching an accuracy of around 50%. This finding suggests that only 20% of the samples are necessary to classify a recording correctly with 50% accuracy.

The relation between model performance and *Volume* exhibited a normal distribution, with little change observed for perturbations close to the seed volume. The model demonstrated robustness to small changes, possibly due to the variations in volume levels in the training examples. Lower volume had a more significant impact on performance than higher volume, likely due to the loss of information resulting from a strong reduction in audio volume, while higher volumes make the recording more difficult to recognize.

The *Echo* perturbator had minimal impact on model performance for all perturbation strengths. This evaluation may not accurately depict the true impact, as the speaker recognition model only analyzes the first second of audio. As a result, the diagram depicting different echo delays appears to be mirrored around the 0.5 second mark, and any echoes with a delay of more than 0.5 seconds are truncated at the end. Moreover, echoes with a delay of one second or more are not included at all. Therefore, an echo delay of 0.5 seconds represents the maximum perturbation strength. Not surprisingly, this also corresponds to the lowest model performance.

Sentiment Analysis. Regarding the sentiment analysis model (right column of Fig. 2), it is evident that performance decreased with increasing perturbation strength for most of the tested perturbators. This is consistent with the findings in [2,10], albeit these studies focused on different NLP tasks.

The *Typo* perturbation strength appeared to have a linear negative relationship with model performance, which was anticipated. As more typos are introduced, less information becomes available for classification, resulting in a gradual decrease in performance.

Likewise, the impact of the *Word Removal* perturbator on model performance exhibited a linear relationship at low and medium parameter values. However, at higher intensities, performance decreased rapidly to around 50% (random guessing). This finding can be attributed to the fact that the sentiment of a document can be inferred from more than just a single word in the document. Therefore, as long as some indicative words remain from the seed text (at lower perturbation strengths), the model's performance remains relatively high. However, once all of these sentiment-indicative words are removed, performance drops drastically.

Interestingly, the *Word Switch* perturbator did not seem to affect model performance, regardless of the perturbation strength. This might be because, at least for this dataset, sentiment classification problems can be largely resolved by simple keyword extraction. Thus, the model likely checks for the presence of certain sentiment-indicating words and ignores word order.

Finally, the *Character Switch* exhibited a linear relationship, with a more rapid decrease at lower perturbation strengths. This result could be explained by the fact that changing more than one character inside a word has little to no impact on performance since the model might not recognize the word in either case. At higher perturbation strengths, the likelihood of switching multiple characters in the same word increases, which reduces the additional performance penalty introduced by the perturbation.

5   Conclusion

According to our experimental findings, it is likely that increasing the strength of data perturbation causes a decline in model performance. This is consistent with the idea that models work best when given data is comparable to training data. Characteristics of models and datasets, as well as tested perturbators, significantly influence the shape of this correlation. While some perturbators showed both linear *and* exponential correlations, others had linear *or* exponential relationships between perturbation strength and model performance. These findings suggest that the type of noise introduced in the data and the model properties can have a significant impact on model performance. Consequently, we recommend researchers and practitioners to conduct comprehensive testing on their model involving various types of perturbators and strength levels to uncover robustness-related issues which could impact real-world performance.

In future work, we plan to expand our experiments by testing a wider range of models, datasets, and perturbation types. Particularly models in the audio and text domain which have not received much research attention yet are of interest. Moreover, we believe that exploring additional rule-based algorithms, as well as perturbators based on neural networks like GANs, could yield more realistic test cases (e.g., by incorporating predetermined rules for creating grammatical errors in genuine text). This could provide more insights into how models behave when faced with more complex and varied forms of data perturbations.

Furthermore, data may be perturbed in multiple ways, such as containing both noise and compression artifacts. Therefore, researching the impact of *combinations* of data perturbations may shed light on whether compounding perturbations causes a proportional or disproportionate decline in model performance.

References

1. Badine, F.: Keras documentation: speaker recognition (2020). www.keras.io/examples/audio/speaker_recognition_using_cnn/
2. Belinkov, Y., Bisk, Y.: Synthetic and natural noise both break neural machine translation (2018). https://doi.org/10.48550/arXiv.1711.02173
3. Deng, J., Dong, W., Socher, R., Li, L.J., Li, K., Fei-Fei, L.: ImageNet: a large-scale hierarchical image database. In: 2009 IEEE Conference on Computer Vision and Pattern Recognition, pp. 248–255 (2009). https://doi.org/10.1109/CVPR.2009.5206848
4. Dodge, S., Karam, L.: Understanding how image quality affects deep neural networks. In: 2016 Eighth International Conference on Quality of Multimedia Experience (QoMEX), pp. 1–6 (2016). https://doi.org/10.1109/QoMEX.2016.7498955
5. Ferràs, M., Madikeri, S., Motlicek, P., Dey, S., Bourlard, H.: A large-scale open-source acoustic simulator for speaker recognition. IEEE Signal Process. Lett. **23**(4), 527–531 (2016). https://doi.org/10.1109/LSP.2016.2537844
6. Karahan, S., Kilinc Yildirum, M., Kirtac, K., Rende, F.S., Butun, G., Ekenel, H.K.: How image degradations affect deep cnn-based face recognition? In: 2016 International Conference of the Biometrics Special Interest Group (BIOSIG), pp. 1–5 (2016). https://doi.org/10.1109/BIOSIG.2016.7736924
7. Kiplagat, E.: Kaggle: speaker recognition dataset (2020). www.kaggle.com/kongaevans/speaker-recognition-dataset
8. Maas, A.L., Daly, R.E., Pham, P.T., Huang, D., Ng, A.Y., Potts, C.: Learning word vectors for sentiment analysis. In: Proceedings of the 49th Annual Meeting of the Association for Computational Linguistics: Human Language Technologies, pp. 142–150. Association for Computational Linguistics, Portland, Oregon, USA (2011). www.aclanthology.org/P11-1015
9. Nouza, J., Cerva, P., Silovsky, J.: Adding controlled amount of noise to improve recognition of compressed and spectrally distorted speech. In: 2013 IEEE International Conference on Acoustics, Speech and Signal Processing, pp. 8046–8050 (2013). https://doi.org/10.1109/ICASSP.2013.6639232
10. Náplava, J., Popel, M., Straka, M., Straková, J.: Understanding model robustness to user-generated noisy texts. In: Proceedings of the Seventh Workshop on Noisy User-generated Text (W-NUT 2021), pp. 340–350. Association for Computational Linguistics (2021). https://doi.org/10.18653/v1/2021.wnut-1.38
11. Omernick, M., Chollet, F.: Keras documentation: text classification from scratch (2020). www.keras.io/examples/nlp/text_classification_from_scratch/
12. Radford, A., Kim, J.W., Xu, T., Brockman, G., McLeavey, C., Sutskever, I.: Robust speech recognition via large-scale weak supervision (2022). https://doi.org/10.48550/arXiv.2212.04356
13. Recht, B., Roelofs, R., Schmidt, L., Shankar, V.: Do ImageNet classifiers generalize to ImageNet? In: Proceedings of the 36th International Conference on Machine Learning, pp. 5389–5400. PMLR (2019). www.proceedings.mlr.press/v97/recht19a.html
14. Roy, P., Ghosh, S., Bhattacharya, S., Pal, U.: Effects of degradations on deep neural network architectures (2023). https://doi.org/10.48550/arXiv.1807.10108
15. Rychalska, B., Basaj, D., Gosiewska, A., Biecek, P.: Models in the wild: on corruption robustness of neural NLP systems. In: Gedeon, T., Wong, K.W., Lee, M. (eds.) Neural Information Processing, pp. 235–247. Lecture Notes in Computer Science. Springer International Publishing, Cham (2019). https://doi.org/10.1007/978-3-030-36718-3

16. Zhang, J.M., Harman, M., Ma, L., Liu, Y.: Machine learning testing: survey, landscapes and horizons. IEEE Trans. Software Eng. (2020). https://doi.org/10.1109/TSE.2019.2962027

17. Zhou, Y., Song, S., Cheung, N.M.: On classification of distorted images with deep convolutional neural networks. In: 2017 IEEE International Conference on Acoustics, Speech and Signal Processing (ICASSP), pp. 1213–1217 (2017). https://doi.org/10.1109/ICASSP.2017.7952349

Vocalization Features to Recognize Small Dolphin Species for Limited Datasets

Luís Rosário[1], Sofia Cavaco[1], Joaquim Silva[1]([✉]), Luís Freitas[2], and Philippe Verborgh[2]

[1] NOVA LINCS, NOVA School of Science and Technology, 2829-516 Caparica, Portugal
l.rosario@campus.fct.unl.pt, {scavaco,jfs}@fct.unl.pt
[2] Madeira Whale Museum, 9200-031 Caniçal, Madeira, Portugal
{luisfreitas,philippeverborgh}@museudabaleia.org

Abstract. Identifying small dolphin species based on their vocalizations remains a challenging task due to their similar vocal signatures and frequency modulation patterns, particularly when the available data sets are relatively limited. To address this issue, a new feature set has been introduced that focuses on capturing both the predominant frequency range of the vocalizations and other higher level details in the spectral contour, which are valuable for distinguishing between small dolphin species. These features are computed from two distinct representations of the vocalizations: the short time Fourier transform and Mel frequency cepstral coefficients. By utilizing these features with two popular classifiers (K-Nearest Neighbors and Support Vector Machines), a model accuracy of 95.47% has been achieved, representing an improvement over previous studies.

Keywords: Bio-acoustic classification · Cetaceans · Bio-acoustic signal processing · Supervised classification

1 Introduction and Related Work

Passive acoustic monitoring (PAM) is a cost-effective method to detect the presence of cetaceans. Long-term deployments in specific areas can inform on the presence of certain species and their activity. However, the inability to confidently identify many cetacean species, based on their vocalizations, has limited its contribution to the research, conservation and management of impacts on cetaceans. The development of automated tools to recognize these cetacean species from acoustic recordings would bring considerable biological value to the

This work is supported by NOVA LINCS (UIDB/04516/2020) with the financial support of FCT.IP. The authors thank Ruth Esteban and Pauline Gauffier for their assistance in the field acoustic recordings in Madeira for Project META (FA 06_2017_017), done by the Madeira Whale Museum.

data collected by PAM and allow the efficient processing of large amounts of data produced by this method.

Signal processing techniques that analyze cetacean vocalizations have been used in tasks ranging from the classification of different calls from a single species [4,16,20], to the distinction between different cetacean species which include whales and dolphins [3,5,9,13]. These works suggest the use of a variety of distinct features such as several statistical acoustic features [3,9] or Mel frequency cepstral coefficients (MFCCs) [17,20]. However, when we focus on dolphin vocalizations alone, these studies miss to achieve an accurate way to properly distinguish the species, as shown by their results, with accuracy ranging from 37.3 to 93% [13], 43.1 to 69.7% [3], 34.1 to 68.4% [9] and 54 to 75% [5]. Recent works present models with better accuracy values (up to 90.4%), although still with some variance among species, based on a limited data set or centered on a single recording location or largely based on an existing software [1,6,17].

In recent years, Convolution Neural Networks (CNN) architectures have been used for bio-acoustic classification. These can be divided into custom architecture or well-defined and trained ones. As an example for a custom, and small, neural network architecture [12] used an Artificial Neural Network (ANN) with a single hidden layer and used time features extracted after applying Wavelet Transform as input data. This implementation achieved accuracy values greater than 95% in the detecting sperm whales and long-finned pilot whales, showing that, as long as the data sets are large enough, high accuracy can be obtained using even simple CNN. As an example of trained architecture, a CNN model [11] was used to classify whale's whistles, achieving 95% accuracy.

This paper proposes a new set of features derived from spectral representations of dolphin vocalizations that is capable of distinguishing four small dolphin species while using recording locations ranging from North America to Southern Europe. This set of features facilitates the distinction of these species, in spite of their underlying similar vocal signatures. This claim is validated by tests made with popular classifiers such as K-Nearest Neighbors (KNN) and Support Vector Machines (SVM). The proposed features are derived from the time-spectral representation of the vocalizations obtained from two different approaches: the first uses the magnitude spectrogram of the short time Fourier transform (STFT); the second uses MFCCs, which have been shown as a viable approach in bio-acoustic classification for several species [8,19], including cetaceans [18,24].

Experimental results show the viability of the proposed feature set in distinguishing small dolphin species, while reaching a global model accuracy of 95.47%. The individual species accuracy ranges from 91.86% to 98.51%, which shows improvement over previous studies. This approach outperforms CNN models when the available datasets are not large enough to train these networks.

2   Features

The proposed feature set is composed of five different features. Their extraction process is performed over the time-frequency representation of the vocalizations. This may be either magnitude spectrograms of the STFT (computed with a

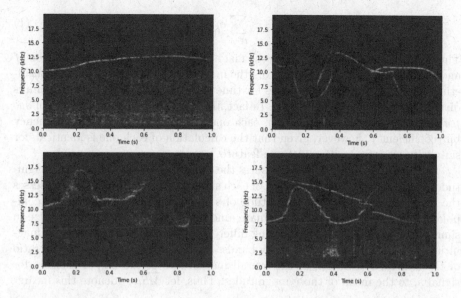

Fig. 1. Spectrograms of samples of four different dolphin species' vocalizations. From left to right, top to bottom: *Delphinus delphis*, *Tursiops truncatus*, *Stenella frontalis*, *Stenella coeruleoalba*.

Hanning window of length 512 and an overlap of 256), or the MFCCs matrix (computed with the same parameters as those used for the STFT).

The proposed features encompass two distinct approaches to the analysis of the vocalizations. The first approach, which culminates in the creation of three **spectral analysis features**, tries to capture what we call *the predominant frequency components*, which can be a good indicator of the frequency distribution and range of the species' vocalizations. However, since the vocalizations of most dolphin species boast a wide frequency range that overlaps among species [2] (Fig. 1), in theory those three features may not be sufficient to properly distinguish vocalizations of distinct dolphin species. To overcome this limitation, we developed two additional features we called the **contour analysis features**, which intent to express some of the higher-level details in the patterns of the vocalization's spectral representation.

2.1   The Spectral Analysis Features

For simplicity, when we need to refer to both the frequency bins in the spectrogram and the coefficients in the MFCC matrix we use the term *bin/coefficient*. Also, the term *vocalization sample* may be referred by *signal* in this paper.

The Spectral Analysis Features (SAF) subset is composed of three distinct features. The first one aims to reflect the magnitude of each vocalization sample s for each bin/coefficient f into which the frequency range is divided. This feature is defined by:

$$MS(s,f) = \sum_{t \in \mathcal{T}} m(s, f, t) \ . \tag{1}$$

Thus, considering that $m(s, f, t)$ is the magnitude of signal s for bin/coefficient f and time slice t, then $MS(s,f)$ mirrors the magnitude sum of signal s in f considering all the individual magnitudes for time slices into which the spectrogram is divided. $\mathcal{T}$ is the set of time slices. In fact, $MS(s,f)$ can be seen as a group of *sub features* that characterize signal s, each one referring to the specific frequency bin/coefficient f, however, given that the calculation of each one is identical, for simplicity we refer to it as just one feature.

The second feature of SAF measures the coefficient of variation of the magnitudes in the spectral representation of each signal s. This feature, $CV(s)$, assesses the relative variation of the magnitude of s along different bin/coefficient components. This may help to discriminate among different species that vocalize in similar frequency bands, but showing different relative global variations of magnitude along the different frequency bands. So, $CV(s)$ is calculated by the ratio of the standard deviation of the overall magnitudes of the bin/coefficients for signal s, to the mean of those magnitudes. Thus, let $\overline{MS(s)}$ denote this mean:

$$\overline{MS(s)} = \frac{\sum\limits_{f=0}^{\|\mathcal{F}\|-1} MS(s,f)}{\|\mathcal{F}\|} \tag{2}$$

where $MS(s,f)$ is calculated by (1) and $\mathcal{F}$ is the set of all considered bin/coefficients. Then,

$$CV(s) = \frac{\sqrt{\frac{1}{\|\mathcal{F}\|} \sum\limits_{f \in \mathcal{F}} \left(MS(s,f) - \overline{MS(s)} \right)^2}}{\overline{MS(s)}} \ . \tag{3}$$

The third feature of SAF intends to highlight the average absolute difference between two consecutive bin/coefficient maximum magnitudes considering all different time slices, for signal s. This is calculated by the following expression:

$$Edginess(s) = \frac{\sum\limits_{f=0}^{\|\mathcal{F}\|-2} |\max_t(m(s, f, t)) - \max_t(m(s, f+1, t))|}{\|\mathcal{F}\| - 1} \ . \tag{4}$$

Again, $m(s, f, t)$ is the magnitude of signal s for bin/coefficient f on time slice t, being f and $f + 1$ adjacent frequency bins or MFCC coefficients. Thus, *Edginess(.)* provides an insight on how edgy/unsmooth the progression of the vocalization magnitude is along the frequency axis. In other words, by averaging the absolute differences between the maximums of contiguous frequency bins, this feature can help to distinguish species that show more interruptions in the vocalization contour over frequency, from others that vocalize more smoothly. Thus, a vocalization with a *steady* pattern (top left Fig. 1) would score a lower *Edginess(.)* than a one with a more *erratic* behaviour (top right Fig. 1); this can help to discriminate vocalizations from different species like these.

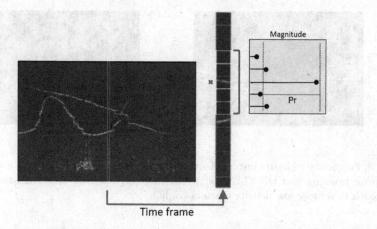

Time frame

Fig. 2. Detection of peak in a time frame with a minimum required prominence. The selected peak (x) will be valid if the prominence (Pr) for the lowest-valued contour of its two immediate neighbors corresponds at least to the 95th percentile of the magnitude present in that time frame. The relative magnitude of the contours within the window to which peak x belongs is represented in the graph on the right part of the figure, although the same relative differences are not noticeable in the spectrogram.

2.2 The Contour Analysis Features

As referred above, the SAF features may not be informative enough to characterize and consequently distinguish dolphin species. Therefore, we developed the subset of the Contour Analysis Features (CAF), which focus on describing the vocalization's contour: (i) the *vocalization slope unsteadiness* ($VSU(s)$), which portrays how unsteady is signal slope in the frequency progression over time; and (ii) the number of inflection points ($InflecNum(s)$) that occur in the frequency contours of signal s, over time.

The first step on the computation of these features, is to detect the vocal contours in the magnitude spectrograms. For this, we apply a peak tracking technique to the magnitude spectrogram based on the MQ modeling and PARSHL techniques [14,15,22]. This process starts by looking for the dominant intensity peaks in each time frame. Due to the characteristics of real-world signals, we cannot simply consider the local maxima in the frame, as too many maxima could be found. Thus, after finding the local maxima, these are filtered out by a peak prominence criterion that compares the height of the peak with the height of its immediate neighbors, which here are the 4 consecutive frequency bins around the peak (Fig. 2). The detection of these local magnitude peaks in successive time frames may still express an unpolished vocalization pattern to which we then apply a clustering algorithm to remove outliers and to obtain clusters of different sections of the vocalization frequency contours. The density-based spatial clustering of applications with noise (DBSCAN) algorithm [7] (with $eps = 11$ and $min\_samples = 12$) is used for this purpose. However, sometimes this approach may still keep some low density clusters which correspond to back-

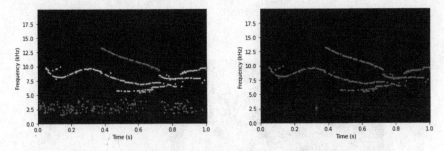

Fig. 3. Frequency contour clusters of a vocalization of *Stenella coeruleoalba* after applying peak tracking and DBSCAN (left) and successive density based cluster filtering approach to remove low density clusters (right).

ground noise and thus, need to be filtered out. To do so, we determine each of the clusters' density by estimating the average number of neighbors within a given radius to each point in the cluster, and then filtering out the clusters that have a bellow average cluster density. Figure 3 shows an example of the outcome of this process.

These clusters will be the foundation for the two features in subset CAF. As both metrics rely on intermediate time instance calculations, the spectrogram is divided into n time segments (which we set to $n = 10$ in our tests) and we compute the slope of each cluster in the segments. For each cluster c of signal s in time segment $[t_i, t_i + \Delta t^*]$, the first active point $(P_{t_i}(c))$ and the last active point $(P_{t_i + \Delta t^*}(c))$ of the cluster in the segment are used as a base to calculate the slope of the cluster in that segment, that is $S_{t_i}(c)$:

$$S_{t_i}(c) = \frac{F_{P_{t_i + \Delta t^*}}(c) - F_{P_{t_i}}(c)}{\Delta t^*} \qquad (5)$$

where Δt^* is an approximate value of time interval $\Delta t = t_{i+1} - t_i$, since the first and the last active points in the cluster may not coincide with those precise time instances, t_i and t_{i+1}. $F_{P_{t_i}}(c)$ is the average frequency value of points within a smaller time window of size $2\frac{t_{i+1} - t_i}{n}$, where $n = 10$, surrounding the closest point P to time instance t, $(t_i$ or $t_{i+1})$. This approach is used as a way to more closely capture the real slope of the cluster, as the true frequency value of the closest point to time instance t could be itself an outlier and misrepresent the true cluster's slope at that time. With this, it is possible to estimate how unsteady is the cluster in the frequency slope progression over time, by calculating the average slope difference from adjacent time segments for cluster c:

$$ClustSlopeUnsteadiness(c) = \frac{\sum\limits_{i=1}^{\|T\|-1} S_{t_{i+1}}(c) - S_{t_i}(c)}{\|T\| - 1} \qquad (6)$$

where T is the set of all time segments into which the spectrogram is divided. Since the vocalization in the spectrogram contains several clusters, the first feature in CAF is expressed by the average *ClustSlopeUnsteadiness(.)* value for each cluster in the spectrogram, expressing how unsteady is vocalization s in the frequency slope progression over time:

$$VSU(s) = \frac{\sum\limits_{c \in C(s)} ClustSlopeUnsteadiness(c)}{\|C(s)\|} \tag{7}$$

where $C(s)$ represents the set of clusters of vocalization s.

The second feature of CAF regards the number of inflection points detected for each cluster, i.e. the number of shifts between up-sweeps and down-sweeps in the cluster curves of vocalization s, which is given by:

$$InflecNum(s) = \sum_{c \in C(s)} \sum_{i=1}^{\|T\|-1} 0^{(S_{t_i}(c) \times S_{t_{i+1}}(c) + |S_{t_i}(c) \times S_{t_{i+1}}(c)|)} . \tag{8}$$

Thus, by using the property that expresses that $0^0 = 1$ and $0^x = 0 \; \forall x \in \mathbb{R}_+^*$, where $\mathbb{R}_+^* = \{x \in \mathbb{R} | x > 0\}$, we add the product of the slopes $S_t(c)$ of adjacent time intervals to the absolute value of that product, and use it as the exponent of base 0. This way, when slopes of adjacent time intervals carry opposite signs, the exponent is 0 and an inflection in the pattern is detected. As it is shown in (8), this is applied to every cluster in signal s, resulting in the final number of inflections in the vocalization.

3 Classification

3.1 Data

In order to train and validate the proposed feature set, we assembled a dataset containing vocalizations of four distinct dolphin species: Short-beaked common dolphin (*Delphinus delphis*), Atlantic spotted dolphin (*Stenella frontalis*), Striped dolphin (*Stenella coeruleoalba*) and Bottlenose dolphin (*Tursiops truncatus*). This dataset comprises 910 one-second recording samples, downsampled to 40 kHz. This particular sampling rate was chosen due to being the minimum sampling rate of the recordings used in our study. This dataset encompasses recordings obtained by the Madeira Whale Museum (MWM) and others from the Watkins Marine Mammal Sound Database (WMMSD)[21].

The small dolphins acoustic recordings from Madeira were collected by the MWM scientific team during dedicated boat surveys. Whenever there were good weather conditions and a group of dolphins of the species of interest was sighted, the boat stopped in the vicinity of the group and a compact self-contained underwater sound recorder (SoundTrap 300 series, model HF, recording the 20 Hz–150 kHz bandwidth) was deployed in continuous recording mode. The device recorded at 10 m depth and was kept floating by a system of buoys of different sizes connected by an elastic rope to the recorder. This layout was used to minimize the waves driven vertical movement of the device which generates noise as the recorder moves through the water. The boat waited 100 m away with the

Table 1. Distribution of recordings by its original source.

Species	WMMSD	MWM	Total
Delphinus delphis (D delphis)	238	164	402
Stenella frontalis (S frontalis)	165	31	196
Stenella coeruleoalba (S coeruleoalba)	134	0	134
Tursiops truncatus (T truncatus)	42	136	178

engine off while the device was recording. To diversify our recording samples, we ensure at least two distinct recording locations for each of the species present in the dataset, which is done by including data from WMMSD. Table 1 shows the source distribution of the recordings among the four species.

In order to reduce low frequency noise, which is predominant in some recordings, a 4th order Butterworth high-pass filter was applied with a cutoff frequency of 1000 Hz. Due to the wide frequency range the vocalizations of these species can reach, a higher cutoff value was not used, as it could have withhold relevant information.

3.2   The Training Phase

Before proceeding to the training of the classification models, as the features span different values of magnitude, they were normalized to become equally weighted. Even though we presented five features, one of them, $MS(s,f)$, can be reflected as a group of *sub features*, as mentioned in Sect. 2.1, in fact up to 257 *sub features* (number of frequency bins in the spectrogram when the STFT representation is used). This led us to use independent component analysis (ICA) for redundancy reduction (with the FastICA algorithm). This reduced the whole feature set into 8 independent components while minimizing the amount of mutual information among them [10]. SVM and KNN classifiers were chosen since they presented the best results during the experiments. Thus, in order to estimate the hyper-parameters of the models (C and *gamma* for SVM with the radial basis function (RBF) kernel, and parameter k for KNN), a grid search approach was used with 5-fold cross-validation. Following the estimation of the optimal hyper-parameters and the parameter, to mitigate the effects of the relatively small dataset, the final training of each model is performed by using leave-one-out cross-validation, from which the final model accuracy is estimated.

4   Results and Discussion

In order to have representative results, we run several tests, each with a given combination of features, a specific spectral representation and classification model. Each test was run 10 times. With the cumulative predictions of those runs, we estimated the general model accuracy (*ModAcc*) and each species accuracy for a given test parameterization. As mentioned in Sects. 1 and 2 we used

Table 2. Accuracy results for KNN. The first column shows the data representation, while the set of features is indicated in the second column.

		D delphis (%)	S frontalis (%)	S coeruleoalba (%)	T truncatus (%)	ModAcc (%)
STFT	*a*	83.51	97.98	88.88	90.30	**90.17**
	b	79.25	93.58	86.34	85.97	**86.28**
	c	80.52	92.98	85.07	85.67	**86.06**
	d	84.18	97.39	88.81	91.11	**90.37**
MFCC₂₀	*a*	85.89	98.36	89.10	90.60	**90.99**
	b	70.00	88.88	89.63	82.83	**82.84**
	c	77.31	93.28	89.85	86.34	**86.70**
	d	77.24	97.84	89.70	90.67	**88.86**
MFCC₄₀	*a*	87.91	97.54	95.15	93.43	**93.51**
	b	74.78	87.31	91.34	85.22	**84.66**
	c	82.39	92.31	94.48	86.94	**89.03**
	d	80.67	95.89	93.66	92.98	**90.80**

distinct representation approaches: (*i*) the STFT, and MFCCs with (*ii*) 20 coefficients, and (*iii*) 40 coefficients. For each of these representations we tested four different combinations of features: (*a*)—the features of subset SAF; (*b*)—all in SAF and the two features of subset CAF; (*c*)—all in SAF and feature *VSU(.)* from CAF; and (*d*)—all in SAF and feature *InflecNum(.)* from CAF. The results of these tests for KNN and SVM can be seen in Tables 2 and 3, respectively.

Table 3. Accuracy results for SVM with RBF kernel. The first two columns indicate the data representation and the set of features.

		D delphis (%)	S frontalis (%)	S coeruleoalba (%)	T truncatus (%)	ModAcc (%)
STFT	*a*	83.73	96.94	93.43	91.11	**91.31**
	b	81.64	95.15	90.82	85.30	**88.23**
	c	82.24	94.78	90.75	86.86	**88.66**
	d	83.13	97.54	92.76	89.70	**90.78**
MFCC₂₀	*a*	90.22	96.64	95.60	91.42	**93.47**
	b	86.49	94.10	95.82	89.25	**91.41**
	c	87.54	95.15	95.07	89.32	**91.77**
	d	89.48	96.34	96.87	93.43	**94.03**
MFCC₄₀	*a*	91.86	96.19	98.51	95.30	**95.47**
	b	85.67	91.94	96.87	92.24	**91.60**
	c	88.43	93.13	97.69	92.91	**93.04**
	d	89.63	94.25	97.23	94.10	**93.80**

Table 4. Model accuracy for each CNN model and different batch sizes.

Species	Batch size	ModAcc (%)
CM_1	64	**81.68**
CM_1	100	**82.78**
CM_2	64	**85.89**
CM_2	100	**75.46**
InceptionV3	64	**80.03**
InceptionV3	100	**73.26**

The results show that using the MFCCs representation produces more accurate models than the STFT while reaching a maximum overall model accuracy of 95.47% (Table 3, test $MFCC_{40} - a$). Also, doubling the number of MFCCs yielded better results with both classifiers for almost all of the shown combination of features. This may be due to the greater detail at high frequencies achieved with the increase in the number of coefficients. Since SAF alone (a) provides better overall results than the joint test with both SAF and CAF (b), at first sight it may seem that CAF brings no new useful information to the classification of the species. However, by analyzing the results when introducing the features of CAF individually $(c$ and $d)$, it is possible to observe instances where some species improved their individual accuracy for a given time-spectral representation. This means that if more species are taken into consideration, the features in CAF may be useful as they can potentially enrich the discrimination capabilities of the whole feature set SAF ∪ CAF. For instance, when introducing the *InflecNum(.)* feature on test $MFCC_{20} - d$ with the SVM classifier, there was an improvement in the individual accuracy for *Stenella coeruleoalba* and *Tursiops truncatus*, by 1.27% and 2.01% respectively. This increase in turn contributed to the the best model accuracy obtained when using $MFCC_{20}$ and second best overall independently of the classifier used.

In order to test Deep Learning CNN models using limited datasets, the same dataset from Table 1 was used. Thus, CNN only receive as input magnitude spectrograms obtained from a STFT time-frequency representation (window and frame size of 512). Three different models of CNN were tested over 50 epochs, while testing two different batch sizes (64 and 100), using a learning rate of 0.0001, a decay of 0.001 and a frame and window size of 512. The tested models consist of two custom made models (CM_1 and CM_2) and the InceptionV3 model [23]. Both custom models are mainly composed by the same layer schematics, however, CM_1 uses even shaped kernels in the convolution layers ($[7 \times 7]$ with stride 4 and $[5 \times 5]$ with stride 2), and CM_2 uses rectangular kernels which are taller than wider ($[10 \times 2]$ with stride 2 and $[20 \times 4]$ with stride 4). Table 4 shows that global accuracy for CNN models ranged from 73.26% (for InceptionV3 using batch size of 100) to 85.89% (for CM_2 using batch size of 64). By comparison with the results of Tables 3 and 2, we can conclude that when the datasets are limited, the proposal presented in this paper outperforms the CNN models.

5 Conclusion

This paper proposes a new set of acoustic features capable of distinguishing small dolphin species by their vocalizations. These features were developed with two objectives in mind: (1) to identify a signal's predominant frequency components and (2) to identify higher-level details in the vocalization patterns. The obtained results suggest that these approaches complement each other as they contribute to an improvement in the accuracy of the models. The best results were obtained using SVM with 40 MFCCs and the features from subset SAF. A global accuracy of 95.47% was achieved, resulting from the following individual accuracy: 91.86% (*Delphinus delphis*); 96.19% (*Stenella frontalis*); 98.51% (*Stenella coeruleoalba*); 95.30% (*Tursiops truncatus*). To the best of our knowledge, these values surpassed the results of previous studies on the task of dolphin classification, for limited datasets thus preventing deep learning approaches from producing high accuracy. The application of these results can be highly relevant in the context of small dolphin PAM taking place in the archipelago of Madeira and worldwide. In spite of the introduction of the features belonging to the contour analysis feature subset (CAF) not being able to consistently outperform the ones from SAF alone, they show promising results as they could enrich the ability to distinguish wider sets of species. Due to this, in future work we plan to extend this study to other cetacean species, as well as other classification approaches such as with deep learning CNN using large datasets.

References

1. Amorim, T.O.S., Castro, F.R.D., Moron, J.R., Duque, B.R., Tullio, J.C.D., Secchi, E.R., Andriolo, A.: Integrative bioacoustics discrimination of eight delphinid species in the western south atlantic ocean. Plos One **14**(6) (2019)
2. Au, W.W.L.: Characteristics of Dolphin sonar signals (Chap. 7). The Sonar of Dolphins, 1st edn, p. 134. Springer, New York (1993)
3. Azzolin, M., Gannier, A., Lammers, M.O., Oswald, J.N., Papale, E., Buscaino, G., Buffa, G., Mazzola, S., Giacoma, C.: Combining whistle acoustic parameters to discriminate mediterranean odontocetes during passive acoustic monitoring. J. Acoust. Soc. Amer. **135**(1), 502–512 (2014)
4. Bahoura, M., Simard, Y.: Blue whale calls classification using short-time fourier and wavelet packet transforms and artificial neural network. Digital Signal Process. **20**(4), 1256–1263 (2010)
5. Baumann-Pickering, S., Wiggins, S.M., Hildebrand, J.A., Roch, M.A., Schnitzler, H.U.: Discriminating features of echolocation clicks of melon-headed whales (peponocephala electra), bottlenose dolphins (tursiops truncatus), and gray's spinner dolphins (stenella longirostris longirostris). J. Acoust. Soc. Amer. **128**(4), 2212–2224 (2010)
6. Erbs, F., Elwen, S.H., Gridley, T.: Automatic classification of whistles from coastal dolphins of the southern african subregion. J. Acoust. Soc. Amer. **141**(4), 2489–2500 (2017)

7. Ester, M., Kriegel, H.P., Sander, J., Xu, X.: A density-based algorithm for discovering clusters in large spatial databases with noise. In: Proceedings of the Second International Conference on Knowledge Discovery and Data Mining, pp. 226–231. KDD'96, AAAI Press (1996)
8. Gatto, B.B., dos Santos, E.M., Colonna, J.G., Sogi, N., Souza, L.S., Fukui, K.: Discriminative singular spectrum analysis for bioacoustic classification. In: Proceeding of the Interspeech 2020, pp. 2887–2891 (2020)
9. Gillespie, D., Caillat, M., Gordon, J., White, P.: Automatic detection and classification of odontocete whistles. J. Acoust. Soc. Amer. **134**(3), 2427–2437 (2013)
10. Hyvärinen, A., Oja, E.: Independent component analysis: algorithms and applications. Neural Netw. **13**(4–5), 411–430 (2000)
11. Jia-Jiang, J., Ran-Bu, L., Jie-Duan, F., Quan-Wang, X., Liu, W., Bo-Sun, Z., Yue-Li, C.: Whistle detection and classification for whales based on convolutional neural networks. Appl. Acoust. **150**, 169–178 (2019)
12. Jia-Jiang, J., Ran-Bu, L., Quan-Wang, X., Yue-Li, C., Bo-Sun, Z., Yan, H., Hua, B., Jie-Duan, F., Yang, J.: Clicks classification of sperm whale and long-finned pilot whale based on continuous wavelet transform and artificial neural network. Appl. Acoust. **141**, 26–34 (2018)
13. Lin, T.H., Chou, L.S.: Automatic classification of delphinids based on the representative frequencies of whistles. J. Acoust. Soc. Amer. **138**(2), 1003–1011 (2015)
14. McAulay, R.J., Quatieri, T.: Speech analysis/synthesis based on a sinusoidal representation. IEEE Trans. Acoust. Speech Signal Process. ASSP **34**(4), 744–754 (1986)
15. McAulay, R.J., Quatieri, T.: Sinusoidal coding (Chap. 4). In: Kleijn, W., Paliwal, K. (eds.) Speech Coding and Synthesis, pp. 121–173. Elsevier Science B.V, Amsterdam (1995)
16. Miralles, R., Lara, G., Carrión, A., Esteban, J.A.: Automatic detection and classification of beluga whale vocalizations. Adv. Appl. Acoust. **2**(2), 61–70 (2013)
17. Nadir, M., Adnan, S.M., Aziz, S., Khan, M.U.: Marine mammals classification using acoustic binary patterns. Arch. Acoust. **45**(4), 721–731 (2020). www.journals.pan.pl/dlibra/publication/135278/edition/118263/content
18. Ness, S.: The Orchive: a system for semi-automatic annotation and analysis of a large collection of bioacoustic recordings. Ph.D. thesis, University of Victoria, 3800 Finnerty Road, Victoria, British Columbia, Canada, V8P 5C2 (2013)
19. Noda, J.J., Sánchez-Rodríguez, D., Travieso-González, C.M.: A methodology based on bioacoustic information for automatic identification of reptiles and anurans. In: Reptiles and Amphibians. InTech (2018)
20. Parada, P.P., Cardenal-López, A.: Using gaussian mixture models to detect and classify dolphin whistles and pulses. J. Acoust. Soc. Amer. **135**(6), 3371–3380 (2014)
21. Sayigh, L., Daher, M.A., Allen, J., Gordon, H., Joyce, K., Stuhlmann, C., Tyack, P.: The Watkins marine mammal sound database: an online, freely accessible resource. Acoust. Soc. Amer. **27**(1), 040013 (2016)
22. Smith, J., Serra, X.: PARSHL: an analysis/synthesis program for non-harmonic sounds based on a sinusoidal representation. In: Proceedings of the International Computer Music Conference, pp. 290–297 (1987)

23. Szegedy, C., Vanhoucke, V., Ioffe, S., Shlens, J., Wojna, Z.: Rethinking the inception architecture for computer vision. In: 2016 IEEE Conference on Computer Vision and Pattern Recognition (CVPR), pp. 2818–2826 (2016)
24. Xian, Y., Thompson, A., Qiu, Q., Nolte, L., Nowacek, D., Lu, J., Calderbank, R.: Classification of whale vocalizations using the weyl transform. In: 2015 IEEE International Conference on Acoustics, Speech and Signal Processing (ICASSP)

Covariance Kernel Learning Schemes for Gaussian Process Based Prediction Using Markov Chain Monte Carlo

Gargi Roy, Kane Warrior, and Dalia Chakrabarty[✉]

Brunel University London, Kingston Lane, London, Uxbridge UB8 3PH, UK
{Gargi.Roy,Kane.Warrior,Dalia.Chakrabarty}@brunel.ac.uk

Abstract. Probabilistic supervised learning within the Bayesian paradigm typically use Gaussian Processes (GPs) to model the sought function, and provide a means for securing reliable uncertainties in said functional learning, while offering interpretability. Prediction of the output of such a learnt function is closed-form in this approach. In this work, we present GP based learning of the functional relation between two variables, using various kinds of kernels that are called in to parametrise the covariance function of the invoked GP. However, such covariance kernels are typically parametric in the literature, with hyperparameters that are learnt from the data. Here, we discuss a new nonparametric covariance kernel, and compare its performance against existing non-stationary and stationary kernels, as well as against Deep Neural Networks. We present results on both univariate and multivariate data, to demonstrate the range of applicability of the presented learning scheme.

Keywords: Covariance kernel hyperparameter · Stationary · Nonparametric · Markov Chain Monte Carlo · Gaussian process

1 Introduction

Prediction or interpolation within any supervised learning setup, is predicated upon the learning of the functional relationship between the response (or target) and the predictor variables (or input variables). For accurate predictions, it is desirable to perform the learning of this sought function as reliably as possible; additionally, one wishes to rely minimally on parametric models of the sought function, to ensure high generalisability of the approach. Predictions following such functional learning have been undertaken in a wide set of application areas, such as epidemiology [6]; underground construction and tunnel making industry [3]; gold mining industry [2]; nuclear power plants [11]; energy storage and management systems [18]; crop yield [1]; species breeding [7] etc. All these applications—including accuracy-sensitive domains such as medicine [4];

Supported by EPSRC DTP Studentship.

information security [17]—require robust; interpretable; and objective uncertainties in the learning of the sought functional relationship, and of the undertaken prediction—given the inherent uncertainty and variability present in the input data [3,11,13,15].

If a parametric form is assigned to a sought function—such as fitting splines/wavelets to the data—then not only does this approach become difficult to generalise to high-dimensional situations, but the method would also neglect the measured observed uncertainties on the output values, at respective designed inputs. Importantly, parametric learning does not capture the correlation structure of the sought function. Given this, we seek nonparametric learning of the sought function, where the very form of the sought function is learnt. In the Bayesian paradigm, the sought function being an unknown, is considered to be random, which is essentially treated as a sample function of a stochastic process. A popular choice of this stochastic process in such nonparametric learning of a sought function is a Gaussian Process (GP) [10], that imposes minimal restrictions on the sought function and allows for simplicity in the computation, as well as generalisability across dimensions. The usage of Bayesian inference techniques towards objective specification of the parameterisation relevant to the invoked GP, is adumbrated by the parametrisation of the covariance function of the GP with covariance kernels. A covariance kernel is a positive-definite function that offers the correlation between two variables that are the outputs at respective inputs, in terms of a distance between these input values. Thus, in the popular Square Exponential (SQE) covariance kernel, the correlation between the standardised outputs of the sought function at two chosen input values, is Normal with zero mean, in the Euclidean distance between these inputs. Variance of this Normal density is driven by the "length scale hyperparameters". Said hyperparameters inform on the scale over which correlation fades along each direction in input space. These are typically treated as unknowns that are learnt from the data. Thus, the data-driven length scale hyperparameters drive the correlation structure of the sought function that represents the relationship between the input and output variables.

Then kernel-based parametrisation of the GP covariance function, needs to be such that (s.t.) these correlation-driving kernel hyperparameters adapt to the unevenness or inhomogeneities in the correlation structure of the available data on the output variable. However, treating the hyperparameters as unknown constants—that are learnt from the data—falls short of the need for such adaptiveness to inhomogeneities in the correlation in this data. This motivates the need for non-stationary of covariance kernels, the very structure of which is s.t. the kernel is specific to a particular location in input space [9,10,12]. Even such non-stationary kernels are however parametric—as are all kernels discussed in the literature, [9,12]—so that the correct implementation of location-specificity in the parametric form of the kernel will demand the learning of a large number of hyperparameters, it would appear. An alternative route is the usage of a kernel that is not parametric, but one which can be shown to adapt to inhomogeneities in the correlation structure of the data. In this paper, we introduce a new nonparametric kernel that demands the learning of a few kernel hyperparameters, given the data at hand, within a Markov Chain Monte Carlo (MCMC) [8] led inferential framework.

The rest of the paper is organized as follows. The model of our proposed nonparametric kernel is briefly stated in Sect. 2. Section 3 presents a detailed case study for empirical illustration of the said methods along with the data and the models for each cases. In the Sect. 4 we present the predictive results for each case along with the comparative results.

2   Model

An MCMC chain is run with the data at hand, to perform inference on all those parameters that contribute to the learning of the sought functional relation between the input and output variables. We refer to this functional relationship as the "mother function" hereon, and refer to the GP that generates it, to be the "mother GP". In our work, each hyperparameter of the new nonparametric kernel function that we introduce, is modelled as a function of the sample function of the "mother GP", with all these hyperparameters embedded within an SQE-looking form that we have chosen to assign to our nonparametric kernel. Of course, with the hyperparameters of such a kernel modelled as random functions—instead of unknown constants—our "SQE-looking" kernel is not parametric, and definitely not SQE in form. Since each sample function of the "mother GP" is generated in an iteration of the MCMC chain, dependence of each hyperparameter on the sample function of the "mother GP" implies that each kernel hyperparameter is a function of the iteration index, where each such function is unknown. We model each such function with a distinct "inner GP". Then any "inner GP" is essentially distinct from the "mother GP" that lies at the outer layer of our learning strategy. Since any real-valued function of the iteration index is continuous—as are all mappings from $\mathbb{N}$ to $\mathbb{R}$—each "inner GP" that generates such a continuous function, can be shown to be stationary. Thus, our new two-layered learning strategy has a non-stationary "mother GP" that nestes within itself, multiple stationary "inner GP"s.

In majority of the GP literature, the kernel hyperparameters are learnt through gradient based optimisation methods for maximisation of the GP marginal likelihood. Then point estimates for the learnt values of the hyperparameters are obtained, which in turn are used to evaluate the posterior predictive distribution. Reference [16] criticises this widely used approach by stating that point estimates of the hyperparameters fail to include comprehensive uncertainties, contributing thereby to over-confident predictions. Non-convexity of the marginal likelihood might also cause unreliable estimates of hyperparameter values at local minima, and presence of multiple modes may affect the interpretability of the kernel hyperparameters. In this work on the other hand, we have used a fully Bayesian setup i.e. Markov Chain Monte Carlo based inference is used to learn uncertainty-included values of the hyperparameters of the covariance kernel. This allows avoidance of the aforementioned shortcomings of optimisation.

3   Empirical Illustration

Often electricity production companies need to know the balance between electricity production, and electricity consumption, as this balance helps determine efficiency of the management and control of relevant resources and involved costs. For this purpose such energy companies require effective predictions of the demand of electricity. This is the context of the empirical illustrations that we discuss in this paper.

We use power consumption data in Tetouan city, that is located in north Morocco [5,14]. The data includes observations from the 1st of January, 2017, to the 31st of December of that year, recorded every 10 minutes. In fact this recorded time series data includes values of five meteorological parameters—including temperature, humidity, wind speed, general diffuse flows and diffuse flows—and the corresponding value of the energy consumption in the three zones that the power distribution in this city is divided into. We however add the power consumption data across these three zones, and refer to our output variable as the "integrated power consumption" in this city. In the univariate setup we model temperature as the input and integrated power consumption as the output variable. In the multivariate set up we have used the four-dimensional input vector consisting of temperature, humidity, wind speeds and diffuse flows along with the same output as in univariate case. Indeed we use only four of the available five input variables in the multivariate model, since wind speed and general diffuse flows are highly correlated variables, that appear as linear transformations of each other. We resample randomly from the full Tetouan City dataset, to construct a training data set of size 203, and a test data set of size 50, while ensuring that no date and no time of observation is replicated amongst the instances at which the observations are considered.

3.1   Model for Univariate Case

Let D_{train} be the training data that consists of pairs of input and output values, i.e. $D_{train} = \{(x_i, y_i)\}_{i=1}^{M}$. We aim to learn the functional relationship $f(\cdot)$ that expresses the relation between input temperature that we denote as X, and the output integrated power consumption, which is denoted by Y. Then $Y = f(X)$ where $f : \mathbb{R} \longrightarrow \mathbb{R}_{\geq 0}$. We seek to learn the sought function $f(\cdot)$ by treating $f(\cdot)$ as an unknown, which in the Bayesian paradigm translates to $f(\cdot)$ being modelled as a function-valued random variable, or rather a random function in this case. Then by definition, $f(\cdot)$ is ascribed a probability distribution. A probability distribution on the space of functions is given by a stochastic process. So we model $f(\cdot)$ as a realisation from a process. For maximal generalisability and ease of computation, we choose this process to be a GP.

So $f(\cdot) \sim GP(\mu(\cdot), cov(\cdot, \cdot))$, where $\mu(\cdot)$ and $cov(\cdot, \cdot)$ are the mean and covariance functions of the GP that generates the sought function $f(\cdot)$. Then by definition, the joint probability of a finite number of realisations of $f(\cdot)$—such as M realisations of $f(\cdot)$ at the M design points $x_1, \ldots, x_M$ in the training data D_{train}—is multivariate Normal, with the M-dimensional mean vector $\boldsymbol{\mu}$ and covariance matrix $\boldsymbol{\Sigma}^{(M \times M)}$. We parametrise matrix $\boldsymbol{\Sigma}$ by saying that the ijth element of this matrix that represents the covariance between the variable Y_i— that represents the output at $X = x_i$—and Y_j, is modelled as a covariance function $K(\cdot, \cdot)$ of a distance between the inputs x_i and x_j at which these output variables are realised. Here $i, j = 1, \ldots, M$. As the joint of $f(x_1), \ldots, f(x_M)$ is multivariate Normal, with mean $\boldsymbol{\mu}$, and covariance matrix $\boldsymbol{\Sigma} = [K(x_i, x_j)]$, it implies that the joint of $Y_1, \ldots, Y_M$ is multivariate Normal. But the joint of these M output variables, is the probability of the data on Y. In fact, it is a conditional probability—conditional on the parameters of the mean and the covariance matrix. As we will parametrise the covariance matrix $\boldsymbol{\Sigma}$ with the kernel function $K(\cdot, \cdot)$ that bears hyperparameters (such as the length scale hyperparameter ℓ that we will soon discuss in detail), the probability of the data on Y is conditional on these kernel hyperparameters. But the probability of the data conditional on model parameters is—by definition—the likelihood. Thus, the likelihood is multivariate Normal with mean $\boldsymbol{\mu}$ and the covariance matrix $\boldsymbol{\Sigma}$ that will be kernel parametrised, with a chosen kernel, parametrised by appropriate hyperparameter(s), i.e. the likelihood is (Eq. 1)

$$\mathcal{L}(\ell | D_{train}) = \frac{1}{\sqrt{(2\pi)^M |\boldsymbol{\Sigma}|}} \exp\left(-\frac{1}{2}(\boldsymbol{Y} - \boldsymbol{\mu})^T \boldsymbol{\Sigma}^{-1}(\boldsymbol{Y} - \boldsymbol{\mu})\right), \tag{1}$$

where $\boldsymbol{Y} = (y_1, \ldots, y_M)^T$. We will learn the hyperparameters of this covariance kernel using Vanilla MCMC in general, with truncated Normal proposal density and generic priors on the unknowns, unless the application is s.t. strong priors are available.

In our empirical illustration, we have used five different stationary covariance kernels [10], inclusive of the Matérn class of kernels with the hyperparameter $\nu = \frac{3}{2}$ and $\nu = \frac{5}{2}$. In these two cases, the remaining kernel hyperparameter— which is the length scale hyperparameter denoted ℓ—is learnt; $\ell > 0$. Equation 2 shows the the Matérn class of covariance kernels with positive hyperparameters ν and ℓ, where $d(\cdot, \cdot)$ is the Euclidean distance between x_i and x_j; $K_\nu(\cdot)$ is the modified Bessel function; and $\Gamma(\cdot)$ is the Gamma function.

$$k(x_i, x_j) = \frac{2^{1-\nu}}{\Gamma(\nu)} \left(\frac{\sqrt{2\nu}}{l} d(x_i, x_j)\right)^\nu K_\nu\left(\frac{\sqrt{2\nu}}{l} d(x_i, x_j)\right) \tag{2}$$

In the third case we learnt both ℓ and ν for this covariance kernel.

Additionally, we have used the Ornstein-Uhlenbeck (OU) kernel in the fourth case. This kernel is a special case of the Matérn class of kernels where ν is set to $\frac{1}{2}$, hence in this case we learn only the hyperparameter ℓ. Finally we have used a composite kernel that is defined as the product of an SQE kernel and the Matérn class of kernels with hyperparameter $\nu = \frac{3}{2}$; this composite kernel is in Eq. 3 and in this case we learn the hyperparameter ℓ.

$$k(x_i, x_j) = \exp\left(-\frac{(x_i - x_j)^2}{2\ell^2}\right) \frac{2^{1-\nu}}{\Gamma(\nu)} \left(\frac{\sqrt{2\nu}}{l} d(x_i, x_j)\right)^\nu K_\nu\left(\frac{\sqrt{2\nu}}{l} d(x_i, x_j)\right) \tag{3}$$

3.2   Model for Multivariate Case

In the multivariate case, the training data is now $D_{train} = \{(\mathbf{x_i}, y_i)\}_{i=1}^{M}$, where, $\mathbf{x_i}$ is now p dimensional vector. In our case, $p = 4$ and the likelihood is again multivariate Normal, as expressed below in Eq. 1. In this case, we employ an SQE-shaped parametric kernel, $K(\mathbf{x_i}, \mathbf{x_j}) := \exp - \left((\mathbf{x_i} - \mathbf{x_j})^T \mathbf{Q} (\mathbf{x_i} - \mathbf{x_j})\right)$, where $\mathbf{Q}$ is the $p \times p$-dimensional diagonal matrix, with the cth diagonal element given as $1/\ell_c$, $\forall c = 1, \ldots p$, with ℓ_c the length scale hyperparameter along the cth direction in the input space. Therefore, in this case we have four length scale hyperparameters, $\ell_1, \ell_2, \ell_3, \ell_4$ that we learn using MCMC, with Gaussian proposal and Gaussian prior densities.

3.3   New Nonparametric Kernel

We will use a newly built nonparametric kernel (called NPK) that is nonparametrically learnt, given the data. This calls for modelling each relevant kernel hyperparameter as an unknown function of an input that we can identify as the time step, at which a new sample path is generated from the GP that underlines the sought function. Essentially we have a "mother GP" that comprises the first layer of our learning strategy, where this "mother GP" is specified with an SQE-looking kernel. When the input is scalar-valued, the sole length scale hyperparameter of this SQE-looking kernel is modelled using another GP that comprises the inner layer of our two-layered learning strategy. While the "mother GP" can be non-stationary in general, the "inner GP" is stationary by design. In fact, the inner GP uses SQE as its covariance kernel. The likelihood is more complicated than a multivariate Normal (given in Eq. 1), since the length scale hyperparameter ℓ is now the output of a random function of the iteration index, s.t. any finite set of such outputs are jointly multivariate Normal. The learning of the functional relation between the length scale hyperparameter ℓ of the covariance kernel of the "mother GP" and the iteration index, is undertaken with a training dataset that comprises pairs of values of iteration index within the previous $n_{lookback}$ number of iterations—from the current iteration within the MCMC chain—and the ℓ value that was current at each such previous iteration, This functional relation between the length scale hyperparameter ℓ and iteration index, is treated as a sample function of the "inner GP". We use Random-Walk-2-block-update Metropolis Hastings for inference in which ℓ is updated in the first block, s.t. in the qth iteration, it is updated to $\ell_{current}^{(q)}$, and then at this updated ℓ, we update the length scale hyperparameter δ of the covariance kernel used to parametrise the covariance function of the "inner GP". For the updating in the first block we use the empirically observed set of pairs of values of X and Y. For the updating in the 2nd block of the qth iteration, we use the lookback data that comprises the $n_{lookback}$-sized, (dynamically-varying) training set $\mathbf{D}_{second}^{(q)} = \{(k, \ell_{current}^{(k)})\}_{k=q-n_{lookback}}^{q-1}$ for $q \geq n_{lookback} + 1$ and $q \leq N_{iter}$. For the first $n_{lookback}$ number of iterations, we perform simple Random Walk (RW) Metropolis Hastings. We use Gaussian priors on the unknowns. In the first block of the undertaken MCMC chain, length scale hyperparameter ℓ of the covariance kernel of the "mother GP" is proposed from a Normal with mean that is the value of ℓ that is current in the previous iteration, and experimentally-fixed variance. Then using the freshly-generated training data $\mathbf{D}_{second}^{(q)}$ in the 2nd block of the qth iteration, we compute the multivariate Normal likelihood of the length scale hyperparameter δ of the kernel that parametrises the covariance function of the "inner GP". This "inner GP" generates the functional relation between ℓ, and the iteration index. We update this hyperparameter δ of the covariance kernel of the "inner GP" and then undertake closed-form prediction of the mean and variance of the output, i.e. the mean value and standard deviation value of ℓ in this iteration. This predicted mean is then recorded as the current value of ℓ at the end of this qth iteration, and the uncertainty in this value in this iteration is the predicted standard deviation of ℓ. Algorithm 1 presents the NPK kernel learning scheme.

Algorithm 1: Nonparametric kernel learning algorithm

---

1 **for** $q \leftarrow 1$ **to** N_{iter} **increment by** 1 **do**
2   **if** $q < n_{lookback}$ **then**
3          $\ell_{current} \leftarrow \ell^{(q-1)}, \ell_{proposed} \sim \mathcal{N}(\ell_{current}, \text{chosen variance})$
4   Compute LogPosterior using D_{train}
5   Update $\ell_{current}$ through accept/reject of $\ell_{proposed}$ using RW MCMC
6   **else**
          /* Block-1   */
7   Repeat line 3 - 5, Generate $\mathbf{D}_{second}$
          /* Block-2   */
8          $\delta_{current} \leftarrow \delta^{(q-1)}, \delta_{prop} \sim \mathcal{N}(\delta_{current}, \text{chosen variance})$
9   Compute LogPosterior using $\mathbf{D}_{second}$
10   Update $\delta_{current}$ through accept/reject of δ_{prop} using RW MCMC
11   Predicted $\ell \leftarrow innerGP(\mathbf{D}_{second}, q, \delta_{current})$
12         $\ell_{current} \leftarrow$ Predicted ℓ
13   Predicted $Y \leftarrow motherGP(D_{train}, \text{empirical test data}, \ell_{current})$

---

4   Results

Figure 1 presents the results of predictions of the integrated power consumption Y plotted against the input temperature X, in five sets of sub-figures, corresponding to five stationary kernels. In the left-most panels of the each sub-figure, results on prediction of Y at test values of X are depicted in red, superimposed with the predicted standard deviation drawn as an error bar on each side of the predicted mean value. The training data points are in the small sized (green) dots, while the blue circles represent the true values of the power consumption at the test inputs. The right panels of sub-figure "(a)" and "(b)" present results of using the Matérn class of kernels with the hyperparameter $\nu = \frac{3}{2}$ and $\nu = \frac{5}{2}$ and length scale hyperparameter ℓ that is learnt to be around 15 and 9 respectively. Right panel of Sub-figure "(c)" depicts results from the Matérn class of kernel in which, both ℓ and ν have been learnt—to be around 25 and 0.11 respectively. Length scale hyperparameter ℓ of the Ornstein-Uhlenbeck (OU) kernel is learnt to be around 27, and this is depicted in the right panel of sub-figure "(d)". Right panel of sub-figure "(e)" shows the learnt length scale hyperparameter ℓ as around 14 for the composite kernel. In addition, traces of the kernel hyperparameters inferred upon by the MCMC technique used in the work, are in the other panels germane to each kernel that we have worked with.

Figure 2 shows the predictive results obtained using the newly developed nonparametric kernel NPK (left panel), along with the traces of learnt length scale hyperparameter of the mother GP and the inner GP, (middle and right panels respectively). The length scale hyperparameter of the mother and inner GP are learnt to be around 5.95 and 1 respectively.

Predictive results of the multivariate model are depicted in Fig. 3a. The left panel of Fig. 3a displays the predictions against the test input index and the right panel of Fig. 3a shows predictions on integrated energy consumption, plotted against test temperature alone, with humidity, wind speeds and diffuse flow values held constant. Figure 4 shows the traces of learnt length scales in the multivariate model along with the traces of the prior and likelihood. From this figure, we note that the four length scale hyperparameters, $\ell_1, \ell_2, \ell_3, \ell_4$ are learnt to be around 16.39, 45.66, 0.151, 0.0001 respectively. Figure 3b presents the predictive results of the univariate model that uses the nonstationary kernel advanced by [9]. We are not including root mean square error (RMSE) for prediction as this scalar summary does not correctly represent the quality of prediction; while predictions made for test inputs in $[a_1, b_1]$ could be quite poor and that over test inputs in $[a_2, b_2]$ could be good, RMSE—or another scalar summary of the results—for such predictions could be similar to that for the case where the predictions are consistently poor over the whole range $[a, b]$ of the test input values, thus suppressing the comparative superiority of the method that produced the better predictions in the interval $[a_2, b_2]$. Here $[a_i, b_i] \subset [a, b]$, $i = 1, 2$. It could even be that a method is more proficient in predicting over intervals in values of the input, within which the inhomogeneities in the correlation of the data are higher, but a scalar summary of the predictions can misdirect attention from such superiority. From a visual inspection of the prediction results, we can see that the nonparametric kernel (NPK) performs best over intervals in input space within which messiness of the real-world dataset is manifest. If a scalar summary of the quality of predictions is anyway sought, we suggest a simple overlap parameter that tells the number of test inputs—out of a total of n—at which the truth lies within the predicted intervals. After all, correct and comprehensive prediction of the uncertainty of the prediction, is also a recommended quality of a learning strategy. The value of the overlap parameter for NPK kernel is 45 (91.84%); for the Matérn class of kernels with the hyperparameter $\nu = \frac{3}{2}$ and $\nu = \frac{5}{2}$ are 7 (14%), 6 (12%) respectively; for the Matérn class of kernel when both the hyperparameters were learnt is 19 (38%); for Ornstein-Uhlenbeck (OU) it is 26 (52%); and for the composite kernel, it is 18 (36%) respectively. Multivariate prediction yields overlap parameter value as 9 (18.37%). However, the uncertainty interval is small for the nonstationary kernel by [9] yielding a zero overlap parameter value.

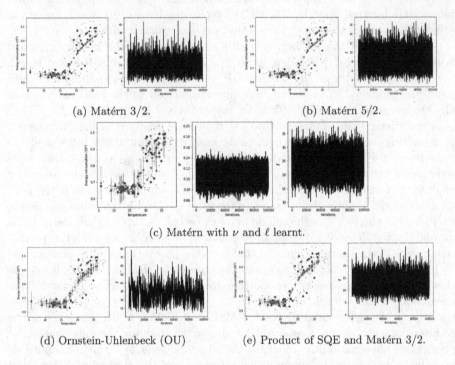

(a) Matérn 3/2.   (b) Matérn 5/2.

(c) Matérn with ν and ℓ learnt.

(d) Ornstein-Uhlenbeck (OU)   (e) Product of SQE and Matérn 3/2.

Fig. 1. Prediction of power consumption plotted at test temperatures in univariate case, (along with uncertainties of prediction), presented as red stars. True values of the output are in blue circles and training points in green dots. Plots include results using five stationary kernels, and traces of learnt kernel hyperparameter(s) are plotted.

We have also implemented Deep Neural Networks with varying architectures to make predictions of the power consumption with gradient descent optimiser, and ReLu activation function. Figure 5, shows the predictive results obtained from the three different DNN architectures. The left-most plot pertains to the DNN architecture that bears two hidden layers with learning rate 0.01 (called NN-1) and the middle panel displays results from using an architecture consisting of two hidden layers with learning rate of 0.3 (called NN-2). The right-most panel depicts results from a DNN that consists of 6 hidden layers (called NN-3). The loss has converged for all these DNNs. The variation in the predictions obtained with the DNNs of varying architecture indicates that even within this small range of architectural parameters scanned, DNN results are sensitive to the choice of the architecture. The choice of the optimal architectural parameters, by minimising the loss function does not appear to resolve the concerns in our experiments. The loss obtained from NN-1, NN-2 and NN-3 after convergence

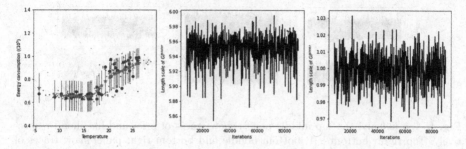

Fig. 2. Prediction of power consumption plotted at test temperatures, as obtained in the univariate case, (along with uncertainties of prediction), presented as red stars. True values of the output are in blue circles and training points in green dots. Plots include results from using nonparametric kernel, NPK (in left), and traces of learnt kernel hyperparameter(s) of mother and inner GP are plotted in the middle and right respectively.

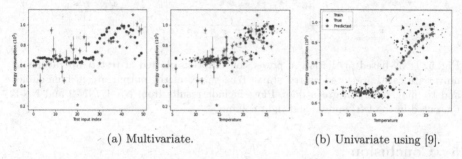

(a) Multivariate.   (b) Univariate using [9].

Fig. 3. Middle panel displays the plot of predicted values of power consumption, plotted (as red stars) against test temperatures in the multivariate case, where the other three inputs are held constant. The uncertainties of prediction are plotted as error bars. True values of the output are in blue circles and training points in green dots. Predicted outputs are plotted against test input index in the left panel. Left and middle panels report results of learning performed using a stationary SQE kernel, with four length scale hyperparameters. The right panel reports results of using the non-stationary kernel of [9] to learn the relation between power consumption and temperature.

are 0.1761, 0.137 and 0.1338 respectively. Also, we see that NN-3 among these DNNs achieves best prediction along with having smallest loss amongst the three. However, loss for NN-2 and NN-3 are very similar in magnitude (∼0.13). Thus, we cannot necessarily extract an intuition about the best architectural choice by looking into the value of the loss function. Also it is unknown what the smallest value of the loss function that can be achieved, for a given data set. Given our experiments, sensitivity to architecture is worrying when we seek reliable and robust implementation of the sought learning.

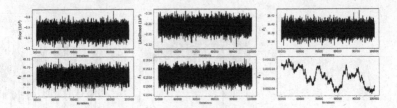

Fig. 4. Top left and the top middle panels show traces of prior and likelihood respectively. Top right, bottom left, bottom middle and bottom right panel show traces of learnt length scales ℓ_1, ℓ_2, ℓ_3, ℓ_4 for the four input variables respectively.

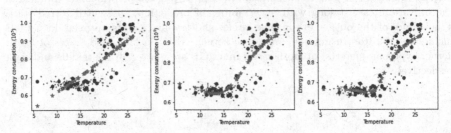

Fig. 5. DNN-based prediction of power consumption plotted at test temperatures in univariate case, presented as red stars. True values of the output are in blue circles and training points in green dots. Plots include results from NN-1, NN-2 and NN-3 presented in the left, middle and right column.

5   Conclusion

In this work we have presented a method that employs a new nonparametric kernel that can be invoked to perform GP-based learning of the functional relation between an input and an output variable, towards prediction of the output at test values of the input. Said kernel helps such sought predictions when the correlation structure of the available data on the output, is not homogeneous. Results from the implementation of this new kernel are compared to results obtained using existing stationary and nonstationary kernels. The presented nonparametric kernel avoids the learning of a large number of hyperparameters, while harbouring the very desirable property that it is dually nonstationary, as we will cultivate in an upcoming contribution.

References

1. Ali, M., Deo, R.C., Downs, N.J., Maraseni, T.: Cotton yield prediction with Markov chain monte Carlo-based simulation model integrated with genetic programing algorithm: a new hybrid copula-driven approach. Agric. Forest Meteorol. **263**, 428–448 (2018)
2. Yan, B., Ren, F., Cai, M., Qiao, C.: Bayesian model based on Markov chain Monte Carlo for identifying mine water sources in submarine gold mining. J. Cleaner Prod. **253**, 120008 (2020)

3. Lu, H., Kim, E., Gutierrez, M.: A probabilistic q-system using the Markov chain to predict rock mass quality in tunneling. Comput. Geotech. **145**, 104689 (2022)
4. Begoli, E., Bhattacharya, T., Kusnezov, D.: The need for uncertainty quantification in machine-assisted medical decision making. Nat. Mach. Intell. **1**(1), 20–23 (2019)
5. Dua, D., Graff, C.: UCI machine learning repository (2017). www.archive.ics.uci.edu/ml
6. Lee, C.H., Chang, K., Chen, Y.M., Tsai, J.T., Chen, Y.J., Ho, W.H.: Epidemic prediction of dengue fever based on vector compartment model and Markov chain Monte Carlo method. BMC Bioinf. **22**(5), 1–11 (2021)
7. Magotra, A., Bangar, Y.C., Yadav, A.: Neural network and Bayesian-based prediction of breeding values in beetal goat. Trop. Anim. Health Prod. **54**(5), 282 (2022)
8. Neal, R.M.: Monte Carlo implementation of gaussian process models for Bayesian regression and classification (1997). arXiv:physics/9701026
9. Paciorek, C., Schervish, M.: Nonstationary covariance functions for gaussian process regression. In: Advances in Neural Information Processing Systems 16 (2003)
10. Rasmussen, C.E., Williams, C.K.I.: Gaussian Processes for Machine Learning. Adaptive Computation and Machine Learning. MIT Press, Cambridge (2006)
11. Rastogi, R., Ghosh, S., Ghosh, A.K., Vaze, K.K., Singh, P.K.: Fatigue crack growth prediction in nuclear piping using Markov chain Monte Carlo simulation. Fatigue & Fract. Eng. Mat. & Struct. **40**(1), 145–156 (2017)
12. Remes, S., Heinonen, M., Kaski, S.: Non-stationary spectral kernels. In: Advances in Neural Information Processing Systems 30 (2017)
13. Roy, G., Chakrabarty, D.: Efficient uncertainty quantification for under-constraint prediction following learning using mcmc. In: Neural Information Processing, pp. 275–287. Springer Nature Singapore, Singapore (2023)
14. Salam, A., El Hibaoui, A.: Comparison of machine learning algorithms for the power consumption prediction:-case study of Tetouan city-. In: 2018 6th International Renewable and Sustainable Energy Conference (IRSEC), pp. 1–5. IEEE (2018)
15. Shen, X., Zhang, Y., Zhang, J., Wu, X.: An interval analysis scheme based on empirical error and mcmc to quantify uncertainty of wind speed. IEEE Trans. Ind. Appl. **58**(6), 7754–7763 (2022)
16. Simpson, F., Lalchand, V., Rasmussen, C.E.: Marginalised gaussian processes with nested sampling. Adv. Neural. Inf. Process. Syst. **34**, 13613–13625 (2021)
17. Smith, H.J., Dinev, T., Xu, H.: Information privacy research: an interdisciplinary review. MIS Q. 989–1015 (2011)
18. Wang, Y., Zhou, C., Chen, Z.: An enhanced approach for load behavior and battery residual capacity prediction using Markov chain and Monte Carlo method. IEEE J. Emerg. Selected Top. Ind. Electr. **4**(1), 159–167 (2023)

Intelligent Robotics

A Review on Quadruped Manipulators

Maria S. Lopes[1,2]([✉])[ID], António Paulo Moreira[1,2][ID], Manuel F. Silva[1,3][ID],
and Filipe Santos[1][ID]

[1] INESC TEC - INESC Technology and Science, Porto, Portugal
[2] Faculty of Engineering of the University of Porto, Porto, Portugal
maria.s.lopes@inesctec.pt
[3] ISEP - Instituto Superior de Engenharia do Porto, Porto, Portugal

Abstract. Quadruped robots are gaining attention in the research community because of their superior mobility and versatility in a wide range of applications. However, they are restricted to procedures that do not need precise object interaction. With the addition of a robotic arm, they can overcome these drawbacks and be used in a new set of tasks. Combining a legged robot's dextrous movement with a robotic arm's maneuverability allows the emergence of a highly flexible system, but with the disadvantage of higher complexity of motion planning and control methods. This paper gives an overview of the existing quadruped systems capable of manipulation, with a particular interest in systems with high movement flexibility. The main topics discussed are the motion planning approaches and the selected kinematic configuration. This review concludes that the most followed research path is to add a robotic arm on the quadrupedal base and that the motion planning approach used depends on the desired application. For simple tasks, the arm can be seen as an independent system, which is simpler to implement. For more complex jobs the coupling effects between the arm and quadruped robot must be considered.

Keywords: Quadruped manipulator · Mobile manipulator ·
Motion-planning · Kinematic redundancy

1 Introduction

Modern developments in science and technology have made it possible to create robotic systems that are more intelligent and have a wider variety of uses. New systems are constantly being developed to overcome human fragilities and bring efficiency and profitability to the processes needed in the industry, agriculture, surveillance and security, and even domestic use [30].

In the past years, the research was focused on mobile robots so that the tasks could be completely autonomous or with reduced human interaction. Standardizing specific tasks can bring health to workers and economic benefits while improving the activity's productivity and performance. Wheeled robots, tracked

N. Moniz et al. (Eds.): EPIA 2023, LNAI 14115, pp. 199–211, 2023.
https://doi.org/10.1007/978-3-031-49008-8_16

200 M. S. Lopes et al.

robots, and legged robots are the three basic categories under which mobile robots can be divided.

Legged robots include quadrupeds, created with four legs that resemble many real animals, like dogs and horses. Compared with the ones from the other categories, these are extremely useful in rough and uneven terrains, which is why they have been gaining much interest in robotics. They are more efficient in dodging obstacles as they can adjust their height and have fewer floor contact areas. However, they brought new challenges derived from the high complexity of the motion planning and controlling algorithms [2].

Quadruped robots, like all other mobile platforms, lack manipulation capabilities. In some applications, that is a significant disadvantage because the possibility of interaction with the environment is crucial in multiple scenarios, not just the ability of localization and navigation that most quadrupeds have. In order to overcome these restrictions, research is progressing by adding manipulation capabilities into these robots, either by using legs with extra flexibility or by adding robotic arms (sometimes more than one, such as centaurs [20]), turning the systems into mobile manipulators.

With robots being able to move in an environment and interact with the present objects, they can be used to perform dangerous or physically demanding activities for workers or others that need precise movements that are hard to do manually. Quadruped manipulators can operate indoors and outdoors in several settings and situations and can be programmed to carry out tasks repeatedly with high accuracy as autonomous or collaborative machines.

The remainder of this paper is structured as follows: Sect. 2 presents the methodology used for this review work. Section 3 the existing quadruped/robotic arm integrations in the literature, followed by their motion planning approaches in Sect. 4. Section 5 details the system's kinematic configuration, and finally, Sect. 6 is an outline of the conclusions taken.

2 Methodology

The review focused on works found in IEEEXplore and SCOPUS that involved quadruped robots capable of manipulation. The review period spanned from 2017 to 2022, and the search was not limited to specific application domains, aiming to encompass a wide range of activities. A more detailed examination was conducted on systems that demonstrated high manipulation capabilities. The following strings were used in the search process:

- ("legged" OR "quadruped*) AND ("manipulator" OR "robot* arm") AND ("dynamics" OR "kinematics" OR "task")
- (("quadruped" OR "legged") AND robot) AND locomotion AND manipulation

After collecting the results, a filtering process was conducted to remove duplicate entries. Additionally, works that solely involved simulation testing, lacked information about the hardware used, or did not provide explicit details about the motion planning approach were excluded from further consideration.

3   Quadruped Manipulators

In the last decades, quadruped robots have gained lots of attention from researchers because of their agility and versatility. Compared to wheeled/tracked robots, these can more easily perform locomotion in unpredictable and unstructured environments and overcome obstacles, like rocks or holes. In recent years, these robots have shown massive potential for real-world applications in areas such as inspection, education, construction surveillance, package delivery, and search and rescue (SaR) [14].

For some of the applications referred, there is no need for substantial manipulation capabilities; however, in other sectors, like agriculture, the possibility of interaction with the environment is a beneficial factor, allowing the expansion of the scope of activities in which quadruped robots can be applied.

3.1   Leg-Arm Approaches

One of the approaches institutions tried to use to overcome manipulation limitations was the leg-arm approach. This means that the legs are multi-modal and capable of some manipulation. When needed, the robots adjust their position so that a leg can reach the desired object.

ETH Zürich implemented this technique on ANYmal (quadruped robot developed by ANYbotics) so that the robot could press elevator buttons [40]. In this case, the robot does the manipulation while still, it cannot walk simultaneously. The manipulation capability is minimal, being restricted to space reachable by the leg. Xin et al. [35] made a similar implementation for pressing buttons, pipe inspection, and bottom sensing.[1] Other similar techniques were followed in [32, 38].

Hooks et al. [17] developed ALPHRED, a quadruped robot that transforms into a tripod or bipod for single-arm or dual-arm manipulation tasks, respectively. The intended application is package delivery, the tripod mode for pushing buttons (like doorbells), and the bipod mode for picking up and transporting boxes. Unlike the ETH example, this robot can walk and manipulate at the same time, a characteristic termed loco-manipulation. However, this change in the kinematic configuration brings considerable challenges to its center of mass (CoM) stabilization and overall system control. Another more complex example is the work done by Hebert et al. [19]. This robot has 7-DoF legs being its behavior more similar to a gorilla. In this case, the robot is capable of dextrous manipulation because the tools and other accessories are not always connected to the end of the limb. However, with legs with many DoF, the motion planner needs a complex optimization process to always give the best solution.[2]

Chen et al. [4] and Whitman et al. [34] used the same technique on a hexapod robot. By allowing two of the legs to do manipulation tasks, the system becomes a dual-arm quadruped manipulator. The implementation was tested to pick up

---

[1] Quadruped robot's foot posture for sensing and manipulation.
[2] RoboSimian: Four-Footed Robot.

and carry boxes lying above tables. Compared with the previously described implementations, this gives the robot more stability.

The leg-arm approach can be used for applications that do not need specific manipulations or specific tools. When the task is straightforward, like painting or cutting, the duality of the leg does not allow a complex end-effector because, above all, it has to be able to walk, so some friction and area of floor contact are restrictions to the end of the limb format. Therefore, in these cases, the most common solution passes through the addition of a robotic arm.

3.2   Robotic Arm Addition

Mobile manipulator is the name given to a system that integrates a robot manipulator with a mobile platform. When the mobile base is a quadruped robot, they can be called quadruped manipulators. A mobile platform has the ability to achieve large work areas but lacks manipulation capabilities, while robotic arms have high manipulation capabilities but are restricted to a fixed workstation. The combination of both (quadruped base and manipulator arm) brings a more advanced system with several advantages (reachability and maneuverability) and disadvantages, such as control complexity due to the high number of degrees of freedom (DoF) and the increased instability of the complete system. A higher number of DoF enables the robot to reach the target with several arm configurations/motions making the design/development of the system control a challenging task. The instability is caused by the arm movement that affects the CoM, moment of inertia, and other parameters that significantly impact the robot's motion control.

Some companies that commercialize quadruped robots started to develop a robotic arm add-on to integrate with their robots. The system was successfully applied in several scenarios, but scientific publications about their systems have yet to be published. That is the case of Boston Dynamics, which equipped Spot [9] with a five-DoF arm (Spot Arm) (1a) capable of opening doors [8], object maneuver/transportation [10] and even dancing [11]. Deep Robotics has also developed a robotic arm for Jueying X20 [26] quadruped robot (1b) used for humanitarian assistance in various task [7]. Finally, Unitree Robotics created the Z1, a 6-DoF robotic arm that can be integrated with some of their quadruped robots (1c) to complete complex tasks and explore various applications scenarios. The application presented was in a fire rescue scenario [28] where the robot (Aliengo) needed to open a door and move a lever.

The majority of the existing applications are made in laboratories, usually by integrating custom-made or commercialized robotic arms into quadruped robots. Some of these examples are referenced and detailed in the following sections.

4   Motion Planning

Due to increased scientific interest in the field, robots have improved their ability to carry out various complex, non-trivial tasks, including running, jumping,

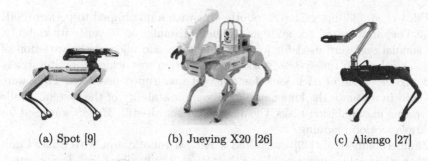

(a) Spot [9]   (b) Jueying X20 [26]   (c) Aliengo [27]

Fig. 1. Examples of commercialized quadruped manipulators

climbing stairs, and manipulating items. However, most of the time, each of these activities is handled separately, which significantly restricts the usage of robots in the actual world, despite simplifying their development. Robots may occasionally surpass humans in a particular task. Still, humans are much better at adapting and integrating actions to complete various jobs, as they can do multiple things simultaneously, like walking while manipulating an object. This makes it possible to carry out several tasks at once. In the past, robots were not capable of such things. However, research has been increasing in the last few years on developing robot controllers to perform several tasks simultaneously.

Besides multi-tasking, there are other difficulties that robots have to overcome, especially the ones with complex systems. Mobile manipulators, for instance, have to take into account the movement of their platform and different constraints depending on the intended objective during the motion planning stage. The robot can not collide with environmental obstacles. Its structure and operation limits must also be considered, like the joint and torque limitations, constraints due to the kinematics depending on the robot's structure, and constraints related to the task to be performed. Because of the high number of DoF that these robots have, they are kinematically redundant, which means that there are a variety of different ways for the manipulator's end-effector to achieve the same pose. This characteristic makes the algorithms more complex because of the infinite number of solutions. These are the main reasons why motion planning is the biggest challenge in achieving loco-manipulation. From the literature reviewed, two different approaches for motion planning of the global system (mobile platform + manipulator) [29] were found: (*i*) separate systems and (*ii*) combined systems.

4.1 Separate Systems (SS)

In this approach, the platform and the manipulator are considered different systems, which means the planning is first done in one and, with that information, the other is planned next. Using this method, the algorithms already used when the systems are separated can be applied here.

Ulloa et al. [33] integrated a robotic arm with a quadruped to perform SaR tasks. They first tested the systems through a simulation to verify its viability. The simulations were used for joint visualization and allowed the variation of the joint values, so the system workspace definition was achieved by iteratively changing the value of each joint for different quadruped positions. They were also used to evaluate the kinematic and dynamic stability of the system. While performing manipulation tasks, the quadruped stands still. *MoveIt* was used for the arm's motion planning.

Zimmermann et al. [39] integrated a Kinova robotic arm with Spot. Compared to others, this quadruped has a limitation, it only allows high-level control, which means that whole-body position/speed is the only possibility, being individual joint control not admissible. This characteristic limits the body movement, so the developers decided to follow a method that separates the body control from the robotic arm control. For the motion planning of the base, they made a simplified dynamic model of the combined system and tuned the parameters using experimental data. However, the control is done separately using a feedforward method. They treat the manipulator as an external force that the base controller has to compensate for. The controllers run in cycles so the base can adapt to the arm's movement.

Ma et al. [22] used reinforcement learning to control the ANYmal quadruped robot with a Kinova Jaco robotic arm, but by separating the system into two parts, it only learns the locomotion policy. The arm controller is implemented with model predictive control (MPC) because it allows the extraction of data needed for the base policy. While the arm is moving, the quadruped adjusts its position to keep the CoM stable.[3]

Guo et al. [15] used self-developed hardware, a quadruped robot with a 5 DoF arm. The vision module provides the target position for the end-effector to the path planning module. The value given to the manipulator's joints is a direct conversion from a 3D point using inverse kinematics (IK). All the manipulation procedure is done while the robot remains stationary.

After the visualization of the fire rescue video [28], it is easy to conclude that the implementation made by Unitree Robotics also followed an approach that viewed the system as two separate sub-systems. This assumption is made due to the fact that while walking, the manipulator stands still, in a resting position, and while performing manipulation tasks, the quadruped stays static, even the torso is not moved.

From the evaluation of the literature that used this approach, some conclusions were achieved: (*i*) a poor placement to one of the subsystems can make the final destination unreachable, (*ii*) an optimal solution to each one of the subsystems might not lead to a globally optimal solution, (*iii*) the control is simpler but does not utilize the system's full capabilities, (*iv*) mutual interferences between the quadruped and the arm are difficult to predict and therefore overcome and (*v*) using this approach, it is easier to obtain a stable robust solution.

---

[3] Combining Learning-based Locomotion with Model-based Manipulation for Legged Mobile Manipulators.

4.2   Combined Systems (CS)

Another approach is to consider the systems integration as a new complex system. This brings the possibility of doing multiple motion tasks at the same time. Manipulator control, torso posture adjustment, joint constraints, and environmental constraints can all be made simultaneously [3]. This approach is much more complex because the system has to deal with the coupling effects between the base and arm and deal with the unknown disturbance provoked by the manipulator.

Bellicoso et al. [1] focused their implementation on the contact forces that the manipulator introduces on the system. Instabilities and subsequent failures could occur if these interaction forces were unaccounted for, while assessing the system's stability. The authors used a whole-body controller (WBC) based on the inverse dynamics (ID), re-planned locomotion continuously using a receding-horizon optimization, and explicitly provided end-effector forces for the controller to track. They ensure the system's stability by using the Zero Moment Point (ZMP) stability criterion, which stabilizes the system by approximating the robot's dynamic model as the one of an inverted pendulum.[4] A similar implementation was done by Ewen et al. [12]. Peng et al. [25] also used WBC based on the kinematics and used the minimization of the sum of the squared joint torques as the objective function.

Hamed et al. [16] developed a controller for dynamical models of quadrupedal robots based on MPC, quadratic programming (QP), and virtual constraints to generate and stabilize locomotion patterns in real-time. The authors also used an inverted pendulum approximation to ensure CoM stability. Morlando et al. [24] and Mittal et al. [23] used similar approaches. Cheng et al. [5] also used MPC in their implementation but developed a feedback system to reduce the computational cost and update rate.

Sleiman et al. [31] proposed a whole-body planning that integrates locomotion and manipulation tasks by formulating a single optimal control problem using MPC. The proposed model is based on the robot's centroidal dynamics, manipulated-object dynamics, and the kinematics of the whole system. The robotic arm is used as a tail to balance the system.[5] Later, Chiu et al. [6] continued their work by updating the model so that the planner would provide collision-free trajectories. The used approach slightly increases the computational complexity of the planner. Jang et al. [18] also used a similar approach with a quadruped manipulator to inspect underground pipelines.

On the other hand, Li et al. [21] implemented a WBC based on the system's ID and used a hierarchical optimization algorithm for task selection. Their system could respond to external disturbances and perform the tracking job even when a precise root dynamics model and the dynamic features of the handled item are undefined.

---

[4] Articulated Locomotion and Manipulation for ANYmal.
[5] A Unified MPC Framework for Whole-Body Dynamic Locomotion and Manipulation.

Yao et al. [37] included reinforcement learning in a MPC approach, using the same system as [33]. The policy is trained while different forces are being applied to the robotic arm, which gives the possibility to change the robotic arm used without having to change the policy implementation.

Boston Dynamics also used a combined systems approach. In their videos [8,10,11] is clear that the manipulation and locomotion movement can be done simultaneously. However, studies were never published about the specific methods used.

Other solutions that created two different modes of operation for the system formed by the quadruped and the manipulator were found in the literature. Xin et al. [36] created a manipulation and a loco-manipulation mode. In the manipulation mode, a hierarchical quadratic programming (HQP) method is used to control the overall system based on the rigid-body dynamics of the robot. This is used in a scenario where the robot has to perform manipulation while standing still. In the loco-manipulation mode, the system is seen as a combination of two sub-systems, the locomotion is controlled with the same HPQ method, using the full dynamic model, but the arm motion is controlled using a proportional-derivative (PD) controller based on the IK. This separation was made because the locomotion and manipulation had the same priority in the HQP, so they opted to separate the modes instead of implementing a more complex system.

Ferrolho et al. [13] made a similar approach by implementing the teleoperated and autonomous modes. The teleoperated is the "locomotion only" mode where the robot moves with the robotic arm in a pre-defined resting position that does not affect the platform's balance. The autonomous mode was used for the manipulation tasks and applied a WBC, with the robot not moving, only adjusting its position to compensate for the alterations of the CoM position.[6]

This approach uses the system's full capabilities allowing complex movements but comes with several significant drawbacks: (i) it requires much more computing power and energy, (ii) the paths generated are not optimized, so the system often needs additional optimization algorithms, (iii) if not properly implemented, solutions are more unstable and less robust to interferences and (iv) it is harder to achieve a granted robust solution, without causing instability in the robot.

4.3 Discussion

Through this, it can be concluded that the system's framework architecture usually follows the diagram of Fig. 2 when a CS approach is chosen. When an SS approach is used, the architecture follows two similar diagrams, one for the body and another for the arm.

The mark "*" in the optimization block means that this is an optional part and is sometimes already included in the motion-planning methods. The inputs (desired position or motion) and joint values depend on the robot model used. If

---

[6] Robust Robot Loco-Manipulation for Industrial Applications.

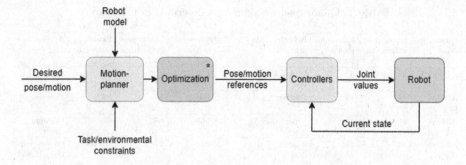

Fig. 2. Simplified framework block diagram

the kinematic model is used, the values produced are joint positions calculated through the desired end-effector position, which can be used later to calculate the needed velocity for each joint (through the Jacobian). On the other hand, if the model is made with robot dynamics, the controller sends torque/voltage commands achieved by the desired input motion. Commonly, the model is based on both dynamics and kinematics.

5   Kinematic Configuration

In robotics, kinematic configurations refer to the positions and orientations of the various parts of a robotic system. The number of DoF and joint types characterize these configurations. All the joints used were revolute for the examples found in the literature. This choice increases the difficulty in motion planning because of the high number of different configuration possibilities for the same tool position, e.g., elbow up and elbow down.

In Table 1 is a compilation of the systems in the reviewed literature. It has information about the quadruped robots used, their weight, and maximum payload. The table focuses on the number of DoF, weight, and continuous payload of the integrated robotic arm. It also indicates the motion planning approach and the applications for which the system was used.

By evaluating the data, it can be concluded that the manipulator has about 20% of the quadruped's weight and does not typically exceed 50% of its maximum payload. Since the arms used were typically commercially available models, the number of DoF was not chosen with the tasks in mind, but depends on the arm's available configuration. However, the number of DoF is related to the motion planning approach used. The standard method for robotic arms with a high DoF number (DoF $\geq$ 5) is the SS because it has a much simpler implementation. For arms with a lower number of DoF, the choice tended to a CS approach to allow the body to perform the movement in specific directions, allowing the system to have more redundancy as it would have if an arm with more DoF was attached. Regarding the payload of the robotic arm, the values are less than 50% of the quadruped's cargo. However, no significant conclusions about how the payload might have been chosen were obtained from the data acquired.

Table 1. Quadruped manipulators described in literature

Quadruped robot	Quadruped's weight (kg)	Maximum payload (kg)	Robotic arm	DoF	Arm's weight (kg)	Continuous payload (kg)	Planning approach	Applications
A1 [33]	12	5	WidowX 250	6	2.63	0.25	SS	SaR
Aliengo [28]	21.5	13	Unitree Z1	6	4.3	2	SS	Fire rescue
Aliengo [21]	21.5	13	ViperX 300	5	3.63	0.75	CS	Opening /doors
ANYmal [1]/[22]	30	15	Kinova Jaco 2	6	4.4	1.6	SS/CS	Object carrying and pulling
ANYmal C [31]	30	15	DynaArm (Custom-made)	4	–	7	CS	Object transport /manuever
Self-designed [36]	25	–	Kinova Jaco 2	6	4.4	1.6	CS	–
Self-designed [15]	205	–	Self-designed	5	35	24	SS	Grasping
Spot [39]	32.7	14	Kinova Gen3	7	8	4	SS	Dynamic grasping
Spot [9]	32.7	14	Spot Arm	5	8	5	CS	Object transport /manuever
Vision 60 [16]	51	10	Kinova Mico 2	4	3.8	5.2	CS	-

6 Conclusions

This article summarizes the current state of the art of quadruped manipulators. From the papers reviewed, two alternatives were evident. One is to use the already available legs to perform manipulation, but this restricts the movement range and the end-effector's shape and characteristics. As the authors were not interested in those types of solutions this topic wasn't discussed in detail. They were, however, interested in significant versatility in manipulation, which was proved possible by adding a robotic arm into the quadrupedal base. This alternative allows much more movement flexibility, therefore those implementations were carefully analyzed. Following the analysis of those systems, it is straightforward to conclude that motion planning is the biggest challenge in achieving an efficient and stable quadruped manipulator.

When the legs are used for manipulation, the hardest part is to keep the robot balanced as the area of contact with the floor is reduced. If the manipulation task requires blunt moves, stability is highly affected. The manipulation flexibility is also reduced because of the fewer possible forms of the leg's end-effector.

With the addition of a robotic arm, the whole system will also be unbalanced but with less intensity. In the literature, two methods have been presented to implement motion planning on quadruped robots with appendices. The first one is to consider the system as two separate subsystems, which simplifies the planning but does not exploit the system's full capabilities. The other one is to evaluate the system as a complex one and use the whole-body model to do the motion planning. In this approach, the robot is treated as a whole, and the motion of each link and joint is analyzed in the context of the entire system. This allows the robot to take advantage of the interactions between its different parts and coordinate its movements more efficiently and effectively. Despite being more complex, this type of planning allows much more motion flexibility.

Other topics accessed were the kinematic configuration adopted in different applications found in the existing literature. The evaluation concluded that most of the developed works opted to use an assembled commercial robotic arm with a controlling interface included. Only one development used a self-designed manipulator. However, all of them considered that the arm should be lightweight (about 20% of the quadruped's weight). Regarding the number of DoF, the only conclusion is that with a low number, the SS method results in substantial movement restrictions.

References

1. Bellicoso, C.D., et al.: Alma - articulated locomotion and manipulation for a torque-controllable robot. In: Proceedings - IEEE International Conference on Robotics and Automation 2019-May, pp. 8477–8483 (2019). https://doi.org/10.1109/ICRA.2019.8794273

2. Biswal, P., Mohanty, P.K.: Development of quadruped walking robots: a review. Ain Shams Eng. J. **12**, 2017–2031 (2021). https://doi.org/10.1016/J.ASEJ.2020.11.005

3. Chai, H., et al.: A survey of the development of quadruped robots: joint configuration, dynamic locomotion control method and mobile manipulation approach. Biomim. Intell. Robot. **2**(1), 100029 (2022). https://doi.org/10.1016/J.BIROB.2021.100029

4. Chen, T., et al.: Design and control of a novel leg-arm multiplexing mobile operational hexapod robot. IEEE Robot. Autom. Lett. **7**, 382–389 (2022). https://doi.org/10.1109/LRA.2021.3127639

5. Cheng, J., Abi-Farraj, F., Farshidian, F., Hutter, M.: Haptic teleoperation of high-dimensional robotic systems using a feedback mpc framework. In: 2022 IEEE/RSJ International Conference on Intelligent Robots and Systems (IROS), pp. 6197–6204 (2022). https://doi.org/10.1109/IROS47612.2022.9981290

6. Chiu, J.R., Sleiman, J.P., Mittal, M., Farshidian, F., Hutter, M.: A collision-free mpc for whole-body dynamic locomotion and manipulation. In: Proceedings - IEEE International Conference on Robotics and Automation, pp. 4686–4693 (2022). https://doi.org/10.1109/ICRA46639.2022.9812280

7. DeepRobotics: Jueying x20: Define a new boundary for quadruped robot industry applications (2021). www.youtube.com/watch?v=w5XCTZjG2qY. Accessed 28 Dec 2022

8. Dynamics, B.: Hey buddy, can you give me a hand? (2018). www.youtube.com/watch?v=fUyU3lKzoio. Accessed 28 Dec 2022

9. Dynamics, B.: Spot *circledR* - the agile mobile robot (2018). www.bostondynamics.com/products/spot. Accessed 28 Dec 2022

10. Dynamics, B.: Spot's got an arm! (2021). www.youtube.com/watch?v=6Zbhvaac68Y&t=1s. Accessed 28 Dec 2022

11. Dynamics, B.: Spot's on it (2021). www.youtube.com/watch?v=7atZfX85nd4. Accessed 28 Dec 2022

12. Ewen, P., Sleiman, J.P., Chen, Y., Lu, W.C., Hutter, M., Vasudevan, R.: Generating continuous motion and force plans in real-time for legged mobile manipulation. In: Proceedings - IEEE International Conference on Robotics and Automation 2021-May, pp. 4933–4939 (2021). https://doi.org/10.48550/arxiv.2104.11685

13. Ferrolho, H., Ivan, V., Merkt, W., Havoutis, I., Vijayakumar, S.: Roloma: robust loco-manipulation for quadruped robots with arms (2022). https://doi.org/10.48550/arxiv.2203.01446

14. George, J.: 5 real-world applications of quadruped robots (2022). www.robotics247.com/article/5_real_world_applications_of_quadruped_robots. Accessed 28 Dec 2022

15. Guo, J., et al.: Research on the autonomous system of the quadruped robot with a manipulator to realize leader-following, object recognition, navigation and operation. IET Cyber-Syst. Robot. 1 (2022). https://doi.org/10.1049/CSY2.12069

16. Hamed, K.A., Kim, J., Pandala, A.: Quadrupedal locomotion via event-based predictive control and qp-based virtual constraints. IEEE Robot. Autom. Lett. 5(3), 4463–4470 (2020). https://doi.org/10.1109/LRA.2020.3001471

17. Hooks, J., et al.: Alphred: a multi-modal operations quadruped robot for package delivery applications. IEEE Robot. Autom. Lett. 5, 5409–5416 (2020). https://doi.org/10.1109/LRA.2020.3007482

18. Jang, Y., Seol, W., Lee, K., Kim, K.S., Kim, S.: Development of quadruped robot for inspection of underground pipelines in nuclear power plants. Electr. Lett. 58, 234–236 (2022). https://doi.org/10.1049/ELL2.12414

19. Karumanchi, S., et al.: Team robosimian: Semi-autonomous mobile manipulation at the 2015 darpa robotics challenge finals. Springer Tracts Adv. Robot. 121, 191–235 (2018). https://doi.org/10.1007/978-3-319-74666-1_6/FIGURES/17

20. Kashiri, N., Baccelliere, L., Muratore, L., Laurenzi, A., Ren, Z., Hoffman, E.M., Kamedula, M., Rigano, G.F., Malzahn, J., Cordasco, S., Guria, P., Margan, A., Tsagarakis, N.G.: Centauro: a hybrid locomotion and high power resilient manipulation platform. IEEE Robot. Autom. Lett. 4(2), 1595–1602 (2019). https://doi.org/10.1109/LRA.2019.2896758

21. Li, J., et al.: Whole-body control for a torque-controlled legged mobile manipulator. Actuators 11, 304 (2022). https://doi.org/10.3390/ACT11110304

22. Ma, Y., Farshidian, F., Miki, T., Lee, J., Hutter, M.: Combining learning-based locomotion policy with model-based manipulation for legged mobile manipulators. IEEE Robot. Autom. Lett. 7, 2377–2384 (2022). https://doi.org/10.48550/arxiv.2201.03871

23. Mittal, M., Hoeller, D., Farshidian, F., Hutter, M., Garg, A.: Articulated object interaction in unknown scenes with whole-body mobile manipulation. In: IEEE International Conference on Intelligent Robots and Systems 2022-October, pp. 1647–1654 (2021). https://doi.org/10.1109/IROS47612.2022.9981779. arXiv:2103.10534v2

24. Morlando, V., Selvaggio, M., Ruggiero, F.: Nonprehensile object transportation with a legged manipulator. In: Proceedings - IEEE International Conference on Robotics and Automation, pp. 6628–6634 (2022). https://doi.org/10.1109/ICRA46639.2022.9811810

25. Peng, K., Haibin, M., Lei, Y., Wenfu, X.: Whole body collaborative planning method for legged locomotion manipulation system in operation process. In: 2022 IEEE International Conference on Robotics and Biomimetics (ROBIO), pp. 2098–2103 (2022). https://doi.org/10.1109/ROBIO55434.2022.10011971

26. Robotics, D.: Jueying x20 (2022). www.deeprobotics.cn/en/products.html. Accessed 28 Dec 2022
27. Robotics, U.: Aliengo (2020). www.shop.unitree.com/products/aliengo. Accessed 28 Dec 2022
28. Robotics, U.: Unitree robotics aliengo + z1 for fire rescue (2022). www.youtube.com/watch?v=7CVwGY65In8. Accessed 28 Dec 2022
29. Sandakalum, T., Ang, M.H.: Motion planning for mobile manipulators-a systematic review. Machines **10** (2022). https://doi.org/10.3390/MACHINES10020097
30. Siciliano, B., Khatib, O.: Springer Handbook of Robotics. Springer (2016). https://doi.org/10.1007/978-3-319-32552-1/COVER
31. Sleiman, J.P., Farshidian, F., Minniti, M.V., Hutter, M.: A unified mpc framework for whole-body dynamic locomotion and manipulation. IEEE Robot. Autom. Lett. **6**, 4688–4695 (2021). https://doi.org/10.48550/arxiv.2103.00946
32. Tsvetkov, Y., Ramamoorthy, S.: A novel design and evaluation of a dactylus-equipped quadruped robot for mobile manipulation. In: 2022 IEEE/RSJ International Conference on Intelligent Robots and Systems (IROS), pp. 1633–1638 (2022). https://doi.org/10.1109/IROS47612.2022.9982229
33. Ulloa, C.C., Domínguez, D., Cerro, J.D., Barrientos, A.: A mixed-reality teleoperation method for high-level control of a legged-manipulator robot. Sensors **22**, 8146 22, 8146 (2022). https://doi.org/10.3390/S22218146
34. Whitman, J., Su, S., Coros, S., Ansari, A., Choset, H.: Generating gaits for simultaneous locomotion and manipulation. In: IEEE International Conference on Intelligent Robots and Systems 2017-September, pp. 2723–2729 (2017). https://doi.org/10.1109/IROS.2017.8206099
35. Xin, G., Smith, J., Rytz, D., Wolfslag, W., Lin, H.C., Mistry, M.: Bounded haptic teleoperation of a quadruped robot's foot posture for sensing and manipulation. In: Proceedings - IEEE International Conference on Robotics and Automation, pp. 1431–1437 (2019). https://doi.org/10.48550/arxiv.1912.07315
36. Xin, G., Zeng, F., Qin, K.: Loco-manipulation control for arm-mounted quadruped robots: dynamic and kinematic strategies. Machines **10**, 719 (2022). https://doi.org/10.3390/MACHINES10080719/S1
37. Yao, Q., et al.: A transferable legged mobile manipulation framework based on disturbance predictive control. In: 2022 IEEE International Conference on Robotics and Biomimetics, ROBIO 2022, pp. 2093–2097 (2022). https://doi.org/10.1109/ROBIO55434.2022.10011816. arXiv:2203.03391v1
38. Zhang, G., Ma, S., Li, Y.: Dynamic modelling and motion planning for the non-prehensile manipulation and locomotion tasks of the quadruped robot. In: 2018 IEEE/RSJ International Conference on Intelligent Robots and Systems (IROS), pp. 1–9 (2018). https://doi.org/10.1109/IROS.2018.8593712
39. Zimmermann, S., Poranne, R., Coros, S.: Go fetch! - dynamic grasps using boston dynamics spot with external robotic arm. In: Proceedings - IEEE International Conference on Robotics and Automation 2021-May, pp. 1170–1176 (2021). https://doi.org/10.1109/ICRA48506.2021.9561835
40. Zürich, E.: Anymal using an elevator (2017). www.youtube.com/watch?v=gM1z60aeunU. Accessed 28 Dec 2022

Knowledge Discovery and Business Intelligence

Pollution Emission Patterns of Transportation in Porto, Portugal Through Network Analysis

Thiago Andrade[1,3](✉) ⓘ, Nirbhaya Shaji[1,3] ⓘ, Rita P. Ribeiro[1,3] ⓘ,
and João Gama[1,2] ⓘ

[1] INESC TEC, Faculty of Engineering, University of Porto, 4200-465 Porto, Portugal
{thiago.a.silva,nirbhaya.shaji}@inesctec.pt
[2] Faculty of Economics, University of Porto, 4200-464 Porto, Portugal
[3] Faculty of Sciences, University of Porto, 4169-007 Porto, Portugal

Abstract. Over the past few decades, road transportation emissions have increased. Vehicles are among the most significant sources of pollutants in urban areas. As such, several studies and public policies emerged to address the issue. Estimating greenhouse emissions and air quality over space and time is crucial for human health and mitigating climate change. In this study, we demonstrate that it is feasible to utilize raw GPS data to measure regional pollution levels. By applying feature engineering techniques and using a microscopic emissions model to calculate vehicle-specific power (VSP) and various specific pollutants, we identify areas with higher emission levels attributable to a fleet of taxis in Porto, Portugal. Additionally, we conduct network analysis to uncover correlations between emission levels and the structural characteristics of the transportation network. These findings can potentially identify emission clusters based on the network's connectivity and contribute to developing an emission inventory for an urban city like Porto.

Keywords: Road emissions · Microscopic emissions model · Vehicle-specific power · Transportation · Climate change · Greenhouse gas · Air pollution · Network analysis · Mobility patterns

1 Introduction

The rapid expansion of urban areas and economic growth worldwide has severely impacted road transport emissions [1,2] which are associated with significant health risks [3–5]. Although the EU's transportation sector emissions steadily increased from 2013 to 2019, they decreased significantly around 2020 due to the COVID-19 pandemic. However, estimates of emissions in 2021 indicate a rebound in transport emissions last year of 7.7% [6]. The same happened in the US: after the emissions fell sharply in 2020 as a result of the pandemic, the values went back up in 2021 according to a CBO recent report [7].

© The Author(s), under exclusive license to Springer Nature Switzerland AG 2023
N. Moniz et al. (Eds.): EPIA 2023, LNAI 14115, pp. 215–226, 2023.
https://doi.org/10.1007/978-3-031-49008-8_17

Air pollution is estimated to cause over 1,200 premature deaths yearly among those under 18 across the EEA's 32 member countries. Air pollution damages health during childhood and increases the risk of disease in later life, according to the 2023 EEA 'Air pollution, and children's health briefing [8]. Children and adolescents are particularly vulnerable to air pollution because their bodies, organs, and immune systems are still developing.

Furthermore, the IPCC's AR6 Synthesis Report on Climate Change 2023 [1] identifies emissions from the transport, industry, and building sectors as the biggest challenge to achieving net zero CO_2 emissions compared to other sectors. It proposes sustainable land use and urban planning as one of the three pathways towards net zero CO_2 by 2100. Detecting and monitoring emissions in urban areas is crucial particularly in countries like Portugal with increasing urban populations that can make cities acting act as pollution clusters.

One of the biggest challenges land use planners and policymakers face in this regard is having methods to understand the current effects of road transport on air pollution and to evaluate the impact after an intervention. A proven approach is to build an Emissions Inventory (EI) of a region, indicating the number of air pollutants in the atmosphere during a year or other period [9,10]. EIs have shown to be an essential input to mathematical models that estimate air pollution [9]. EIs also help understand vehicle emissions' temporal and spatial distribution at the landscape scale. It has allowed the study of the influence of site-specific factors on urban road emissions [11].

This paper explores how emission models can be used along with road network analysis for the development of an EI framework for the city of Porto. It highlights the application of network science techniques to analyze emissions in an urban environment. Alongside exploring how to map road emissions across the city's transportation network, we also demonstrate how network structure matrices, which assess the importance of players solely on their position, can provide valuable insights into identifying high-emission clusters within the city.

The paper is organized as follows. Section 2 briefly reviews the related works in this area and the city decomposition methods we used to map the emissions over the study region. Section 3 explains the data set and the methods used in detail. Section 4 describes the experimental setup and discusses the factors that may have constrained the study. Conclusions and suggestions for further research are presented in Sect. 5.

2   Related Work

A previous study [12] using data from Porto, Portugal, examined the impact of traffic emissions on air pollution and its harmful effects on historical landmarks. The study monitored the levels of pollutants for 40 days during the autumn-winter season of 2008 and collected samples in December of the same year to determine the damage to the buildings. It was discovered that traffic emissions were the primary source of polycyclic aromatic hydrocarbons (PAHs) in the air, and the health risk analysis showed that the estimated values of lifetime lung cancer risks exceeded the health-based guideline level. The study confirmed that historical monuments in urban areas could act as passive repositories for air pollutants, making them interesting spots for further research on the effects of urban air pollution.

Manizales, Colombia, was the area of study for Gonzalez et al.'s [13]. They worked on an emissions inventory using the Vehicle Specific Power (VSP) model [14] to get realistic emission estimates for creating a baseline in atmospheric modeling and urban air quality indexes. The VSP method was shown to be effective in detecting the high emissions in the city as the method uses road inclination to measure pollution. The authors conclude that this happens due to the unique characteristics dominated by a complex topography with hills that put more stress on the vehicle engines, which results in higher fuel emissions.

Global Positioning System (GPS) trajectory data from a taxi fleet were analyzed with the aim of predicting air pollution emissions for Singapore [15]. The proposal is for the quantification of instantaneous drive cycle parameters in high spatiotemporal resolution. The authors were able to identify highly localized areas of elevated emissions levels. The idea is to use the method as a complement to traditional emission estimates in emerging cities and countries where reliable fine-grained urban air quality data is not easily available.

Some researchers were interested in studying the structural properties of complex relational networks. In [16], the work focuses on how centrality is relevant to various spatial factors affecting human life and behaviors in cities. The authors present a comprehensive study of centrality distributions over geographic networks of urban streets using five different measures of centrality: degree, closeness, betweenness, straightness, and information. They compared these measures over various samples of different world cities. These samples are represented as primal geographic graphs, i.e., valued graphs defined by metric rather than topological distance where intersections are turned into nodes and streets into edges.

In this study, we explore how real-world road transport data can derive insights aiding in creating an urban EI by constructing a graph with nodes as road intersections and its edges weighted with the emissions. We employ two methods to identify emission indicators from real-world traffic data: Vehicle-specific power (VSP) [14] and Microscopic Instantaneous Emissions (MIE) [17]. Our work differs from previous ones concerning the mixture of MIE and VSP models while leveraging network analysis to identify the pollution hot spots over a region.

3   Data and Methods

The data we used is a subset of the dataset available at Kaggle [18], which contains 1,704,759 trajectories from 442 taxis during the period from 2013-07-01 to 2014-06-30 over the metropolitan region of Porto, Portugal. For the work described in this paper, we used a subset of trips from Porto inner city over the duration of the whole month of August 2013, containing 4,736,978 points organized in 119,474 trajectories over 429 vehicles. The data prepossessing and filtering are described in detail in Sect. 3.1. Later, using OSMnx [19] and OSM,[1] these trajectories and their corresponding emissions are map-matched over the city of Porto and a road network structure is constructed with vertices (nodes) as the intersections and edges as the roads connecting them. For calculating the emission from road trips, we use VSP and MIE. While VSP is a generalized method frequently used to map instantaneous vehicle engine power to emission estimates, MIE gives pollutant-specific microscopic emissions. Finally, we analyze the network structure and the emission behaviors over the network to understand road emissions in the area of study.

The features from the original dataset that we used for this work are the following: TRIP ID—a unique identifier for each trip; TAXI ID—a unique identifier for each taxi; TIMESTAMP—a Unix Timestamp (in seconds) identifying the trip's start; and POLYLINE—a list of GPS coordinates (i.e. WGS84 format) mapped as a string; this list contains one pair of coordinates for every 15 s of the trip; the last list item corresponds to the trip's destination, while the first one represents its start.

3.1   Data Pre-processing

The dataset, which can be found in detail at [20,21] for a similar use case, was cleaned to remove outliers and noise, following the methods used by [22,23]. Unlike other datasets with variable granularity, here the data sampling rate is regular through all the data points, having an interval of 15 s between the points.

Data Cleaning To obtain the trajectories, we need to get the values from the column 'POLYLINE' in the taxi dataset. Each row contains the GPS coordinates we will need to form the trajectories to compute the emissions.

The first step is the preprocessing task that includes, among other activities, the data cleaning process where we perform outliers and noise removal [22,23]. We look for duplicate data in the dataset and remove it. We also look for null data where we cannot use the latitude or longitude to create new features in the next step. Due to the influence of GPS signal loss and data drift, several unwanted points show up in the trajectories during the data acquisition. To delete these inconsistent data and improve data reliability a median smoothing filter is applied to each set of five GPS points to remove the noise [24].

Feature Extraction For the taxi data, we used the latitude, longitude, and timestamp to generate new features (speed, acceleration, and road inclination) that are further used to calculate the VSP and the MIE emission values [21].

Vehicle Specific Power (VSP) is conventionally defined as instantaneous vehicle engine power. It has been widely utilized to reveal the impact of vehicle operating conditions on emission and energy consumption estimates dependent

---

[1] https://www.openstreetmap.org/.

upon speed, roadway grade, and acceleration or deceleration based on the vehicle operation [14], as shown in the formula (1).

$$\mathrm{VSP} = v[1.1a + 9.81\sin(\arctan(grade)) + 0.132] + 0.000302v^3 \qquad (1)$$

where VSP is vehicle specific power $[KW/ton]$; v is vehicle speed $[m/s]$ each second; a is acceleration $(+)$ or deceleration $(-)$ $[m/s^2]$ each second; and $grade$ is terrain gradient $[\pm\%]$. The elevation ($grade$) for the data points was obtained using Open-Elevation API.[2]

The calculation of VSP allows for obtaining the vehicle's power distribution throughout a trip. To ease the visualization and the analysis, it is then possible to group VSP points into 14 classes of required power, as shown in table "Energy range distribution" from the paper [25]. This power range division allows vehicle fuel consumption and emissions mapping according to the VSP category as done by [25]. This work uses VSP modes as an indicator of vehicle emission, with a higher VSP mode corresponding to higher emission potential.

Microscopic Instantaneous Emissions (MIE) Model we also employ a second approach for microscopically calculating the instantaneous emissions. We used the formula proposed by [17] that analyses every pair of points in the trajectories dataset and consider four types of pollutants: Carbon Dioxide (CO_2), Nitrogen Oxides (NO_x), Particulate Matter (PM), and Volatile Organic Compounds (VOC). The model uses as a reference table a group of values obtained from an extensive experiment with different types of vehicles and categories, including the fuel type (Petrol, Diesel, Liquefied Petroleum Gas (LPG)). The following formula (2) is used to calculate the instantaneous microscopic emissions $E_p^{j,u}$ of pollutant (j) (any of the four types of pollutants) from the vehicle's (u) speed (s_p) and acceleration (a_p) at point (p). The values for the emission factors (f) come from the reference table "Emission functions for the 2010 fleet of urban traffic" in the paper [17].

$$E_p^{j,u} = f_1^{j,u} + f_2^{j,u}s_p + f_3^{j,u}s_p^2 + f_4^{j,u}a_p + f_5^{j,u}a_p^2 + f_6^{j,u}s_pa_p \qquad (2)$$

while for the pollutants CO_2 and PM, the acceleration is neglected. For NO_x and VOC, the emission factors must consider acceleration with values smaller, greater, or equal to $-0.5\,m/s^2$.

Portuguese Fleet by Fuel Type According to the Microscopic Instantaneous Emissions (MIE) model, the vehicle's fuel type is one of the main factors for emissions. To have more fidelity in the results, we obtained a dataset from the Portuguese official statistics agency (INE/PORDATA)[3] that contains the values of these components along the recent years (from 2010 to 2020). We assign the

---

[2] https://open-elevation.com/.

[3] https://www.pordata.pt/en/portugal/motor+vehicles+in+circulation+total+ and+by+type+of+fuel+used-3101.

fuel type to each car proportionally in the dataset for 2013, which is the matching year of our taxi fleet dataset. In this way, we set 60.5% of the taxi fuel types to be diesel oil, 38.6% as gasoline, and joined the rest of 0.7% from LPG and 0.2% from others as a single category to represent both LPG and others (can include electrical) with 0.9%. Although the dataset represents the whole country data, we used it as a generalization for the city of Porto as it is the second largest city and has the second larger fleet, thus, we can assume is roughly following the data distribution for the whole dataset.

3.2   Road Transportation and Emission Network

As our idea is to compute the emissions from vehicles that are constrained in a road, the strategy of map matching the GPS logged points with the most probable street is fair and used in the literature [15]. To perform this task, we used a Python library called Open Street Maps Network (OSMnx) [19] jointly with the Open Street Maps (OSM)[4] collaborative project. Based on this idea, we snap the points to the closest road returned from the libraries and use the values for each road to calculate the emissions in each of them.

A network structure consists of nodes and edges, where nodes represent the objects to analyze while edges represent the relationships between those objects. For this particular scenario, the OSMnx [19] can be seen as an extra layer for the OSM where it converts the roads and their junctions into a multigraph representation where the vertices (V) are the road junctions/intersections, and the edges (E) are the roads connecting them.

Before entering into details of the analysis method, it is important to clarify a few network terminologies.

Definition 1. A network is a graph $G = (V, E)$ where $V = \{v_1, v_2, ..., v_n\}$, is the set of vertices (intersections) and $e \in E$ is an edge between any two vertices (a road). An adjacency matrix A defines the connectivity of G, $A_{ij} = 1$ if v_i and v_j are connected, else $A_{ij} = 0$ [16].

Definition 2. A homogeneous network is a network $G = (V, E)$, where each node $v_i \in V$ belongs to the same type and each edge $e_{ij} \in E$ also belongs to the same type [16].

Definition 3. An attribute network can be defined as $G = (V, E, A, F)$ where V is the set of vertices, E is the set of edges, A is the adjacency matrix, and ith row of F denotes the k dimensional attribute vector of node i [16].

The network centrality measures are among the most widely used indices based on network data [16]. They generally reflect a unit's prominence; this may be its structural power, status, prestige, or visibility in different substantive settings. In this work, we have focused on three of the most important centrality measures: degree centrality, closeness centrality, and betweenness centrality.

---

[4] https://www.openstreetmap.org/.

Degree centrality is a network metric that measures how many direct neighbors a node has. It is the number of connections a node has to other nodes, and the degree distribution is the probability distribution of these degrees over the whole network.

Closeness centrality is a network metric that measures the closeness of a node to all other nodes in the network. In other words, it measures how easily a node can access all other nodes in the network. A node with high closeness centrality is considered to be more central to the network because it can reach other nodes more quickly and efficiently than a node with low closeness centrality.

Betweenness centrality is a network metric that measures the degree to which a node acts as a bridge or mediator between other nodes in the network. It quantifies the number of shortest paths between pairs of nodes in the network that pass through a given node. A node with high betweenness centrality plays a critical role in maintaining the connectivity of the network because it lies on many of the shortest paths between other nodes. Removing a node with high betweenness centrality from the network can significantly disrupt the flow of information or resources between other nodes.

We calculate the road emission levels from raw GPS data by summing all the emissions in a given edge (road) between two nodes (intersection) and then compute the network metrics.

4   Experimental Results

This section presents the outcomes of the study. Initially, in Sect. 4.1, we delve into the insights gained from mapping emissions across city roads. The road network is created with nodes as road intersections and edges as roads connecting them as described previously in Sect. 3.2. Later in Sect. 4.2, we explore how these mapping can aid in identifying properties of the road network structure that indicate higher emission regions or roads.

4.1   Emissions over Porto

As the original data could be seen as a time series where each day is transformed into one observation, a subset of trips from Porto's inner city over the duration of a day was used for the examples in this experiment. These also helped faster data processing while using Gephi for the network analysis. The final data has 3,342 trajectories from 398 different vehicles for the day 2013-08-01.

Figure 1 shows the emission values obtained from the VSP and MIE methods. As expected, the MIE has a level of detail for each of the pollutants resulting in a more specific scenario for each studied area. Conversely, VSP depicts the pollution levels in a broader way, disregarding the particularities of the pollutants.

Although the techniques used to analyze emissions may differ, it is evident from the visual results (cf. Fig. 1) that roads with higher emissions share a commonality across the city for various pollutants and methodologies. In the case of CO_2 emissions, one can notice two main roads with maximum emission values

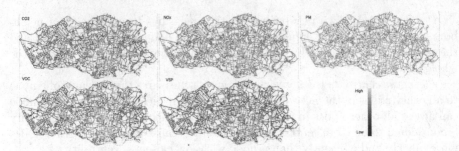

Fig. 1. Emissions calculated using MIE (four first images from top left to bottom right) and VSP (bottom center) models for 2013-08-01.

(yellow) on the city ring. The inner city has more data ranging on medium emission (green values), and the peripheral areas are low CO_2 emission areas (blue). Similarly, for the NO_x values, we see most of the data with medium emissions (green) while the city ring has high emissions (yellow). For the PM emissions, we see higher levels (yellow) in the inner city (inside of the ring) as well as the road that connects to the airport (yellow portion lined on top towards north-west direction). The rest of the area is medium (green), with very few areas with low-emission roads (blue). Finally, for the VOC, the values are similar to the CO_2 with a few more roads with high emissions (yellow) in the inner city. The VSP produces emission distribution results over the city that are very similar to those of MIE methods, with comparable contrast. The inner city shows a clear pattern with higher emission values with the highlight of a large part of the road that goes by the river (southeast) in yellow and green colors. The peripheral parts have the lowest values with the exception of the green/yellow part of the city ring that falls over the highway that connects Porto city with Porto airport (yellow portion lined on top towards north-west direction).

4.2   Road Network Analysis

The road emission network comprises 1,525 nodes (intersections) connected by 1,157 edges (or roads). Figure 2 shows images of five different types of emissions over the Porto inner city network. The nodes in the network signify intersections, while the edges represent the roads connecting them. The edge length in the image is proportional to the actual edge length. The nodes differ in color and size, representing their respective closeness and betweenness centrality. The edge color represents the emission value on that edge/road. The color scale for node closeness and edge emission is purple (low) to orange (high).

In Fig. 2, closeness and betweenness centrality of nodes in network metrics provide information on the network structure. They are independent of the emission values displayed by the edge color.

The network section with more prominent orange nodes (indicating high closeness and betweenness centrality) is mainly connected by green to orange edges. This suggests that roads with higher emission values surround the network's most central nodes/intersections. Almost all of the higher centrality nodes fall on the north part of the city along the highway connecting the city. In a way, higher centrality indicates higher importance of the intersection, especially in the case of a road network where commuters often prefer the shortest routes.

We can see the betweenness of the nodes (larger nodes) and the emissions of the edges connecting them are. related, i.e. the emission on roads connecting intersections (nodes) with high betweenness (bigger nodes) are the highest emissions in the network. Also, the orange nodes, which are the nodes with higher closeness, fall on the part of the roads that recorded higher emissions in most of the emissions. It is interesting to note a high emission area at the bottom of the city on one of the larger roads. This is consistent in all of the emission measures. It could be because of the higher length of roads, but this needs to be further studied.

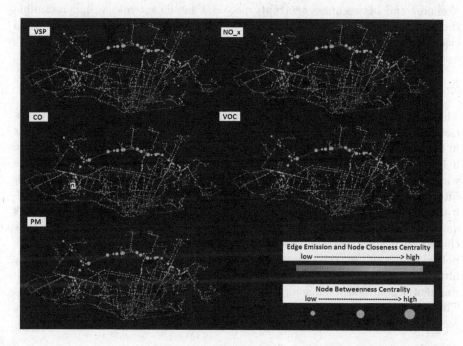

Fig. 2. Five instances of the same road network with nodes representing the intersections and edges representing the roads between them. The color and size of the nodes represent the closeness and betweenness centrality, respectively, which are network structure metrics independent of the emission values represented as the edge color. The part of the network with larger orange color nodes (with high closeness and betweenness centrality) is connected mainly through green to orange edges (higher emission values), indicating the occurrence of higher emission roads around nodes/intersections most central to the network.

4.3 Discussion

The VSP and MIE models provide evidence to support the hypothesis that simple GPS data, which is becoming widely available with the advent of the Internet of Things (IoT), can be used to develop an EI. These methods can help get emission indicators that could be used further to study urban road network characteristics contributing to higher emissions. Hence, policymakers no longer need to continually invest in heavy equipment and surveillance to understand the emissions associated with transport data.

We have shown that by overlaying emission data onto the road network, we can obtain valuable insights into emission distribution and patterns in the city. By analyzing these network structures, we can better understand how the road network contributes to overall emissions.

The network analysis allowed us to investigate the relationship between roads in the city network and their corresponding emissions. Among the measures, closeness and betweenness centrality played a significant role in understanding the importance of a road and its emission levels. Our results section shows a clear positive correlation between betweenness centrality and emissions.

5 Conclusion and Future Work

This work demonstrates the potential for using raw GPS data to measure pollution and emission levels in a region, specifically in the context of a fleet of taxis in Porto, Portugal. Using feature engineering and high-spatial emissions models, it is possible to identify areas with higher emissions levels and correlate these with centrality measures of nodes/intersections in the city's road network. For future work, we intend to perform more extensive experiments on different real-world datasets around various cities and vehicles and provide detailed network analysis. This can branch out to study not only the effects of varying vehicle characteristics but also the effects of urban landscape patterns [26] and driving behaviors of the user [11]. These potential extensions can offer valuable insights into the intricate connections between transportation, urban design, and environmental pollution, enhancing the richness of the region's emission inventory. This information is particularly valuable for organizations in the transportation sector as they seek to monitor and manage their carbon footprint effectively.

Acknowledgement. This work is financed by National Funds through the Portuguese funding agency, FCT—Fundação para a Ciência e a Tecnologia, within project LA/P/0063/2020. This work was developed under the project "City Analyser" (POCI-01-0247-FEDER-039924), financed by European Regional Development Fund (ERDF), through the Research and Technological Development Incentive System, within the Portugal2020 Competitiveness and Internationalization Operational Program. Thiago Andrade is also financed by National Funds through the Portuguese funding agency, FCT—Fundação para a Ciência e a Tecnologia within the grant: UI/BD/152697/2022.

References

1. Zhongming, Z., Linong, L., Xiaona, Y., Wangqiang, Z., Wei, L., et al.: Ar6 synthesis report: climate change 2022 (2022). https://www.ipcc.ch/report/sixth-assessment-report-cycle/
2. European Environment Agency: Decarbonising road transport - the role of vehicles, fuels and transport demand. Transport and environment report 2021 (2021)
3. Borrego, C., Tchepel, O., Costa, A.M., Amorim, J.H., Miranda, A.I.: Emission and dispersion modelling of Lisbon air quality at local scale. Atmos. Environ. **37**(37), 5197–5205 (2003). 11th International Symposium, Transport and Air Pollution
4. Tchepel, O., Dias, D.: Quantification of health benefits related with reduction of atmospheric PM10 levels: implementation of population mobility approach. Sci. World J. **21**(3), 189–200 (2011)
5. Dias, D., Tchepe, O., Carvalho, A., Miranda, A.I., Borrego1, C.: Particulate matter and health risk under a changing climate: assessment for Portugal. Int. J. Environ. Health Res. **2012**, Article ID 409546 (2012)
6. European Environment Agency. Greenhouse gas emissions from transport in Europe (2021). https://www.eea.europa.eu/ims/greenhouse-gas-emissions-from-transport
7. CBO. Emissions of carbon dioxide in the transportation sector (2022). https://www.cbo.gov/publication/58861
8. European Environment Agency. Air pollution and children's health (2023). https://www.eea.europa.eu/publications/air-pollution-and-childrens-health
9. Ntziachristos, L., Gkatzoflias, D., Kouridis, C., Samaras, Z.: Copert: a European road transport emission inventory model. In: Information Technologies in Environmental Engineering, pp. 491–504. Springer, Berlin, Heidelberg (2009). ISBN 978-3-540-88351-7
10. Deng, F., Lv, Z., Qi, L., Wang, X., Shi, M., Liu, H.: A big data approach to improving the vehicle emission inventory in China. Nat. Commun. **11**(1), 1–12 (2020)
11. Shaji, N.: Spatio-temporal clustering to study vehicle emissions and air quality correlation at Porto. MSc. Thesis (2022). https://hdl.handle.net/10216/147251
12. Slezakova, K., Castro, D., Begonha, A., Delerue-Matos, C., da Conceição Alvim-Ferraz, M., Morais, S., do Carmo Pereira, M.: Air pollution from traffic emissions in Oporto, Portugal: health and environmental implications. Microchem. J. **99**(1), 51–59 (2011)
13. González, C.M., Gómez, C.D., Rojas, N.Y., Acevedo, H., Aristizábal, B.H.: Relative impact of on-road vehicular and point-source industrial emissions of air pollutants in a medium-sized andean city. Atmos. Environ. **152**, 279–289 (2017)
14. Frey, H.C., Unal, A., Chen, J., Li, S., Xuan, C.: Methodology for developing modal emission rates for EPA's multi-scale motor vehicle & equipment emission system. US Environmental Protection Agency, Ann Arbor, Michigan (2002)
15. Nyhan, M., Sobolevsky, S., Kang, C., Robinson, P., Corti, A., Szell, M., Streets, D., Lu, Z., Britter, R., Barrett, S.R.H., et al.: Predicting vehicular emissions in high spatial resolution using pervasively measured transportation data and microscopic emissions model. Atmos. Environ. **140**, 352–363 (2016)
16. Crucitti, P., Latora, V., Porta, S.: Centrality in networks of urban streets. Chaos: Interdiscip. J. Nonlinear Sci. **16**(1), 015113 (2006)
17. Panis, L.I., Broekx, S., Liu, R.: Modelling instantaneous traffic emission and the influence of traffic speed limits. Sci. Total Environ. **371**(1–3), 270–285 (2006)

18. Moreira-Matias, L., Gama, J., Ferreira, M., Mendes-Moreira, J., Damas, L.: Predicting taxi-passenger demand using streaming data. IEEE Trans. Intell. Transp. Syst. **14**(3), 1393–1402 (2013)
19. Boeing, G.: Osmnx: new methods for acquiring, constructing, analyzing, and visualizing complex street networks. Comput. Environ. Urban Syst. **65**, 126–139 (2017)
20. Shaji, N., Andrade, T., Ribeiro, R.P., Gama, J.: Study on correlation between vehicle emissions and air quality in Porto. In: Machine Learning and Principles and Practice of Knowledge Discovery in Databases, pp. 181–196. Springer Nature Switzerland (2023). ISBN 978-3-031-23618-1
21. Andrade, T., Gama, J.: Estimating instantaneous vehicle emissions. In: Proceedings of the 38th ACM/SIGAPP Symposium on Applied Computing, pp. 422–424 (2023)
22. Andrade, T., Gama, J., Ribeiro, R.P., Sousa, W., Carvalho, A.: Anomaly detection in sequential data: principles and case studies. Wiley Encyclopedia of Electrical and Electronics Engineering, pp. 1–14 (2019)
23. Gama, J., de Leon Carvalho, A.C.P., Faceli, K., Lorena, A.C., Oliveira, M., et al.: Extração de conhecimento de dados: data mining, 3rd edn. Edições Sílabo, Lisboa (2017)
24. Andrade, T., Cancela, B., Gama, J.: From mobility data to habits and common pathways. Expert. Syst. **37**(6), e12627 (2020)
25. Rodríguez, R.A., Virguez, E.A., Rodríguez, P.A., Behrentz, E.: Influence of driving patterns on vehicle emissions: a case study for Latin American cities. Transp. Res. Part D: Transp. Environ. **43**, 192–206 (2016)
26. Li, S., Zhou, C., Wang, S., Jincan, H.: Dose urban landscape pattern affect CO_2 emission efficiency? empirical evidence from megacities in China. J. Clean. Prod. **203**, 164–178 (2018)

Analysis of Dam Natural Frequencies Using a Convolutional Neural Network

Gonçalo Cabaço[1], Sérgio Oliveira[2], André Alegre[2,3], João Marcelino[4],
João Manso[4], and Nuno Marques[1(✉)]

[1] NOVA LINCS, NOVA School of Science and Technology, Campus da Caparica,
2829-516 Caparica, Portugal
nmm@fct.unl.pt
[2] Concrete Dams Department, National Laboratory for Civil Engineering (LNEC),
Av. do Brasil 101, 1700-075 Lisboa, Portugal
soliveira@lnec.pt
[3] Civil Engineering Department, Instituto Superior de Engenharia de Lisboa -
Instituto Politécnico de Lisboa (ISEL-IPL), R. Conselheiro Emídio Navarro 1,
1959-007 Lisboa, Portugal
[4] Geotechnics Department, National Laboratory for Civil Engineering (LNEC),
Lisbon, Portugal

Abstract. The accurate estimation of dam natural frequencies and their
evolution over time can be very important for dynamic behaviour analysis and structural health monitoring. However, automatic modal parameter estimation from ambient vibration measurements on dams can be
challenging, e.g., due to the influence of reservoir level variations, operational effects, or dynamic interaction with appurtenant structures. This
paper proposes a novel methodology for improving the automatic identification of natural frequencies of dams using a supervised Convolutional
Neural Network (CNN) trained on real preprocessed sensor monitoring
data in the form of spectrograms. Our tailored CNN architecture, specifically designed for this task, represents the first of its kind. The case study
is the 132 m high Cabril arch dam, in operation since 1954 in Portugal;
the dam was instrumented in 2008 with a continuous dynamic monitoring
system. Modal analysis has been performed using an automatic modal
identification program, based on the Frequency Domain Decomposition
(FDD) method. The evolution of the experimental natural frequencies of
Cabril dam over time are compared with the frequencies predicted using
the parameterized CNN based on different sets of data. The results show
the potential of the proposed neural network to complement the implemented modal identification methods and improve automatic frequency
identification over time.

Keywords: Dams · Vibration analysis · Natural frequencies ·
Convolutional neural network · Machine learning · Structural health
monitoring

© The Author(s), under exclusive license to Springer Nature Switzerland AG 2023
N. Moniz et al. (Eds.): EPIA 2023, LNAI 14115, pp. 227–238, 2023.
https://doi.org/10.1007/978-3-031-49008-8_18

1   Introduction

Concrete dams are structures that have always played an important role in our society, creating water reservoirs, allowing fresh water supply to the population, flood control, and energy generation. Due to the natural ageing of concrete, the varying forces that dams are subjected to and the possibility of being exposed to the effects of natural events such as earthquakes, these structures may present a certain level of deterioration that needs to be monitored. To achieve this goal, the safety control of large concrete dams tends to rely on Seismic and Structural Health Monitoring (SSHM) systems. These systems are designed to continuously measure vibrations as there is a correlation between the deterioration state and the way dams vibrate: natural frequencies and vibration modes are affected by structural changes induced by eventual damage. Modal configurations of the main vibration modes may be affected" The dam vibrations are usually measured through the use of accelerometers, located at specific points along the dam body [7]. Amplitude spectra are then calculated from the measured acceleration records using the Fast Fourier Transform (FFT) algorithm using taylor-made software that automatically performs the analysis of the collected data [7].

In an attempt to improve the existing software, the National Laboratory for Civil Engineering (LNEC) is interested in studying how a machine learning approach could complement it, primarily through the identification of the natural frequencies of the dam. These frequencies can be later used to establish a relationship with water level and/or seasonal variations so that structural changes due to material deterioration can be detected. As a result, we propose a pioneering methodology for the automatic identification of natural frequencies of dams. Our approach leverages a Convolutional Neural Network (CNN) architecture specifically designed for this task, as previous studies in frequency-based analysis have provided limited guidance. To generate a visual representation of the data, similar to spectrograms, we utilize real data collected from a dam over a decade.

2   Case Study: Cabril Dam

The case study of this work is the iconic Cabril dam, a large arch dam in operation since 1954 on the Zêzere River, in the center of Portugal. This is the highest dam in Portugal and an essential part of the country's power supply infrastructure.

2.1   Dam Description

Cabril dam is a 132 m high double curvature arch dam, with a 290 m long crest. As seen in Fig. 1, the dam was designed with a unique geometry, namely with a thicker crest; in the central cantilever, the cross-section thickness varies between a maximum of 20 m, near the dam base, to a minimum of 4.5 m, around el. 290 m, increasing again to about 6 m at the crest level (el. 297 m). The reservoir water level usually ranges from a minimum at el. 265 m to the normal water level at el. 294 m. As for appurtenant works, reference should be made to the intake tower, a reinforced concrete structure that is connected to the crest of the central cantilever of the dam through a concrete walkway, with a joint in the dam-tower contact surface. The hydro power plant, with a total installed capacity of 97 MW, is located at the downstream base of the dam.

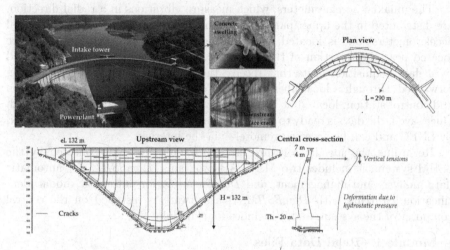

Fig. 1. Cabril dam, Portugal. Upstream, central cross-section and plan views, and detected deterioration phenomena.

Built almost 70 years ago, the Cabril dam presents some deterioration problems. During the first filling of the reservoir, horizontal cracks appeared on the downstream face of the dam, in several blocks between el. 280 and el. 290 m; according to specific computational studies, this phenomenon occurred due to the tensile stresses originated by the dam deformation under the hydrostatic pressure, and it was clearly conditioned by the cross-section geometry with a thicker crest. In addition, concrete swelling phenomena due to alkali-aggregate reactions were detected in the 1990s. However, dam behaviour has been thoroughly monitored over the years, and normal operating conditions have not been affected; recent studies, based on dynamic monitoring data, seem to indicate that the structural integrity of the dam has not been affected by the existing deterioration process [1].

2.2   Continuous Vibration Monitoring System

In 2008, the National Laboratory for Civil Engineering (LNEC) and Energias de Portugal (EDP), decided to install a pioneer Seismic and Structural Health Monitoring (SSHM) system to monitor the dynamic behaviour of the Cabril dam over time. Since then, similar systems have been installed in other large dams across Portugal given the good results that were obtained [7]. The particular system at Cabril dam was designed to measure accelerations in the upper zone of the dam and at the dam-foundation interface (near the abutments), at a sampling rate of 1000 Hz (in general the acceleration records are stored after decimation for a sampling frequency of 50 Hz; only for seismic events the acceleration records are stored at 1000 Hz). Overall, the system includes 16 uniaxial accelerometers, and 3 triaxial accelerometers.

The uniaxial accelerometers, which measure vibrations in a radial direction, are distributed in the upper part of the dam by two galleries. As for the triaxial accelerometers, one is located in the upper gallery, whilst the other two are located near the insertion of the dam base. The accelerometers are controlled by 4 data acquisition units that receive the recorded data. This data is then forwarded, through a local fiber optical network, to a server in the observation and control station, located at the dam power station, so that it can be stored. Once saved, the data is ready to be fed into the data collection software developed by LNEC and can be accessed remotely via the internet.

Regarding the specific software used to handle the data collected by the SSHM system, it includes two MATLAB programs: *DamSSHM*, for automatic data analysis and management, and *DamModalID*, for automatic modal identification. Starting with *DamSSHM*, this software is installed on the central computer of the system, and it includes four modules [1]:

- **Module 1—Read Data Files**
  The data continuously recorded with the measuring sensors is received by 4 data acquisition units and sent to the central computer. This data is then stored in 4 binary files, one for each unit, every hour. This first module of *DamSSHM* was specifically prepared to read these 4 binary files to create matrices in MATLAB with all acceleration records.
- **Module 2—Automatic Data Analysis and Management**
  The second module of *DamSSHM* was developed both to analyse the acceleration records, with the purpose of detecting corrupt files or potential measurement errors, and to manage the generated data files. This management is done by creating new data files containing decimated records with an artificial sampling rate of 50 Hz (instead of the original sampling rate of 1000 Hz). By doing this, the size of the files is greatly reduced, saving storage space. This module can also send a daily monitoring summary by email.
- **Module 3—Automatic Detection of Vibrations during Seismic Events**
  The third module does exactly what its name says: automatic detection of vibrations induced by seismic events. The module evaluates specific parameters and patterns in the acceleration records and is able to distinguish possible seismic vibrations from those induced by operational sources.
- **Module 4—Automatic Maintenance of the Server Storage**
  As previously mentioned, the software creates files with decimated records, which are much smaller in size than the original binary files. However, these files continue to be stored on the central server. The fourth and last module

of *DamSSHM* selects a single hour from a predefined time period and saves a backup of the original files. The remaining files are deleted.

Moving on to *DamModalID*, this program was developed to perform modal analysis on the collected data, to determine the natural frequencies and modal configurations of the main vibration modes (Fig. 2). It is based on the Frequency Domain Decomposition (FDD) method, that consists in the analysis of the singular value decomposition (SVD) of the power spectral density (PSD) matrix, which in turn is estimated from the measured outputs (discrete time series) using the Welch method. Moreover, it also has an interactive graphical interface, allowing a more detailed analysis of both the acceleration records and the modal identification results.

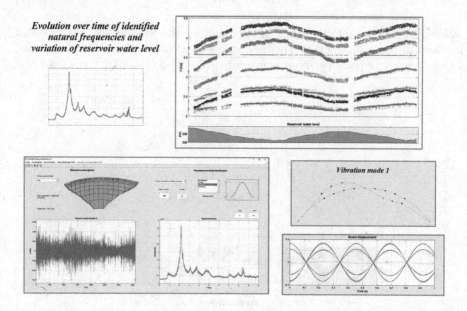

Fig. 2. *DamModalID.* Automatic modal identification results and graphical interface.

3 Supervised Convolutional Neural Network (CNN) Proposed for the Analysis of Dam Natural Frequencies

This work involves the use of the machine learning algorithm Convolutional Neural Network (CNN). Since the proposed model expects to receive labeled data, it falls into the supervised learning category. As the main goal is to identify natural frequencies (continuous values), we are facing a regression problem.

3.1   Dataset

To conduct our research, a real dataset provided by LNEC was used. The data composing the dataset started to be collected at the Cabril dam, through the continuous dynamic monitoring system described in Sect. 2.2. The data is already in the frequency domain [7].

Figure 3 shows a graphical representation of an entry from the initial dataset, which has over 27000 h. It comprises the average amplitudes for each frequency value in the range of 0–6 Hz, calculated hourly from the records of all available accelerometers. To calculate the number of pairs ($frequency, amplitude$) per hour, the following equation can be applied:

$$n = \frac{f_{\max} - f_{\min}}{\frac{1}{ws}} + 1, \tag{1}$$

where f represents the frequency interval and ws the window size of the Welch method. In this case, the Welch method was used with 400-second data segments, so the number of pairs per hour is given by: $(6 - 0) \div (1 \div 400) + 1 = 2401$.

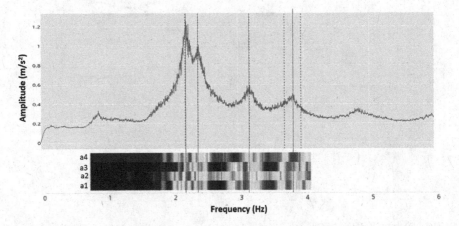

Fig. 3. Average spectral amplitudes in the range of 0–6 Hz and the first five natural frequencies (which will be used as CNN target values during training) for a specific hour of the dataset and input example (spectrogram with 4 accelerometers).

In addition, we also have access to the estimated values of the first five natural frequencies, which should coincide with certain amplitude peaks. The dam's natural frequencies, obtained from measurements as the frequencies of the main spectral peaks, are dependent on the reservoir water level, as can be confirmed by results obtained using software developed in LNEC based on the Finite Element Method (FEM). Such dependencies adjusted based on the water level, and different smoothing techniques were applied in a semi-manual way [7]. It should be noted that the dataset has a very high level of noise and there is always some error associated with these estimates, causing some frequencies to deviate from the most accurate value. Despite this fact, these pre-identified natural frequency values were still be used as ground truth.

The spectral data illustrated in Fig. 3 together with the semi-manual estimated natural frequency annotated values produced a first dataset labeled ds-1D containing the average spectral amplitudes calculated from all the accelerometers.

A more elaborated composed representation was also prepared by representing the spectrograms as 2D images (e.g., [2]). The major differences between these datasets and the previous one are that instead of one-dimensional arrays, we now have spectrograms, as illustrated in Fig. 3. To generate the spectrograms, the dataset was expanded not only to include the average amplitudes, but also the amplitudes measured by the four most relevant specific accelerometers as dataset labeled ds-2D4. The choice made was to associate the frequency range with the width of the spectrogram, the number of accelerometers with its height, and the amplitude values with its colour. First, the amplitudes recorded by the four sensors for the same hour are selected. Those values are then normalized with the following formula:

$$x'_i = \frac{x_i - x_{\min}}{x_{\max} - x_{\min}},\tag{2}$$

where $x_\square$ represents the set of amplitude values for a given hour (e.g., each value i is normalized by corresponding minimum and maximum observed values). This ensures consistency across spectrograms, by using a fixed colour scale to all images.

In an attempt to add even more information to the spectrograms, we believed it was worth trying to use all sixteen uniaxial accelerometers instead of just four. Furthermore, we also decided to switch to a frequency range of 1 to 5 Hz and use only 200-second data segments to produce this dataset variation. By adopting this approach, the five distinct natural frequencies not only retain their identifiable characteristics but also contribute to further compactness in the images. The full set of sixteen accelerometers is labelled as dataset ds-2D16. The process results in one spectrogram per hour of data in our dataset and contains thousands of spectrograms, each representing different conditions based on the water level in the reservoir and the state of the dam's deterioration, as illustrated in Fig. 4. So, over the course of more than a decade, a spectrogram has been generated every hour.

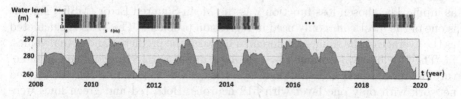

Fig. 4. Spectrogram generation for CNN training.

3.2 Main Model

To build and train our CNN model, we will be using Keras [3]. Keras is an open-source deep learning Python API that was designed with a focus on enabling fast experimentation, providing essential abstractions and building blocks for developing and shipping machine learning solutions. We did not find any previous work that specifically utilizes spectrograms for dam vibration analysis (there are datasets, but without frequency data[1]). However, there have been works in the area of vibration analysis using 2D-CNNs, as exemplified in medical domain for ECG analysis [4], and sound analysis [2]. In these works, 2D-CNNs for image processing [5] have been shown to be effective when adapted to processing time-frequency spectrograms. Therefore, we chose to base our main model on a combination of standard CNN models and the model introduced by Anjos et al. [2] for sibilant consonants classification using log Mel filter banks and a 2D CNN, which has shown remarkable performance in signal processing and classification tasks based on time-frequency spectrograms. However, for more complete testing, the input layer was adapted to receive the different dataset input shapes. For example, when the `ds-1D` dataset (Sect. 3.1) is used, the model directly uses 1D convolutional layers.

Spectrograms, like the one in Fig. 3, are illustrative of $2D$ inputs. The main model has four convolutional layers, each followed by a pooling layer and a dropout of 20%. The number of filters in the convolutional layers increases by a factor of 2, assuming the values 32, 64, 128, and 256. All these layers use filters of size 3×3 with a stride of 1. Both pooling layers perform the max pooling operation with a 2×2 window and a stride of 2.

The output of the last pooling layer is flattened and fed to a fully connected network with three hidden layers with 1000, 500, and 100 neurons, respectively. Lastly, a dropout of 50% is applied before the final output layer, which consists of 5 neurons, since we are aiming to identify exactly five natural frequencies. The convolutional and hidden layers use the ReLu activation function, while the output layer uses the linear activation, as it is the most suitable for regression problems.

3.3 CNN Hyperparameter Tuning

We have tested different model hyperparameters based on experimental evidence. Figure 5 compares the validation loss values per epoch, on the logarithmic scale (base e), for four preliminary tests performed using dataset `ds-2D4` spectrograms as input. The chosen loss function was the Mean-Squared Error (MSE), since it is one of the most commonly used in regression problems. The MSE is calculated as the average of the squared differences between the predicted and actual values.

The blue line was obtained by training a model with a less complex architecture, featuring three convolutional layers instead of four, and a fully connected network with only one layer with 512 neurons. Both red and green lines were

---

[1] https://www.kaggle.com/datasets/konivat/three-gorges-dam-water-data.

obtained by training a model with the architecture presented in the previous section. Lastly, the purple line was obtained by training a model with a more complex architecture, featuring five convolutional layers and a fully connected network with four hidden layers with 1000, 500, 100, and 10 neurons, respectively. Another difference between these tests was the value used for the *learning_rate* hyperparameter of the Adam optimizer. An optimizer is one of the two arguments required to compile a Keras model (the other one being the loss function) and its *learning_rate* hyperparameter defaults to 0.001. That said, both the first and second tests (blue and red lines, respectively) were conducted with the default value, whereas the third and fourth tests (green and purple lines, respectively) were conducted with the value set to 0.0001. Once again, since there are so many different combinations that can be put together, we decided to save time by stopping at 200 epochs.

As seen in the figure, lowering *the learning_rate* mitigated the steep decline of the loss curve during the first training epochs by slowing down the training process, and even though it initially led to higher validation errors, it paid off later on as shown by the third test. On the other hand, increasing complexity only helped to a certain extent, as the last test ended up with a higher final error than the previous two. So the set of hyperparameters from test 3 was selected as our main model.

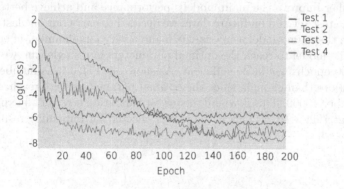

Fig. 5. Model loss comparison (log scale).

4   Results: Analysis of Natural Frequencies of Cabril Dam

Experiments were conducted using the three datasets from the previous section to achieve high accuracy. They compared the impact of utilizing spectrograms versus not using them on CNN performance. Different methods of generating spectrograms and testing various model architectures were explored. The behavior of the best-performing model was studied under simulated damage conditions. The different encodings of the dataset using the previously described (Sect. 3.1) direct encoding of 1D spectral amplitudes and the different 2D Spectrograms (with 4 and 16 sensors) were provided as input to our models. To ensure we achieved the best possible results, we have also tested the VGG19 [8], one of the most well-known CNN architectures. We chose to freeze the layers of the base model, and then replaced the three fully connected layers with the same fully connected network that we used in the main model. This model managed to perform worse than all previous experiments, and it was also the most time-consuming to execution, given the complexity of the network.

The Table 1 summarizes the experiments up to this point (all experiments were set to go through exactly 300 epochs).

Table 1. Summary of experiments.

Model	Description	Input Size	Loss $(\times 10^{-4})$
1D main model	ds-1D—Raw Data (1D arrays)	$2401 \times 1 \times 3$	2.82
4D main model	ds-2D4—Four-Sensor Spectrograms	$1201 \times 4 \times 3$	1.34
16D main model	ds-2D16—Sixteen-Sensor Spectrograms	$801 \times 16 \times 3$	1.28
Modified VGG19	ds-2D16—Sixteen-Sensor Spectrograms	$801 \times 32 \times 3$	4.69

To further improve the main model's performance and achieve better results both on the test set and on future data, we decided to carry out one last training round with the main model using ds-2D16 and a very large number of epochs. In order for the model to reach the optimal parameters in a single run, we believed that 100000 epochs would be sufficient. As shown in Fig. 6, this number turned out to be more than enough, since the optimal parameters were reached around epoch number 10000. This is where the lowest validation error of all experiments occurred, at 7.44×10^{-5}. This is the model selected for remaining results.

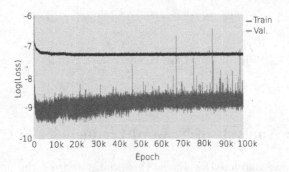

Fig. 6. Best model loss (zoomed log scale, weight regularization turned off for testing).

We can also verify how the model behaves on the test set, by comparing its predictions with the original natural frequency values. Figure 7a illustrates this

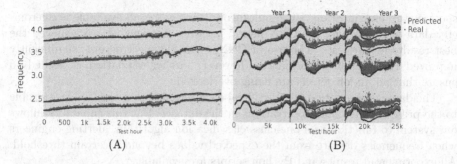

Fig. 7. Comparison between the real natural frequency values (in blue) and the values predicted by the best model (in red) for: **A**—Real data **B**—Simulated data.

comparison. In this example, the test set includes the last six months of available data, arranged chronologically, which is roughly 20% of the entire dataset. Naturally, we want the points to overlap as much as possible, because the closer they are, the more accurate the prediction.

To conclude our analysis, a final experiment was performed to evaluate the model's behaviour in case the dam starts to show some level of deterioration, as one of the main uses of dynamic monitoring systems is the detection of structural damage due to progressive material deterioration over time. Since no real data is available, we had to simulate the gradual decline in concrete stiffness ourselves.

With that aim, we stipulated a decrease of 0.2 Hz over a three-year period. To do so, we grabbed the data from the last available year (2020) and gradually shifted the amplitude values to the left. After producing the artificial data for the next three years, we generated the respective sixteen-sensor spectrogram for each hour. Figure 7b shows the comparison between the artificial natural frequencies and the values predicted by our best model via such spectrograms on each test year. For the three simulated years, it can be observed that the lower the frequencies, the harder it is for the model to make the right prediction.

5   Conclusion and Future Work

This work presents a machine learning approach utilizing Convolutional Neural Networks (CNNs) and preprocessed sensor data collected from the Cabril dam. Through various experiments, we explored different model architectures, hyperparameters, and input shapes to enhance the identification of the main natural frequencies of concrete dams. The choice of CNNs was motivated by their proven effectiveness in vibration analysis and signal processing tasks, as demonstrated by studies in image classification tasks, e.g. by Krizhevsky et al. [5] and Nielsen [6]. Our findings highlight the potential of CNNs in accurately identifying the main natural frequencies of concrete dams, contributing a significant advancement to the field of dam vibration analysis.

No previous work exists on analyzing dam frequency using machine learning methods and our main model is based on state-of-the-art CNN models for spectrogram classification. By simultaneously including all available accelerometer data while keeping the CNN neural network manageable, we achieved the best results in our tests. The use of CNNs with 2D spectrograms significantly improved the overall performance. However, further validation is needed to ensure that no major details are being overlooked.

The damage simulation with artificial data revealed that the CNN is sensible to the presence of similar observations in the dataset. But this capability allows our system to function as a one-class classification algorithm, alerting engineers when frequencies deviate from the expected values beyond a certain threshold. All experimental results and Python scripts are available.[2]

While water level and air temperature have a correlation with the natural frequencies being analyzed, they were not included as input features to avoid bias and a skewed outcome. However, the potential usefulness of incorporating these variables in future work should not be dismissed. Additionally, exploring unsupervised methods based on current encodings and incorporating additional variables like water level or air temperature holds promise for further advancements in dam vibration analysis.

Acknowledgements. The authors thank Energias de Portugal (EDP) for their support in the installation and maintenance of the dynamic monitoring system installed in Cabril dam and for allowing the use of collected monitoring data. This research was funded by the Portuguese Foundation for Science and Technology (FCT) in the framework of the project PTDC/ECI-EGC/5332/2020—Seismic Monitoring and Structural Health of Large Concrete Dams (SSHM4Dams).

References

1. Alegre, A.: Modelling and monitoring the dynamic behaviour of concrete dams. Modal Analysis and Seismic Response. Ph.D. Thesis, Instituto Superior Técnico (2021)
2. Anjos, I., Eskenazi, M., Marques, N., Grilo, M., Guimarães, I., Magalhães, J., Cavaco, S.: Detection of voicing and place of articulation of fricatives with deep learning in a virtual speech and language therapy tutor. In: Proceedings Interspeech 2020. pp. 3156–3160 (2020). https://doi.org/10.21437/Interspeech. 2020–2821
3. About keras. https://keras.io/about/. Accessed 06 Aug 2022
4. Huang, J., Chen, B., Yao, B., He, W.: ECG arrhythmia classification using STFT-based spectrogram and convolutional neural network. IEEE Access **7**, 92871–92880 (2019)
5. Krizhevsky, A., Sutskever, I., Hinton, G.E.: Imagenet classification with deep convolutional neural networks. In: Proceedings of the 25th NIPS, pp. 1097–1105 (2012)
6. Nielsen, M.A.: Neural Networks and Deep Learning. Determination Press (2019), http://neuralnetworksanddeeplearning.com
7. Oliveira, S., Alegre, A.: Seismic and structural health monitoring of dams in Portugal. In: Limongelli, M., Çelebi, M. (eds.) Seismic Structural Health Monitoring From Theory to Successful Applications, pp. 87–113. Springer, Berlin (2019)
8. Simonyan, K., Zisserman, A.: Very deep convolutional networks for large-scale image recognition. In: International Conference on Learning Representations (2015)

---

[2] https://bit.ly/CNN-Dam-Analysis23.

Imbalanced Regression Evaluation Under Uncertain Domain Preferences

Nuno Costa[1](✉) and Nuno Moniz[2]

[1] INESC TEC, Porto, Portugal
nuno.m.costa@inesctec.pt
[2] Lucy Family Institute for Data and Society, University of Notre Dame, Notre Dame, USA
nuno.moniz@nd.edu

Abstract. In natural phenomena, data distributions often deviate from normality. One can think of cataclysms as a self-explanatory example: rarely occurring events differ considerably from common outcomes. In real-world domains, such tail events are often the most relevant to anticipate, allowing us to take adequate measures to prevent or attenuate their impact on society. However, mapping target values to particular relevance judgements is challenging and existing methods do not consider the impact of bias in reaching such mappings—relevance functions. In this paper, we tackle the issue of uncertainty in non-uniform domain preferences and its impact on imbalanced regression evaluation. Specifically, we develop two methods for assessing the volatility of model performance when dealing with uncertainty regarding the range of target values that are more important to the underlying problem. We demonstrate the importance of our proposed methods in capturing the impact of small changes in relevance assessments of target values and how they may impact experimental conclusions.

1 Introduction

A common assumption in statistical-based learning is the premise of normality. However, real-world domains commonly present departures (even if slightly) from normality, raising two critical caveats for machine learning. First, cases framed within the central tendency of the distributions are the most well-represented in the data. Thus, resulting models will be better at recognising and anticipating such cases. Second, cases with extreme/rare values are often associated with high-impact events, e.g., fraud. Therefore, in certain situations, such cases should be prioritised and not under-valued w.r.t the ability to anticipate them.

Imbalanced learning focuses on modelling and predicting rare and extreme events. A challenging machine learning task [5], it mostly focuses on classification tasks, facing issues such as identifying small disjunct areas, lacking density and information in training data, overlapping classes, noisy data and data set

© The Author(s), under exclusive license to Springer Nature Switzerland AG 2023
N. Moniz et al. (Eds.): EPIA 2023, LNAI 14115, pp. 239–250, 2023.
https://doi.org/10.1007/978-3-031-49008-8_19

shift [9]. Work concerning regression is residual, but it has received increasing interest recently, including contributions on task formalisation for different data scenarios [10,13] and proposals for pre-processing strategies [11,19]. However, its major challenge remains in correctly mapping target values to their predictive importance and evaluating models' performance towards relevant values.

Relevance functions [20] are the core concept in imbalanced regression, mapping domain values, i.e., target values, and their importance (usually measured between 0 and 1) to the user in obtaining an accurate prediction. Although this mapping should be a user-defined process, we often lack such domain knowledge and thus rely on distribution inference methods. Essentially, values in the centre of the distribution are associated with relevance near 0, and as those values separate from such centre, their relevance approximates (or assumes the value of) 1. Most importantly, this process assumes that available data is a representative sample of the underlying data domain, which is not always true.

We identify three scenarios of relevance function usage when tackling scientific problems in regression subject to skewed domain preferences:

1. The underlying phenomena and the most relevant range of target values have been studied, e.g. the Beaufort wind scale connecting wind speed ranges and physical consequences felt on the sea and land [7];
2. Domain-knowledge experts disagree on which target value range is more relevant, leading to multiple relevance functions, e.g. biomarker concentration for characterisation of neuro-degenerative disease stages [3];
3. Insufficient scientific efforts to establish a domain preference.

In this paper, we propose two sensitivity evaluation methods that allow users to quantify the impact of *counterfactual* relevance functions in imbalanced regression evaluation of predictive models. In all three cases presented above, the methods (convolution and elastic) allow us to understand how different models perform under different (although similar) relevance criteria. Critically, this contribution bridges an important gap in the evaluation and robustness assessment of models in imbalanced regression tasks.

The remainder of the paper is organised as follows. Section 2 describes the task of imbalanced regression, followed by introducing the proposed methods in Sect. 3. An experimental evaluation is presented and thoroughly discussed in Sect. 4, followed by conclusions and future work in Sect. 5.

2   Imbalanced Regression

Standard regression tasks assume that a function $f()$ maps predictor variables to a continuous target variable. Such function is formalised as $Y = f(X_1, X_2, \ldots, X_p)$, where Y is a numerical target variable, and features describing each case are denoted with $X_1, X_2, \ldots, X_p$. An approximation $h()$ (a model) to this function is obtained by using a data set with examples of the function mapping (known as a training set), i.e., $\mathcal{D} = \{\langle \mathbf{x}_i, y_i \rangle\}_{i=1}^n$. Here, our objective is to optimise models using a certain loss function, $L(\hat{y}, y)$, such as the absolute or the squared error of estimations w.r.t. the true values. When all target values are considered equally important, i.e., uniform domain preferences, standard regression tasks assume that the utility U of the estimations is a function of the estimation error $L(\hat{y}, y)$ and that it is inversely proportional to the loss function, $U \propto L^{-1}$. However, this is not the case for learning tasks confounded by varying user preferences across a range(s) of target values or in scenarios where estimation error may not be a helpful metric across all possible target values.

2.1 Relevance Functions

Imbalanced regression faces the challenge of providing a formal approach that describes non-uniform preferences over continuous domains. Figure 1 illustrates the difference between the standard assumption of uniform vs non-uniform preferences. Ideally, users or domain experts should carry out the specification of domain preferences. When not possible, we can rely on distribution-based statistics to automatically infer a suitable relevance function in such cases.

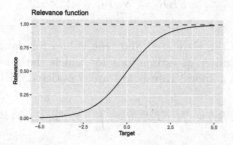

Fig. 1. Example of target values' relevance for a specific domain preference. The dashed magenta line represents the case where no preferences are given; therefore, all values are considered equally important.

Definition A relevance function $\phi(Y) : Y \rightarrow [0, 1]$ is a continuous function that encodes a user-defined domain preference Y by mapping it into a $[0, 1]$ scale of relevance, where 0 and 1 represent the minimum and maximum relevance, respectively [17].

The relevance function construction starts with control points mapping to regions where relevance is known, ideally provided by domain experts. These are either specified by users or automatically derived from the data. When the latter is carried out, such a process relies on using the adjusted box-plot method [18], as suggested by Ribeiro and Moniz [17]. From the control points, an interpolation method approximates a continuous function ready to use in potentially infinite domains. For this occasion, we will use Piecewise Cubic Hermite Interpolating Polynomials [6], as suggested by Ribeiro [16].

2.2 Evaluation

Evaluation metrics for numerical prediction tasks commonly assume that all domain values have equal importance, i.e., uniform domain preferences. Several metrics have been proposed for learning settings where non-uniform preferences apply, i.e., a different level of relevance is associated with distinct ranges of the target variable. These range from asymmetrical approaches, common in finance, e.g., LIN-LIN [4], to adaptations of well-known metrics for classification tasks, such as the utility-based F-Score [2,12,16]. More recently, Ribeiro and Moniz [17] provide a thorough discussion on the limitations of existing metrics in the scope of learning with non-uniform preferences and propose the Squared Error-Relevance Area (SERA) metric, which tackles several shortcomings in previous work. In this paper, we will focus on the use of SERA.

Definition For a given data set D and a relevance function ϕ, consider the subset D^t where the relevance of the target value is above or equal to a cutoff t. Thus, it's possible to obtain an estimate of the Squared Error-Relevance of a model as:

$$SER_t = \sum_{i \in D^t} (\widehat{y}_i - y_i)^2 \tag{1}$$

where $\widehat{y}_i$ and y_i are the estimated and true values for data point i. For this estimate, only the subset of estimations for which the relevance of the true target value is above a known threshold t are considered. SERA is defined as:

$$SERA = \int_0^1 SER_t dt = \int_0^1 \sum_{i \in D^t} (\widehat{y}_i - y_i)^2 dt \tag{2}$$

As such, the smaller the area under the curve (SERA), the better the model's performance. In a situation where no domain preferences are defined, i.e. $\phi(Y) = 1$, SERA converges to the sum of squared errors [17].

3 Sensitivity Evaluation and Relevance Uncertainty

The formal definition for imbalanced regression tasks [17] provides the basis for tackling the first issue in this project: how to evaluate and compare solutions for which the relevance of obtaining correct estimations in different target values is different. By having a more appropriate metric for evaluating regression models on extreme values, we are left with a second challenge: in situations of uncertainty concerning the range of predictive focus, what is the best solution to ensure robust predictive power?

We propose two methods that can be applied with a SERA-based evaluation of predictive solutions. Such methods are based on the simulation of neighbouring configurations of the relevance function based on the initial input, i.e., *counterfactual* relevance functions. Our intuition is that evaluating models in similar configurations (w.r.t the original input) makes it possible to understand the behaviour of different strategies under uncertainty and identify the most robust models. Our proposed methods simulate two degrees of freedom concerning relevance functions: *i)* x-axis displacement and *ii)* slope incline., which we deem as a good as a first exploration.

- **Convolution.** First (Algorithm 1), we can think of the situation in which the hint regarding the shape is correct but inaccurate concerning which are the most relevant values. By shifting the relevance function across a certain range—much like a convolution—, it is possible to collect the performance of models for an additional number of similarly derived relevance functions;
- **Elastic.** Second (Algorithm 2), we consider a situation where the relevance function derived from the original data is correct about which values are the most relevant but not correct about the shape. It consists of fixing the point where the relevance is larger than 0 while varying the first point where the relevance is equal to 1.

For both methods, we first determine the target variable $Y \in \mathcal{Y}$ range and obtain a relevance function $\phi(Y)$. Next, we define the peak relevance π_{max} for $\phi(Y)$ as the minimum value for which $\phi(Y) = 1$, i.e. the first maxima encountered. Similarly, we define the base relevance, π_{min}, as the largest target value for which $\phi(Y) = 0$, i.e. the point immediately before the slope of $\phi(Y)$. σ stands for standard deviation. Figure 2 illustrates the transformations performed on a sigmoid relevance function: a) refers to Convolution, while b) refers to Elastic. Note that, within the scope of our work, we are dealing with the one-tail right distribution of values. When a distribution is skewed left, the peak and base relevance values are exchanged.

Result: Performance for Convolution method
Y = training set target variable;
δ = search step size;
$\phi()$ =initial relevance function;
π_{max} =initial peak relevance;
π_{min} =initial base relevance;
$n = \frac{range(Y)}{\delta}$;
for i *in* n **do**
  update relevance function $\phi()$ s.t. $\pi_{max} = \pi_{max} + \delta$ and $\pi_{min} = \pi_{min} + \delta$;
  evaluate the model using SERA with $\phi()$ as the criterion;
end

Algorithm 1: Convolution simulation for relevance function

4 Experimental Study

In this section, we present an experimental study concerning the usefulness of our sensitivity assessment approaches, guided by our main research question: how robust are the conclusions concerning the performance of predictive models in imbalanced regression when accounting for relevance uncertainty?

Result: Performance for Elastic method

Y = training set target variable;

δ = search step size;

$\phi()$ =initial relevance function;

π_{max} =initial peak relevance;

π_{min} =initial base relevance;

$M = \tilde{Y}$, median Y;

$\mathbf{n} = \frac{range(M, M+\sigma(Y))}{\delta}$;

for i in $\mathbf{n}$ **do**

    update relevance function $\phi()$ s.t. $\pi_{max} = \pi_{max} + \delta$ and $\pi_{min} = \pi_{min}$;

    evaluate the model using SERA with $\phi()$ as the criterion;

end

Algorithm 2: Elastic simulation for relevance functions.

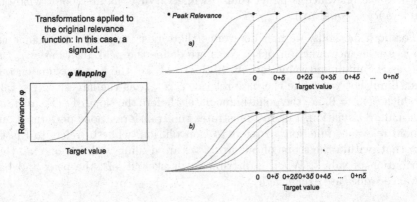

Fig. 2. Left—Original relevance function (in the example, a sigmoid). The dashed line is the inflexion point. Right—**a** Convolution. The relevance function maintains the same sigmoid shape but is continuously transferred across a range in n steps. Right—**b** Elastic. The relevance function's inflection point is fixed in the same place, but its extremities get compressed/stretched, thus becoming narrower/wider.

4.1   Methods

This subsection provides experimental details concerning the adopted methodology, learning algorithms, and estimation procedures.

Learning Algorithms For this study, we consider the following algorithms: Multivariate Adaptive Regression Splines (*mars*), Extreme Gradient Boosting (*xgboost*), and Random Forest. These are listed in Table 1, with the respective hyperparameter grid and implementation details. The hyperparameters of *xgboost* and Random Forest are chosen using a random search. From the high-dimensional grid space, 15 random combinations are considered. On the other hand, MARS evaluates 24 fixed combinations.

Table 1. Parameters considered for grid search during model training

Algorithm	Grid size	Parameters	R Package
Mars	24	Degree $\in \{1, 2, 3\}$ Nprune $\in \{1, 2, 3, 4, 5, 6, 7, 8\}$	Earth
Xgboost	50	Nrounds $\in \{1 : 1000\}$ Max depth $\in \{1 : 10\}$ eta $\in \{0,001 : 0,6\}$ gamma $\in \{0 : 10\}$	Xgboost
Random forest	60	Mtry—10 value sequence $\in \{0 : ncol(data)\}$ Min node size $\in \{1, 3, 5\}$ Split rule $\in \{variance, extratrees\}$ n.trees = 500	Ranger

Estimation Concerning estimation methodologies for validation, we adopt a 10-fold cross-validation method [8] on the train set for hyperparameter optimisation. Models are evaluated using the input relevance function and then calculating the error on an out-of-sample test set using the SERA metric.

Relevance function. The data sets used in this study come from different domains, and apart from their title and features' names, we cannot introduce any domain expertise to build a guess of what the relevance profile should look like. Therefore, we assume the automatic relevance function generated according to Ribeiro and Moniz [17] as our reference. The exception is for the Germany, Beijing, and Norway datasets, which deal with particulate matter concentration, and where the Standard international guidelines provide an initial relevance function for PM10 concentration levels on the atmosphere [15].

For the Convolution technique, *counterfactual* relevance functions are drawn from an initial relevance function, using one standard deviation to the left and right of the automatically generated points. For example, for a function with peak relevance at 100, i.e. $\phi(100) = 1$, we simulate relevance functions where values between $100 - \sigma$ and $100 + \sigma$ will be reference points for peak relevance. In short, the relevance function is incrementally shifted to both sides in its original form. For the Elastic technique, we apply it in the same range, but this time moving the left extremity further to the left while the right extremity moves to the right, and vice-versa. A good analogy is as if one would stretch or shrink the original relevance function by pulling/pushing its peaks (for 1 and 0).

Optimisation criteria. Given the context of imbalanced regression tasks, previous work has demonstrated how using traditional optimisation criteria within this scope may be misleading [17]. Accordingly, our analysis concerning the best hyper-parameter combinations within the scope of this experimental study is based on the use of the SERA metric (Sect. 2.2).

4.2   Results

In this section, our goal is to demonstrate that the techniques proposed in this paper can properly assess the robustness of predictive models' performance in the context of uncertainty in imbalanced regression tasks. Accordingly, we divide this section into two parts:

1. Case-study analysis of the Convolution and Elastic techniques applied to three air pollution data sets and the indicator $PM10$ to grasp the impact of using such techniques with policy-informed control points;
2. Evaluation of prediction models in all the remaining available data sets, to which we don't possess target value preferences concerning the robustness of their performance when applying our proposed techniques;

Concerning the first part, a note on the data sets used. The first data set concerns hourly averages of concentration levels in Beijing (China) from August 2012 to March 2013 [21]; the second, daily averages for rural background stations in Germany from 1998 to 2009 [14]; and, finally, hourly values for a station in Alnabru, Oslo (Norway), between October 2001 and August 2003 [1]. The benefit of using these data sets is that we can base the set of control points used on official recommendations per the World Health Organisation [15] for denoting 24-hour averages as normal or dangerous: $\phi(50\mu g/m) = 0$ and $\phi(150\mu g/m) = 1$, respectively. Figure 3 illustrates the outcomes for the best models of each learning algorithm used, estimated according to the methodology described in Sect. 4.1. The scenario corresponding to the x-axis value of 0 concerns the relevance function using policy-informed control points.

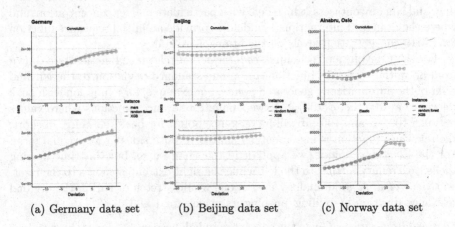

(a) Germany data set   (b) Beijing data set   (c) Norway data set

Fig. 3. Pollution data sets where the scientific community provides relevance guidelines. The vertical dashed line in each chart corresponds to the nearest approximation of the domain knowledge relevance function. The bigger circles represent the best model for each relevance function adaptation.

A careful analysis of the results provides interesting insights concerning possible scenarios. For example, concerning the first data set (left), we observe that, when applying both techniques, there is a considerable performance overlap despite different underlying relevance functions. In the second data set (centre), we notice a consistent distinction between these models throughout the entire set of neighbouring relevance functions. As for the third (right), we understand how conclusions concerning a certain relevance function may be brittle. Small shifts in the reference points for relevance judgements may greatly impact model evaluation and comparison. It also illustrates how different shapes of the underlying relevance function may have distinct impacts—comparison of Convolution and Elastic techniques.

Concerning the second part, we test the Convolution and Elastic techniques in the 29 data sets,[1] having as reference the relevance function defined by the automatic method proposed by Ribeiro and Moniz [17]. The experimental resolution for neighbouring configurations when applying our proposed techniques is 19 steps for Convolution and 19 steps for the Elastic technique. Results are presented in two distinct manners. First, illustrating an overview of the experimental results, Fig. 4 describes the rank shift probability for the prediction models estimated as the best (best rank) among all candidates. The rank shift probability translates as the percentage of neighbouring scenarios where the best model, according to the automatic relevance function, did not remain the best. In other words, a robust scenario would describe a near 0% of rank shift probability, meaning that the best model according to initial performance rank remained as such in all neighbouring scenarios tested, and vice-versa. Second, by analysing concrete cases that demonstrate the usefulness of using the proposed techniques based on interesting scenarios from the first set of results—see Fig. 5.

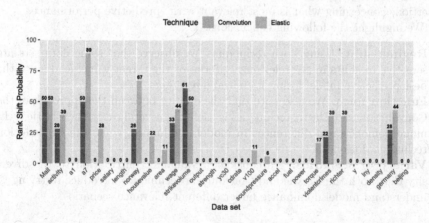

Fig. 4. Rank shift probability for all data sets according to applying the Convolution and Elastic techniques.

Overall, we observe the same scenarios as in the first part of our experimental results—see Fig. 4. In almost half of the data sets used (14), neither proposed

---

[1] Data sets are made available in https://github.com/nunompmoniz/IRon.

technique demonstrated performance rank shifts for the best model w.r.t the reference relevance function. Around a quarter of the data sets demonstrated varying levels of rank shift probability when applying both the Convolution and Elastic techniques. We should highlight cases at both extremes, such as with the data sets *a7* and *violentcrimes*. The former presents probabilities of 50 and 89% for Convolution and Elastic techniques, respectively, and, for the latter, 17 and 22%. Finally, we observe 6 cases where only applying the Elastic technique rendered a positive probability. No cases with such behaviour were observed when applying the Convolution technique. In this aspect, we should mention the case of the data set *Richter*, with 39% of rank shift probability for the Elastic technique and 0% for the Convolution technique.

To better grasp the usefulness of the proposed techniques, we propose to look closer at the results (Fig. 5) from three data sets and their illustrative scenarios: the *Output, Richter* and *a7* data sets. In the *Output* data set, we find a scenario of robustness in terms of performance, where simulations based on both techniques conclude that the best initial performer (in this case, a Random Forest model) stays as such all neighbouring configurations. As for the *Richter* data set, we observe a good example where, if the relevance function is convoluted to the right, models present a similar performance, but when the relevance function is convoluted to the left, the best model (from the *mars* algorithm) is no longer the best option for the particular imbalanced regression task. Finally, regarding the *a7* data set, we observe a considerable discrepancy between results for Convolution and Elastic techniques when contracting/expanding the form of the relevance function or when sliding it right or left. This impact raises concrete issues on the particular sensitivity of some domains to small changes in assertions concerning what is most relevant w.r.t. predictive performance.

We highlight the following conclusions.

- **Regime shift.** Using both techniques, we observe that some data sets are sensitive to shifts in the relevance criteria for the target value, leading to the best predictive model losing its initial advantage.
- **Function form.** We also note that the duality between the approach in the Convolution and Elastic techniques is useful: in several cases, the Elastic technique demonstrates differences in model dominance, while the Convolution technique does not;
- **Variety of scenarios.** We consider a valuable contribution to the diversity that both the Elastic and Convolution techniques introduce in trying to understand model dominance under different relevance scenarios.

5   Conclusions and Future Work

In this paper, we propose two simulation-based techniques that allow key insights into the robustness of prediction models in imbalanced regression tasks. This is a prevalent scenario where domain knowledge regarding which target values are more important is unavailable. The two proposed methods, Convolution and

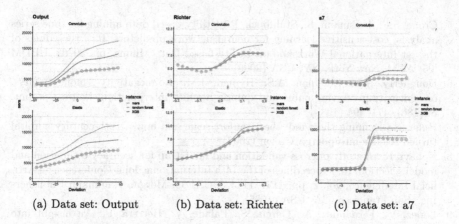

(a) Data set: Output   (b) Data set: Richter   (c) Data set: a7

Fig. 5. Performance of models in experimental data sets under applying the Convolution and Elastic techniques. The bigger circles represent the best model for each relevance function adaptation.

Elastic, extend the traditional performance evaluation process using multiple relevance functions to simulate neighbourhood scenarios of the target value's relevance regions. Altogether, these methods have allowed us to evaluate better each model's performance on the relevant target value band, and by extending the analysis to multiple relevance configurations, we can identify the most consistent and robust model, i.e. the ones that will consistently perform better than others regardless of which target value range is deemed the most relevant. Based on the experimental analysis of the methods proposed in this paper, we demonstrate how they can be useful in solving imbalanced regression problems and how their adoption may impact the future development of this research topic, particularly concerning evaluation efforts.

For the sake of reproducible science, all data sets and code necessary to reproduce the results presented in this paper are available in (removed for anonymous submission).

References

1. Aldrin, M.: Improved predictions penalizing both slope and curvature in additive models. Comput. Stat. Data Anal. **50**(2), 267–284 (2006)
2. Branco, P.: Re-sampling approaches for regression tasks under imbalanced domains. Ph.D. thesis, Universidade do Porto (2014)
3. Chen, T.B., Lai, Y.H., Ke, T.L., Chen, J.P., Lee, Y.J., Lin, S.Y., Lin, P.C., Wang, P.N., Cheng, I.H.: Changes in plasma amyloid and tau in a longitudinal study of normal aging, mild cognitive impairment, and alzheimer's disease. Dement. Geriatr. Cogn. Disord. **48**(3–4), 180–195 (2019)
4. Christoffersen, P.F., Diebold, F.X.: Further results on forecasting and model selection under asymmetric loss. J. Appl. Econ. **11**(5), 561–571 (1996)

5. Crone, S.F., Lessmann, S., Stahlbock, R.: Utility based data mining for time series analysis: cost-sensitive learning for neural network predictors. In: Proceedings of the 1st International Workshop on Utility-based Data Mining, pp. 59–68. UBDM '05, ACM, New York, NY, USA (2005)

6. Dougherty, R.L., Edelman, A.S., Hyman, J.M.: Nonnegativity-, monotonicity-, or convexity-preserving cubic and quintic hermite interpolation. Math. Comput. **52**(186), 471–494 (1989)

7. Huler, S.: Defining the wind: the Beaufort scale and how a 19th-century admiral turned science into poetry. Crown (2007)

8. Kohavi, R.: A study of cross-validation and bootstrap for accuracy estimation and model selection. In: Proceedings of the 14th International Joint Conference on Artificial Intelligence, vol. 2, pp. 1137–1143. IJCAI'95, Morgan Kaufmann Publishers Inc., San Francisco, CA, USA (1995)

9. López, V., Fernández, A., García, S., Palade, V., Herrera, F.: An insight into classification with imbalanced data: empirical results and current trends on using data intrinsic characteristics. Inf. Sci. **250**, 113–141 (2013)

10. Moniz, N., Branco, P., Torgo, L.: Evaluation of ensemble methods in imbalanced regression tasks. In: Torgo, L., Krawczyk, B., Branco, P., Moniz, N. (eds.) Proceedings of the First International Workshop on Learning with Imbalanced Domains: Theory and Applications. Proceedings of Machine Learning Research, vol. 74, pp. 129–140. PMLR, ECML-PKDD, Skopje, Macedonia (2017), 'proceedings.mlr.press/v74/moniz17a.html'

11. Moniz, N., Ribeiro, R.P., Cerqueira, V., Chawla, N.: Smoteboost for regression: improving the prediction of extreme values. In: 2018 IEEE 5th International Conference on Data Science and Advanced Analytics (DSAA), pp. 150–159 (2018)

12. Moniz, N., Torgo, L., Eirinaki, M., Branco, P.: A framework for recommendation of highly popular news lacking social feedback. NGC **35**(4), 417–450 (2017)

13. Oliveira, M., Moniz, N., Torgo, L., Santos Costa, V.: Biased resampling strategies for imbalanced spatio-temporal forecasting. JDSA **12**(3), 205–228 (2021)

14. Pebesma, E.: spacetime: spatio-temporal data in R. JSS **51**, 1–30 (2012)

15. Press, W.: Who air quality guidelines for particulate matter, ozone, nitrogen dioxide and sulfur dioxide. World Health Organization. 'whqlibdoc.who.int/hq/2006/WHO_SDE_ PHE_OEH_06. 02_eng.pdf'. Accessed 25 (2014)

16. Ribeiro, R.: Utility-Based Regression. Ph.D. thesis, Department Computer Science, Faculty of Sciences—University of Porto (2011)

17. Ribeiro, R.P., Moniz, N.: Imbalanced regression and extreme value prediction. Mach. Learn. **109**(9–10), 1803–1835 (2020)

18. Rousseeuw, P.J., Hubert, M.: Robust statistics for outlier detection. WIREs Data Min. Knowl. Discov. **1**(1), 73–79 (2011). https://doi.org/10.1002/widm.2

19. Torgo, L., Branco, P., Ribeiro, R.P., Pfahringer, B.: Resampling strategies for regression. Expert. Syst. **32**(3), 465–476 (2015)

20. Torgo, L., Ribeiro, R.: Utility-based regression. In: Proceedings of the 11th European Conference on Principles and Practice of Knowledge Discovery in Databases, pp. 597–604. ECMLPKDD'07, Springer, Berlin, Heidelberg (2007)

21. Zheng, Y., Liu, F., Hsieh, H.P.: U-air: when urban air quality inference meets big data. In: Proceedings of the 19th ACM SIGKDD International Conference on Knowledge Discovery and data Mining, pp. 1436–1444 (2013)

Studying the Impact of Sampling
in Highly Frequent Time Series

Paulo J. S. Ferreira[1]([✉]) [ID], João Mendes-Moreira[1] [ID], and Arlete Rodrigues[2]

[1] INESC TEC, Faculty of Engineering, University of Porto, R. Dr. Roberto Frias s/n, 4200-465 Porto, Portugal
up201305617@fe.up.pt, jmoreira@fe.up.pt
[2] Bosch Security Systems - Sistemas de Segurança, S.A., Estrada Nacional 109/IC 1 - Zona Industrial de Ovar, Pardala, S. João, 3880-728 Aveiro, Portugal
Arlete.Rodrigues@pt.bosch.com

Abstract. Nowadays, all kinds of sensors generate data, and more metrics are being measured. These large quantities of data are stored in large data centers and used to create datasets to train Machine Learning algorithms for most different areas. However, processing that data and training the Machine Learning algorithms require more time, and storing all the data requires more space, creating a Big Data problem. In this paper, we propose simple techniques for reducing large time series datasets into smaller versions without compromising the forecasting capability of the generated model and, simultaneously, reducing the time needed to train the models and the space required to store the reduced sets. We tested the proposed approach in three public and one private dataset containing time series with different characteristics. The results show, for the datasets studied that it is possible to use reduced sets to train the algorithms without affecting the forecasting capability of their models. This approach is more efficient for datasets with higher frequencies and larger seasonalities. With the reduced sets, we obtain decreases in the training time between 40 and 94% and between 46 and 65% for the memory needed to store the reduced sets.

Keywords: Time series · Forecasting · Data reduction · Numerosity reduction · Big data · Machine learning · Holt-winters

1 Introduction

With the rapid advancement of data acquisition technologies, such as cloud data centers, sensors, personal computers, and smartphones, these devices collect an

This work is a result of the project Safe Cities - Inovação para Construir Cidades Seguras, with the reference POCI-01-0247-FEDER-041435, co-funded by the European Regional Development Fund (ERDF), through the Operational Programme for Competitiveness and Internationalization (COMPETE 2020), under the PORTUGAL 2020 Partnership Agreement.

© The Author(s), under exclusive license to Springer Nature Switzerland AG 2023
N. Moniz et al. (Eds.): EPIA 2023, LNAI 14115, pp. 251–262, 2023.
https://doi.org/10.1007/978-3-031-49008-8_20

enormous volume of data. These devices automate the data collection and storage processes, resulting in the continuous accumulation of massive datasets for future data mining tasks [1].

It become common practice to utilize data-driven models for asset and system condition monitoring [16,20,21]. However, to train these models, a dataset is required. With the increasing digitization in various fields, a growing amount of sensor-collected data is being recorded and stored in databases. These databases serve as the foundation for creating datasets used in model training. The size of these datasets can vary depending on the number of sensors, measured metrics, and the specific use case. Dataset sizes can range from a few samples to several million samples [25]. This can pose a Big Data problem.

To Fisher et al. [4], Big Data means that the data cannot be handled and processed straightforwardly by most current information systems or methods because this kind of data becomes too big to be handled by a single machine. An extensive dataset will not fit in memory, and computations will take a long time. New data may constantly stream, so the processing system must decide which part of the stream to capture. This type of dataset probably will not fit on a single hard drive; as a result, it will be stored on several hard drives. They are stored in databases that grow massively and become difficult to store, manage, share, analyze, and visualize via traditional database software tools [19].

According to Wu et al. [27], there are three main issues when dealing with Big Data. The first is related to data acquisition. Collecting large volumes of data necessitates significant energy consumption for data collection and transfer through networks to store data in data centers and databases. Second, storing all the data has called for more advanced technologies that are inefficient energy and resources. Third, the process of analytics and data mining of big data is usually computationally expensive, consuming time, energy, and memory. However, this paper will only focus on the third issue with Big Data.

Even though the resources for storing and processing data are becoming more affordable and more advanced, it is often advisable to reduce the dataset to make the data processing and the training and deployment of the model more accessible, cheaper, and faster. A large dataset usually leads to a significantly more computational effort to train the models. This requires either more processing time or more powerful computers. However, not all training samples may provide equally helpful information for training: some examples may have higher or lower training value than others. For instance, mislabeled or inaccurately demarcated samples may negatively affect the model's performance and thus be less valuable during the training phase [10].

This paper proposes a data reduction approach to create a smaller dataset version. To reduce the data this approach reduces the frequency of the dataset. However, in time series, when the frequency of data is changed, the algorithm will also provide forecasted values in the same frequency as the data used to train the algorithm. For example, if we had a 30 min frequency dataset and reduced the frequency to 60 min, the algorithm would provide forecasted values with a frequency of 60 min. The advantage of our approach is maintaining the forecasting frequency equal to the original frequency of the dataset. Our approach has linear complexity and can be used to reduce large datasets, which later could be used for model training. Our approach can reduce the data storage space and achieve faster training times. The approach is based on numerosity reduction and data aggregation.

The remainder of the paper is organized as follows. Section 2 of this paper covers related works and the position of the proposed method. Section 3 presents our approach and the methodology followed. Section 4 presents the Experimental Setup, including the algorithm, software, datasets, and evaluation metrics. Section 5 describes the experiments. Section 6 presents and discusses the results. Finally, in Sect. 7, we conclude this paper and describe open points to be closed in future work.

2 Related Work

Techniques for data reduction can be employed to obtain a condensed representation of the dataset that significantly reduces its volume while preserving the essential characteristics of the original data [7]. By doing so, mining the reduced dataset becomes more efficient while producing similar or nearly identical results.

According to Han et al. [7], data reduction methods can be classified into five categories: data aggregation, feature selection, numerosity reduction, dimensionality reduction, and discretization.

Data aggregation involves consolidating data and presenting it in a summarized form. It includes activities such as summarizing monthly data when only annual data are required or merging data from multiple sources [9,14].

Feature selection aims to identify and eliminate irrelevant, weakly relevant, or redundant features from the dataset [13,23,29].

Dimensionality reduction involves reducing the number of random variables or attributes under consideration. Techniques such as Discrete Wavelet Transforms (DWT) [28] and Principal Components Analysis (PCA) [2,24] are used to transform or project the original data onto a lower-dimensional space.

Data discretization entails converting continuous data into a finite set of intervals to reduce the number of distinct values. Labels are then used to simplify the representation by replacing the actual values. Most data discretization algorithms require specifying parameters, which can be challenging without prior time series analysis to determine suitable values for obtaining a good discrete representation of the data [11,17].

Numerosity reduction techniques replace the original data volume with alternative, more compact representations. These techniques can be parametric or nonparametric. Parametric methods employ models to estimate the data, storing only the data parameters instead of the actual data. Nonparametric approaches to reduced data representation include histograms [25], clustering [3,22], and sampling [15]. Sampling allows a large dataset to be represented by a smaller random subset, serving as an effective data reduction technique.

Our approach aims to generate a reduced version of the original data with fewer samples. Based on the analysis of related work, our data reduction approach falls within the category of Numerosity reduction (specifically sampling) and Data aggregation.

3 Methodology

We will reduce the number of samples in the dataset to decrease the data volume. We have established two levels of reduction. At Level 1, we decrease the samples by half, while at Level 2, we reduce the samples by one-third. We employ two distinct approaches to achieve sample reduction: elimination and aggregation. In the elimination approach, specific samples are removed, whereas, in the aggregation approach, the samples are consolidated using the mean function (see Table 1).

Table 1. Reduction strategies.

Timestamps	Original	Elimination	Aggregation
t1	V1	V1	(V1 + V2)/2
t2	V2		
t3	V3	V3	(V3 + V4)/2
t4	V4		
t5	V5	V5	(V5 + V6)/2
t6	V6		

When we reduce the data, the frequency of forecasted values also decreases. For instance, if we initially have data spaced at 30-minute intervals and apply Level 1 reduction, the resulting data will be spaced at 60-minute intervals. Consequently, the generated model will only forecast hourly data instead of data for every half hour. However, it is our intention for our approach to predict values with the same frequency as the original sensor. To achieve this, we implemented post-processing techniques on the forecasted values.

For Level 1 reduction, we utilized the average of the previous and next values to bridge the gap between these two points (see Table 2). In the case of Level 2 reduction, we employed interpolation techniques to fill in the gaps in the forecasted values. The interpolation techniques are: linear, spline, and polynomial interpolation [18].

4 Experimental Setup

4.1 Algorithm

The Holt-Winters (HW) [26] is an extension of Holt's method, to capture seasonality and was proposed by Holt and Winters. HW is applied whenever the data

Table 2. Post-processing for the Level 1 reduction.

Timestamps	Original	Level 1	Forecasted	Post-Processed
t1	V1	V1	F1	F1
t2	V2			F2 = (F1 + F3)/2
t3	V3	V3	F3	F3
t4	V4			F4 = (F3 + F5)/2
t5	V5	V5	F5	F5

exhibits both a trend and a seasonal variation [12]. The HW seasonal method comprises the forecast equation and three smoothing equations: one for the level, one for the trend, and one for the seasonal component [8]. There are two variations to this method that differ in the nature of the seasonal component: additive and multiplicative [8]. We use the implementation of the Holt-Winters from the RAPIDS[1] package.

4.2 Datasets

In our experiments, we use two types of datasets: private and public datasets. The private dataset, SC, contains information on physical building conditions. As for the public datasets, we accessed them from the Monash Time Series Forecasting Repository [6], a publicly available repository. Each dataset available at the Monash Time Series Forecasting Repository has several time series. In this paper, we only use one of the time series. Table 3 provides an overview of the datasets used in this paper, including the selected time series and its main characteristics. Additionally, Fig. 1 illustrates the behavior of the selected time series for each dataset.

Table 3. Characteristics of the selected time series.

Dataset	Frequency	Seasonality	Selected time series
Melbourne pedestrian count	60 min	Weekly	15
Electricity	60 min	Annual	5
San francisco traffic	60 min	Weekly	49
SC	30 min	Annual	N/A

4.3 Missing Data

The authors have already prepared the public datasets, ensuring their readiness for use. For datasets with missing values, the authors employed the Last Observation Carried Forward (LOCF) method to replace the missing values. However,

---

[1] https://rapids.ai/.

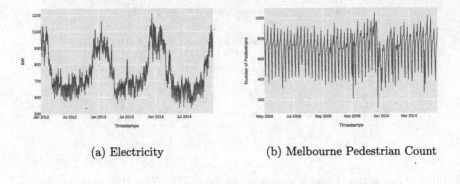

(a) Electricity   (b) Melbourne Pedestrian Count

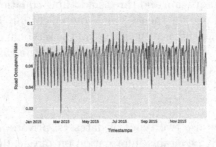

(c) San Francisco Traffic

Fig. 1. Behaviour of the selected time series.

addressing the issue of missing values required a specific approach for the SC dataset.

To tackle this, we experimented to determine the most suitable imputation method for replacing the missing values in the SC dataset. After thorough research, we assessed the effectiveness of several simple imputation methods, including Mean, Median, Backward Fill, Forward Fill, and Random Sampling. Upon analyzing the results obtained from the experiment, we concluded that the Random Sampling method yielded the lowest calculated error. Based on these findings, we selected Random Sampling as the imputation method for the SC dataset.

4.4   Evaluation

We use a sliding window approach to iterate over the data and evaluate our models. In this approach, a fixed-size training window slides over the entire time series history with a fixed step. The model is repeatedly tested against a forecasting window, where older data points are dropped, and the forecasting window is incorporated into the training window in the next iteration.

We use the entire last year for testing. We use the remaining data for the training window. We select a forecasting window of one week with a step of one week, resulting in 52 iterations (52 weeks of a year). In each iteration, we calculate the error to analyze the error's evolution over time.

To evaluate the performance of our approach, we employ the Root Mean Square Error (RMSE). RMSE is a widely used metric for quantifying the error of a model in predicting quantitative data. Equation 1 presents the formula for calculating RMSE, where n represents the number of fitted points, At denotes the actual value, and Ft represents the forecast value.

$$RMSE = \sqrt{\sum_{t=1}^{n} \frac{(Ft - At)^2}{n}} \tag{1}$$

To evaluate the evolution of the RMSE over time, we use and adapt the Prequential Error Estimator algorithm, developed by Gama et al. [5], and update the error as new data becomes available. In addition to assessing the performance of the generated models using various metrics, we also measure the training time and the disk space occupied by the dataset files.

5   Experiments

Firstly, it is necessary to establish a baseline that will serve as a reference for comparing the results of the data reduction experiments. The baseline we intend to utilize does not involve data reduction; we employ the complete and original dataset. This initial experiment aims to generate predictions from the algorithms without any data manipulation, i.e., we do not reduce the data. This approach allows us to assess the algorithm's original predictive capacity when using the entire dataset. Once we establish the baseline, we run the experiments using the reduced datasets and compare the results against the baseline. All experiments follow the same procedure and evaluation protocol (refer to Sect. 4.4); the only difference is the dataset version (original or reduced) employed for training the algorithm.

6   Results and Discussion

To condense the information, we have summarized the results in Table 4 (results for the SC and San Francisco Traffic datasets) and Table 5 (results for the Electricity and Melbourne Pedestrian Count datasets). These tables display the RMSE values for iterations 1, 13, 26, 29, and 52. To ensure readability, we include results only for every 13th iteration, preserving the essential information. For Level 2 reduction, we only present the results of the post-processing method that yielded the best outcomes. Regarding the SC dataset, Spline Interpolation proved to be the most effective post-processing method for Aggregation and Elimination. For the San Francisco Traffic dataset, both Linear and Polynomial Interpolation methods produced identical results in Aggregation and Elimination. The Electricity dataset showcased superior results with the Linear Interpolation method in Aggregation and Elimination. Similarly, the Linear

Interpolation method yielded better outcomes in both Aggregation and Elimination for the Melbourne Pedestrian Count dataset. Tables 4 and 5 illustrate the RMSE progression for the selected datasets.

Table 4. RMSE values for iterations 1, 13, 26, 39, and 52 for datasets SC and San Francisco Traffic.

		SC					Traffic				
		1	13	26	39	52	1	13	26	39	52
Baseline		2.38	2.49	2.38	2.39	2.39	0.019	0.017	0.017	0.017	0.018
Level 1	Agg	2.15	2.08	2.00	2.00	2.00	0.025	0.017	0.016	0.017	0.018
	Elim	2.13	2.31	2.22	2.23	2.33	0.018	0.017	0.015	0.016	0.016
Level 2	Agg	1.90	1.84	1.80	1.80	1.80	0.022	0.019	0.018	0.018	0.019
	Elim	1.98	2.24	2.17	2.16	2.16	0.016	0.017	0.015	0.015	0.016

Analyzing Table 4, we can observe that, for the SC and San Francisco Traffic datasets, the Level 1 reduction did not negatively impact the generated model's performance. We can even observe a decrease in the model error over time when using our reduction approach compared to the baseline. The Aggregation strategy led to a greater error reduction for SC, while the Elimination strategy was more effective for the San Francisco Traffic dataset. Additionally, we observe a reduction in the error when applying the Level 2 reduction to the same datasets. The Level 2 reduction with Aggregation allowed us to achieve lower error estimations over time for the SC dataset (see Fig. 2a), and the Elimination strategy yielded favorable results for the San Francisco Traffic dataset. For these datasets, it is possible to utilize a smaller amount of data to train the Holt-Winters algorithm without compromising the forecasting capability of the resulting model.

Table 5. RMSE values for iterations 1, 13, 26, 39, and 52 for datasets Electricity and Melbourne Pedestrian Count dataset.

		Electricity					Pedestrian				
		1	13	26	39	52	1	13	26	39	52
Baseline		262.75	169.82	158.68	147.71	151.30	121.08	106.74	146.72	168.64	162.18
Level 1	Agg	268.50	183.79	171.70	159.17	162.50	207.59	220.94	235.31	256.97	253.32
	Elim	281.06	182.86	177.58	165.80	167.69	174.10	181.17	202.38	227.31	222.22
Level 2	Agg	287.50	191.90	177.49	164.18	170.41	274.88	288.06	294.01	314.72	313.07
	Elim	265.49	162.42	142.44	134.17	140.48	213.70	211.74	229.13	248.64	243.12

For datasets Electricity and Melbourne Pedestrian Count (see Table 5), using the Level 1 reduction and employing both Aggregation and Elimination, there is an increase in the error of the models. However, the algorithm error increase is more pronounced for the Melbourne Pedestrian Count dataset than for the Electricity dataset. This behavior is even more evident when using Level 2 reduction for the Melbourne Pedestrian Count (see Fig. 2b), where we can detect a higher error increase. As for the Electricity dataset, we can see that the Level 2 reduction with Aggregation negatively impacted the model's performance. However, using Elimination, there was a decrease in the error and an improvement in the model's performance. Overall, and unlike the other datasets analyzed, the Melbourne Pedestrian Count dataset was the one where our approach to reducing the data achieved the worst results. The model's capability to generate good forecasted values is compromised using our approach for this dataset.

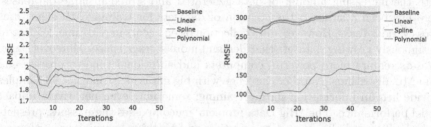

(a) Evolution of the RMSE for the best test scenario.

(b) Evolution of the RMSE for the worst test scenario.

Fig. 2. Evolution of the RMSE for the best and worst test scenarios.

We also measure the memory occupied and the time needed to train the algorithm Holt-Winters using the reduced sets. We measure the memory in bytes and the training time in seconds. Figure 3a shows the memory occupied by the baseline and reduced sets. Figure 3b shows the time needed to train Holt-Winters using the baseline and reduced sets.

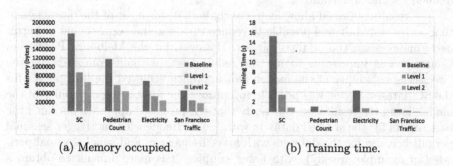

(a) Memory occupied.

(b) Training time.

Fig. 3. Computational cost.

Analyzing Fig. 3a, we can see a reduction in the memory needed to store the reduced sets compared to the baseline. We decrease approximately 50% for

Level 1 and 63% for Level 2 in the memory required to keep the reduced sets. Figure 3b also shows a reduction in the time needed to train Holt-Winters using the reduced sets instead of the original dataset. It was possible to reduce the training time by approximately 70% when using the reduced set obtained from Level 1 and 90% when using the reduced set obtained from Level 2. Overall, we can conclude that when using fewer data to train the Holt-Winters algorithm, it is possible to achieve lower training times, and less memory is required to store these reduced sets.

7   Conclusion and Future Work

With the increasing amount of data generated and stored in large databases, there has been a surge in the creation of datasets for training ML algorithms across various tasks. However, data collection often occurs in real-time, leading to continuously growing datasets that demand more storage space. Moreover, large datasets require more powerful computers and additional time to process and train ML algorithms. Another challenge with big datasets is that not all samples provide helpful information during training; some may even negatively impact model performance. The "Big Data problem" encompasses these issues, presenting a significant challenge to data scientists and Machine Learning practitioners. To overcome these challenges, practitioners employ data filtering, sampling, and dimensionality reduction techniques to optimize training processes and enhance model performance.

In this paper, we propose two simple techniques to reduce large datasets to obtain a smaller version of the original dataset without compromising the forecasting capability of the model and, at the same time, reduce the training time and the space required to store the data. We used as reduction techniques the elimination and aggregation of samples. We also propose two levels of reduction. In Level 1, we reduce the data by half; in Level 2, we reduce the data by one-third. We tested this approach on four datasets with different sampling frequencies and seasonalities.

The results obtained allow us to conclude that, for most of the datasets and time series tested, it was possible to reduce the data and secure equal or better performance than the original dataset. However, for the Melbourn Pedestrian Count, it was impossible to use the reduced sets without compromising the forecasting capability of the model. Our approach achieved the best results for the SC dataset, i.e., it was possible to improve the forecasting capability of the model. From the results, we can verify that the proposed approach obtained the best results for the studied datasets with higher frequencies and bigger seasonal periods because for the datasets with lower frequencies and small seasonal periods (for example, weekly), with fewer samples, it is more difficult to obtain a reasonable calculation of the seasonal component during the training stage. With the reduced sets, we reduced the time needed to train the algorithm (reductions between 40 and 82% for Level 1 and between 53 and 94% for Level 2) and the storage space required to store the reduced sets (between 46 and 49% for Level 1 and between 60 and 65% for Level 2) compared with the original dataset.

This paper shows that it is possible to obtain similar model performance when using a reduced version of the original dataset and simultaneously reduce the training time and memory needed to store these smaller versions. We obtained these results by employing simple and naive techniques to reduce the original dataset, specifically by eliminating and aggregating samples. The results show the importance of investigating new and more complex techniques to reduce big datasets. In future work, we intend to use these results to research more advanced techniques to reduce the datasets and test with other forecasting algorithms (for example, SARIMA and LSTM).

References

1. Bawaneh, M., Simon, V.: A novel time series representation approach for dimensionality reduction. Infocommunications J. **14**(2), 44–55 (2022)
2. Benocci, R., Potenza, A., Bisceglie, A., Roman, H.E., Zambon, G.: Mapping of the acoustic environment at an urban park in the city area of Milan, Italy, using very low-cost sensors. Sensors **22**(9) (2022)
3. Choi, Y., An, N., Hong, S., Cho, H., Lim, J., Han, I.S., Moon, I., Kim, J.: Time-series clustering approach for training data selection of a data-driven predictive model: application to an industrial bio 2,3-butanediol distillation process. Comput. Chem. Eng. **161**, 107758 (2022)
4. Fisher, D., DeLine, R., Czerwinski, M., Drucker, S.: Interactions with big data analytics. Interactions **19**(3), 50–59 (2012)
5. Gama, J., Sebastião, R., Rodrigues, P.: On evaluating stream learning algorithms. Mach. Learn. **90**, 317–346 (2013)
6. Godahewa, R., Bergmeir, C., Webb, G.I., Hyndman, R.J., Montero-Manso, P.: Monash time series forecasting archive. In: Neural Information Processing Systems Track on Datasets and Benchmarks (2021)
7. Han, J., Kamber, M., Pei, J.: Data Mining, 3rd edn. The Morgan Kaufmann Series in Data Management Systems, Morgan Kaufmann, Boston (2012)
8. Hyndman, R., Athanasopoulos, G.: Forecasting: Principles and Practice, 2nd edn. OTexts, Australia (2018)
9. Kotzur, L., Markewitz, P., Robinius, M., Stolten, D.: Impact of different time series aggregation methods on optimal energy system design. Renew. Energy **117**, 474–487 (2018)
10. Lapedriza, À., Pirsiavash, H., Bylinskii, Z., Torralba, A.: Are all training examples equally valuable? (2013). arXiv:abs/1311.6510
11. Li, Y., Jann, T., Vera-Licona, P.: Benchmarking time-series data discretization on inference methods. Bioinformatics **35**(17), 3102–3109 (2019)
12. Lima, S., Gonçalves, A.M., Costa, M.: Time series forecasting using holt-winters exponential smoothing: an application to economic data. In: AIP Conference Proceedings, vol. 2186, p. 090003. AIP Publishing LLC (2019)
13. Ma, D., Ren, W., Han, M.: A two-stage causality method for time series prediction based on feature selection and momentary conditional independence. Phys. A **595**, 126970 (2022)
14. Mamingi, N.: Beauty and ugliness of aggregation over time: a survey. Rev. Econ. **68**(3), 205–227 (2017). https://doi.org/10.1515/roe-2017-0027

15. Nascimento, G.L., Freitas, C.G.S., Rosso, O.A., Aquino, A.L.L.: Data sampling algorithm based on complexity-entropy plane for smart sensing applications. IEEE Sens. J. **21**(22), 25831–25842 (2021)

16. Nejad, E.B., Silva, C., Rodrigues, A., Jorge, A., Dutra, I.: Autosw: a new automated sliding window-based change point detection method for sensor data. In: 2022 IEEE International Conference on Industry 4.0, Artificial Intelligence, and Communications Technology (IAICT), pp. 235–241 (2022)

17. Pal, S.S., Kar, S.: Time series forecasting for stock market prediction through data discretization by fuzzistics and rule generation by rough set theory. Math. Comput. Simul. **162**, 18–30 (2019)

18. Phillips, G.M.: Interpolation and Approximation by Polynomials. CMS Books in Mathematics, Springer (2003)

19. Sagiroglu, S., Sinanc, D.: Big data: a review. In: 2013 International Conference on Collaboration Technologies and Systems (CTS), pp. 42–47 (2013)

20. Silva, C., Rodrigues, A., Jorge, A., Dutra, I.: Sensor data modeling with Bayesian networks. In: 2022 IEEE International Conference on Industry 4.0, Artificial Intelligence, and Communications Technology (IAICT), pp. 261–267 (2022)

21. Silva, C., da Silva, M.F., Rodrigues, A., Silva, J., Santos Costa, V., Jorge, A., Dutra, I.: Predictive maintenance for sensor enhancement in industry 4.0. In: Hong, T.P., Wojtkiewicz, K., Chawuthai, R., Sitek, P. (eds.) Recent Challenges in Intelligent Information and Database Systems, pp. 403–415. Springer Singapore, Singapore (2021)

22. Teichgraeber, H., Lindenmeyer, C.P., Baumgärtner, N., Kotzur, L., Stolten, D., Robinius, M., Bardow, A., Brandt, A.R.: Extreme events in time series aggregation: a case study for optimal residential energy supply systems. Appl. Energy **275**, 115223 (2020)

23. Tuominen, J., Lomio, F., Oksala, N., Palomäki, A., Peltonen, J., Huttunen, H., Roine, A.: Forecasting daily emergency department arrivals using high-dimensional multivariate data: a feature selection approach. BMC Med. Inform. Decis. Mak. **22**(1) (2022)

24. Wan, X., Li, H., Zhang, L., Wu, Y.J.: Dimensionality reduction for multivariate time-series data mining. J. Supercomput. **78**(7), 9862–9878 (2022)

25. Wibbeke, J., Teimourzadeh Baboli, P., Rohjans, S.: Optimal data reduction of training data in machine learning-based modelling: a multidimensional bin packing approach. Energies **15**(9) (2022)

26. Winters, P.R.: Forecasting sales by exponentially weighted moving averages. Manage. Sci. **6**(3), 324–342 (1960)

27. Wu, J., Guo, S., Li, J., Zeng, D.: Big data meet green challenges: greening big data. IEEE Syst. J. **10**(3), 873–887 (2016)

28. Yang, L., Zhai, Y., Zhang, Y., Zhao, Y., Li, Z., Xu, T.: A new methodology for anomaly detection of attacks in IEC 61850-based substation system. J. Inf. Secur. Appl. **68**, 103262 (2022)

29. Yun, K.K., Yoon, S.W., Won, D.: Interpretable stock price forecasting model using genetic algorithm-machine learning regressions and best feature subset selection. Expert Syst. Appl. **213**, 118803 (2023)

Mining Causal Links Between TV Sports Content and Real-World Data

Duarte Melo[1]([✉]) [iD], Jessica C. Delmoral[1] [iD], and João Vinagre[2,3,4] [iD]

[1] NOS SGPS, Porto, Portugal
duartemelo4@gmail.com, https://joint-research-centre.ec.europa.eu
[2] Joint Research Centre - European Commission, Seville, Spain
https://www.inesctec.pt,https://www.fc.up.pt
[3] INESC TEC, Porto, Portugal
[4] FCUP - University of Porto, Porto, Portugal

Abstract. This paper analyses the causal relationship between external events and sports content TV audiences. To accomplish this, we explored external data related to sports TV audience behaviour within a specific time frame and applied a Granger causality analysis to evaluate the effect of external events on both TV clients' volume and viewing times. Compared to regression studies, Granger causality analysis is essential in this research as it provides a more comprehensive and accurate understanding of the causal relationship between external events and sports TV viewership. The study results demonstrate a significant impact of external events on the TV clients' volume and viewing times. External events such as the type of tournament, match popularity, interest and *home team effect* proved to be the most informative about the audiences. The findings of this study can assist TV distributors in making informed decisions about promoting sports broadcasts.

Keywords: Data fusion · Granger causality · Sports broadcast

1 Introduction

In recent years, the distribution of TV content has seen an increase in terms of diversification of channels, programmes and viewing options. This new reality has created increasingly fragmented audiences, with more diverse and personal visualisation patterns, making the task of anticipating customer preferences for TV content distributors more difficult [13]. Although the distribution of TV content has suffered a decrease in demand, especially with the emergence of media on the internet, sports live content are still very popular nowadays and immune to this TV decrease [16].

The drivers that lead people to see sports live content can be categorised into two different types: individual and structural variations [17]. In the first case, the drivers of TV consumption are linked to individual characteristics. For

---

This work is part of the first author's MSc dissertation at the University of Porto.

instance, people who have a more active social life are not expected to have the same viewing patterns as people who have fewer outside contacts. Even though individual analysis is useful in controlled environments, as it allows explaining the consequences of exposure to TV, it is not so effective when the intention is to unveil mass behaviour, generally of greater value to the industry [17]. The structural variation perspective ignores the individual characteristics and uses aggregated audience measurements. It is an approach more focused on finding structural patterns about audience behaviour (e.g., the impact of the scheduling of a program on audience behaviour).

Recently, we have witnessed a growing interest in research that aims to develop tools for real-world event detection and characterization (e.g., *Social Media Sentiment Analysis*), however, it is yet unclear the effect of external events on people's engagement in TV visualisation. Uncovering this effect can have several important implications: (1) TV distributors may be willing to adjust the content and advertisements to the target audiences; (2) TV recommender systems may leverage this knowledge and adapt their recommendations accordingly; (3) regardless of the dynamics of football competition, it is possible to automate the application of recommendation systems. Although many existing expert and intelligent systems for determinants of sports TV viewership enable computers to analyse the correlation between real-world events and TV viewership, limited contributions have been made to analyse the causal effects of real-world events on TV viewership. This study seeks to provide a new understanding of TV viewership presenting data-driven conclusions of the external events that have the most significant impact on TV viewership, using a Granger causality analysis framework.

The remainder of the paper is organized as follows: Sect. 2 presents a literature review of the determinants of sports TV viewership. Section 3 outlines the review and preparation of the behavioural data used in this study. In Sect. 4 the causal analysis methodology is presented. Section 5 presents the study's findings, specifically the impact of external events on football TV viewership in a popular Portuguese tournament. Finally, in Sect. 6 the conclusions and future work are presented.

2   Literature Review

Sports broadcast are known to have the largest share of TV audiences [16], despite their importance, few studies investigate the factors of demand for sports events, measured by TV viewership. The literature on TV audience demand is still relatively underdeveloped compared to the literature analysing live attendance [3,7]. One study that investigates determinant of TV demand is presented in [8], where the authors analyse all the TV broadcasts of the German national football team from January 1993 to June 2008. The analysis is based on TV ratings generated by the *Growth from Knowledge*[1] (GfK). Non-sporting deter-

---

[1] This data source estimates viewership from a representative panel of 5,640 households that contain approximately 13,000 people.

minants of viewing like weather conditions, the broadcasting network, and student holidays were used. The study aims to build a bridge between determinants of demand from the sports economic perspective and determinants of demand from a classical critical success factor analysis, and from a media economics perspective. A regression analysis was applied, and with this, it has concluded that the demand for a sportscast depends mostly on the sporting competition of the match and its relevance within the context of the tournament. Moreover, viewers prefer a national team with more experienced players and matches with an opponent of high quality with a greater reputation. This study also showed that some sport-unrelated factors have explanatory powers, such as kickoff time and weather conditions.

In [16] four FIFA World Cup competitions (2002, 2006, 2010, 2014) have been used to evaluate the determinants of their TV audience size. Through multiple regression analyses, the study tested the explanatory power of independent variables to predict TV audience size. The results showed that when a national team qualifies for the tournament, the *home team effect* (the connection of audiences to a team) is the most relevant predictor of audience size, followed by match quality and scheduling variables.

From the above two studies we can conclude that the main determinants of sports TV viewership are elements associated with the attractiveness of the match, namely: the match quality and importance, the outcome uncertainty, and audience identification with a team.

The present research study adds to the existing literature by addressing some gaps and limitations by (1) utilizing data on traditional sports-related explanatory variables, including outcome uncertainty, match quality, and match importance, as well as less conventional sports-indirect factors, such as news generated by a football match, Twitter teams' popularity, and meteorological factors, and (2) employing a causality analysis to identify influential real-world events on the volume and view patterns of television clients.

3 Data

For this study, conducting an exhaustive review of a wide range of web APIs that collect relevant data on external events was essential. This data, when combined with the measurement of sports TV audience data, would provide us with the necessary information to investigate the impact of external events, such as holidays, weather, and major news events, on both the number of clients and the viewing time of sports TV content.

To learn how football external events affect TV audiences, we use five types of data in this work:

1. *TV demand*—To support the development of this work, a TV content provider in Portugal supplied us with a TV viewership database containing TV program records, with information about the number of viewers and total viewing time between March 2019 and March 2021.

2. *Competition characteristics*—Following the discoveries in [2,8,16], where it was shown that factors inherent to competition (e.g., outcome uncertainty and match quality) can affect viewing patterns, we leverage data from the football betting portal *Football-Data*, which provides historical data on football matches results and odds. However, to ensure we can account for any missing tournaments in *Football-Data*, it was also incorporated data from the *Sports DB* data source. This open crowd-sourced database of sports artwork and metadata offers a free API built by its users and provides us with additional information to enrich our analysis. Furthermore, we use ESPN's Soccer Power Index (SPI), an international and club rating system designed to be the best possible representation of a team's current overall skill level. It has rating data back to 1888 (from more than 550,000 different matches).
3. *Match interest*—Inspired by the findings of [12], where has been shown that the use of Google search trends can provide relevant information about mass behaviours, we use the same Google tool to find the popularity of match-related search terms. In addition, we also explore the impact of the number of news in the viewing patterns through *Público* newspapers (one of the most popular local newspapers).
4. *Match popularity*—To measure the impact that teams' popularity has on TV patterns, we use the Twitter API to extract the number of followers for each team.
5. *Weather conditions*—Weather factors are also believed to have an impact on viewing patterns [4,8], so we extract weather data from 675 different geographic points. As TV demand data is related to Portuguese audiences, weather data is collected from Portuguese weather stations.

Once we had completed the selection of relevant APIs and extracted the raw data from external sources, we faced the challenge of integrating multiple datasets collected under heterogeneous conditions. To guide our implementation of data fusion, we first explored the structure and organization of the platforms and identified two major tasks:

1. Merge the viewership TV data (using the electronic program guide - EPG) with the football match information to create a unified dataset that captures both the viewing patterns and match characteristics.
2. Merge the remaining external datasets to incorporate additional relevant information that can enhance our understanding of the impact of external events on sports TV audiences.

The pie chart in Fig. 1 provides an insightful visualisation of the percentage of merged football matches with sports EPG data and those left out. This visualisation reveals that 40% of the games were successfully linked to the EPG metadata. These findings are particularly noteworthy considering the diverse range of match competitions and the fact that we sourced data from different data providers. Even more, compared to the state of the art, where only 5% of external data were successfully linked to EPG metadata [14]. These results offer new opportunities to enrich sports data analytics and to provide more comprehensive insights into sports media consumption patterns.

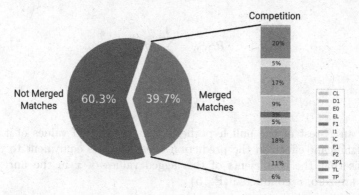

Fig. 1. Percentage of Merged Football Matches with Sports EPG Data: 20% of these matches are related to *La Liga (SP1)*, 18% to *Premier League (E0)*, 17% to *Liga NOS (P1)*, 11% to *Bundesliga (D1)*, 9% to *Serie A (I1)*, while the remaining matches are distributed evenly across other competitions.

4   Methods

4.1   Granger Causality Test

To establish whether or not real-world event data can affect and hence predict future football TV viewership fluctuations, we use a Granger causality test [10].

The essential principle of Granger causality analysis is to test if the past values of one variable x (the driving variable) help to explain the current values of another variable y (the response variable).

There are many ways to apply a Granger causality test, in our specific case we follow an approach in [11] that uses a bivariate vector autoregression. This assumes a lag length p, and estimates the restricted by ordinary least squares(OLS). The restricted Eq. (1) only includes the lagged values of the response variable y, while the unrestricted Eq. (2) includes both the lagged values of y and the lagged values of the driving variable x,

$$y_t = c_0 + \sum_{i=1}^{p} \gamma_i y_{t-i} + e_t \tag{1}$$

$$y_t = c_1 + \sum_{i=1}^{p} \alpha_i y_{t-i} + \sum_{i=1}^{p} \beta_i x_{t-i} + u_t \tag{2}$$

where y_t represents the response variable at time t, x_{t-i} represents the predictor variable at time $t - i$, c_0, c_1, γ_i, α_i and β_i are coefficients to be estimated and e_t and u_t are the prediction errors.

To test for Granger causality, we compare the residual sum of squares (RSS) of two models: one that includes only past values of the response variable (Eq. 3) and one that includes past values of both variables (Eq. 4).

$$RSS_0 = \sum_{t=1}^{T} \hat{e}_t^2 \tag{3}$$

$$RSS_1 = \sum_{t=1}^{T} \hat{u}_t^2 \tag{4}$$

Then an F-test of the null hypothesis that the lagged values of x do not have a significant effect on the prediction of y, which is equivalent to the null hypothesis that the coefficients of the lagged values of x in the unrestricted equation are zero, is conducted (Eq. 5)

$$H_0 : \beta_1 = \beta_2 = \cdots = \beta_p = 0 \tag{5}$$

To test this hypothesis, we perform an F-test on the difference in RSS of the two models. (Eq. 6)

$$F = \frac{(RSS_0 - RSS_1)/p}{RSS_1/(T - 2p - 1)} \tag{6}$$

If the critical value of F at 95% probability level is lower than the observed value of F (6), we reject the null hypothesis(H_0). The significance level we use is 5% and if the p-value of a pair of variables is smaller than 0.05, we could say with 95% confidence that a predictor x causes a response y. The null hypothesis test (H_0) is that the lagged values of x does not Granger cause y.

For this problem, we run the Granger test with only one lag ($p=1$). We opted for this test because by using a single lag we can more accurately capture the immediate influence of the football match external factors on the subsequent viewing behaviour.

The Granger causality test assumes series stationarity. In order not to have false estimates, before conducting causality tests, we first test whether the series are stationary or not. For this purpose, we use the augmented Dickey Fuller unit root test [6]. In the case of non-stationarity, differentiation is applied to the series in order to make them stationary:

$$y_t' = y_t - y_{t-1} \tag{7}$$

This results in $T - 1$ values, since the first value cannot be differentiated.

4.2   Causal Analysis of TV Viewership in Liga NOS

We apply a set of case studies to explore the causal relationship between real-world data and TV viewership. The chosen tournament, Liga NOS, was selected due to its significant impact on TV audiences and its large number of matches. The 19/20 season was selected as it is the only season that brings together all matches from an entire season, providing a comprehensive dataset for analysis. However, it should be noted that the latter part of this season occurred during the initial phase of the COVID pandemic, and as such, we need to take that into account when interpreting the results.

Despite the fact that we only use one competition (*Liga NOS*), it should be noted that this methodology is generalisable and applicable to other sports tournaments.

Based on prior knowledge, it was hypothesized that:

1. Match result uncertainty Granger causes TV viewership [9];
2. Participant teams' quality Granger causes TV viewership;
3. Participant teams' interest Granger causes TV viewership;
4. Participant teams' popularity Granger causes TV viewership [12];
5. Weather conditions Granger causes TV viewership;
6. Scheduling Granger causes TV viewership;
7. TV-network Granger causes TV viewership [14].

In order to make a better assessment of these hypotheses, a set of variables were selected within the scope of each external factor (see Table 1).

Table 1. Summary of the external variables used for the causality analysis.

Factor	Variable	Description
Outcome uncertainty	'probtie'	Match tie probability
	'b365_d'	Match draw odds
Match quality	'goals_diff_match'	The average goals difference for the home and away team
	'goals_a_match'	The average goals against for the home and away team
	'losses_match'	The average number of losses for the home and away team
	'rank_match'	The average raking of the match
	'spi_match'	The average strength of the home and away team
	'importance_match'	The average importance of the home and away team
Match interest	'counted_news'	Number of news in the days before the match
	'week_interest'	Number of google searches in the week preceding the match
	'day_interest'	Number of google searches in the day preceding the match
	'hour_interest'	Number of google searches in the hour preceding the match
Match popularity	'followers_count_match'	Sum of the number of followers of the home and away team on twitter
Weather	'wind_speed'	Atmospheric quantity just before the start of the match
	'temp'	
	'precipitation'	
Scheduling	'day_of_week'	Day of the week
	'hour'	Hour
TV-network	'counted_channels'	Number of channels a match was broadcast live

The outcome uncertainty is referred to as one of the most important factors in public forecasting of sporting events [9]. To quantify the impact of this factor, we use two measures in our analysis. Firstly, we consider the draw projection generated by the *Sports Power Index* (*SPI*), and the draw odd offered by the *bet365* bookmakers.

The match quality and the match popularity are other factors that possibly influence the number of TV audiences [7,16]. In order to obtain these match values, we follow the implementation in [5] and grouped the features referring to the home and away team into a single feature. In this study, n teams are considered. The ranking of each team based on performance is $\{T_1, T_2, T_3, \ldots, T_n\}$, where T_i identifies the ranking of the ith team i. Knowing that the success of competing teams can be measured by rank-order of each team, (e.g., T_i, T_j) the quality of the match can be expressed by the average rank-order of competing teams [5].

$$(T_i + T_j)/2 \qquad (8)$$

Search patterns also proved to be useful in giving information about mass behaviour [12]. Therefore, we use Google search trends match features. In addition, the number of news in the 5 days preceding the game is also used as an interest factor.

Broadcast related factors are also considered to have an impact in terms of TV audiences [14]. Thus, we used the day of the week and the game time as scheduling factors and the number of channels that broadcast the game as a broadcast factor. The resulting time series plot of some external factors and TV viewership features, which will serve as the basis for our Granger causality test, can be seen in Fig. 2. Although all the external factors for a given match occur before the time of the match, our data did not hold this property. Therefore, we applied a shift in external factors (from time T to time T-1) to capture any causal relationships between the external factors and TV viewership. Creating a lag of 1 allowed us to examine whether past values of the independent variable (external factors) were predictive of the current value of the dependent variable

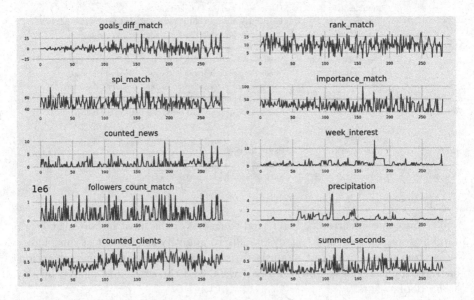

Fig. 2. Liga NOS time series plot.

(TV viewership). By doing so, we could investigate whether there was a delayed effect of the external factors on TV viewership.

To verify the proposed methodology we use seven cases studies. On one hand, a general case study with all Portuguese league matches validates whether or not external events have predictive power on sports TV viewership. On the other hand, six different teams case studies evaluate the external events predictive power across different teams context, providing more accurate information about the Portuguese TV audience behaviour. For this purpose, we select two teams with big TV customer engagement (*FC Porto* and *Sporting CP*), two teams with medium customer engagement (*Sp Braga* and *Famalicão FC*) and two teams with low customer engagement (*Rio Ave* and *CD Aves*). The average viewing time and the volume of customers per team in Liga NOS in the 19/20 season is shown in Fig. 3.

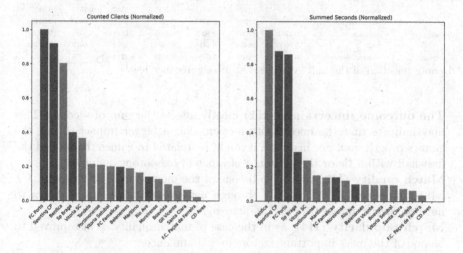

Fig. 3. TV viewing time and client volume for Liga NOS 19/20 teams. The red bars represent the six teams' case studies selected.

5   Results and Discussion

Tables 2 and 3 present the results of the p-values for Granger causality tests performed on various external factors affecting TV clients' volume and viewing times, respectively. The columns represent different football clubs, while the rows represent the various variables tested. The results elucidate on two crucial issues. First, when we look at all Portuguese league matches, it appears that at the significance level of 5%, with the exception of precipitation and the day of the week, all the other external events have predictive power on TV clients' volume and viewing times. Second, the number of external events that have predictive power on TV clients' volume and viewing times is higher in teams with lower customer engagement.

Table 2. Counted Clients Granger causality tests.

Factor	Variables	All p-value	FC Porto p-value	Sporting CP p-value	Sp Braga p-value	Famalicão FC p-value	Rio Ave p-value	CD Aves p-value
Outcome uncertainty	'probtie'	0.0000*	0.0867	0.6143	0.8870	0.0034*	0.1921	0.0004*
	'b365_d'	0.0001*	0.1024	0.2384	0.9503	0.0466*	0.2165	0.0019*
Match quality	'goals_diff_match'	0.0000*	0.0295*	0.1620	0.7904	0.0128*	0.0006*	0.0033*
	'goals_a_match'	0.0000*	0.7543	0.7006	0.8435	0.0662	0.0003*	0.1893
	'losses_match'	0.0000*	0.4064	0.6864	0.7200	0.0109*	0.0049*	0.0097*
	'rank_match'	0.0000*	0.2069	0.7721	0.5389	0.0755	0.0114*	0.0004*
	'spi_match'	0.0000*	0.0189*	0.1661	0.1338	0.0549	0.0001*	0.0000*
	'importance_match'	0.0000*	0.4718	0.0616	0.2455	0.6542	0.0410*	0.7404
Match interest	'counted_news'	0.0000*	0.0712*	0.8655	0.4417	0.0074*	0.0101*	0.0080*
	'week_interest'	0.0174*	0.0463*	0.0294*	0.4990	0.6846	0.1537	0.2734
	'day_interest'	0.0217*	0.5412	0.3345	0.7482	0.6846	0.0044*	0.1663
	'hour_interest'	0.0011*	0.8177	0.1920	0.7616	0.6846	0.1719	0.8842
Match popularity	'followers_count_match'	0.0000*	0.9855	0.0015*	0.0334*	0.0092*	0.0001*	0.0000*
Weather	'wind_speed'	0.0406*	0.6981	0.8237	0.8694	0.4784	0.7426	0.3271
	'temp'	0.0002*	0.1423	0.4837	0.7689	0.3547	0.1547	0.0461*
	'precipitation'	0.7665	0.2098	0.3977	0.9242	0.2605	0.0460*	0.6049
Scheduling	'day_of_week'	0.1271	0.7066	0.8005	0.8991	0.6788	0.5085	0.9602
	'hour'	0.0000*	0.0439*	0.4416	0.3463	0.9038	0.0679	0.0356*
TV-network	'counted_channels'	0.0000*	0.3661	0.0751	0.3118	0.2214	0.7996	0.1803

* Denote rejection of the null hypothesis at 5% significance level

- **The outcome uncertainty (H1)** mostly affects the sum of seconds. This may indicate that the uncertainty measure has a bigger impact during the game's progression. For instance, it might be related to games that ended the first half with a tie or the existence of a penalty shootout definition [1];
- **Match quality (H2)** proved to be one of the most important factors;
- **Match interest (H3)**, mainly through news counting, has also shown to have predictive power over TV audiences.
- **Match popularity (H4)**, as in the case of match quality, it also proved to be one of the most important factors in TV audiences;
- **The weather factor (H5)** only in the case of teams with low customer engagement it has shown to have a predictive effect. This may suggest that fans of teams with less engagement do not have a stronger bond with their team and let themselves be carried away by external events;
- **Scheduling (H6)** showed to have an impact only on the counting of clients xof two teams (a team with high customer engagement and other with low customer engagement). These results are not surprising given that we are only considering games from one competition, the game schedule is very similar throughout the league;
- **Channel counting (H7)** proved to be an irrelevant factor in predicting TV audiences. This suggests that when a game is played on more than one channel, people spread across different channels.

Table 3. Summed seconds Granger causality tests.

Factor	Variables	All	FC Porto	Sporting CP	Sp Braga	Famalicão FC	Rio Ave	CD Aves
		p-value	p-value	p-value	p-value	p-value	p-value	p-value
Outcome uncertainty	'probtie'	0.0000*	0.0182*	0.3254	0.9719	0.0018*	0.0317*	0.0008*
	'b365_d'	0.0000*	0.0229*	0.6316	0.3151	0.0509	0.0602	0.0093*
Match quality	'goals_diff_match'	0.0000*	0.0012*	0.1322	0.0494*	0.0006*	0.0000*	0.0015*
	'goals_a_match'	0.0000*	0.5233	0.8175	0.2116	0.0060*	0.0000*	0.1572
	'losses_match'	0.0000*	0.2266	0.5867	0.1566	0.0006*	0.0004*	0.0014*
	'rank_match'	0.0000*	0.0574	0.5626	0.0879	0.0031*	0.0012*	0.0007*
	'spi_match'	0.0000*	0.0001*	0.0677	0.0005*	0.0009*	0.0000*	0.0001*
	'importance_match'	0.0000*	0.4289	0.0207*	0.0090*	0.8476	0.0076*	0.9655
Match interest	'counted_news'	0.0000*	0.2665	0.8224	0.2365	0.0048*	0.0013*	0.0266*
	'week_interest'	0.0018*	0.0435*	0.0019*	0.8584	0.7787	0.0145*	0.5736
	'day_interest'	0.0005*	0.2743	0.5419	0.7161	0.7787	0.0669	0.5039
	'hour_interest'	0.0018*	0.4230	0.3488	0.7097	0.7787	0.2556	0.8311
Match popularity	'followers_count_match'	0.0000*	0.7152	0.0001*	0.0000*	0.0008*	0.0000*	0.0000*
Weather	'wind_speed'	0.0661*	0.5088	0.9282	0.6149	0.7900	0.2108	0.1525*
	'temp'	0.0004*	0.1188	0.4082	0.5284	0.5312	0.3216	0.3206*
	'precipitation'	0.8115	0.0687	0.0645	0.9183	0.7712	0.0487*	0.1143
Scheduling	'day_of_week'	0.0550	0.2471	0.7584	0.3185	0.5503	0.6911	0.3115
	'hour'	0.0000*	0.0894	0.2426	0.6625	1.0000	0.0726	0.1062
TV-network	'counted_channels'	0.0005*	0.9896	0.4560	0.8331	0.4655	0.8014	0.7287

* Denote rejection of the null hypothesis at 5% significance level

6 Conclusion

The results revealed a high connection rate between external data and EPG metadata data and a large number of events detected as having a cause-and-effect relationship in sports TV audiences. Our findings further support the usefulness of online data to understand TV behaviours. Data sources such as news, Twitter API and Google trends proved to be of the greatest value in predicting TV audiences. Despite that, some limitations should be noted, which also suggest future research directions. The causality analysis results are based on bivariate time series models. Future research should investigate causal relationships between external real-world events and TV viewing patterns within a multivariate framework. In addition, the use of a different causal discovery framework can bring more confidence in the obtained results. A possible alternative to the Granger causality test is PCMCIplus [15], a conditional independence (CI) based method for linear and nonlinear, lagged and contemporaneous causal discovery from observational time series. Finally, we only incorporate data from Portugal. In future research, including data from multiple countries or regions will enable finding important patterns or differences that exist in other parts of the world.

Acknowledgements. The third author contributed to the technical work in this paper while affiliated with INESC TEC and the University of Porto and to the writing of the paper while affiliated with the Joint Research Centre of the European Commission.

References

1. Abell, J., Condor, S., Lowe, R.D., Gibson, S., Stevenson, C.: Who ate all the pride? patriotic sentiment and English national football support. Nations Natl. **13**(1), 97–116 (2007)
2. Alavy, K., Gaskell, A., Leach, S., Szymanski, S.: On the edge of your seat: demand for football on television and the uncertainty of outcome hypothesis. Int. J. Sport Financ. **5**(2), 75 (2010)
3. Baimbridge, M., Cameron, S., Dawson, P.: Satellite television and the demand for football: a whole new ball game? Scott. J. Polit. Econ. **43**(3), 317–333 (1996)
4. Barnett, G.A., Chang, H.J., Fink, E.L., Richards, W.D., Jr.: Seasonality in television viewing: a mathematical model of cultural processes. Commun. Res. **18**(6), 755–772 (1991)
5. Borland, J., Macdonald, R.: Demand for sport. Oxf. Rev. Econ. Policy **19**(4), 478–502 (2003). http://www.jstor.org/stable/23606855
6. Dickey, D.A., Fuller, W.A.: Distribution of the estimators for autoregressive time series with a unit root. J. Am. Stat. Assoc. **74**(366a), 427–431 (1979). https://doi.org/10.1080/01621459.1979.10482531
7. Downward, P., Dawson, A., Dejonghe, T.: The Demand for professional team sports: attendance and broadcasting 261–300 (2009). https://doi.org/10.1016/B978-0-7506-8354-8.00010-7
8. Feddersen, A., Rott, A.: Determinants of demand for televised live football: features of the German national football team. J. Sports Econ. **12**(3), 352–369 (2011). https://doi.org/10.1177/1527002511404783
9. Forrest, D., Simmons, R.: Outcome uncertainty and attendance demand in sport: the case of English soccer. J. R. Stat. Soc. Ser. D (The Statistician) **51**(2), 229–241 (2002). http://www.jstor.org/stable/3650322
10. Granger, C.W.J.: Investigating causal relations by econometric models and cross-spectral methods. Econometrica **37**(3), 424–438 (1969). http://www.jstor.org/stable/1912791
11. Hamilton, J.D.: Time series analysis. Princeton University Press (2020)
12. Mesquita, S., Vieira, C.H., Perfeito, L., Gonçalves-Sá, J.: Learning from pandemics: using extraordinary events can improve disease now-casting models. CoRR (2021). arXiv:abs/2101.06774
13. Napoli, P.M.: The unpredictable audience: an exploratory analysis of forecasting error for new prime-time network television programs. J. Advert. **30**(2), 53–60 (2001). https://doi.org/10.1080/00913367.2001.10673637
14. Nixon, L., Ciesielski, K., Philipp, B.: Ai for audience prediction and profiling to power innovative tv content recommendation services. In: Proceedings of the 1st International Workshop on AI for Smart TV Content Production, Access and Delivery, pp. 42–48. AI4TV '19, Association for Computing Machinery, New York, NY, USA (2019). https://doi.org/10.1145/3347449.3357485
15. Runge, J.: Discovering contemporaneous and lagged causal relations in autocorrelated nonlinear time series datasets. In: Conference on Uncertainty in Artificial Intelligence, pp. 1388–1397. PMLR (2020)
16. Uribe, R., Buzeta, C., Manzur, E., Alvarez, I.: Determinants of football tv audience: the straight and ancillary effects of the presence of the local team on the FIFA world cup. J. Bus. Res. **127**, 454–463 (2021). https://doi.org/10.1016/j.jbusres.2019.10.064
17. Webster, J.G., Wang, T.Y.: Structural determinants of exposure to television: the case of repeat viewing. J. Broadcast. Electron. Media **36**(2), 125–136 (1992)

Hybrid SkipAwareRec: A Streaming Music Recommendation System

Rui Ramos[1](✉) , Lino Oliveira[1] , and João Vinagre[1,2,3]

[1] INESC TEC, Porto, Portugal
`rui.j.ramos@inesctec.pt`
[2] Joint Research Centre - European Commission, Seville, Spain
[3] Faculty of Sciences - University of Porto, Porto, Portugal

Abstract. In an automatic music playlist generator, such as an automated online radio channel, how should the system react when a user hits the skip button? Can we use this type of negative feedback to improve the list of songs we will playback for the user next? We propose SkipAwareRec, a next-item recommendation system based on reinforcement learning. SkipAwareRec recommends the best next music categories, considering positive feedback consisting of normal listening behaviour, and negative feedback in the form of song skips. Since SkipAwareRec recommends broad categories, it needs to be coupled with a model able to choose the best individual items. To do this, we propose Hybrid SkipAwareRec. This hybrid model combines the SkipAwareRec with an incremental Matrix Factorisation (MF) algorithm that selects specific songs within the recommended categories. Our experiments with Spotify's Sequential Skip Prediction Challenge dataset show that Hybrid SkipAwareRec has the potential to improve recommendations by a considerable amount with respect to the skip-agnostic MF algorithm. This strongly suggests that reformulating the next recommendations based on skips improves the quality of automatic playlists. Although in this work we focus on sequential music recommendation, our proposal can be applied to other sequential content recommendation domains, such as health for user engagement.

Keywords: Sequential recommendation · Next best action recommendation · Implicit negative feedback · Reinforcement learning

1 Introduction

Music helps in our intellectual development, stimulating creativity, and provides a means of expressing ourselves.[1] Humans spend a lot of time listening to it,[2] and the songs that we choose to listen to are influenced by a number of factors, but the most obvious are our individual taste and preferences. However, given

---

[1] https://www.betterup.com/blog/benefits-of-music. Accessed: 2023-03-27.
[2] https://musicalpursuits.com/music-streaming/. Accessed: 2023-03-27.

© The Author(s), under exclusive license to Springer Nature Switzerland AG 2023
N. Moniz et al. (Eds.): EPIA 2023, LNAI 14115, pp. 275–287, 2023.
https://doi.org/10.1007/978-3-031-49008-8_22

the huge music catalogues available today in most music streaming services, choosing the next song to listen to is not always easy.

Our contribution, Hybrid SkipAwareRec, is a proposal of a next-action recommendation system for music that interacts in real time with the user. It is divided in two parts: (1) SkipAwareRec, a Reinforcement Learning (RL) Recommender System whose objective is to recommend the best possible next music categories, by collecting user feedback—positive and negative—during the interaction of the recommender agent with the user, and (2) Hybrid SkipAwareRec, that combines SkipAwareRec with an incremental Matrix Factorisation (MF) algorithm that selects the items belonging to the recommended category that best match user preferences. Figure 1 illustrates how these two components are combined in an RL setting. In our problem, Actions correspond to music categories composed of subsets of items, and ISGD is an incremental MF algorithm for personalised item recommendation. The figure illustrates our final setting—Hybrid SkipAwareRec—, in which we use SkipAwareRec to predict the best next category in the streaming session. We then reduce the candidate space such that ISGD considers only items belonging to that category. To account for errors of SkipAwareRec in category prediction, we add to the resulting recommended items some additional recommendations obtained from ISGD considering the whole item space. We provide further details of this hybrid setting in Sect. 3.3.

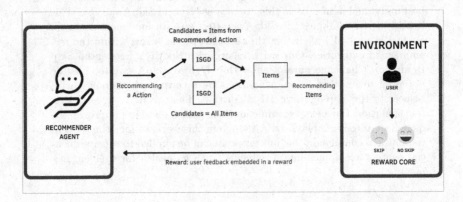

Fig. 1. Hybrid SkipAwareRec overview

In the remainder of the paper we provide an overview of related work in Sect. 2, followed by the description of our methodology and proposed solution in Sect. 3. Our results are presented and briefly discussed in Sect. 4. Section 5 summarises the main conclusions and indicates future research directions.

2 Related Work

The ability of recommender systems to adapt their behaviour to individual preferences is becoming more and more valuable [3]. Recently, the iterative recommendation approach has been successfully applied to different real-world recommendation tasks in several specific scenarios, such as e-learning, recommendation of music, movies, news, and professional skills [7]. It has also been shown that exploiting negative feedback can be beneficial in music recommendation [1,8].

2.1 Recommendations with Negative Implicit Feedback

There are several types of user feedback that can be used to update the models responsible for generating recommendations. Most existing contributions exploit explicit feedback—which effectively demonstrates the user's feelings towards the recommendations—and positive implicit feedback—users' positive interests acquired through indirectly monitoring its behaviour. When it comes to negative implicit feedback, there are few works that cover this type of user response. Furthermore, the few contributions that cover this type of feedback use it in boolean form, that is, without quantification, just existence or not.

Regarding non-sequential recommendation paradigms, there are some works that focus on natural—not artificial—negative implicit feedback. Peska and Vojtáš [9] studied the implication of using implicit negative feedback in e-commerce oriented recommendation systems, using page visits, mouse movements, scrolling, among others. In all test cases of their work, the combined negative preferences were superior to other methods for larger train sets, suggesting that negative preferences may become important while trying to sort already good objects. Lee et al. [5] introduced a mechanism to infer negative implicit feedback and test the feasibility of this type of user response as a way to represent what users want in the context of a job recommendation system, using as negative implicit feedback the action of opening a job offer and closing it, rather than saving it. Compared to cases using only positive preferences, the distinction between good and bad jobs was significantly clear when using negative preferences.

Regarding sequential recommendation using negative implicit feedback, Zhao et al. [12] proposed a pairwise Deep RL for the recommendation framework with the ability to continuously improve its strategies during interactions with users by collecting both positive and negative feedback. In their work, authors separated negative and positive items during learning—they model the sequential interactions between users and a recommender system as an Markov Decision Process (MDP) and leverage RL to automatically learn the optimal strategies by recommending items on a trial-error basis and receive reinforcement of these items from user feedback.

2.2 Sequential Music Recommendation

The vast majority of contributions in sequential music recommendation are based on RL. The problem is modelled as a MDP with the goal of obtaining a controlled environment to apply an RL task. Contributions differ through different components of the MDPs and stages of the algorithm they use to recommend.

In the work of Hu et al. [4], each state represents a sequence of songs clusters listened by the user, and listening to a song is considered an action. As a reward, authors used a function of user listening, collecting, and downloading songs, and the RL algorithm used was Q-Learning. Similarly, Chi et al. [2] also use clusters of songs—researchers categorised all the songs in the experimental dataset into four classes manually pre-annotated by users with correspondence to their emotion class. Authors also used implicit feedback in their work, with its reward function consisting of implicit feedback—listening time and number of replays—and explicit feedback—ratings. The algorithms used were SARSA and Q-Learning. There are two contributions that are quite similar, both Wang [11] and Liebman [6] use song sequence to represent states, the listening of a song as a representation of an action and a function of user's preferences over individual songs and song transitions as a reward function. Wang uses a tree-search heuristic algorithm, while Liebman uses a Policy-gradient algorithm.

3   Methodology and Proposed Solution

Hybrid SkipAwareRec is divided into three main tasks: the generation of a set of actions that are used for recommendation, the recommendation of an action and the recommendation of specific items.

3.1   Action Set Generation

In a recommendation problem, one of the most important tasks is to learn user preferences. The tastes of each user can be represented by topics, or categories, that represent sets of similar specific items in a given context. For example, in a TV content recommendation context, it is important to understand what the users favourite topics are, such as comedy, sports, action, among others.

An RL approach with all available items represents a giant action space and is therefore very difficult to model. The task of grouping similar items into categories also greatly reduces the search space, enabling the RL algorithm to work with a small action set.

To generate the action set that correspond to musical categories, we use standard K-Means, because of its scalability and convergence guarantees. Through various song attributes, such as duration, year of release, acoustics, beat strength, resonance, danceability, among many others that can be chosen by whoever performs the task, it is possible to create a set of categories resulting from the grouping of songs.

3.2   Next Best Action Recommendation

In a real scenario, a recommender system is in constant interaction with a user. The recommendation task can be seen as an iterative process in which the user receives a recommended item and provides feedback to the system, allowing that in the next iteration the recommendation model incorporates the feedback received and makes a new recommendation, closer to the user's current preferences.

When listening to music, the choice of the next song to listen to is conditioned by several factors, with user preferences being the most important one to consider. With this in mind, the goal of this stage is to use negative implicit feedback, more specifically song skips, to train an RL algorithm that learns user preferences during music streaming sessions and generates good category recommendations based on this learning. Figure 2 shows the general diagram of this process.

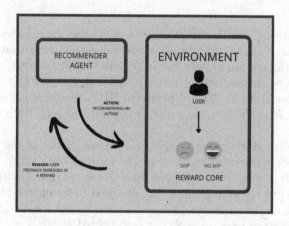

Fig. 2. Iterative Learning via Implicit Negative Feedback

In an RL problem, there is a learner and decision maker—the agent—that interacts with the environment. In our case, the environment is the user of the system that receives and reacts to recommendations—provides rewards and a new state based on the agent's actions. Thus, in this type of learning, we do not explicitly fit an agent to a dataset such as in a supervised learning task, but rather present it with rewards that can be either positive, neutral or negative.

Agent and Environment In our MDP, the environment is completely observable, i.e., the agent directly observes the state of the environment. This allows us to make the analogy to a recommender system that directly observes user's behaviour. The agent is the recommender system whose actions correspond to recommendations to the user. The user observes this action and provides implicit feedback, which is used as input to a function that outputs a reward. After an action has been performed, a new state is transitioned to and the process repeats until the session is over.

States and Actions The set of states S_n in an MDP defines the context of the environment, i.e., it is a set of tokens that represent every state S_i that the agent can be in. An action A, on the other hand, is what causes the environment to change its state. In our problem setting, an action represents the listening of a song from a certain musical category. We define the states as the set of the previous K actions performed by the user—i.e. the categories of the previous songs. This way, we can preserve historical information regarding the transition between musical categories by the user, and at the same time be able to focus on recent actions. Our model also allows state resets, to account for context switches in which the session is interrupted—a situation where the sequence of actions is uninformative to the recommender. An example of a context switch is the change of playlist or streaming source.

Reward The goal of an RL algorithm is to maximise the accumulated reward. Rewards are given by the output of a real-valued function that models how good or promising certain actions are in certain states. Essentially, it indicates "how good it is to choose/be in a certain state". A Reward R_{S_t} is received for transitioning to a state S_t. The objective in RL is to choose action A so as to maximise $R_{t+1}, R_{t+2}, R_{t+3}, \ldots$ in order to get the best long-term accumulation of rewards.

In our problem setting, the central element and focus of the reward function is the implicit negative feedback in the form of song skips. Furthermore, this information is quantified, since we have access to different types of skips, depending on when the skip is made. We assigned different weights to the feedback depending on its moment of skip—we gave higher reward values to skips that were transmitted later, or even not transmitted at all.

Two analyses were conducted on data from the Spotify Sequential Skip Prediction Challenge,[3] which showed that skip behaviour is not related to the time of day or type of music listening context. In addition, a survey was conducted which confirmed the intuition that the value of a skip in a user's own private playlist is different from a skip in other playlists (e.g. public or other users'). Only 2.4% of users who responded to the survey stated that they skip a song in their own private collection because they do not like it. The remaining respondents gave reasons such as "I do not want to listen to that specific song at the moment" and "I am trying to find a specific song through the jumps between songs" to skip songs in this type of context. Thus, we used this insight to shape our reward function differently for the user's own collections and for other contexts.

Table 1 shows the values of the reward function defined for the problem.

---

[3] https://www.aicrowd.com/challenges/spotify-sequential-skip-prediction-challenge. Accessed: 2023-03-28.

Table 1. Reward function output

Skip moment	Reward—user collection	Reward—other context
1	0.7	0.1
2	0.7	0.3
3	0.7	0.7
4	0.9	0.9
Not skipped	1	1

Reinforcement Learning Algorithm To solve the problem of sequentially choosing the next music category, from which the recommendations will arise, we used Q-Learning, a value-based off-policy temporal-difference (TD) RL algorithm whose goal is to learn the value of an action in a given state, by learning the action-value function. This algorithm finds an optimal policy to maximise the expected value of the total reward over any and all successive steps from the current state.

This algorithm was chosen because of its great advantage of being able to compare the expected utility of available actions without requiring a model of the environment. With this type of model-free approaches, we can update the whole value function and policy with every new sample.

Reinforcement Learning Mechanism In an iterative and sequential application it is mandatory that the model is constantly updated with each new iteration. To do this, we use the properties of RL to update our model each time the user transmits feedback on a given item. Whenever an information is read or received that a user has chosen an action, in addition to the state transition performed in the MDP, the Q-Table in Q-Learning is also updated. The Next Best Action (NBA) recommendation at step is obtained by choosing the action with the highest Q-value in a certain state.

In order to solve the Exploration vs Exploitation problem, an ϵ-Greedy strategy is used to balance the two techniques during recommendations. This paradigm consists of randomly selecting, with a defined probability, whether to exploit or explore: 1-ϵ of the time the algorithm exploits and ϵ of the time the algorithm explores. With this, the user will receive recommendations aligned with their already demonstrated preferences, as well as new and different recommendations that allow the agent to discover new information about his/her preferences.

Recommendation Strategy There are two stages involved in our algorithm for recommending the NBA. In an initial phase, the algorithm is only fed with data in order to build its Q-Table. Considering that there is enough real data to perform a good learning, it is valuable not to start recommendations right away after the start of learning because, as the name of the approach suggests, the algorithm learns by reinforcement, and with little interaction, its performance will not produce good results. It is preferable to have an initial training phase with real historical data, rather than using the approach right away to generate recommendations with few interactions performed.

In a second phase of the RL approach, the connection of the model is now only and exclusively with a specific user. This way, the algorithm when it is framed with a single user already has a good basis of how to recommend, and starts to mould itself to that user in the long term.

3.3   Next Best Items Recommendation

In Sect. 3.2, we describe SkipAwareRec, an RL algorithm that recommends the next best item category that corresponds to the action, at each state, that maximises the expected accumulated reward. The idea is then to use this category to narrow down the recommendation candidates space. For the actual item recommendation, any general-purpose collaborative filtering algorithm that learns from implicit feedback can be used in our problem. In this work, we use ISGD [10], an incremental MF algorithm for implicit positive-only feedback. The ability to learn incrementally fits well with our sequential learning setting, since both the RL and the MF algorithms can learn online, in parallel, from the same sequence of user actions.

Hybrid SkipAwareRec The most straightforward combination of SkipAwareRec with ISGD would be to simply have the latter recommend items from within the category recommended by the first. However, as we show in Table 2, this is not the best approach. For example, let us imagine a hypothetical scenario where actions/categories correspond to music genres and SkipAwareRec recommends Jazz. There may be songs from the Blues genre that are also good recommendations for the user. Solely using the NBA approach, all Blues songs will be simply ignored. Maybe more importantly, if SkipAwareRec fails to predict the correct category, the recommendation is guaranteed to fail.

To address this, we adapt the use of the ISGD algorithm to generate a Top K recommendations, whose K/2 recommendations come from the recommended NBA and K/2 recommendations from all existing items in the data space, as illustrated in Fig. 3. If the recommendations of the two ISGDs differ, we have a total of K recommendations. Otherwise, no recommendations are added, and we recommend only the unique ones in the list resulting from the junction of the two sets, resulting in a total of recommendations between K/2 and K-1. This way, we present the user with less limited and concentrated recommendations. We call this approach Hybrid SkipAwareRec.

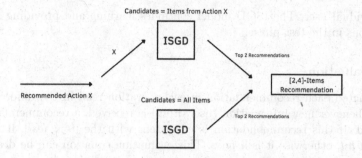

Fig. 3. Example of Hybrid SkipAwareRec with K = 4

Recommendation Strategy Similarly to the algorithm proposed to recommend the NBA, this paradigm also has 2 stages. In the first stage, the recommendation model is fed only with historical data from several users. This first phase runs in parallel with the first phase of SkipAwareRec.

The second stage starts when the algorithm is delivered to online users. ISGD continues to recommend and collect information about user iterations with items, in order to update its model in real time, thus preserving the incrementality of the solution overall.

4 Experiments and Results

4.1 Data Setup and Model Training

To evaluate our solution, we used data from the Spotify Sequential Skip Prediction Challenge—1,000,003 entries, where each entry represents the listening of a song in a given session, 59,062 sessions, of a length between 10 and 20 songs each, and a total of 174,768 individual songs associated with all these sessions. We only use data from premium sessions, since only these users are allowed to control the order of songs. We performed clustering to generate the set of possible actions/categories, resulting in a total of 23 categories, chosen using the Elbow Method. With this categorisation, there is a mode of 4 clusters per session.

To train the SkipAwareRec and ISGD models, we broke the sessions data into a training set with 85% of the data and a test set with the other 15%. We feed SkipAwareRec with the training data containing skip information. With this, we build sequential states, for each session, and update our Artificial Intelligence (AI) model. In parallel, the same training dataset was used to build the ISGD model—but without skip information—that will also be incrementally updated in a next stage.

The dataset contains 5 different types of skip, relating to different moments of the songs, which were used for the definition of the MDP reward function. After this learning stage, the RL-based model is ready to recommend personalised actions by reading an initial action by a given user. After connecting to a single user, the algorithm starts to learn his/her preferences and adapting to the individual user. The ISGD model continues learning and providing recommendations in the test phase.

4.2   Evaluation

We evaluated each recommendation in each iteration read in the different sessions. Whenever new information (user, item) is received, a recommendation is generated. If this recommendation is consistent with the item read, it is considered a *hit*, otherwise it is a *miss*. This evaluation equation can be described by:

$$Hit\ Ratio\ (HR) = \frac{\#\ Guessed\ Recommendations}{\#\ Recommendations} * 100$$

Table 2 demonstrates the results of two ISGD models. The first ISGD recommends 2 items only from the category generated by SkipAwareRec, while the second recommends 2 items from the entire universe of songs. The ISGD algorithm that recommends from the whole item set performs better. This happens because when the NBA recommendation fails, the entire recommendation fails.

Table 2. Iterative items recommendations results in all recommendations moments

Recommendation algorithm	Guessed recommendations	Number of recommendations	HR (%)
ISGD with SkipAwareRec items	6626	107864	6.14
ISGD with all items	8043	107864	7.46

Given this result, we wanted to check the results of the SkipAwareRec+ISGD combination only when SkipAwareRec hits the right category—Table 3 shows these results. In this scenario, the ISGD algorithm that recommends only items from the generated NBA is much higher (almost double) than the ISGD that recommends items from the entire universe of songs.

Table 3. Iterative items recommendations results when SkipAwareRec guesses the next action

Recommendation algorithm	Guessed recommendations	Number of recommendations	HR (%)
ISGD with SkipAwareRec items	6626	31398	21.10
ISGD with all items	3493	31398	11.12

This insight is what has driven us to devise Hybrid SkipAwareRec. Given that when getting the category right, the ISGD that recommends only items from that same category is much better, and that overall, the ISGD that recommends items from the music universe is slightly better, we decided to create the hybrid strategy. We put together the recommendations from both ISGDs presented and arrive at the results in Table 4. As can be seen, the Hybrid SkipAwareRec had a performance of 10.36%, considerably higher than standalone ISGD in Table 2. The chart in Fig. 4 presents a performance comparison of the three different approaches.

Table 4. Iterative items recommendations results with Hybrid SkipAwareRec

Recommendation algorithm	Guessed recommendations	Number of recommendations	HR (%)
Hybrid SkipAwareRec	11176	107864	10.36

Finally, it is important to note that we are recommending a maximum of 4 songs, out of a universe of a total of 174,768 songs. For reference, a random recommender would have a hit probability of 0.0023%.

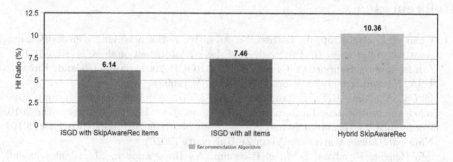

Fig. 4. Performance comparison of the different approaches

5   Conclusions and Future Work

We present in this paper a sequential recommendation algorithm for music that relies on real time user feedback in the form of song listens and song skips. Our algorithm is divided in two parts: (1) SkipAwareRec, a sequential NBA recommendation algorithm based on RL that selects the best actions corresponding to item categories, and (2) Hybrid SkipAwareRec, that combines SkipAwareRec with ISGD, an incremental MF algorithm that selects the items belonging to the recommended category that best match user preferences.

Our offline results show that our approach clearly outperforms a standalone version of the MF algorithm. This result encourages many future work directions. One research path would be to experiment with more publicly available datasets—unfortunately not abundant—, preferably with longer sessions that allow the algorithm to learn more about the users. Another direction would be to focus on the algorithmic approach, such as studying the impact of the design choices of the reward function, using different RL approaches, clustering algorithms with different levels of granularity, as well as experimenting with other incremental baseline algorithms. Finally, we would like to evaluate SkipAwareRec online, with real users.

An adaptation of SkipAwareRec is also being implemented with the goal of recommending customised content to individual users in a healthcare use case.

Acknowledgements. This work is co-financed by Component 5—Capitalisation and Business Innovation, integrated in the Resilience Dimension of the Recovery and Resilience Plan within the scope of the Recovery and Resilience Mechanism (MRR) of the European Union (EU), framed in the Next Generation EU, for the period 2021–2026, within project HfPT, with reference 41.

The third author contributed to the technical work in this paper while affiliated with INESC TEC and the University of Porto and to the writing of the paper while affiliated with the Joint Research Centre of the European Commission.

References

1. Chao, D.L., Balthrop, J., Forrest, S.: Adaptive radio: achieving consensus using negative preferences. In: Proceedings of the 2005 International ACM SIGGROUP Conference on Supporting Group Work, GROUP 2005, Sanibel Island, Florida, USA, November 6–9, 2005, pp. 120–123. ACM (2005)
2. Chi, C.-Y., Tsai, R.T.-H., Lai, J.-Y., Hsu, J.Y.J.: A reinforcement learning approach to emotion-based automatic playlist generation. In: Proceedings of the 2010 Conference on Technologies and Applications of Artificial Intelligence TAAI2010. National Taiwan University, Yuan Ze University (2010)
3. den Hengst, F., Grua, E.M., el Hassouni, A., Hoogendoorn, M.: Reinforcement learning for personalization: a systematic literature review. Data Sci. **3**(2), 107–147 (2020)
4. Hu, B., Shi, C., Liu, J.: Playlist recommendation based on reinforcement learning. In: Intelligence Science I—Second IFIP TC 12 International Conference, ICIS 2017, Shanghai, China, 25–28 Oct 2017, Proceedings, volume 510 of IFIP Advances in Information and Communication Technology, pp. 172–182. Springer, Berlin (2017)
5. Lee, D.H., Brusilovsky, P.: Reinforcing recommendation using implicit negative feedback. In: User Modeling, Adaptation, and Personalization, 17th International Conference, UMAP 2009, formerly UM and AH, Trento, Italy, 22–26 June 2009. Proceedings, Vol. 5535 of Lecture Notes in Computer Science, pp. 422–427. Springer, Berlin (2009)
6. Liebman, E., Saar-Tsechansky, M., Stone, P.: DJ-MC: a reinforcement-learning agent for music playlist recommendation. In: Proceedings of the 2015 International Conference on Autonomous Agents and Multiagent Systems, AAMAS 2015, Istanbul, Turkey, 4–8 May 2015, pp. 591–599. ACM (2015)
7. Lin, Y., Liu, Y., Lin, F., Wu, P., Zeng, W., Miao, C.: A survey on reinforcement learning for recommender systems. CoRR (2021). arXiv:abs/2109.10665
8. Park, M., Lee, K.: Exploiting negative preference in content-based music recommendation with contrastive learning. In: RecSys '22: Sixteenth ACM Conference on Recommender Systems, Seattle, WA, USA, 18–23 Sept 2022, pp. 229–236. ACM (2022)

9. Peska, L., Vojtás, P.: Negative implicit feedback in e-commerce recommender systems. In: 3rd International Conference on Web Intelligence, Mining and Semantics, WIMS '13, Madrid, Spain, 12–14 June 2013, p. 45. ACM (2013)
10. Vinagre, J., Jorge, A.M., Gama, J.: Fast incremental matrix factorization for recommendation with positive-only feedback. In: User Modeling, Adaptation, and Personalization - 22nd International Conference, UMAP 2014, Aalborg, Denmark, 7–11 July 2014. Proceedings, Vol. 8538 of Lecture Notes in Computer Science, pp. 459–470. Springer, Berlin (2014)
11. Wang, Y.: A hybrid recommendation for music based on reinforcement learning. In: Advances in Knowledge Discovery and Data Mining—24th Pacific-Asia Conference, PAKDD 2020, Singapore, 11–14 May 2020, Proceedings, Part I, Vol. 12084 of Lecture Notes in Computer Science, pp. 91–103. Springer, Berlin (2020)
12. Zhao, X., Zhang, L., Ding, Z., Xia, L., Tang, J., Yin, D.: Recommendations with negative feedback via pairwise deep reinforcement learning. In: Proceedings of the 24th ACM SIGKDD International Conference on Knowledge Discovery & Data Mining, KDD 2018, London, UK, 19–23 Aug 2018, pp. 1040–1048. ACM (2018)

Interpreting What is Important: An Explainability Approach and Study on Feature Selection

Eduardo M. Rodrigues[1]([:envelope:]) [iD], Yassine Baghoussi[1,2] [iD],
and João Mendes-Moreira[1,2] [iD]

[1] Praça de Gomes Teixeira, Universidade do Porto, 4099-002 Porto, Portugal
up201700176@up.pt, {baghoussi,jmoreira}@fe.up.pt
[2] LIAAD - INESC TEC, Rua Dr. Roberto Frias, 4200-465 Porto, Portugal

Abstract. Machine learning models are widely used in time series forecasting. One way to reduce its computational cost and increase its efficiency is to select only the relevant exogenous features to be fed into the model. With this intention, a study on the feature selection methods: Pearson correlation coefficient, Boruta, Boruta-Shap, IMV-LSTM, and LIME is performed. A new method focused on interpretability, SHAP-LSTM, is proposed, using a deep learning model training process as part of a feature selection algorithm. The methods were compared in 2 different datasets showing comparable results with lesser computational cost when compared with the use of all features. In all datasets, SHAP-LSTM showed competitive results, having comparatively better results on the data with a higher presence of scarce occurring categorical features.

Keywords: XAI · Explainability · Feature selection

1 Introduction

Artificial Intelligence (AI) has revolutionized the way we make predictions and decisions, especially in the field of time series forecasting. With the increasing availability of data and the development of sophisticated AI algorithms [8,10], we can now make highly accurate predictions on various time series datasets [5,13]. However, building accurate and reliable AI models for time series forecasting is often a computationally expensive task, especially when dealing with multivariate time series with a high number of features that requires an increase in the complexity of the models. This computational cost can be a major challenge for many organizations, as it can slow down the predictions, require larger computational infrastructure, and increase the overall cost of developing and deploying AI models.

To address this issue, feature selection techniques can be used to identify the most important features that significantly impact the target variable and

Supported by Wysupp (https://www.wysupp.com).

eliminate the irrelevant ones. Feature selection is a critical step in model development, as it not only reduces the complexity of the model but also improves its interpretability, generalizability, and accuracy [12]. There are several feature selection techniques available, such as filter methods, wrapper methods, and embedded methods [1]. These techniques work, in its majority, by evaluating the importance of each feature based on their contribution to the target variable and selecting the most relevant ones.

In this article, we make a study on prediction's quality and performance based on the applied feature selection method and introduce an Explainability approach to feature extraction utilizing SHapley Additive exPlanations (SHAP) [9], a game-theoretic approach to explain the output of any machine learning model, paired with a Long Short-Term Memory (LSTM) algorithm. SHAP is a model-agnostic technique, meaning it can be applied to any machine learning algorithm, regardless of its complexity or structure. While the LSTM model, as a deep learning model, is capable of differentiating the relevant and irrelevant features during its training process.

Our results demonstrate that selecting the most important features by their SHAP values can have varying performance depending on whether it is applied to an instance-based, or global average-based threshold. By applying an instance-based threshold our models can achieve comparable performance with significantly reduced complexity without miss-categorizing important features, resulting in faster and more efficient predictions when compared to the original dataset. Our approach, SHAP-LSTM, is also more interpretable than other methods, as it provides insights into the underlying relationships between the features and the target variable. We believe that SHAP-LSTM can have significant practical applications in many fields, such as finance, healthcare, retail, and energy, where accurate and efficient time series forecasting with interpretable results is critical for decision-making.

2   Related Works

Several methods have been developed to increase human trust in deep learning models by making them more interpretable. One such approach is the Interpretable Multivariate Long Short-Term Memory (IMV-LSTM) model framework proposed by Guo et al. [6]. This framework is based on a unique update scheme that associates each element of the model's hidden state matrix with information from a specific input variable. The framework was applied to several datasets, including hourly PM2.5 data and associated meteorological data in Beijing, time series of energy production from a photo-voltaic power plant in Italy, and a public dataset used for indoor temperature forecasting, demonstrating comparable performance to standard LSTM models while offering interpretable insights into the underlying factors guiding the model's decision-making process.

Marco Tulio et al. [11] introduced Local Interpretable Model-agnostic Explanations (LIME), an algorithm for explaining the predictions made by any classifier or regressor. To explain a specific instance, the algorithm perturbs the feature values of the instance while maintaining the label, creating a set of "neighbor" instances. The original model is then used to predict the labels of the neighbor instances. An interpretable model is fitted to the set of neighbor instances and their predicted labels. Finally, the interpretable model is used to explain the prediction for the original instance by identifying the most important features and their contribution to the prediction. The authors evaluate LIME on several datasets and show that it can generate informative explanations.

Another model agnostic interpretability contender is SHAP. Proposed by Scott et al. [9], SHAP is based on the idea of Shapley values, a concept from cooperative game theory. The method assigns each feature of a given input a Shapley value, which represents the average marginal contribution of the feature across all possible coalitions of features. The Shapley values are then used to calculate the contribution of each feature to the prediction made by the model. This method is capable of giving local interpretability, while it can be lacking in a global scenario as shown by the experiments performed in the next sessions of this paper.

3   Datasets and Methods

For this article two multivariate time-series datasets were used to validate the proposed method, those being Rossmann Store Sales [4], and Bike Sharing Dataset [3].

3.1   Rossmann Store Sales

Contains as target variable the daily total sales of 1115 Rossmann stores, as well as 27 exogenous features after executing one-hot encoding: store number, date, year, month, week of the year, day of the month, day of week, if the store is open or not, if the store is running a promotion in a given day, school holiday, if it takes part in a recurring promotion, if it has competition nearby and since when has it being open, year and month, and its distance, the store type as one of 4 categorical values, the store assortment as one of 3 categorical values, if it's a public holiday, Easter holiday or Christmas and if the recurring promotion is active or not. It encapsulates a historic period of 3 years for each store while some were closed for a period of 6 months for refurbishment. The most recent 90 days were used for testing and validation, while the remaining data was used for training.

3.2   Bike Sharing Dataset

Contains a total count of rented bicycles as the target variable and 26 exogenous features after executing one-hot encoding: date, year, month, day of the month, an identifier of each record corresponding to days elapsed since the first record, temperature, feeling temperature, humidity, wind speed, seasons of the year as categorical values, if it's a working day or not, if it's a holiday or not, if it had a sunny, cloudy or heavy rain weather as categorical values and days of the week as categorical values. The core data set is related to the two-year historical log corresponding to the years 2011 and 2012 from the Capital Bikeshare system. The most recent 90 days were used for testing and validation while the remaining 1 year and 9 months of data were used for training.

3.3 Data Exploration

An exploratory analysis was conducted in each of the datasets to find the evident relationships between features.

Rossmann Store Sales For this dataset, it was possible to identify a strong relationship to the target variable for holidays, day of the week, and year. Meaning that a good method for feature selection should identify them as important features, and if a model would identify the week of the year as important it should not select the month as well, and vice versa, due to their high correlation.

Bike Sharing Dataset For this dataset it was possible to identify a strong relationship to the target variable for months, season, weather, year, temperature, feeling temperature, and wind speed. Meaning that a good method for feature selection should identify them as important features, and if a model would identify temperature as important it should not select feeling temperature as well, and vice versa, due to their high correlation.

3.4 LSTM Hyperparameter Tunning

As previously mentioned, to use the proposed method it is required to have a trained LSTM model, and in order to obtain the best hyperparameters, a grid search was performed in a single-layer LSTM. The number of hidden cells was altered in order of powers of 2 ranging from 2^3 to 2^7; the learning rate was altered in order of 0.0001 from 0.0001 to 0.005. It was set with training patience of 50 with a maximum number of epochs of 10001.

The LSTM model was trained using the training data, but only saved when the loss over a one-step ahead prediction of the test data had an improvement.

3.5 SHAP Method Implementation

SHAP is a common method used to explain local decisions taken by black box machine learning models, such as LSTM, and the existent *Python* implementation developed by Lundberg et al. [9] was used. This is a robust library with various visualization tools, capable of handling single and multiple instance interpretation and returning the features by order of importance determined by the calculated SHAP value or average calculated SHAP value over all instances respectively.

Since this is a method aimed at local interpretation, in cases of exogenous features with sparse occurrence it tends to underestimate their importance. The proposed method aims to handle this case by setting an instance-based threshold to the matrix of SHAP values calculated by Lundberg's implementation, this way detecting the feature's importance regardless of its rate of occurrence.

4 Experiments, Results, and Discussion

4.1 Experimental Setup

To test the computational cost reduction with features selection, a set of different methods were implemented as well as SHAP-LSTM, with their results stored, to have the features used on a LSTM model, and processing times for comparison between methods. A monolayer LSTM model with 32 hidden cells and a learning rate of 0.005 was trained to obtain the feature importance through LIME and SHAP.

All processes were executed using CPU Intel(R) Core(TM) i7-8565U 1.80 GHz, in a 16 GB RAM device.

Feature Selection Methods The Feature selection methods implemented were:

Pearson Correlation Coefficient (PCC). The most commonly used method for feature selection, uses Pearson Correlation to identify the best features based on a set threshold [2].

Boruta. Uses the training of many tree-based models with permuted feature values to, then, perform statistical tests and determine if each feature is important, unimportant or tentative [7].

Boruta-Shap. A combination of Boruta feature selection algorithm with Shapley values, with better speed, and quality of the feature subset produced.

LIME. An Explainability algorithm with a good global interpretation, applied to the same trained model as SHAP and making the use of thresholds to select features [11].

IMV-LSTM. Another Explainability algorithm with two variations, Full and Tensor, where each element of the model's hidden state matrix is updated with information from a specific input variable, and this is used as weights of importance [6].

4.2 Experimental Procedure

Initially, the *Python Pandas* library implementation of the correlation calculation algorithm was used, and 5 thresholds for correlation coefficient acceptance were set. The Boruta method, following its *Python* implementation, was then applied with a gradient boosting explainer and a random forest explainer, analog to the Boruta-Shap method implemented under the context of this experiment. A search for better parameters on the explainer model to Boruta, as well as on Boruta itself took place, although the results did not suffer noticeable changes.

Using the trained LSTM model, LIME was applied to explain 90 instances on the training data due to its inherent random nature, the numerical importance evaluation of each feature was then averaged by the number of instances and thresholds put in place to select the most significant exogenous time-series. Again with the same trained model, the *Python* SHAP implementation by Lundberg et al. [9] was used to interpret a period of 365 days in each dataset, and the feature importance extracted based on the average value of the SHAP value calculated or the maximum SHAP value calculated. To select the features for PCC, average SHAP-LSTM, instance SHAP-LSTM and LIME thresholds were chosen in an attempt to have a homogeneous distribution of features for each interval.

To use both variations of IMV-LSTM all it required was to train the models using the IMV-Full and IMV-Tensor architectures with the same hyper parameters as stipulated before. Due to the very high importance differentiation a single threshold was set for both variations of the method.

With the selected features for each method, a monolayer LSTM model with 32 hidden cells and a 0.005 learning rate was trained and used to predict a 90-day forecast using the test portion of the data. The processing time of every run was recorded and the errors were measured according to the mean absolute scaled error (MASE) because it is scale independent. A random seed was reset to the same value after every training to increase the fairness between the models.

4.3   Results

Feature Selection Computational Cost The computation time for each of the implemented feature selection methods for the Bike Sharing Dataset (BSD) and 30 randomly selected stores from the Rossmann Store Sales (RSS) dataset are shown in Table 1.

Table 1. Computation time for feature selection methods for each dataset. $\overline{time}$ is the average computational time, $\widetilde{time}$ the median and $\sigma(t)$ the standard deviation.

	BSD	RSS		
Methods	$\overline{time}$	$\widetilde{time}$	$\overline{time}$	$\sigma(t)$
Correlation	0.17	0.19	0.11	0.2
Boruta GB	50.38	89.20	59.19	52.55
Boruta RF	62.48	132.40	80.70	85.52
Boruta-SHAP GB	156.83	261.90	211.98	99.06
Boruta-SHAP RF	186.14	218.84	180.08	73.53
Tensor IMV-LSTM	507.30	696.13	468.64	572.84
Full IMV-LSTM	3807.70	666.16	472.92	469.90
LIME-LSTM	340.98	553.46	606.98	135.85
SHAP-LSTM	2678.22	1161.61	831.25	874.79

Bike Sharing Dataset The results of the forecasting are shown in Table 2.

Important to notice that even though the errors show a comparable result for the univariate case, the model was incapable of learning any seasonality or trend as can be seen in Fig. 1. For all applied methods, not once the same subset of exogenous features was selected.

Table 2. Results for 90 step ahead forecast on test portion of Bike Sharing dataset using a monolayer LSTM model with 32 hidden cells and learning rate of 0.005.

Method	Threshold	MASE	Training Time (s)	Features Used
Standard LSTM	–	2.00	204	0
All features	–	2.10	119.20	27
PCC	0.05	1.99	133	19
	0.10	1.61	133	13
	0.15	2.13	208	11
	0.20	1.94	148	10
	0.25	2.48	142	8
Boruta GB	–	3.24	401	1
Boruta RF	–	1.88	165	5
Boruta-Shap GB	–	1.93	192	3
Boruta-Shap RF	–	1.82	170	5
Tensor IMV-LSTM	0.045	2.04	229	8
Full IMV-LSTM	0.060	3.14	251	11
LIME-LSTM	0.0020	1.66	123	23
	0.0025	2.34	155	19
	0.0030	2.21	237	12
	0.0035	1.72	214	8
	0.0040	1.80	228	7
Average	0.01	2.01	112	13
SHAP-LSTM	0.02	2.64	121	10
	0.03	1.89	211	2
	0.04	1.89	204	1
Instance	0.05	2.19	145	24
SHAP-LSTM	0.06	1.72	149	24
	0.07	2.30	123	19
	0.08	2.86	352	10
	0.09	2.75	116	3

Rossmann Store Sales The results of the forecasting over 30 randomly chosen stores are shown in Table 3.

4.4 Discussion

For the Bike Sharing Dataset when applying the Random Forest explainer, Gradient Boosting Shap, and Random Forest Shap Boruta methods, the model trained with the chosen features showed a good data trend understanding while the results left to be desired when forecasting the seasonality. The opposite is true for the Gradient Boosting explainer Boruta, as can be seen in Fig. 2.

For PCC, LIME, Average SHAP-LSTM, and Instance SHAP-LSTM with lower threshold values the trained model will predict seasonality with higher accuracy while for higher values the trend will be better understood by the

Table 3. Results for 90 step ahead forecast on test portion of Rossmann Store Sales dataset, for 30 randomly chosen stores, using a monolayer LSTM model with hidden size 32 and learning rate of 0.005. Th is the threshold set, $\overline{MASE}$ and $\overline{Time}$ are the averaged values, $\widetilde{Time}$ and $\widetilde{MASE}$ the median, $\sigma(MASE)$ the standard deviation and $N.F.$ the average number of features selected by each method.

Method	Th	$\overline{MASE}$	$\widetilde{MASE}$	$\sigma(MASE)$	$\overline{Time(s)}$	$\widetilde{Time(s)}$	$N.F.$
Standard LSTM	–	1.13	1.15	0.12	475	437	0
All features	–	0.94	0.94	0.10	257	230	27
PCC	0.05	0.96	0.96	0.11	305	294	10
	0.10	0.99	0.98	0.10	351	366	8
	0.15	1.00	1.01	0.12	326	321	6
	0.20	1.00	1.01	0.11	348	334	5
	0.25	1.00	0.98	0.11	323	310	5
Boruta GB	–	0.95	0.94	0.10	242	208	4
Boruta RF	–	0.94	0.95	0.11	239	194	5
Boruta-Shap GB	–	0.94	0.95	0.10	211	182	5
Boruta-Shap RF	–	0.94	0.95	0.10	209	191	5
Tensor IMV-LSTM	0.045	0.98	0.96	0.12	330	283	9
Full IMV-LSTM	0.060	0.96	0.95	0.11	281	234	10
LIME-LSTM	0.007	1.01	1.00	0.13	282	237	7
	0.008	1.01	1.00	0.12	310	285	6
	0.009	1.03	1.02	0.15	302	283	5
	0.010	1.04	1.05	0.14	353	341	4
Average	0.01	0.96	0.96	0.10	215	185	9
SHAP-LSTM	0.02	0.96	0.98	0.11	215	186	8
	0.03	0.96	0.96	0.09	223	154	7
	0.04	0.96	1.00	0.11	235	193	4
Instance	0.05	0.97	0.98	0.10	230	195	12
SHAP-LSTM	0.10	0.97	0.99	0.11	228	207	11
	0.15	0.95	0.96	0.10	296	219	6
	0.20	0.98	0.98	0.10	299	238	3

LSTM. Although these methods require a threshold to be set by the user, in the Bike Sharing dataset, LIME, and Average SHAP-LSTM showed a tendency to not have big variable weight differentiation, complicating the user's task. Meanwhile Instance SHAP-LSTM shows a higher weight difference between variables as well as a more accurate depiction of scarce occurrence variable importance such as weather_condition3 (Thunderstorm, light snow or light rain) shown in Fig. 3a.

The same issue was noticed for the Rossmann Store Sales dataset. For LIME and Average SHAP-LSTM the feature importance is not differentiated by large margins, complicating the task to set a threshold. On the other hand, Instance SHAP-LSTM shows a higher weight difference between variables as well as a more accurate depiction of importance for scarce occurrence variables such as the StateHoliday_(a: public holiday, b: Easter holiday, c: Christmas) as shown in Fig. 3b.

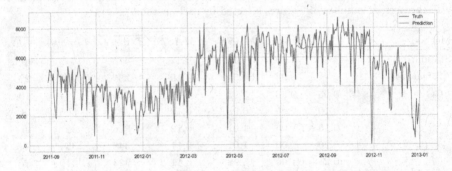

Fig. 1. Univariate 90 step ahead forecasting of the Bike Sharing test dataset.

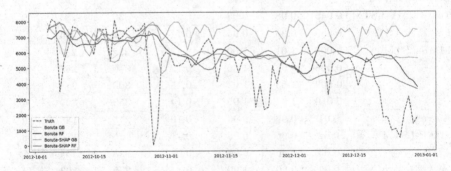

Fig. 2. Forecast using the Boruta GB, Boruta RF, Boruta-SHAP GB, Boruta-SHAP RF feature selection method.

PCC, LIME, Average SHAP-LSTM, and Instance SHAP-LSTM were also the only methods capable of consistently identifying the importance of the features with noticeable relationship with the target variable determined during the data exploration process. Neither of these methods was capable of rejecting exogenous features highly correlated to each other. By the other hand, for the Rossmann dataset, the Tensor IMV-LSTM and Full IMV-LSTM considered features with static values such as store assortment and store type as important, being the only methods to do so.

5   Conclusion and Future Work

In this paper, a study on the effects of feature selection over the forecast of time series using an LSTM has taken place, as well as the, to the best of our knowledge, proposition of a new feature selection method SHAP-LSTM. The feature selection methods studied were the Pearson correlation coefficient, Boruta, Boruta-Shap, IMV-LSTM, LIME, and the proposed method, SHAP-LSTM.

To implement the proposition, an LSTM model was trained with the best set of hyperparameters found through a grid search, subsequently, a Python SHAP implementation was used to obtain local explanations over a span of 365 instances on the training data. With the SHAP values matrix, an instance-based threshold was set to correctly evaluate the importance of each feature regardless of their rate of occurrence.

To compare each feature selection method against each other and without any selection, a 90 step ahead prediction was made with an LSTM model over

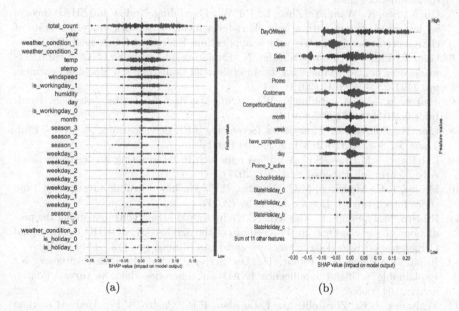

(a)   (b)

Fig. 3. SHAP values for Bike Sharing Dataset (**a**) and Rossmann Store Sales (Store 266) (**b**). Red dots represent the effects of a high feature value on the forecast, while blue represent the effect of a low value.

the test data on two datasets, with the same set of hyperparameters, using: the features selected by each method, all features, and only the target variable. Their errors were measured using MASE and the computation time for the training as well as the feature selection method displayed.

A natural evolution from this paper is to prove the applicability of features selected using Instance SHAP-LSTM on different regression models, such as ARIMAX, as well as develop an ensemble method for feature selection using the proposed algorithm.

Overall, it was shown an improvement in computational cost due to feature selection, while maintaining comparable results over the forecast. Instance SHAP-LSTM proved itself to be an improvement on Average SHAP-LSTM for global interpretation and a competitive method for feature selection.

References

1. Brouard, C., Mariette, J., Flamary, R., Vialaneix, N.: Feature selection for kernel methods in systems biology. NAR Genomics Bioinform. **4**(1), lqac014 (2022)
2. Chen, H., Chang, X.: Photovoltaic power prediction of LSTM model based on Pearson feature selection. Energy Rep. **7**, 1047–1054 (2021)
3. Fanaee-T, H., Gama, J.: Event labeling combining ensemble detectors and background knowledge. Prog. Artif. Intell. 1–15 (2013). https://doi.org/10.1007/s13748-013-0040-3, [Web Link]
4. FlorianKnauer, W.C.: Rossmann store sales (2015), 'kaggle.com/competitions/rossmann-store-sales'
5. Gu, X., See, K., Wang, Y., Zhao, L., Pu, W.: The sliding window and SHAP theory-an improved system with a long short-term memory network model for state of charge prediction in electric vehicle application. Energies **14**(12), 3692 (2021)
6. Guo, T., Lin, T., Antulov-Fantulin, N.: Exploring interpretable LSTM neural networks over multi-variable data. In: International Conference on Machine Learning, pp. 2494–2504. PMLR (2019)
7. Jankowski, M.K.A., Rudnicki, W.: Boruta-a system for feature selection. Fund. Inform. **101**(4), 271–285 (2010)
8. Lim, B., Zohren, S.: Time-series forecasting with deep learning: a survey. Phil. Trans. R. Soc. A **379**(2194), 20200209 (2021)
9. Lundberg, S.M., Lee, S.I.: A unified approach to interpreting model predictions. Adv. Neural Inf. Process. Syst. **30** (2017)
10. Masini, R.P., Medeiros, M.C., Mendes, E.F.: Machine learning advances for time series forecasting. J. Econ. Surv. **1**, 36 (2021)
11. Ribeiro, M.T., Singh, S., Guestrin, C.: Why should i trust you? explaining the predictions of any classifier. In: Proceedings of the 22nd ACM SIGKDD International Conference on Knowledge Discovery and Data Mining, pp. 1135–1144 (2016)
12. Rojat, T., Puget, R., Filliat, D., Del Ser, J., Gelin, R., Díaz-Rodríguez, N.: Explainable artificial intelligence (XAI) on timeseries data: a survey (2021). arXiv:2104.00950
13. Velasquez, C.E., Zocatelli, M., Estanislau, F.B., Castro, V.F.: Analysis of time series models for Brazilian electricity demand forecasting. Energy **247**, 123483 (2022)

Time-Series Pattern Verification in CNC Machining Data

João Miguel Silva[1,2]([📧]), Ana Rita Nogueira[1,2], José Pinto[1],
António Correia Alves[1], and Ricardo Sousa[1,2]

[1] INESC TEC, Rua Dr Roberto Frias, 4200 - 465 Porto, Portugal
[2] Faculdade de Engenharia da Universidade do Porto, Rua Dr Roberto Frias,
4200 - 465 Porto, Portugal
joao.p.silva@inesctec.pt

Abstract. Effective quality control is essential for efficient and successful manufacturing processes in the era of Industry 4.0. Artificial Intelligence solutions are increasingly employed to enhance the accuracy and efficiency of quality control methods. In Computer Numerical Control machining, challenges involve identifying and verifying specific patterns of interest or trends in a time-series dataset. However, this can be a challenge due to the extensive diversity. Therefore, this work aims to develop a methodology capable of verifying the presence of a specific pattern of interest in a given collection of time-series. This study mainly focuses on evaluating One-Class Classification techniques using Linear Frequency Cepstral Coefficients to describe the patterns on the time-series. A real-world dataset produced by turning machines was used, where a time-series with a certain pattern needed to be verified to monitor the wear offset. The initial findings reveal that the classifiers can accurately distinguish between the time-series' target pattern and the remaining data. Specifically, the One-Class Support Vector Machine achieves a classification accuracy of 95.6 % ± 1.2 and an F1-score of 95.4 % ± 1.3.

Keywords: Industry 4.0 · Quality control · CNC turning machining · Cutting insert · One-class classification · Linear frequency cepstral coefficients

1 Introduction

Industry 4.0 and Quality 4.0 represent a paradigm shift in manufacturing to achieve smarter, more efficient, and integrated manufacturing processes. Combining the Internet of Things (iot) with Machine Learning (ml) offers unprecedented opportunities to reduce downtime, improve product quality control and system design in real time [1,4,7,17,26,28,30].

ML offers many advantages when applied to manufacturing. First, ML models can learn patterns and relationships between variables, enabling predictions of intervention outcomes and identification of areas for improvement, with its ability to process multiple complex data sources, including sensors, logs, and processes [20]. Second, ML can facilitate real-time analysis and decision-making, allowing manufacturers to react quickly to changes in system conditions and prevent issues before they occur [25]. Third, highly complex and dynamic environments such as industrial contexts require constant actualisation, in which ML models can be refined to adapt to changes [27]. Finally, ML allows for greater automation, which reduces the need for manual intervention, limiting human error, improving system efficiency, and cutting labour costs. By leveraging these advantages, ML can dramatically improve product quality control, increasing efficiency and product quality [6,12].

Computer Numerical Control (CNC) machining is an industrial manufacturing process that uses computer software to control cutting tools and workpieces to create precise and complex shapes. ML has had a high impact on CNC machining, enabling efficient production of parts with various specifications [2,16,18,22]. Turning and milling are two main types of CNC machining processes, which are essential in manufacturing and used to create a variety of precision components and products such as automotive parts, aerospace components, medical devices, and consumer products [16,18]. Generally, those types involve two stages: rough and finishing machining. In the finishing stage, small variations in tool wear can significantly affect the quality of the finished product. Therefore, wear adjustments are often necessary to maintain the desired accuracy of the finished pieces. These adjustments are recorded in the CNC machine at the tool level [10]. In this scenario, a vast amount of times series are produced.

Despite this large amount of available data, sometimes, only a few time-series have the proper patterns to be used in the industrial-specific analysis (for example, monitoring the wear offset of a given tool). This raises the need for a system that can effectively detect these desired patterns in the data, which is the main challenge of this work.

In general, our approach is based on the application of discriminating features that can differentiate patterns in the time-series and a model that can separate one known pattern from any arbitrary one. For this purpose, a Linear Frequency Cepstral Coefficients (LFCC) and One-Class Classification (OCC) models were used, respectively. The LFCC feature extraction is based on the spectral representation using Discrete Fourier Transform (DFT) and Discrete Cosine Transform (DCT), where the underlying patterns (which may not be apparent in the time domain) are easily described. These are spectral descriptors that present high discriminating properties regarding information. Another important property is noise/data perturbation resilience. Moreover, these features are computationally efficient and allow the models to be applied in real-time or online scenarios where efficiency is important [5]. OCC is a ML methodology that aims to identify whether a new observation belongs to a specific class with no information about other classes. It is commonly used in anomaly detection and class verification [24].

This methodology is suitable to solve the problem due to the possibility of determining whether a time-series belongs or not to the same type of suitable for monitoring algorithm (includes algorithms that predict the best tool change instant) stages. The primary objective of this research work is the development of a methodology for time-series verification applied to CNC machining data that verifies one particular type of time-series from a large set. The secondary objective of this research is to create a function that can assist in monitoring time-series data related to wear offset adjustments, which were previously verified as having the target pattern. It is important to note that the successful accomplishment of the secondary objective is contingent upon the successful attainment of the primary objective.

The main contribution is a robust methodology capable of discriminating the types of the time-series (same type, not the same type) with a relevant performance. We also contribute with a reproducible benchmarking focused on the OCC methods that used highly discriminating LFCC features. For the application context, a function capable of verifying offset adjustment time-series was integrated into a system that supports the correct cutting tool use.

The remainder of this paper is organised as follows: Sect. 2 presents the background. Section 3 illustrates the problem and the proposed solution, and Sect. 4 the results obtained in the tests. Finally, Sect. 5 presents the main findings and overall conclusions regarding the developed work.

2 Background

In this section, we provide a brief background on CNC machining and offset adjustment in turning, LFCC, and OCC.

2.1 CNC Machining and Offset Adjustment in Turning

CNC machining, one of the areas in which ML is having an high impact [2,22], is an industrial manufacturing process that utilises computer software to control the movement of cutting tools and workpieces to create precise, complex shapes and components.

Milling and turning are the two primary types of CNC machining processes, which are crucial in manufacturing and used to produce a wide range of precision components and products, including automotive parts, aerospace components, medical devices, and consumer products. In addition, CNC machining offers several advantages over traditional machining methods, including increased accuracy, faster production times, and the ability to produce complex shapes and parts with greater efficiency.

Milling involves rotating a cutting tool while it moves along multiple axes to remove material from a workpiece. The cutting tool is typically mounted on a spindle that can move in three directions (X, Y, and Z), allowing it to cut into the workpiece from various angles. This process is beneficial for creating complex shapes, such as gears or parts with intricate curves, and quickly removing large amounts of material.

Conversely, turning involves rotating the workpiece and using a cutting tool to remove material. The cutting tool is typically stationary, moving along a

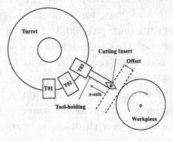

(a) An example of a CNC machine with two turrets.

(b) Illustration of the wear offset on T03.

Fig. 1. Real case of a CNC and an illustration of T03 wear offset.

single axis to cut into the spinning workpiece. This process is commonly used for creating cylindrical shapes, such as shafts or tubes, and achieving tight tolerances on parts requiring high accuracy.

A turret in CNC machining is a tool-holding device that can rotate to bring different cutting tools into the working position. The tool-holder is the component of the CNC machine that securely holds the cutting tool in place during the machining process.

CNC machines can have several turrets, each with multiple tool holders, which allows for the efficient production of parts with different geometries and specifications [16,18].

Figure 1 illustrates a real example of a CNC machine with two turrets Fig. 1a and an illustration of the wear offset of T03 Fig. 1b.

Several tools in each turret play a crucial role in the manufacturing process of high-precision metallic pieces. These tools are involved in two main manufacturing stages: rough machining and finishing machining. The rough machining stage removes excess material from the piece, while the finishing machining stage fine-tunes the shape and dimensions of the piece to meet the tight tolerance requirements.

Considering the precision required in the final product, even small variations in the tool wear can significantly impact the quality of the finished product. This is particularly true for tools involved in the finishing machining stage, where the tolerances are even tighter. As a result, operators often need to perform wear adjustments to maintain the desired accuracy of the finished pieces.

2.2 Feature Extraction and Linear Frequency Cepstral Coefficients

Feature extraction is a crucial step in many ML applications, where the objective is to identify patterns in data. The process selects informative features and removes irrelevant or redundant information to improve the accuracy and efficiency of ML models, and various methods such as statistical techniques, wavelet transforms, Principal Component Analysis (PCA), LFCC, and deep learning can be used depending on the data and application [9,23].

LFCC are commonly used in audio signal processing for speech recognition and speaker identification tasks [31]. However, the underlying concept of the cepstrum, which is used to extract the LFCC, can be applied to other types of signals beyond audio, such as vibration analysis [23], image processing [11], and electrocardiogram signals [19].

The method is based on the concept of cepstrum, which involves taking the logarithm of the magnitude of the DFT of a signal. This process effectively separates the spectral envelope and the fine spectral structure of the signal. The LFCC can then be obtained by taking the DCT of the log spectrum after removing the spectral envelope. The resulting coefficients are informative features for ML algorithms.

2.3 One-Class Classification

OCC is a ML technique that aims to identify instances that belong to a single class based on their similarity to previously observed instances of that class. It is advantageous when the number of examples of the target class is limited or when the instances of other classes need to be better defined.

In OCC, the algorithm is trained on a set of examples from a single class, and the objective is to identify instances that deviate from that class. This approach is often used in anomaly detection, which aims to identify rare or unexpected events in a dataset.

The One-class Support Vector Machine (OCSVM) [21] is a type of OCC used for unsupervised anomaly and novelty detection. It constructs a hyperplane that maximizes the margin and captures only a small fraction of data points. It works well with high-dimensional and nonlinear data with sparse and unbalanced features but requires many training samples and can be sensitive to kernel functions and hyperparameters.

Local Outlier Factor (LOF) [29] detects outliers by measuring local deviation and assigning anomaly scores. It works well for global and local outliers, non-uniform datasets, and noise but not high-dimensional datasets.

Isolation Forest (IF) [14] detects outliers by isolating them in fewer dataset partitions. It is efficient with high-dimensional datasets but not with low-dimensional datasets.

Stochastic Gradient Descent One-class Support Vector Machine (SGDOCSVM) [15] is a variant of OCSVM that optimizes hyperparameters using stochastic gradient descent. It is ideal for large-scale datasets with high-dimensional and sparse features but may not perform as well as OCSVM on small datasets or complex nonlinear relationships.

In the industrial context, OCC can be used to identify when the wear offset of a tool deviates from a known pattern, indicating that it may need to be replaced or adjusted [3]. This approach is instrumental because it allows us to detect tool wear without explicit labels indicating when it is worn out. It can also identify early signs of wear, allowing us to take preventive measures before the tool fails.

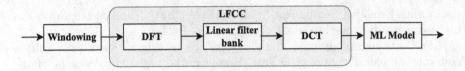

Fig. 2. Overview of the feature extraction methodology applied.

Kampelopoulos et al. [8] proposed using OCC for leak detection in pipeline systems. They trained classifiers on a noise class of normal signals from acoustic sensors during normal pipeline operation and evaluated the classifiers' predictions on test measurements, including artificially generated leaks. This promising approach also has applications in fault and novelty detection.

Finally, Lee et al. [13] proposed a fault-detection module for manufacturing sites using one-class learning from imbalanced industrial data. The study used deep-learning time-series predictions for feature extraction and tested four deep-learning architectures with actual mass production data.

3   Methodology

Throughout the developed methodology, data-driven methods are central to our approach. To provide such methods with the required data, a dataset was collected from Jasil, a Portuguese company specialising in high-precision metallic workpieces using CNC technology. The data was collected from three distinct CNC turning machines that operated continuously six days a week, twenty-four hours a day, with exceptions for maintenance and customer demand. During this period, two distinct products were manufactured: $P1$ and $P2$. The data was gathered over four months, from October 2022 to February 2023, with a sampling rate of 1.25 Hz (approximately 150 k data points per series). After thorough analysis, we concluded that missing values, outliers, and measurement errors are absent in this dataset.

Figure 2 represents the feature extraction overview.

The collected variables came from two turrets of the CNC machine, including temperature, spindle torque, spindle speed, wear offset X, and the working tool and corresponding turret. It is important to note that for the following statistical analysis, we focused on the wear offset of the X-axis as the studied variable and on one of the turrets.

Jasil's department of quality control and maintenance has communicated to us that, for this work, tool 3 (T03) from turret 1 is being utilised to compensate for any offset variations that may arise during the machining process concerning the relevant dimensions.

This situation has arisen since the tolerances associated with the measurement involving T03 are the narrowest. It is important to note that the design of this tool will vary depending on the product being manufactured.

Table 1. Manufacturing comparison of two products across three CNC machines. These time-series correspond to the desired pattern to train the OCC for the T03.

Machine	Product	Total units	Cutting changes	μ units manufactured	μ offset adjustments	μ cutting insert wear [mm]
56	$P1$	4869	96	50 ± 36	9 ± 6	0.423 ± 0.153
	$P2$	1460	42	35 ± 27	9 ± 5	0.421 ± 0.187
57	$P1$	4538	100	45 ± 29	9 ± 6	0.404 ± 0.194
	$P2$	1863	59	31 ± 22	8 ± 5	0.407 ± 0.159
217	$P1$	5796	129	44 ± 28	4 ± 3	0.399 ± 0.125
	$P2$	2953	63	45 ± 32	4 ± 3	0.399 ± 0.081

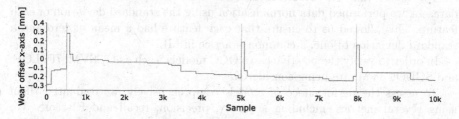

Fig. 3. An example of wear offset from the X-axis of tool T03. The blue line represents the wear offset and the magenta vertical lines correspond to the cutting insert changes across the production process.

Table 1 summarises the statistical measures of the data collected in T03. Several statistical parameters are presented, including the number of units manufactured, the number of cutting insert changes, the average units produced per cutting insert, the average offset adjustments, and the average cutting insert wear. It is important to note that from now on, this data will be considered positive examples to be used to train a ML model.

These statistical results will help the quality and maintenance department to get useful insights into the production process of each machine and product.

Figure 3 shows an example of the wear offset a CNC machine used on the analysis for product $P1$.

The cutting insert change algorithm is based on a 2nd order *Butterworth* digital high-pass filter and 0.125 Hz as cutoff frequency, which can capture sudden variations of the wear-off set in the X-axis (T03). Subsequently, an adaptive threshold is applied across the resulting signal to determine the peaks accurately. The described method assumes that the time-series being analysed exhibits specific characteristics (positive cases).

To detect these potential desired patterns in the studied time-series, we divided them into different, same-sized overlapped sliding windowing (multiplied by a Hamming window). To each frame, the LFCC feature extraction technique was applied to transform the raw data into a set of features to feed to ML models.

Table 2. OCC metrics comparison.

	Accuracy	Precision	Recall	F1-score
OneClassSVM	95.63 ± 1.20	100.00 ± 0.00	91.26 ± 2.41	95.41 ± 1.32
IsolationForest	85.20 ± 0.96	100.00 ± 0.00	70.40 ± 1.91	82.62 ± 1.32
LocalOutlierFactor	92.98 ± 5.48	88.97 ± 8.98	99.27 ± 0.21	93.63 ± 4.92
SGDOneClassSVM	72.14 ± 22.30	87.93 ± 25.45	64.28 ± 16.55	71.00 ± 18.24

Each window consisted of 2048 samples, and we used a hop size of 512 samples to ensure overlap between windows. In our implementation, we used 22 cepstral coefficients.

To ensure that the resulting features were comparable across different datasets, we performed data normalisation using the standard deviation of each feature. This allowed us to ensure that each feature had a mean of zero and a standard deviation of one, a common practice in ML.

In order to verify the positive cases OCC models, such as OCSVM, IF, LOF, and SGDOCSVM, are being considered.

To assess the performance of models comprehensively, we evaluated them using several metrics, including accuracy, precision, recall and F1-score. We implemented a series of experiments under the following configuration, beginning with a dataset comprising a positive and a negative set. The positive set (2993 instances) was randomly partitioned into 70% training data (2095 instances) and 30% testing data (assuming the independence between different windows), and we derived ten different datasets by randomly sampling the positive set. Using the 70% training data, we trained these four methods and evaluated their performance using the 30% testing data (898 instances) and the negative set (898 instances). The latter corresponds to the wear offset of another set of tools that was confirmed as not having the desired pattern.

We conducted hyperparameter tuning through a grid search, resulting in the following parameter configurations: for OCSVM, *nu=0.1, gamma='scale', and kernel='rbf'*; for LOF, *contamination=0.01, algorithm='auto', leaf_size=30, and novelty=True*; for IF, *n_estimators=100, max_features=1.0, and contamination=0.3*; and for SGDOCSVM, *nu=0.5, tol=1 ×10⁻³, and max_iter=1000*.

4   Results and Discussion

The results and discussion section presents the findings and analysis of the study, aiming to provide a comprehensive understanding of the research problem and its implications.

We compared all OCC methods to better understand how the models perform in this industrial situation where several machines produce data. If we analyse Table 2, which represents the mean accuracy, precision, recall and F1-score, it is possible to see that, in general, OCC can effectively distinguish the desired

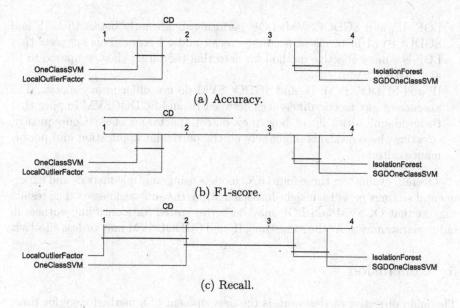

Fig. 4. Critical difference diagram for accuracy, F1-score and recall (Nemenyi test)

pattern in the data. Moreover, in this same table, it is possible to spot that OCSVM has better results than the remaining methods.

To understand if the differences between these models are significant, we compared them in terms of critical difference using the Nemenyi test (with 5% significance). After conducting the Nemenyi test, which indicated a significant difference between the methods, we generated a critical difference diagram to assess and compare these observed differences. For example, in Fig. 4, which represents the critical difference diagrams for the accuracy, F1-score, and recall, respectively, it is possible to see that the method with the better results is OCSVM.

Based on the given information, several differences exist among the methods regarding their performance metrics. Here are some of the key divergences:

- OCSVM and IF: According to the diagram, OCSVM performs significantly better than IF in terms of accuracy, and F1-score. This suggests that OCSVM is a more effective method for detecting the target class compared to IF;
- OCSVM and SGDOCSVM: OCSVM performs significantly better than SGDOCSVM in terms of accuracy, F1-score and recall. This suggests that OCSVM is a more accurate and precise method for detecting the target class compared to SGDOCSVM;
- LOF and OCSVM: According to the diagram, LOF is not significantly different from OCSVM in any metric. This suggests that LOF and OCSVM are both effective methods for detecting the target class, and there is no significant difference between them in terms of performance;

– LOF, IF, and SGDOCSVM: LOF performs significantly better than IF and SGDOCSVM in terms of accuracy, recall and F1-score. This suggests that LOF is a more effective method for detecting the target class compared to IF and SGDOCSVM;
– IF and SGDOCSVM: IF and SGDOCSVM do not differ in any metric. The absence of any metric differences between IF and SGDOCSVM implies that their dissimilarities lie in how they detect the target class. Consequently, selecting these methods might rely on the particular application and performance criteria.

Overall, evaluating these four OCC models using multiple metrics and experimental settings provides insight into their strengths and weaknesses. The results suggest that OCSVM and LOF may be better suited for identifying outliers in industrial scenarios. At the same time, IF and SGDOCSVM may be less effective.

5   Conclusion

The main objective of this work is the development of a methodology for time-series verification applied to CNC machining data that verifies one particular type of time-series from a large set. In addition, we also aim to create a function that can assist in monitoring time-series data related to wear offset adjustments, which were previously verified as having the target pattern.

For this, we compared four OCC models, namely OCSVM, IF, LOF, and SGDOCSVM, to evaluate their performance in detecting the desired pattern in the time-series. We used various metrics such as accuracy, precision, recall and F1-score to assess their performance comprehensively. Our results show that OCSVM and LOF are better suited for identifying outliers in this industrial scenario. In conclusion, our study highlights the importance of using appropriate time-series pattern verification to improve the reliability and safety of industrial systems.

Acknowledgments. This work is co-financed by the ERDF - European Regional Development Fund, through the Operational Programme for Competitiveness and Internationalisation - COMPETE 2020 Programme under the Portugal 2020 Partnership Agreement within project PRODUTECH4SC, with reference POCI-01-0247-FEDER-046102 and through the Norte Portugal Regional Operational Programme - NORTE 2020 under the Portugal 2020 Partnership Agreement, within project SAD-CoPQ, with reference NORTE-01-0247-FEDER-069725, and co-financed by Component 5 - Capitalization and Business Innovation, integrated in the Resilience Dimension of the Recovery and Resilience Plan within the scope of the Recovery and Resilience Mechanism (MRR) of the European Union (EU), framed in the Next Generation EU, for the period 2021–2026, within project Produtech_R3, with reference 60. Additionally, we thank Jasil and Vanguarda for the data and data infrastructure provided.

References

1. Ayvaz, S., Alpay, K.: Predictive maintenance system for production lines in manufacturing: a machine learning approach using iot data in real-time. Expert Syst. Appl. **173**, 114598 (2021)
2. Brillinger, M., Wuwer, M., Hadi, M.A., Haas, F.: Energy prediction for CNC machining with machine learning. CIRP J. Manuf. Sci. Technol. **35**, 715–723 (2021)
3. Du, X.: Fault detection using bispectral features and one-class classifiers. J. Process Control **83**, 1–10 (2019)
4. Dutta, G., Kumar, R., Sindhwani, R., Singh, R.K.: Digitalization priorities of quality control processes for smes: a conceptual study in perspective of industry 4.0 adoption. J. Intell. Manufact. **32**(6), 1679–1698 (2021)
5. Han, J.H., Chi, S.Y.: Consideration of manufacturing data to apply machine learning methods for predictive manufacturing. In: 2016 Eighth International Conference on Ubiquitous and Future Networks (ICUFN), pp. 109–113. IEEE (2016)
6. Hesser, D.F., Markert, B.: Tool wear monitoring of a retrofitted CNC milling machine using artificial neural networks. Manufact. Lett. **19**, 1–4 (2019)
7. Javaid, M., Haleem, A., Singh, R.P., Suman, R.: Significance of quality 4.0 towards comprehensive enhancement in manufacturing sector. Sensors Int. **2**, 100109 (2021)
8. Kampelopoulos, D., Kousiopoulos, G.P., Karagiorgos, N., Konstantakos, V., Goudos, S., Nikolaidis, S.: Applying one class classification for leak detection in noisy industrial pipelines. In: 2021 10th International Conference on Modern Circuits and Systems Technologies (MOCAST), pp. 1–4. IEEE (2021)
9. Khalid, S., Khalil, T., Nasreen, S.: A survey of feature selection and feature extraction techniques in machine learning. In: 2014 Science and Information Conference, pp. 372–378 (2014). https://doi.org/10.1109/SAI.2014.6918213
10. Khan, S.S., Madden, M.G.: A survey of recent trends in one class classification. In: Artificial Intelligence and Cognitive Science: 20th Irish Conference, AICS 2009, Dublin, Ireland, August 19–21, 2009, Revised Selected Papers 20, pp. 188–197. Springer (2010)
11. Kılıç, R., Kumbasar, N., Oral, E.A., Ozbek, I.Y.: Drone classification using rf signal based spectral features. Eng. Sci. Technol. Int. J. **28**, 101028 (2022)
12. Lee, C., Lim, C.: From technological development to social advance: A review of industry 4.0 through machine learning. Technol. Forecasting Soc. Change **167**, 120653 (2021)
13. Lee, J., Lee, Y.C., Kim, J.T.: Fault detection based on one-class deep learning for manufacturing applications limited to an imbalanced database. J. Manuf. Syst. **57**, 357–366 (2020)
14. Liu, F.T., Ting, K.M., Zhou, Z.H.: Isolation forest. In: 2008 Eighth IEEE International Conference on Data Mining, pp. 413–422 (2008). https://doi.org/10.1109/ICDM.2008.17
15. Mutlu, G., Acı, Ç.İ: Svm-smo-sgd: a hybrid-parallel support vector machine algorithm using sequential minimal optimization with stochastic gradient descent. Parallel Comput. **113**, 102955 (2022)
16. Okokpujie, I.P., Bolu, C., Ohunakin, O., Akinlabi, E.T., Adelekan, D.: A review of recent application of machining techniques, based on the phenomena of CNC machining operations. Proc. Manuf. **35**, 1054–1060 (2019)
17. Peres, R.S., Jia, X., Lee, J., Sun, K., Colombo, A.W., Barata, J.: Industrial artificial intelligence in industry 4.0-systematic review, challenges and outlook. IEEE Access **8**, 220121–220139 (2020)

18. Plaza, E.G., López, P.N., González, E.B.: Efficiency of vibration signal feature extraction for surface finish monitoring in CNC machining. J. Manuf. Process. **44**, 145–157 (2019)

19. Quiceno-Manrique, A., Alonso-Hernandez, J., Travieso-Gonzalez, C., Ferrer-Ballester, M., Castellanos-Dominguez, G.: Detection of obstructive sleep apnea in ECG recordings using time-frequency distributions and dynamic features. In: 2009 Annual International Conference of the IEEE Engineering in Medicine and Biology Society, pp. 5559–5562. IEEE (2009)

20. Sarker, I.H.: Machine learning: algorithms, real-world applications and research directions. SN Comput. Sci. **2**(3), 160 (2021)

21. Schölkopf, B., Platt, J.C., Shawe-Taylor, J., Smola, A.J., Williamson, R.C.: Estimating the support of a high-dimensional distribution. Neural Comput. **13**(7), 1443–1471 (2001)

22. Soori, M., Arezoo, B., Dastres, R.: Machine learning and artificial intelligence in CNC machine tools, a review. Sustainable Manuf. Ser. Econ. 100009 (2023)

23. Sousa, R., Antunes, J., Coutinho, F., Silva, E., Santos, J., Ferreira, H.: Robust cepstral-based features for anomaly detection in ball bearings. Int. J. Adv. Manuf. Technol. **103**, 2377–2390 (2019)

24. Swersky, L., Marques, H.O., Sander, J., Campello, R.J., Zimek, A.: On the evaluation of outlier detection and one-class classification methods. In: 2016 IEEE International Conference on Data Science And Advanced Analytics (DSAA), pp. 1–10. IEEE (2016)

25. Tien, J.M.: Internet of things, real-time decision making, and artificial intelligence. Ann. Data Sci. **4**, 149–178 (2017)

26. Turkyilmaz, A., Dikhanbayeva, D., Suleiman, Z., Shaikholla, S., Shehab, E.: Industry 4.0: challenges and opportunities for kazakhstan smes. Proc. CIRP **96**, 213–218 (2021)

27. Usuga Cadavid, J.P., Lamouri, S., Grabot, B., Pellerin, R., Fortin, A.: Machine learning applied in production planning and control: a state-of-the-art in the era of industry 4.0. J. Intell. Manuf. **31**, 1531–1558 (2020)

28. Wang, J., Xu, C., Zhang, J., Zhong, R.: Big data analytics for intelligent manufacturing systems: a review. J. Manuf. Syst. **62**, 738–752 (2022)

29. You, L., Peng, Q., Xiong, Z., He, D., Qiu, M., Zhang, X.: Integrating aspect analysis and local outlier factor for intelligent review spam detection. Futur. Gener. Comput. Syst. **102**, 163–172 (2020)

30. Zheng, T., Ardolino, M., Bacchetti, A., Perona, M.: The applications of industry 4.0 technologies in manufacturing context: a systematic literature review. Int. J. Prod. Res. **59**(6), 1922–1954 (2021)

31. Zhou, X., Garcia-Romero, D., Duraiswami, R., Espy-Wilson, C., Shamma, S.: Linear versus mel frequency cepstral coefficients for speaker recognition. In: 2011 IEEE Workshop on Automatic Speech Recognition & Understanding, pp. 559–564. IEEE (2011)

A Comparison of Automated Machine Learning Tools for Predicting Energy Building Consumption in Smart Cities

Daniela Soares[1(✉)], Pedro José Pereira[1,2], Paulo Cortez[2], and Carlos Gonçalves[3]

[1] EPMQ - IT Engineering Maturity and Quality Lab, CCG ZGDV Institute, Guimarães, Portugal
{daniela.soares,pedro.pereira}@ccg.pt
[2] ALGORITMI Center/LASI, Department of Information Systems, University of Minho, Braga, Portugal
pcortez@dsi.uminho.pt
[3] ISEP, Polytechnic of Porto, rua Dr. António Bernardino de Almeida, 4249-015 Porto, Portugal
cag@isep.ipp.pt

Abstract. In this paper, we explore and compare three recently proposed Automated Machine Learning (AutoML) tools (AutoGluon, H2O, Oracle AutoMLx) to create a single regression model that is capable of predicting smart city energy building consumption values. Using a recently collected one year hourly energy consumption dataset, related with 29 buildings from a Portuguese city, we perform several Machine Learning (ML) computational experiments, assuming two sets of input features (with and without lagged data) and a realistic rolling window evaluation. Furthermore, the obtained results are compared with a univariate Time Series Forecasting (TSF) approach, based on the automated FEDOT tool, which requires generating a predictive model for each building. Overall, competitive results, in terms of both predictive and computational effort performances, were obtained by the input lagged AutoGluon single regression modeling approach.

Keywords: Automated machine learning · Smart cities · Regression

1 Introduction

Due to advances in Information Technology (IT) and Artificial Intelligence (AI), nowadays it is easy to collect, store and process data that reflect relevant phenomena within the context of smart cities [13]. In particular, the efficient and environmentally responsible use of energy resources has become an important concern of smart cities decision makers, which aim to create ecological and sustainable environments for its citizens. Following this need, several works have

© The Author(s), under exclusive license to Springer Nature Switzerland AG 2023
N. Moniz et al. (Eds.): EPIA 2023, LNAI 14115, pp. 311–322, 2023.
https://doi.org/10.1007/978-3-031-49008-8_25

been proposed regarding the usage of ML to predict energy consumption and demand, aiming to improve energy efficiency and sustainability [7,11,14–16,20].

In this paper, as a real-world demonstration use case, we address the prediction energy consumption of several buildings from a Portuguese city. Following a typical smart city context, energy consumption data is collected on a regular basis with an associated timestamp, thus its prediction can be addressed as a univariate Time Series Forecasting (TSF) task [12]. However, this TSF approach implies modeling each building separately, which can lead to a vast amount of forecasting models (one for each building), increasing the difficulty of ML model maintenance and monitoring. A different approach is to use a single regression model capable of predicting the energy consumption of any building, increasing the learning task difficulty but simplifying the ML deployment phase, since only one model is maintained.

Regarding the related works, the usage of a single regression building energy prediction model approach is a recent trend (e.g., [7,14,17]). Nevertheless, the majority of these related works do not adopt an Automated ML (AutoML) model selection and tuning. AutoML is particularly valuable for smart cities, allowing non-experts to more easily create and maintain ML predictive models [13]. In effect, the related works typically adopt a manual tuning of ML algorithms, performing some trial-and-error comparison performances on a particular dataset. Within our knowledge, there are only two studies that have employed AutoML tools for building energy consumption prediction, addressing this goal as a regression [19] or TSF [12] tasks. Yet, in these two studies, the authors have modeled each building separately, resulting in one ML model for each building. In contrast, in this work we target a single energy consumption prediction ML model for all buildings. In particular, we empirically compare 3 distinct and recent AutoML tools (AutoGluon, H_2O, Oracle AutoMLx), using two sets of input features. The comparison assumes both predictive and computational effort performances measures, under a realistic and robust rolling window scheme [18]. Moreover, we also compare the single AutoML regression approach with an individual building ML modeling, obtained by using the FEDOT Automated TSF (AutoTSF) tool [12].

The remainder of the paper is organized as follows. Section 2 presents the related work. Then, Sect. 3 describes the datasets used, the AutoML and AutoTSF tools and the adopted evaluation procedure. Next, Sect. 4 presents and discusses the obtained empirical results. Finally, Sect. 5 presents the main conclusions and future work directions.

2   Related Work

Most related studies address the energy consumption prediction using one of the following approaches: (1) build a ML model to each building for which they want to predict future consumption [12,19,20]; or (2) model all public building using a single, and consequently more complex, ML model [3,4,7,14,15,17]. In most cases, the former approach involves having dozens or hundreds of models, increasing the complexity of ML deployment and monitoring tasks. Nevertheless, modeling the pattern from a specific building can simplify the training process and potentially lead to better predictions. On the other hand, the latter single model approach simplifies the deployment phase. For the multiple learning models approach, the previous works assumed an univariate TSF [12] or a regression task [19,20]. Regarding the single model approach, most works address assume a regression task (e.g., [7,17]).

In terms of the modeling phase, most of related works perform the ML model selection process manually, by implementing and comparing several ML algorithms [15,20]. Given the extensive set of models used in previous studies, in [16], the authors proposed a framework for selecting the most appropriate ML model for energy consumption prediction, based on multiple factors (e.g., size of dataset, number of attributes). Regarding the ML algorithms, the relevant recent studies that assumed regression tasks used: Artificial Neural Networks (ANN) [1,3,15,17,20], including Long Short-Terms Memory (LSTM) ANN [7]; Decision Trees (DT) [3,7]; Support Vector Machines (SVM) [3,7,15,17,20]; K-Nearest Neighbours (kNN) [3,17]; Linear Regression (LR) [15,20]; Ridge [3]; and Ensemble methods [3], including Random Forest (RF) [14,20], eXtreme Gradient Boosting (XGBoost) and Adaptative Boosting (Adaboost) [15]. It should be noted that all these research studies performed a ML algorithm selection without tuning its hyperparameters, thus no hyperparameter selection was executed.

In a different approach, in [12,19] the authors applied AutoML algorithms for data preprocessing, model selection and tuning. AutoML compares several algorithms with different hyperparameters values, returning the configuration with the best predictive performance. Recent studies have shown the value of these algorithms in the smart cities domain [13]. In particular, Wang et al. [19] apply two AutoML algorithms, namely auto-sklearn and TPOT, for electric load forecasting, comparing them with LR, RF, SVM, XGBoost and Gradient Boost Machines (GBM) using two different datasets. The data was modeled as a regression task and the TPOT algorithm presented the best overall results. In another study [12], the authors tested several Automated TSF (AutoTSF) algorithms under 9 time-series smart cities open datasets, 3 of which were related to energy consumption. The best overall results were achieved by FEDOT framework. Yet, both these studies using automated approaches modeled each building separately.

In this paper, we address the building energy consumption prediction task by using automated modeling tools, implementing and comparing two different approaches: (1) modeling all buildings with a single regression model, comparing 3 different and popular AutoML tools: AutoGluon, H$_2$O and Oracle AutoMLx; and (2) modeling each building separately, using the AutoTSF FEDOT tool that provided the best overall results in [12]. Within our knowledge, this is the first study comparing these different approaches based on automated tools for model selection and tuning. To evaluate our models, we used a real-world dataset of energy consumption from 29 buildings from a Portuguese city. Furthermore, we employ a robust Rolling Window evaluation procedure [18] with statistical tests to validate our results.

3   Materials and Methods

3.1   Data

In this work, we explore energy consumption data that was provided by a Portuguese company. Due to commercial privacy concerns, several data details (e.g., geographic location, specific time stamps or individual energy consumption values) are not disclosed. The data were recently collected, corresponding to around one year of records. In total, we had access to 29 distinct energy consumption files, each including the consumption values from a public building that were recorded every 15 min during the collected time period. The data records contained several attributes, including the building unique delivery point identifier, the consumption time and date and the average energy consumed in kW. It is worth noting that the data correspond to the energy consumption of special low voltage connection, that is, buildings with contracted power equal to or less than 45 kVA, which are associated with small buildings or residential customers. Additionally, a supplementary dataset was provided, containing specific information about the buildings, namely the address, typology (e.g., school, administrative, cultural, parking lot, civil protection), useful area in m^2, year of construction and the delivery point identifier.

In terms of data preprocessing, the 29 energy consumption files were firstly integrated into a single Comma-Separated Values (CSV) file. Then, we merged the additional building attributes (provided in the supplementary dataset) into the same CSV file. Next, following a feedback that was obtained from the private company experts, the 15 min values were aggregated into an hourly scale, by summing four consecutive consumption values for each building. Then, aiming to improve the predictive performance of the ML models, we generated three new lagged inputs, related to energy consumption values for the same building, as recorded in three distinct time periods: the previous hour; the previous day at the same hour; and the previous week at the same hour. The rationale of the lagged inputs is to allow an autoregressive ML modeling for the regression approach, as typically performed by univariate TSF models [12]. To verify the impact of the lagged attributes, we designed two input feature scenarios, described on Table 1. Scenario A includes only features related to the time and hour of the targeted energy consumption and contextual building information, while scenario B complements these inputs with the three additional lagged energy consumption values. It should be noted that Scenario B does not require a large storage of historical data to perform predictions on new buildings (only one week of data is needed).

3.2   AutoML Methods

As previously explained, in this work we explore two main ML approaches to predict energy consumption data: **regression**, assuming a single prediction model

Table 1. List of analyzed data attributes.

Context	Name	Description	Scenarios
Time	Hour	Consumption time	A,B
	Weekday	Day of the week of consumption.	
Building	Typology	Building type, one of the 6 levels {administrative, cultural, school, parking lot, civil protection, others})	A,B
	Useful area	Building floor area (in m^2).	
Energy	Previous hour	Consumption in the previous hour	B
	Previous day	Consumption in the previous day and same hour	
	Previous weekday	Consumption in the previous weekday and same hour.	
Target	Consumption	Energy consumption (in kW).	–

that is capable of predicting the hourly energy consumption for all buildings; and pure univariate **TSF**, generating an individual prediction model for each building (total of 29 models). For both approaches, we selected automated tools for the model selection and hyperparameter tuning.

The tool selection for the regression approach, is based on our previous work, published in 2023 [13], in which we developed an AutoML platform for smart cities (AI4CITY) that automatically creates full ML pipelines, choosing data preprocessing steps and AutoML tools based on the data characteristics and the ML task. The AI4CITY plaform makes use of H_2O and AutoGluon AutoML search engines. In [13], it was shown that the automatic AI4CITY ML pipelines produced better results for 15 of the 26 analyzed smart city datasets when compared with the direct usage of the H_2O and AutoGluon tools. Following this result, in this paper we adopt the AI4CITY tool under two variants, where the AutoML is executed using the H_2O or AutoGluon algorithms. Additionally, by requirement of the private company that provided the data, we also explore the recently proposed Oracle AutoMLx tool [21] for the regression ML approach and that works under a computational cloud infrastructure. Regarding the univariate TSF approach, a recent study compared 8 distinct AutoTSF open-source tools under 9 smart city time series, 3 of which were related to energy consumption [12]. The FEDOT tool presented the best overall results and, therefore, we selected it for our TSF experimentation.

In terms of ML models tested by each AutoML tool, we used the default settings (in order to achieve an unbiased comparison). When available in the tool documentation, we detail the searched ML algorithms and the number of hyperparameters ($\mathcal{H}$) tuned by the AutoML:

- **H_2O**—Generalized Linear Model (GLM) ($\mathcal{H} = 1$), RF ($\mathcal{H} = 0$), Extremely Randomized Trees (XRT) ($\mathcal{H} = 0$), GBM ($\mathcal{H} = 8$), XGBoost ($\mathcal{H} = 9$),

Deep Learning Neural Network (DLNN) ($\mathcal{H} = 7$) and two Stacked Ensembles (all – uses all base learners; and best – uses the best model per searched ML algorithm, total of 6 individual models). The Stacked Ensembles adopt a second-level GLM learner that weights the individual base learner predictions.

- **AutoGluon**—assumes the tabular prediction feature, which first executes several ML algorithms under a default hyperparameter grid search: GBM ($\mathcal{H} = 2$), CatBoost Boosted Trees ($\mathcal{H} = 0$), RF ($\mathcal{H} = 1$), Extra Trees ($\mathcal{H} = 1$), kNN ($\mathcal{H} = 1$), and a DLNN ($\mathcal{H} = 0$). Then, a Stacked Ensemble is created and returned as the global prediction model. The Stacked Ensemble works as special DLNN, in which the individual ML models are stacked in multiple layers and trained in a layer-wise manner, such as detailed in [6].

- **Oracle AutoMLx**—AdaBoost ($\mathcal{H} = 2$), DT ($\mathcal{H} = 4$), Extra Trees ($\mathcal{H} = 6$), ANN, kNN ($\mathcal{H} = 2$), Light GBM ($\mathcal{H} = 9$), Linear SVM ($\mathcal{H} = 2$), LR ($\mathcal{H} = 3$), RF ($\mathcal{H} = 4$), SVM ($\mathcal{H} = 3$), and XGBoost ($\mathcal{H} = 8$).

As for the automatic preprocessing, both AI4CITY and Oracle AutoMLx use standard z-score scaling for numeric features and one-hot encoding for the categorical attributes (generation of binary value for each categorical level). However, the Oracle tool uses a maximum limit of 5 unique levels, after which a label encoding is applied, instead of one hot encoding. On the other hand, AI4CITY sets this limit as 50, after which the Inverse Document Frequency (IDF) transformation is applied. In the analyzed building energy consumption dataset, the typology attribute is the only categorical feature, with 6 unique values. Consequently, AI4CITY applies one hot encoding transformation to this column, while Oracle AutoML applies a label encoding. Lastly, for the univariate TSF approach, no preprocessing is applied to the dataset by the AI4CITY tool, thus it directly feeds the time series data into the FEDOT AutoTSF tool. Furthermore, to ensure a fair comparison between these tools, we used all AutoML search default values, except for two aspects. Firstly, the maximum execution time was set to 60 min, in order to prevent an excessive computational execution time. Secondly, all default internal cross validation procedures were disabled, being replaced by an internal time ordered holdout split scheme, since time matters in this domain, i.e., all prediction models should be trained using older data and validate or tested using more recent data records [18].

3.3   Evaluation

In order to develop a realistic and robust comparison, a Rolling Window (RW) procedure was developed to simulate several training and testing iterations over time [5,18]. The RW iteratively trains the ML models, using a window W of the oldest data observations, to perform H-ahead predictions. Then, for the next iteration, the window rolls a step of S, by discarding the S oldest data observations from the training data and updating it with the S newest records, during a total of U iterations. In this work, aiming to achieve a reasonable amount of $U = 20$ iterations, we have set $W = 5,760$ hours (approximately 8 months) and $H = 24$ hours (corresponding to one day), while $S = 144$ hours

(6 days) was calculated according to the formula $S = D - (W + H)/U$, where $D = 8,760$ hours is the length of the full dataset. For a particular RW iteration, for the AutoML tools (Gluon, H2O and Oracle), the available training data is further split by using a time ordered holdout split method, producing validation (with $V = 12$ most recent records, corresponding to half a day) and fitting (with the remainder older examples). The fitting set is used to train the ML models, while the validation set is used to rank the ML algorithms and guide the AutoML search. As for the FEDOT tool, we used its default internal time series validation scheme, similarly to the setup adopted in [12].

Both the predicted performance and the computing effort required by the AutoML tools were taken into consideration during the evaluation process. To measure the accuracy of a predictive model, we use two popular regression measures, namely the Mean Absolute Error (MAE) and Root Mean Square Error (RMSE). To evaluate the computational effort, two temporal measures were used, namely the time to train the model (in minutes) and the test time (in milliseconds). The results that are shown in the next section correspond to the median values of the $U = 20$ RW iteration executions. We used the median aggregation function since it is less sensitive to outliers when compared with the average function. Regarding the specific FEDOT tool, it performs a pure TSF modeling for each of the 29 buildings, thus generating 29 distinct forecasting models. The FEDOT results were thus aggregated by first computing the median of the $U = 20$ RW iterations for each individual TSF model and then computing the overall median for all buildings. Statistical significance is measured by using the nonparametric Wilcoxon test [9].

4   Results

All experiments were executed using code written using the Python programming language. The FEDOT, H2O, and AutoGluon computational experiments were executed using a Linux virtual machine with 12 cores and 64 Gb of RAM. As for the Oracle AutoMLx, the tool license we had access only runs in a cloud system with 16 Gb of RAM and a VM.Standard.E4.Flex computational environment which includes one GPU.

The overall results are presented in Table 2, in terms of the median values of the $U = 20$ RW iterations. From the table, it becomes clear that scenario B performance values are much improved, demonstrating the importance of time-dependent (lagged) factors. For the B scenario, the Gluon model obtained the most accurate prediction measures, exhibiting MAE and RMSE values of 3.38 kW and 7.57 kW, followed by H2O and Oracle. As for the computational effort, the Oracle tool provided the most computationally efficient results. Yet, it should be noted that the Oracle results were obtained by using a different (and better) computational cloud infrastructure. Thus, the computational measures cannot be directly compared with the ones obtained by Gluon and H2O. When using the same computational environment, Gluon required less computational effort, in terms of both training and prediction times, when compared with the

H2O tool and for both scenarios (A and B). Regarding FEDOT, which performs the pure TSF modeling approach, the obtained predictive performance values are significantly worse (for both MAE and RMSE) when compared with all scenario B AutoML executions. As for the computational effort, FEDOT requires a median computational effort (when modeling just one building) that is higher when compared with the AutoML tools. This is a relevant issue, since the actual FEDOT running time for all buildings 29 times higher (e.g., the total FEDOT RW median training time for all 29 buildings is around 2,175 min). Thus, considering the obtained results, it becomes clear that the usage of a single regression model for scenario B is the best energy consumption modeling approach, since it produces a single ML model that requires less computation and provides better predictive performances.

Table 2. Comparison of results (median RW values; best values in **bold**).

Scenario	ML Model	MAE (kW)	RMSE (kW)	Train Time (min)	Prediction Time (ms)
A	Gluon	14.33	25.56	27.0	0.39
	H2O	15.56	27.63	60.0	1.23
	Oracle	14.11	25.76	**1.0**	**0.02**
B	Gluon	**3.38***	**7.57**	42.0	0.83
	H2O	3.51†	7.81	60.0	1.15
	Oracle	3.60†	9.26	9.0	0.11
TSF	FEDOT	6.89	15.96	75.0	12.99

*—Statistically significant under a paired comparison with all other methods.
$\dagger$—Statistically significant under a paired comparison with FEDOT.

Further scenario B result comparison details are provided in Table 3, which shows the median values of the predictive performance measures for each tool and building typology type, comparing the AutoML results with the FEDOT tool. The last row shows the average values, when considering all six building types. Overall, Table 3 favors the Gluon tool, which obtains the best median MAE values for 4 building types (Schools, Parking lots, Civil Protection, and Others) and the best median RMSE values for 3 types (Administrative, Parking lots and Civil protection), while also presenting the lowest average (last row) MAE (5.68 kW) and RMSE (9.83 kW) values. In terms of the distinct Gluon performances, the predictive errors are substantially higher for the parking lots (median MAE of 12.66 kW), civil protection (9.13) and administrative buildings (6.58 kW). In contrast, high quality predictions were obtained for the cultural buildings (median MAE of 0.90 kW), schools (2.44 kW) and others (2.38 kW).

For demonstration purposes, the left of Fig. 1 plots the median of the Regression Error Characteristic (REC) curves [2] for all RW interactions with their respective Wilcoxon 95% confidence intervals. For all absolute tolerance values (x-axis) the Gluon results are significantly better when compared with FEDOT. For instance, when assuming a tolerance of 5 kW, Gluon correctly predicts 80% of the records while FEDOT only predicts 60%. The middle of Fig. 1 exemplifies

Table 3. Comparison of results by building typology (median rolling window values; best values in **bold**).

Typology	Gluon		H2O		Oracle		FEDOT	
	MAE	RMSE	MAE	RMSE	MAE	RMSE	MAE	RMSE
Administrative	6.58	**15.64**	6.97	18.20	**6.53**	15.89	18.61	35.48
Cultural	0.90	1.29	**0.83**	**1.25**	0.96	1.40	1.26	1.96
Schools	**2.44**	4.49	2.45	**4.24**	2.46	4.27	5.10	9.21
Parking lots	**12.66**	**20.37**	14.61	22.95	13.32	20.68	20.79	27.52
Civil protection	**9.13**	**13.63**	10.39	15.11	13.17	17.58	16.50	20.35
Others	**2.38**	3.54	2.71	3.78	2.44	**3.51**	4.68	5.88
Average	**5.68**	**9.83**	6.33	10.92	6.48	10.56	11.16	16.73

the quality of the obtained Gluon forecasts for the last RW $U = 20$ iteration and one administrative building. Finally, the right of Fig. 1 plots the full RW Gluon results in terms of a regression scatter plot (x−axis denotes the target values and y−axis represents the predictions). The predictions, shown in terms of blue colored points, are close to the perfect prediction diagonal line.

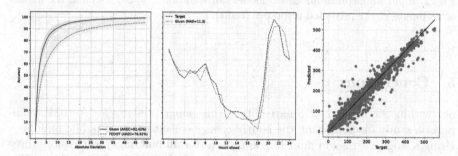

Fig. 1. RW median REC curve with Wilcoxon 95% confidence intervals (left), example of Gluon predictions for an Administrative building (middle) and Gluon RW regression scatter plot results (right).

Additionally, we performed an explainable AI (XAI) analysis by applying the SHapley Additive exPlanation (SHAP) method [10] (as implemented in the shap Python package) on the best ML model obtained by Gluon in the last RW iteration, which was a Weighted Ensemble (see Sect. 3.2). Figure 2 presents the top 5 features in terms of their importance (left) and the SHAP values (right). Regarding the feature importance, the consumption from the previous hour is the predominant attribute, with a relative importance of 55%, followed by the consumption in the previous day and same hour (8%), the hour of consumption (8%), the consumption in the previous weekday and same hour (7%) and the

building useful area (2%). These results prove the relevance of newly lagged engineered features, since they correspond to 3 of the top 5 predominant attributes,
demonstrating the relevance of an autoregressive modeling. The right of Fig. 2
shows the overall impact of each input in the predicted result. As an example, a
decrease on the first input (consumption of the previous hour) reflects a decrease
on the predicted consumption (denoted by the blue dots).

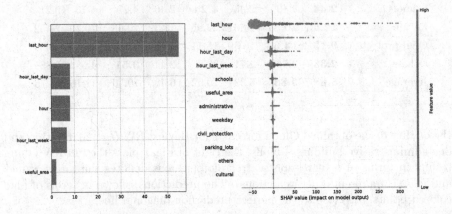

Fig. 2. Input importance for Gluon model (for iteration $U = 20$, left) and the impact
of its inputs in the predicted responses (right).

5   Conclusions

Set within the context of Smart Cities, this paper presents an AutoML comparison study for predicting the hourly energy consumption of public buildings.
Using a single regression modeling approach (for all buildings), we explore three
recently proposed AutoML tools: AutoGluon, H2O and Oracle AutoMLx. The
analyzed data was related with a one year collection period, related with 29
buildings from a Portuguese city. Several computational experiments were held,
assuming a realistic rolling window evaluation, two input sets (with and without lagged attributes) and both predictive and computational effort measures.
Furthermore, we also tested a univariate TSF approach that generates a predictive model for each building, using the FEDOT AutoTSF tool. The best
overall results were obtained by the single regression AutoGluon lagged predictive method, returning a median MAE value of 3.38 kilowatts and requiring a
reasonable computational effort. In future work, we intend to incorporate more
building specific attributes, aiming to further improve the predictive results. We
also plan to explore other AutoML tools (e.g., TPOT, TransmogrifAI) [8].

Acknowledgments. This work has been supported by FCT – Fundação para a
Ciência e Tecnologia within the R&D Units Project Scope: UIDB/00319/2020.

References

1. Bagnasco, A., Fresi, F., Saviozzi, M., Silvestro, F., Vinci, A.: Electrical consumption forecasting in hospital facilities: an application case. Energy Build. **103**, 261–270 (2015)

2. Bi, J., Bennett, K.P.: Regression error characteristic curves. In: Fawcett, T., Mishra, N. (eds.) Machine Learning, Proceedings of the Twentieth International Conference (ICML 2003), August 21–24, 2003, Washington, DC, USA, pp. 43–50. AAAI Press (2003)

3. Burger, E.M., Moura, S.J.: Gated ensemble learning method for demand-side electricity load forecasting. Energy Build. **109**, 23–34 (2015). https://doi.org/10.1016/j.enbuild.2015.10.019

4. Chou, J.S., Tran, D.S.: Forecasting energy consumption time series using machine learning techniques based on usage patterns of residential householders. Energy **165**, 709–726 (2018). https://doi.org/10.1016/j.energy.2018.09.144

5. Cortez, P., Matos, L.M., Pereira, P.J., Santos, N., Duque, D.: Forecasting store foot traffic using facial recognition, time series and support vector machines. In: Graña, M., López-Guede, J.M., Etxaniz, O., Herrero, Á., Quintián, H., Corchado, E. (eds.) International Joint Conference SOCO'16-CISIS'16-ICEUTE'16 - San Sebastián, Spain, October 19th-21st, 2016, Proceedings. Advances in Intelligent Systems and Computing, vol. 527, pp. 267–276 (2016). https://doi.org/10.1007/978-3-319-47364-2_26

6. Erickson, N., Mueller, J., Shirkov, A., Zhang, H., Larroy, P., Li, M., Smola, A.J.: Autogluon-tabular: Robust and accurate automl for structured data. CoRR abs/2003.06505 (2020)

7. Faiq, M., Tan, K.G., Liew, C.P., Hossain, F., Tso, C.P., Lim, L.L., Wong, A.Y.K., Shah, Z.M.: Prediction of energy consumption in campus buildings using long short-term memory. Alex. Eng. J. **67**, 65–76 (2023)

8. Ferreira, L., Pilastri, A.L., Martins, C.M., Pires, P.M., Cortez, P.: A comparison of automl tools for machine learning, deep learning and xgboost. In: International Joint Conference on Neural Networks, IJCNN 2021, Shenzhen, China, July 18–22, 2021, pp. 1–8. IEEE (2021). https://doi.org/10.1109/IJCNN52387.2021.9534091

9. Hollander, M., Wolfe, D.A., Chicken, E.: Nonparametric Statistical Methods. Wiley, NJ, USA (2013)

10. Lundberg, S.M., Lee, S.: A unified approach to interpreting model predictions. In: Guyon, I., von Luxburg, U., Bengio, S., Wallach, H.M., Fergus, R., Vishwanathan, S.V.N., Garnett, R. (eds.) Advances in Neural Information Processing Systems 30: Annual Conference on Neural Information Processing Systems 2017, December 4–9, 2017, Long Beach, CA, USA, pp. 4765–4774 (2017)

11. Mosavi, A., Salimi, M., Faizollahzadeh Ardabili, S., Rabczuk, T., Shamshirband, S., Varkonyi-Kóczy, A.R.: State of the art of machine learning models in energy systems, a systematic review. Energies **12**(7) (2019). https://doi.org/10.3390/en12071301

12. Pereira, P.J., Costa, N., Barros, M., Cortez, P., Durães, D., Silva, A., Machado, J.: A comparison of automated time series forecasting tools for smart cities. In: Marreiros, G., Martins, B., Paiva, A., Ribeiro, B., Sardinha, A. (eds.) Progress in Artificial Intelligence - 21st EPIA Conference on Artificial Intelligence, EPIA 2022, Lisbon, Portugal, August 31 - September 2, 2022, Proceedings. Lecture Notes in Computer Science, vol. 13566, pp. 551–562. Springer (2022). https://doi.org/10.1007/978-3-031-16474-3_45

13. Pereira, P.J., Gonçalves, C., Nunes, L.L., Cortez, P., Pilastri, A.: AI4CITY - An Automated Machine Learning Platform for Smart Cities. In: SAC '23: The 38th ACM/SIGAPP Symposium on Applied Computing, Tallinn, Estonia, March 27–31, 2023, pp. 886–889. ACM (2023). https://doi.org/10.1145/3555776.3578740

14. Pham, A.D., Ngo, N.T., Truong, T.T.H., Huynh, N.T., Truong, N.S.: Predicting energy consumption in multiple buildings using machine learning for improving energy efficiency and sustainability. J. Clean. Prod. **260**, 121082 (2020)

15. Robinson, C., Dilkina, B., Hubbs, J., Zhang, W., Guhathakurta, S., Brown, M.A., Pendyala, R.M.: Machine learning approaches for estimating commercial building energy consumption. Appl. Energy **208**, 889–904 (2017)

16. Seyedzadeh, S., Rahimian, F.P., Glesk, I., Roper, M.: Machine learning for estimation of building energy consumption and performance: a review. Vis. Eng. **6**, 1–20 (2018)

17. Shapi, M.K.M., Ramli, N.A., Awalin, L.J.: Energy consumption prediction by using machine learning for smart building: case study in Malaysia. Dev. Built Environ. **5**, 100037 (2021)

18. Tashman, L.J.: Out-of-sample tests of forecasting accuracy: an analysis and review. Int. J. Forecast. **16**(4), 437–450 (2000)

19. Wang, C., Bäck, T., Hoos, H.H., Baratchi, M., Limmer, S., Olhofer, M.: Automated machine learning for short-term electric load forecasting. In: IEEE Symposium Series on Computational Intelligence, SSCI 2019, Xiamen, China, December 6–9, 2019, pp. 314–321. IEEE (2019). https://doi.org/10.1109/SSCI44817.2019.9002839

20. Wu, Z., Chu, W.: Sampling strategy analysis of machine learning models for energy consumption prediction. In: 2021 IEEE 9th International Conference on Smart Energy Grid Engineering (SEGE), pp. 77–81. IEEE (2021)

21. Yakovlev, A., Moghadam, H.F., Moharrer, A., Cai, J., Chavoshi, N., Varadarajan, V., Agrawal, S.R., Karnagel, T., Idicula, S., Jinturkar, S., Agarwal, N.: Oracle automl: A fast and predictive automl pipeline. Proc. VLDB Endow. **13**(12), 3166–3180 (2020). https://doi.org/10.14778/3415478.3415542

Measuring Latency-Accuracy Trade-Offs in Convolutional Neural Networks

André Tse[1]([✉])(iD), Lino Oliveira[1](iD), and João Vinagre[1,2](iD)

[1] INESC TEC, Porto, Portugal
andre.tse@inesctec.pt
[2] Faculty of Sciences - University of Porto, Porto, Portugal

Abstract. Several systems that employ machine learning models are subject to strict latency requirements. Fraud detection systems, transportation control systems, network traffic analysis and footwear manufacturing processes are a few examples. These requirements are imposed at inference time, when the model is queried. However, it is not trivial how to adjust model architecture and hyperparameters in order to obtain a good trade-off between predictive ability and inference time. This paper provides a contribution in this direction by presenting a study of how different architectural and hyperparameter choices affect the inference time of a Convolutional Neural Network for network traffic analysis. Our case study focus on a model for traffic correlation attacks to the Tor network, that requires the correlation of a large volume of network flows in a short amount of time. Our findings suggest that hyperparameters related to convolution operations—such as stride, and the number of filters—and the reduction of convolution and max-pooling layers can substantially reduce inference time, often with a relatively small cost in predictive performance.

Keywords: Convolutional neural network · Inference time · Network traffic analysis

1 Introduction

Multiple applications involving machine learning have strict response time requirements. This is for example the case of predictive maintenance, network traffic analysis, energy or transport control systems. In such applications, machine learning models may have to answer a large amount of queries in a short amount of time, which means that the latency at inference time—i.e. at prediction—is critical.

Our goal in this work is to study model latency during the prediction phase, focusing particularly on Convolutional Neural Networks (CNNs). Our focus is on helping practitioners to make models both responsive and accurate. Architecture design, weight initialization, pruning and regularization strategies are a few of the possible ways to reduce the prediction time of these networks. The challenge is to having negligible loss, or even no loss in predictive ability. We evaluate various changes to model architecture and hyperparameters, and illustrate the trade-off between accuracy and prediction time of the models in a network traffic analysis task. The machine learning model consists of a CNN designed to correlate encrypted network traffic flows in the TOR network. CNNs have become an effective method for analyzing network data, but they are not without challenges. The issue of inference time is one of the major problems. Although there have been several studies focused on making machine learning models faster in the training phase, there are very few contributions regarding the reduction of inference times in the prediction phase.

Besides analysing this accuracy versus inference time trade-off, we also aim at finding consistent strategies to reduce time under low-latency requirements.

In short, this paper presents as main contributions:

- A methodology to develop and evaluate Machine Learning (ML) methods within low latency constraints;
- An analysis of the various hyperparameters and various architectures that make up a Convolutional Neural Network (CNN), to understand how these influence the prediction times of the network.

This paper is divided into 5 sections. Section 2 contains a comprehensive state-of-the-art and literature review while Sect. 3 presents the proposed methodology used, as well as an explanation of the dataset used for the experiments that were performed. In Sect. 4, we present all the tests and experiments performed using the proposed methodology. Finally, in Sect. 5 are the conclusions obtained along with possible lines of development that may be applied in future work.

2   Related Work

Convolutional Neural Networks (CNNs) excel at prediction tasks but their high computational requirements can make them challenging to use on devices with constrained resources. This section discusses related studies on approaches to apply CNNs more efficiently and how it affects the accuracy and prediction time of CNN.

Lebdev and Lempitsky [7] explain the steps and approaches of the *pruning* process, while LeCun et al. [8] were the first to investigate pruning neural networks in 1989. By eliminating unnecessary weights from the network, this method improves generalization, speeds up learning rates and reduces the need for comprehensive training data. Then, Molchanov et al. [9] presented an iterative pruning method that removes the least important parameters based on heuristic selection criteria. Lastly, through removing the least significant filters from each convolution layer, Houdhary et al. [3] automatic method for determining the ideal number of filters has produced encouraging results on a variety of datasets.

Putra and Leu [12] suggest a multilevel neural network architecture to reduce the expected inference time of a larger network by stacking a smaller network where sensor data is initially passed, and its predicted value is then passed into a decider algorithm. Meanwhile, Teerapittayanon et al. [13] report BranchyNet which improves the conventional deep network structure by enabling accurate classification of samples in the network's early stages to exit and preventing needless processing in later network layers, resulting in faster inference. More recently, Bolukbasi et al. [1] describe two methods in which the first is also an adaptive early-exit strategy that allows easy examples to bypass some of the network's layers, while the second involves an adaptive network selection method that arranges pre-trained Deep Neural Networks (DNNs) with different cost/accuracy trade-offs in a directed acyclic graph. Fu et al. [5] suggest a novel approach that takes into account both algorithm and hardware architecture design principles for accelerating Binarized Neural Networks (BNNs) with Field-Programmable Gate Arrays (FPGAs) by using similarities between input and kernel weights, the aim of decreasing the latency and power consumption of BNNs is possible.

Quantization is a simple technique for increasing processing speed, memory efficiency and compression for neural networks as mentioned by Lebdev and Lempitsky [7]. Hessian AWare Quantization (HAWQ) is a quantization method presented by Dong et al. [4] based on systematic selection of the order for block-wise fine-tuning as well as the quantization accuracy from second-order (Hessian) information. To reduce complexity and memory usage, Hacene et al. [6] suggest combining a new pruning method that effectively prunes connections in a CNN convolutional layers with a quantization scheme that does so by substituting the convolutional operation for a low-cost multiplexer. Finally, Chang et al. [2] suggest the first solution, which uses various quantization schemes for different rows of the weight matrix to achieve a better distribution of weights in different rows that are not the same and a better utilization of heterogeneous FPGA hardware resources.

The methodology developed in this paper differs from the approaches presented as it focus on reducing the prediction time in the test phase rather than the training phase.

3   Proposed Methodology

The architecture of a standard CNN (Fig. 1) can be quite complex as it consists several layers and the input undergoes several transformations until it is translated into an output.

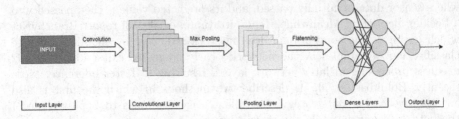

Fig. 1. Simple scheme of how a CNN works

Achieving a good trade-off between prediction time and accuracy, i.e., the shortest possible prediction time without degrading accuracy can become possible by changing some hyperparameters that make up the network or changing the architecture of the network itself.

Table 1 provides a list of the hyperparameters of a CNN. The goal is be to make individual tests of each hyperparameter by changing them and comparing accuracy. For each hyperparameter, we will have as many models as the different values we experiment with. After training the models we generate a plot with two vertical axes, one representing the model's accuracy and the other the model's prediction time. Thus, we can observe the influence of the variation of the values of each hyperparameter and from there draw elations that contribute to our study.

However, some hyperparameters—such as Padding or Activaction Functions—do not allow a plot construction, as they are discrete variables that can only take on a limited range of predefined values. For example, Padding can only take on the values of "VALID" or "SAME" with that being said, the relationship between the hyperparameter value and the model's accuracy and inference time cannot be represented by a line. In such cases, a table will be produced in order to compare the different attributes of that hyperparameter. Regarding the changes in the network architecture, in most of the tests, these will be performed by making the changes in the architecture and then varying the values similarly to the tests on the hyperparameters.

To obtain accurate time measurements, these are taken 10 times and the minimum time is chosen, to avoid interference problems from other processes on the machine, which can be quite noticeable because the prediction times are already relatively short.

4   Results and Analysis

4.1   Case Study: Traffic Correlation

The most well-known anonymizing network is The Onion Router (Tor), with millions of users everyday [10, 11]. By tunneling payload traffic through multiple-layered encrypted channels known as circuits, Tor accomplishes client-side anonymity. Entry, middle, and exit nodes are the three relay nodes that serve as

Table 1. List of hyperparameters of a CNN [14]

	Parameters	Hyperparameters
Convolutional layer	Kernels	Kernel size
		Number of kernels
		Stride
		Padding
		Activation function
Pooling layer	None	Pooling method
		Filter size
		Stride
		Padding
Dense layer	Weights	Number of weights
		Activation function

client proxies in each route. Furthermore, Tor can offer server-side privacy via Onion Services (OS).

Tor's vulnerability to flow correlation attacks, in which an adversary attempts to link the egress and ingress portions of a Tor connection by comparing its traffic characteristics such as packet timings and sizes, is extremely challenging [10] given the large amount of traffic on Tor and its world-wide distributed nature.

For a deanonymization attack to be successful, it is therefore extremely important to be able to correlate as many ingress and egress segments as possible in a short amount of time.

Dataset In order to test the methodology developed we used a dataset that provides CNN traffic data as input which in a similar way to DeepCorr [10], a CNN-based deep learning architecture that learns a flow correlation function tailored to TOR's network. The CNN built for this problem will receive as input raw flow features. A single bidirectional network flow i is represented by the following vector array:

$$F_i = [T_i^u; S_i^u; T_i^d; S_i^d]$$

where T represents the vector of Inter-Packet Delays (IPD) of the flow i, S is the vector of i'th packet sizes, and u and d superscripts represent "upstream" and "downstream" sides of bidirectional flow i. In the instance where that is intended to correlate two flows i and j, this pair of flows with the following two-dimensional matrix consisting of 8 rows is represented as follows:

$$F_{i,j} = [T_i^u; T_j^u; T_i^d; T_j^d; S_i^u; S_j^u; S_i^d; S_j^d]$$

where the lines of the array are taken from the flow representations F_i and F_j. Summarizing, traffic is transformed into a multivariate time series for input to a CNN.

4.2   Results

To perform the tests, we used a scaled-down version of DeepCorr [10]. The structure of our model can be seen in Table 2. The only difference between this model and the original DeepCorr model is the reduce_factor with a value of 16, which significantly reduces the complexity of the network and allows to make the experiments feasible and faster on the available hardware.

Table 2. Network architecture used in the correlation stage

Layer	Details
Input layer	Size: 8 * Flow length
Convolutional layer 1	Kernel num: 2000/reduce_factor
	Kernel size: (2, 30)
	Stride: (2, 1)
	Activation: ReLU
Max Pool 1	Window size: (1, 5)
	Stride: (1, 1)
Convolutional layer 2	Kernel num: 1000/reduce_factor
	Kernel size: (4, 10)
	Stride: (4, 1)
	Activation: ReLU
Max Pool 2	Window Size: (1, 5)
	Stride: (1, 1)
Fully connected 1	Size: 3000, Activation: ReLU
Fully connected 2	Size: 800, Activation: ReLU
Fully connected 3	Size: 100, Activation: ReLU
Output layer	Size: 1, Activation sigmoid

In the model shown, input vectors consisting of two TOR flows that will be tested for correlation are captured by the first convolution layer. Thus, the second convolution layer uses a combination of timing and size information to capture aspects of the overall traffic flow.

Next, we show how changing the configuration of the CNN impacts the time-accuracy trade-off.

Kernel size To find out the impact on prediction time and accuracy our experiments varied the kernel width in two CNN layers, which can be seen in Fig. 2. High prediction times were produced by the first layer's kernel width of 15 to 31, which then experienced a sharp decline while maintaining high precision throughout the whole experiment. Moreover, with a lowest prediction time of 0.18 s and high accuracy, the second layer's kernel size had a greater influence

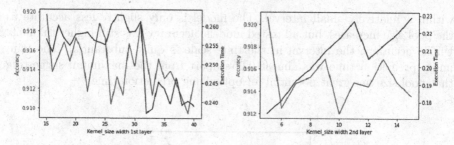

Fig. 2. Trade-off between accuracy and prediction time with varying kernel width in 1st and 2nd layers

on prediction time. From the results analysis our perspective is that varying the kernel size can shorten the prediction times but we must be able to ensure that the kernel is not too large, taking too long to perform the convolution operations, or too small, taking too long to go through the entire input.

Filters The number of filters is an important setting in the convolution process and as such we carried out experiments to vary the values of the number of filters in both layers. A difference of 42% was found between the maximum and minimum values obtained and a somewhat predictably increasing trend in prediction time as the number of filters increased. Accuracy showed some irregularities but remained consistently high—above 0.91—as shown in Fig. 3. From our perspective, reduced prediction time in CNNs can be achieved by lowering the number of filters.

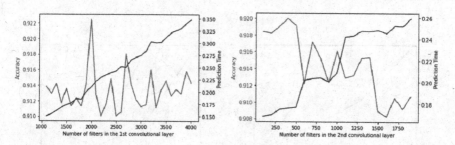

Fig. 3. Trade-off between accuracy and prediction time by varying the size of the filters in 1st and 2nd layers

Pool_Size The experiment was conducted to determine how the pool_size affected the model's prediction time. The original pool_size in DeepCorr was (1, 5). We varied the width from 1 to 31 while the height remained at 1. Figure 4 shows that as pool_size width expanded there was clearly an increase in prediction time, while results for accuracy showed no obvious trends and remained within a relatively small interval. The model is only slightly less accurate as the pool_size increases, but all tested models' accuracy was still higher than 0.9. Unlike accuracy, the interval in the time scale is quite substantial. The minimum prediction time was almost 0.25 s apart from the maximum, suggesting that pool_size has great potential for optimizing prediction time.

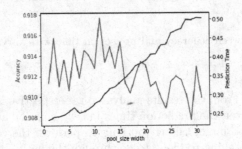

Fig. 4. Trade-off between accuracy and prediction time by varying the pool_size width in both max pooling layers

Strides in Max Pooling layer Figure 5 shows the graphics of both experiments and the first layer stride had a significant impact on prediction time but had lower accuracy, while the second layer showed little variation in prediction time but had a more significant impact on accuracy, according to our two experiments that varied the stride in the first and second layers of a CNN. Faster prediction times are achieved with bigger strides but because the output shape is so small in the second layer, this effect is minimal.

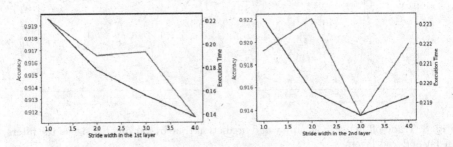

Fig. 5. Trade-off between accuracy and prediction time by varying the stride width in 1st and 2nd layers

Number of Convolutional/Max Pooling Layers Convolution and max-pooling layers were removed from the network architecture as part of the experiments. This experiment involved readjusting the values of the kernel size and stride in the new network structure. Using only one convolutional and max pooling layer, the kernel demonstrated an increasing trend while strides showed a decreasing trend in prediction times. Having said that, when the effects of the strides and kernel were examined, it became clear that the strides hyperparameter had a bigger influence on prediction time. In order to achieve a good trade-off between low prediction times and high accuracy, removing convolutional and max pooling layers appears to be an effective approach.

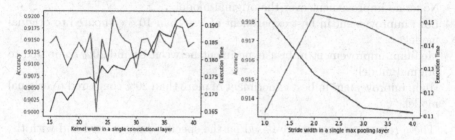

Fig. 6. Trade-off between accuracy and prediction time using only one convolutional/pooling layer and varying the kernel and the stride

The experiment of increasing the number of convolution/max pooling layers to 3 was tested, resulting in a slightly changed network architecture. However, this resulted in a similar accuracy to the original model's, but a slower prediction time of 0.05 s (a 19% increase).

Absence of Max Pooling layer Without the existence of a max pooling layer there is no downsampling which makes the process of training a CNN more difficult. Since prediction time in the testing phase is the main concern, we took two pooling layers out of the original network and contrasted the outcomes. The resulting model architecture with fewer layers resulted in a difference in time of 0.03 s (Table 3). In general, if training time is not a problem, removing pooling layers has some potential for speeding up CNNs.

Table 3. Comparison table between the original model and a model with no max pooling layers

Model	Accuracy	Prediction time
Original Model	0.9110	0.2110
Model without Max pooling layers	0.9120	0.1864

4.3 Result Analysis

Although they are not extensively illustrated in Sect. 4.2, tests were performed involving all the hyperparameters in Table 1 and also some changes in the network architecture. All are summarized in Table 4. This table categorizes all the experiments as hyperparameters and CNN architecture, and includes an assessment, based on the experiments in our dataset, of the potential to reduce prediction times. We use 4°C of potential improvement:

- None: no improvement over the original model;
- Low: improvement in best experiment of less than 10% compared to original model;
- Medium: improvement in best experiment between 10 and 20% compared to original model;
- High: improvement in best experiment of more than 20% compared to original model.

These relevance degrees are based on the specific dataset used and with the original model in Table 2 as comparison. Note that pool_size was set to $(1, 5)$ in the original model but showed a significant difference of 50% between minimum and maximum times in Fig. 4, potentially indicating that a larger pool_size may prove more significant in different circumstances.

Table 4. Summary of performed tests with corresponding influence in prediction time

Hyperparameters	CNN architecture	Positive influence on prediction time
Kernel		Medium
Strides in convolutional layer		High
Filters		High
Pool_Size		Low*
Strides in max pooling layer		High
Padding		Low
Activation functions		None
Dropout		Low
Number of neurons		Low
	Add convolutional/Max pooling layers	None
	Remove convolutional/Max pooling layers	High
	Add dense layers	None
	Remove dense layers	Low
	Remove Max Pooling layer	Medium

*Depends on the circumstance

5 Conclusions and Future Work

This work offers a thorough analysis of reducing the prediction of a CNN and its trade-off with accuracy. To assess the effect of network architectures and hyperparameters on the prediction and accuracy of CNN predictions a novel methodology was created. The most crucial hyperparameters and network changes were found through multiple experiments and analysis. According to the results in our case study, the convolution and max pooling layers as well as the quantity of filters were the most important hyperparameters in influencing how well a CNN performed. Additionally, it was discovered that eliminating layers was a successful strategy for lowering CNNs prediction time.

The results of this work have important implications for the use of CNNs and contribute to a deeper understanding of the underlying mechanisms that govern their performance.

Future work involves expanding the research to test the approach on datasets from other areas, such as image classification or recommendation systems. Furthermore, it would also be valuable to test other approaches in changing the architecture of CNNs, also using larger networks. Multiple changes of hyperparameters and architectures could also be tested simultaneously to determine the best results. Additionally, creating a metric that reflects the trade-off between accuracy and model prediction time would allow for even more accurate analysis of a model. The results achieved in this paper are being applied for the development and integration of digital contents as well as providing intelligence in process management solutions for the footwear industry.

Acknowledgements. This work is co-financed by Component 5—Capitalization and Business Innovation, integrated in the Resilience Dimension of the Recovery and Resilience Plan within the scope of the Recovery and Resilience Mechanism (MRR) of the European Union (EU), framed in the Next Generation EU, for the period 2021–2026, within project FAIST, with reference 66. This work was also partially supported by Fundação para a Ciência e Tecnologia (FCT), under project DAnon with grant CMU/TIC/0044/2021.

References

1. Bolukbasi, T., Wang, J., Dekel, O., Saligrama, V.: Adaptive neural networks for efficient inference. In: International Conference on Machine Learning, pp. 527–536. PMLR (2017)
2. Chang, S.E., Li, Y., Sun, M., Shi, R., So, H.K.H., Qian, X., Wang, Y., Lin, X.: Mix and match: a novel FPGA-centric deep neural network quantization framework. In: 2021 IEEE International Symposium on High-Performance Computer Architecture (HPCA), pp. 208–220. IEEE (2021)
3. Choudhary, T., Mishra, V., Goswami, A., Sarangapani, J.: Inference-aware convolutional neural network pruning. Futur. Gener. Comput. Syst. **135**, 44–56 (2022)
4. Dong, Z., Yao, Z., Gholami, A., Mahoney, M.W., Keutzer, K.: Hawq: Hessian aware quantization of neural networks with mixed-precision. In: Proceedings of the IEEE/CVF International Conference on Computer Vision, pp. 293–302 (2019)

5. Fu, C., Zhu, S., Su, H., Lee, C.E., Zhao, J.: Towards fast and energy-efficient binarized neural network inference on FPGA (2018). arXiv:1810.02068

6. Hacene, G.B., Gripon, V., Arzel, M., Farrugia, N., Bengio, Y.: Quantized guided pruning for efficient hardware implementations of deep neural networks. In: 2020 18th IEEE International New Circuits and Systems Conference (NEWCAS), pp. 206–209. IEEE (2020)

7. Lebedev, V., Lempitsky, V.: Speeding-up convolutional neural networks: a survey. Bull. Pol. Acad. Sci.: Tech. Sci. **66**(6) (2018)

8. LeCun, Y., Denker, J., Solla, S.: Optimal brain damage. In: Advances in Neural Information Processing Systems, vol. 2 (1989)

9. Molchanov, P., Tyree, S., Karras, T., Aila, T., Kautz, J.: Pruning convolutional neural networks for resource efficient inference (2016). arXiv:1611.06440

10. Nasr, M., Bahramali, A., Houmansadr, A.: Deepcorr: strong flow correlation attacks on tor using deep learning. In: Proceedings of the 2018 ACM SIGSAC Conference on Computer and Communications Security, pp. 1962–1976 (2018)

11. Panchenko, A., Lanze, F., Engel, T.: Improving performance and anonymity in the tor network. In: 2012 IEEE 31st International Performance Computing and Communications Conference (IPCCC), pp. 1–10. IEEE (2012)

12. Putra, T.A., Leu, J.S.: Multilevel neural network for reducing expected inference time. IEEE Access **7**, 174129–174138 (2019)

13. Teerapittayanon, S., McDanel, B., Kung, H.T.: Branchynet: Fast inference via early exiting from deep neural networks. In: 2016 23rd International Conference on Pattern Recognition (ICPR), pp. 2464–2469. IEEE (2016)

14. Yamashita, R., Nishio, M., Do, R.K.G., Togashi, K.: Convolutional neural networks: an overview and application in radiology. Insights Imaging **9**(4), 611–629 (2018)

MultiAgent Systems: Theory and Applications

Machine Learning Data Markets: Evaluating the Impact of Data Exchange on the Agent Learning Performance

Hajar Baghcheband[1,2($\boxtimes$)] , Carlos Soares[1,2,3] , and Luís Paulo Reis[1,2]

[1] FEUP - Faculty of Engineering University of Porto, Porto, Portugal
{csoares,lpreis}@fe.up.pt
[2] LIACC-Artificial Intelligence and Computer Science Laboratory (member of LASI LA), Porto, Portugal
h.baghcheband@fe.up.pt
[3] Fraunhofer AICOS Portugal, Porto, Portugal

Abstract. In recent years, the increasing availability of distributed data has led to a growing interest in transfer learning across multiple nodes. However, local data may not be adequate to learn sufficiently accurate models, and the problem of learning from multiple distributed sources remains a challenge. To address this issue, Machine Learning Data Markets (MLDM) have been proposed as a potential solution. In MLDM, autonomous agents exchange relevant data in a cooperative relationship to improve their models. Previous research has shown that data exchange can lead to better models, but this has only been demonstrated with only two agents. In this paper, we present an extended evaluation of a simple version of the MLDM framework in a collaborative scenario. Our experiments show that data exchange has the potential to improve learning performance, even in a simple version of MLDM. The findings conclude that there exists a direct correlation between the number of agents and the gained performance, while an inverse correlation was observed between the performance and the data batch sizes. The results of this study provide important insights into the effectiveness of MLDM and how it can be used to improve learning performance in distributed systems. By increasing the number of agents, a more efficient system can be achieved, while larger data batch sizes can decrease the global performance of the system. These observations highlight the importance of considering both the number of agents and the data batch sizes when designing distributed learning systems using the MLDM framework.

Keywords: Machine learning · Data market · Data exchange · Collaborative agent-based learning · Multi-agent system

1 Introduction

The increasing availability of distributed data has led to a growing interest in developing efficient and effective methods for distributed machine learning. However, the quality of the data can be insufficient, which may affect the accuracy

N. Moniz et al. (Eds.): EPIA 2023, LNAI 14115, pp. 337–348, 2023.
https://doi.org/10.1007/978-3-031-49008-8_27

of the models. A promising approach that has gained significant attention is the use of multi-agent systems (MAS) for collaborative learning [22,23]. MAS can provide a framework for distributed learning, where agents communicate with each other to improve the accuracy and efficiency of machine learning models [5]. Several studies have explored the potential of multi-agent systems and distributed machine learning in various contexts, including individual [20] and global learning objectives [4,7], data set improvement [18], and model performance enhancement [23]. The interaction with other agents usually involves negotiation and exchanging data. During the interaction, agents could exchange data to create reliable systems and reduce human intervention [3]. Additionally, data markets have been proposed as a means for agents to exchange relevant data for money in a cooperative relationship to improve their models [1,11,13].

The Machine Learning Data Market (MLDM) framework has been proposed to simulate cooperative relationships among agents, allowing them to exchange data to improve model performance.[1] The MLDM framework operates in a distributed environment, where each agent learns a personalized model without a global model and negotiates with other agents to maximize its utility function. However, since data holds economic value, the agents have limited budgets to acquire data. Therefore, exchanging adequate data is critical for all agents.

Previous research has demonstrated that exchanging data can lead to better models, albeit based on a system with only two agents. Therefore, our objective is to investigate the behavior of the system; analyze the impact of data exchange in a distributed environment; provide further evidence supporting the efficacy of the MLDM. The purpose of this paper is to evaluate the behavior of the framework under various configurations by examining the effects of data batch size and population size. The framework is tested over a sequence of datasets, and the results are averaged across datasets for a comprehensive understanding of the system behavior. Our findings show that exchanging data gradually enhances the learning performance of the agents by improving their local datasets. Furthermore, we find that increasing the number of agents exchanging data is positively correlated with performance gain while increasing the batch size has a negative effect on performance gain. Our study provides evidence of the effectiveness of MLDM and the importance of exchanging adequate data.

To provide context, Sect. 2 reviews related work on distributed machine learning in MAS and data markets. In Sect. 3, we explain the proposed MLDM framework in detail, highlighting the negotiation process among agents. We then describe the experimental setup and present the results in Sect. 4. Finally, we conclude the paper and suggest future work in Sect. 5.

2   State of the Art

In this section, we will explore the intersection of Multi-Agent Systems (MAS) and Distributed Machine Learning (DML) by reviewing the state of the art in

---

[1] The work was presented at the 11th International Workshop on Intelligent Data Processing (IDP)—special session—Niagara Falls, Canada, 17 November 2022.

the field. This will include a comparison between some distributed technologies and the MAS in machine learning tasks such as clustering, classification, and prediction. Additionally, we will look at the emergence of Machine Learning Data Markets (MLDM) as a way to facilitate the exchange of data between agents. We will discuss the reasons why data markets are necessary and review some of the papers.

2.1 Multi-agent Systems and Machine Learning

Multi-agent systems (MAS) offer several advantages over other distributed machine learning approaches such as federated learning, peer-to-peer, and mobile edge computing. MAS provides a flexible and scalable architecture for distributed machine learning, allowing the system to learn from one another and make decisions based on local knowledge, interact with each other, and adapt to changing network conditions, data availability, and system requirements. In contrast, peer-to-peer systems [17] rely on direct communication between neighbors. Federated learning [6,15] is limited by the centralized server's computing power and network bandwidth. Mobile edge computing may be constrained by device capabilities and battery life [12]. In federated learning, each client learns independently and sends model updates to the central server, which aggregates the updates and sends back a new global model. This process can lead to communication bottlenecks and potential data privacy concerns. In contrast, MAS can allow agents to learn collaboratively [16] while maintaining data privacy by exchanging only relevant information.

In recent years, MAS has emerged as a promising approach for solving complex distributed machine learning (DML) tasks such as classification, clustering, and predictions. In a MAS-based DML scenario, autonomous agents use communication to learn from each other's experiences and improve their individual models. For instance, Bazzan [4] proposed a distributed problem-solving scenario in which multiple agents collaborated to solve a classification problem by utilizing distributed data. The agents used different machine learning methods, and they shared their knowledge to improve their models. The multi-agent reinforcement learning (MARL) approach was used in conjunction with the classification process. The agents assessed whether their classes were correct or not based on the reward signal. In another study, Chaimontree et al. [7] proposed a multi-agent data mining (MADM) framework to determine the best set of clusters. The agents communicated with each other in a collaborative relationship to produce the best learning cluster. Several other approaches have been proposed in prediction problems such as agent-based machine learning in transportation [2], Multi-agent and machine learning in the oil and gas industry [10], in network security [14].

2.2 Data Markets

However, in recent years, there has been a growing interest in the intersection of Multi-Agent Systems (MAS) and Distributed Machine Learning (DML). A key challenge in this area is finding the best combination of agents to learn from, as agents may have varying capabilities. To address this, researchers have proposed the use of Data Markets (DM) [1,11,18,19], which enable agents to exchange relevant data for monetary compensation to improve their models.

While the concept of trading data in a market may seem straightforward, there are several challenges that make it a complex task. For example, data is not a conventional commodity, as it possesses unique properties that must be considered. It is easily replicable; has combinatorial nature (i.e., features have overlapping information); its value is time-dependent; and is dependent on who has access to the data set [1,11]. To tackle these challenges, some researchers have proposed data valuation methods based on the usefulness of data in improving machine learning models [8,9,11,18]. One popular approach is to use the Shapley value [11], which rewards data that furthers the market's goals and distributes rewards fairly among all contributors. Other researchers have proposed data valuation methods based on information gain [18] and designed novel reward schemes to maintain fairness while trading off incentives.

The role of a central entity in data markets has been a topic of discussion among researchers. Some papers propose a central entity that determines the value of rewards and distributes them among contributors [18], adjusts the price of data [1], or authorizes verification [11]. While centralization can provide a level of control and regulation to the market, it can also lead to issues such as bias, censorship, and lack of transparency. Decentralized data markets can potentially offer greater privacy and security, as well as more democratic control over the market. However, designing effective incentive mechanisms and ensuring the quality of data in a decentralized environment remain significant challenges. Overall, the debate on the role of a central entity in data markets reflects the larger tension between centralized and decentralized approaches to digital platforms and networks.

3   Machine Learning Data Market

Generally, the effectiveness of machine learning algorithms depends on the quality of the training data. However, obtaining relevant training data can be very difficult, especially in distributed environments. This challenge becomes worse in real-time prediction problems where data gets outdated quickly. Therefore, exchanging the right data at the right price is the main issue in data markets.

Intelligent agents gradually gather data and exchange it in MLDM to improve their predictive performance. The agent can gain a better awareness of its surroundings and ultimately develop stronger decision-making by incorporating the exchanged data into its training set. This section focuses on providing a thorough overview of the negotiation technique and agent architecture within the MLDM framework. Without any central authority, each agent individually chooses the best time and price for exchanging data. As a result, the MLDM functions as a decentralized system, with all agents making data trading decisions on their own.

3.1 MLDM Architecture

The MLDM consists of the society of agents A that $A_i \in A = \{A_1, A_2, ..., A_n\}$. They exchange data to improve their local model performance regarding its trading strategies set S and set of available learning algorithms L, therefore in other words $MLDM = \{A, S, L\}$. Agents may be heterogeneous which means they can have different learning algorithms and trading strategies.

The assumptions are as follows:

- Data is horizontally distributed in the environment (the agent has access to all the features of a given instance, but not all the instances)
- Agents are only able to access small parts of the complete data set. Each agent collects a batch of data during the time, learns its model, and utilizes the prediction results for decision-making. Agents are motivated to exchange data in order to increase their learning performance and improve their decision-making.
- Data collected by agents are mutually different which makes the data of the agent a unique and valuable commodity. But it is not entirely independent, therefore, the agent's data could be helpful for others to model their learning, in this case, data exchange makes sense. For example, drivers in different cities collect various data related to location, but some data relevant to time and climate can be similar in all cities.
- Using open data sources does not pose any privacy concerns.

The configuration for agents is defined as $A_i = \{Bg_i, S_i, L_i\}$ where Bg_i is the maximum budget, $S_i \in S$ is the trading strategy that agent A_i is going to utilize in the negotiation and $L_i \in L$ is the agent's learning algorithm. As part of the data market proposed in this paper, each agent A_i will perform the following procedures at time t (see Fig. 1):

- *The Modeling Component (MC)* that learns a model $M_{i,t} = L_i(TnB_{i,t})$ applying the learning algorithm L_i on the available training batch at that time, $TnB_{i,t}$;
- *The Prediction Component (PC)* $P_{i,t} = M_{i,t}(TsB_{i,t})$ evaluates the performance of the model $M_{i,t}$ on the available test batch $TsB_{i,t}$;
- *The Negotiation and Exchange Component (NEC)* $N_{i,t} = S_i(TrB_{i,j,t})$ to exchange data with other agents A_j based on its budget at that time $Bg_{i,t}$ and the negotiation strategy S_i; trade batch of data $TrB_{i,j,t}$
- *The Evaluation Component (EC)* to evaluate the predictive performance of the traded batch on the model improvement $M_{i,t} = L_{i,t}(TnB_{i,t} \cup Tr_{i,j,t})$ and $P_{i,t} = M_{i,t}(TsB_{i,t})$.

To summarize, all agents will develop their models, $M_{i,t}$, based on collected data along with exchanged data (if any), then evaluate the model based on a new batch of data ($TsB_{i,t} = Bt_{i,t}$ as test batch), and calculate the performance $P_{i,t}$. Therefore the status of agents A_i at time t is defined as $A_{i,t} = \{Bt_{i,t}, M_{i,t}, P_{i,t}, PA_{j,t}, Bg_{i,t}\}$.

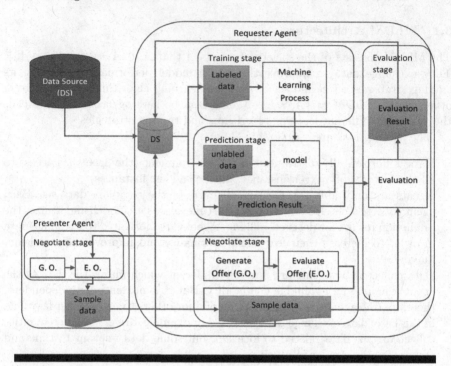

Fig. 1. Components in agent architecture

3.2   Simple Negotiation Strategy

In our first approach to MLDM, we decided to use a very simple negotiation strategy. Agents have a limited budget and their goals are increasing predictive performance and trading revenue. So they must decide who they will exchange data with and how much they are willing to pay/receive for it. Each agent informs all others of the predictive performance of its model. At time t, based on the perceived performance of other agents, $PA_{j,t}$ and budget, $Bg_{i,t} \geq 0$ ($Bg_{i,t} \leq Bg_i$), an agent A_i will decide to exchange data with the other agents. The agent with the highest performance receives offers for the most recent batch of data. Since data is valuable, after the payment, the agent sends the requested data. Therefore, if A_j has the highest learning performance, agent A_i should pay the cost of traded data $(TrB_{i,j,t})$, $C_{i,t}$, as follows:

$$C_{i,t} = \begin{cases} size(TrB_{i,j,t}) * DC & if \quad C_{i,t} \leq B_{i,t} \\ B_{i,t} & otherwise \end{cases} \tag{1}$$

where $size(Tr_{i,j,t})$ is the amount of traded data (number of records) and DC is the data cost per record.

After negotiation, the traded batch will be appended to the agent's data; agent A_i will learn its model based on a new data source, $M_{i,t+1} = L_i(Tnb_{i,t+1} \cup TrB_{i,j,t})$, then evaluate the new model accuracy, $P_{i,t+1} = M(TsB_{i,t+1})$.

4   Experimental Result

In this paper, we try to investigate the efficiency of data exchange, therefore we simplify the MLDM architecture. Agents are considered to have the same learning algorithm and trading strategy to simplify the evaluation.

The goal of the experiments in this paper is to assess how the simple MLDM proposed behaves, especially in comparison to a centralized learning process (i.e. simply running the algorithm on all the training data). In these experiments, we vary the number of agents as well as the size of the batches of data.

4.1   The Experimental Setup

The experimental Assumptions are as follows:

- Evaluation of the MLDM framework was conducted by selecting a set of 45 data sets from the OpenML platform [21].
- In terms of the learning algorithm, the K-Nearest Neighborhood (KNN) is selected as the machine learning (ML) algorithm for all agents. As mentioned in Sect. 3.1, different agents can run different ML algorithms. However, to simplify, we selected the same learning algorithm for all agents. We use KNN because it is a simple and well-known algorithm.
- In terms of budget, all agents have a constant initial budget for all agents A_i ($Bg_i = 1000$). During the negotiation, they are going to spend/receive money, therefore, their budget is decreased/increased.
- To simplify in this paper, the data cost ($DC = 1$) is the same for all types of sample data.

As discussed in Sect. 3.2, the negotiation strategy is based on each agent estimating the predictive performance of the model it generated. This is done by splitting its local data into training and test sets ($DB_{i,0} = TnB_{i,0} \cup TsB_{i,0}$). We refer to this as *Local Evaluation* ($P_{i,t} = M_{i,t}(TsB_{i,t})$). Given that these estimates are obtained on separate data, it makes the comparison between agents less reliable. Therefore, we also estimate the predictive performance of the models on a separate set of data (TsG). We refer to this as *Global Evaluation* ($P_{i,t} = M_{i,t}(TsG)$). It provides a more global perspective of the whole system. The results discussed in this paper are based on the global evaluation as $H(\theta|E)$. The estimated performance is averaged across all datasets for all agents in the MLDM scenario.

To assess the effect of exchanging data on the performance of ML models, we compare MLDM with a baseline version of MLDM without data exchange (i.e. all agents use only their local data to develop their models). In the baseline version, $H(\theta)$ is considered for the performance averaged across all datasets. It is useful to represent the accuracy of the model before and after exchanging data, respectively. If the exchanged data can induce a greater performance, Accuracy gain (AG) will be as follows:

$$AG(\theta; E) = H(\theta|E) - H(\theta). \tag{2}$$

4.2   Results

The main goal of this part is to study the MLDM behavior under different configurations. We start by discussing the effect of the size of the data batch on both the predictive performance and the economic value. Then we carry out a similar analysis concerning the number of agents.

Data Batch Size The size of the batch size determines the proportion of data that is collected by each agent from the data source in each iteration. In these experiments, three different values are considered $Bt = \{0.01, 0.025, 0.05\}$. This means that we simulate that 100, 40, and 20 batches are generated with 1%, 2.5%, and 5% of the datasets except for the global test set, respectively. Smaller batch sizes mean that the agents start with a smaller training set and its size increases slowly.

We will study if the agent has a small dataset, exchanging data may improve its model. The goal of this experiment is to investigate the effect of different batch sizes on predictive accuracy.

Figure 2a, b, and c, depict the gain in accuracy (see Eq. 2) for different batch sizes, in scenarios with two, three, and five agents respectively. The results conclude that when the batch size increases, the gain in accuracy is smaller. It is shown that in a case the local data is low, exchanging data helps to improve learning accuracy.

When we have two agents, the gain in accuracy is almost the same, but in the other populations, the gap between gained accuracy in different local data sizes is a little more impressive. Nevertheless, It is concluded that in a case the local data is low, exchanging data helps to improve learning accuracy. For example, considering the batch size is 0.01, it means that all agents have a small local data set, and results show they can learn a slightly accurate model by exchanging data.

Population Size In this experiment, we simulate three different values as population size $Population = \{2, 3, 5\}$. Figure 3a, b, and c show the gain in accuracy (see Eq. 2) for different numbers of agents, in scenarios with different batch sizes. The figures show that the gain in accuracy increases with the number of agents. By increasing the number of agents, the probability of finding higher-quality data is increased, and exchanging high-quality data may result in higher-performance models.

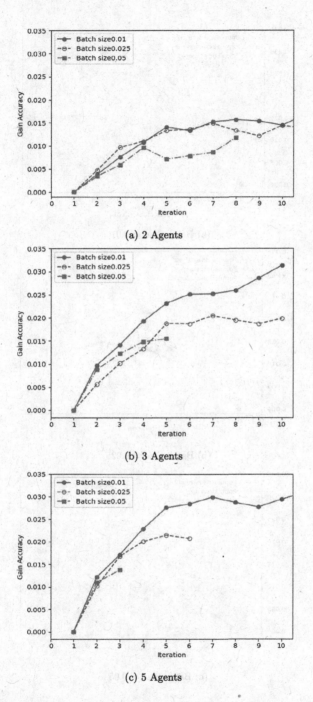

(a) 2 Agents

(b) 3 Agents

(c) 5 Agents

Fig. 2. Gain in accuracy over different batch sizes during the time

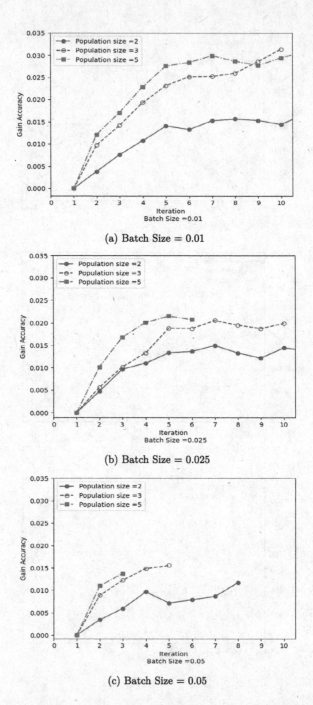

(a) Batch Size = 0.01

(b) Batch Size = 0.025

(c) Batch Size = 0.05

Fig. 3. Gain in accuracy over different Population sizes during the time

5   Conclusion

In simple distributed ML systems, agents learn a personalized model according to their own learning objectives using local data. However, the lack of volume and representativeness of that data may affect the quality of the model significantly. Therefore, exchanging data between agents is expected to improve their predictive performance. In this paper, we empirically analyze the behavior of MLDM, a MAS framework to exchange data between agents that learn ML models. The agents negotiate data to improve their models. We studied the effect of both the batch size as well as the population size on the predictive performance of MLDM. It is concluded that improvements in learning accuracy can be observed even using simple negotiation. Accuracy gains are directly related to the number of agents, but the gains decrease as batch sizes increase.

Although the simplicity of the configuration of MLDM used in this study was important to illustrate the potential of the framework, we expect that better results can be obtained with more complex negotiation strategies. We will value data based on gained accuracy in negotiation strategies among agents, involving sending offers/counteroffers and accepting/rejecting negotiations, taking into account the characteristics of the data exchanged.

Acknowledgements. This work was financially supported (or partially financially supported) by Base Funding—UIDB/00027/2020 of the Artificial Intelligence and Computer Science Laboratory—LIACC—funded by national funds through the FCT/MCTES (PIDDAC) and by a PhD grant from Fundação para a Ciência e Tecnologia (FCT), reference SFRH/BD/06064/2021.

References

1. Agarwal, A., Dahleh, M., Sarkar, T.: A marketplace for data: an algorithmic solution. In: ACM EC 2019 - Proceedings of the 2019 ACM Conference on Economics and Computation, pp. 701–726 (2019)
2. Arel, I., Liu, C., Urbanik, T., Kohls, A.G.: Reinforcement learning-based multi-agent system for network traffic signal control. IET Intel. Transp. Syst. 4(2), 128–135 (2010)
3. Assoudi, H., Lounis, H.: A multi-agent-based approach for autonomic data exchange processes. In: Proceedings of the International Conference on Software Engineering and Knowledge Engineering, SEKE 2014-January, pp. 334–337 (2014)
4. Bazzan, A.L.: Cooperative induction of decision trees. In: Proceedings of the 2013 IEEE Symposium on Intelligent Agents, IA 2013–2013 IEEE Symposium Series on Computational Intelligence, SSCI 2013, pp. 62–69 (2013)
5. Bazzan, A.L.: Beyond reinforcement learning and local view in multiagent systems. KI - Kunstliche Intelligenz **28**(3), 179–189 (2014)
6. Brendan McMahan, H., Moore, E., Ramage, D., Hampson, S., Agüera y Arcas, B.: Communication-efficient learning of deep networks from decentralized data. In: Proceedings of the 20th International Conference on Artificial Intelligence and Statistics, AISTATS 2017 54 (2017)

7. Chaimontree, S., Atkinson, K., Coenen, F.: Clustering in a multi-agent data mining environment. Lecture Notes in Computer Science (including subseries Lecture Notes in Artificial Intelligence and Lecture Notes in Bioinformatics) 5980 LNAI, pp. 103–114 (2010)

8. Ghorbani, A., Zou, J.: Data shapley: equitable valuation of data for machine learning. In: 36th International Conference on Machine Learning, ICML 2019 2019-June, pp. 4053–4065 (2019)

9. Ghorbani, A., Zou, J., Esteva, A.: Data Shapley Valuation for Efficient Batch Active Learning. IEEE, pp. 1456–1462 (2023)

10. Hanga, K.M., Kovalchuk, Y.: Machine learning and multi-agent systems in oil and gas industry applications: a survey. Comput. Sci. Rev. **34**, 100191 (2019)

11. Kharman, A.M., Jursitzky, C., Zhou, Q., Ferraro, P., Marecek, J., Pinson, P., Shorten, R.: On the design of decentralised data markets, pp. 1–26 (2022). arXiv:2206.06299

12. Lim, W.Y.B., Luong, N.C., Hoang, D.T., Jiao, Y., Liang, Y., Yang, Q., Niyato, D., Miao, C.: Federated learning in mobile edge networks: a comprehensive survey (2019). arXiv:1909.11875

13. Lorenzo, B., Gonzalez-Castano, F.J.: A matching game for data trading in operator-supervised user-provided networks. In: 2016 IEEE International Conference on Communications, ICC 2016 (2016)

14. Louati, F., Ktata, F.B.: A deep learning-based multi-agent system for intrusion detection. SN Appl. Sci. **2**(4), 675 (2020)

15. McMahan, H.B., Moore, E., Ramage, D., y Arcas, B.A.: Federated learning of deep networks using model averaging (2016). arXiv:1602.05629

16. Panait, L., Luke, S.: Cooperative multi-agent learning: the state of the art. Auton. Agent. Multi. Agent. Syst. **11**(3), 387–434 (2005)

17. Sattler, F., Wiegand, T., Samek, W.: Trends and advancements in deep neural network communication (2020). arXiv:2003.03320

18. Sim, R.H.L., Zhang, Y., Chan, M.C., Low, B.K.H.: Collaborative machine learning with incentive-aware model rewards. In: 37th International Conference on Machine Learning, ICML 2020 PartF16814(Ml), pp. 8886–8895 (2020)

19. Stahl, F., Schomm, F., Vossen, G.: Data marketplaces: an emerging species. Front. Artif. Intell. Appl. Databases **2013**, 145–158 (2014)

20. Vanhaesebrouck, P., Bellet, A., Tommasi, M.: Decentralized collaborative learning of personalized models over networks. In: Proceedings of the 20th International Conference on Artificial Intelligence and Statistics, AISTATS 2017 (2017)

21. Vanschoren, J., van Rijn, J., Bischl, B., Torgo, L.: Openml: networked science in machine learning. SIGKDD Explor. **15**(2), 49–60 (2013). https://doi.org/10.1145/2641190.2641198

22. Wang, G., Yin, J., Hossain, M.S., Muhammad, G.: Incentive mechanism for collaborative distributed learning in artificial intelligence of things. Futur. Gener. Comput. Syst. **125**, 376–384 (2021)

23. Wang, H., Liu, C., Jiang, D., Jiang, Z.: Collaborative deep learning framework for fault diagnosis in distributed complex systems. Mech. Syst. Signal Process. **156**, 107650 (2021)

Multi-robot Adaptive Sampling
for Supervised Spatiotemporal
Forecasting

Siva Kailas[1]([✉]) [ID], Wenhao Luo[2] [ID], and Katia Sycara[1] [ID]

[1] Carnegie Mellon University, Pittsburgh, PA 15213, USA
skailas@andrew.cmu.edu
[2] University of North Carolina at Charlotte, Charlotte, NC 28223, USA

Abstract. Learning to forecast spatiotemporal (ST) environmental processes from a sparse set of samples collected autonomously is a difficult task from both a sampling perspective (collecting the best sparse samples) and from a learning perspective (predicting the next timestep). Recent work in spatiotemporal process learning focuses on using deep learning to forecast from dense samples. Moreover, collecting the best set of sparse samples is understudied within robotics. An example of this is robotic sampling for information gathering, such as using UAVs/UGVs for weather monitoring. In this work, we propose a methodology that leverages a neural methodology called Recurrent Neural Processes to learn spatiotemporal environmental dynamics for forecasting from selective samples gathered by a team of robots using a mixture of Gaussian Processes model in an online learning fashion. Thus, we combine two learning paradigms in that we use an active learning approach to adaptively gather informative samples and a supervised learning approach to capture and predict complex spatiotemporal environmental phenomena.

Keywords: Adaptive sampling · ST forecasting · Neural process

1 Introduction

A notable challenge in multi-robot systems is the multi-robot information gathering problem, which encompasses a variety of formulations including multi-robot adaptive sampling [15,22], multi-robot sensor coverage [8,10], and multi-robot informative path planning [3]. However, learning to forecast spatiotemporal (ST) environmental processes is relatively understudied within the context of robotics, let alone multi-robot systems. While there is prior work in deep learning for spatiotemporal process learning in domains such as high-frequency trading and video surveillance, these works often investigate learning from a set of timesteps where each timestep contains the entire spatial context [13,17,18,20]. These cannot be used when we can only gather sparse amounts of data at each timestep.

This material is based upon work supported by the AI Research Institutes program supported by NSF and USDA-NIFA under AI Institute: for Resilient Agriculture, Award No. 2021-67021-35329.

In this work, we are particularly interested in such a variant of the multi-robot adaptive sampling problem, in which a group of robots are deployed in an environment from random initial configurations and then seek to gather the best samples in the environment for learning a parametric (i.e. deep learning-based) spatiotemporal forecasting model. This problem formulation possesses a few differences compared to the prior work. Firstly, we address the problem of multi-robot adaptive sampling, which involves coordinating a team of robots effectively to sample an environmental phenomena. Most of the prior work in adaptive sampling has been limited to single robot [1,4,11,12,19]. Secondly, we consider an environment with an arbitrary spatiotemporal process. Spatiotemporal processes depend on both the spatial features and temporal evolution of the underlying phenomena, but a large amount of prior work in multi-robot adaptive sampling only addresses spatially correlated time-invariant processes [6,8,10,14]. Thirdly, we consider determining samples for learning a parametric spatiotemporal model for forecasting. Recent work in adaptive sampling often rely solely on non-parametric learning methods for modelling the environment phenomena, which is often restrictive and can only handle limited spatiotemporal evolution rates [1,6,8,10–12,14]. Moreover, parametric learning methods often scale better with data and have powerful representational capacity, making them an interesting modelling approach for arbitrary spatiotemporal environment phenomena.

Our **main contribution** in this work is an end-to-end methodology that starts with effective and coordinated multi-robot information gathering to adaptively sample and procure a collection of samples as a dataset used to train a parametric spatiotemporal model. Our approach is able to select highly informative samples that improve the predictive performance of the spatiotemporal model. To the best of our knowledge, this is the first work to address integrating multi-robot information gathering with deep learning for spatiotemporal model learning. The paper is organized as follows: Sect. 2 formally introduces the problem, Sect. 3 introduces the overall approach and detailed remarks about each component in the approach, Sect. 4 describes the evaluation of the approach, and Sect. 5 summarizes this work and potential future work.

2   Problem Formulation

Consider a set of n robots moving in a bounded environment $Q \subset \mathbb{R}^2$ and assume the environment can be discretized into a set of points $q \in Q$. Moreover, let $T \subset \mathbb{R}$ be the time range of interest and assume that this has been discretized into a set of timesteps $t \in T$. With this, the position of each robot $i \in \{1, \ldots, n\}$ at timestep t can be denoted by $x_i^t \in Q$. We assume the environment is free of obstacles and can be partitioned into n Voronoi cells at any timestep t where each Voronoi cell V_i^t is defined in (1).

$$V_i^t = \{q \in Q : ||q - x_i^t||_2 \leq ||q - x_j^t||_2 \forall j \neq i\} \tag{1}$$

This is a common assumption made in robotic information gathering that is reasonable for most situations in robot exploration [6,8,10]. Each Voronoi cell

V_i^t corresponds to robot i, meaning robot i is allocated that space at timestep t. This will be leveraged in the proposed active learning methodology to avoid collisions and improve initial environmental modelling. The current location of the robot x_i is sampled and added to its local dataset, which is then used to adaptively choose the next sampling locations.

Regarding the distribution of environmental phenomenon at each point of interest q at time t, there exists an unknown density function $\phi(q, t) : Q \times T \to \mathbb{R}$ that maps the location q and time t to the scalar value of the phenomena $\phi(q, t)$. That is, the unknown environmental phenomena is both spatial and time varying since it maps each spatial location q and timestep t to a real-valued density value, such as air temperature, animal presence, etc.

Let $X_t = \{q_1, \ldots q_m\}$ be the set of candidate sampling locations recommended at timestep t and $X_{\{t_p : t_{p+k}\}} = \bigoplus_{t \in \{t_p : t_{p+k}\}} X_t$ represent a set of m candidate sampling locations chosen at each of the k timesteps from timestep t_p and t_{p+k} where $\bigoplus$ represent vector concatenation. Furthermore, let $F_X(t_p : t_{p+k}, q) : X_{\{t_p : t_{p+k}\}} \to \mathbb{R}$ be a parametric model trained on data X that estimates $\phi(q, t_{p+k+1})$. In our case, the function F is a neural model and X is the dataset that F is trained on. Moreover, the parameter k indicates that we are allowed to explore and sample in a window of k consecutive timesteps, and F is responsible for using those collected samples to predict the environment on the $k + 1$ timestep. Thus, we propose to address the optimization problem shown in (2).

$$\underset{X}{\mathrm{argmin}} \sum_{q \in Q} \sum_{p \in T} (F_X(t_p : t_{p+k}, q) - \phi(q, t_{p+k+1}))^2 \tag{2}$$

Note that the robots must procure the data X in a single-shot manner, which is akin to actual robotic information gathering. That is, given a window of timesteps in the spatiotemporal environment, each robot only gets to collect m samples at each timestep in the environment, and the robots must proceed sequentially in time (i.e. they cannot revisit a previous timestep). Thus, it is imperative that the robots coordinate with one another in order to choose the best samples given a miniscule amount of initial data.

We choose to parameterize F as a recurrent neural process (RNP), an extension of neural processes for handling spatial and temporal dependencies in data [7]. However, any parametric model designed for spatiotemporal modelling can be chosen if desired. Yet, the question to address is *how to coordinate a team of robots to choose a good set of samples at each timestep to collect into dataset X that will likely improve forecasting performance for a parametric spatiotemporal model.* We hypothesize that if we use an active learning approach that refines a rudimentary working environment model and then utilizes the rudimentary working model to adaptively sample and procure a dataset X, then a spatiotemporal deep learning model F would perform better. However, using simple or naive heuristics such as random sampling or uncertainty-based sampling, which are commonly used in prior work, will not effectively procure an appropriate dataset for improved forecasting. Thus, we propose specific augmentations and design choices in this integrated approach to ensure the two components we use are compatible and complement one another.

To address this, we propose to use a spatiotemporal mixture of Gaussian Processes (STMGP) where each Gaussian Process component uses a squared exponential kernel with automatic relevance determination to gather data in an adaptive sampling manner to approximately solve the optimization problem shown in (2). At each timestep, the robots use the STMGP model to inform the next timestep sampling locations and move towards those locations. The STMGP model then updates itself with the collected samples in a distributed manner and produces a set of samples to the RNP to learn a forecasting model.

Thus, we start with an active learning methodology (robotic information gathering) and then leverage a supervised learning approach (use of gathered data for model learning) to capture the spatiotemporal dynamics of the environment for forecasting. This ultimately provides a step towards bridging the gap between robotic information gathering and powerful parametric models for spatiotemporal environment modelling.

3   Proposed Approach

We now present a high-level representation of our approach described in Algorithm 1.

Given 1% of the data as initial data randomly (Line 1) and random starting configurations (Lines 2–3), the robots first sample their current location (Line 8), collect that sample into their local datasets (Line 9), update their local GP components (Line 10), and compute a mixture of their local GP parameters (Line 12). The robots use the spatiotemporal mixture of GPs to infer the mean and variance of each location in the environment at the current timestep (Line 13), and use this inference to determine where to sample in the next timestep (Line 14). The new sampling locations are used to adjust the Voronoi partitions and the local datasets of each robot (Lines 16–17) via communication. The robots also use a uni-model GP to compute an approximate covariance matrix across all locations at the current timestep (Line 18), which is used to inform which samples to procure as part of the dataset for training the RNP (Line 19). This is repeated for the allotted number of timesteps in the environment, where the environment changes after each timestep in accordance to ϕ. Finally, the procured dataset is used to train the RNP to accurately forecast (Line 21). The RNP is then evaluated on unseen timesteps in the environment to determine how well the RNP captured the spatiotemporal phenomena for forecasting (Line 22). This approach modifies and integrates various components, and we describe each component, its modifications, and its role in the integrated system in the subsections below. Algorithm 1 also details where each subsection corresponds to in the integrated system.

3.1   Spatiotemporal Mixture of Gaussian Processes (STMGP)

We first briefly describe the uni-model spatiotemporal GP and then introduce the mixture of GPs model. Let $\mathbf{X}$ be the locally collected data consisting of the sampling location and timestep for a given robot and $\mathbf{Y}$ be the corresponding environment values for the (location, time) in $\mathbf{X}$. We can represent the mean vector $\mu_{\mathbf{X}} = [\mu(q,t)]_{(q,t)\in\mathbf{X}}$ and positive definite symmetric covariance matrix $K_{\mathbf{X},\mathbf{X}} = [\mathbf{k}((q,t),(q',t'))]_{(q,t),(q',t')\in\mathbf{X}}$ where $\mathbf{k}(\cdot)$ is the kernel function. The posterior mean vector is given as $\mu_{\mathbf{X}^*|\mathbf{X},\mathbf{Y}} = K_{\mathbf{X}^*,\mathbf{X}}K_{\mathbf{X},\mathbf{X}}^{-1}\mathbf{Y}$ and the posterior covariance matrix is given as $K_{\mathbf{X}^*|\mathbf{X},\mathbf{Y}} = K_{\mathbf{X}^*,\mathbf{X}^*} - K_{\mathbf{X}^*,\mathbf{X}}K_{\mathbf{X},\mathbf{X}}^{-1}K_{\mathbf{X}^*,\mathbf{X}}^{\top}$ where $\mathbf{X}^*$ is all possible locations $q \in Q$ for the next timestep. This serves as the local GPs in the methodology described below.

We now outline the active learning methodology used to procure a set of samples used for learning a parametric spatiotemporal environment model for forecasting. The mixture of Gaussian Processes was first introduced by [21], and has been used in sensor coverage of static environments by [8, 10] due to its improved representational capacity. We modify the mixture of Gaussian

---

Algorithm 1 STMGP + RNP

Require: k {k is time window size}
Require: m {m is number of samples per timestep to provide to RNP}
1: $\mathbf{X}_i, \mathbf{Y}_i \leftarrow$ GetRandomInitialData(1%)
2: $q_t =$ GetRandomStartingLocations()
3: $V_t =$ UpdateVoronoiPartitions(q_t)
4: $X_C, Y_C \leftarrow \emptyset, \emptyset$
5: $\hat{\gamma}_t \leftarrow 0$ {$\hat{\gamma}_t(i)$ is the mutual information lower bound for robot i}
6: **for** $t = t_p : t_{p+k}$ **do**
7:     **for** each robot i **do**
8:         $x_i, y_i \leftarrow$ SampleLocation($q_t(i)$) {returns $\phi(q_t(i),t) + \epsilon$}
9:         $\mathbf{X}_i, \mathbf{Y}_i \leftarrow \mathbf{X}_i \cup x_i, \mathbf{Y}_i \cup y_i$
10:        $GP_i \leftarrow$ FitGP($\mathbf{X}_i, \mathbf{Y}_i$)
11:    **end for**
12:    $MGP_t =$ MixGPs(GP_i) {Sect. 3.1}
13:    $\mu_{q_i^*|\mathbf{X}_i,\mathbf{Y}_i}^*, \sigma_{q_i^*|\mathbf{X}_i,\mathbf{Y}_i}^* \leftarrow MGP_t.\mu, MGP_t.\sigma$ {Sect. 3.1}
14:    $q_t \leftarrow \text{argmax}_{q_i^*} \sqrt{\sigma_{q_i^*|\mathbf{X}_i,\mathbf{Y}_i}^* + \hat{\gamma}_{t-1}} - \sqrt{\hat{\gamma}_{t-1}}$ {Sect. 3.2}
15:    $\hat{\gamma}_t \leftarrow \hat{\gamma}_{t-1} + \sigma_{q_t^*|\mathbf{X}_i,\mathbf{Y}_i}^*$ {Sect. 3.2}
16:    $V_t =$ UpdateVoronoiPartitions(q_t)
17:    $\mathbf{X}_i, \mathbf{Y}_i \leftarrow$ ExchangeSamplesBasedOnVoronoiPartitions($\mathbf{X}_i, \mathbf{Y}_i, V_t$)
18:    $\tilde{K} \leftarrow$ FitGP($\bigcup_i \mathbf{X}_i, \bigcup_i \mathbf{Y}_i$).$K$
19:    $X_C(t), Y_C(t) \leftarrow$ StreamSubmodularSecretary($\tilde{K}, m$) {Sect. 3.2}
20: **end for**
21: $F_{X_C,Y_C} \leftarrow$ AddSamplesToDatasetAndTrainRNP($\{X_C, Y_C\}$)
22: EvaluateOnUnseenData(F_{X_C,Y_C})

Processes approach for spatiotemporal environments by utilizing the aforementioned spatiotemporal GP components. We present the salient aspects of the mixing process, as well as modification to the sampling strategy as well.

Our distributed approach leverages a Spatiotemporal Mixture of Gaussian Processes (STMGP) for adaptive sampling in an environment Q. Here, each robot i has a learned local Gaussian Process component GP_i, which yields a set of n GP components $\{GP_1, \ldots GP_n\}$ and an associated probability function $P(q, i_g) = P(q \in Q$ is best described by $GP_{i_g})$. Suppose the robot i has sampled locations $\mathbf{X}_i$ and suppose $\mathbf{Y}_i$ are the associated ground-truth values sampled from locations $\mathbf{X}_i$. Moreover, suppose robot i has a mean $\mu_{\mathbf{X}^*_i|\mathbf{X}_i,\mathbf{Y}_i}$ and covariance matrix $K_{\mathbf{X}^*_i|\mathbf{X}_i,\mathbf{Y}_i}$ as well. Now, let $x^* \in \mathbf{X}^*_i$. Furthermore, let $\mu_{x_i^*|\mathbf{X}_i,\mathbf{Y}_i} \in \mu_{\mathbf{X}^*_i|\mathbf{X}_i,\mathbf{Y}_i}$ and $\sigma_{x_i^*|\mathbf{X}_i,\mathbf{Y}_i} \in \text{diag}(K_{\mathbf{X}^*_i|\mathbf{X}_i,\mathbf{Y}_i})$. We can represent the local conditional posterior mixture mean $\mu_{x_i^*|\mathbf{X}_i,\mathbf{Y}_i}^*$ and local conditional posterior mixture variance $\sigma_{x_i^*|\mathbf{X}_i,\mathbf{Y}_i}^*$ as shown in Eqs. (3) and (4) respectively where $\textit{diff} = (\mu_{x_i^*|\mathbf{X}_{i_g},\mathbf{Y}_{i_g}} - \mu_{x_i^*|\mathbf{X}_i,\mathbf{Y}_i}^*)^2$.

$$\mu^*_{x^*_i|\mathbf{X}_i,\mathbf{Y}_i} = \sum_{i=1}^{m} P(q, i_g) * \mu_{x^*_i|\mathbf{X}_{i_g},\mathbf{Y}_{i_g}} \tag{3}$$

$$\sigma^*_{x^*_i|\mathbf{X}_i,\mathbf{Y}_i} = \sum_{i=1}^{m} P(q, i_g) * (\sigma_{x^*_i|\mathbf{X}_{i_g},\mathbf{Y}_{i_g}} + diff) \tag{4}$$

Here, $\mathbf{X}_{i_g} \subset \mathbf{X}_i$ and $\mathbf{Y}_{i_g} \subset \mathbf{Y}_i$, and each represents the set of samples and ground-truth values that can be best described by GP_{i_g} (i.e. $\mathbf{X}_{i_g} = \{q \in \mathbf{X}_i : \arg\max_{i'_g} P(q, i'_g) = i_g\}$. The mixing probabilities are determined via a distributed EM procedure, and we modify $\mathbf{X_i}$ and $\mathbf{Y_i}$ based on the Voronoi tessellation induced by the current location of each robot. The above procedure is carried out in a decentralized manner using the method in [8].

Depending on the goal of the adaptive sampling, we may either wish to maximize the mean ($q^* = \arg\max \mu^*_{x^*_i|\mathbf{X}_i,\mathbf{Y}_i}$), variance ($q^* = \arg\max \sigma^*_{x^*_i|\mathbf{X}_i,\mathbf{Y}_i}$), or a combination of the two similar to an upper confidence bound heuristic ($q^* = \arg\max \mu^*_{x^*_i|\mathbf{X}_i,\mathbf{Y}_i} + \beta\sigma^*_{x^*_i|\mathbf{X}_i,\mathbf{Y}_i}$). Since we wish to address reducing the mean squared error as shown in Eq. (2), we choose to leverage mutual information as our sampling heuristic. We describe this in Sect. 3.2.

3.2   Mutual Information for Sampling

There are two sampling aspects that are occurring. The first is to choose which sample to collect for updating the spatiotemporal mixture of GPs model. The second is to choose which samples to recommend for collection to provide to the parametric spatiotemporal model for training. We inform both sampling aspects using mutual information-based criteria, but require different approaches to do so since each sampling aspect involves a different sampling problem formulation.

Mutual Information for Updating the STMGPs: Calculating mutual information is known to be difficult, but in order to have the most accurate representation of the environment, each robot should choose the most informative sample. Thus, for optimizing each local Gaussian Process component, we choose a sample that optimizes for a lower bound on the mutual information between the current local Gaussian Process GP_i and the noisy observations to be collected $\mathbf{Y}_i$ from the sampling locations $\mathbf{X}_i$ at timestep t. Let $\gamma_t = \max_{\mathbf{X}_i} I_t(\mathbf{X}_i, \phi|GP_i)$ where $I(\cdot)$ is the mutual information. For Gaussian Processes, the lower bound $\hat{\gamma}_t = \sum_{t'=1}^{t} \sigma^2_{t'}(x_{t'}) \leq \frac{2}{\log(1+\sigma_n^{-2})}\gamma_t$ holds [2].

The lower bounded quantity $\hat{\gamma}_t$ can be computed as shown in Eq. (5), and optimizing for the lower bounded quantity $\hat{\gamma}_t$ yields the optimization strategy shown in Eq. (6) for each robot [2].

$$\hat{\gamma}_t = \hat{\gamma}_{t-1} + \sigma^*_{x^*|\mathbf{X}_i,\mathbf{Y}_i} \tag{5}$$

$$x^* = \underset{x^*_i}{\arg\max} \sqrt{\sigma^*_{x^*_i|\mathbf{X}_i,\mathbf{Y}_i} + \hat{\gamma}_{t-1}} - \sqrt{\hat{\gamma}_{t-1}} \tag{6}$$

Mutual Information for Recommending Samples: At each timestep t, the robots must determine which sampling locations to sample and collect as data for training the parametric spatiotemporal model. We rely on utilizing mutual information to maximize the informativeness of the samples chosen. Once again, computation of mutual information is difficult. Moreover, instead of determining the mutual information with respect to a function (which was the case in Sect. 3.2), we have to find the subset of locations that provides the maximal informativeness with respect to one another. Let $\Phi_t = \{\phi(q,t) : \forall q \in Q\}$ be the set of environment values at all the locations in the environment Q at timestep t. Let R_t be a set of c sampling points to procure for the dataset for learning the parametric spatiotemporal model and their associated environment density values. We wish to solve the optimization problem posed in Eq. (7).

$$R_t^* = \operatorname*{argmax}_{R_t} \mathcal{I}(R_t, \Phi_t \setminus R_t) = \operatorname*{argmax}_{R_t} \mathcal{H}(\Phi_t \setminus R_t) - \mathcal{H}(\Phi_t \setminus R_t | R_t) \qquad (7)$$

The problem in Eq. (7) is a combinatorial, intractable problem [23]. However, mutual information gain is a monotone and submodular function [9,23]. As a result, we leverage submodular function optimization to find a selection of sampling locations that is a provably good approximation to the optimal choice. Similar to [9,23], we employ a greedy-based approach to avoid the combinatorial complexity of this optimization problem. In particular, we employ a stream-based secretary algorithm to approximately solve for the optimal R_t^* at each timestep t based on the methodology in [9] shown in Algorithm 2.

This ensures that a set of candidate samples can be chosen quickly and in a tractable manner prior to the next timestep. We compute a near-optimal approximation of the mutual information $\tilde{\mathcal{I}}(\cdot)$ using submodular function optimization. To compute the approximation of mutual information via submodular function optimization in Algorithm 2, the covariance matrix $\tilde{K} = \left[\tilde{\mathbf{k}}(q_i, q_j)\right]_{\forall q_i, q_j \in Q}$ is needed. We approximate this covariance matrix via a uni-model GP.

Algorithm 2 Stream Submodular Secretary Algorithm [9]

Require: $\tilde{\mathcal{I}}(\cdot | \tilde{K})$ {$\tilde{K}$ is a covariance matrix used to approximate the mutual information}
Require: c {number of samples to return}
1: $R_t \leftarrow \emptyset$
2: $r \leftarrow 0, n \leftarrow |\{q : q \in Q\}|$
3: **for** each segment $S_l = \{q_i \in Q : \frac{n(l-1)}{c} < i \le \frac{nl}{c}\} \forall l = 1, \ldots, c$ **do**
4:    **for** each $q_i \in S_l$ **do**
5:       **if** $\frac{n(l-1)}{c} < i < \frac{n(l-1)}{c} + \frac{n}{c*\exp(1)}$ and $\tilde{\mathcal{I}}(R_t \cup q_i) > r$ **then**
6:          $r \leftarrow \tilde{\mathcal{I}}(R_t \cup q_i)$
7:       **else if** $\tilde{\mathcal{I}}(R_t \cup q_i) > r$ or $i == \frac{nl}{c}$ **then**
8:          $R_t \leftarrow R_t \cup q_i$
9:          $r \leftarrow 0$
10:          **break**
11:       **end if**
12:    **end for**
13: **end for**
14: **return** R_t {return dataset R_t of size c}

3.3 Training Local Gaussian Processes

We now specify the kernel function for each local GP model. We use a squared exponential kernel, which we augment with automatic relevance determination structure to compute a length hyperparameter for each input dimension. Let $x_a = \begin{bmatrix} q_a \; t_a \end{bmatrix}$ and $x_b = \begin{bmatrix} q_b \; t_b \end{bmatrix}$. Let $d = \dim(x_a) = \dim(x_b)$ and let $x(i)$ denote the i-th element in vector x. Then, we can represent the squared exponential kernel with automatic relevence determination as shown in Eq. (8).

$$\mathbf{k}(x_a, x_b | \theta = \begin{bmatrix} \sigma \; \sigma_f \; \sigma_n \end{bmatrix}) = \sigma_f^2 \exp \left[-\frac{1}{2} \sum_{m=1}^{d} \frac{(x_a(m) - x_b(m))^2}{\sigma(m)^2} \right] \qquad (8)$$

We can optimize for the parameters in θ in a Bayesian framework by maximizing the natural logarithm of the marginal likelihood [16]. The optimization problem to compute the optimal θ^* can be posed as $\theta^* = \text{argmax}_\theta \log \mathbb{P}(\mathbf{Y}|\mathbf{X}, \theta)$, where $\log \mathbb{P}(\mathbf{Y}|\mathbf{X}, \theta) = -\frac{N}{2} \log(2\pi) - \frac{1}{2} \log |K_{\mathbf{X},\mathbf{X}}| - \frac{1}{2} \mathbf{Y}^\top K_{\mathbf{X},\mathbf{X}}^{-1} \mathbf{Y}$.

4 Empirical Evaluation

We evaluated our approach on a spatiotemporal dataset to demonstrate the efficacy of our methodology. We describe the empirical evaluation below.

4.1 Experimental Setup

We test our methodology on a spatiotemporal air temperature dataset [5]. This dataset contains monthly air temperature readings from 1948 to near present in $2.5°$ latitude $\times$ $2.5°$ longitude discretization. We test on a 45×21 size grid with the same discretization, yielding an area of $112.5°$ latitude by $50°$ longitude area. Figure 1 shows a visualization of the dataset for a couple of consecutive timesteps to demonstrate qualitatively the spatial and temporal correlation present within the data.

We test three different sampling strategies for recommending samples to the RNP for training: (1) Pure random sampling, which is the common sampling strategy used in most prior work that use deep learning for spatiotemporal modelling; (2) Choosing the samples with the highest uncertainty or variance based on the mixture of Gaussian Processes model, which is the common sampling strategy used in active learning for static spatiotemporal modelling; and (3) Choosing samples based on the largest mutual information gain, which is our proposed approach. Our primary metric for analysis is the root mean square error (RMSE), since this is the most common metric used in adaptive sampling and reconstruction literature. We set $k = 6$ and $m = 10$ (Sect. 2, Algorithm 1).

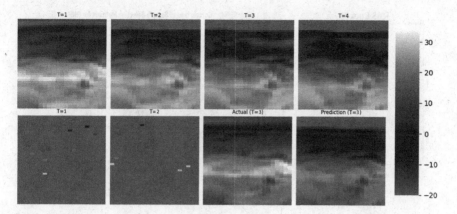

Fig. 1. (Top) Visualization of the ground truth air temperature data across 4 consecutive timesteps. (Bottom) Visualization of an example RNP inference for a time window of two timesteps. The first two frames with 10 samples selected are provided as input to the RNP, third frame is the ground truth, and the fourth frame is the RNP prediction

4.2 Results

We first evaluate the performance of the spatiotemporal mixture of GPs model on forecasting the next timestep after collecting samples and updating the STMGP model in the current timestep. Figure 2 (left) shows that with less than 1% of the spatiotemporal dataset provided as initial data per robot, the STMGP model is able to converge within 5 timesteps to a model that can accurately forecast the next timestep with an RMSE between 4 and 6. Note that the RMSE fluctuates due to the environment changing at each timestep and the STMGP forecasting the next timestep given only the data it has seen until that timestep. The maximum and minimum air temperature in this dataset are -45.76 and 42.15, so this RMSE is quite low (normalized RMSE $= 0.0683$). This demonstrates that the STMGP is accurately predicting the air temperature distribution for the next timestep, so the STMGP model is clearly choosing appropriate samples to ensure that it maintains a representative model. This validates the use of mutual information as the sampling heuristic for updating the STMGP model.

However, there is clearly a limit to the achievable RMSE using a nonparametric model such as the STMGP in a pure active learning scheme. From Fig. 2 (right), we can see that the recurrent neural process (RNP) is able to achieve a better RMSE regardless of the sampling strategy used. This demonstrates the gap between the use of nonparametric models and parametric models, especially powerful function approximators that are common in deep learning. This further motivates finding an end-to-end methodology for integrating multi-robot information gathering and adaptive sampling with powerful parametric or deep learning methodologies for spatiotemporal forecasting and model learning.

We compare the performance of the recurrent neural process on three different sampling strategies: (1) Random Sampling, (2) Maximum Variance, and (3)

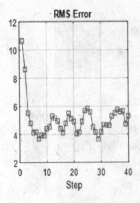
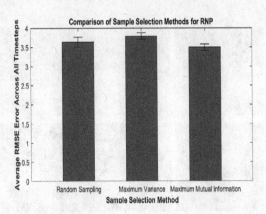

Fig. 2. (Left) RMSE of forecasting the next timestep at each timestep in the environment using only the STMGPs. (Right) Average RMSE of forecasting on an evaluation dataset of unseen timesteps in the environment using the RNP with various sampling strategies

Maximum Mutual Information **(our approach)**. We first train an RNP using the samples procured by each of the sampling strategies until convergence (50 epochs), and then evaluate the RNP on unseen time windows in the environment for forecasting. Table 1 shows the results of the achieved RMSE of the RNP on 11 different seeds. The random seeds randomize the initial configurations of the robots, the initial data given to the mixture of GPs (only applicable for (2) and (3)), the random noise added to the observation, and the train-evaluation dataset generation. The results demonstrate that using maximum mutual information produces the lowest RMSE error along with the lowest variance in the RMSE error in comparison to the other two sampling strategies. Using maximum variance produces consistent, low variance RMSE results in comparison to random sampling, which has high variance in the average RMSE. This is likely due to the larger volatility present in sampling randomly. However, using maximum uncertainty or variance as the sampling strategy produces a higher average RMSE than simple random sampling. However, using the combination of using mutual information for updating the MGP model as well as using mutual information for selecting candidate samples for the RNP yields both low average and variance in the RMSE, outperforming the other two strategies. We validate this difference is statistically significant with a 2-sample t-test to determine if the results are statistically significant. We find that using the maximum mutual information gain sampling strategy reports a p-value of 0.00394 when compared to using the random sampling strategy and reports a p-value of 3.9363e-08 when compared to using maximum variance sampling strategy, which indicates that our approach is statistically significantly better than alternative approaches based on prior work under a significance value of 0.01.

Table 1. (Left Col.) Sampling method used to procure data for RNP. (Center Col.) Average RMSE across 11 different seeds for training the RNP. The use of the MGPs with mutual information provided statistically significantly better RMSE error for forecasting. (Right Col.) Average number of epochs needed to achieve RMSE < 4.

Comparison of RMSE and convergence for RNP under different sampling methods		
Sampling method	Mean RMSE ± StdDev	Mean epoch ± StdDev
Random sampling	3.635091 ± 0.130838	31.363636 ± 5.31550
Max variance (STMGP)	3.788727 ± 0.082061	36.454545 ± 6.743346
Max mutual information (STMGP)	3.492363 ± 0.087282	27.636363 ± 3.170890

Finally, we analyze the convergence properties of the RNP under the various sampling strategies. In particular, we investigate how many epochs it takes on average for the RNP to outperform the RMSE achieved by Mixture of GPs for forecasting. Table 1 demonstrates that the RNP is able to achieve an RMSE less than 4 in the least number of epochs when using maximum mutual information, followed by random sampling and maximum variance. Thus, not only does our methodology provide an end-to-end approach that achieves more accurate spatiotemporal forecasting, but does so in an efficient manner such that model training is effective and converges faster compared to other strategies and approaches. We once again validate that this difference is statistically significant with a 2-sample t-test. We find that using the maximum mutual information gain sampling strategy reports a p-value of 0.03154 when compared to using the random sampling strategy and reports a p-value of 0.00076 when compared to using maximum variance sampling strategy, which indicates that our approach is statistically significantly better than alternative sampling approaches based on prior work under a significance value of 0.05.

5   Concluding Remarks

In this work, we present an end-to-end methodology that starts with effective and coordinated multi-robot information gathering to adaptively sample and procure a collection of samples as a dataset used to train a parametric spatiotemporal model. To the best of our knowledge, this is the first work to address integrating multi-robot information gathering with deep learning for spatiotemporal model learning, as prior work often chooses to focus on one or the other. By using a parametric model as the basis of modelling the spatiotemporal phenomena, we achieve more accurate results in forecasting as compared to nonparametric methodologies. Moreover, we show that we can enable these powerful parametric or deep learning methods for spatiotemporal modelling and forecasting to be used in robotic environment monitoring contexts by integrating multi-robot adaptive sampling with supervised spatiotemporal environment learning. As future work, we plan to investigate different kernels that can be used for improving the performance of the STMGP in adaptive sampling. We also plan to investigate incorporating constrained informative path planning to this methodology.

References

1. Binney, J., Sukhatme, G.S.: Branch and bound for informative path planning. In: 2012 IEEE International Conference on Robotics and Automation, pp. 2147–2154. IEEE (2012)
2. Contal, E., Perchet, V., Vayatis, N.: Gaussian process optimization with mutual information. In: International Conference on Machine Learning, pp. 253–261. PMLR (2014)
3. Dutta, A., Ghosh, A., Kreidl, O.P.: Multi-robot informative path planning with continuous connectivity constraints. In: 2019 International Conference on Robotics and Automation (ICRA), pp. 3245–3251 (2019)
4. Hollinger, G.A., Sukhatme, G.S.: Sampling-based robotic information gathering algorithms. Int. J. Robot. Res. **33**(9), 1271–1287 (2014)
5. Kalnay, E., Kanamitsu, M., Kistler, R., Collins, W., Deaven, D., Gandin, L., Iredell, M., Saha, S., White, G., Woollen, J., et al.: The ncep/ncar 40-year reanalysis project. Bull. Am. Meteor. Soc. **77**(3), 437–472 (1996)
6. Kemna, S., Rogers, J.G., Nieto-Granda, C., Young, S., Sukhatme, G.S.: Multi-robot coordination through dynamic voronoi partitioning for informative adaptive sampling in communication-constrained environments. In: IEEE International Conference on Robotics and Automation (ICRA), pp. 2124–2130. IEEE (2017)
7. Kumar, S.: Spatiotemporal modeling using recurrent neural processes (2019)
8. Luo, W., Nam, C., Kantor, G., Sycara, K.: Distributed environmental modeling and adaptive sampling for multi-robot sensor coverage. In: Proceedings of the 18th International Conference on Autonomous Agents and MultiAgent Systems, pp. 1488–1496 (2019)
9. Luo, W., Nam, C., Sycara, K.: Online decision making for stream-based robotic sampling via submodular optimization. In: 2017 IEEE International Conference on Multisensor Fusion and Integration for Intelligent Systems (MFI), pp. 118–123 (2017)
10. Luo, W., Sycara, K.: Adaptive sampling and online learning in multi-robot sensor coverage with mixture of gaussian processes. In: 2018 IEEE International Conference on Robotics and Automation (ICRA), pp. 6359–6364 (2018)
11. Ma, K.C., Liu, L., Heidarsson, H.K., Sukhatme, G.S.: Data-driven learning and planning for environmental sampling. J. Field Robot. **35**(5), 643–661 (2018)
12. Ma, K.C., Liu, L., Sukhatme, G.S.: An information-driven and disturbance-aware planning method for long-term ocean monitoring. In: IEEE/RSJ International Conference on Intelligent Robots and Systems (IROS), pp. 2102–2108. IEEE (2016)
13. McDermott, P.L., Wikle, C.K.: Bayesian recurrent neural network models for forecasting and quantifying uncertainty in spatial-temporal data. Entropy **21**(2) (2019)
14. Ouyang, R., Low, K.H., Chen, J., Jaillet, P.: Multi-robot active sensing of nonstationary gaussian process-based environmental phenomena. In: Proceedings of the 2014 International Conference on Autonomous Agents and Multi-Agent Systems. pp. 573–580. AAMAS '14, International Foundation for Autonomous Agents and Multiagent Systems, Richland, SC (2014)

15. Pan, L., Manjanna, S., Hsieh, M.A.: Marlas: multi agent reinforcement learning for cooperated adaptive sampling (2023)
16. Rasmussen, C.E., Nickisch, H.: Gaussian processes for machine learning (gpml) toolbox. J. Mach. Learn. Res. **11**, 3011–3015 (2010)
17. Shi, X., Chen, Z., Wang, H., Yeung, D.Y., Wong, W.k., Woo, W.c.: Convolutional lstm network: a machine learning approach for precipitation nowcasting. In: Proceedings of the 28th International Conference on Neural Information Processing Systems, vol. 1, pp. 802–810. NIPS'15, MIT Press, Cambridge, MA, USA (2015)
18. Shi, X., Gao, Z., Lausen, L., Wang, H., Yeung, D.Y., Wong, W.k., Woo, W.c.: Deep learning for precipitation nowcasting: a benchmark and a new model. In: Proceedings of the 31st International Conference on Neural Information Processing Systems, pp. 5622–5632. NIPS'17, Curran Associates Inc., Red Hook, NY, USA (2017)
19. Singh, A., Krause, A., Kaiser, W.J.: Nonmyopic adaptive informative path planning for multiple robots. In: Proceedings of the 21st International Joint Conference on Artificial Intelligence, pp. 1843–1850 (2009)
20. Srivastava, N., Mansimov, E., Salakhutdinov, R.: Unsupervised learning of video representations using lstms. In: Proceedings of the 32nd International Conference on International Conference on Machine Learning, vol. 37, pp. 843–852. ICML'15, JMLR.org (2015)
21. Tresp, V.: Mixtures of gaussian processes. In: Advances in Neural Information Processing Systems 13 (2000)
22. Zhang, B., Sukhatme, G.S.: Adaptive sampling for field reconstruction with multiple moblie robots. In: Sukhatme, G. (ed.) The Path to Autonomous Robots, pp. 1–13. Springer, US, Boston, MA (2009)
23. Zhong, H., Balakrishnan, G., Bowen, R.S., Zabih, R., Freeman, W.T.: Finding maximally informative patches in images. In: NeurIPS 2021 Workshop on Deep Generative Models and Downstream Applications (2021)

Natural Language Processing, Text Mining and Applications

Topic Model with Contextual Outlier Handling: a Study on Electronic Invoice Product Descriptions

Cesar Andrade[1]([✉]), Rita P. Ribeiro[1,3], and João Gama[2,3]

[1] Department of Computer Science, Faculty of Sciences, University of Porto,
4169-007 Porto, Portugal
goersch@hotmail.com
[2] Faculty of Economics, University of Porto, 4200-464 Porto, Portugal
[3] INESC TEC, 4200-465 Porto, Portugal

Abstract. E-commerce has become an essential aspect of modern life, providing consumers worldwide with convenience and accessibility. However, the high volume of short and noisy product descriptions in text streams of massive e-commerce platforms translates into an increased number of clusters, presenting challenges for standard model-based stream clustering algorithms. This is the case of a dataset extracted from the Brazilian NF-e Project containing electronic invoice product descriptions, including many product clusters. While LDA-based clustering methods have shown to be crucial, they have been mainly evaluated on datasets with few clusters. We propose the Topic Model with Contextual Outlier Handling (TMCOH) method to overcome this limitation. This method combines the Dirichlet Process, specific word representation, and contextual outlier detection techniques to recycle identified outliers aiming to integrate them into appropriate clusters later on. The experimental results for our case study demonstrate the effectiveness of TMCOH when compared to state-of-the-art methods and its potential for application to text clustering in large datasets.

Keywords: Short text stream clustering · Contextual outliers · Bert

1 Introduction

The rapid growth of e-commerce and digital transactions has led to an increasing need for efficient and accurate methods to organize and classify large amounts of product information. Product descriptions, in particular, play a crucial role in the success of online businesses as they directly impact customer decision-making and overall user experience. However, managing product descriptions can be challenging, as they are often unstructured, noisy, and vary in length.

Robust clustering algorithms are necessary to efficiently group similar product descriptions and filter out outliers, which can aid in detecting anomalies and potential frauds by analyzing patterns and trends in grouped transaction data.

© The Author(s), under exclusive license to Springer Nature Switzerland AG 2023
N. Moniz et al. (Eds.): EPIA 2023, LNAI 14115, pp. 365–377, 2023.
https://doi.org/10.1007/978-3-031-49008-8_29

Recently, model-based stream clustering algorithms have been developed to address the challenges of clustering short text streams, including Latent Dirichlet Allocation (LDA) [2] and its extensions. These methods have been extensively evaluated on datasets from Tweets and News. However, it's important to note that despite the real-world data from tweets and news being vast, these evaluations often utilize smaller, more manageable datasets.[1] Therefore, the effectiveness of these approaches in clustering short text on truly massive datasets remains largely unexplored, to the best of my knowledge.

Motivated by the Brazilian NF-e Project, an electronic invoicing initiative with challenges akin to e-commerce platforms handling unstructured, noisy, short-text data, we propose the Topic Model with Contextual Outlier Handling (TMCOH). This new method leverages LDA-based methods to cluster product descriptions, furthermore handling contextual outliers. Our approach combines the strengths of existing algorithms such as MStream [18] while incorporating additional steps to treat the outliers.

Our main contributions are as follows. We provide a broad understanding of LDA methods [9,13,17,18], assessing their applicability and effectiveness within a large-scale e-commerce database abundant with clusters. To tackle the challenges posed by short, noisy text streams, we introduce TMCOH, a novel technique that converts data into a specific word representation and identifies contextual outliers. This method manages small clusters and contextual outliers by anticipating that subsequent data batches will re-evaluate certain documents, potentially identifying more fitting clusters and ensuring more precise clustering outcomes. Also, we demonstrate the effectiveness of our approach in normalizing product descriptions. We employ a Neural Machine Translation (NMT) model with a transformer architecture, resulting in a semantically richer dataset.

This paper is organized as follows. Section 2 reviews related work in similarity-based and model-based stream clustering. Section 3 presents our approach, TMCOH. Section 4 details the case study, dataset, and lexical normalization process. Section 5 presents the experimental study, including the experimental setup, and reports the results. Section 6 discusses various aspects of the experiment. Finally, Sect. 7 concludes the paper and suggests future research directions.

2   Related Work

Similar and model-based approaches are two prominent related areas of study in the context of clustering short text streams. Similarity-based clustering groups data points by considering pairwise similarity, whereas model-based clustering organizes data based on underlying statistical models that describe the data distribution. Recent advancements in pre-trained language models, such as BERT [5], coupled with clustering algorithms like HDBSCAN [3], have revealed promising results in various text clustering tasks using similarity-based

---

[1] For instance, the Tweets and Tweets-T dataset contains 30,322 entries, and the News & News-T dataset contains 11,109 entries.

approaches. BERT generates contextualized embeddings, opening new opportunities for understanding word context and modeling language structures [6]. These embeddings can then serve as input for clustering algorithms. In studies [1,7], combining BERT embeddings and HDBSCAN for short text clustering has improved performance over traditional methods. In ELINAC [15], the authors introduced an autoencoder-based method for clustering electronic invoices.

Latent Dirichlet Allocation (LDA) [2] is a model-based stream clustering technique that has inspired several extensions. Examples include MStream [18], which uses Gibbs Sampling for single-pass or iterative clustering; FastStream [13] that employs an inverted index and various similarity measures to calculate the similarity between texts and clusters; DCSS [17] that considers topic distribution correlations at neighboring time points; and OSDM [9] that integrates word-occurrence semantic information into a new graphical model for online clustering of short texts. However, these approaches struggle with massive datasets and do not address outliers effectively. To overcome this challenge, Rakib et al. [14] enhanced MStream and OSDM by detecting outliers and dynamically reassigning them to appropriate clusters using similarity thresholds that adapt over time. Two more approaches cover LDA with outlier detection techniques. DPMM [19] considers the cluster with one element as an outlier but doesn't handle contextual outliers, and ODSE [16] presents an online Dirichlet model for noisy short text stream clustering, combining sentence embeddings and DBSCAN, which treat outliers as noisy and exclude them from further analysis.

Murshed et al. conducted a comprehensive study on short text topic modeling [11]. They highlighted the primary datasets used in this field, which include DBLP, Web Snippet, Google News, BaiduQA, and various Twitter datasets such as Tweets2011, Tweets, and Tweetset. However, it is worth noting that e-commerce datasets are not among those mentioned in the study.

Nevertheless, none of these approaches considers the potential for subsequent data batches to improve cluster identification for specific documents when dealing with large datasets. This aspect motivated our proposal for a new method that uniquely combines the strengths of the MStream model and contextual outlier detection, offering an adaptable, efficient solution for handling massive datasets with many clusters. By addressing the challenges of short text streams and contextual outlier detection, our method sets itself apart from other models in the field, providing a scalable approach to managing complex data landscapes.

3   Topic Model with Contextual Outlier Handling

We propose TMCOH—Topic Model with Contextual Outlier Handling, a new method that combines the Dirichlet process based on the MStream model with contextual outlier detection. Our idea is that by reprocessing contextual outliers and small clusters, it is likely that the subsequent batch will help identify a more suitable cluster for these documents, ensuring a more accurate clustering outcome. Figure 1 depicts the main steps of our method. The process starts with selecting a batch of documents and applying the one-pass DPMM technique to create clusters. The method then verifies cluster size against a predefined threshold. Descriptions in smaller clusters are considered outliers, while larger clusters are encoded and submitted for contextual outlier detection. Detected outliers are re-incorporated into the batch of documents to be processed. Outliers are data points that deviate considerably from the majority. Contextual outlier detection aims to identify data points considered outliers within certain contexts, such as specific subsets of data or combinations of attributes [4].

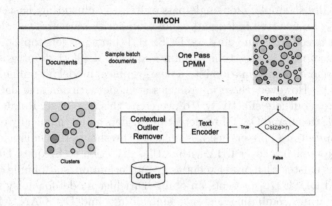

Fig. 1. TMCOH Method.

Similar to MStream [18], TMCOH assumes that documents are generated by the Dirichlet Process Multinomial Mixture (DPMM) model [19], applies a collapsed Gibbs sampling algorithm for the DPMM model for static text clustering. Accordingly, it defines a Cluster Feature (CF) vector for a cluster z as a tuple $\{\vec{n}_z, m_z, n_z\}$, where $\vec{n}_z$ contains a list of word frequencies, m_z is the number of documents, and n_z is the number of words. The CF vector exhibits addible properties [18], allowing for a document d to be efficiently added to cluster z by updating its CF vector as follows $\{n_z^w + N_d^w \; \forall w \in d, m_z + 1, n_z + N_d\}$, where N_d^w and N_d are the number of occurrences of word w in document d and the total number of words in document d, respectively.

Our proposed TMCOH method, as presented in Algorithm 1, begins by applying the one-pass clustering from MStream [18] to a batch of documents, creating an initial set of cluster assignments $\vec{z}_t$. The algorithm proceeds to the post-processing phase to refine the clustering results by iterating through each cluster z in the set of clusters $\vec{z}_t$. During the post-processing phase, if a cluster is considered too small (i.e. smaller than a predefined threshold c_{size}), all documents within it are returned to the main set of documents, deleting the current cluster. For clusters equal to or larger than the threshold, their text is encoded using the ENCODING() function, representing the cluster as $zEncoded$. After encoding, the OUTLIERDETECTION() function is conducted on the encoded text, identifying atypical documents. Initially, these outliers are removed from their

Algorithm 1: TMCOH($\vec{d}, c_{size}, b_{size}$)—based on MStream [18]

Input : $\vec{d}$—documents, c_{size}—threshold for cluster size, b_{size}—initial batch size
Output : $\vec{z}$—cluster assignments for documents
begin
    while $|\vec{d}| > 0$ **do**
        $\vec{d}_t$ = Sample b_{size} from $\vec{d}$
        Remove $\vec{d}_t$ from $\vec{d}$
        $\vec{z}_t$ = MSTREAM($\vec{d}_t$) // cluster assignments for documents in bach t
        for *each cluster* $z \in \vec{z}_t$ **do**
            if $|z| < c_{size}$ **then**
                for *each document* $d \in z$ **do**
                    Append d to $\vec{d}$
                    Remove z from $\vec{z}_t$
                end
            else
                $zEncoded$ = ENCODING(z)
                $outliers$ = OUTLIERDETECTION($zEncoded$)
                for *each document* $d \in outliers$ **do**
                    Append d to $\vec{d}$
                    Remove d from $\vec{z}_t$
                end
            end
        end
        b_{size} = ADAPTATIVEBATCHSIZE()
        Append $\vec{z}_t$ to $\vec{z}$
    end
    return $\vec{z}$
end

---

respective clusters and reintegrated into the main document set. The process is repeated until all batches are processed. At this point, the remaining outliers are returned to the main set of documents.

The TMCOH algorithm employs an adaptive batch size strategy, implemented through the ADAPTIVEBATCHSIZE() function, to manage the prevalence of small clusters in the final stages. This function adjusts the batch size based on the mean number of outliers in recent batches, dynamically adapting to the data distribution and mitigating potential issues. This ensures smooth processing throughout, effectively addressing small cluster concentrations. The process concludes with the return of the refined cluster assignments.

4   Case Study on Electronic Invoice Product Descriptions

The Brazilian NF-e Project was established in 2006 to modernize tax documentation by shifting from paper-based documents to a national electronic system. As a result, massive data has been gathered, comprising details of invoices, sellers, buyers, and products. In this context, leveraging machine learning algorithms can prove invaluable for detecting tax fraud and evasion. As the NF-e project generates an immense volume of data, it is crucial to identify abnormal patterns in invoice descriptions. This dataset is particularly significant as it shares similarities with e-commerce platforms, which manage extensive databases consisting of both structured and unstructured data generated by users.

For this case study, we used an extract from the NF-e dataset for November 2021, provided by the Amazonas State Department of Finance. The dataset contained 475,565 samples and included the features described below.

- GTIN: a unique identifier assigned to a product, usually represented as a bar code or a QR code.
- NCM: a code used to classify goods for customs purposes.
- Product Description: a free text field used by the invoice's issuer to describe the product being sold, often containing short and noisy text.

According to Muller et al. [10], lexical normalization (LN) can enhance Natural Language Processing systems by standardizing text data, thereby addressing variations that do not contribute to its meaning. In our approach to LN, we collected 6.5 million full product descriptions from http://shopping.google.com and generated abbreviated versions to create a diverse training dataset of 120 million entries. We then trained a Neural Machine Translation (NMT) model with a transformer architecture [20] on this dataset, enabling the model to discern patterns and relationships between the original and abbreviated texts. This training equipped the model to process and normalize text data. We employed this LN model to expand abbreviations into their full forms, yielding a dataset with normalized descriptions.

Following this process, we generated six different datasets for this study by combining the cluster labels: GTIN, NCM4, NCM8, and the two types of product descriptions: the original and the normalized ones. The NCM code is used in two formats: NCM4 and NCM8. NCM4 refers to the first four digits of the NCM code, representing the broad category or chapter of the product. In contrast, NCM8 refers to the full eight-digit NCM code, providing a more specific product classification. We generated six different datasets, Table 1, for this study by attaching additional information to the Product Description: GTIN, NCM4, NCM8, GTIN-LN, NCM4-LN, and NCM8-LN.

Table 1. Datasets characteristics of the six datasets, including the number of instances, corpus length, mean words per description, and numbers of clusters.

	GTIN	NCM4	NCM8	GTIN-LN	NCM4-LN	NCM8-LN
Number of instances	475,565	475,565	475,565	475,565	475,565	475,565
Corpus length	3,076,252	3,076,252	3,076,252	3,220,158	3,220,158	3,220,158
Mean number of words	6.47	6.47	6.47	6.77	6.77	6.77
Number of clusters	104,536	706	2404	104,536	706	2404

5   Experimental Study

This section details our experimental setup and presents the outcomes of our case study, comparing the performance of state-of-the-art LDA techniques with our TMCOH approach.

5.1 Experimental Setup

We considered several techniques and methods to assess their effectiveness in clustering product descriptions. Among those, LDA methods require tuning parameters, such as α and β, to obtain the desired clustering performance. Adjusting these parameters, which influence the number of clusters and word distribution across topics, along with the number of iterations that affect the convergence and stability of the Gibbs sampling algorithm, is crucial for achieving optimal clustering performance and results. We inspected the clustering performance of various LDA methods in our case study, including MStream [18] with $\alpha = 0.07$, $\beta = 0.002$, and the number of iterations equal to 1; FastStream [13]; DCSS [17] with $\alpha = 0.07$, $\beta = 0.002$; and OSDM [9] with $\alpha = 0.002$ and $\beta = 0.0004$. This experiment employs an MStream code[2] proposed by Rakib and Asaduzzaman in [13], which implements an inverted index-based searching technique. In all experiments, a consistent batch size of 1000 instances was utilized.

To evaluate our experimental results, we resorted to the following metrics widely used in the literature: Homogeneity (H), Completeness (C), Normalized Mutual Information (NMI), and Purity (P) metrics. Homogeneity measures how well each cluster contains only members of a single class, while completeness evaluates how well each class is represented within a single cluster. NMI is a score combining homogeneity and completeness, measuring the similarity between the true class labels and the assigned cluster labels. Purity assesses the clustering quality by calculating the proportion of the dominant class in each cluster [16].

Regarding our proposed TMCOH, first, we compared two text encoding methods: BERT embeddings using sentence transform from HuggingFace (neural- mind/bert-base-portuguese-cased) and TFIDF. The experiment aimed to determine which approach would improve better the clustering of product descriptions. Second, we assessed three outlier detection algorithms for their effectiveness in clustering: HDBSCAN, K-means, and iForest. The aim was to establish which technique would be most effective for outlier detection when clustering product descriptions. Clusters with up to three elements are considered outliers, i.e. $c_{size} = 3$. We set $\alpha = 0.07$, $\beta = 0.002$, and an initial batch size $b_{size} = 1000$.

5.2 Obtained Results

Table 2 displays the results from the LDA methods across all datasets. MStream consistently outperforms other methods in all metrics, showcasing its superior clustering performance. Furthermore, applying lexical normalization to product descriptions improved all metrics across all experiments.

Table 3 presents the results of the TMCOH method with different clustering outlier methods (HDBSCAN, K-Means, and iForest) and text encoding (TFIDF

---

[2] https://github.com/rashadulrakib/short-text-streamclustering/tree/master/Fast-BatchClustering.

and BERT) applied to all datasets. The results indicate that the TMCOH method applied to K-Means data consistently outperforms other methods in all metrics and across all datasets.

In summary, the TMCOH method with K-Means consistently exhibits superior performance, achieving higher values in all metrics and for all datasets compared to other methods. The performance of the TMCOH method with TFIDF text encoding is comparable to that of BERT encoding. And the normalized dataset obtained the highest scores.

Table 2. Homogeneity (H), Completeness (C), Normalized Mutual Information (NMI) and Purity (P) measures per dataset and by LDA method.

Dataset	LDA Method	H	C	NMI	P	Dataset	LDA Method	H	C	NMI	P
GTIN	FastStream	0.759	0.998	0.862	0.386	GTIN-LN	FastStream	0.844	0.998	0.914	0.631
	OSDM	0.433	0.894	0.583	0.032		OSDM	0.473	0.914	0.624	0.037
	DCSS	0.408	0.999	0.573	0.117		DCSS	0.497	0.999	0.661	0.123
	MStream	**0.947**	**0.999**	**0.972**	**0.783**		MStream	**0.957**	**0.897**	**0.922**	**0.837**
NCM4	FastStream	0.703	0.626	0.662	0.499	NCM4-LN	FastStream	0.818	0.655	0.728	0.716
	OSDM	0.569	0.506	0.536	0.511		OSDM	0.672	0.551	0.606	0.599
	DCSS	0.337	0.552	0.413	0.224		DCSS	0.448	0.605	0.512	0.284
	MStream	**0.969**	**0.690**	**0.806**	**0.916**		MStream	**0.972**	**0.746**	**0.843**	**0.916**
NCM8	FastStream	0.731	0.750	0.740	0.481	NCM8-LN	FastStream	0.833	0.770	0.800	0.703
	OSDM	0.552	0.597	0.574	0.421		OSDM	0.643	0.642	0.642	0.496
	DCSS	0.372	0.706	0.482	0.201		DCSS	0.480	0.749	0.582	0.252
	MStream	**0.968**	**0.795**	**0.873**	**0.899**		MStream	**0.970**	**0.798**	**0.876**	**0.905**

Table 3. Homogeneity (H), Completeness (C), Normalized Mutual Information (NMI) and Purity (P) measures of TMCOH method per dataset and by outlier detection method and text encoding strategy (BERT and TFIDF).

Dataset	Outlier detection	BERT				TFIDF			
		H	C	NMI	P	H	C	NMI	P
NCM4	HDBSCAN	0.828	0.772	0.799	0.597	0.812	0.775	0.793	0.582
	K-Means	0.835	0.770	0.801	0.601	**0.831**	**0.773**	**0.801**	**0.602**
	iForest	0.816	0.772	0.793	0.582	0.818	0.770	0.793	0.585
NCM4-LN	HDBSCAN	0.864	0.797	0.829	0.681	0.853	0.799	0.825	0.666
	K-Means	0.867	0.792	0.828	0.675	**0.866**	**0.795**	**0.829**	**0.678**
	iForest	0.852	0.795	0.822	0.663	0.850	0.794	0.821	0.658
NCM8	HDBSCAN	0.831	0.861	0.845	0.557	0.815	0.865	0.839	0.541
	K-Means	**0.838**	**0.860**	**0.849**	**0.565**	0.834	0.861	0.847	0.565
	iForest	0.820	0.861	0.839	0.540	0.822	0.860	0.840	0.544
NCM8-LN	HDBSCAN	0.858	0.878	0.868	0.631	0.849	0.879	0.863	0.618
	K-Means	0.864	0.875	0.869	0.631	**0.863**	**0.876**	**0.869**	**0.634**
	iForest	0.847	0.877	0.862	0.612	0.846	0.876	0.861	0.609

6   Discussion

To better understand the findings and what they could mean, we now discuss some of those we considered essential aspects of our study. These include examining the formation of small clusters, exploring LDA methodologies, comparing the performance of different clustering techniques, analyzing the differences between NCM4 and NCM8, scrutinizing the differences between BERT and TFIDF, investigating batch evolution, and examining lexical normalization.

Small Clusters Formation. FastStream and MStream show different clustering performances for the GTIN dataset, with MStream outperforming FastStream regarding all metrics scores. Both algorithms have high completeness scores (C = 0.999 for MStream and C = 0.998 for FastStream), indicating that elements belonging to the same class are mostly grouped within the same cluster. However, the lower purity score for FastStream (P = 0.386) compared to MStream (P = 0.783) suggests more class mixing within clusters for FastStream.

Additionally, a common issue observed is the formation of single-element clusters, an issue particularly prevalent in the NCM4 and NCM8 datasets, which hampers the overall quality of results. Our barplot analysis, as shown in Fig. 2, illustrates this problem, revealing a dominance of single-class data points in clusters formed by the MStream and FastStream methods. This motivated the creation of the TMCOH method, designed specifically to tackle this issue. However, it's important to note that TMCOH faces its own challenges, notably in forming larger clusters. We acquired the true labels for evaluation by randomly sampling 475 rounds, each selecting 1000 unique instances of true labels.

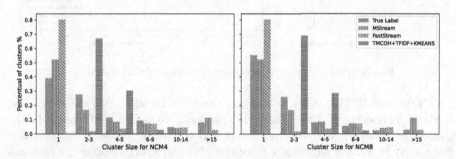

Fig. 2. The proportion of clusters by size, comparing the True Label, MStream, Fast-Stream, and TMCOH results at all batches for NCM4 and NCM8 datasets.

LDA Methods. After analyzing the clustering methods used for the dataset, it was found that DCSS and OSDM performed poorly compared to other methods. MStream, on the other hand, displayed a high level of performance as it is capable of detecting single-class clusters, which are abundant in the dataset. However, FastStream still struggles with the issue of single-class cluster dominance, which has a negative impact on its overall performance.

Clustering Performance. K-Means clustering outperforms other algorithms on all datasets and their normalized versions, achieving comparable values of H, C, NMI and P. Conversely, iForest shows slightly lower performance than both K-Means and HDBSCAN across all metrics. K-Means assumes the data are evenly distributed in the input space and form convex shapes. HDBSCAN posits that clusters exhibit varying densities. Iforest primarily concentrates on isolating anomalies without explicitly assuming any data distribution. Thus, treating the datasets as convexly distributed yields a more accurate approach.

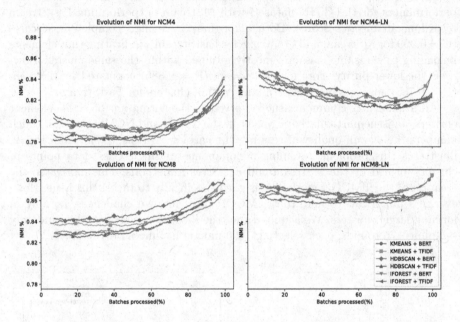

Fig. 3. NMI as TMCOH processes batches on NCM datasets.

NCM4 Versus NCM8. When comparing the NCM4 and NCM8 datasets using K-Means clustering and the TMCOH approach, we notice a difference in the number of clusters, with 706 for NCM4 and 2,404 for NCM8. This increased granularity in NCM8 suggests a more complex clustering structure, which can impact the performance of the algorithms. We observe improvements in the C metric, while H and P values show mixed results across both datasets. These variations in performance metrics highlight the influence of dataset granularity and clustering structure on the chosen clustering methods.

BERT Versus TFIDF. Both text encoding methods show comparable performance for the TMCOH method. TFIDF offers slightly higher metric scores. Therefore, using a generalist BERT model for sentence transformation from HuggingFace (neuralmind/bert-base-portuguese-cased) does not seem to contribute positively to the results. The analysis is even worse considering BERT's computational cost and longer processing time.

Batches Evolution. The graphs shown in Fig. 3 display the NMI metrics' progression as batches are processed for NCM-related datasets. Generally, the NMI increases as more data batches are processed. However, after further inspection, we noticed that there was a slight decrease in NMI due to a gradual decline in homogeneity. This decline may occur due to an increase in the number of instances in the batches, which was promoted by the adaptive batch size strategy. The increased number of instances could lead to a higher likelihood of overlapping or merging clusters, ultimately resulting in reduced homogeneity. On a positive note, the final batches improved H, C, and NMI. This suggests that the clusters are becoming more complete as more members of the same class are grouped, thereby enhancing the overall quality of the clustering.

Lexical Normalization. Comparing the results of the original and normalized datasets, we find that both algorithms generally perform better on normalized data. The normalization process increases the corpus length from 3,076,252 to 3,220,158 words by reducing abbreviation ambiguity. This enhanced clarity and quality of the text allow clustering algorithms to focus more effectively on the core content, thereby leading to more accurate clusters.

Execution Time. Experiments on clustering 475,656 instances showed FastStream as the fastest method, taking 1.93 minutes. In contrast, MSTREAM, despite its performance, took about 16.8 hours, while TMCOH varied between 8.83 and 12.23 hours. Results were consistent across a server with 256 GB RAM and 48 Xeon cores, and a virtual machine with four cores and 16 GB RAM.

7   Conclusions

The era of big data is producing massive datasets containing unstructured, noisy, and diverse information, which poses challenges in organizing and classifying this crucial data. To address this, there is a need for robust clustering algorithms that efficiently group similar data points and filter out outliers. This study proposes the TMCOH method for clustering short text streams, explicitly focusing on product descriptions as a representative case of massive data clustering.

The TMCOH method has shown to be effective in clustering short text streams, particularly in product descriptions. It maintains coherence and stability even when processing large batches of over 475k instances in the dataset. However, the superiority of TMCOH or MStream as a clustering method depends on the specific application. While single-element clusters can be important in identifying unique or outlier data points in certain scenarios, they may not be as useful or even problematic in situations where the main goal is to identify broader patterns or trends in the data.

Future work can explore bi-terms in clustering algorithms to enhance TMCOH's performance and investigate the impact of different fine-tuned BERT encodings specially trained with e-commerce data.

References

1. Asyaky, M.S., Mandala, R.: Improving the performance of HDBSCAN on short text clustering by using word embedding and UMAP. In: 8th International Conference on Advanced Informatics: Concepts, Theory, and Applications (ICAICTA), pp. 1–6. IEEE (2021)
2. Blei, D.M., Ng, A.Y., Jordan, M.I.: Latent dirichlet allocation. J. Mach. Learn. Res. **3**, 993–1022 (2003)
3. Campello, R.J.G.B., Moulavi, D., Sander, J.: Density-based clustering based on hierarchical density estimates. In: Pacific-Asia Conference on Knowledge Discovery and Data Mining, pp. 160–172. Springer (2013)
4. Chandola, V., Banerjee, A., Kumar, V.: Anomaly detection: a survey. ACM Comput. Surv. (CSUR) **41**(3), 1–58 (2009)
5. Devlin, J., Chang, M.-W., Lee, K., Toutanova, K.: BERT: Pre-training of deep bidirectional transformers for language understanding. arXiv preprint arXiv:1810.04805 (2018)
6. Dai, Z., Callan, J.: Deeper text understanding for IR with contextual neural language modeling. In: Proceedings of the 42nd International ACM SIGIR Conference on Research and Development in Information Retrieval (2019)
7. Eklund, A., Forsman, M.: Topic modeling by clustering language model embeddings: human validation on an industry dataset. In: Proceedings of the 2022 Conference on Empirical Methods in Natural Language Processing: Industry Track, pp. 635–643 (2022)
8. Kenter, T., De Rijke, M.: Short text similarity with word embeddings. In: Proceedings of the 24th ACM Int. Conf. on Information and Knowledge Management, pp. 1411–1420. ACM (2015)
9. Kumar, J., Shao, J., Uddin, S., Ali, W.: An online semantic-enhanced Dirichlet model for short text stream clustering. In: Proceedings of the 58th Annual Meeting of the Association for Computational Linguistics, pp. 766–776. Association for Computational Linguistics (2020)
10. Muller, B., Sagot, B., Seddah, D.: Enhancing BERT for lexical normalization. In: The 5th Workshop on Noisy User-generated Text (W-NUT), pp. 1–10. Association for Computational Linguistics (2019)
11. Murshed, B.A.H., Mallappa, S., Abawajy, J., Saif, M.A.N., Al-Ariki, H.D.E., Abdulwahab, H.M.: Short text topic modelling approaches in the context of big data: taxonomy, survey, and analysis. Artificial Intelligence Review, pp. 1–128. Springer (2022)
12. Paalman, J., Mullick, S., Zervanou, K., Zhang, Y.: Term based semantic clusters for very short text classification. In: International Conference on Recent Advances in Natural Language Processing (RANLP 2019), pp. 878–887. INCOMA Ltd. (2019)
13. Rakib, M.R.H., Asaduzzaman, M.: Fast clustering of short text streams using efficient cluster indexing and dynamic similarity thresholds. CoRR abs/2101.08595 (2021)
14. Rakib, M.R.H., Zeh, N., Milios, E.: Short text stream clustering via frequent word pairs and reassignment of outliers to clusters. In: Proceedings of the ACM Symposium on Document Engineering 2020, pp. 1–4. ACM (2020)
15. Schulte, J.P., Giuntini, F.T., Nobre, R.A., Nascimento, K.C.D., Meneguette, R.I., Li, W., Gonçalves, V.P., Rocha Filho, G.P.: ELINAC: Autoencoder approach for electronic invoices data clustering. Appl. Sci. 12(6), 3008 (2022)

16. Si, X., Li, P., Hu, X., Zhang, Y.: An online Dirichlet model based on sentence embedding and DBSCAN for noisy short text stream clustering. In: 2022 International Joint Conference on Neural Networks (IJCNN), pp. 1–8. IEEE (2022)
17. Xu, Y., Wang, S., Zhang, S., Wang, F.: Dynamic clustering for short text stream based on Dirichlet process. IEEE Access **10**, 22852–22865 (2022)
18. Yin, J., Wang, J., Xu, W., Gao, M.: Model-based clustering of short text streams. In: 27th ACM International Conference on Information and Knowledge Management, pp. 697–706. ACM (2018)
19. Yin, J., Wang, J.: A model-based approach for text clustering with outlier detection. In: 2016 IEEE 32nd International Conference on Data Engineering (ICDE), pp. 625–636. IEEE (2016)
20. Ye, Q., Sachan, D., Felix, M., Padmanabhan, S., Neubig, G.: When and Why are pre-trained word embeddings useful for Neural Machine Translation. In: HLT-NAACL. ACM (2018)

Tweet2Story: Extracting Narratives from Twitter

Vasco Campos[1]([✉]) [iD], Ricardo Campos[2] [iD], and Alípio Jorge[1] [iD]

[1] INESC TEC and Faculdade de Ciências da Universidade do Porto, Porto, Portugal
vasco.m.campos@inesctec.pt, ricardo.campos@ubi.pt
[2] INESC TEC and University of Beira of Interior, Porto, Portugal
amjorge@fc.up.pt

Abstract. Topics discussed on social media platforms contain a disparate amount of information written in colloquial language, making it difficult to understand the narrative of the topic. In this paper, we take a step forward, towards the resolution of this problem by proposing a framework that performs the automatic extraction of narratives from a document, such as tweet posts. To this regard, we propose a methodology that extracts information from the texts through a pipeline of tasks, such as co-reference resolution and the extraction of entity relations. The result of this process is embedded into an annotation file to be used by subsequent operations, such as visualization schemas. We named this framework **Tweet2Story** and measured its effectiveness under an evaluation schema that involved three different aspects: (i) as an Open Information extraction (OpenIE) task, (ii) by comparing the narratives of manually annotated news articles linked to tweets about the same topic and (iii) by comparing their knowledge graphs, produced by the narratives, in a qualitative way. The results obtained show a high precision and a moderate recall, on par with other OpenIE state-of-the-art frameworks and confirm that the narratives can be extracted from small texts. Furthermore, we show that the narrative can be visualized in an easily understandable way.

Keywords: Narrative extraction · Open information extraction · Twitter

1 Introduction

Modern social media platforms are used to discuss current topics (e.g., a football game) in real time. *Twitter*, in particular, is a valuable platform for common people, but even more so for journalists [11]. Given the nature of tweets, individually they can contain relevant information, but stacked together they can be cumbersome and redundant. In addition to this, they are often written in colloquial language, which makes it hard to follow up on the different dimensions of topics and opinions revolving around them.

N. Moniz et al. (Eds.): EPIA 2023, LNAI 14115, pp. 378–388, 2023.
https://doi.org/10.1007/978-3-031-49008-8_30

Motivated by this, we take a step towards helping to comprehend the narratives behind a set of documents related to a given topic. A narrative is a formal representation of the relationships that exist between the textual elements of a document. A set of documents is a collection of texts that relate to the same topic, like a set of tweets or a news article. With this in mind, we set a goal to propose a methodology to automatically extract narratives from a set of documents and formulate a central research question: *Can a set of tweets help to reconstruct a news article about related topics?*. In order to answer to this question, we define an information extraction pipeline consisting of 5 steps: Named Entity Recognition, Temporal Entity Extraction, Co-Reference Resolution, Event Extraction and Entity Relation Extraction, which set the ground for the narrative extraction process and define the use of a set of rules devised to extract the narrative. Finally, the results are automatically transformed into brat[1] annotation files, thus giving the narrative a formal schema. To evaluate our methodology, we considered a collection of tweet posts and related news articles and try to infer whether there are connection points between the two. In particular, we perform three types of evaluation: (i) we compare the triples extracted by our methodology with OpenIE state-of-the-art models using the CaRB standard benchmark task and their dataset [2]; (ii) we use the Signal1M-tweetir dataset [14], which links news articles to tweets about the same topic, and compare their narratives; (iii) finally, we make a qualitative analysis of the Knowledge Graphs produced by our methodology.

The main contributions of this paper are: (i) a methodology that automatically extracts the narrative of a set of documents into a brat style annotation file, which can be later used as an entry point to visualization tools; (ii) a gold annotation dataset with 48 news articles annotated in brat format by an expert linguist, which we believe can foster the emergence of works in this area; and (iii) an open source implementation of our methodology available in Github repository.[2]

While our approach can be applied to texts of any nature it particularly suits the case of short texts such as tweets posts which form a big part of our daily-life communication. Based on this, we named our methodology Tweet2Story. Though we cannot claim the proposal of any new information extraction method, we may argue that integrating this components into one such pipeline and coming up with an annotation schema as a first step for visualization purposes, is an innovative methodology in the process of automatically extracting narratives from short texts, that has not been considered in the past.

The remainder of this article is organized as follows. Section 2 shows a study of the related literature. Section 3 gives a detailed explanation of the proposed solution for automatic narrative extraction. Section 4 analyses the results obtained in the course of the designed evaluation. Finally, Sect. 5 concludes the article by summarizing its main contributions with eyes set on the future.

---

[1] https://brat.nlplab.org/standoff.html.
[2] https://github.com/LIAAD/Tweet2Story.

2   Related Work

The process of extracting narratives from texts is an emerging area which only recently has gained attention from the research community [3]. The work of Metilli et al. [10] is an example of the research in this direction, by proposing a fully integrated narrative construction solution. In their paper, the authors identify 8 different steps (including event detection, named entity recognition and relation extraction) to successfully extract knowledge from a text and build a narrative. A training and a testing model is provided for the first two steps.

Other works focus on the narrative extraction aspects of long texts. Eisenberg [6], for instance, focuses on understanding parts of the narrative structure of a story, such as the narrative point of view and the diegesis. Vargas [15], on the other hand, explores the automatic extraction of narrative information for the task of story generation and shows how to improve the performance of information extraction tools. To train the models, Russian folktale stories are used.

Progress has also been made on the parallel area of Open Information Extraction (OpenIE) which sets ground for a few automatic narrative extraction subsequent tasks. Cassirer et al. [7] for example, introduced ReVerb, a syntactic constraint to help extract triples (relations between entities) from a text. A few years later, Del Corro et al. [4] presented ClausIE, which improved OpenIE SOTA results by simplifying complex sentences with multiple clauses (clause-based). More recently, Angeli et al. [1] presented Stanford OpenIE, a clause-based approach that makes use of natural logic inference to shorten the clauses with higher effectiveness when compared to the previous systems.

3   Tweet2Story: Automatic Extraction of Narratives

In the following, we describe the methodology devised to extract narratives from texts related to a given topic. Section 3.1 introduces the IE (Information Extraction) pipeline designed to identify the main elements and relationships found in the narrative. Section 3.2 highlights a set of rules defined to complement the information extracted from pre-trained IE models. The end result of our methodology is an annotation schema file, a formal abstract representation of the narrative, that gives meaning to the stack of documents that form the story. This will be presented in Sect. 3.3.

3.1   Identifying Narrative Elements and Relationships

We begin by defining an information extraction pipeline, consisting of 5 steps, that set the ground for the narrative extraction process by identifying elements and relationships between elements in the text. Details of each of the steps are given below.

1. **Named Entity Recognition.** Retrieve named entities from the text and place them in pre-defined categories. For example, in the tweet "Tropical Storm Grace forms in Eastern Atlantic", the entity "Eastern Atlantic" fits the category of "location". This step takes advantage of a pre-trained model for named entity recognition[3], trained on blogs and comments;

2. **Temporal Entity Extraction.** Focuses solely on retrieving temporal information and mapping it into a context-independent representation. For example, the expression "last week" would be parsed as "07-02-2022". To accomplish this task we make use of the HeidelTime [13] tool;

3. **Co-reference Resolution.** Aims to find co-references about actors in the entire document and to group them into clusters. Co-references are usually nouns or pronouns that refer to the same entity in a text. For example, in the tweet "ts fred continues to weaken as it moves away from the cape verde islands.", both "ts fred" and "it" refer to the same entity and, therefore, belong to the same cluster. To perform this task, we resort to the AllenNLP[4] pre-trained model for co-reference resolution [8];

4. **Event Extraction.** Detects events in the text, typically through verbs and modifiers. For example, in the tweet "Tropical Storm Grace forms in Eastern Atlantic", the event is expressed through the verb **"forms"**. This step also uses a pre-trained model trained by AllenNLP, but for the task of semantic role labelling [12];

5. **Entity Relation Extraction.** Using the semantic role classification of each word/expression on a tweet, it extracts relations between entities (triples). The relations are always between an actor and an event and fit into a given category. For example, "Tropical Storm Grace forms in Eastern Atlantic" produces the triple 'Tropical Storm Grace - forms - in Eastern Atlantic', which is categorized as a **location** triple, due to "Eastern Atlantic" being classified as a "Location Modifier". As in our previous step, this task is performed using the AllenNLP semantic role labelling model [12].

3.2 Narrative Extraction Rules

In addition to the use of pre-trained models, we make use of a set of rules devised to extract the narrative. In this section, we describe the most important ones. First, we decided, as in Dutkiewicz's work [5, p. 7], that **verbs** are most likely the cause of events or relations between arguments. Therefore, in our work, all events **must** contain a verb. Additionally, two different verbs that are linked by **one** other argument are also considered part of the same event, as exemplified in Table 1. In this table, *tag* represents the output of the Semantic Role Labelling AllenNLP model for the triple "he–was meant to be–a surgeon", extracted from a tweet. While the *ann.* row represents the way Tweet2Story annotates it.

Secondly, the subject of the sentence (e.g., "he") represents the person/thing that is performing the event in it and is therefore the agent of the sentence. For

---

[3] https://github.com/explosion/spacy-models/releases/tag/en_core_web_md-3.1.0.
[4] https://allennlp.org/.

this reason, we define the "ARG0" tags (subjects) as "AGENT" relations. Other arguments such as "ARG1" (e.g., "a surgeon") and "ARG2" are also considered to develop "theme" relations with the event, since they are more generic. A "theme" relation occurs when the subject is describing its position. In this case, the subject is describing that he was meant to have the position of surgeon.

Finally, we also map the modifier arguments ("ARGM") into specific categories supported by our annotation system. For example, "direction" modifiers ("The man throws the ball **up**") are mapped as "path" relations (caused by motion verbs, like "throw").

Table 1. Semantic roles for the triple "he–was meant to be–a surgeon"

word	he	was	meant	to	be	a	surgeon
tag	B-ARG0	B-V	B-V	B-ARG1	B-V	B-ARG1	I-ARG1
ann.	T1	EVENT	EVENT	EVENT	EVENT	T2	T2

3.3 Annotation Schema

After the execution of each of the five tasks that constitute our pipeline, results are automatically annotated using the brat format, thus giving the narrative a formal schema. Figure 1 illustrates this process for our running example "he was meant to be a surgeon". In the figure, the word "he", extracted as a person by the named entity recognition task, is turned into an "ACTOR" annotation.

T42	ACTOR 840 842	he
T76	ACTOR 859 868	a surgeon
T102	EVENT 843 858	was meant to be
E12	EVENT:T102	
R51	SEMROLE_agent Arg1:E12 Arg2:T42	
R52	SEMROLE_theme Arg1:E12 Arg2:T76	

Fig. 1. Brat annotation example

Each row has an identifier (T42), the entity role ("ACTOR"), the character span where the entity can be found in the text (840 842) and the actual entity ("he"). The last two lines represent a relation between entities. In this case, the entity "he" is connected to "was meant to be", which is connected to "a surgeon". This annotation depicts the triple "he–was meant to be–a surgeon" and categorizes the semantic relation as a thematic relation (a general semantic role), while showing that "he" is the agent of the relation.

In conclusion, defining the rules allows the framework to fully extract a narrative from a document, by annotating it using the brat format. The end product

Table 2. CaRB benchmark–Results for the optimal threshold

System	Precision	Recall	F1	AUC
Ollie	0.505	0.346	0.411	0.224
PropS	0.34	0.3	0.319	0.126
OpenIE4	0.553	0.437	**0.488**	**0.272**
OpenIE5	0.521	0.424	0.467	0.245
ClausIE	0.411	**0.496**	0.45	0.224
Tweet2Story	**0.561**	0.271	0.365	0.211

is a ".ann" file with a structure similar to the one in Fig. 1, but scaled for a whole document (e.g. a set of tweets). The ".ann" file may then be used to produce visualizations through Knowledge Graphs (see Figs. 4 and 5, used here for evaluation purposes).

4   Analysis of Results

4.1   As an OpenIE Tool

The evaluation as an OpenIE tool consisted on the evaluation of the task of extracting entity relations (triples), against OpenIE state-of-the-art models using CaRB [2]–a Crowdsourced Benchmark for OpenIE - that uses a standard OpenIE task and a gold benchmark corpus of triples.

Figure 2 shows a precision-recall curve for each of the SOTA systems present in CaRB (Ollie, PropS, OpenIE4, OpenIE5, ClausIE) plus Tweet2Story. The results are complemented in Table 2. Both the figure and the table show that Tweet2Story does fairly well against state-of-the-art OpenIE models, despite not being designed for OpenIE specifically.

In particular, Table 2 shows that Tweet2Story has the best precision out of all models, but dips on recall. According to the CaRB framework, this confirms that the Tweet2Story framework is capable of extracting triples without noise (high precision), at the expense of sometimes overlooking important information (moderate recall).

These results were slightly surprising, since Tweet2Story was not optimized to perform an OpenIE task. Its innovation is more related to the pipeline and to the automatic annotation and visualization process rather than the steps themselves. Our objective with this evaluation was showing that Tweet2Story could extract fairly robust triples and these results prove that it can.

4.2   With Manually Annotated Data

In this section, we evaluate the appropriateness of our methodology on extracting narratives from tweets and comparing them against reference news articles. To this regard, we make use of the Signal1M-tweetir dataset [14], which links a set

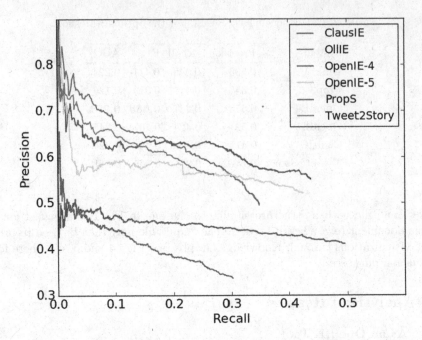

Fig. 2. CaRB framework–Tweet2Story vs. state-of-the-art

of tweets to a news article about the same topic. To cope with this, we asked a linguistic expert to formally annotate 48 news articles narratives. Each article has an average of 12 tweets linked to them. In total, we accounted for 564 tweets linked to the news articles. A deeper description of the annotation process is out of the scope of this work due to space limitations. However, we should call attention to the fact that making these annotations available to the community is the result of a considerable effort and an important step that should foster the emergence of other proposals lacking reference datasets.

To conduct the evaluation, we make use of the ROUGE-1 metric [9] to compare the triples extracted from the tweets (using Tweet2Story) with the triples extracted from the news article (manually annotated by expert). We compare the results of our framework against OpenIE state-of-the-art models (ClausIE, StanfordIE, ReVerb) and a baseline (entitled "complete"), which limits itself to extract one triple for each sentence, while disregarding any semantic relations that may occur between entities. By looking at Fig. 3, we conclude that our methodology extracts the most similar narratives between tweets and news articles out of all models, thus showing that it is able to extract the most important parts of the tweets, while still performing a complete narrative extraction pipeline. Overall, results are low due to the fact that the tweets only contain certain parts of the news story. A preliminary study conducted on top of the SignalMedia dataset shows that, on average, only **37%** of the information in the news article can be found on the tweets. This supports the fact that specifically curated datasets for this evaluation task are lacking and should be devised in the future.

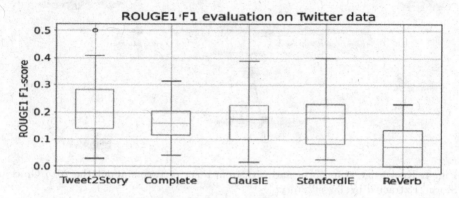

Fig. 3. ROUGE-1 results on Signal1M-tweetir data

4.3   Empirical Comparison of Visualizations

Lastly, we performed a qualitative analysis of our methodology over two knowledge graphs obtained by a set of tweets about the Grace storm occurred in 2015 and its related news article. The first (see Fig. 4) was automatically obtained by our methodology. The second (see Fig. 5) was manually annotated by a linguistic expert, thus resembling the evaluation procedure previously described in the course of Sect. 4.2. All in all, Fig. 4 shows that our methodology is capable of extracting a narrative from a set of documents, namely a set of tweets. Here, we can see the different topics that were discussed, such as the speed of the storm, place it might or might not pass through and even predictions about its dissipation.

If we compare Fig. 4 with Fig. 5, we can also see that the tweets only partially reconstruct the news article. However, most parts of the tweets narrative is complementary and adds something to the reference news text. Therefore a journalist could use this visualization to gather new information or understand the public opinion about the topic. Some more local stories not covered by journalists, could also be automatically constructed and explored by knowledge-graphs, timelines, or other tools (including plain text). This shows that, while tweets may not be a replacement for a news article in its entirety, they are certainly helpful to complement the story and to get new insights from it. This answers our research question. It also makes an important point on the fact that automatically devising a formal representation of a narrative is the first, and an important step, to explore large-scale built stories.

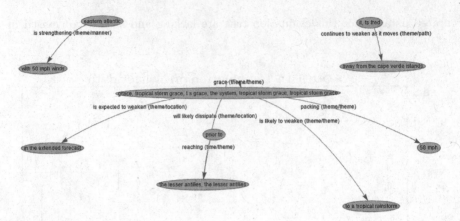

Fig. 4. Knowledge graph of a narrative from a set of tweets about the 2015 Grace Storm. Extracted by Tweet2Story

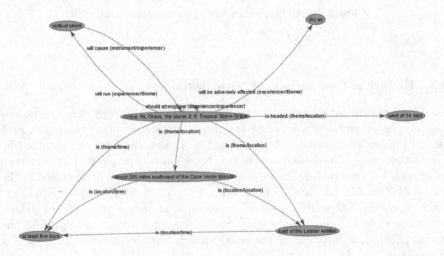

Fig. 5. Knowledge graph of a narrative from a news article about the 2015 Grace Storm. Manually annotated by an expert

5   Conclusion

In this paper, we took a step towards automating the process of narrative extraction from a document, such as a set of tweets. The results obtained show that our methodology can extract triples similarly to what is done by state-of-the-art models, while innovating by providing a complete pipeline that produces annotations and visualizations of the narrative. Tweet2Story is a first step in the direction of automatic narrative extraction, therefore it still has room for improvements. One possible future direction would be to improve the entity relation extraction mechanism (Table 1), which sometimes overlooks important parts of the narrative.

Acknowledgment. This work is financed by National Funds through the Portuguese funding agency, FCT–Fundação para a Ciência e a Tecnologia, within project UIDB/50014/2020 and LA/P/0063/2020. The authors of this paper were financed by National Funds through the FCT–Fundação para a Ciência e a Tecnologia, I.P. (Portuguese Foundation for Science and Technology) within the project StorySense, with reference 2022.09312.PTDC).

References

1. Angeli, G., Johnson Premkumar, M.J., Manning, C.D.: Leveraging linguistic structure for open domain information extraction. In: Proceedings of the 53rd Annual Meeting of the Association for Computational Linguistics and the 7th International Joint Conference on Natural Language Processing (Volume 1: Long Papers), pp. 344–354. Association for Computational Linguistics, Beijing, China (Jul 2015). https://doi.org/10.3115/v1/P15-1034, https://aclanthology.org/P15-1034
2. Bhardwaj, S., Aggarwal, S., Mausam, M.: CaRB: A crowdsourced benchmark for open IE. In: Proceedings of the 2019 Conference on Empirical Methods in Natural Language Processing and the 9th International Joint Conference on Natural Language Processing (EMNLP-IJCNLP), pp. 6263–6268. Association for Computational Linguistics, Hong Kong, China (Nov 2019). 10.18653/v1/D19-1651, https://www.aclweb.org/anthology/D19-1651
3. Campos, R., Jorge, A., Jatowt, A., Bhatia, S., Litvak, M.: The 6th international workshop on narrative extraction from texts: Text2story 2023. In: Kamps, J., Goeuriot, L., Crestani, F., Maistro, M., Joho, H., Davis, B., Gurrin, C., Kruschwitz, U., Caputo, A. (eds.) Advances in Information Retrieval, pp. 377–383. Springer Nature Switzerland, Cham (2023)
4. Del Corro, L., Gemulla, R.: Clausie: Clause-based open information extraction. In: Proceedings of the 22nd International Conference on World Wide Web, p. 355–366. WWW'13, Association for Computing Machinery, New York, NY, USA (2013). 10.1145/2488388.2488420, https://doi.org/10.1145/2488388.2488420
5. Dutkiewicz, J., Nowak, M., Jedrzejek, C.: R2e: Rule-based event extractor. In: Proceedings of the RuleML 2014 Challenge and the RuleML 2014 Doctoral Consortium hosted by the 8th International Web Rule Symposium (RuleML 2014), pp. 1–13. Poznań University of Technology, Prague, Czech Republic (2014)
6. Eisenberg, J.D.: Automatic Extraction of Narrative Structure from Long Form Text. Ph.D. thesis, Florida International University (2018)
7. Fader, A., Soderland, S., Etzioni, O.: Identifying relations for open information extraction. In: Proceedings of the 2011 Conference on Empirical Methods in Natural Language Processing, pp. 1535–1545. Association for Computational Linguistics, Edinburgh, Scotland, UK. (Jul 2011). https://aclanthology.org/D11-1142
8. Lee, K., He, L., Zettlemoyer, L.: Higher-order coreference resolution with coarse-to-fine inference. In: Proceedings of the 2018 Conference of the North American Chapter of the Association for Computational Linguistics: Human Language Technologies, Volume 2 (Short Papers), pp. 687–692. Association for Computational Linguistics, New Orleans, Louisiana (Jun 2018). https://doi.org/10.18653/v1/N18-2108, https://aclanthology.org/N18-2108

9. Lin, C.Y.: ROUGE: A package for automatic evaluation of summaries. In: Text Summarization Branches Out, pp. 74–81. Association for Computational Linguistics, Barcelona, Spain (Jul 2004). https://aclanthology.org/W04-1013

10. Metilli, D., Bartalesi V., Meghini C.: Steps towards a system to extract formal narratives from text. In: Text2Story 2019-Second Workshop on Narrative Extraction From Texts, pp. 53–61. CEUR-WS.org, Aachen, DEU, Cologne, Germany (April 2019)

11. MuckRack: The state of journalism 2021. MUCK RACK Blog (Mar 15 2021). https://muckrack.com/blog/2021/03/15/state-of-journalism-2021

12. Shi, P., Lin, J.: Simple Bert models for relation extraction and semantic role labeling (2019). arXiv:abs/1904.05255

13. Strötgen, J., Gertz, M.: Heideltime: High quality rule-based extraction and normalization of temporal expressions. In: Proceedings of the 5th International Workshop on Semantic Evaluation, p. 321–324. SemEval'10, Association for Computational Linguistics, USA (2010)

14. Suarez, A., Albakour, D., Corney, D., Martinez, M., Esquivel, J.: A data collection for evaluating the retrieval of related tweets to news articles. In: 40th European Conference on Information Retrieval Research (ECIR 2018), pp. 780–786. Springer, Cham, Grenoble, France (March 2018). https://link.springer.com/chapter/10.1007/978-3-319-76941-7_76

15. Vargas, J.V.: Narrative Information Extraction with Non-Linear Natural Language Processing Pipelines. Ph.D. thesis, Drexel University (2017)

Argumentation Mining from Textual Documents Combining Deep Learning and Reasoning

Filipe Cerveira do Amaral[1,2(✉)], H. Sofia Pinto[1,2], and Bruno Martins[1,2]

[1] Instituto Superior Técnico, Universidade de Lisboa, Lisboa, Portugal
{filipe.amaral,sofia.pinto,bruno.g.martins}@tecnico.ulisboa.pt
[2] INESC-ID, Lisboa, Portugal

Abstract. Argumentation Mining (AM) is a growing sub-field of Natural Language Processing (NLP) which aims at extracting argumentative structures from text. In this work, neural learning and symbolic reasoning are combined in a system named N-SAUR, that extracts the argumentative structures present in a collection of texts, and then assesses each argument's strength. The extraction is based on Toulmin's model and the result quality surpasses previous approaches over an existing benchmark. Complementary scores are also extracted and combined with a set of rules that produce the final calculation of argument strength. The performance of the system was evaluated through human assessments. Users can also interact with the system in various ways, allowing for the strength calculation to change through user-cooperative reasoning.

Keywords: Natural language understanding · Machine learning · Neural-symbolic approaches · Argumentation mining

1 Introduction

Argumentation and debate constitute a vital part of human societies. Recent developments in artificial intelligence are being applied to analyzing and simulating this human cognitive activity. In particular, Argumentation Mining (AM) is a growing sub-field of Natural Language Processing (NLP) with many practical applications in areas that include law, healthcare, and e-government [1], aiming at the extraction of the argument structures present in text. This includes perceiving the core idea of a document, and further distinguishing relevant from irrelevant segments of text (i.e., the Argumentative Discourse Units (ADUs) [13]) with respect to that idea, together with the relations that may exist among them, according to a chosen argumentation model.

Understanding whether a given piece of evidence supports a given claim, or whether two claims attack each other, are complex problems that humans can address thanks to their ability to exploit commonsense knowledge to perform reasoning and inference. Despite the remarkable impact of deep neural networks in NLP, these techniques alone will likely not suffice to address the complex issues associated with AM, motivating the development of techniques that explicitly consider knowledge expressed in the form of rules and constraints.

This paper presents a Neural-Symbolic Argumentation Mining system with User-Cooperative Reasoning (N-SAUR), which uses neural technology to extract and label ADUs from texts, based on the Toulmin argumentation model [15], followed by a symbolic AI approach to reason about the previously collected information. Reasoning is performed through a set of Problog rules, which attempt to calculate how strong a given claim is, in regards to its argumentative power.

2   Related Work

We now present relevant sub-symbolic and neural-symbolic approaches, previously described in the literature.

Sub-Symbolic Methods to Argumentation Mining: In [16], two types of Argumentation Mining (AM) are defined: close-domain discourse level and information-seeking. The former refers to identifying the structure of the arguments, and the latter to extracting the implicit meaning of the arguments, as well as the claims they are defending. The authors defined an argument as an atomic piece of text, thus not requiring any context. Using BERT and FLAIR models to implement a slot-filling approach based on token-level annotations, they were able to extract ADUs. Data supporting the experiments consisted of a large amount of text on controversial topics, so that discussion was present and arguments from different points of view would appear.

Open-domain AM was tackled in [11], searching in a pool of documents for arguments on a given topic, both supporting and refuting the main topic. The results emphasize the importance of (1) using contextualized word embeddings (e.g., from BERT), and (2) the need for clustering similar arguments, to simplify the argumentative structure before classification. An approach to AM across different languages was described in [3], emphasizing the importance of training on same-domain corpora, as the context and the theme of an argumentative text are crucial for it to be understood.

Regarding argumentative models, in [16] the authors used a simple binary PRO/CON classification scheme, in which ADUs are either for or against the topic of the text at hand. In [9], the authors used a slightly more complex structure, in which an ADU could either be a premise, a claim, or a major claim. Premises support claims, which in turn either support or attack major claims, of which a text can have just a few. Other authors have instead used a modified Toulmin model [7], represented on the right-hand side of Fig. 1 and based on the original model shown at the left-hand side. This model features claims, that can be supported by either backing or grounds, and attacked by rebuttals, which can, in turn, be attacked by refutations.

Neural-Symbolic Methods to Argumentation Mining: An extensive analysis on the combination of learning and reasoning is described in [6]. The former

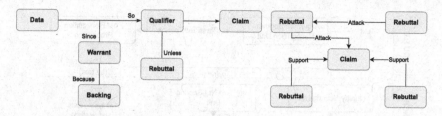

Fig. 1. Toulmin's original model and the modified Toulmin model [7], respectively on the left and right-hand sides. Both diagrams are adapted from [7].

is usually implemented with neural techniques and the latter with symbolic approaches. The authors propose the combination of both approaches, naming it neural-symbolic computing. On the other hand, the authors of [5] called for a *"leap forward"* in Argumentation Mining (AM) by integrating both sub-symbolic and symbolic approaches. They showed some examples of logical inference tools (including defeasible inference and DeepProbLog [10]).

A new task, Argument Explicitation (AE), was proposed in [9]. Besides detecting the arguments present in a text, AE also (a) tries to explain them (i.e., enhancing them with knowledge that is retrieved on-the-fly), (b) tries to make the missing premises (called enthymemes) explicit, and (c) assesses the arguments' validity, by either fact-checking or, in case of a subjective conclusion, performing enthymeme reconstruction, making it evident for the user that the argument that is being made assumes a given implicit premise, and making it the user's responsibility to assess its validity. In the same paper, a framework for the task is proposed, combining different kinds of explicitation.

3 The N-SAUR System

We propose a Neural-Symbolic Argumentation Mining with User-Cooperative Reasoning (N-SAUR) system, which receives as input a collection of argumentative texts that fall into a single topic of discussion, and then calculates the strength of each claim that is present in the documents, scoring them with a value from 0 to 1 that can be read as the likelihood of each claim being a strong one, with regard to its argumentative power.

N-SAUR is divided into three tasks (see left-hand side of Fig. 2), namely (a) recognition of all the ADUs in the document collection, and (b) complementary ADU scoring, which is itself composed of (b1) quality and natural language inference scoring, and (b2) the final logical calculation.

ADU Recognition and Expression: After receiving the text collection as input, the first task the system performs is individual to each text, and concerns detecting and classifying all relevant spans of text for the argumentation that is taking place in every single document. The encoded information includes each ADU's text content, as well as their classifications and relations, according to the modified Toulmin model (right-hand side of Fig. 1).

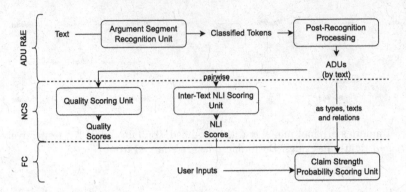

Fig. 2. The N-SAUR system architecture.

Neural Complementary Scoring: With all ADUs extracted and their classifications and relations encoded, the next components of the system aim at perceiving how strong, with regard to its argumentative power, each claim is. The local context of an argument, i.e. all the argumentative structure leading to the final idea, i.e., the claim, is represented by the expressed classifications and relations among the extracted ADUs. The more a claim is supported or attacked, the stronger or weaker it is, respectively. Each extracted ADU will be scored according to its inherent argumentative power, by the **Quality Scoring Unit**. The stronger the quality of an ADU that is supporting or attacking a claim, the stronger or weaker that claim should be, respectively.

Additionally, the system will assess the relations between all the ADUs from documents about the same topic. For that, all possible pairs of ADUs are scored by the **Inter-Text Natural Language Inference Scoring Unit**. This information enables N-SAUR to derive additional support/attack relations, thus getting more data to assess a claim's strength. A claim will be supported or attacked by an ADU if that ADU is entailed by another one that in turn supports or attacks the claim, respectively.

Final Calculation: With all the previously gathered scores, the system is now able to calculate the argumentative strength of each claim in the collection of input documents, using a set of rules and probabilistic logic. Additionally, N-SAUR enables users' input for a claim's strength calculation. We call this ability user-cooperative reasoning.

Argument Segment Recognition Unit: The first component in the N-SAUR pipeline aims at detecting the relevant spans for the argumentative structure of each text, as well as the corresponding classifications. All word tokens are classified using a BIO encoding (Beginning, Inside, Outside) for the classes claim, grounds, backing, rebuttal, or refutation. Several deep learning BERT-based models from the HuggingFace Transformers library were tested, fine-tuning them to this task with the Argumentation in User-Generated Content Dataset [7]. The best model, BERT Large Cased [2], was chosen.

Post-Recognition Processing: With all tokens classified, the next module in the pipeline aggregates the tokens into the spans of text with a classification, expressing the ADUs. Afterwards, according to the modified Toulmin model, the system encodes the relations that exist among all ADUs from the same text. For a relation to occur, the distance between the given ADUs is not taken into consideration, and if a backing and a claim are detected in the same text they have a relation of support. If there is more than one possible relation, then all of them are encoded with equal probability for each target (e.g., two claims and one premise means that there is a 50% chance of the premise supporting either of the claims). This is the first part of the pipeline that introduces probabilistic logic, using Problog, which will then be propagated forward.

Natural Language Inference Scoring: All the extracted ADUs, as well as their classifications and relations, are organized into all possible inter-text pairs, in order to perform Natural Language Inference (NLI). This task takes two sentences and determines if there is a relation of entailment, contradiction, or neutrality between them. For that, a DeBERTa model [8] from the HuggingFace Transformers library, which is already fine-tuned for the NLI task, was used. The model produces, for each pair, a probability distribution for the three classes - neutrality, entailment, or contradiction. From all these results, the pairs for which neutrality has the highest probability are discarded. A sample of pairs is then drawn according to the highest majority probability, balanced according to the entailment and contradiction classes.

Quality Scoring Unit: In addition to the support it has, a claim's strength is also influenced by its own inherent quality. Besides that, it is also possible to consider the inherent quality of its supporters and attackers. This way, any given ADU that is a source of a relation to a given claim can have its quality measured and used as a weight of that relation.

Given the aforementioned ideas, all extracted ADUs, and not only claims, are scored for quality. Experiments were made with several other BERT-based models from the HuggingFace Transformers library (including RoBERTa) and BERT was chosen. This model was trained for quality scoring using the IBM-Rank [14] dataset, which contains statements and their corresponding scores, from 0 to 1. In order to perform the fine-tuning, a regression head was added to the output of BERT, so that the neural model outputs a score between 0 and 1. All ADUs already mined by the pipeline are scored in this way.

Claim Strength Probability Scoring: With all the previously gathered information, N-SAUR can now calculate how strong each of the extracted claims is, using Problog, which is used to encode all the information to be given as input to probabilistic reasoning. There are three sources of data to be expressed in Problog facts, namely the ADU extractions per se, and the results from the two scoring units.

Both classifications and relations are extracted simultaneously, since the latter are implicit in the former, given the argumentation model being used. The following code snippet shows an example of the Problog encoding for a document with two claims. The predicate support(XX, YY) means XX supports YY.

```
1       claim(c1).
2       claim(c2).
3       grounds(g1).
4       0.5::support(g1, c1).
5       0.5::support(g1, c2).
```

For the other sub-processes of data, Problog facts are also used. In the following code snippet, the probability of each fact is given by the quality score and from the NLI result (i.e., the probability of the most likely label from the neural model, given that it is not neutral), respectively. The predicates entail(XX, YY) and contradict(WW, ZZ) mean XX entails YY and WW contradicts ZZ.

```
1       0.87::quality(c1).
2       0.78::quality(c2).
3       0.33::quality(g1).
4       0.85::quality(g2).
5       0.54::entail(g1, g2).
6       0.38::contradict(g2, c2).
```

The Problog facts are fed into the final calculation unit, which joins them with the strength calculation program. The following set of rules makes it possible to derive a support/attack relation from a combination of entailment and other support/attack relations, to which we add the quality score of the newly created relation's source.

```
1       support(A,C) :- support(A,B), entail(B,C), quality(A).
2       support(A,C) :- support(B,C), entail(B,A), quality(A).
```

Given all facts from previous code snippets, we can derive a support relation between $g2$ and $c1$, because of the entailment between $g1$ and $g2$.

The following code snippet shows the next abstraction level in the strength calculation. It is possible to compute how much a given claim is opposed by other ADUs, as given by how much it is attacked, and also according to whether there is a contradiction in the ADUs that support it (Lines 1–2). This is then used to calculate how much the claim is endorsed (Line 3). Furthermore, a claim can also be supported by user input, under a support form, being expressed as a different kind of endorsement (Line 4).

```
1       oppose(C) :- claim(C), attack(A,C), not(attack(_,A)).
2       oppose(C) :- claim(C), support(A,C), contradict(A,C).
3       endorse(C) :- claim(C), support(_,C), not(oppose(C)).
4       user_endorse(C) :- claim(C), user(A), support(A,C).
```

Finally, the claim's strength is given by combining the endorsement, the quality of the claim itself, and, if there is any, the users' inputs:

```
1       strength(C) :- endorse(C), quality(C); endorse(C),
                quality(C), user_endorse(C).
```

It is worth noting that although the previous rules are not assigned to any probabilities, the probabilistic facts will propagate them, yielding very expressive results. As such, each claim's strength will be calculated with regard to several probabilistic facts. Moreover, a user can change each fact's probability in order to check the results yielded by the change. It is also possible to vote directly on how strong a claim is. With several votes, expressed as a number from 0 to 1, N-SAUR will, arguably, get closer to the real strength of a given claim.

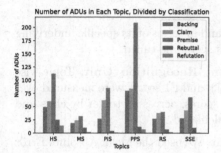

Fig. 3. The AUGC dataset distribution of ADU classes.

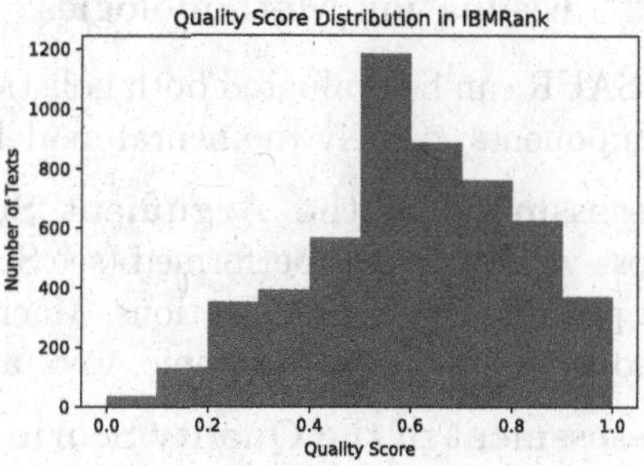

Fig. 4. Quality score distribution on the IBMRank dataset [14].

4 Experimental Setup

This section provides a characterization of the data supporting our experiments, together with the evaluation methodology and the corresponding results.

4.1 Data

N-SAUR has three neural units, two of which were fine-tuned before their usage: the Argument Segment Recognition and the Quality Scoring units. The Argumentation in User-Generated Content (AUGC) dataset [7] was used to fine-tune the BERT Large model used for argument span recognition. The dataset is divided into three parts: an unlabeled raw corpus, a version with annotations regarding persuasiveness, and a version with annotations regarding argument structures. For this work, only the last part was used. It contains 340 small texts about six different controversial topics relating to education: homeschooling, mainstreaming (including children with special needs into regular classes), prayer in schools, public versus private schools, redshirting (postponing children's kindergarten entrance), and single-sex education. All these texts were collected from internet users' posts on blogs or forums, comments, or articles. The distribution of the ADU classifications is represented in Fig. 3.

In turn, the IBMRank dataset [14] was used to train the model for quality scoring. To create this dataset, human annotators were asked to label sentences as good or bad, as well as to decide what was the best one out of a random pair. These results were then converted into a numerical label and the data was cleansed according to factors such as the annotator agreement and the difference in quality between arguments. The IBMRank dataset contains 5297 sentences with lengths between 36 and 275 characters, which were split into training and testing folds of 90% and 10% of sentences, respectively. The quality score distribution across the data is shown in Fig. 4.

4.2 Evaluation Methodologies

N-SAUR can be evaluated both holistically and in terms of its specific underlying components, namely the neural models that were fine-tuned.

Assessment of the Argument Segment Recognition Unit: Topic-wise cross-validation was performed (see Sect. 4.1), and F1 scores were measured over all possible token classifications. Macro-F1 scores, across all topics by class and also across all classes by topic, were also calculated.

Assessment of the Quality Scoring Unit: We used the Mean Absolute Error (MAE) for model assessment, given by:

$$\text{MAE}(r, p) = \frac{1}{n} \sum_{i=1}^{n} |r_i - p_i|, \tag{1}$$

where r_i and p_i refer to each n real and predicted values, respectively.

Holistic Assessment: To evaluate the final results, the performance of N-SAUR was compared to real people's assessments. To do that, the *public vs private schools* topic was chosen, since it was thought to be a topic most people have already an opinion about, and requires no further explanation. A sample of 30 claims was drawn from the total set of claims collected by N-SAUR. The participants were asked to compare pairs of claims and indicate which one was the best. Many times, however, the claim text itself is not enough, so a context was added, composed of all the ADUs that had a relation (attack or support) with the claim. Given this information, the goal was to get the ranking of 30 claims with pairwise comparisons. A reasonable number of pairs to sample was between 86 and 138, to have correct results with a probability of 2/3 [12]. Hence, 104 unique pairs were divided into 13 surveys of 8 questions each.

Two experiments were made with the gathered data. The first one aimed at contrasting the performance of N-SAUR with the annotators in regard to pairwise comparisons. For each pair of claims, the annotators' and N-SAUR's picks as the stronger claim were compared. The annotators' pick is determined by a majority vote, and the system's pick is the claim with the highest strength score. To refine the results, the pairs are organized by how much consensus there was among the annotators, namely from 50 to 66.7%, from 66.7 to 83.3%, and from 83.3 to 100%. For each bin, an accuracy score can be calculated by considering pairs in which both the annotators' and the system's picks for the stronger claim are the same, as successful.

The second experiment started by producing a ranking of all 30 claim pairs. To do so, each of the pair's majority stance was used for a Borda count method [4], in order to score each claim. On the other hand, N-SAUR also produces a ranking, by means of its assigned strength scores. The two rankings were compared with the Normalized Discounted Cumulative Gain (NDCG) [17], considering the result of the Borda count method as a relevance score. The NDCG value for a list of results p is given by:

$$nDCG_p = \frac{\sum_{i=1}^{p} \frac{2^{rel_i}-1}{\log_2(i+1)}}{\sum_{i=1}^{|REL_p|} \frac{2^{rel_i}-1}{\log_2(i+1)}}, \tag{2}$$

where rel_i is the relevance of the given item, and $|REL_p|$ is the ordered list of relevant items.

Table 1. Fine-tuning results of BERT Large Cased using the AUGC dataset.

Tags	MS	RS	HS	PPS	SSE	PIS	Macro-F1
O	0.957	0.999	0.994	0.988	0.993	0.999	0.988
B-Backing	0.872	0.966	0.898	0.922	0.967	0.947	0.929
I-Backing	0.941	0.997	0.994	0.983	0.988	0.95	0.976
B-Claim	0.788	0.857	0.949	0.841	0.929	0.903	0.878
I-Claim	0.853	0.918	0.986	0.933	0.939	0.927	0.926
B-Premise	0.886	0.932	0.934	0.959	0.919	0.942	0.929
I-Premise	0.957	0.996	0.986	0.984	0.985	0.989	0.983
B-Rebuttal	0.583	0.400	0.557	0.615	0.700	0.800	0.609
I-Rebuttal	0.929	0.847	0.841	0.869	0.952	0.729	0.861
B-Refutation	0.000	0.000	0.000	0.000	0.000	0.000	0.000
I-Refutation	0.000	0.442	0.806	0.879	0.065	0.000	0.365
Macro-F1	0.706	0.759	0.813	0.816	0.767	0.744	0.768
AUGC	0.188	0.257	0.197	0.203	0.194	0.166	0.201

4.3 Experimental Results

We now present and discuss the results obtained for each of the parts.

Assessment of the Argument Span Recognition Unit: The results of the fine-tuning for argument span recognition are presented in Table 1, divided into the 6 topics of the AUGC dataset, that constituted the folds for cross-validation training of a BERT Large Cased model. It is worth pointing out that our approach yielded better results than those presented for the original benchmark, which used an SVM classifier [7] in the same cross-domain setting.

The *public vs private schools* topic was chosen for subsequent analysis, and a confusion matrix for its results is presented in Fig. 7.

It is also possible to draw a comparison between the number of examples for each ADU class (see Fig. 3) and result quality. Even though state-of-the-art neural models surpassed the previous benchmark, the argumentation model is perhaps too complex to perform this kind of automated recognition, especially regarding the refutation class, thus justifying the tendency for choosing simpler models. On the other hand, the poor performance on some classes may be due to a lack of enough data (e.g., for the neural models to distinguish premises and refutations/rebuttals effectively).

Assessment of the Quality Scoring Unit: We measured an MAE of 0.173, which represents a small difference between predictions and real scores, yielding a good determinant of each ADU's quality, and consequently an accurate contribution to the pipeline.

Holistic Assessment: For the human vs N-SAUR performance comparison, 50 people responded to the aforementioned surveys. Almost all the participants (94%) were between 18 and 29 years old, and only a small minority (8%) claimed not to have previously watched nor participated in any debates. All pairs of claims were evaluated at least three times.

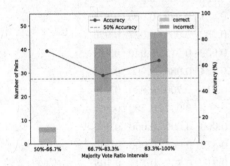 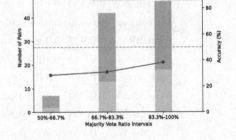

Fig. 5. N-SAUR pairwise performance by consensus.

Fig. 6. N-SAUR pairwise performance without quality scoring.

Accuracy for the first experiment is presented in Fig. 5. It is possible to see that for all bins, there was a majority of correctly classified pairs, which is then reflected in the accuracy (curve in blue), being always above the 50% mark (grey dashed line). This measure is higher on the first bin, perhaps because of its small amount of pairs. On the other hand, with the remaining two bins, the system's performance goes up with the consensus of annotators' votes, as can be seen by the accuracy increase from the second to the third bin. In the second experiment, the overall ranking of N-SAUR, contrasted with the one produced by the annotations as the ground-truth, yielded an NDCG score of 0.830.

In order to further validate the previous results, another experiment was carried out, in which quality scoring was removed and the aforementioned assessment metrics were calculated. Rankings by the system were in this case performed according to rules without a quality predicate. The pairwise comparison results are represented in Fig. 6, which shows that the results are worse than the original N-SAUR. The NDCG experiment, however, measured a value of 0.853, being slightly better. These results show that sometimes a single measure may not be enough, and perhaps the NDCG is better because the sample size of 30 claims may have been too little. Nevertheless, further analysis with a larger quantity of annotations is required.

Overall, the experiments suggest that N-SAUR was capable of perceiving some of the same patterns humans use to make their judgments. The results also open the door for further investigation, aiming at establishing benchmarks considerably higher than 50% on the claim's strength prediction task.

5   Conclusions and Future Work

We presented a Neural-Symbolic Argumentation Mining with User–Cooperative Reasoning (N-SAUR) system, following the argument made in [5] for combining both symbolic and sub-symbolic techniques (with the additional optional user interaction) to perform Argumentation Mining (AM) and further reasoning with the results. We used state-of-the-art neural methods for NLP to extract the argumentative structures from text documents and classify them formally, followed by the gathering of natural language inference relations and quality scores. All

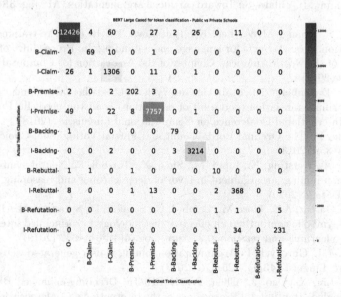

Fig. 7. Confusion matrix for the public vs private schools topic.

this information is encoded in Problog, and claim strength scores are calculated through probabilistic reasoning, with the option of user participation.

N-SAUR is innovative in various ways: it combines two approaches of AI, which are usually separate, applying them to an NLP sub-field of growing importance. It also used a complex argumentative model, surpassing existing benchmarks. Moreover, it embodies a framework in which more models, complementary scores, and even user votes can be added, with the end goal of coming increasingly closer to the real strength prediction of an argument clause.

Future work in neural-symbolic AM should consider tackling the problem with a more complex set of rules, attempt to cluster similar claims [11], and add more complementary neural scores (e.g., probabilities associated with ADU recognition), so as to yield more fine-grained results. Future work should also further investigate the calibration of the probability scores output by the neural models and add the user-cooperative aspect to the experiments. Moreover, a full integration of DeepProbLog [10], allowing for all the probabilities used in Problog to be computed end-to-end by a neural network, should be attempted.

Acknowledgements. This research was supported by Fundação para a Ciência e Tecnologia (FCT), through the INESC-ID multi-annual funding with reference UIDB/50021/2020 and by CHIST-ERA within the CIMPLE project (CHIST-ERA-19-XAI-003) which corresponds to the FCT reference CHIST-ERA/0001/2019.

References

1. Atkinson, K., Baroni, P., Giacomin, M., Hunter, A., Prakken, H., Reed, C., Simari, G., Thimm, M., Villata, S.: Towards artificial argumentation. AI Mag. **38**(3), 25–36 (2017)
2. Devlin, J., Chang, M.W., Lee, K., Toutanova, K.: BERT: Pre-training of deep bidirectional transformers for language understanding. In: Proceedings of the Conference of the North American Chapter of the Association for Computational Linguistics (2019)
3. Eger, S., Daxenberger, J., Stab, C., Gurevych, I.: Cross-lingual argumentation mining: Machine translation (and a bit of projection) is all you need! In: Proceedings of the International Conference on Computational Linguistics (2018)
4. Emerson, P.: The Original Borda Count and Partial Voting. Soc. Choice Welfare **40**, 353–358 (2013)
5. Galassi, A., Kersting, K., Lippi, M., Shao, X., Torroni, P.: Neural-symbolic argumentation mining: an argument in favor of deep learning and reasoning. Frontiers in Big Data 2 (2020)
6. d'Avila Garcez, A.S., Gori, M., Lamb, L.C., Serafini, L., Spranger, M., Tran, S.N.: Neural-symbolic computing: an effective methodology for principled integration of machine learning and reasoning. J. Appl. Log. **6**(4), 611–632 (2019)
7. Habernal, I., Gurevych, I.: Argumentation mining in user-generated web discourse. Comput. Linguist. **43**(1), 125–179 (2017)
8. He, P., Liu, X., Gao, J., Chen, W.: DeBERTa: Decoding-enhanced BERT with disentangled attention. In: Proceedings of the International Conference on Learning Representations (2021)

9. Hulpus, I., Kobbe, J., Meilicke, C., Stuckenschmidt, H., Becker, M., Opitz, J., Nastase, V., Frank, A.: Towards explaining natural language arguments with background knowledge. In: Joint Proceedings of the International Workshop on Dataset PROFILing and Search, and the Workshop on Semantic Explainability, co-located with the International Semantic Web Conference (2019)

10. Manhaeve, R., Dumančić, S., Kimmig, A., Demeester, T., De Raedt, L.: Neural probabilistic logic programming in DeepProbLog. Artif. Intell. **298** (2021)

11. Reimers, N., Schiller, B., Beck, T., Daxenberger, J., Stab, C., Gurevych, I.: Classification and clustering of arguments with contextualized word embeddings. In: Proceedings of the Annual Meeting of the Association for Computational Linguistics (2019)

12. Ren, W., Liu, J., Shroff, N.: Sample complexity bounds for active ranking from multi-wise comparisons. In: Proceedings of the Annual Meeting on Neural Information Processing Systems (2021)

13. Stede, M., Schneider, J.: Argumentation mining. Synth. Lect. Hum. Lang. Technol. **11**, 1–191 (2018)

14. Toledo, A., Gretz, S., Cohen-Karlik, E., Friedman, R., Venezian, E., Lahav, D., Jacovi, M., Aharonov, R., Slonim, N.: Automatic argument quality assessment-new datasets and methods. In: Proceedings of the Conference on Empirical Methods in Natural Language Processing (2019)

15. Toulmin, S.E.: The Uses of Argument. Cambridge University Press (2003)

16. Trautmann, D., Daxenberger, J., Stab, C., Schutze, H., Gurevych, I.: Fine-grained argument unit recognition and classification. In: Proceedings of the AAAI Conference on Artificial Intelligence (2020)

17. Wang, Y., Wang, L., Li, Y., He, D., Liu, T.Y., Chen, W.: A theoretical analysis of NDCG type ranking measures. In: Proceedings of the Conference on Learning Theory (2013)

Event Extraction for Portuguese: A QA-Driven Approach Using ACE-2005

Luís Filipe Cunha[1,2,4(✉)], Ricardo Campos[1,3], and Alípio Jorge[1,2]

[1] LIAAD-INESC TEC, Porto, Portugal
lfc@di.uminho.pt, ricardo.campos@ubi.pt, amjorge@fc.up.pt
[2] FCUP-University of Porto, Porto, Portugal
[3] University of Beira Interior, Covilhã, Portugal
[4] University of Minho, Braga, Portugal
http://www.inesctec.pt

Abstract. Event extraction is an Information Retrieval task that commonly consists of identifying the central word for the event (trigger) and the event's arguments. This task has been extensively studied for English but lags behind for Portuguese, partly due to the lack of task-specific annotated corpora. This paper proposes a framework in which two separated BERT-based models were fine-tuned to identify and classify events in Portuguese documents. We decompose this task into two sub-tasks. Firstly, we use a token classification model to detect event triggers. To extract event arguments, we train a Question Answering model that queries the triggers about their corresponding event argument roles. Given the lack of event annotated corpora in Portuguese, we translated the original version of the ACE-2005 dataset (a reference in the field) into Portuguese, producing a new corpus for Portuguese event extraction. To accomplish this, we developed an automatic translation pipeline. Our framework obtains F1 marks of 64.4 for trigger classification and 46.7 for argument classification setting, thus a new state of the art reference for these tasks in Portuguese.

Keywords: Event extraction · Question answer · Corpus translation

1 Introduction

Over the years, event extraction has been extensively studied and found to be a difficult information extraction task [17]. It aims to extract structured data regarding "something that happens" in a text, often understood as a specific occurrence involving one or more participants. According to the Automatic Content Extraction (ACE) 2005 annotation guidelines [1], this involves an event mention, trigger, type, argument and corresponding role:

- **Event mention**: a phrase or sentence in which an event occurs, including one trigger and an arbitrary number of arguments.
- **Event trigger**: the word that expresses an event occurrence.

N. Moniz et al. (Eds.): EPIA 2023, LNAI 14115, pp. 402–414, 2023.
https://doi.org/10.1007/978-3-031-49008-8_32

- **Event type**: represents a high-level categorization of events based on their general semantic meaning. It can be composed of sub-types that provide a more specific categorization of events.
- **Event argument**: an entity mention, temporal expression or value that serves as a participant or attribute with a specific role in an event mention.
- **Argument role**: indicates the semantic relationship of the argument within the event, such as the agent that performs the action, the time or location of the event, etc.

Typically, event mentions consist of an event trigger and their corresponding event arguments. Consider the following sentence, which illustrates the process of automatically identifying and classifying the event triggers and their corresponding arguments found in the text.

"Elvis Presley morreu de ataque cardíaco em 1977, Memphis, Tennessee."
(Elvis Presley died of a heart attack in 1977, Memphis, Tennessee.)

In this example, the word *"morreu"* (died) is an event trigger of type Life.Die and "Elvis Presley" is an event argument with role Victim.

While several English event extraction systems already exist [2,25,36], they reveal poor portability to other languages due to dependencies on English annotated textual resources. In this paper, we aim to tackle this problem in the context of the Portuguese language.

In particular, we aim to develop a method that allows for the extraction of event mentions by leveraging the power of Transformers-based models [34]. To address this problem, we divided the event extraction task into two sub-tasks: Trigger extraction and Argument Extraction.

We approach trigger identification and classification as a Token Classification task. Then for the Argument extraction, we use a Question Answering (QA) model (inspired by Du et al. [9]) where we question the event trigger about its corresponding event argument roles. To perform these tasks, we used BERTimbau [33], a BERT [6] model pre-trained on Portuguese textual data. We fine-tuned this model with event annotations from a Portuguese translated version of ACE-2005 [7], containing textual data annotated with event triggers and corresponding arguments. For the QA task, we also experimented with the SQuAD [30] dataset in order to train our model to perform extractive QA.

Since ACE-2005 was not available in Portuguese, and the Portuguese annotated corpora we found [4,10] did not contain explicit annotations for both event triggers and arguments, we decided to automatically translate the ACE-2005 corpus from English to Portuguese. For this purpose, we developed a translation pipeline that enabled us to automate the translation and alignment tasks. This translated dataset is an important contribution to this current work.

The main **contributions** of this work are listed below:

- A pipeline for dataset translation and annotation alignment that allows the translation of annotated datasets to the Portuguese language.

- Based on this pipeline, we produced a new dataset by translating ACE 2005 for Portuguese, which is already in the process of being accepted at the Linguistic Data Consortium (LDC) repository.
- Using the Portuguese version of ACE-2005 corpus, we produced and deployed event extraction models. These models correspond to a baseline for Portuguese event extraction.
- Based on the produced models, we developed and made available on Huggingface Hub, an event extraction framework for the Portuguese language.

2   Related Work

Event extraction is a fundamental task in Natural Language Processing (NLP) that has been widely researched in recent years mainly for English and with less attention to other languages. Over the years, several approaches have been proposed to tackle this task, ranging from traditional rule-based methods to more advanced machine learning and deep learning techniques [14, 18].

Recent works Du et al. [9] have demonstrated promising results using QA models in event extraction. The authors leveraged BERT [6] models fine-tuned on the ACE-2005 corpus, to identify event triggers and corresponding arguments.

Huang et al. [13] addressed event extraction by using Zero-Shot Learning to handle the scarcity of annotated data and the limited range of event types, which constrains the applicability of this task to certain domains. They drew inspiration from Pustejovsky et al. [26], who proposed that the semantics of an event structure can be generalized to different event mentions. Following this idea, they used an event ontology that defines structures for each event type. The authors used Abstract Meaning Representations (AMR) [3] to identify the event triggers and argument candidates, constructing a structure for each event.

Although event argument extraction has been primarily approached as a sentence-level task, it should be noted that in real-world scenarios, the arguments of an event can be dispersed across multiple sentences. To address this problem, Li et al. [19] propose a document-level approach for argument extraction. They use a generative model (BART [16], T5 [28]) that is conditioned by the input sequence and unfilled templates created from an event ontology. The model is responsible for filling those templates with a limited vocabulary in order to prevent it from "hallucinating".

Despite the advances in this particular area, little has been done for the Portuguese language. Quaresma et al. [27] implemented an Event Extraction framework for the Portuguese language, focused on the crime investigation domain. Their framework relied on Semantic Role Labeling to extract event arguments and was validated on PropBank [10] corpus. The authors did not classify events by type and instead focused on the roles provided by the SRL schema, such as Actor, Place, Time, and Object. Consequently, it would be difficult to compare their work with ours as ACE-2005 contains 33 different event types.

The same applies to the work developed by Costa and Branco [5]. They used feature engineering combined with a decision tree trained on the TimeBankPT corpus to extract events from Portuguese texts. However, the TimeBankPT corpus event annotations only contain the following event types: REPORTING, OCCURRENCE, STATE, I_STATE, and I_ACTION. These annotations lack detail on event structure compared to ACE-2005, specifically the event arguments and roles.

3 Methodology

This section will discuss the methodologies used to extract event triggers (Sect. 3.1) and event arguments (Sect. 3.2). To achieve this, we fine-tune a Portuguese BERT model [33] with a Portuguese-translated version of the ACE-2005 corpus (more details in Sect. 4.1). We fine-tined the model for token classification and Question Answer tasks to extract event triggers and event arguments, respectively.

3.1 Trigger Extraction

For the first task, we train a model that identifies and classifies event triggers. The task is formulated as a token classification one. Given a sequence of N_1 tokens $W = [w1, w2, ..., wN_1]$ and a fixed set of event types (None type included) of length N_2 $A = [a1, a2, ..., aN_2]$ our model assigns each token from W to their corresponding label from A.

To perform this task we used BERTimbau [33], a BERT-based model that was pre-trained on Portuguese texts. We fine-tuned this model on token classification using the Portuguese-translated version of the ACE-2005 corpus. For that, we converted the translated corpus to the IOB scheme [31] (**B**eginning, **I**nside and **O**utside) where a label is assigned to each token of the text sequence. We consider the 9 event types and 33 event sub-types contained in ACE-2005 as labels for token classification task.

3.2 Argument Extraction

To extract arguments from the text, we used extractive QA, where we formulated questions about the event to obtain the argument roles. These questions are influenced by each specific trigger word. Given a sentence S and a question Q, this task aims to find the token span offsets where the corresponding answer a lies in S. In order to accomplish this objective, we fine-tuned the BERTimbau model in a QA task.

The input sequence format is described below:

$$[\textbf{CLS}] \text{ question}(\textbf{Q}) \text{ } [\textbf{SEP}] \text{ sentence } (\textbf{S})[\textbf{SEP}]$$

In this format, we have the BERT classification token CLS and the SEP token that separates the S and Q input text sequences. The model outputs logits for the start (a_{start}) and end (a_{end}) positions of the answer to each token of the input sequence. Before selecting the most probable answer offsets, several validations must be performed to ensure that the answer span is valid. For instance, the answer a should be fully contained within the sentence S and not part of the question Q; The start offset a_{start} cannot be greater than the end offset a_{end}, etc. These validations are common procedures in the QA task.

Questions Generation In the following, we outline how we generated the actual questions for fine-tuning the model. We adopted a template-based approach, similar to Du et al. [9] and Lyu et al. [22]. Based on the event type, we can determine the appropriate questions to ask in order to extract specific arguments. In ACE-2005, each event type has a predetermined set of argument roles. We generated a question template for each event type by creating a set of questions (in Portuguese) based on the event type's corresponding roles. Each question of the template expects to obtain as an answer the argument associated with each role. We referred to the argument roles description provided in the ACE-2005 annotation guidelines to generate these questions.

Table 1 contains the questions used to extract the arguments of an event type LIFE.DIE. Following the guidelines [1], we know that this event type can have five different argument roles: Agent, Victim, Instrument, Time and Place.

Table 1. Question templates for the event type LIFE.DIE.

Role	Question (Portuguese)	Question (English)
Agent	*Quem é o assassino?*	Who is the assassin?
Victim	*Quem morre?*	Who died?
Instrument	*Qual é o instrumento utilizado?*	What is the used instrument?
Time	*Quando ocorre a morte?*	When is the death?
Place	*Onde ocorre a morte?*	Where is the death?

Then, to contextualize the question within the event mention, we concatenate it with the event trigger word, a method that has shown to improve the model results [9]. We use the following question format: {question} + in {trigger}?. For instance, in our example of Sect. 1, we have an event of type LIFE.DIE. In order to extract the argument role Time, the following question is generated:

Quando ocorre a morte + em morreu?
(When is the death + in died?)

Given this prompt, the model should output the answer span corresponding to "*em 1977*" (in 1997). The model uses the generated questions to extract each argument role from the text. Given an event mention and an event trigger, we replicate this procedure for all the event arguments.

Impossible Answer It's important for the model to be able to identify questions that do not have a correct answer. In fact, not all event argument roles can be found in every event mention. For instance, in the example provided, the `Agent` argument role cannot be found in the text, which implies that the question "Who is the assassin?" should not have a correct answer.

To address this problem, we trained the model to predict the "impossible" answer. During the training phase, we gave the model several questions without any answer. In these cases, the answer span offsets are assigned to the index 0 of the input sequence corresponding to the BERT CLS token. By doing so, during inference, our model is able to filter out the roles that may not be present in the text by giving the highest probability to the CLS token. In that case, we consider that the argument role is not present in the current event mention.

4 Data

When it comes to the event extraction task, ACE-2005 is considered the standard corpus in this field. While other corpora such as PropBank focus on the annotation of predicate-argument structure, ACE-2005 goes beyond this by providing information on the overall event structure, including the event type and its corresponding argument roles. It is available in English, Chinese, and Arabic, however, there is no version of this dataset in Portuguese. We decided to take the effort of translating the dataset, thus being able to work with this valuable resource for Portuguese. In this work, we used a translated version of ACE-2005 in Portuguese, which contains 5 526 event mentions consisting of 5 526 event triggers and 9 649 corresponding event arguments.

We have also used the well known SQuAD corpus [30] for training an extractive question answering model. It consists of articles obtained from Wikipedia and a set of corresponding questions and answers about each article. In this work, we used two versions of this dataset: SQuAD1.1, which contains 100 000 questions and respective answers; SQuAD2.0 [29], which contains 150 000 questions and answers. The latter version contains all the questions from version 1.0, however, it contains 50 000 additional questions that have no correct answers. In version 2.0, one must consider the impossible answer scenario when finding the correct answer, creating a more challenging QA task. A Portuguese version of SQuAD 1.0 was already available from the Deep Learning Brasil Group[1], however, we took the effort of translating version 2.0.

4.1 ACE-2005 Translation

In this section, we provide an overview of the ACE-2005 corpus translation process. Although we use automatic translation, translating an annotated dataset can become particularly challenging when it comes to aligning its annotations. In fact, mismatches can occur between the annotations and their occurrences in

---

[1] http://www.deeplearningbrasil.com.br/.

the corresponding sentence. For instance, in sentence "The troops land on the shore", ACE-2005 states that the trigger "land" should be extracted. However, the word "land" is translated to *"terra"* (land as a noun) in isolation and to *"desembarcam"* (land as a verb) in context.

In the pre-processing[2] of ACE-2005, each event annotation was assigned to its corresponding text sentence. Then, we automatically translated each sentence, its corresponding triggers and arguments. These translations resulted in annotations' miss-alignments i.e., translated annotations that were not contained in the translated sentences. In order to align these cases, we developed an alignment pipeline that is composed of four components: lemmatization, multiple translations, a BERT-based world aligner and fuzzy string similarity.

Regarding lemmatization, instead of directly matching the annotations to their respective sentence, we calculated lemma tokens from both the translated sentence and the corresponding translated annotations. Then, we performed the matching process using these lemma tokens. If that method was not able to find a match, we proceed to the next element of the pipeline. In particular, we used Microsoft Dictionary Lookup API to retrieve alternative translations of the event annotations and tried to match them in their sentences.

The third component of our pipeline involved aligning the annotations with a parallel corpus word aligner, proposed in Dou et al. [8]. In practice, we used the embeddings retrieved from the BERT-Multilingual model [6] in order to compute the correspondence between each token of the source sentences (English) and the translated sentences (Portuguese). Then by looking at the English annotations words, we calculated the corresponding Portuguese annotations.

Finally, if the previous approaches could not solve the miss-alignment, we used character-level similarity algorithms such as Levenshtein distance [15] and Gestalt pattern matching [32]. This approach allowed us to identify the substring within the sentence that was most similar to the annotations.

4.2 SQuAD Translation

In this work, we used a version of SQuAD1.1 that had been previously translated into Portuguese. To create a Portuguese version of the SQuAD2.0 dataset, we automatically translated the additional 50,000 impossible questions. Since these questions do not have a valid answer within the article's text, performing annotation alignments to this dataset was unnecessary.

5 Modeling

To validate our approach we use the translated ACE-2005 corpus for training and testing, as well as the translated SQuAD datasets for modeling question-answering. We aim to assess the following: (1) the success of the trigger identification and classification approach; (2) the success of the question answering

---

[2] https://github.com/nlpcl-lab/ace2005-preprocessing.

approach for argument classification; (3) the impact of training the model to detect the absence of event arguments. Given the lack of other works in Portuguese, we compare our work with the results obtained by state of the art approaches for the same tasks on the original ACE-2005 corpus.

Our first setup was to fine-tune the BERTimbau model [33] with the train split from our translated version of ACE-2005 (BERT-PT-ACE05). We used the event trigger annotations to train the token classification model and the argument annotations to train the QA model.

Then, for the argument extraction task, we used an existing Portuguese QA model [12] (pre-trained on SQuAD1.1 dataset) and fine-tune it with the ACE-2005 data (BERT-PT-SQuAD1.1-ACE05). The motivation of this approach consisted of teaching the model to answer general questions first and then using that knowledge to answer our event-driven questions to extract the event arguments. Due to the nature of the SQuAD1.1 dataset, the Portuguese QA model [12] is not able to output impossible answers.

Next, we tested a similar approach, but instead of using a QA model based on SQuAD1.1, we fine-tuned the BERTimbau model with SQuAD2.0 so the model could learn how to identify impossible answers. Subsequently, we used ACE-2005 data so the model learns how to extract the event arguments (BERT-PT-SQuAD2.0-ACE05). As stated before, dealing with impossible answers is important because not all event argument roles are present in every event.

6   Results

Our models were validated on the test split of ACE-2005 containing 422 event triggers and 892 arguments. We ensured a fairer comparison with state-of-the-art in English by using the same data splits and evaluation criteria as previous works [9,17]. A correct identification and classification of an event trigger requires matching its offsets and event type with the gold-standard. An event argument's correct identification and classification demands matching its offsets with the ACE-2005 annotations and ensuring its semantic role is accurate. In other words, matching between extracted elements and ground truth must be exact.

On Table 2 is presented a comparison of our results using the ACE in Portuguese against SOTA event extraction methods using the original ACE 2005. The evaluation metrics are Precision (P), Recall (R) and F1 scores. Looking at the trigger extraction task, our F1 for Portuguese is about 10% below F1 for English. This superiority, also observable for argument extraction (nearly 15%), is probably due to the translation effects and language specifics. As for the arguments, one can observe a slightly positive impact of using question-answering and a clearer impact of allowing non-answers (more details in Sect. 7).

Finally, for direct qualitative evaluation, we developed and deployed a Web application[3] that functions as an interface for the proposed event extraction framework making our models accessible and usable.

---

[3] https://hf.co/spaces/lfcc/Event-Extractor.

Table 2. Event Extraction results on ACE-2005 dataset.

Model	Trigger classification			Argument classification		
	P	R	F1	P	R	F1
English ACE-2005						
JRNN 2016 [25]	73.0	66.0	69.3	56.7	54.2	55.4
JointEntityEvent 2016 [36]	75.1	63.3	68.7	70.6	36.9	48.4
GAIL-ELMo 2019 [37]	74.8	69.4	72.0	61.6	45.7	52.4
BERT_QA_Arg 2020 [9]	71.1	73.7	72.4	56.8	50.2	53.3
OneIE 2020 [20]	–	–	74.7	–	–	56.8
Text2Event 2021 [21]	69.6	74.4	71.9	52.5	55.2	53.8
FourIE 2021 [23]	–	–	75.4	–	–	58.0
GraphIE 2022 [24]	–	–	**75.7**	–	–	**59.4**
Portuguese ACE-2005						
BERT-PT-ACE05	63.6	65.3	64.4	46.3	45.1	45.7
BERT-PT-SQuAD1.1-ACE05	–	–	–	45.7	46.3	46.0
BERT-PT-SQuAD2.0-ACE05	–	–	–	46.8	46.6	**46.7**

7   Discussion

Our models for Portuguese were trained using automatically translated data. However, the automatic translation still faces many challenges, including accurately capturing the nuances of language, handling idiomatic expressions, and dealing with cultural language differences. Therefore, it is important to be aware of these limitations and expect some noise in the translated data.

Another limitation we found was the annotation alignment. In fact, we used several techniques to improve our results in the alignment of the trigger and argument span annotations. Despite that, we know there are still alignment errors, causing triggers and arguments to be wrongly annotated. Consider the following sentence "We discussed the Middle East peace process" and the corresponding translation "*Discutimos o processo de paz no Médio Oriente*". In this sentence, the word "discussed" is an event trigger of type `Contact.Meet` while the word "We" corresponds to an event argument playing the role `Entity`. However, in the Portuguese translation, the sequence "We discussed" was translated into "*Discutimos*" (the verb was conjugated in the first person plural). The argument "We" became implicit, making the annotation hard to align.

Furthermore, in addition to the translation noise, we believe that the event extraction difficulty for English and Portuguese languages is not the same. For instance, the Portuguese language has a greater diversity of words. This is the case of the conjugation of verbs. Looking at the trigger words, the ACE-2005 corpus has about 1237 different trigger words in total, while the Portuguese translated version has 1900 trigger words. Although we show comparative results of our work against SOTA English models, it is not entirely fair to make a direct comparison given the differences in language and cultural context.

As for the results, our validation data was translated in the exact same manner as our training data, which means that it also contains the translation and alignment noise we mentioned above. It would be interesting to validate our models against data revised by humans, ensuring a higher data quality.

In fact, we employed identical metrics as previous works to compare our outcomes. Nonetheless, the strict evaluation metrics hide many near misses. Consider the following example:

Gold Argument: *ex-banqueiro sênior Callum McCarthy*
Predicted Argument: *O ex-banqueiro sênior Callum McCarthy*
(The former senior banker Callum McCarthy)

In this case, our model prediction closely matches the ground truth but receives no credit for it because it fails to identify the determinant "O" (the).

Finally, another limitation of our method is that ACE-2005 annotations are sentence-level, causing our models to have difficulties extracting cross-sentence event arguments. In order to attenuate this problem, our deployed framework uses a context window that works as a hyperparameter allowing us to consider more than one sentence as context for the QA task.

8   Conclusion

This work proposes a novel method for extracting events from Portuguese text. Our approach involves two tasks: first, we classify and identify event triggers using token classification; Then, we extract event arguments using extractive QA. To train models capable of performing those tasks, we fine-tune the BERTimbau model with SQuAD and ACE-2005 datasets, the latter being a reference in the event extraction field. Since these datasets were not available in Portuguese, we developed a translation pipeline to automatically translate them. We present a new event extraction baseline for Portuguese using the ACE-2005 dataset translated into Portuguese. As we could not find any comparable works in Portuguese, we used existing English event extraction works as a benchmark. While our models achieved lower results compared to the English models, we believe the comparison cannot be made directly due to language differences.

For future work, considering the lack of extensive research on this task for Portuguese, there are numerous suitable approaches that could improve our results. For example, expanding our data domain by incorporating other event-driven datasets, such as TAC KBP 2015 [11] and MINION [35]. We could also leverage Semantic Role Labeling for Portuguese in order to enhance the performance of event argument extraction.

Acknowledgments. The authors of this paper were financed by National Funds through the FCT–Fundação para a Ciência e a Tecnologia, I.P. (Portuguese Foundation for Science and Technology) within the project StorySense, with reference 2022.09312.PTDC)

References

1. English annotation guidelines for events. Linguistic Data Consortium (2005). https://www.ldc.upenn.edu/sites/www.ldc.upenn.edu/files/english-events-guidelines-v5.4.3.pdf
2. Balali, A., Asadpour, M., Campos, R., Jatowt, A.: Joint event extraction along shortest dependency paths using graph convolutional networks. Knowl. Based Syst. **210**, 106492 (2020). https://doi.org/10.1016/j.knosys.2020.106492
3. Banarescu, L., Bonial, C., Cai, S., Georgescu, M., Griffitt, K., Hermjakob, U., Knight, K., Koehn, P., Palmer, M., Schneider, N.: Abstract Meaning Representation for sembanking. In: Proceedings of the 7th Linguistic Annotation Workshop and Interoperability with Discourse, pp. 178–186. Sofia, Bulgaria (Aug 2013)
4. Costa, F., Branco, A.: Temporal information processing of a new language: fast porting with minimal resources. In: Proceedings of the 48th Annual Meeting of the Association for Computational Linguistics, pp. 671–677. Sweden (July 2010)
5. Costa, F., Branco, A.: Lx-timeanalyzer: a temporal information processing system for Portuguese (2012). http://hdl.handle.net/10455/6796
6. Devlin, J., Chang, M., Lee, K., Toutanova, K.: BERT: pre-training of deep bidirectional transformers for language understanding (2018). CoRR arXiv:abs/1810.04805
7. Doddington, G., Mitchell, A., Przybocki, M., Ramshaw, L., Strassel, S., Weischedel, R.: The automatic content extraction (ACE) program-tasks, data, and evaluation. In: Proceedings of the Fourth International Conference on Language Resources and Evaluation (LREC'04). European Language Resources Association (ELRA), Lisbon, Portugal (May 2004)
8. Dou, Z.Y., Neubig, G.: Word alignment by fine-tuning embeddings on parallel corpora. EACL 2021–16th Conference of the European Chapter of the Association for Computational Linguistics, Proceedings of the Conference, pp. 2112–2128 (2021)
9. Du, X., Cardie, C.: Event extraction by answering (almost) natural questions. EMNLP 2020–2020 Conference on Empirical Methods in Natural Language Processing, Proceedings of the Conference, pp. 671–683 (2020)
10. Duran, M.S., Aluísio, S.M.: Propbank-br: a brazilian treebank annotated with semantic role labels. In: LREC, pp. 1862–1867 (2012)
11. Ellis, J., Getman, J., Fore, D., Kuster, N., Song, Z., Bies, A., Strassel, S.: Overview of linguistic resources for the tac kbp 2015 evaluations: methodologies and results
12. Guillou, P.: Portuguese bert base cased qa (question answering), finetuned on squad v1.1 (2021)
13. Huang, L., Ji, H., Cho, K., Voss, C.R.: Zero-shot transfer learning for event extraction (2017). CoRR arXiv:abs/1707.01066
14. Lai, V.D.: Event extraction: a survey (2022)
15. Levenshtein, V.I.: Binary codes capable of correcting deletions, insertions, and reversals **163**(4), 845–848 (1965)
16. Lewis, M., Liu, Y., Goyal, N., Ghazvininejad, M., Mohamed, A., Levy, O., Stoyanov, V., Zettlemoyer, L.: Bart: Denoising sequence-to-sequence pre-training for natural language generation, translation, and comprehension (2019)
17. Li, Q., Ji, H., Huang, L.: Joint event extraction via structured prediction with global features. In: Proceedings of the 51st Annual Meeting of the Association for Computational Linguistics (Volume 1: Long Papers), pp. 73–82. Bulgaria (2013)
18. Li, Q., Li, J., Sheng, J., Cui, S., Wu, J., Hei, Y., Peng, H., Guo, S., Wang, L., Beheshti, A., Yu, P.S.: A survey on deep learning event extraction: approaches and applications (2022)

19. Li, S., Ji, H., Han, J.: Document-level event argument extraction by conditional generation (2021). CoRR arXiv:abs/2104.05919
20. Lin, Y., Ji, H., Huang, F., Wu, L.: A joint neural model for information extraction with global features. In: Proceedings of the 58th Annual Meeting of the Association for Computational Linguistics, pp. 7999–8009 (Jul 2020)
21. Lu, Y., Lin, H., Xu, J., Han, X., Tang, J., Li, A., Sun, L., Liao, M., Chen, S.: Text2Event: controllable sequence-to-structure generation for end-to-end event extraction. In: Proceedings of the 59th Annual Meeting of the Association for Computational Linguistics and the 11th International Joint Conference on Natural Language Processing (Volume 1: Long Papers), pp. 2795–2806 (Aug 2021)
22. Lyu, Q., Zhang, H., Sulem, E., Roth, D.: Zero-shot event extraction via transfer learning: Challenges and insights. In: Proceedings of the 59th Annual Meeting of the Association for Computational Linguistics and the 11th International Joint Conference on Natural Language Processing (Volume 2: Short Papers) (Aug 2021)
23. Nguyen, M.V., Lai, V.D., Nguyen, T.H.: Cross-task instance representation interactions and label dependencies for joint information extraction with graph convolutional networks. In: Proceedings of the 2021 Conference of the North American Chapter of the Association for Computational Linguistics: Human Language Technologies, pp. 27–38 (Jun 2021). https://doi.org/10.18653/v1/2021.naacl-main.3
24. Nguyen, M.V., Min, B., Dernoncourt, F., Nguyen, T.: Joint extraction of entities, relations, and events via modeling inter-instance and inter-label dependencies. In: Proceedings of the 2022 Conference of the North American Chapter of the Association for Computational Linguistics: Human Language Technologies, pp. 4363–4374. United States (Jul 2022). https://doi.org/10.18653/v1/2022.naacl-main.324
25. Nguyen, T.H., Cho, K., Grishman, R.: Joint event extraction via recurrent neural networks. In: Proceedings of the 2016 Conference of the North American Chapter of the Association for Computational Linguistics: Human Language Technologies, pp. 300–309. California (Jun 2016). https://doi.org/10.18653/v1/N16-1034
26. Pustejovsky, J.: The syntax of event structure. Cognition **41**(1), 47–81 (1991). https://doi.org/10.1016/0010-0277(91)90032-Y
27. Quaresma, P., NogueDu2020ira, V.B., Raiyani, K., Bayot, R.: Event extraction and representation: a case study for the Portuguese language. Information (2019)
28. Raffel, C., Shazeer, N., Roberts, A., Lee, K., Narang, S., Matena, M., Zhou, Y., Li, W., Liu, P.J.: Exploring the limits of transfer learning with a unified text-to-text transformer (2020)
29. Rajpurkar, P., Jia, R., Liang, P.: Know what you don't know: Unanswerable questions for squad
30. Rajpurkar, P., Zhang, J., Lopyrev, K., Liang, P.: Squad: 100,000+ questions for machine comprehension of text. In: EMNLP 2016-Conference on Empirical Methods in Natural Language Processing, Proceedings, pp. 2383–2392 (Jun 2016)
31. Ramshaw, L.A., Marcus, M.P.: Text chunking using transformation-based learning (1995). CoRR arXiv:cmp-lg/9505040
32. Ratcliff, J.W., Metzener, D.E.: Pattern-matching-the gestalt approach. Dr Dobbs J. **13**(7), 46 (1988)
33. Souza, F., Nogueira, R., Lotufo, R.: Bertimbau: pretrained bert models for Brazilian Portuguese. In: Cerri, R., Prati, R.C. (eds.) Intelligent Systems, pp. 403–417. Springer International Publishing, Cham (2020)
34. Vaswani, A., Shazeer, N., Parmar, N., Uszkoreit, J., Jones, L., Gomez, A.N., Kaiser, L., Polosukhin, I.: Attention is all you need (2017)
35. Veyseh, A.P.B., Nguyen, M.V., Dernoncourt, F., Nguyen, T.H.: MINION: a large-scale and diverse dataset for multilingual event detection. CoRR (2022)

36. Yang, B., Mitchell, T.M.: Joint extraction of events and entities within a document context (2016). CoRR arXiv:abs/1609.03632
37. Zhang, T., Ji, H., Sil, A.: Joint entity and event extraction with generative adversarial imitation learning. Data Intell. **1**(2), 99–120 (2019)

Symbolic Versus Deep Learning Techniques for Explainable Sentiment Analysis

Shamsuddeen Hassan Muhammad[1,3]([✉]), Pavel Brazdil[2,3], and Alípio Jorge[1,3]

[1] FCUP, U.Porto, Porto, Portugal
shamsuddeen2004@gmail.com, amjorge@fc.up.pt
[2] FEP, U.Porto, Porto, Portugal
pbrazdil@inesctec.pt
[3] INESCTEC, Porto, Portugal

Abstract. Deep learning approaches have become popular in many different areas, including sentiment analysis (SA), because of their competitive performance. However, the downside of this approach is that they do not provide understandable explanations on how the sentiment values are calculated. In contrast, previous approaches that used sentiment lexicons can do that, but their performance is normally not high. To leverage the strengths of both approaches, we present a neuro-symbolic approach that combines deep learning (DL) and symbolic methods for SA tasks. The DL approach uses a pre-trained language model (PLM) to construct sentiment lexicon. The symbolic approach exploits the constructed *sentiment lexicon* and manually constructed *shifter patterns* to determine the sentiment of a sentence. Our experimental results show that the proposed approach leads to promising results with the additional advantage that sentiment predictions can be accompanied by understandable explanations.

Keywords: Sentiment analysis · Shifter patterns · Neuro-symbolic approach

1 Introduction

Sentiment analysis is an important task in Natural Language Processing that computationally determines the sentiment expressed in a text. Approaches to sentiment analysis include lexicon-based, machine learning-based, and recently deep learning (DL) approaches that achieve state-of-the-art performance [24]. However, DL has the limitation of not providing satisfactory explanations for how sentiment values are derived. In contrast, lexicon-based sentiment analysis systems can do that, but generally perform poorly compared to DL approaches. Therefore, it is worth exploring whether these two approaches can be combined

N. Moniz et al. (Eds.): EPIA 2023, LNAI 14115, pp. 415–427, 2023.
https://doi.org/10.1007/978-3-031-49008-8_33

to leverage their respective strengths [2, 4, 16], following the recent trend in neuro-symbolic research [3, 15]. Symbolic approaches refer to methods that rely on high-level symbolic (human-readable) representations of problems and their solutions, using, for instance, rules or similar constructs.

Neuro-symbolic approaches to sentiment analysis can be divided into two main groups. The first and most widely used approach involves works that aim to improve the performance of the deep learning approach by providing external additional information in a symbolic form, such as sentiment lexicons. The other, group involves works whose focus is to provide explanations regarding how the sentiment predictions are obtained while leveraging deep learning approaches to attain better performance. Our approach falls into the latter group.

We propose a combined approach that leverages symbolic and deep learning (DL) approaches to enhance the performance of symbolic approaches to sentiment analysis (SA) tasks. To be competitive, the symbolic system uses, besides the sentiment lexicon, also *shifter patterns*. Shifters are specific terms that change the polarity of associated words or phrases and so capture certain contextual information, leading to enhanced performance. The experimental results show that the proposed approach leads to promising results, substantially better than the results of a pure lexicon-based approach.

2   Related Work

There are many approaches to sentiment analysis, including lexicon-, machine learning-, and in particular, deep learning-based approaches.

Lexicon-based approaches to sentiment analysis can be divided into different groups based on the lexicon construction approach used. It can be manual, semi-automated, or automatic [11, 20]. The disadvantage of manual approaches is that the preparation of the lexicon requires a considerable effort. On the other hand, *Semi-automatic approaches* to lexicon enhancement start with a relatively small lexicon that contains certain important *seed words* provided manually. The process of label propagation is used to transfer the values from the seed words to other terms with similar meaning [14, 21]. *Automatic approaches* construct sentiment lexicon automatically from annotated texts [1, 4, 23].

It is well known that the same word may convey different sentiment values in different domains. For example, the word *grow* in *the share has grown* has a positive orientation, as is the case in the financial domain. On the other hand, the same word that appears in a sentence like *the tumour has grown*, from the medical domain, has a negative semantic orientation. Therefore, there is a need to consider a specific context. One way to achieve this is by employing so-called *sentiment shifters*, discussed further on.

Deep learning (DL) approaches use neural network architectures to automatically learn features and provide state-of-the-art performance [4, 9, 19, 22, 31]. State-of-the-art DL approaches use the transformer architecture and exploit the idea of self-attention and positional encoding [30]. Transformers have the ability to use as input longer word sequences and so can learn from larger contexts.

Transformer-based pre-trained models, such as *BERT* [8] and *RoBERTa* [18], are used in many NLP tasks, including, e.g., text classification and machine translation. The multilingual variants of these models, such as, *mBERT* [8], can adapt to other languages that were not included in pre-training [13,22]. Recently, some research has focused on combining symbolic and deep learning-based approaches—a neuro-symbolic approach.

The aim of some **neuro-symbolic approaches** approaches that exploit DL is to enhance its performance by providing additional information in a symbolic form, such as *Concept Net* [12,17]. Ghosal et al. [12] addressed the problem of cross-domain sentiment analysis, by exploring ConceptNet to enrich the given text. This was done by providing both information about domain-general and domain-specific concepts. Kocoń et al. [16] used information from different knowledge bases to feed into their DL models.

Various authors compared different approaches to SA. Atteweldt et al. [2] compared different approaches for SA on a Dutch corpus in economic domain. The study showed that a given off-the-shelf sentiment lexicons did not perform well, when compared to machine learning (ML) methods, particularly DL methods (CNN). Tavares et al. [28] explored the classification of sentiment from economic news headlines in Portuguese newspapers. Among the ML approaches, the best results were obtained by SVM but these were surpassed by a rule-based approach that was developed manually. The work discussed in [4] compared a lexicon-based approach enhanced with shifters with the DL approach (BERT-based). This paper continues with this work and extends it, for instance, by extending the types of shifters used. Catelli et al. [6] also compared lexicon-based and deep learning-based approaches. They used a network of local grammars to compute the sentiment values of words surrounded by contexts. Although the results of DL approach were better, the difference from the symbolic approach was not very high. The fact that the enhanced lexicon-based approach provided competitive performance to deep learning encouraged us to seek further improvements, which are discussed in the next section.

3 Combining Symbolic and Deep Learning for SA

The design of the proposed approach reflected the following objectives: (1) provide good performance in SA tasks, and (2) provide explainable solutions. To achieve the second objective, we exploit a symbolic system at the top level. As DL systems often achieve better performance, a DL system was used to generate a sentiment lexicon. The general architecture of the proposed system is illustrated in Fig. 1. We note that we exploit two alternative ways of generating the sentiment lexicon. One uses labelled sentence fractions supplied to a learning system to create a lexicon (Ecolex), following [4]. The second one uses the same input to fine-tune a pre-trained language model and is subsequently used to construct a sentiment lexicon (DeepLex).

The performance of the chosen sentiment lexicon is further enhanced by exploiting *shifter patterns* that capture some interrelationships between individual words in the target text. Currently, they were designed manually, but as

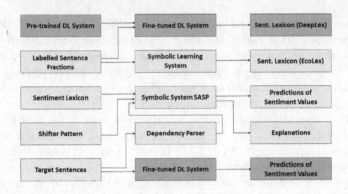

Fig. 1. Architecture of the proposed neuro-symbolic approach to sentiment analysis

Schulder et al. [25] have shown, automatic methods could be used to extend a relatively small set of given *seed shifters* further. The application of shifter patterns requires that the given target text is preprocessed by a chosen dependency parser. Our proposed approach offers a good performance in the chosen specific domain of economics and finance. The methodology can, however, be reused for other languages and domains. In the following subsections, we provide more details on different aspects of the proposed approach.

3.1 Corpus Used and its Annotation

We used the same corpus as in [4], that includes nearly 400 sentences from different articles in online Portuguese newspapers discussing issues from the areas of finance and economics. Each sentence was labelled manually with a sentiment value on a scale of -3 to 3. Table 1 shows examples of some sentences in this corpus.

Table 1. Examples of some sentences and ratings

Sentence	Translation	Val.
Portugal **não pode estar a governar só para os mercados**, ou seja, para tentar demonstrar que o défice está melhor.	Portugal **cannot govern only for the markets**, that is, try to demonstrate that the deficit is better.	−1
O saldo positivo das nossas trocas compensa largamente o financiamento das atividades do país.	The positive balance of our exchanges largely compensates for the financing of the country's activities.	2

We notice that many sentences include both positive and negative segments. This was one of the reasons why we decided to split the given sentences into shorter sentence fractions, following [4]. The sentence fractions were used as training data for the construction of the sentiment lexicon. Having shorter sentence fractions that are labelled facilitates this process. Parts of the sentences that appeared to be irrelevant were dropped. To illustrate the process of generating sentence fractions, let us consider the first sentence in Table 1. This sentence was divided into several fractions, such as the ones shown below. Each fraction was attributed a rating that seemed appropriate:

- *governar só para os mercados* (govern only for the markets)/ −1,
- *défice* (deficit)/−2,
- *o défice está melhor* (the deficit is better)/1.

This process was manual and gave rise to about 1700 sentence fractions. The division of the given sentences and the corresponding fractions into train and test subsets was similar to the scheme of N-fold (N = 6) cross validation (CV). The existing data was separated into N partitions, while the data of one partition was used as test data. The data of the other partitions was used as *training data*.[1] As there are N different ways of selection a partition for testing, we obtain N (here N = 6) different setups, i.e., pairs of training and testing datasets, and hence also, N separate results.

3.2 Generation of Sentiment Lexicons

As we have pointed out, in this work we consider two different ways of generating sentiment lexicon in an automatic manner. Both use the training data in the form of labelled sentence fractions as input. One approach follows the approach discussed in [4], which constructs, for each possible sentiment-bearing word encountered in the training data, a distribution of ratings. This process takes into account the length of each sentence fraction. The resulting lexicon is referred to as EcoLex. This lexicon can be regarded as a domain-specific lexicon that in our case is oriented towards economics and finance.

Previous work has shown that it is advantageous to combine a given domain-specific lexicon with a general-purpose lexicon. We have therefore followed this strategy also here. For this, we have chosen *SentiLex'*, which was obtained from *SentiLex-PT* [5,26], an off-the-shelf general purpose lexicon for Portuguese, by eliminating all entries with the neutral class and idiomatic expressions. A combination of the two lexicons mentioned above, referred to as *EcoSentiLex*. It includes all entries in the domain-specific lexicon and a subset of entries in the general-purpose lexicon *SentiLex'* that do not appear in the domain-specific lexicon.

The second approach uses the labelled training data (sentence fractions) to fine-tune a pre-trained Portuguese language model—BERTimbau [27]. The fine-tuned model was used to create a sentiment lexicon called *DeepLex* by predicting the sentiment of words.

---

[1] The method used here is similar to, but not the same as N-fold CV. The main difference is that we do not start with a single pool of data, but rather N (6) different sets of sentences and the corresponding sentence fractions.

Table 2 shows some sentiment values in the sentiment lexicons discussed. We note that some of the words shown in the columns *EcoLex* and *DeepLex* are specific to economics and finance, which is the specific domain considered here (e.g., *competitivo/Adj* (competitive), *consolidação/N* (consolidation), etc.). The average lexicon sizes across all setups are shown in the last line of the table. The size of *DeepLex* is shown as *undefined*, as it is not a real lexicon, but a "virtual" one. The trained DL system can be queried and returns, for any set of words, the sentiment values.

Table 2. Examples of some sentiment values in different lexicons

Word	Class	EcoLex	SentiLex'	EcoSentiLex	DeepLex
Competitivo (competitive)	Adj	1.33	–	1.33	1.86
Adequado (adequate)	Adj	0.40	1	0.40	1.84
Consolidação (consolidation)	N	0.58	–	0.58	1.54
Absurdo (absurd)	Adj	–	–1	–1	–1.53
Agressivo (agressive)	Adj	–0.93	–1	–0.93	–2.05
No. entries		1236	5497	6504	undef.

3.3 Shifter Patterns

Lexicon-based approaches that include only single words (unigrams) have one major shortcoming—they do not capture contextual information. For example, the sentiment conveyed by *inverte o crescimento de economia* (inverts the growth of the economy) is negative, even if the sentiment value of some of the words in this phrase is positive. One way to resolve this is employing the so-called *sentiment shifters*, sometimes called also *valence shifters*. A shifter is a word or expression that changes the polarity of another word or expression [4, 25, 29].

In our example above, the word *inverte* (inverts) is a shifter that changes the polarity of the sentence *o crescimento de economia* (growth of the economy). The word or phrase affected by the shifter is referred to here as the *focal element*. The focal element may include other shifters. The word *crescimento* (growth) that appears in the above phrase is an example. It can be considered as an *intensifier* of its focal element *economia (economy)*. In earlier works, the *sentiment shifters* were normally identified manually [4, 29], although some authors explored automatic ways to extend a given set of *seed shifters* [25]. In this work, we manually construct shifters.

We have considered the following shifter types: *reversal/inversion, intensification, attenuation/downtoning* and *ignore/omit*. More details on each are given further on, including the *ignore* type, which - to the best of our knowledge - has not yet been used in SA. For each particular shifter category (e.g. reversal/inversion), we define several patterns, depending on the syntactic class of the focal element (e.g., V, Adj, N) and its role in dependency relationships, i.e., whether the shifter is the *head token* or a *dependent* one. Table 3 shows some shifter patterns for reversal/inversion.

Table 3. Some shifter patterns that include reversal/inversion

Id	Shifter pat.	Token 1	Token 2	|S|
RAV+	$S^R \rightarrow F_V^+$	S=não (not)	(F=crescer (grow))	12
RAV-	$S^R \rightarrow F_V^-$	S=não (not)	(F=prejudicar (harm))	12
RAJ+	$S^R \rightarrow F_{ADJ}^+$	S=não (not)	(F=satisfatório (satisfactory))	6
RAJ-	$S^R \rightarrow F_{ADJ}^-$	S=não (not)	(F=mau (bad))	6
RAN+	$S^R \rightarrow F_N^+$	S= não (no)	(F=crescimento (growth))	7
RAN-	$S^R \rightarrow F_N^-$	S= não (no)	(F=crise (crisis))	7
RV'N+	$S^R \leftarrow F_N^+$	S=inverter (reverse)	(F=crescimento (growth))	22
RV'N-	$S^R \leftarrow F_N^-$	S=inverter (reverse)	(F=crise (crisis))	13
RVN+	$F_N^+ \leftarrow S^R$	(F=crescimento (growth))	S=invertido (reversed)	22
RVN-	$F_N^- \leftarrow S^R$	(F=crise (crisis))	S=reduzida (reduced)	13
RN'N+	$S^R \leftarrow F_N^+$	S=inversão (reversal)	(F=crescimento (growth))	21
RN'N-	$S^R \leftarrow F_N^+$	S=redução (reduction)	(F=despesa (expenditure))	12
RNN+	$F_N^+ \leftarrow S^I$	(S=crescimento (growth))	F=reduzido (reduced)	5
RNN-	$F_N^- \leftarrow S^I$	(S=dívida (debt))	F=reduzido (reduced)	5
RVV+	$S^R \leftarrow F_V^-$	S=faltar (fail to)	(F=crescer (grow))	1

The first shifter pattern in this table is identified as *RAV+*. The shifter pattern can be described using the expression $S^R \rightarrow F_V^+$, showing that the shifter S^R is a reversal shifter. Besides, the pattern stipulates that the focal element F_V^+ should be a verb (V) with positive polarity. As the arrow points to this focal element, this signifies that it should be the head token. The column $|S|$ in Table 3 identifies the number of shifters associated with each rule, which are stored in an auxiliary table. The pattern *RAV+* includes various shifters, some of which are: *não* (not), *demais* (too much), *demasiado* (too much), *incapacidade* (inability), *insuficientemente* (insufficiently), *mal* (badly), *nada* (not at all), *nem* (neither), *nunca* (never) and *sem* (without).

As the name suggests, *intensifiers* augment the sentiment value of the focal element and *attenuators* decrease it. For instance, the intensifier *muito* (very) in the phrase *muito bom* (very good), augments the positive sentiment value of *bom* (good). Intensifiers may intensify also negative sentiment value, as in *muito mal* (very bad). For each of these types is accompanied by a set of shifter patterns, similar to the ones in Table 3. They are not shown here due to space limitations. However, interested readers can consult [4] for more details.

As for the *ignore/omit* type, this category includes the shifters *apesar* (despite), *embora* (although). These appear in constructions of the form *apesar p1 p2* (despite *p1 p2*), where *p1* and *p2* are phrases (e.g., *p1=aumento de produção* (increased production), *p2=os salários não aumentaram* (the salaries did not increase)). We notice that the phrases *p1* and *p2* have usually opposite polarity. In our example, *p1* has a positive polarity and *p2* a negative one. However, the overall polarity of the composite phrase is determined by the phrase *p2*. The sentiment value of the phrase *p1* is ignored.

System SASP that Derives Sentiment Values

System SASP uses the given shifter patterns together with the given sentiment lexicon to derive the sentiment values of given target texts. The rules are somewhat different for each shifter category, as Table 4 shows.

Table 4. Calculation of the sentiment value for different shifter types

Shifter type	Rule	Setting of C
Reversal/Inversion of F^+	$SV(F^+, S^R) = C_{R+} * SV(F^+)$	$C_{R+} = -0.8$
Reversal/Inversion of F^-	$SV(F^-, S^R) = C_{R-} * SV(F^-)$	$C_{R-} = -0.2$
Intensification	$SV(F^+, S^I) = C_I * SV(F)$	$C_I = 2$
Attenuation	$SV(F^+, S^A) = C_A * SV(F)$	$C_A = 0.5$
Ignore/Omit	$SV(F^+, S^O) = C_O * SV(F)$	$C_O = 0$

The symbol S^X represents a shifter of certain type (e.g., $S^R=$ reversal/inversion) and F the focal element. Each rules shows how to calculate the final sentiment value of the focal element. This is done by multiplying the value of the focal element retrieved from the lexicon (e.g., $SV(F^+)$) by an appropriate constant (e.g., $C_{R+} = -0.8$). In case of inversion, the result depends on whether the focal element has positive or negative sentiment value. In the positive case, the constant C_{R+} is set to -0.8 which reverses the polarity of the focal element. For the negative case, the constant C_{R-} is set to -0.2, which reverses the negative value to a value near 0. This seems to work well with examples, such as *não é mau* (it is not bad), which is not really equivalent to *bom* (good).[2]

Let us use the text *inverte o crescimento de economia* (inverts the growth of economy) as an example to explain how the shifter rules and patterns are invoked when trying to determine the sentiment value of some given target text. The SASP system goes through the list of shifters that appear in different patterns with the objective of determining which ones appear in the target text. We note that the shifter *inverter* (to invert) appears, for instance, in pattern *RV'N+*. The system uses the dependency links provided by the dependency parser to identify the focal element. Considering our example, the focal element is *crescimento de economia* (the growth of economy). So, the next aim is to verify whether

---

[2] The authors of [4] have experimented with different values for C_R, etc. (all except C_O which is new). The values shown were selected by taking into account previous work [28] and tests on a given validation set.

all the conditions specified by the pattern $S^R \leftarrow F_N^+$ are verified in the target text. For instance, the focal element must be a noun or a noun phrase with the positive polarity (F_N^+). Besides, it must figure as the dependent token (the arrow originates in the dependent token and points to the head token).

Some phrases include more than one shifter. Our previous example is an example of this phenomenon. The focal element *crescimento de economia* (the growth of economy) includes the word *crescimento* (the growth), which is also a shifter, namely an intensifier. The system SASP processes the syntactic elements bottom-up, starting with the rightmost element in the dependency tree. This strategy guarantees that the shifter *crescimento* (the growth) is processed before the shifter *inverter* (to invert).

Providing explanations showing how the sentiment value was obtained is important for users [10]. Our approach retrieved explanations from the symbolic part of the system. The format of the explanations adopted lists all words in the given text and accompanies them by other information. Consider, for instance, the explanation for two different phrases, *crescer muito* (grow very much) and *não funciona mal* (does not work badly).

crescer/*0.642/1.285/D muito/IAV+
não/*−0.401/0.001/RAV- funciona/0.625/D mal/−0.286/D/RAV+

The explanation of the first example includes the following elements: sentiment value(s) retrieved from the sentiment lexicon identified by "*" ("*0.642"); the sentiment values that were derived using the shifter patterns and the values in its scope ("1.285"); identifier of the shifter pattern(s) invoked ("IAV+"); symbol "D" that accompanies all dependent tokens in the scope of the shifter.

The explanation of the second example shows that two shifters have been applied here. First the shifter *mal* (badly) is identified as inversion/reversal shifter and hence the corresponding pattern RAV+ is applied. The final value of this phrase is then reversed again thanks to the shifter *não* which invokes the patterns RAV-. The final sentiment value of this phrase is slightly positive (0.001), which seems correct. This type of explanation appears to be richer than that the ones provided by model-agnostic approaches, which capture the degree of influence between inputs and outputs [7,10].

3.4 Experimental Setup and Results

The setup used here includes the following systems used to predict the sentiment values on the test set:

- *SASP-EcoSentiLex* - Symbolic system SASP that uses symbolic shifter rules in conjunction with the sentiment lexicon *EcoSentiLex*.
- *SASP-DeepLex* - Symbolic system that uses symbolic shifter patterns in conjunction with the sentiment lexicon *DeepLex*.
- *DeepLearn* - Deep learning system obtained by fine-tuning a pre-trained DL system (BERTimbau), as discussed in Sect. 3.2).

Table 5. Weighted F1-score results on sentence fractions (Frac) long sentences (Sents) and an ablation study relative to different shifter types.

Setup	$Fracts$	$Sents$	$Sents_{-R}$	$Sents_{-I}$	$Sents_{-A}$	$Sents_{-O}$
SASP-EcoSentiLex	71.8	64.3	−2.7	1.0	−0.8	−1.0
SASP-DeepLex	78.3	55.4	–	–	–	–
DeepLearn	91.0	66.8	–	–	–	–

Previous results reported in [4] have shown that it is advantageous to use shifter patterns together with the sentiment lexicon, so the results that include just the sentiment lexicons are not shown. Also, the values for the individual setups are not shown due to space limitations. The values shown represent mean weighted F1 value across six different setups.

The results are presented in Table 5. Column *Fracts* shows the results on sentence fractions. The symbolic system *SASP-EcoSentiLex* achieves 71.8%. The system *SASP-DeepLex* that uses both symbolic shifter patterns and *DeepLearn* lexicon achieves a still higher performance of 78.3%. The performance of the DL system (*DeepLearn*) is the highest of all the alternatives (91.0%).

The results of different systems on long sentences are shown in column *Sents*. We note that all the results are substantially lower than those obtained on sentence fractions. The system that degraded least is *SASP-EcoSentiLex*. The good results of *SASP-DeepLex* and *DeepLearn* on sentence fractions are not maintained on long sentences. It is likely that the amount of training fractions is not sufficient to capture the intricate relationships among the different parts of the sentences used in the tests. We are planning to investigate this issue in the future.

Table 5 includes also the results of *ablation study* carried out in conjunction with *SASP-EcoSentiLex* system. For instance, the column $Sents_{-R}$ shows the effect of omitting all reverse shifters on performance. As we can see, the performance drops by 2.7%. The columns $Sents_{-I}$, $Sents_{-A}$ and $Sents_{-O}$ show the effect of omitting the intensification, attenuation and ignore/omit shifters respectively on performance.

There are some cases where the prediction of *SASP-EcoSentiLex* does not have the right polarity and hence results in an error. First, some errors are caused by the dependency parser used. It indicates wrongly the words within the scope of the head token. These errors could be avoided by using a more reliable dependency parser. Other errors arise because the entries in sentiment lexicon are missing or incorrect. Then, when the shifter is applied, this does not lead to the expected outcome. For example, when the shifter *não* is detected in *não desfavorecido* (not underprivileged), no impact may be observed if the sentiment value of *desfavorecido* were absent in the sentiment lexicon and hence the system would assume that its value of 0. Inverting 0 produces again 0. Another class of errors is caused by the fact that the existing shifter patterns do not cover the current case. This happens, for instance, with the phrase *impostos sobre rendimentos* (taxes on income). As *rendimentos* (income) is normally attributed a positive value, the whole phrase could be attributed wrongly a positive value.

4   Conclusions

We show that it is beneficial to exploit the so-called neuro-symbolic approach to achieve both explanation and performance in sentiment analysis tasks. The proposed system *SASP-EcoSentiLex* uses the symbolic part for overall control, and for providing explanations accompanying the predictions of sentiment values. The DL system is used for various subtasks, such as, construction of the sentiment lexicon.

The DL system involved *BERTimbau* pre-trained on Portuguese texts which was further fine-tuned on our training data, namely the sentence fractions obtained from texts in Portuguese. The predictive power of the sentiment lexicon was enhanced by additional shifter patterns and rules. Both of these were used by the symbolic system (SASP) to generate the predictions.

The results indicate that the proposed neuro-symbolic system *SASP-DeepLex* achieves good performance on data consisting of sentence fractions. The performance of this system is lower than the performance of the pure DL system (*DeepLearn*). However, considering that it could still be improved, it is an interesting alternative.

The results of all systems considered here were much lower on long sentences. The advantage of using a DL system over the SASP system is not really very large. As we have pointed out, it is likely that the amount of training fractions was not sufficient to capture the intricate relationships among the different parts of the sentences used in the test set. We are planning to investigate this issue in the future. It would also be interesting to examine when the symbolic and DL approach fail and how this knowledge could be used to improve the system(s).

The great advantage of the proposed approach is that it provides understandable explanations about how the predictions are obtained. More work is, however, needed to evaluate whether the format of explanations is understandable to different users and whether this could be improved.

The results also confirm that the use of shifter patterns, in conjunction with the given sentiment lexicon, normally leads to better results than the use of the lexicon alone. This probably happens because the shifter patterns capture some context information, similarly as DL systems do.

Acknowledgements. This work is financed by National Funds through the Portuguese funding agency, FCT - Fundação para a Ciência e a Tecnologia, within project LA/P/0063/2020 of INESC TEC and project UIDB/00022/2020 of CLUP. We wish to thank our colleagues from FLUP, U. Porto for permitting to exploit the corpus and labelled sentence fractions elaborated earlier [4]. Finally, we wish to express our gratitude to the anonymous reviewers to his/her useful comments.

References

1. Almatarneh, S., Gamallo, P.: Automatic construction of domain-specific sentiment lexicons for polarity classification. In: Proceedings of the of the International Conference on Practical Applications of Agents and Multi-Agent Systems, pp. 175–182. Springer (2017). https://doi.org/10.1007/978-3-319-61578-3-17
2. van Atteveldt, W., van der Velden, M.A., Boukes, M.: The validity of sentiment analysis: comparing manual annotation, crowd-coding, dictionary approaches, and machine learning algorithms. Commun. Methods Meas. **15**(2), 121–140 (2021)
3. Besold, T.R., d'Avila Garcez, A., Bader, S., Bowman, H., Domingos, P., Hitzler, P., Kühnberger, K.U., Lamb, L.C., Lima, P.M.V., de Penning, L., Pinkas, G., Poon, H., Zaverucha, G.: Neural-Symbolic Learning and Reasoning: A Survey and Interpretation, pp. 1–51. IOS Press (2022)
4. Brazdil, P., Muhammad, S.H., Oliveira, F., Cordeiro, J., Silva, F., Silvano, P., Leal, A.: Semi-automatic approaches for exploiting shifter patterns in domain-specific sentiment analysis. Mathematics **10**(18) (2022). https://www.mdpi.com/2227-7390/10/18/3232
5. Carvalho, P., Silva, M.J.: Sentilex-pt: Principais características e potencialidades. Oslo Stud. Lang. **7**(1), 425–438 (2015)
6. Catelli, R., Pelosi, S., Esposito, M.: Lexicon-based vs. bert-based sentiment analysis: a comparative study in Italian. Electronics **11**(3) (2022). https://www.mdpi.com/2079-9292/11/3/374
7. Datta, A., Sen, S., Zick, Y.: Algorithmic transparency via quantitative input influence: theory and experiments with learning systems. In: 2016 IEEE Symposium on Security and Privacy (SP), pp. 598–617 (2016)
8. Devlin, J., Chang, M.W., Lee, K., Toutanova, K.: Bert: pre-training of deep bidirectional transformers for language understanding. arXiv preprint arXiv:1810.04805 (2018)
9. Dogra, V., Verma, S., Kavita, Chatterjee, P., Shafi, J., Choi, J., Ijaz, M.: A complete process of text classification system using state-of-the-art NLP models. Comput. Intell. Neurosci. (2022)
10. Došilović, F., Brčić, M., Hlupić, N.: Explainable artificial intelligence: a survey. In: MIPRO 2018-41st International Convention Proceedings (2018)
11. Forte, A.C., Brazdil, P.B.: Determining the level of clients' dissatisfaction from their commentaries. In: Proceedings of the International Conference on Computer. Processing of the Portuguese Language, pp. 74–85. Springer (2016)
12. Ghosal, D., Hazarika, D., Roy, A., Majumder, N., Mihalcea, R., Poria, S.: KinG-DOM: Knowledge-guided DOMain adaptation for sentiment analysis. In: Proceedings of the 58th Annual Meeting of the Associate for Computer Linguistics, pp. 3198–3210. ACL (2020). https://www.aclanthology.org/2020.acl-main.292
13. Grote, H., Schmidt, F.: Mad-x-an upgrade from mad8. In: Proceedings of the 2003 Particle Accelerator Conference, vol. 5, pp. 3497–3499. IEEE (2003)
14. Hamilton, W.L., Clark, K., Leskovec, J., Jurafsky, D.: Inducing domain-specific sentiment lexicons from unlabeled corpora. In: Proceedings of the Conference on Empirical Methods in NLP, pp. 595–605. NIH Public Access (2016)
15. Hitzler, P., Sarker, M.K.: Neuro-symbolic Artificial intelligence: State of the Art. IOS press (2022)
16. Kocoń, J., Baran, J., Gruza, M., Janz, A., Kajstura, M., Kazienko, P., Korczyński, W., Miłkowski, P., Piasecki, M., Szołomicka, J.: Neuro-symbolic models for sentiment analysis. In: Computational Science - ICCS 2022: 22nd International Conference, pp. 667–681 (2022)

17. Liu, H., Singh, P.: ConceptNet - a practical commonsense reasoning tool-kit. BT Technol. J. **22**(4), 211–226 (2004)
18. Liu, Y., Ott, M., Goyal, N., Du, J., Joshi, M., Chen, D., Levy, O., Lewis, M., Zettlemoyer, L., Stoyanov, V.: RoBERTa: A robustly optimized BERT pretraining approach. arXiv preprint arXiv:1907.11692 (2019)
19. Minaee, S., Kalchbrenner, N., Cambria, E., Nikzad, N., Chenaghlu, M., Gao, J.: Deep learning based text classification: a comprehensive review. arXiv preprint arXiv:2004.03705 (2021)
20. Moreno-Ortiz, A., Fernández-Cruz, J., Hernández, C.P.C.: Design and evaluation of SentiEcon: a fine-grained economic/financial sentiment lexicon from a corpus of business news. In: Proceedings of the 12th Language Resources and Evaluation Conference, pp. 5065–5072 (2020). https://www.aclweb.org/anthology/2020.lrec-1.623.pdf
21. Muhammad, A., Wiratunga, N., Lothian, R., Glassey, R.: Domain-based lexicon enhancement for sentiment analysis. In: Proceedings of the BCS SGAI Workshop on Social Media Analysis, pp. 7–18. Citeseer (2013), https://www.ceur-ws.org/Vol-1110/paper1.pdf
22. Muhammad, S.H., Adelani, D.I., Ahmad, I.S., Abdulmumin, I., Bello, B.S., Choudhury, M., Emezue, C.C., Aremu, A., Abdul, S., Brazdil, P.: NaijaSenti: a Nigerian Twitter sentiment corpus for multilingual sentiment analysis. LREC 2022, arXiv preprint arXiv:2201.08277 (2022)
23. Muhammad, S.H., Brazdil, P., Jorge, A.: Incremental approach for automatic generation of domain-specific sentiment lexicon. In: Proceedings of Advances in Information Retrieval, LNCS. vol. 12036, pp. 619–623. Springer (2020)
24. Muhammad, S.H., Yimam, S., Abdulmumin, I., Ahmad, I.S., Ousidhoum, N., Ayele, A., Adelani, D., Ruder, S., Beloucif, M., Bello, S.B., Mohammad, S.M.: SemEval-2023 task 12: sentiment analysis for african languages (AfriSenti-SemEval). In: Proceedings of the 17th International Workshop on Semantic Evaluation (SemEval-2023) (2023)
25. Schulder, M., Wiegand, M., Ruppenhofer, J.: Automatic generation of lexica for sentiment polarity shifters. Nat. Lang. Eng. **27**(2), 153–179 (2021)
26. Silva, M.J., Carvalho, P., Sarmento, L.: Building a sentiment lexicon for social judgement mining. In: Proceedings of the International Conference on Computational Processing of the Portuguese Language (PROPOR), pp. 218–228. Springer (2012)
27. Souza, F., Nogueira, R., Lotufo, R.: BERTimbau: pretrained BERT models for Brazilian Portuguese. In: Brazilian Conference on Intelligent Systems, pp. 403–417. Springer (2020)
28. Tavares, C., Ribeiro, R., Batista, F.: Sentiment analysis of Portuguese economic news. In: Proceedings of the 10th Symposium on Languages, Applications and Technologies (SLATE 2021), Article 17. vol. 94, pp. 17:1–17:13. Schloss Dagstuhl-Leibniz-Zentrum für Informatik (2021)
29. Trnavac, R., Das, D., Taboada, M.: Discourse relations and evaluation. Corpora **11**(2), 169–190 (2016)
30. Wolf, T., Debut, L., Sanh, V., Chaumond, J., Delangue, C., Moi, A., Cistac, P., Rault, T., Louf, R., Funtowicz, M., et al.: Transformers: State-of-the-art natural language processing. In: Proceedings of the 2020 Conference on Empirical Methods in Natural Language Processing: System Demonstrations, pp. 38–45 (2020)
31. Yadav, A., Vishwakarma, D.K.: Sentiment analysis using deep learning architectures: a review. Artif. Intell. Rev. **53**(6), 4335–4385 (2020)

Assessing Good, Bad and Ugly Arguments Generated by ChatGPT: a New Dataset, its Methodology and Associated Tasks

Victor Hugo Nascimento Rocha[1]([✉]) [iD], Igor Cataneo Silveira[2] [iD],
Paulo Pirozelli[3] [iD], Denis Deratani Mauá[2] [iD], and Fabio Gagliardi Cozman[1] [iD]

[1] Escola Politécnica, São Paulo, Brazil
`{victor.hugo.rocha,fgcozman}@usp.br`
[2] Instituto de Matemática e Estatística, São Paulo, Brazil
`igorcs@ime.usp.br, denis.maua@usp.br`
[3] Instituto de Estudos Avançados Universidade de São Paulo, C4AI
(c4ai.inova.usp.br) Av. Prof. Lúcio Martins Rodrigues, 370, São Paulo, SP 05508-020,
Brazil
`paulo.pirozelli.silva@usp.br`

Abstract. The recent success of Large Language Models (LLMs) has sparked concerns about their potential to spread misinformation. As a result, there is a pressing need for tools to identify "fake arguments" generated by such models. To create these tools, examples of texts generated by LLMs are needed. This paper introduces a methodology to obtain good, bad and ugly arguments from argumentative essays produced by ChatGPT, OpenAI's LLM. We then describe a novel dataset containing a set of diverse arguments, *ArGPT*. We assess the effectiveness of our dataset and establish baselines for several argumentation-related tasks. Finally, we show that the artificially generated data relates well to human argumentation and thus is useful as a tool to train and test systems for the defined tasks.

Keywords: Argument classification · Argument mining ·
Argumentation mining · ChatGPT · Automatic essay scoring · NLP

1 Introduction

Recently we have witnessed the popularization of large language models (LLMs). OpenAI's ChatGPT,[1] for instance, has garnered considerable media attention and public interest due to its impressive linguistic abilities and wide range of knowledge. This has led many people to use it as an alternative to traditional search engines for gathering information. However, LLMs are not at this point reliable tools for knowledge-related tasks. In particular, given that their main

---

[1] https://openai.com/blog/chatgpt.

N. Moniz et al. (Eds.): EPIA 2023, LNAI 14115, pp. 428–440, 2023.
https://doi.org/10.1007/978-3-031-49008-8_34

goal is to model the joint probability distribution of tokens, they tend to produce grammatically sound and realistic texts that can be problematic in a number of ways, such as producing convincing arguments to justify false claims. This is particularly worrisome considering that even hand-made datasets are getting more and more contaminated by the use of LLMs [20].

It is that unintended aspect of LLMs that we investigate in this work. We focus on ChatGPT, even though we expect our conclusions to be representative of any similar LLM. To the best of our knowledge, this is the first study in the literature with this specific aim.

Given the complexity of LLMs, such a study must be based on empirical investigation, by extracting and analyzing a diverse set of arguments. To this end, our first contribution is a methodology to generate arguments that are representative of ChatGPT's skills. Our second contribution is the dataset itself, ArGPT, a curated set of argumentative essays that have been annotated by human experts with carefully selected labels. We expect this dataset to be a useful resource in our quest to understand the behavior of LLMs as regards to argumentation. To validate this effort and to indicate how the dataset can be employed in practice, our third contribution is a well defined set of tasks and corresponding baselines; namely, Argument Quality Classification, Span Identification, Component Classification, Relation Classification, and Essay Scoring. Finally, we show that our LLM argumentation dataset is sufficiently similar to human-made datasets, suggesting that our method is scalable for argument mining in general, enabling faster and lower-cost generation of data.

The paper is divided as follows. Section 2 summarizes the needed background. Section 3 presents the methodology used to create the dataset. Section 4 introduces the annotation process and statistics for ArGPT. Section 5 defines the tasks proposed for our dataset and presents their respective baselines. In Sect. 6, we show that the arguments generated with our methodology are similar to traditional, human-made Argument Mining datasets. Finally, Sect. 7 concludes and presents ideas for future work.[2]

2   Background

Our investigation about the quality of arguments provided by LLMs is informed by two proxy tasks: Argument(ation) Mining (AM) and Automatic Essay Scoring (AES), topics that we now briefly review.

2.1   Argument(ation) Mining

Argument Mining (AM) is interested in extracting arguments, their relations and structures from natural language texts [10]. It is usually divided into three different subtasks: span detection, component classification and relation classification. The first task finds the parts of an input text that are argumentative; the

---

[2] All code, data, and experiments for this paper are available at: https://github.com/C4AI/ArGPT.

second classifies those components into argumentative entities (such as premises, claims, etc.); and the third task classifies the relations among components (support, attack, etc.) [10,14]. Earlier methods in AM adopted algorithms based on hand-crafted features and rules, but recently the use of contextual language models, such as transformers, has gained prominence [7,13].

One of the major problems in AM is the heterogeneity of the existing datasets. Each corpus is based on a particular methodology and takes a different terminology to label arguments. On top of that, the size of the existing datasets tend to be limited when compared to datasets found in other NLP tasks, possibly due to the difficulty in generating and annotating arguments [1]. Despite this, important efforts have been undertaken to create AM datasets. We can mention a solid corpus about the medical field [13]; another one that tries to solve the lack of annotated data in the scientific domain [1]; a corpus that contains user comments about policy proposals [15]; a smaller corpus that is based on student argumentation [16]; and the dataset constructed by the Project Debater by the IBM Corporation.[3] A particularly valuable resource is a corpus consisting of 402 annotated student essays about controversial themes [17], where argumentative parts are associated with one of the labels "MajorClaim", "Claim" and "Premise", and each "Premise" is related to other components through an "Attack" or "Support" relation.

One significant feature that seems to be lacking in existing AM corpora is the annotation of texts containing flawed arguments. Arguments in datasets are commonly written by well-educated people and in contexts that have no correct answer (e.g., "Life in a city is much better than life in the countryside" [17]). This tends to result in argumentations that are almost always adequate. A dataset with flawed arguments is a key step in building detectors for such arguments.

2.2   Automatic Essay Scoring

Automatic Essay Scoring (AES) aims to automatically assign a grade to an essay [9]. Argumentative essays are found in student exams worldwide, such as in TOEFL,[4] and play a significant role in education as they require students to engage with a subject matter; analyze different perspectives; construct logical arguments; and support their viewpoints with evidence. AES is a valuable tool to understand the quality of arguments. Essays with high scores are those that meet basic requirements, such as presenting a clear and concise claim, and providing strong and logical premises to support it. On the other hand, essays that receive low scores may indicate that the argumentative structure is flawed or incomplete.

AES datasets are mostly based on exams. The standard dataset, ASAP,[5] comprises eight different prompts answered by 7th to 10th grade students, with two of them being argumentative [12]. The TOEFL dataset [3] is made of essays written by non-native English speakers and is sadly not publicly available. One

---

[3] https://research.ibm.com/interactive/project-debater/.

[4] https://www.ets.org/toefl/test-takers/ibt/about/content/writing.html.

[5] https://www.kaggle.com/c/asap-aes.

Themes	Student prompt	Professor prompt
	Suppose you're a student taking an exam and you're faced with the following question: "**Explain why it is said that Miles Davis was a major inspiration for Wolfgang Amadeus Mozart**". Can you write a text using the argumentative essay structure to answer this question as if you were the student and without mentioning yourself?	Suppose you are a professor correcting a test and you come across the wrong answer above. Can you write a text in third person using the argumentative essay structure to respond to the wrong argument of the answer as if you were the professor, without mentioning yourself, the test or the answer itself?

Fig. 1. Generating ArGPT. We selected several themes for argumentative essays based on false or self-contradictory ideas. We gave ChatGPT a first prompt (the *student* prompt), instructing it to create an argumentative essay about a selected theme. In the following round, we provided a second prompt (the *professor* prompt) instructing it to write an essay correcting the student's argumentation. If the produced essays did not follow our requirements, we repeated the process.

final dataset is ArgRewrite V.2 [8]. Its smaller size is compensated by having different levels of annotation, which are useful for a wide range of NLP tasks.

3 Generating Argumentative Essays with ChatGPT

As with any other empirical investigation, our study about the validity and quality of argumentations produced by LLMs starts with the acquisition of data. This data must properly represent all the scenarios we may be interested in, with examples of both good and bad argumentation containing both real and fake claims.

In order to collect such data, we established some main guidelines for our interaction with ChatGPT. To start, we decided that the texts should be argumentative essays, as those usually involve a straightforward argumentation structure and are common both in AM and AES [12,16,17]. To induce contradictions or other forms of bad argumentation, we selected only fake or contradictory claims as themes for the essays. We make use of ChatGPT's propensity to produce justifications, even when facing clearly wrong propositions [4]. This way, we led ChatGPT to produce several contradictory arguments. Finally, to speed up the process, we framed the interaction with ChatGPT as an academic setting where a student must write an essay about a topic and a professor must correct it with a second essay. The dataset acquisition methodology is summarized in Fig. 1 and consists of the following three steps:

1. **Themes.** The themes for the essays were chosen as to induce flawed argumentation by presenting contradictory or false ideas. We selected themes from several areas, including art, history, philosophy and science. All themes were expressed in English and are available with the dataset.
2. **Student Essay.** In order to induce the writing of the first argumentative essay, we fed ChatGPT the prompt: *Suppose you're a student taking an exam*

and you're faced with the following question: "Explain [THEME]". Can you write a text using the argumentative essay structure to answer this question as if you were the student and without mentioning yourself?.

3. **Professor Essay.** In a second round of the same dialogue section, we asked ChatGPT to correct the first essay playing the role of a professor. The goal of this second interaction was to get one of two outcomes: (i) if the student had created a flawed argument, the professor would write an essay with the correct argumentation; or (ii) if the student's argument was reasonable, the professor would produce a flawed argument. The professor prompt was: *Suppose you are a professor correcting a test and you come across the wrong answer above. Can you write a text in third person using the argumentative essay structure to respond to the wrong argument of the answer as if you were the professor, without mentioning yourself, the test or the answer itself?.*

After collecting the essays, we checked whether they followed our requirements; i.e., whether the texts attended to an essay structure and tackled the proposed theme. When that was not the case, we re-prompted the themes in a new dialogue section until we got a pair of adequate argumentative essays. No theme required more than a single re-promting. We note that prompts had to be finely engineered through a relatively long trial and error process to produce the desired results.

4   ArGPT: Dataset Annotation and Statistics

To produce a dataset that can in fact be used to study how ChatGPT argues, all generated arguments must be annotated in meaningful ways. To check the essays argumentative structure, we first annotated them for the three standard AM tasks (span identification, component classification, relation classification). Next, as we wanted to assess the overall quality of the written material, we also annotated texts for AES.

To guide the AM annotations, we mostly followed the methodology by Stab and Gurevych [17].[6] However, our approach to classifying argumentative components and relations was more minimalist. While they differentiated three types of argumentative components (premises, claims, and major claims), we only distinguished between major claims—the central viewpoints argued in the essays—and premises, which supported or attacked other components, whether major claims or premises. We adopted this approach due to several reasons. Firstly, most of premises in our essays were related to major claims. Secondly, it was more important to establish the components' relations than to categorize them. Finally, we wanted to simplify the annotation process so as to annotate many arguments. The types of relations between arguments are two: attack, when the source component contradicted or weakened the target component, and support, when the source strengthened or justified the target.

---

[6] For the sake of space, we discuss only the differences of our methodology in respect to theirs.

Table 1. List of criteria for Automatic Essay Scoring and the corresponding scores. "Interm." gives the score for each minor criteria, whereas "Final" gives the score for the major criteria. The AES score is an average of the four major criteria.

Major criteria	Minor criteria	Interm.	Final
Structure	Clearly states a major claim	2.5	10
	Introduces the theme	2.5	
	Develops the arguments throughout the text	2.5	
	Recapitulates the arguments in the conclusion	2.5	
Writing	Adherence to standard language norms	5	10
	Correct use of argumentative connectives	5	
Coherence	Adherence to the theme	2.5	10
	No repetition of arguments	2.5	
	No contradictions	2.5	
	No beating around the bush	2.5	
Truthfulness	States true or plausible arguments	10	10

We also had to accommodate for the idiosyncrasies of texts produced by ChatGPT. In argumentative essays, it is a common practice to repeat the main claim several times. ChatGPT's texts also followed this pattern; however, since we fed it with claims that likely went against its knowledge base, it occasionally contained contradictory major claims in the same text. Therefore, we established that all occurrences of a major claim in an essay should be annotated separately and that the annotator should establish the relation (attack or support) among them. We also pointed to annotators that some premises might not be linked (directly or indirectly) to one of the major claims, as ChatGPT sometimes presents irrelevant information or is unable to connect some of the premises to the rest of the argumentative graph.

As for the AES annotation, ArGPT's argumentative essays were evaluated with respect to quality and correctness. To ensure consistency in our assessment, we developed a comprehensive list of criteria, modeled after evaluations from standard exams. Our list is organized into four main criteria: structure, writing, coherence, and truthfulness. *Structure* measures whether the essay attends to the necessary structure of an argumentative essay; *Writing* evaluates linguistic correctness; *Coherence* evaluates the essay's argumentative structure; and *Truthfulness* evaluates the veracity of the presented information. Each of these criteria is further divided into one or more subcriteria. As a final score, we take the arithmetic mean between these four criteria. Table 1 displays the full set of criteria and the points associated with them.

Based on our methodology, 84 themes were selected, resulting in 168 argumentative essays. Each essay was generated in about 8 minutes (16 minutes per theme). As a matter of comparison, according to testing services such as TOEFL, a person takes between 30 and 50 minutes to write an essay. Hence we can see that a state-of-art conversational agent indeed operates quickly for the purposes of dataset generation. The full annotation process was carried out by an experienced annotator specifically hired for this (not an author of this paper), who spent around 20 minutes in each essay. ArGPT is split into training (80%), validation (10%) and test (10%) sets.[7]

Table 2. Statistics for ArGPT and similar AM and AES datasets. Statistics for ArGPT are for the full dataset. "Average Number of Words" is not reported for the AM datasets that do not provide the full text. Information on "Structure Type", "Number of Components", and "Number of Relations" are not available for AES datasets.

	ArGPT	[17]	[16]	[15]	[13]	[1]	[12]	[3]	[8]
Corpus type	AM+AES	AM	AM	AM	AM	AM	AES	AES	AES
Structure type	graph	tree	tree	graph	graph	tree	–	–	–
Num. texts	168	402	112	731	659	60	3600	12000	258
Num. components	2730	6089	576	4779	4198	353	–	–	–
Num. relations	2713	3832	464	1353	2601	293	–	–	–
Avg. Num. Words	380	366	–	–	337	134	350	348	582

Statistics for ArGPT are shown in Table 2, as well as for similar AM and AES datasets (see Sect. 2). The average word count per essay in ArGPT (380) is in line with the other datasets. The statistics also show that our dataset has a higher rate of relations per component; a side effect of annotating the relations between the multiple major claims. Regarding the essay scores, they ranged from 5.25 to 9.75, with an average of 7.76 and standard deviation of 0.96.

Given annotations for AM and AES, ChatGPT produced mostly high-quality essays, with well-distributed scores and which seem to follow an argumentative structure. Based on that, particularly the third[8] and fourth criteria from Table 1, we defined a typology for the argumentation quality of the essays. Essays with a solid argumentation (high coherence) and which argued in support of a true claim were labeled "Good". Essays that exhibited a flawed argumentation were labeled "Bad", regardless of whether they defended something that was true or not. Finally, texts that did a quite good job in defending false claims were labeled "Ugly". We consider this to be a particularly dangerous class of arguments, since it has the potential to successfully convince people to accept a false claim. Out of the 168 essays, 81 were categorized as "Bad", 50 were labeled as "Good", and 37 were marked as "Ugly" (the training, validation and

---

[7] ChatGPT has emerged as a valuable annotation tool, often outperforming manual annotations. (e.g., [6,19]). Nonetheless, despite our best efforts, we could not teach ChatGPT to generate annotations adhering to our methodology. This limitation is reasonable, considering that even human annotators require training to perform such tasks effectively.

[8] We excluded "Adherence to the theme" from this account.

test sets all closely follow that proportion of labels). These numbers show that our methodology, which involved simulating a student-teacher interaction and prompting false claims, was successful in producing diverse arguments.

5 Using ArGPT: Supported Tasks and Their Baselines

The purpose of building a LLM-based argumentation dataset was to obtain a resource for detecting and evaluating arguments produced by these models. These processes range from identifying the individual components in an argument up to assessing its global structure. For this reason, we defined five tasks that together account for the whole process of argument identification and classification. The first is a novel task of argument quality evaluation, the next three are typical within AM [14], and the last is simply AES:

1. *Argumentation Quality Evaluation*: In this task, a model receives an essay as input and has to predict the quality of the argumentation. There are three possible labels: Good, Bad, and Ugly.
2. *Span Identification*: Given an essay, a model has to predict the correct BIO tag (Beginning, Inside, Outside) for each token in the text.
3. *Component Classification*: In this task, components are classified as Premise or Major Claim. The input is a concatenation of the component and the text ("component + [SEP] + text"), and the output is one of the two labels. We provide the full text together with the component because the role of an argumentative component depends on the context.
4. *Relation Classification*: Given two argument components, a model needs to determine their relation, using one of three possible labels: Attack, Support, and None. The input for this task is a concatenation of the two components ("source-component + [SEP] + target-component").
5. *Essay Scoring*: This is modeled as a regression task. A model receives an argumentative essay as an input and must predict its score.

For each of these tasks, we establish a couple of baselines, based on two standard transformer-based architectures: BERT [5] and RoBERTa [11] base. After some initial tests, all the models were trained using the same hyperparameter configurations: 15 epochs, batch size of 8 and learning rate of 2e-5. This decision, along with the one to model the tasks as described above, was taken for simplicity's sake, since our goal in this paper is to study our dataset, with the construction of a more complex model being the subject of future work.

5.1 Evaluation Metrics

To evaluate the first four tasks, we utilize F1-score micro and macro as our metrics. To make their utilization in AM tasks clear, we follow the definitions by Morio et al. [14]. The first task (Span Identification) predicts a set of spans, defined as a pair (s, e), where s represents the span's start token and e the end token. The second task (Component Classification) predicts a set of components (s, e, c), where s and e have the same meaning as before and c is the component's label. Lastly, the third task (Relation Classification) predicts a set of relations, with each one defined as $(s_{src}, e_{src}, s_{tgt}, e_{tgt}, r)$, where s_{src} and e_{src} represent the source component's span, s_{tgt} and e_{tgt} the target's span and r the relation label. Given this, the evaluation metrics for the AM tasks can be defined. Consider $\mathcal{G}_{task}$ the set of gold outputs of a certain AM task and $\mathcal{S}_{task}$ the set of system outputs for the same task. The precision metric is defined as $P = |\mathcal{G}_{task} \cap \mathcal{S}_{task}|/|\mathcal{S}_{task}|$, the recall metric is $R = |\mathcal{G}_{task} \cap \mathcal{S}_{task}|/|\mathcal{G}_{task}|$ and, finally, the F1-score is $F = 2PR/P + R$.

Table 3. Baseline results for ArGPT's test set. The first two rows report the values for models trained in individual tasks (no error propagation). The last row shows the result achieved in each step of an end-to-end AM pipeline allowing the error to propagate and using the RoBERTa models trained for each individual task.

BERT	Arg. Qual.		Span	Component		Relation		AES	
	F1 (%)	Macro (%)	F1 (%)	F1 (%)	Macro (%)	F1 (%)	Macro (%)	MSE	QWK
	56.25	40.40	50.56	90.87	78.74	**93.91**	36.81	0.58	0.53
RoBERTa	**56.25**	54.97	**77.35**	92.34	81.67	92.36	44.18	0.44	0.65
Pipeline	–	–	77.35	71.07	71.46	52.89	37.58	–	–

For the AES task, we utilize two metrics. The first is the Quadratic Weighted Kappa (QWK), which measures the degree of agreement between two graders. The QWK score ranges from -1 to 1, where 0 indicates random agreement, 1 indicates perfect agreement, and -1 indicates perfect disagreement. Although the effectiveness of QWK is debated [21], it is widely used in the AES field due to the influence of the ASAP dataset. The second metric employed in this task is the Mean Squared Error (MSE), usually used for regression tasks.

5.2   Results and Discussion

Table 3 illustrates the results achieved in the different tasks for ArGPT's test set. The first two lines report the values for BERT and RoBERTa models in the individual tasks, with RoBERTa performing better in all tasks.

The RoBERTa model achieved an F1-macro score of 54.97% in the Argument Quality task. This is evidence that, to some extent, our models were able to differentiate the good, bad and ugly arguments produced by ChatGPT. It should be noted however that while our models do contain some form of knowledge in their parametrization, their ability to fact-check claims is limited, since they do not have access to up-to-date knowledge databases. This shortcoming is part of the reason why the results were not better in certain cases.

For AM, in addition to the individual tasks, we simulated an end-to-end pipeline, i.e. from raw texts to the argumentation graphs, in which errors are able to propagate between tasks. For each part of the pipeline, we took the model that performed better in the standalone task (shown in bold in Table 3), which was RoBERTa in all cases. The pipeline starts with the trained span identification model. The output from this model (the identified components), instead of the gold-standard spans, are then separately passed to the component classifier and to the relation classifier. The "Pipeline" row in Table 3 reports the values achieved by the simulation. As expected, the performances for both the component and relation classifiers were worse when the error was allowed to propagate. Nonetheless, the results were comparable to those found in the literature for similar datasets, both with and without error propagation [7,14]. We also note that the results obtained by our models in AES were similar to others in the literature [12].

Table 4. The first three rows bring the results for the Stab & Gurevych's dataset [17], for three models: (i) a pretrained model (no fine-tuning); (ii) a model fine-tuned on this dataset [14]; (iii) and the best models trained on ArGPT. The last row presents the results of a model trained on Stab & Gurevych's dataset and tested on ArGPT.

	Span	Component		Relation	
	F1 (%)	F1 (%)	Macro (%)	F1 (%)	Macro (%)
Pretrained Model	0	12.09	10.78	0.02	0.03
Recent result [14]	85.20	87.68	80.37	66.91	55.84
Our best model	53.48	91.63	76.31	92.98	34.11
Model trained in [17]	48.51	87.23	55.84	86.85	34.26

6 The Connection with Human Argumentation

The arguments generated by ChatGPT resemble those found in human argumentation. Yet, one might wonder whether ArGPT dataset is useful for performing AM for human-generated texts.

To verify that hypothesis we designed two experiments. In the first, we tested whether models trained on ArGPT generalize to the dataset by Stab & Gurevych [17]. The rationale is that if a model trained in ArGPT performs well in human-generated essays, then we can leverage ChatGPT for cheaper training of AM systems. For consistency, we modified the target dataset annotations by changing "Claim" labels to "Premise", and applying our changes to "Major Claims". The results, in Table 4, are compared to both a pretrained model (RoBERTa with no fine-tuning) and the results by Morio et al. [14] (even if this comparison is limited due to methodological changes). Compared to a pretrained model, our model did learn to solve tasks related to human argumentation and very decently performed them. And, although the results achieved by our model were far from state of the art approaches, we must remember that it was not fine-tuned in the target dataset and still got some decent F1-metrics.

For the second experiment, we took the opposite route. We trained a model (RoBERTa with the same hyperparameters as before) in Stab & Gurevych's dataset and tested it on ArGPT's test set. The results, shown in the last row of Table 4, were similar.

Together, the two experiments strongly suggest that ArGPT (and our methodology in general) can be effectively used to learn AM models that emulate human datasets, with two clear advantages. First, text generation by ChatGPT is significantly faster and cheaper than by (paid) humans. Secondly, one can produce texts containing features that are difficult for non-expert human annotators to intentionally produce, such as contradictions, defenses of false claims and so on. Those advantages can mitigate the current poverty of annotated data in AM.

7   Conclusions and Future Work

We have developed a number of techniques to assess the ability of LLMs to argue, in particular looking at OpenAI's ChatGPT; we thus introduced a new dataset, ArGPT, consisting of essays that argue over false claims following a teacher-professor dialogue simulation. The dataset is annotated in a number of structural and qualitative ways, following a purposefully-developed methodology. We also defined five tasks related to argumentation and provided baselines for them. Our results indicate that it is possible to differentiate, at least to some extent, between good, bad and ugly arguments produced by ChatGPT. Additionally, we have shown that our method is also useful to support AM and AES applications. Indeed, ArGPT and its associated methodology can be used to (i) develop systems capable of identifying problematic argumentation generated by LLMs, (ii) train and evaluate AM and AES systems, and (iii) speed up the generation of data for these and related tasks.

As our methods should be applicable to any LLM, it is still necessary to actually investigate how the arguments produced by other LLMs differ from the ones created by ChatGPT. This is particularly important as new open-source LLMs are now released almost every day [2,18]. Contrary to ChatGPT, not all LLMs have carefully curated data or enforce content barriers; thus, our methods can be even more valuable in those cases.

In future work we will increase the size of ArGPT and improve baseline models for all tasks. We plan to create a larger ArGPT by an improved annotation process, where two annotators will combine their annotations into a consensus. To create more robust baselines, we intend to explore models that can deal with structured knowledge or that can incorporate the argumentation structures extracted by the AM tasks. We also plan to deal with pieces other than essays, to make our dataset more diverse and applicable to a broader range of research.

Acknowledgments. This work was carried out at the Center for Artificial Intelligence (C4AI-USP), with support by FAPESP grant 2019/07665-4 and by the IBM Corporation. Victor Hugo is partially supported by the Coordenação de Aperfeiçoamento de Pessoal de Nível Superior - Brasil (CAPES) grant 88887.616392/2021-00. Paulo is supported by the FAPESP grant 2019/26762-0. Denis is partially supported by grants FAPESP #2022/02937-9 and CNPq #305136/2022-4. Fabio is partially supported by CNPq #305753/2022-3. Igor is partially supported by CAPES grant 88887.635492/2021-00. We acknowledge support by CAPES - Finance Code 001.

References

1. Accuosto, P., Saggion, H.: Mining arguments in scientific abstracts with discourse-level embeddings. Data Knowl. Eng. **129**, 101840 (2020)
2. Anand, Y., Nussbaum, Z., Duderstadt, B., Schmidt, B., Mulyar, A.: Gpt4all: training an assistant-style chatbot with large scale data distillation from gpt-3.5-turbo. github.com/nomic-ai/gpt4all (2023)
3. Blanchard, D., Tetreault, J., Higgins, D., Cahill, A., Chodorow, M.: Toefl11: A corpus of non-native english. ETS Research Report Series **2013**, i–15 (2013)
4. Bubeck, S., Chandrasekaran, V., Eldan, R., Gehrke, J., Horvitz, E., Kamar, E., Lee, P., Lee, Y.T., Li, Y., Lundberg, S., Nori, H., Palangi, H., Ribeiro, M.T., Zhang, Y.: Sparks of Artificial General Intelligence: Early Experiments with gpt-4 (2023)
5. Devlin, J., Chang, M.W., Lee, K., Toutanova, K.: BERT: Pre-training of deep bidirectional transformers for language understanding. In: NAACL HLT 2019–2019 Conference of the North American Chapter of the Association for Computational Linguistics: Human Language Technologies—Proceedings of the Conference, vol. 1, pp. 4171–4186. Association for Computational Linguistics (ACL) (2019)
6. Gilardi, F., Alizadeh, M., Kubli, M.: Chatgpt outperforms crowd-workers for text-annotation tasks (2023)
7. Hidayaturrahman, Dave, E., Suhartono, D., Arymurthy, A.M.: Enhancing argumentation component classification using contextual language model. J. Big Data **8**(1), 103 (2021)
8. Kashefi, O., Afrin, T., Dale, M., Olshefski, C., Godley, A., Litman, D., Hwa, R.: ArgRewrite vol. 2: an annotated argumentative revisions corpus. Lang. Res. Eval. **56**(3), 881–915 (2022)
9. Lagakis, P., Demetriadis, S.: Automated essay scoring: a review of the field. In: 2021 International Conference on Computer, Information and Telecommunication Systems (CITS), pp. 1–6 (2021)
10. Lawrence, J., Reed, C.: Argument mining: a survey. Comput. Linguist. **45**(4), 765–818 (2020)
11. Liu, Y., Ott, M., Goyal, N., Du, J., Joshi, M., Chen, D., Levy, O., Lewis, M., Zettlemoyer, L., Stoyanov, V.: Roberta: A Robustly Optimized BERT Pretraining Approach (2019). arxiv:abs/1907.11692
12. Mathias, S., Bhattacharyya, P.: ASAP++: enriching the ASAP automated essay grading dataset with essay attribute scores. In: International Conference on Language Resources and Evaluation (LREC 2018). European Language Resources Association (ELRA), Miyazaki, Japan (2018)
13. Mayer, T., Cabrio, E., Villata, S.: Transformer-based argument mining for health-care applications. In: Frontiers in Artificial Intelligence and Applications. vol. 325, pp. 2108–2115. IOS Press BV (2020)
14. Morio, G., Ozaki, H., Morishita, T., Yanai, K.: End-to-end Argument Mining with Cross-corpora Multi-task Learning. Trans. Assoc. Comput. Linguist. **10**, 639–658 (2022). https://doi.org/10.1162/tacl_a_00481

15. Park, J., Cardie, C.: A corpus of eRulemaking user comments for measuring evaluability of arguments. In: International Conference on Language Resources and Evaluation (LREC 2018). European Language Resources Association (ELRA), Miyazaki, Japan, May 2018
16. Peldszus, A., Stede, M.: An annotated corpus of argumentative microtexts. European Conference on Argumentation (ECA'16), pp. 801–816 (2016)
17. Stab, C., Gurevych, I.: Parsing argumentation structures in persuasive essays. Comput. Linguist. **43**(3), 619–659 (2017)
18. Taori, R., Gulrajani, I., Zhang, T., Dubois, Y., Li, X., Guestrin, C., Liang, P., Hashimoto, T.B.: Stanford Alpaca: An Instruction-Following LLaMA Model (2023)
19. Törnberg, P.: Chatgpt-4 outperforms experts and crowd workers in annotating political twitter messages with zero-shot learning (2023)
20. Veselovsky, V., Ribeiro, M.H., West, R.: Artificial artificial artificial intelligence: Crowd workers widely use large language models for text production tasks (2023)
21. Yannakoudakis, H., Cummins, R.: Evaluating the performance of automated text scoring systems. In: Workshop on Innovative Use of NLP for Building Educational Applications, pp. 213–223. Association for Computational Linguistics, Denver, Colorado, Jun 2015

Advancing Neural Encoding of Portuguese with Transformer Albertina PT-*

João Rodrigues[1]([✉]), Luís Gomes[1], João Silva[1], António Branco[1],
Rodrigo Santos[1], Henrique Lopes Cardoso[2], and Tomás Osório[2]

[1] NLX—Natural Language and Speech Group, University of Lisbon, Faculty of
Sciences (FCUL), Dept. Informatics, Campo Grande, 1749-016 Lisboa, Portugal
{jarodrigues,luis.gomes,jsilva,antonio.branco,rsdsantos}@fc.ul.pt
[2] Laboratório de Inteligência Artificial e Ciência de Computadores (LIACC)
Faculdade de Engenharia da Universidade do Porto (FEUP), Rua Dr. Roberto Frias,
4200-465 Porto, Portugal
hlc@fe.up.pt
tomas.s.osorio@gmail.com

Abstract. To advance the neural encoding of Portuguese (PT), and
a fortiori the technological preparation of this language for the digital
age, we developed a Transformer-based foundation model that sets a
new state of the art in this respect for two of its variants, namely European Portuguese from Portugal (PT-PT) and American Portuguese from
Brazil (PT-BR). To develop this encoder, which we named Albertina
PT-*, a strong model was used as a starting point, DeBERTa, and its
pre-training was done over data sets of Portuguese, namely over a data
set we gathered for PT-PT and over the brWaC corpus for PT-BR.
The performance of Albertina and competing models was assessed by
evaluating them on prominent downstream language processing tasks
adapted for Portuguese. Both Albertina versions are distributed free of
charge and under a most permissive license possible and can be run on
consumer-grade hardware, thus seeking to contribute to the advancement
of research and innovation in language technology for Portuguese.

Keywords: Portuguese · Large language model · Foundation model ·
Encoder · Albertina · DeBERTa · BERT · Transformer · Deep learning

1 Introduction

In recent years, the field of Artificial Intelligence has come to successfully exploit
the paradigm of deep learning, a machine learning approach based on large artificial neural networks [17]. Applied to Natural Language Processing (NLP), deep
learning gained outstanding traction with notable breakthroughs under the distributional semantics approach, namely with word embedding techniques [19]
and the Transformer neural architecture [28]. These neural models acquire

N. Moniz et al. (Eds.): EPIA 2023, LNAI 14115, pp. 441–453, 2023.
https://doi.org/10.1007/978-3-031-49008-8_35

semantic representations from massive amounts of data in a self-supervised learning process that ultimately results in the so-called *Foundation Models* [4].

Self-supervision is accomplished in NLP through language modeling [3] and was initially adopted in shallow neural models such as Word2Vec [19] for word embeddings. Over time, this approach was scaled beyond the single-token level to sequence transduction with encoding-decoding models based on recurrent [27] or convolution networks and occasionally supported by attention mechanisms [2].

A particular neural network architecture, the Transformer, has stood out among all others, showing superior performance by a large margin, sometimes even surpassing human-level performance [30,31], and became mainstream in virtually every NLP task and application [4]. Several variants have spun out from the base Transformer architecture (encoder-decoder), including the landmark encoder BERT [7] and the outstanding decoder GPT [5], which have been most successfully adapted to downstream tasks, complemented with techniques such as transfer learning [21], fine-tuning [22] or few-shot prompting [5].

The large scale of foundation models is crucial to their strength and successful deployment. Adding to the difficulty of accessing sufficiently large computational resources, most NLP research is focused on the English language, which is just one of the around 7,000 idioms on the planet. Consequently, there is a lack of competitive and openly available foundation models specifically developed for the vast majority of languages other than English, which happens to be also the case for Portuguese. This restrains the scientific progress and the innovative pace related to those languages, as well as curtailing other societal benefits, further enlarging the digital divide between English and other languages.

To the best of our knowledge, there are a couple of publicly published models that were developed specifically for Portuguese, namely for its European variant from Portugal (PT-PT) and for its American variant from Brazil (PT-BR). However, they present considerable drawbacks, namely in what concerns their suboptimal performance level and the non-existent public distribution of encoders for the PT-PT variant.

Accordingly, there is important motivation and considerable room for improvement in creating new and better encoders for Portuguese, which we developed and present in this paper—and named as Albertina PT-*.[1] On a par with an encoder for PT-BR that sets a new state of the art for this language variant, its twin PT-PT version is an original contribution to the state-of-the-art concerning Portuguese: a freely available neural encoder specifically developed for its European variant with highly competitive performance, whose reporting publication is publicly available and which is openly distributed.

The remainder of this paper is organized as follows. Section 2 provides an overview of existing models with support for Portuguese, with a particular focus on the pre-existing BERTimbau, for PT-BR. The data sets used in pre-training and evaluating our model are presented in Sect. 3. Section 4 describes Albertina

---

[1] The models can be obtained here: The Albertina-PT-PT model can be obtained at https://huggingface.co/PORTULAN/albertina-ptpt and the Albertina-PT-BR model can be obtained at https://huggingface.co/PORTULAN/albertina-ptbr.

PT-* and its pre-training and fine-tuning procedures. The evaluation results of its versions on downstream tasks are discussed in Sect. 5. Section 6 closes the paper with concluding remarks.

2 Related Work

Regarding related work, we consider Transformer-based encoder models that, to the best of our knowledge, are concerned with the Portuguese language. Accordingly, besides searching the literature, we also screened the Hugging Face [13] model repository, as it has become the main source of NLP models.

Multiple studies [6,7,18,25] have shown that language-specific foundation models perform better than multilingual ones. This realization has thus led to a few initiatives that created language-specific encoders, trained from scratch for a single language, such as ERNIE for Chinese [26], BERTje for Dutch [6], CamemBERT for French [18], and MarIA for Spanish [10], among others.

Nevertheless, given it is not always viable to create a model specifically for a given language due to a lack of available data or computing resources, multilingual models have been resorted to as a temporary yet common mitigation for this problem for many languages. These are models that are pre-trained on data that include a mix of languages—albeit English is typically present in a greater amount—and are thus capable of modeling multiple languages.

2.1 Encoders Whose Multilingual Data Set Included Portuguese

Taking the number of Hugging Face downloads as a proxy for popularity and user base size, the stand-out models that support Portuguese are multilingual, namely XML-Roberta, available in Base and Large sizes, Multilingual BERT (mBERT) Base Cased, and DistilBERT Base.

Several task-specific or domain-specific models have been built upon these multilingual foundations. For instance, BioBERTpt (Portuguese Clinical and Biomedical BERT) [24] was created by fine-tuning mBERT on clinical notes and biomedical literature in Portuguese.

2.2 Encoders Specifically Concerned with Portuguese

To the best of our knowledge, for PT-PT there is the encoder presented in [20], but it is not possible to find therein clear evaluation results against downstream tasks and, most importantly, the distribution of that model is not announced.

As for PT-BR, there are a couple of encoders publicly distributed. That is the case of BERTabaporu,[2] which is of limited interest though, given its quite narrow domain, as it is a BERT-based encoder trained on Twitter data. The most popular of these two encoder models for PT-BR, by far, is BERTimbau [25].

BERTimbau is available in two model sizes, Base, with 110 million parameters, and Large, with 330 million parameters. In both cases, the authors took

---

[2] https://huggingface.co/pablocosta/bertabaporu-base-uncased.

an existing BERT-based model as starting point and, after discarding the word embeddings and the masked language modeling head layers, performed a hefty 1 million steps of additional pre-training on the brWaC corpus (see Sect. 3.1).

- BERTimbau Base took multilingual mBERT Base [7] as its starting point. It was pre-trained with a batch size of 128 and sequences of 512 tokens during 4 days on a TPU v3-8, performing about 8 epochs on the corpus [25, §5.1].
- BERTimbau Large took the monolingual English BERT Large [7] as the starting point, given there was no multilingual mBERT available in Large size. It was pre-trained with sequences of 128 tokens in batches of size 256 for the first 900,000 steps and sequences of 512 tokens in batches of size 128 for the final 100,000 steps. Its pre-training took 7 days on a TPU v3-8 instance and performed about 6 epochs on the corpus [25, §5.1].

Both the Base and Large variants of BERTimbau outperform mBERT in a couple of downstream tasks in Portuguese, with the Large variant being better [25]. Given this was an inaugural general-domain encoder for Portuguese, it set the state of the art for those tasks in Portuguese.[3]

Since the creation of BERTimbau, improved Transformer-based architectures have been developed that, together with more efficient training techniques, should allow better-performing models to be developed. This strengthens the motivation to develop alternative, state-of-the-art encoders also for PT-BR.

3   Data Sets

We proceed now with presenting the data sets used to pre-train Albertina PT-* and the data sets used to fine-tune it for the downstream tasks where it was extrinsically evaluated, for both PT-PT and PT-BR variants.

3.1   Data Sets for the Pre-training Stage

To secure conditions for comparability with BERTimbau, for the pre-training of Albertina PT-BR we resorted to the same data set, the brWaC corpus (Brazilian Portuguese Web as Corpus) [29]. It contains 2.7 billion tokens in 3.5 million documents and was obtained from crawling many different sites to ensure diversity. The authors report that some effort was made to remove duplicated content.

As for the pre-training of the Albertina PT-PT, we resorted to a data set that resulted from gathering some openly available corpora of European Portuguese from the following sources:

---

[3] As such, BERTimbau has come to serve as the basis for several other task-specific models available in Hugging Face. These task-specific models, however, appear to be unpublished, unnamed, or provide no information on their Hugging Face page; as such, they will not be covered in the present paper.

- OSCAR [1]: the OSCAR data set includes documents in more than one hundred languages, including Portuguese, and it is widely used in the literature. It is the result of a selection performed over the Common Crawl[4] data set, crawled from the Web, that retains only pages whose metadata indicates permission to be crawled, that performs deduplication, and that removes some boilerplate, among other filters. Given that it does not discriminate between the Portuguese variants, we performed extra filtering by retaining only documents whose meta-data indicate the Internet country code top-level domain of Portugal. We used the January 2023 version of OSCAR, which is based on the November/December 2022 version of Common Crawl.
- DCEP [11]: the Digital Corpus of the European Parliament is a multilingual corpus including documents in all official EU languages published on the European Parliament's website. We retained its Portuguese portion.
- Europarl [14]: the European Parliament Proceedings Parallel Corpus is extracted from the proceedings of the European Parliament from 1996 to 2011. We retained its Portuguese portion.
- ParlamentoPT: the ParlamentoPT is a data set we obtained by gathering the publicly available documents with the transcription of the debates in the Portuguese Parliament.

We filtered these data using best practice in the literature, resorting to BLOOM [16] pre-processing pipeline,[5] resulting in a data set of 8 million documents, containing around 2.2 billion tokens.

The number of documents from each source—Europarl, DCEP, ParlamentoPT, and OSCAR data—corresponds approximately to 15%, 20%, 31%, and 34% of the entire data set for PT-PT, respectively. All these data sets are publicly available, including ParlamentoPT.[6]

3.2 Data Sets for the Fine-tuning Concerning Downstream Tasks

We organized the data sets used for downstream tasks into two groups. In one group, we have the two data sets from the ASSIN 2 benchmark, namely STS and RTE, that were used to evaluate BERTimbau [25].

In the other group of data sets, we have the translations into PT-BR and PT-PT of the English data sets used for a few of the tasks in the widely-used GLUE benchmark [31], which allowed to test both Albertina variants on a wider variety of downstream tasks.

---

[4] https://commoncrawl.org/.

[5] We skipped the default filtering of stopwords since it would disrupt the syntactic structure, and also the filtering for language identification given the corpus was pre-selected as Portuguese.

[6] ParlamentoPT was collected from the Portuguese Parliament portal in accordance with its open data policy (https://www.parlamento.pt/Cidadania/Paginas/DadosAbertos.aspx, and can be obtained here: https://huggingface.co/datasets/PORTULAN/parlamento-pt.

ASSIN 2

ASSIN 2 [23] is a PT-BR data set of approximately 10,000 sentence pairs, split into 6,500 for training, 500 for validation, and 2,448 for testing, annotated with semantic relatedness scores (range 1 to 5) and with binary entailment judgments. This data set supports the task of semantic text similarity (STS), which consists of assigning a score of how semantically related two sentences are, and the task of recognizing textual entailment (RTE), which given a pair of sentences, consists of determining whether the first entails the second.

We did not create a PT-PT version of ASSIN 2. That would require transposing the data set, which is PT-BR, into PT-PT; however, to the best of our knowledge, there is no automatic translation system for direct translation between those variants. One solution would be to translate through an intermediate language, say English or Spanish, and then translate the result into PT-PT, but doing this would likely highly degrade the quality of the resulting benchmark by a factor that would not be possible to determine.

GLUE Tasks Translated

GLUE [31] has become a standard benchmark for model evaluation on downstream tasks. As the original GLUE is in English, we resort to PLUE [8] (Portuguese Language Understanding Evaluation), a data set that was obtained by automatically translating GLUE [31] into PT-BR. We address four tasks from those in PLUE, namely:

- two similarity tasks: MRPC, for detecting whether two sentences are paraphrases of each other, and STS-B, for semantic textual similarity;
- and two inference tasks: RTE, for recognizing textual entailment,[7] and WNLI, for coreference and natural language inference.

To obtain the PT-PT version of this benchmark, we automatically translated the same four tasks from GLUE using DeepL Translate,[8] which specifically provides translation from English to PT-PT as an option.[9]

4   Albertina PT-* Model

We describe the pre-training of the Albertina language model for Portuguese, in its two PT-PT and PT-BR versions, as a continuation of the pre-training of DeBERTa with our data sets. We also address its fine-tuning for the downstream tasks considered for its extrinsic evaluation.

---

[7] This is the same task as the ASSIN 2 RTE, but on different source data.
[8] https://www.deepl.com/.
[9] This is distributed at https://huggingface.co/datasets/PORTULAN/glue-ptpt.

4.1   The Starting Encoder

We take DeBERTa [12] as our starting encoder since it is reported to improve on multiple strong encoders and surpass human performance on the SuperGLUE benchmark. The main novelty in DeBERTa comes from two techniques, namely *disentangled attention* and *enhanced mask decoder*, which are related to how information about the relative and the absolute positions of tokens is encoded and handled by the model.

In other BERT-like encoders and Transformers in general, information about the position of tokens is represented as a vector, such as, for instance, a sinusoidal embedding, that is added to the content embedding of the token. The disentangled attention mechanism in DeBERTa uses separate content (H) and relative position (P) embeddings, and the attention mechanism attends separately to these embeddings. So, when calculating the cross attention $A_{i,j}$ between tokens i and j, the disentangled attention mechanism incorporates not only the usual content-to-content attention $H_i H_j^T$ but also content-to-position $H_i P_{j|i}^T$ attention and position-to-content $P_{i|j} H_j^T$ attention.

The second specific mechanism in DeBERTa, the enhanced mask decoder, incorporates information about the absolute position of tokens right before the softmax layer to predict the masked tokens. Usually, all three inputs (Query, Key, and Value) to the self-attention calculation come from the hidden states in the preceding layer, but in the enhanced mask decoder of DeBERTa the Query input is based on the absolute position of the token.

As codebase, we resorted to the DeBERTa V2 XLarge, for English, that is available from Hugging Face.[10] We use the Transformers [32] library with Accelerate [9]. The model has 24 layers with a hidden size of 1536, and a total of 900 million parameters. This version brings some changes to the original DeBERTa paper [12]. In particular: (i) it uses a vocabulary size of 128,000 and the *sentencepiece* tokenizer [15], (ii) it adds an additional convolution layer to the first Transformer layer, and (iii) it shares the position projection and content projection matrices in the attention layer.

4.2   Pre-training Albertina PT-BR

For the training of Albertina PT-BR, the brWaC data set was tokenized with the original DeBERTa tokenizer with a 128-token sequence truncation and dynamic padding. The model was trained using the maximum available memory capacity[11] resulting in a batch size of 896 samples (56 samples per GPU without gradient accumulation steps). We chose a learning rate of 1e-5 with linear decay and 10k warm-up steps based on the exploratory experiments. In total, around 200k training steps were taken across 50 epochs. Additionally, we used the standard BERT masking procedure with a 15% masking probability.

---

[10] https://huggingface.co/microsoft/deberta-v2-xlarge.
[11] The PT-BR model was trained for 1 day and 11 hours on a2-megagpu-16gb Google Cloud A2 VMs with 16 GPUs, 96 vCPUs and 1.360 GB of RAM.

4.3   Pre-training Albertina PT-PT

To train Albertina PT-PT, the data set was tokenized with the original DeBERTa tokenizer. The sequences were truncated to 128 tokens and dynamic padding was used during the training. The model was trained using the maximum available memory capacity[12] resulting in a batch size of 832 samples (52 samples per GPU and applying gradient accumulation in order to approximate the batch size of the PT-BR model). Similarly to the PT-BR variant above, we opted for a learning rate of 1e-5 with linear decay and 10k warm-up steps. However, since the number of training examples is approximately twice of that in the PT-BR variant, we reduced the number of training epochs to half and completed only 25 epochs, which resulted in approximately 245k steps.

4.4   Fine-tuning Albertina and BERTimbau

Albertina PT-BR and BERTimbau Large were fine-tuned for each of the 6 tasks described above (4 from GLUE and 2 from ASSIN 2), while Albertina PT-PT was fine-tuned on the 4 GLUE tasks only (as ASSIN-2 is for PT-BR). Each of these model-task combinations was fine-tuned for a range of sets of hyperparameter values, with the purpose of selecting the best-performing set of hyperparameters for each combination. Specifically, we experimented with dropout 0 and 0.1, learning rate 1e-6, 5e-6 and 1e-5, 32bit and 16bit floating point precision, and random seeds 41, 42, and 43. When combined, these ranges resulted in a considerable experimental space, with 36 experiments for each model-task pair. In every such experiment, the whole model was fine-tuned (not just its output head), for 5 epochs with batches of 16 examples.

5   Experimental Results

The experimental results obtained are reported in this section. Every score reported is the average of three runs with different seeds. The set of hyperparameters that produced the highest score on the development data for a given model/task was selected to subsequently evaluate it. It is the corresponding score over the test data that is reported.

Table 1. Performance on the ASSIN 2 tasks RTE (Accuracy) and STS (Pearson). Higher values indicate better performance, with the best results in bold.

	RTE	STS
Albertina PT-BR	**0.9130**	**0.8676**
BERTimbau Large	0.8913	0.8531

---

[12] The PT-PT model was trained for 3 days on a2-highgpu-8gb Google Cloud A2 VMs with 8 GPUs, 96 vCPUs and 680 GB of RAM.

5.1   Improving the State of the Art on ASSIN 2 Tasks

The performance scores of Albertina PT-BR and BERTimbau Large on the RTE task and STS task of ASSIN 2 are displayed in Table 1. Our model improves the state of the art for PT-BR on these two tasks by a quite competitive margin.

5.2   Setting the State of the Art on Portuguese GLUE Tasks

The performance of Albertina and BERTimbau Large are compared again, this time on the four tasks from PLUE, in PT-BR. As displayed in Table 2, our model continues to show superior performance, in three of these four tasks.

Table 2. Performance on the PLUE tasks, for PT-BR, namely RTE and WNLI (Accuracy), MRPC (F1) and STS-B (Pearson)

	RTE	WNLI	MRPC	STS-B
Albertina PT-BR	0.7545	0.4601	0.9071	**0.8910**
BERTimbau Large	0.6546	**0.5634**	0.8873	0.8842
Albertina PT-PT	**0.7960**	0.4507	**0.9151**	0.8799

Table 3 shows the performance of Albertina on the same four tasks from GLUE as before, but now automatically translated to PT-PT.

Table 3. Performance on the GLUE tasks translated into PT-PT, namely RTE and WNLI (Accuracy), MRPC (F1) and STS-B (Pearson)

	RTE	WNLI	MRPC	STS-B
Albertina PT-PT	**0.8339**	**0.4225**	**0.9171**	0.8801
Albertina PT-BR	0.7942	0.4085	0.9048	**0.8847**

5.3   Discussion

In this study, we present a Transformer-based foundation model that establishes a new state-of-the-art performance for multiple benchmark data sets in Portuguese. It is worth noting that the better efficacy of our model, compared to the pre-existing BERTimbau, goes on par with its better efficiency, as efficacy is achieved with significantly reduced computational requirements compared to pre-existing models. In particular, while the BERTimbau model was trained over one million steps, our model required less than a quarter of a million steps. Our model's ability to achieve superior performance with less training time/computation likely results from resorting to all pre-trained layers, including the first layer, concerning word embeddings, and the last layer, concerning masked token prediction (the masked language modeling head), in contrast to the common practice in the literature of resetting these two layers to random weights to continue the pre-training.

With the cross-evaluation, the motivation for the creation of separated versions for the two language variants PT-PT and PT-BR is somewhat empirically justified: when evaluated on PT-PT tasks, Albertina PT-PT outperforms Albertina PT-BR in all tasks except one, where it is only marginally inferior, cf. Table 3; conversely, when evaluated on PT-BR data, Albertina PT-BR outperforms Albertina PT-PT in half of the tasks, cf. Table 2.

Although not directly comparable, the state-of-the-art English models using the original GLUE data sets[13] show performance results that are slightly superior to the results with Albertina. We hypothesized that this is due mainly to the fact that the English models were evaluated on the respective GLUE test sets (by being submitted to the automatic GLUE benchmark online), while Albertina was not. The reason was that the GLUE online service for testing was not available when we needed it and provided no notice about whether it would reopen. We had thus to evaluate our model offline, and thus on a different split of the data. We used the original development set for evaluation, and from the original training set, we used 10% for development and the rest for actual training. Moreover, we consider that the WNLI task was particularly affected by this difference in data partition given its limited sample size.

6   Concluding Remarks

In this paper, we presented Albertina PT-*, a state-of-the-art foundation model for Portuguese with 900 million parameters, of the encoder class, available in two versions, one for the European Portuguese variant from Portugal (PT-PT), and one for the American Portuguese variant from Brazil (PT-BR). To the best of our knowledge, there is no pre-existing encoder specifically developed for PT-PT that has been made publicly available and distributed for reuse. Hence, our Albertina PT-PT is a contribution in that direction and thus sets the state of the art for this variant of Portuguese. As for PT-BR, our Albertina encoder improves the state of the art, taking into account the previous level that was set by the pre-existing encoder BERTimbau, with 330 million parameters, showing superior performance in five out of six downstream tasks used for extrinsic evaluation.

As future work, we will be seeking to progress along a number of directions that may help to secure improvements in the performance of Albertina PT-*. We will experiment with training our encoder versions from scratch on Portuguese data only. It will be important to keep searching for and using better data in terms of quality (boilerplate cleaning, etc.), coverage of different genres, domains and registers, and coverage of additional Portuguese variants. And last but not least, we will be trying to obtain better encoders for Portuguese by virtue of

---

[13] https://gluebenchmark.com/leaderboard.

improved design, increasing their size, experimenting with more architectures, or finding better hyper-parameters.

Acknowledgments. This research was partially supported by: PORTULAN CLARIN—Research Infrastructure for the Science and Technology of Language, funded by Lisboa 2020, Alentejo 2020 and FCT (PINFRA/22117/2016); ACCELERAT.AI— Multilingual Intelligent Contact Centers, funded by IAPMEI (C625734525-00462629); ALBERTINA—Foundation Encoder Model for Portuguese and AI, funded by FCT (CPCA-IAC/AV/478394/2022); and LIACC—Artificial Intelligence and Computer Science Laboratory (FCT/UID/CEC/0027/2020).

References

1. Abadji, J., Ortiz Suarez, P., Romary, L., Sagot, B.: Towards a cleaner document-oriented multilingual crawled corpus. In: Proceedings of the Thirteenth Language Resources and Evaluation Conference (LREC), pp. 4344–4355 (2022)
2. Bahdanau, D., Cho, K., Bengio, Y.: Neural machine translation by jointly learning to align and translate. In: 3rd International Conference on Learning Representations (ICLR) (2015)
3. Bengio, Y., Ducharme, R., Vincent, P.: A neural probabilistic language model. Adv. Neural Inf. Process. Syst. **13** (2000)
4. Bommasani, R., Hudson, D.A., Adeli, E., Altman, R., Arora, S., von Arx, S., Bernstein, M.S., Bohg, J., Bosselut, A., Brunskill, E., et al.: On the opportunities and risks of foundation models (2021). arXiv:2108.07258
5. Brown, T., Mann, B., Ryder, N., Subbiah, M., Kaplan, J.D., Dhariwal, P., Neelakantan, A., Shyam, P., Sastry, G., Askell, A., et al.: Language models are few-shot learners. Adv. Neural. Inf. Process. Syst. **33**, 1877–1901 (2020)
6. De Vries, W., van Cranenburgh, A., Bisazza, A., Caselli, T., van Noord, G., Nissim, M.: BERTje: A Dutch BERT model (2019). arXiv:1912.09582
7. Devlin, J., Chang, M.W., Lee, K., Toutanova, K.: BERT: Pre-training of deep bidirectional transformers for language understanding. In: Proceedings of the 2019 Conference of the North American Chapter of the Association for Computational Linguistics, pp. 4171–4186 (2019)
8. Gomes, J.R.S.: PLUE: Portuguese language understanding evaluation. github.com/ju-resplande/PLUE (2020)
9. Gugger, S., Debut, L., Wolf, T., Schmid, P., Mueller, Z., Mangrulkar, S.: Accelerate: Training and inference at scale made simple, efficient and adaptable (2022). github.com/huggingface/accelerate
10. Gutiérrez-Fandiño, A., Armengol-Estapé, J., Pàmies, M., Llop-Palao, J., Silveira-Ocampo, J., Carrino, C.P., Armentano-Oller, C., Rodriguez-Penagos, C., Gonzalez-Agirre, A., Villegas, M.: MarIA: Spanish language models. Procesamiento del Lenguaje Natural, pp. 39–60 (2022)
11. Hajlaoui, N., Kolovratnik, D., Väyrynen, J., Steinberger, R., Varga, D.: DCEP -digital corpus of the European parliament. In: Proceedings of the Ninth International Conference on Language Resources and Evaluation (LREC) (2014)
12. He, P., Liu, X., Gao, J., Chen, W.: DeBERTa: Decoding-enhanced BERT with disentangled attention. In: International Conference on Learning Representations (2021)
13. Hugging Face. huggingface.co/ Accessed Apr. 2023

14. Koehn, P.: Europarl: A parallel corpus for statistical machine translation. In: Proceedings of Machine Translation Summit X: Papers, pp. 79–86 (2005)
15. Kudo, T., Richardson, J.: SentencePiece: A simple and language independent subword tokenizer and detokenizer for neural text processing. In: Proceedings of the 2018 Conference on Empirical Methods in Natural Language Processing: System Demonstrations, pp. 66–71 (2018)
16. Laurençon, H., Saulnier, L., Wang, T., Akiki, C., del Moral, A.V., Scao, T.L., Werra, L.V., Mou, C., Ponferrada, E.G., Nguyen, H., et al.: The BigScience ROOTS corpus: A 1.6TB composite multilingual dataset. In: Thirty-sixth Conference on Neural Information Processing Systems Datasets and Benchmarks Track (2022)
17. LeCun, Y., Bengio, Y., Hinton, G.: Deep learning. Nature **521**(7553), 436–444 (2015)
18. Martin, L., Muller, B., Ortiz Suárez, P.J., Dupont, Y., Romary, L., de la Clergerie, É., Seddah, D., Sagot, B.: CamemBERT: a tasty French language model. In: Proceedings of the 58th Annual Meeting of the Association for Computational Linguistics, pp. 7203–7219 (2020)
19. Mikolov, T., Chen, K., Corrado, G., Dean, J.: Efficient estimation of word representations in vector space (2013). arXiv:1301.3781
20. Miquelina, N., Quaresma, P., Nogueira, V.B.: Generating a European Portuguese BERT based model using content from Arquivo.pt archive. In: Proceedings of the Intelligent Data Engineering and Automated Learning 23rd International Conference (IDEAL), pp. 280–288 (2022)
21. Pan, S.J., Yang, Q.: A survey on transfer learning. IEEE Trans. Knowl. Data Eng. **22**(10), 1345–1359 (2010)
22. Peters, M.E., Ruder, S., Smith, N.A.: To tune or not to tune? adapting pretrained representations to diverse tasks. In: Proceedings of the 4th Workshop on Representation Learning for NLP (RepL4NLP), pp. 7–14 (2019)
23. Real, L., Fonseca, E., Gonçalo Oliveira, H.: The ASSIN 2 shared task: a quick overview. In: 14th International Conference on the Computational Processing of the Portuguese Language (PROPOR), pp. 406–412. Springer (2020)
24. Schneider, E.T.R., de Souza, J.V.A., Knafou, J., Oliveira, L.E.S., et al.: BioBERTpt–a Portuguese neural language model for clinical named entity recognition. In: Proceedings of the 3rd Clinical Natural Language Processing Workshop, pp. 65–72. Association for Computational Linguistics (2020)
25. Souza, F., Nogueira, R., Lotufo, R.: BERTimbau: pretrained BERT models for Brazilian Portuguese. In: Intelligent Systems: 9th Brazilian Conference (BRACIS), pp. 403–417. Springer (2020)
26. Sun, Y., Wang, S., Feng, S., Ding, S., Pang, C., Shang, J., Liu, J., Chen, X., Zhao, Y., Lu, Y., et al.: Ernie 3.0: Large-scale knowledge enhanced pre-training for language understanding and generation (2021). arXiv:2107.02137
27. Sutskever, I., Vinyals, O., Le, Q.V.: Sequence to sequence learning with neural networks. Adv. Neural Inf. Process. Syst. **27** (2014)
28. Vaswani, A., Shazeer, N., Parmar, N., Uszkoreit, J., Jones, L., et al.: Attention is all you need. Adv. Neural Inf. Process. Syst. **30** (2017)
29. Wagner Filho, J.A., Wilkens, R., Idiart, M., Villavicencio, A.: The brWaC corpus: a new open resource for Brazilian Portuguese. In: Proceedings of the 11th International Conference on Language Resources and Evaluation (LREC) (2018)
30. Wang, A., Pruksachatkun, Y., Nangia, N., Singh, A., Michael, J., Hill, F., et al.: Superglue: A stickier benchmark for general-purpose language understanding systems. Adv. Neural Inf. Process. Syst. **32** (2019)

31. Wang, A., Singh, A., Michael, J., et al.: GLUE: A multi-task benchmark and analysis platform for natural language understanding. In: Proceedings of the EMNLP Workshop BlackboxNLP, pp. 353–355 (2018)
32. Wolf, T. et al.: Transformers: State-of-the-art natural language processing. In: Proceedings of the 2020 Conference on Empirical Methods in Natural Language Processing: System Demonstrations, pp. 38–45 (2020)

OSPT: European Portuguese Paraphrastic Dataset with Machine Translation

Afonso Sousa[1,2]([✉]) and Henrique Lopes Cardoso[1,2][iD]

[1] Faculdade de Engenharia, Universidade do Porto, Porto, Portugal
ammlss@fe.up.pt, hlc@fe.up.pt
[2] Laboratório de Inteligência Artificial e Ciência de Computadores (LIACC),
Porto, Portugal

Abstract. We describe OSPT, a new linguistic resource for European Portuguese that comprises more than 1.5 million Portuguese-Portuguese sentential paraphrase pairs. We generated the pairs automatically by using neural machine translation to translate the non-Portuguese side of a large parallel corpus. We hope this new corpus can be a valuable resource for paraphrase generation and provide a rich semantic knowledge source to improve downstream natural language understanding tasks. To show the quality and utility of such a dataset, we use it to train paraphrastic sentence embeddings and evaluate them in the ASSIN2 semantic textual similarity (STS) competition. We found that semantic embeddings trained on a small subset of OSPT can produce better semantic embeddings than the ones trained in the finely curated ASSIN2's training data. Additionally, we show OSPT can be used for paraphrase generation with the potential to produce good data augmentation systems that *pseudo*-translate from Brazilian Portuguese to European Portuguese.

Keywords: Paraphrastic dataset · Semantic embeddings · Paraphrase generation · European portuguese

1 Introduction

Paraphrase generation[1] transforms a natural language text into a new text with the same semantic meaning but a different syntactic or lexical surface form [7]. This is a challenging problem commonly approached using supervised learning [2,17].

While this task has been extensively explored for English, few works have been developed for other languages, namely Portuguese. We are aware of one work exploring paraphrase generation for (Brazilian) Portuguese [28]. There is no existing work targeting paraphrase generation for European Portuguese, and

---

[1] The code and data are available at https://github.com/afonso-sousa/pt_para_gen

N. Moniz et al. (Eds.): EPIA 2023, LNAI 14115, pp. 454–466, 2023.
https://doi.org/10.1007/978-3-031-49008-8_36

only two small phrasal datasets of aligned paraphrases are available [4,5], which are not publicly accessible. For English, however, approaches have been developed for generating freely-available datasets with millions of sentential paraphrase pairs [12,37].

In this paper, we describe the creation of a dataset containing more than 1.5 million sentential paraphrase pairs. We use neural machine translation (NMT) to translate the English side of a large English-Portuguese parallel corpus, namely OpenSubtitles [23]. We pair the Portuguese translations with the European Portuguese references to form paraphrase pairs. We call this dataset OSPT, as an abbreviation of OpenSubtitles for Portuguese. This dataset covers a broad range of paraphrase phenomena (we cover this analysis in more detail in Sect. 3).

We show the utility of the dataset by using it to train paraphrastic sentence embeddings. We primarily evaluate our sentence embeddings on the ASSIN2 [29] semantic textual similarity (STS) competition. Despite being built for Brazilian Portuguese, for a lack of a better alternative, we deem this competition a good option to evaluate the quality of our data intrinsically. We compare sentence embeddings trained on the official training set from the competition against sentence embeddings trained with a small subset of OSPT. We found the embeddings trained with our dataset outperform those trained from a curated training split.

Lastly, we show that our dataset can be used in paraphrase generation. Having the European Portuguese sentences as targets in fine-tuning a multilingual pre-trained language model produces a *pseudo*-translation effect. The generations are much more European Portuguese-like than the sources, which exhibited Brazilian-like features.

We release our dataset, trained sentence embeddings, paraphrase generators, and all the code to do so. As far as we know, OSPT is the most extensive collection of Portuguese sentential paraphrases released to date. We hope it can motivate new research directions in Portuguese and be used to create powerful Natural Language Processing models while adding robustness to existing ones by incorporating paraphrastic knowledge.

2 Related Work

We discuss work in automatically building paraphrase corpora using parallel text for learning sentence embeddings and similarity functions, and paraphrase generation in Portuguese.

Paraphrase Discovery and Generation
Many methods have been developed for generating or finding paraphrases, including using multiple translations of the same source material [6], using comparable articles from multiple news sources [10], crowdsourcing [18], using diverse machine translation systems to translate a single source sentence [34], and using tweets with matching URLs [21].

Besides all these techniques, the most influential prior work uses bilingual corpora. Bannard, and Callison-Burch [3] used methods from statistical machine translation to find lexical and phrasal paraphrases in parallel text. Ganitkevitch et al. [13] scaled up these techniques to produce the Paraphrase Database (PPDB), which has then been extended for many languages [12] since it only needs parallel text. Wieting et al. [38] used NMT to translate the non-English side of sentential parallel texts to get English-English paraphrase pairs and claimed their data quality to be on par with manually-written English paraphrase pairs. The same authors then scale up the method to produce a larger dataset [37]. We intend to do the same but produce Portuguese-Portuguese paraphrase pairs.

Sentence Embeddings
As in Wieting and Gimbel's work [37,38], we train sentence embeddings to demonstrate the quality of the dataset. These works trained models on noisy paraphrase pairs and evaluated them primarily on semantic textual similarity (STS) tasks. Prior work in learning general sentence embeddings has used autoencoders [16], encoder-decoder architectures [11], and other learning frameworks [1,9,27]. More recently, there are approaches leveraging the embeddings of pretrained language models, like SimCSE [14] or Sentence-BERT (SBERT) [30]. We use the latter for our STS task.

Parallel Text for Learning Embeddings
Prior work has shown that parallel text, and resources built from parallel text like NMT systems and PPDB, can be used to learn word and sentence embeddings. Some works have used PPDB as a knowledge resource for training or improving embeddings [26,36]. Others have used NMT architectures and training settings to obtain better embeddings, like Mallinson et al. [25] that adapted trained NMT models to produce sentence similarity scores in semantic evaluations, or Wieting and Gimpel [37] that proposed mega-batches to expand the search space for selecting negative examples for each paraphrase pair to then compute a margin triple loss [30]. In this work, we opt to use a multiple negative loss [15] because we do not have negative examples. This loss assumes that every other target sentence (aside from the target sentence from the pair being evaluated) in the batch is a negative example.

3   The Dataset

To create our dataset, we used back-translation [38]. We used an English-Portuguese NMT system to translate English sentences from the training data into Portuguese. We paired the translations with the European Portuguese references to form Portuguese-Portuguese paraphrase pairs (i.e., $\langle MixedPortuguese, EuropeanPortuguese \rangle$ pairs).

Throughout the document, we refer to Portuguese as a mixture of European and Brazilian Portuguese, as most pre-trained multilingual models do not distinguish between the two variants. To refer to a specific variant, we explicitly say so.

Table 1. Examples from source dataset machine-translated sentences that build into paraphrase pairs for our dataset. Each entry consists of the original English sentence ("en-XX"), its Portuguese machine translation ("MT pt-XX") and the European Portuguese reference ("pt-PT"). These pairs have varying lexical diversity.

en-XX	MT pt-XX	pt-PT
That's for someone else to judge	É para outra pessoa julgar.	Não é a nós que cabe julgar isso
What are you doing with those people, I wondered	O que estão a fazer com essas pessoas, perguntei-me	O que fazes com estas pessoas, perguntei-me eu
You wouldn't want me to pretend	Vocês não querem que eu finge.	Vais querer que eu finja?
But I was able to find out that her area of expertise was gerontology	Mas pude descobrir que a sua área de especialidade era a geronologia.	Mas eu consegui descobrir que a sua área profissional era a gerontologia
You all right?	Está bem?	Estás bem?
Guys, it was like a circus out there	Rapaces, era como um circo lá fora	Rapazes, estava muita confusão

Because pivot translation can potentially diminish the fidelity of the information forwarded into the target language, we chose parallel data containing text in European Portuguese, from which we can translate the side which is not European Portuguese. This is the approach from [37]. Additionally, in [38], the authors found little difference among Czech, German, and French as source languages for back-translation from English. As for Portuguese, we did not find prior work focusing on the best source language to translate from. As such, to maximize performance, we chose English as our language to translate from and an English-centric multilingual pre-trained language model, such as mBART-50 [35]. This model extends the original mBART [24] to encompass more languages, including Portuguese.

3.1 Choosing a Data Source

As far as we know, the two primary publicly available datasets with European Portuguese bitext are Europarl [20] and OpenSubtitles [23]. As per the study conducted in [37], Europarl exhibits low diversity in terms of rare word usage, vocabulary entropy, and parse entropy, mainly due to the formulaic and repetitive nature of speech in a Parliament. In [37], the authors chose the CzEng dataset [8], of which a significant portion is movie subtitles which tend to use a vast vocabulary and have a diversity of sentence structures. This serves as a strong motivation for conducting our experiments using OpenSubtitles.

The OpenSubtitles dataset has over 33 million English-European Portuguese bitext pairs. Because of the computational expense of translating such an extensive dataset, we sample 3 million entries. When translating the English sentences to Portuguese, we used beam search with a beam size of 5 and selected the highest-scoring translation. We show illustrative examples in Table 1. Note the matching is not always perfect, mainly because the original bitext pairs not being perfect translations (there are instances where the meaning is significantly different). The translations are of very high quality, with sporadic errors like gender-mismatch due to English having no gendered nouns, or translations failing to discern whether a second person pronoun ("you") is singular or plural.

3.2 Automatic Quality Assessment, Cleaning, and Filtering

As manually evaluating such an extensive dataset is very expensive and time-consuming, we resort to automatic mechanisms to assess the dataset's quality and clean and filter uninteresting information.

We found recurring problems on manual inspection, like close captions, start hyphenation, and sentence misalignment. For example, "(vomita) Tu queres saber o que é de loucos?" has a close caption that should be removed. Similarly, in "- Deem-me dois minutos.", the hyphen should be removed to match the target sentence. An example of the misalignment is 'E Dr^a. Lin, tente não me chamar." → "Sim.", where the two sentences do not share the same meaning. To find these pairs, we search for big differences in token size between source and target. We use the following equation to prune heavily uneven word counts while normalizing for text sizes:

$$|n\_tokens_{src} - n\_tokens_{tgt}| / \max(n\_tokens_{src}, n\_tokens_{tgt}) > 0.5$$

We arbitrate the threshold value to be 0.5 based on a few empirical experiments. For a random sample of 100 000 entries, we find around 3 500 entries that do not match the above equation (are deemed unfit to keep). The mean SBERT score for this sample is 81.69, a low value for SBERT, indicating that these pairs with heavily uneven word counts have a low semantic similarity.

Finally, we remove sentence pairs that are exactly the same. This behavior occurs most prominently for very small sentences (<4 tokens).

3.3 Data Analysis

We further analyze the relevance of the data. As per Li et al. [22], relevance regards how semantically close the paraphrase text is to the original text. We study the semantic similarity resorting to Sentence BERT [30] (SBERT). Specifically, we conduct preliminary testing with multilingual SBERT (mSBERT) [31], and a Brazilian Portuguese SBERT[2] trained on ASSIN2 [29]. Despite being more general-purpose, we found mSBERT performs better than the latter. Using

---

[2] This model can be found on the HuggingFace as "ricardo-filho/bert-base-portuguese-cased-nli-assin-2".

mSBERT and normalizing the scores in the range of $[0, 1]$, we get an average value of 87.724, which suggests the majority of the pairs have high semantic similarity between them. Nonetheless, we prune pairs with semantic scores lower than 80. From empirical assessment, from this threshold on, most sentence pairs are misaligned.

We do not conduct any particular study regarding fluency (the syntactic and grammar correctness of the paraphrased text [22]), relying on the assumption that pre-trained language models are inherently good grammar inductors [19].

OSPT has 1 519554 pairs. For reference, two widely used English sentential parallel paraphrase datasets, QQP[3] and PAWS [39] have respectively 1 49263 and 2 8904 paraphrase pairs. TaPaCo [32], a corpus of sentential paraphrases for various languages, has 3 6451 Brazilian Portuguese paraphrase pairs. The OSPT averages 8 words for both source and target sentences, as subtitles are rarely long. QQP averages around 11 words per sentence, PAWS around 21, and TaPaCo around 7.

4 Learning Sentence Embeddings

We assess the quality of the dataset intrinsically, using it to train sentence embeddings.

4.1 Experimental Setup

We fine-tune a mSBERT [31] model. We train the model for 10 epochs with a batch size of 64, a learning rate of 2e-5, AdamW optimizer and a linear scheduler with 100 warmup steps. As referred to in Sect. 2, the training loss we use allows for training good quality sentence embeddings without negative examples. The training data for the loss consists of sentence pairs $[(a_1, b_1), \ldots, (a_n, b_n)]$ where we assume that (a_i, b_i) are similar sentences and (a_i, b_j) are dissimilar sentences for $i \neq j$. It minimizes the distance (cosine similarity) between a_i and b_i while maximizing the distance between a_i and b_j for all $i \neq j$.

We evaluate sentence embeddings using the ASSIN2 semantic textual similarity (STS) tasks [29]. Given two sentences, the aim of the STS tasks is to predict their similarity on a 0-5 scale, where 0 indicates the sentences are on different topics and 5 means they are entirely equivalent. To fairly compare OSPT with ASSIN2's official training data (with 6 500 pairs), we randomly sampled a subset of 6.5K pairs from our dataset. We further compare with a 6500-pair subset of the TaPaCo dataset.

---

[3] https://quoradata.quora.com/First-Quora-Dataset-Release-Question-Pairs.

4.2   Results

In Table 2, we report the scores for the official task's evaluation metrics.

Table 2. Results for STS on the ASSIN2 test set. We compare three fine-tuned SBERT models, one using the ASSIN2 training data (has 6 500 pairs), other using a random subset of 6 500 samples from TaPaCo [32], and the other using a random subset of 6 500 samples from OSPT. We report the official metrics from the STS tasks of the ASSIN2 competition. The best results are in **bold**.

	Pearson's r	MSE
SBERT-ASSIN2	0.711	0.03
SBERT-TaPaCo	0.763	**0.02**
SBERT-OSPT	**0.780**	**0.02**

The results reported compare the same model trained under the same conditions, and with the same amount of data, only changing the data source. The mSBERT trained with a subset of OSPT performed the best for the task, achieving the highest Pearson's r and MSE values. Assuming the randomly sampled subsets to be good representations of the data as a whole (which is hard to assess if this is true for sentences), we can conclude the data to be of good quality, or at least, to be good enough to produce good quality sentence embeddings.

5   Paraphrase Generation

Besides creating state-of-the-art paraphrastic sentence embeddings, we show our dataset can help produce interesting paraphrase generators for data augmentation.

5.1   Experimental Setup

We fine-tune three mBART [24] models, two on subsets of OSPT and another on the TaPaCo dataset. Since our dataset is so large, it is computationally demanding to train paraphrase generation models in its entirety. As such, we filter the data to create a training set of 240K samples, 30K samples for validation, and 30K for testing. Additionally, we build a subset of OSPT of 36451 training pairs (the same size as TaPaCo) for fair comparison. We train both models for four epochs, with a batch size of 64, a learning rate of 1e-4, AdamW optimizer, and a linear scheduler with 100 warmup steps.

Following recent work [17], we use as our primary evaluation metric the **iBLEU** [33] score:

$$\text{iBLEU} = \alpha \cdot \text{BLEU}(outputs, references)$$
$$- (1 - \alpha) \cdot \text{BLEU}(outputs, inputs)$$

iBLEU measures the fidelity of generated outputs to reference paraphrases as well as the level of diversity introduced. We set α as 0.7 per the original paper [33]. Additionally, to probe the semantic retention of the generations, we measure the semantic similarity using mSBERT [30]. We chose this metric because it was found to have the lowest coupling between semantic similarity and linguistic diversity [2].

5.2   Results

We evaluate paraphrase generation using the ASSIN2 competition's test set.

Table 3. Top-1 results for automatic evaluation on the ASSIN2 test set. The **Source as prediction** baseline serves as a dataset quality indicator. The naming convention matches the number of pairs used to train the models. The best results are in **bold**.

	iBLEU↑	SBERT↑
Source as prediction	−9.9	74.876
mBart-OSPT-240k	−2.5	70.476
mBart-OSPT-36k	**−2.3**	69.324
mBart-TaPaCo	−3.6	**71.048**

Table 3 shows the performance of the two mBART-based models we fine-tuned. The results are bound to the basic statistics of the data, hence why we report the *source as prediction*, that is, using the source sentences as predictions. The ASSIN2 pairs have high word overlap, expressed as a low iBLEU score in the *source as prediction* baseline. Consequently, models trained on that data will produce sentences similar to the sources. That is why the iBLEU scores are low across the board. These iBLEU values could be made higher by increasing the α hyper-parameter, but we would be reducing the contribution of lexicon diversity for the results. Nevertheless, we can see that we can improve diversity by having more diverse generations (expressed as a higher iBLEU score) with a drop in the semantics (even though the metric is not fully decoupled from the vocabulary used). The model trained on OSPT-36k achieves the highest diversity but at the cost of some semantic preservation. Ramping up the number of training examples to 240k has a minimal decrease in diversity with increased semantic fidelity, much closer to the model trained on TaPaCo. Note that we did not fiddle with hyper-parameters, and four epochs may not be sufficient for achieving optimal performance considering the complexity and size of our model, hence why the larger model is not clearly better than the smaller one. Notice that TaPaCo is a Brazilian Portuguese dataset, such as ASSIN2, making it likely to perform better in this specific context, as we are trying to produce European Portuguese text. Moreover, this ASSIN2 test set contains texts with low syntactic diversity and many uses of the gerund form of the verbs, a pattern most prevalent in Brazilian Portuguese.

A. Sousa and H. L. Cardoso

Table 4. Example generations from the mBART-OSPT-240k model on the ASSIN2 test set illustrating the *pseudo*-translation.

Original	Generation
Alguém está tocando um piano	Está alguém a tocar piano
O homem está falando ao telefone	O homem está a falar ao telefone
Um homem negro está andando no pavimento	Está um negro a caminhar no chão
Duas mulheres estão dançando	Duas mulheres dançam

Table 4 shows some examples of these sentences and the respective generations from the mBart-OSPT-240k model. We can produce European Portuguese paraphrases by building the training pairs with the European Portuguese as targets, even when paraphrasing from Brazilian Portuguese. Our model performs a *pseudo*-translation from Brazilian Portuguese to European Portuguese.

Future work could use the properties mentioned above of the paraphrase generator to further denoise the dataset we present in this paper. We could use the generations of this paraphrase generator to convert the source sentences of our dataset into European-like Portuguese. We can also consider generalizing the approach and employing this technique to convert any Brazilian Portuguese text into European Portuguese.

6 Conclusion

We described the creation of a dataset of more than 1.5M Portuguese sentential paraphrase pairs. We showed how to use this dataset to train paraphrastic sentence embeddings that outperform systems trained with other data on STS tasks, as well as how it can be used for generating paraphrases for purposes of data augmentation and *pseudo*-translate from Brazilian Portuguese to European Portuguese.

The key advantage of our approach is that it only requires parallel text and a translation system. There are hundreds of millions of parallel sentence pairs, and more are being generated continually. Our procedure immediately applies to the wide range of languages for which we have parallel text. Additionally, the quality of the datasets generated using this approach will increase in parallel with improvements in Machine Translation.

We release our dataset, code, and pre-trained sentence embeddings.[4]

This work is supported by LIACC, funded by national funds through FCT/MCTES (PIDDAC), with reference UIDB/00027/2020.

Acknowledgments. The first author is supported by a PhD studentship with reference 2022.13409.BD from Fundação para a Ciência e a Tecnologia (FCT).

---

[4] We will release code and embeddings under the permissive MIT license.

References

1. Arora, S., Liang, Y., Ma, T.: A simple but tough-to-beat baseline for sentence embeddings. In: International Conference on Learning Representations (2017)
2. Bandel, E., Aharonov, R., Shmueli-Scheuer, M., Shnayderman, I., Slonim, N., Ein-Dor, L.: Quality controlled paraphrase generation. In: Proceedings of the 60th Annual Meeting of the Association for Computational Linguistics (Volume 1: Long Papers), pp. 596–609. Association for Computational Linguistics, Dublin, Ireland, May 2022. https://doi.org/10.18653/v1/2022.acl-long.45
3. Bannard, C., Callison-Burch, C.: Paraphrasing with bilingual parallel corpora. In: Proceedings of the 43rd Annual Meeting of the Association for Computational Linguistics (ACL'05), pp. 597–604. Association for Computational Linguistics, Ann Arbor, Michigan, Jun 2005. https://doi.org/10.3115/1219840.1219914
4. Barreiro, A., Mota, C.: e-pact: esperto paraphrase aligned corpus of en-ep/bp translations. Traduçao em Revista 1(22), 87–102 (2017)
5. Barreiro, A., Mota, C., Baptista, J., Chacoto, L., Carvalho, P.: Linguistic resources for paraphrase generation in portuguese: a lexicon-grammar approach. Lang. Resour. Eval. (2021)
6. Barzilay, R., McKeown, K.R.: Extracting paraphrases from a parallel corpus. In: Proceedings of the 39th Annual Meeting of the Association for Computational Linguistics, pp. 50–57. Association for Computational Linguistics, Toulouse, France, Jul 2001. https://doi.org/10.3115/1073012.1073020
7. Bhagat, R., Hovy, E.: Squibs: what is a paraphrase? Comput. Linguist. 39(3), 463–472 (2013)
8. Bojar, O., Dušek, O., Kocmi, T., Libovický, J., Novák, M., Popel, M., Sudarikov, R., Variš, D.: Czeng 1.6: enlarged czech-english parallel corpus with processing tools dockered. In: Text, Speech, and Dialogue: 19th International Conference, TSD 2016, Brno, Czech Republic, 12–16 Sept. 2016, Proceedings 19. pp. 231–238. Springer (2016)
9. Conneau, A., Kiela, D., Schwenk, H., Barrault, L., Bordes, A.: Supervised learning of universal sentence representations from natural language inference data. In: Proceedings of the 2017 Conference on Empirical Methods in Natural Language Processing, pp. 670–680. Association for Computational Linguistics, Copenhagen, Denmark, Sept. 2017. https://doi.org/10.18653/v1/D17-1070
10. Dolan, W.B., Brockett, C.: Automatically constructing a corpus of sentential paraphrases. In: Proceedings of the Third International Workshop on Paraphrasing (IWP2005) (2005)
11. Gan, Z., Pu, Y., Henao, R., Li, C., He, X., Carin, L.: Learning generic sentence representations using convolutional neural networks. In: Proceedings of the 2017 Conference on Empirical Methods in Natural Language Processing, pp. 2390–2400. Association for Computational Linguistics, Copenhagen, Denmark, Sept. 2017. https://doi.org/10.18653/v1/D17-1254
12. Ganitkevitch, J., Callison-Burch, C.: The multilingual paraphrase database. In: Proceedings of the Ninth International Conference on Language Resources and Evaluation (LREC'14), pp. 4276–4283. European Language Resources Association (ELRA), Reykjavik, Iceland, May 2014
13. Ganitkevitch, J., Van Durme, B., Callison-Burch, C.: PPDB: the paraphrase database. In: Proceedings of the 2013 Conference of the North American Chapter of the Association for Computational Linguistics: Human Language Technologies, pp. 758–764. Association for Computational Linguistics, Atlanta, Georgia, Jun 2013

14. Gao, T., Yao, X., Chen, D.: SimCSE: simple contrastive learning of sentence embeddings. In: Proceedings of the 2021 Conference on Empirical Methods in Natural Language Processing, pp. 6894–6910. Association for Computational Linguistics, Online and Punta Cana, Dominican Republic, Nov 2021. https://doi.org/10.18653/v1/2021.emnlp-main.552

15. Henderson, M., Al-Rfou, R., Strope, B., Sung, Y.H., Lukács, L., Guo, R., Kumar, S., Miklos, B., Kurzweil, R.: Efficient natural language response suggestion for smart reply (2017). arXiv:1705.00652

16. Hill, F., Cho, K., Korhonen, A.: Learning distributed representations of sentences from unlabelled data. In: Proceedings of the 2016 Conference of the North American Chapter of the Association for Computational Linguistics: Human Language Technologies, pp. 1367–1377. Association for Computational Linguistics, San Diego, CA, June 2016. https://doi.org/10.18653/v1/N16-1162

17. Hosking, T., Tang, H., Lapata, M.: Hierarchical sketch induction for paraphrase generation. In: Proceedings of the 60th Annual Meeting of the Association for Computational Linguistics (Volume 1: Long Papers), pp. 2489–2501. Association for Computational Linguistics, Dublin, Ireland, May 2022. https://doi.org/10.18653/v1/2022.acl-long.178

18. Jiang, Y., Kummerfeld, J.K., Lasecki, W.S.: Understanding task design trade-offs in crowdsourced paraphrase collection. In: Proceedings of the 55th Annual Meeting of the Association for Computational Linguistics (Volume 2: Short Papers), pp. 103–109. Association for Computational Linguistics, Vancouver, Canada, Jul 2017. https://doi.org/10.18653/v1/P17-2017

19. Kim, T., Choi, J., Edmiston, D., Goo Lee, S.: Are pre-trained language models aware of phrases? Simple but strong baselines for grammar induction. In: International Conference on Learning Representations (2020)

20. Koehn, P.: Europarl: a parallel corpus for statistical machine translation. In: Proceedings of Machine Translation Summit X: Papers, Phuket, Thailand, pp. 79–86, 13–15 Sept. 2005

21. Lan, W., Qiu, S., He, H., Xu, W.: A continuously growing dataset of sentential paraphrases. In: Proceedings of the 2017 Conference on Empirical Methods in Natural Language Processing. pp. 1224–1234. Association for Computational Linguistics, Copenhagen, Denmark, Sept. 2017. https://doi.org/10.18653/v1/D17-1126

22. Li, Z., Jiang, X., Shang, L., Li, H.: Paraphrase generation with deep reinforcement learning. In: Proceedings of the 2018 Conference on Empirical Methods in Natural Language Processing, pp. 3865–3878. Association for Computational Linguistics, Brussels, Belgium, Oct.–Nov. 2018. https://doi.org/10.18653/v1/D18-1421 ¡error l="308" c="Invalid command: paragraph not started." /¿

23. Lison, P., Tiedemann, J.: OpenSubtitles2016: extracting large parallel corpora from movie and TV subtitles. In: Proceedings of the Tenth International Conference on Language Resources and Evaluation (LREC'16), pp. 923–929. European Language Resources Association (ELRA), Portorož, Slovenia, May 2016

24. Liu, Y., Gu, J., Goyal, N., Li, X., Edunov, S., Ghazvininejad, M., Lewis, M., Zettlemoyer, L.: Multilingual denoising pre-training for neural machine translation. Trans. Assoc. Comput. Linguist. **8**, 726–742 (2020)

25. Mallinson, J., Sennrich, R., Lapata, M.: Paraphrasing revisited with neural machine translation. In: Proceedings of the 15th Conference of the European Chapter of the Association for Computational Linguistics: Volume 1, Long Papers, pp. 881–893. Association for Computational Linguistics, Valencia, Spain, Apr 2017

26. Mrkšić, N., Ó Séaghdha, D., Thomson, B., Gašić, M., Rojas-Barahona, L.M., Su, P.H., Vandyke, D., Wen, T.H., Young, S.: Counter-fitting word vectors to linguistic constraints. In: Proceedings of the 2016 Conference of the North American Chapter of the Association for Computational Linguistics: Human Language Technologies, pp. 142–148. Association for Computational Linguistics, San Diego, CA, June 2016. https://doi.org/10.18653/v1/N16-1018

27. Pagliardini, M., Gupta, P., Jaggi, M.: Unsupervised learning of sentence embeddings using compositional n-gram features. In: Proceedings of the 2018 Conference of the North American Chapter of the Association for Computational Linguistics: Human Language Technologies, Volume 1 (Long Papers), pp. 528–540. Association for Computational Linguistics, New Orleans, Louisiana, June 2018. https://doi.org/10.18653/v1/N18-1049

28. Pellicer, L.F.A.O., Pirozelli, P., Costa, A.H.R., Inoue, A.: PTT5-paraphraser: diversity and meaning fidelity in automatic portuguese paraphrasing. In: Computational Processing of the Portuguese Language: 15th International Conference, PROPOR 2022, Fortaleza, Brazil, 21–23 Mar. 2022, Proceedings, pp. 299–309. Springer (2022)

29. Real, L., Fonseca, E., Oliveira, H.G.: The ASSIN 2 shared task: a quick overview. In: International Conference on Computational Processing of the Portuguese Language, pp. 406–412. Springer (2020)

30. Reimers, N., Gurevych, I.: Sentence-BERT: sentence embeddings using siamese BERT-networks. In: Proceedings of the 2019 Conference on Empirical Methods in Natural Language Processing. Association for Computational Linguistics, Nov. 2019

31. Reimers, N., Gurevych, I.: Making monolingual sentence embeddings multilingual using knowledge distillation. In: Proceedings of the 2020 Conference on Empirical Methods in Natural Language Processing. Association for Computational Linguistics, Nov. 2020

32. Scherrer, Y.: TaPaCo: a corpus of sentential paraphrases for 73 languages. In: Proceedings of the Twelfth Language Resources and Evaluation Conference, pp. 6868–6873. European Language Resources Association, Marseille, France, May 2020

33. Sun, H., Zhou, M.: Joint learning of a dual SMT system for paraphrase generation. In: Proceedings of the 50th Annual Meeting of the Association for Computational Linguistics (Volume 2: Short Papers), pp. 38–42. Association for Computational Linguistics, Jeju Island, Korea, July 2012

34. Suzuki, Y., Kajiwara, T., Komachi, M.: Building a non-trivial paraphrase corpus using multiple machine translation systems. In: Proceedings of ACL 2017, Student Research Workshop, pp. 36–42. Association for Computational Linguistics, Vancouver, Canada, Jul 2017

35. Tang, Y., Tran, C., Li, X., Chen, P.J., Goyal, N., Chaudhary, V., Gu, J., Fan, A.: Multilingual translation with extensible multilingual pretraining and finetuning (2020). arXiv:2008.00401

36. Wieting, J., Bansal, M., Gimpel, K., Livescu, K.: From paraphrase database to compositional paraphrase model and back. Trans. Assoc. Comput. Linguist. **3**, 345–358 (2015)

37. Wieting, J., Gimpel, K.: ParaNMT-50M: Pushing the limits of paraphrastic sentence embeddings with millions of machine translations. In: Proceedings of the 56th Annual Meeting of the Association for Computational Linguistics (Volume 1: Long Papers), pp. 451–462. Association for Computational Linguistics, Melbourne, Australia, July 2018. https://doi.org/10.18653/v1/P18-1042

38. Wieting, J., Mallinson, J., Gimpel, K.: Learning paraphrastic sentence embeddings from back-translated bitext. In: Proceedings of the 2017 Conference on Empirical Methods in Natural Language Processing, pp. 274–285. Association for Computational Linguistics, Copenhagen, Denmark, Sept. 2017. https://doi.org/10.18653/v1/D17-1026

39. Zhang, Y., Baldridge, J., He, L.: PAWS: Paraphrase adversaries from word scrambling. In: Proceedings of the 2019 Conference of the North American Chapter of the Association for Computational Linguistics: Human Language Technologies, Volume 1 (Long and Short Papers), pp. 1298–1308. Association for Computational Linguistics, Minneapolis, Minnesota, June 2019. https://doi.org/10.18653/v1/N19-1131

Task Conditioned BERT for Joint Intent Detection and Slot-Filling

Diogo Tavares[1]([⊠]), Pedro Azevedo[2], David Semedo[1], Ricardo Sousa[2], and João Magalhães[1]

[1] Universidade NOVA de Lisboa, Lisbon, Portugal
dc.tavares@campus.fct.unl.pt, {df.semedo,jm.magalhaes}@fct.unl.pt
[2] Farfetch, Lisbon, Portugal

Abstract. Dialogue systems need to deal with the unpredictability of user intents to track dialogue state and the heterogeneity of slots to understand user preferences. In this paper we investigate the hypothesis that solving these challenges as one unified model will allow the transfer of parameter support data across the different tasks. The proposed principled model is based on a Transformer encoder, trained on multiple tasks, and leveraged by a rich input that conditions the model on the target inferences. Conditioning the Transformer encoder on multiple target inferences over the same corpus, i.e., intent and multiple slot types, allows learning richer language interactions than a single-task model would be able to. In fact, experimental results demonstrate that conditioning the model on an increasing number of dialogue inference tasks leads to improved results: on the MultiWOZ dataset, the joint intent and slot detection can be improved by 3.2% by conditioning on intent, 10.8% by conditioning on slot and 14.4% by conditioning on both intent and slots. Moreover, on real conversations with Farfetch costumers, the proposed conditioned BERT can achieve high joint-goal and intent detection performance throughout a dialogue.

Keywords: Dialogue state tracking · Intent detection · Slot filling · BERT

1 Introduction

Conversational assistants need to explicitly maintain information about user goals by tracking the user intent and storing a set of *slot-value pairs*. This is critical to ensure the smoothness of user-agent interaction leading to frustration-free outcomes. Both dialogue state and slot values can be used as a way to provide a general initial product suggestion [13], before more fine-grained attributes are requested by the system. Hence, keeping the dialogue agent up-to-date with user's perception of the current conversation is a critical, yet, non-trivial task [12].

Algorithms that support more natural conversations need to tackle complex phrasal constructions [3] and dialogue contextual information [11]. Each

N. Moniz et al. (Eds.): EPIA 2023, LNAI 14115, pp. 467–480, 2023.
https://doi.org/10.1007/978-3-031-49008-8_37

user utterance conveys multiple and intertwined hints leading to very rich language structures and possible co-references to the dialogue history. Recent approaches [3,11,12,25], explored the Transformer model in this context and leveraged the attention mechanisms to tackle the above challenges. A common practice is to use the control token to detect intent [4,20,22] or presence of a slot span [3,17,23]. Recent works extend the Transformer with new heads [4,20,22], tackling both intent detection and slot filling in a multi-task setting. While these works capture the dependencies between intent detection and slot-filling, all the inferences are solely conditioned on the dialogue utterances, without accounting for each target inference task.

Our research hypothesis is that jointly learning dialogue inference tasks while conditioning the Transformer on the aforementioned dialogue state-tracking (DST) tasks, will lead to more precise joint-inferences of user intent and slot filling, i.e., more accurate dialogue state inferences. This hypothesis is supported by the way BERT [7] attends to different tokens [5]—the [CLS] token, retaining a global sequence embedding, can leverage a number of language tasks [7], by functioning as an attention hub, contextualizing the whole input sequence. Extra special attention hub tokens can then be added and learned through fine-tuning. Hence, we argue that introducing new task-specific tokens, acting as task-specific attention hubs, alongside Transformer heads, could allow for the introduction of additional domain-specific operations. We argue that these empirical observations are all rooted on the same principle: *when the Transformer encoder is conditioned on the target task, the self-attention mechanism across all layers becomes aware of the target inference operation.* Thus, the conditioning input can steer the inferences across all layers. This forms the base assumption of our work.

In the following section we discuss the related work. In Sects. 3 and 3.1 we describe the proposed approach. Section 4 presents and discuss experimental results.

2   Related Work

Dialogue State Tracking (DST) refers to the act of maintaining a set of user goals or preferred attributes by performing slot-filling in task-oriented dialogues, which can be either single or multi-domain. Span-based slot-filling approaches have been widely explored with promising results, as seen in [23], [3], [17], with the first employing RNN encoding and the latter two using a BERT-based encoder. Extracting spans may sometimes be sufficient to attain good performance, but, in open-ended dialogues, may prove insufficient when facing values implicitly mentioned by the user or values which refer to previously filled slots. To remedy this, work towards introducing other types of information has been developed, maintaining the same BERT encoder setup. [11] proposed to directly refer the previously made slot assignments or system suggestions, depending on the output of the slot-gate, which is extended so as to perform a more fine-grained classification. Other approaches, such as [26], make use of predefined ontologies when slots are considered categorical. While non-categorical slots are classified by detecting relevant spans in the dialogue, categorical slots use a fixed BERT model to encode all possible slot key-value combinations in the ontology, and use cosine similarity matching with the [CLS] token output of both BERT instances. While this work is similar in spirit to ours, we directly adapt BERT-DST [3] to develop our models, as was previously attempted by [11].

BERT-DST [3] classifies each slot independently from one another in two steps: first, using BERT's [CLS] token embeddings, it classifies whether a slot is or is not present in the utterances, or whether the user expressed no interest in its value; referred to as a **slot-gate**. Second, for each slot where the slot-gate output is positive, using the embedding of each token, attempts to extract the dialogue span in which its value is mentioned.

Intent Detection requires analyzing a user utterance and classifying it, as a whole, given a set of possible user intents. Transformer encoder-based approaches are especially adept at this task, performing the classification step using sentence embeddings. Intent detection data is limited in task-oriented datasets, and most approaches [4,14,16] focus on single-utterance queries for voice assistants [6,9], forgoing multi-turn interactions.

Recently developed **DST datasets**, such as [17,24], have attempted to account for the fact that real-world systems will contain categorical and non-categorical slots. Alongside this notion, they also push the relevance of intent detection, with [17] supplying intent annotations and [24], an update to Multi-WOZ [2], updating the annotation set with user intent annotations.

3   Proposed Model

Slot-filling and intent detection are natural language processing tasks associated to the understanding of a sequence $\mathcal{D} = \{(u_1, a_1), ..., (u_T, a_T)\}$, of T dialogue turns, where each turn i is represented by a tuple (u_i, a_i) composed of user and system utterances, respectively. First, given the user utterance u_{T+1} and a set of M possible intents $\mathcal{I} = \{I_1, ..., I_M\}$, our goal is to infer the correct intent I_m of the user utterance. Second, given all dialogue utterances up to turn T and a set of N slot-keys $\mathcal{S} = \{s_1, ..., s_N\}$, the goal is to assign a slot-value $v \in \{v_1, ..., v_i, ...\}$ to every slot-key s_k which was, explicitly or otherwise, accepted or suggested by the user in the turns present in $\mathcal{D}$. A slot-value can be anything from a *hotel location* to the *number of people* in a restaurant reservation. The act of maintaining all relevant slot key-value pairs in a dialogue $\mathcal{D}$ is referred to as *Dialogue State Tracking* (DST).

3.1   Dialogue Task Conditioned Encoder

Conditioning the Transformer encoder on dialogue data can be achieved by considering the entire sequence of dialogue utterances. We can consider the independent probabilities of user intent $p(I_m|u_T, \mathcal{H}_c)$ and slot key-value

$p(s_k = v_i | u_T, \mathcal{H}_c)$ where u_T stands for the current user utterance, and $\mathcal{H}_c = \{u_{T-c}, \ldots, u_{T-1}\}$ is the set of past dialogue utterances. Alternatively to the independent modes, the joint-inferences of intent and slot filling is an explicitly dependency-based model, $p(I_m, s_k = v_i | u_T, \mathcal{H}_c)$ where the joint inference is, again, conditioned on the dialogue history $\mathcal{H}_c$. We extend these variables and investigate how different conditioning assumptions affect the Transformer inference performance for joint slot-filling and intent detection. In practice, we enrich the conditional probability with dialogue task information DT,

$$p(I_m, s_k = v_i | u_T, \mathcal{H}_c, DT), \tag{1}$$

which brings a series of advantages to Transformer-based implementations of the above model.

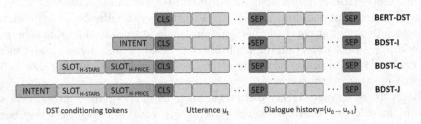

Fig. 1. The dialogue target task is explicitly passed to the encoder to condition its inferences.

3.2   Dialogue Task Conditioning

Large Transformer models [12, 20] are able to singlehandedly model complex tasks within dialogues, such as next sentence prediction, intent detection, and ontology-based slot-filling. Even though intent detection in TOD-BERT [20] is performed by leveraging the [CLS] token, both SimpleTOD [12] and TOD-BERT prepend user and assistant utterances with special tokens that denote the speaker. In DST, user and assistant turns should be attended differently: in order to perform slot-filling on a slot key, the user must either state it (explicitly or otherwise) or agree with an assistant suggestion. The aforementioned tokens can *condition* the Transformer into performing slot-filling appropriately in each situation. SimpleTOD [12] further makes use of tokens to delineate the start and end of each dialogue subtask, such as slot-filling and response generation.

Hence, in light of what we know [20] regarding special token usage on vanilla BERT ([CLS], [SEP]) and pre-trained TOD systems (utterance source tokens, subtask delineation), we pass dialogue specific tokens to the encoder to condition its inference operations (Fig. 1). Each one of these dialogue specific tokens is then fine-tuned on the corresponding target inference tasks. This is extremely important since now, all encoder layers will have explicit information regarding the required output task.

3.3 BERT-DST: Span Slots

First, we build on the BERT-DST [3] model and leverage the fact that BERT overly attends to special tokens [5]. This baseline model uses the standard input formatting [7] (first row of Fig. 1), where each input token is mapped to an h dimensional internal representation. The output $\mathbf{O} \in \mathbb{R}^{L \times h}$ comprises contextualized embedding representations of the input tokens.

As previously described, the [CLS] token feeds the slot-gate *softmax* layer, and the slot values are extracted using a span-based approach over $\mathcal{D}$. The span detection is implemented as two classification layers, one for the *span-start* and one for the *span-end*, see Fig. 2. All these layers are trained under a common loss function

$$\mathcal{L}_{slot} = \alpha \cdot \mathcal{L}_{slot\_gate} + \frac{1-\alpha}{2} \cdot (\mathcal{L}_{span\_start} + \mathcal{L}_{span\_end}), \qquad (2)$$

a convex combination parameterized by α.

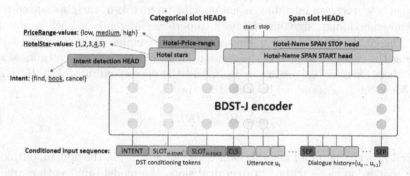

Fig. 2. The BDST-J architecture explicitly conditions the dialogue state inference operations in an end-to-end fashion over the intent and domain-slots.

3.4 BDST-I: Intent Detection

Our first take towards conditioning the Transformer encoder in the target inference task is to introduce an [INTENT] token to the sequence input. This new token embedding is used by a linear classification layer head to detect the intent.

Introducing the aforementioned token is feasible as both tasks are inherently related—in fact, recent DST approaches [17] attempt to consolidate intent detection and slot-filling within the same model. We also argue that slot classification is inherently coupled with the current user intent. When users *intend* to, for instance, request hotel information, it is more likely that they would mention the *number of people* than also request a *restaurant location* in the same turn. This is also shown by a strong Cramer's V correlation [1] between utterances of a specific intent and mentioned slots, on all considered datasets (discussed in Sect. 4.1). Specifically, the MultiWOZ and Farfetch-Costumers datasets both exhibit a 0.62, Farfetch-Sim 0.53, and Sim-R with 1.

We fine-tune BDST-I to both slot-filling and intent detection, adding $\beta \cdot \mathcal{L}_{intent}$ to the BERT-DST loss function (Eq. 2), with $\mathcal{L}_{intent}$ as the cross entropy loss for the intent prediction target, and β is a convex combination constants:

$$\mathcal{L}_{BDST-I} = \beta \cdot \mathcal{L}_{intent} + (1 - \beta) \cdot \mathcal{L}_{slot} \tag{3}$$

The embedding weights of the [INTENT] token are initialized with the [CLS] weights and are then fine-tuned to the intent detection task. β was determined experimentally on the validation set.

3.5   BDST-C: Categorical Slots

The search for the presence of slots is usually focused on the ones that make sense for the current dialogue stage—in real world scenarios, it is not plausible to search for all slots in all dialogue stages. Thus, for each categorical slot that we wish to detect, we introduce a slot-specific input token, each initialized with random embeddings, signaling we need to perform inference on each mentioned slot. The BERT model input is shown in Fig. 1: assuming *hotel-stars* and *hotel-price* as the categorical slots in the domain. In such cases, given a categorical slot [cs], whose possible values are in $V_{[cs]}$, and the corresponding token $BERT_{cs}$, the slot value is determined by a classifier head,

$$\arg\max_{V_{cs}} W_{cs} \cdot BERT_{cs} + b_{cs} \tag{4}$$

where V_{cs} is the set of all possible values for slot key [cs] in the domain ontology. Note that in domains without categorical slots, the model input is the same as vanilla BERT-DST.

BDST-C uses a different classification strategy depending on the slot type, so special considerations must be taken. We use a weighted sum for the loss, as follows:

$$\mathcal{L}_{BDST-C} = \beta \cdot \mathcal{L}_{cat} + (1 - \beta) \cdot \mathcal{L}_{slot} \tag{5}$$

Following the assumption that each slot is of equal importance to the final result, we fix β to (#*categorical slots*)/(#*total slots*).

3.6   BDST-J: Joint Intent and Multiple-Slots

As previously mentioned, both extensions attempt to exploit BERT being capable of assigning operations to special tokens. Similarly to how [CLS] is known to contain an aggregate sequence representation for NSP, it is easy to see how an [INTENT] token could also contain an aggregate representation based on all the possible intents. The same rationale applies to the extra categorical tokens, potentially containing sentence-level representations weighted on the semantic classification of specific slot-keys. Hence, we generalize the above approaches and introduce a fully flexible input sequence for the joint task, BDST-J, Fig. 1. It follows that, when training BDST-J, the loss function is:

$$\mathcal{L}_{BDST-J} = \alpha \cdot \mathcal{L}_{BDST-I} + (1 - \alpha) \cdot \mathcal{L}_{BDST-C} \qquad (6)$$

All parameters are determined on the validation set.

4 Evaluation

In this section we evaluate the vanilla BERT-DST model, BDST-I, BDST-C, and BDST-J on Sim-M, Sim-R, MultiWOZ 2.2 benchmarks, and on the Farfetch dataset, with real testers. All the baselines we tested are encoder-only architectures and have a similar number of parameters for a fair comparison, with the exception of the low-parameter TRADE-DST [21]. Other architectures require more training time and are more complex to deploy.

4.1 Datasets

M2M (Sim-M + Sim-R). Sim-R and Sim-M [18], respectively focusing on the restaurant and movie ticket domains, use crowdsourced paraphrasing of template utterances to simulate both user and agent. *All slots are non-categorical*, which biases the dialogue towards simple and direct conversations where slot values are *always* explicit in utterances. Dialogues are also noiseless, which may not reflect some of the challenges of an in production, robust DST system. Both datasets have a high proportion of out of vocabulary values, meaning that several test set slot values are absent during training. These values are contained in the *restaurant_name* and *movie* slots. Sim-R contains coarse-grained intent detection, with two possible intent values: *find* and *reserve restaurant*. Compared to other datasets used in this work, the amount of dialogues is relatively low—to perform well on M2M, models must develop a robust understanding of the semantics of slot-filling with sparse data.

MultiWOZ 2.2 (MW) MultiWOZ [2] is a widely used DST dataset which follows a standard human-to-human Wizard of Oz approach, spanning several domains. This allows for significantly higher language variety and more complex dialogues, as there are little to no restrictions put on the users when creating data. The lack of language restrictions and the *explicit usage of categorical slots* requires inferring values in turns, alongside extractively collecting slot values from utterances. An extra challenge is entity bias and misannotations, which have been approached by multiple works [8,10,15,24]. For training and evaluation, we use the 2.2 variant [24] supported by the original MW authors.[1] MW 2.2 extends the 2.1 version by cleaning some annotations and, not only introducing categorical slot annotations, but also introducing a set of *active user intents* per user turn. We follow the assumption that the *current user intent* is the next to

---

[1] https://github.com/budzianowski/multiwoz.

be fulfilled in the active user intent set (i.e. when an intent is removed from the active intent set, the user had been working towards fulfilling it). We use this assumption to retrieve a *single intent* per user utterance.

Farfetch Simulated Dialogues (Farfetch-Sim). This dataset comprises dialogues that simulate a fashion concierge [19] that understands customer needs and provides the correct answers. These were created in a way that reflects past real user experiences on the Farfetch platform, with a massive number of users. The simulated dialogues cover the complete customer journey: greeting, product search and exploration, to checkout. Throughout the different conversational journeys, users engage in product-grounded conversations, across different scenarios. We defined a range of scenarios and flows that reproduce real-world client-assistant interactions and introduce novel fashion-specific sub-dialogues that combine language and product metadata. From a total of 39,956 simulated dialogues, we extract 236,072 annotated utterances (slot-filling and intent) for training, 48,427 for validation and 48,097 testing.

Farfetch User Dialogues (Farfetch-Costumers). This set of real and authentic dialogues was obtained during a user testing session of a Farfetch's in-house conversational shopping assistant prototype. Users (actual costumers) were sampled based on device (desktop or mobile chat), and clothing gender (men or women), and had no prior experience using a conversational agent for product discovery. A total of 85 complete dialogues were annotated with slot-filling and intent detection information, and used for testing.

Table 1. Results on the M2M datasets.

Model	Sim-M		Sim-R	
	JG	Int. Acc.	JG	Int. Acc.
BERT-DST [3]	81.9	–	88.6	–
BDST-C	82.6	–	86.1	–
BDST-I	83.3	100.0	**91.3**	99.9
TripPy [11]	**83.5**	–	90.0	–

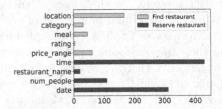

Fig. 3. Slot key distribution on the Sim-R train split, by intent

4.2 Training

Similarly to vanilla BERT-DST, we train the models using randomly sampled batches of size 32. Unless otherwise stated, we used the [BERT base, Uncased] architecture and weights and train for 100 epochs—except for the Farfetch dialogues, which we train for 20 epochs, due to their large amount. We set the learning rate to $2e^{-6}$ and use ADAM optimizer.

4.3 Metrics and Evaluation Methodology

We evaluate slot-filling using the standard **joint-goal accuracy** (JG) metric. Joint-goal accuracy is calculated as follows: in dialogue turn T, update a set of active slots S (initialized as $\emptyset$ when the dialogue begins) by adding all (*slot key, slot value*) pairs present in T so that S contains at most one of each slot keys, replacing ones that were previously present. The joint-goal score for turn T is 1 if S is equal to the ground truth, which is updated in a similar manner. (i.e. *active slots for all current and previous turns have been correctly classified*), and 0 otherwise. The final value is the average of the joint-goal scores of every dialogue turn. The joint-goal score tends to accumulate errors from earlier dialogue turns, unless the system is able to reclassify. We evaluate single-turn dialogues using the slot F1 score, as per JointBERT [4].

To evaluate in the M2M dataset, we use the provided BERT-DST [3] evaluation script. In the MultiWOZ dataset, we use the recommended TRADE-DST [21] pre-processing and evaluation scripts (we refrain from using the special pre-processing considerations for plural nouns). We use different evaluation scripts to ensure that comparisons with other works are adequate. We adapt the TRADE-DST evaluation scripts for the Farfetch dialogues.

4.4 General Results

In this section we analyze the performance of the proposed approach under different conditions: *no overlap of slots per intent* and *multi-slot per intent*.

No Overlap of Slots Per Intent: M2M Table 1 displays the evaluation metrics on the M2M datasets of our two proposals alongside vanilla BERT-DST performance. To generate an ontology for categorical slots, we use a similar heuristic to the one used for the SGD dataset [17]: slots which refer to a range of values or a small amount of discrete elements which can easily be listed are categorical, while slots with continuous, uncountable or several values are non-categorical. In Sim-M, we consider the slot *num_tickets* as categorical—in Sim-R, we consider the *num_people, price_range, meal* and *rating* slots.

The BDST-C performance on Sim-M is quite close to the vanilla model, as expected. This is due to only one slot being considered categorical. It is also important to note that the data was not created with categorical slots in mind—since all slots are explicitly present in dialogue spans, moving away from them may not be ideal for performance; especially relevant in SIM-R. On the other hand, the joint-goal score of BDST-I was higher than anticipated, showing itself to be competitive with the state-of-the-art [11]. By analyzing the coarse-grained intent information contained in the data (*none, BUY_MOVIE_TICKETS* in Sim-M; *none, FIND_RESTAURANT, RESERVE_RESTAURANT* in Sim-R). We find that, in M2M, the user intent directly correlates with the slots that are being mentioned, containing no overlap of mentioned slots, per intent (Fig. 3). The general performance improvement when introducing intent information supports our claim that *jointly training a model on both slot-filling and intent detection tasks can improve performance*.

Table 2. Joint-goal and intent detection accuracy scores on MultiWOZ 2.2 dataset. Values with * are reported by [24]. It should be noted that the DS-DST model uses two BERT models.

Model	MW 2.2	
	JG	Int. Acc.
BERT-DST [3]	33.0	–
BERT-DST (w/ dialogue history)	37.6	–
BDST-I	40.8	88.4
BDST-C	48.4	–
BDST-J	49.0	87.9
BDST-C^{LARGE}	48.6	–
BDST-J^{LARGE}	49.8	87.7
Systems		
SGD Baseline [17]	42.0*	–
TRADE-DST [21]	45.4*	–
DS-DST [26]	51.7*	–

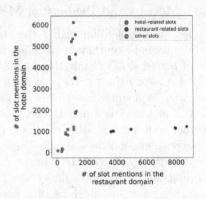

Fig. 4. Cross-domain slot mentions on the MultiWOZ 2.2 in the *hotel* versus *restaurant* domains

Multi-slot Per Intent: MultiWOZ Leveraged by the insights from the previous experiments and the results on the MultiWOZ dataset (Table 2), we reached several conclusions. First, we observed that training a model for both intent detection and slot-filling improves slot-filling performance. MultiWOZ 2.2, similarly to Sim-R, displays a high correlation between the active intent and the slots that are being mentioned. Second, the proposed conditioning architecture, i.e. tokens and corresponding heads, enabled our models to approach state-of-the-art performance. When compared with TRADE-DST, our model performs significantly better, proving to be a solid alternative for real-world systems where probabilistic outputs are preferred. Third, introducing more domain information improves overall performance. The joint-goal score largely increases by simply *introducing categorical slot tokens*. This can be seen when evaluating BERT-DST instances versus their BDST-C counterparts. A similar result can be seen when introducing intent information—in MultiWOZ, the result of the intent detection task can inform slot-filling modules of the domain relevant to the current utterance. Then, we show how the domain of the classified user intent is directly related to the frequency of mentioned slots (Fig. 4). When the current domain is restaurant, the **slot-gate** for hotel related slots is more likely to be correct when outputting *none*, while slot-gates related to restaurant slots are likely to output *span*. Finally, we also observed that increasing the model size slightly improves performance. In our tests using BERT-large, which contains about 3 times more trainable parameters than BERT-base (345 million vs. 110 million), shows a limited, but consistent, performance gain of less than 1% in all situations.

Table 3. Joint-goal and intent detection accuracy scores on Farfetch dialogues.

Model	Farfetch-Sim		Farfetch-Costumers		
	Slot F1	Int. Acc.	Slot F1	Int. Acc.	JG
JointBERT [4]	93.5	96.7	83.2	93.8	54.9
BDST [3]	94.2	–	85.0	–	65.1
BDST-I	**94.6**	**98.1**	**87.3**	**95.4**	**71.0**

Farfetch Dialogues Finally, we evaluated the proposed model in an online shopping assistant with both simulated and real costumer dialogues. For this experiment, models are trained solely on simulated dialogues. Table 3 reports the obtained results. First, in the simulated dialogues (Farfetch-Sim), we observe that BDST-I can successfully detect both intents and slot-values, with significant improvements in slot F1 and intent accuracy. When we consider dialogues with real costumers, the robustness of BDST-I becomes more evident: the gap in slot-F1, intent accuracy and, more importantly, the joint-goal accuracy between BDST-I and the other two baselines increase considerably. In particular, joint-goal accuracy is 71.0% and intent accuracy reaches 95.4%, which confirms that performing both tasks simultaneously and conditionally inferring slot values and intents provides the model with more information to improve its performance.

5 Conclusion

In the context of this work, we explicitly assumed that there are strong dependencies among language tokens, and that these dependencies become even more salient when the Transformer is conditioned on the dialogue data and on the dialogue state. We proposed an extension to a well-established model, which takes advantage of introducing extra dialogue information and multi-task learning, significantly increasing performance in all cases. Our contributions are as follows:

- **DST inference task conditioning architecture**: The multi-head architecture and the corresponding tokens elegantly extends the Transformer encoder architecture to facilitate joint slot-filling and intent detection. We also observed that training on the different tasks also improved results, thus leveraging the multi-task parameter sharing nature.
- **Multiple slot-filling across domains**: The proposed architecture nicely supports the MultiWOZ 2.2 scenarios where multiple heterogeneous slots co-occur in data, e.g. restaurant span-based slots with hotel categorical slots.
- **State of the art competitive results across heterogeneous domains**: Our models which perform intent detection and slot-filling outperform strong baselines [21] of equivalent complexity, by learning the intrinsic correlations between the user intent and the slots which are currently being mentioned.

- **Generalization to realistic domain-specific dialogues**: Experiments show that BDST-I effectively generalizes in state-tracking for domain-specific and real scenarios, outperforming the compared approaches.

To sum up, we proposed a principled and theoretically well grounded approach to dialogue state tracking that significantly improves performance. The model is flexible enough be augmented with external heuristics [11], and generalizes to multiple domains.

References

1. Akoğlu, H.: User's guide to correlation coefficients. Turkish J. Emerg. Med. **18**, 91–93 (2018)
2. Budzianowski, P., Wen, T.H., Tseng, B.H., Casanueva, I., Stefan, U., Osman, R., Gašić, M.: Multiwoz - a large-scale multi-domain wizard-of-oz dataset for task-oriented dialogue modelling. In: EMNLP (2018)
3. Chao, G.L., Lane, I.: BERT-DST: Scalable end-to-end dialogue state tracking with bidirectional encoder representations from transformer. In: INTERSPEECH (2019)
4. Chen, Q., Zhuo, Z., Wang, W.: Bert for joint intent classification and slot filling. arXiv:abs/1902.10909 (2019)
5. Clark, K., Khandelwal, U., Levy, O., Manning, C.D.: What does BERT look at? an analysis of BERT's attention. In: Proceedings of the 2019 ACL Workshop BlackboxNLP: Analyzing and Interpreting Neural Networks for NLP, pp. 276–286 (2019)
6. Coucke, A., Saade, A., Ball, A., Bluche, T., Caulier, A., Leroy, D., Doumouro, C., Gisselbrecht, T., Caltagirone, F., Lavril, T., et al.: Snips voice platform: an embedded spoken language understanding system for private-by-design voice interfaces. arXiv preprint arXiv:1805.10190 pp. 12–16 (2018)
7. Devlin, J., Chang, M.W., Lee, K., Toutanova, K.: BERT: Pre-training of deep bidirectional transformers for language understanding. In: Proceedings of the 2019 Conference of the North American Chapter of the Association for Computational Linguistics: Human Language Technologies, Volume 1 (Long and Short Papers), pp. 4171–4186 (2019)
8. Eric, M., Goel, R., Paul, S., Sethi, A., Agarwal, S., Gao, S., Kumar, A., Goyal, A.K., Ku, P., Hakkani-Tür, D.: Multiwoz 2.1: A consolidated multi-domain dialogue dataset with state corrections and state tracking baselines. In: Calzolari, N., Béchet, F., Blache, P., Choukri, K., Cieri, C., Declerck, T., Goggi, S., Isahara, H., Maegaard, B., Mariani, J., Mazo, H., Moreno, A., Odijk, J., Piperidis, S. (eds.) Proceedings of The 12th Language Resources and Evaluation Conference, LREC 2020, Marseille, France, May 11–16, 2020, pp. 422–428. European Language Resources Association (2020). https://aclanthology.org/2020.lrec-1.53/
9. Hakkani-Tur, D., Tur, G., Celikyilmaz, A., Chen, Y.N., Gao, J., Deng, L., Wang, Y.Y.: Multi-domain joint semantic frame parsing using bi-directional rnn-lstm. In: Proceedings of Interspeech (2016)
10. Han, T., Liu, X., Takanobu, R., Lian, Y., Huang, C., Wan, D., Peng, W., Huang, M.: Multiwoz 2.3: A multi-domain task-oriented dialogue dataset enhanced with annotation corrections and co-reference annotation. In: Proceedings of the 10th CCF International Conference on Natural Language Processing and Chinese Computing, pp. 206–218. CCF (2021)

11. Heck, M., van Niekerk, C., Lubis, N., Geishauser, C., Lin, H., Moresi, M., Gasic, M.: Trippy: A triple copy strategy for value independent neural dialog state tracking. In: Pietquin, O., Muresan, S., Chen, V., Kennington, C., Vandyke, D., Dethlefs, N., Inoue, K., Ekstedt, E., Ultes, S. (eds.) Proceedings of the 21th Annual Meeting of the Special Interest Group on Discourse and Dialogue, SIGdial 2020, 1st virtual meeting, July 1–3, 2020, pp. 35–44. Association for Computational Linguistics (2020). https://aclanthology.org/2020.sigdial-1.4/

12. Hosseini-Asl, E., McCann, B., Wu, C.S., Yavuz, S., Socher, R.: A simple language model for task-oriented dialogue. NeurIPS 2020-December (5 2020)

13. Manku, G., Lee-Thorp, J., Kanagal, B., Ainslie, J., Feng, J., Pearson, Z., Anjorin, E., Gandhe, S., Eckstein, I., Rosswog, J., Sanghai, S., Pohl, M., Adams, L., Sivakumar, D.: Shoptalk: A system for conversational faceted search. CoRR (2021), arxiv.org/abs/2109.00702

14. Pouran Ben Veyseh, A., Dernoncourt, F., Nguyen, T.H.: Improving slot filling by utilizing contextual information. In: Proceedings of the 2nd Workshop on Natural Language Processing for Conversational AI, pp. 90–95 (2020)

15. Qian, K., Beirami, A., Lin, Z., De, A., Geramifard, A., Yu, Z., Sankar, C.: Annotation inconsistency and entity bias in MultiWOZ. In: Proceedings of the 22nd Annual Meeting of the Special Interest Group on Discourse and Dialogue, pp. 326–337 (2021)

16. Qin, L., Che, W., Li, Y., Wen, H., Liu, T.: A stack-propagation framework with token-level intent detection for spoken language understanding. In: EMNLP-IJCNLP, pp. 2078–2087 (2019)

17. Rastogi, A., Zang, X., Sunkara, S., Gupta, R., Khaitan, P.: Towards scalable multi-domain conversational agents: the schema-guided dialogue dataset. In: AAAI (2020)

18. Shah, P., Hakkani-Tür, D., Liu, B., Tür, G.: Bootstrapping a neural conversational agent with dialogue self-play, crowdsourcing and on-line reinforcement learning. In: NAACL, pp. 41–51 (2018)

19. Sousa, R.G., Ferreira, P.M., Costa, P.M., Azevedo, P., Costeira, J.P., Santiago, C., Magalhaes, J., Semedo, D., Ferreira, R., Rudnicky, A.I., Hauptmann, A.G.: Ifetch: multimodal conversational agents for the online fashion marketplace. In: Proceedings of the 2nd ACM Multimedia Workshop on Multimodal Conversational AI, pp. 25–26. MuCAI'21, Association for Computing Machinery, New York (2021). https://doi.org/10.1145/3475959.3485395

20. Wu, C.S., Hoi, S.C., Socher, R., Xiong, C.: TOD-BERT: Pre-trained natural language understanding for task-oriented dialogue. In: EMNLP, pp. 917–929 (2020)

21. Wu, C.S., Madotto, A., Hosseini-Asl, E., Xiong, C., Socher, R., Fung, P.: Transferable multi-domain state generator for task-oriented dialogue systems. In: Proceedings of the 57th Annual Meeting of the Association for Computational Linguistics, pp. 808–819 (2019)

22. Wu, D., Ding, L., Lu, F., Xie, J.: SlotRefine: A fast non-autoregressive model for joint intent detection and slot filling. In: EMNLP, pp. 1932–1937 (2020)

23. Xu, P., Hu, Q.: An end-to-end approach for handling unknown slot values in dialogue state tracking. In: Proceedings of the 56th Annual Meeting of the Association for Computational Linguistics (Volume 1: Long Papers), pp. 1448–1457 (2018)

24. Zang, X., Rastogi, A., Sunkara, S., Gupta, R., Zhang, J., Chen, J.: Multiwoz 2.2: A dialogue dataset with additional annotation corrections and state tracking baselines. In: Proceedings of the 2nd Workshop on Natural Language Processing for Conversational AI, ACL 2020, pp. 109–117 (2020)

25. Zeng, Y., Nie, J.Y.: Multi-domain dialogue state tracking - a purely transformer-based generative approach (2020)
26. Zhang, J., Hashimoto, K., Wu, C., Wan, Y., Yu, P.S., Socher, R., Xiong, C.: Find or classify? dual strategy for slot-value predictions on multi-domain dialog state tracking. CoRR (2019). arxiv.org/abs/1910.03544

Planning, Scheduling and Decision-Making in AI

Data-driven Single Machine Scheduling Minimizing Weighted Number of Tardy Jobs

Nikolai Antonov$^{(\boxtimes)}$, Přemysl Šucha , and Mikoláš Janota

Czech Technical University in Prague, Prague, Czech Republic
antonni1@fel.cvut.cz

Abstract. We tackle a single-machine scheduling problem where each job is characterized by weight, duration, due date, and deadline, while the objective is to minimize the weighted number of tardy jobs. The problem is strongly NP-hard and has practical applications in various domains, such as customer service and production planning. The best known exact approach uses a branch-and-bound structure, but its efficiency varies depending on the distribution of job parameters. To address this, we propose a new data-driven heuristic algorithm that considers the parameter distribution and uses machine learning and integer linear programming to improve the optimality gap. The algorithm also guarantees to obtain a feasible solution if it exists. Experimental results show that the proposed approach outperforms the current state-of-the-art heuristic.

Keywords: Data-driven · Heuristic · Machine learning · Scheduling

1 Introduction

We address an optimization problem with a number of practical applications in everyday life, including parcel delivery, crop harvesting, and customer service [6]. To illustrate the problem's essence, imagine a production line that produces various orders or batches, which we call *jobs*. Assume that the technical process imposes limitations that only one item can be produced at a time, and no interruptions are allowed until a product is completed. The production of every particular good is assigned with two deadlines: soft (also known as *due date*) and hard. Missing the due date is allowed but results in a loss or a penalty. However, failing to meet the hard deadline is strictly unacceptable and may result in catastrophic failures on other production lines or even bring the entire

This work was supported by the Czech MEYS under the ERC CZ project POSTMAN no. LL1902, by the Grant Agency of the Czech Technical University in Prague, grant No. SGS22/167/OHK3/3T/13 and by the Grant Agency of the Czech Republic under the Project GACR 22-31670S. This article is part of the RICAIP project that has received funding from the EU's Horizon 2020 research and innovation programme under grant agreement No 857306.

© The Author(s), under exclusive license to Springer Nature Switzerland AG 2023
N. Moniz et al. (Eds.): EPIA 2023, LNAI 14115, pp. 483–494, 2023.
https://doi.org/10.1007/978-3-031-49008-8_38

production to a halt. The goal is to manufacture all products before their hard deadline while minimizing the total penalty incurred. In scheduling theory, the problem is known as $1|\tilde{d}_i| \sum w_i U_i$ in Graham's notation [5].

The problem is typically addressed in the literature using two common methods. The first involves creating an integer linear programming (ILP) model and handling it with a general solver. Another option is to use the state-of-the-art exact branch-and-bound algorithm by Baptiste et al. [1], developed specifically for this problem. Since both approaches have their limitations, heuristics can be a suitable alternative. Indeed, solving the ILP model may have volatile running times, while a heuristic works quickly and reliably. An efficient heuristic can also improve the branch-and-bound technique by providing tighter bounds for quicker solutions. Although the state-of-the-art approach can handle up to 30,000 jobs within an hour, we observed that the algorithm struggles with smaller instances of 1000–5000 jobs, exceeding a one-hour time limit. The literature also reports specific instances of 250 jobs that the algorithm was unable to solve within the same time limit [7]. This paradox is primarily due to the heuristic algorithm inside the branch-and-bound, which may not provide a tight enough bound on the objective. The fact that a heuristic method can be efficient for some instances but not others inspired us to create an algorithm that will benefit from the distribution of job parameters.

Problem Formulation. Let us have a machine (system) capable of doing some work divided into pieces, which we call *jobs*. The machine follows three basic assumptions: it handles a single job at a time, never interrupts a started job and does not idle, i.e., after processing a job, it immediately moves to the next one until all the assigned jobs are completed. We are given a set of jobs $N = \{1, 2, ..., n\}$ with *durations* p_i, *due dates* d_i and *deadlines* $\tilde{d}_i$ for all $i \in N$. We assume that p_i, d_i, $\tilde{d}_i$ are positive integers and $p_i \leq d_i \leq \tilde{d}_i$ for all $i \in N$. In addition, each job has a *weight* (or *cost*), which is a positive integer w_i, $i \in N$ that represents how valuable a particular job is. All the jobs are available from the very beginning (time moment 0). Let the jobs be processed according to the permutation π of N and completed at time moments C_i^π, $i \in N$. In scheduling terminology, π is called a *schedule*. We define the set of *early* jobs $E_\pi = \{i \in N \mid C_i^\pi \leq d_i\}$ completed before the due date, and the set of *tardy* jobs $T_\pi = \{i \in N \mid d_i < C_i^\pi \leq \tilde{d}_i\}$ completed after the due date, but before the deadline. A schedule π is called *feasible*, if $C_i^\pi \leq \tilde{d}_i$ for every job $i \in N$, and in terms of introduced sets that is equivalent to $E_\pi \cup T_\pi = N$. Following [1], we assume an equivalent *maximization* problem instead of minimization. Our goal is to maximize the weighted number of early jobs while every job must meet its deadline. That means we want to find a schedule π^* maximizing $f(\pi) = \sum_{i \in E_\pi} w_i$, so that $E_\pi \cup T_\pi = N$.

Literature Review. The problem is known to be strongly NP-hard [13]. The state-of-the-art exact method for solving the problem is the algorithm proposed by Baptiste et al.[1]. As it is mentioned above, the efficiency of this algorithm varies for different types of instances; for example, for one class of specific instances, it faces difficulties solving instances with 250 jobs. This class was studied in [7], where the authors improved the algorithm from [1] such that it can solve 5000 jobs within the same time limit.

The state-of-the-art heuristic for the studied problem is also proposed by Baptiste et al. [1]. Essentially, it is a part of the exact algorithm presented there. It starts by solving a max-profit flow relaxation of the original problem and then determines if a job is early or tardy using ILP and variable fixing techniques. A common rule-based heuristics for solving $1|\tilde{d_i}|\sum w_i U_i$ are *EDF (Earliest Deadline First)*, *EDD (Earliest Due Date first)* and *ATC (Apparent Tardiness Cost)* [12]. Although they are fast and easy to implement, they show a large optimality gap in practice, and only *EDF* can guarantee meeting all job deadlines if a solution exists. According to [1], exact algorithms and relaxation heuristics are the primary sources of improvements for the studied problem. Although meta-heuristic applications have been mentioned in the past for related problems, the literature on this topic is significantly outdated, and therefore we do not discuss them further.

Our approach is based on supervised machine learning (ML) and inspired by the work [2] who have demonstrated the remarkable benefits of applying ML to a wide range of combinatorial optimization problems. However, we are not aware of any ML applications to the studied problem. The closest related work is [3], which addresses the $1||\sum T_i$ problem of minimizing the total violation of due dates. The authors propose to estimate the objective value using LSTM-based neural networks. However, their problem does not assume deadlines, and the approach depends on Lawler's decomposition, which cannot be applied to our case. In addition, a standard LSTM-based neural network requires significant running time. Structured learning is highlighted in [11] for minimizing the completion time of jobs with release times, and [9] addresses online single-machine scheduling using Q-learning techniques. Many applications of reinforcement learning to combinatorial optimization problems are described in the survey by [10]. For a simple setup of supervised machine learning, refer to [8].

Our Contributions. We introduce a novel scheduling heuristic to minimize the weighted number of tardy jobs on a single machine. Our approach consists of three interconnected components that work in synergy to achieve optimal or near-optimal results. The first component leverages machine learning as a decision-making oracle. Unlike traditional methods that rely on a single neural network to predict directly from extracted features, we use two separate networks to estimate different aspects of the problem, achieving more accurate results. Secondly, we refine our predictions through ILP, using an empirically proven job selection strategy. Lastly, we develop a framework based on the fundamental problem properties that can transform any sequence of predictions into a feasible solution if one exists. Our experiments demonstrate that the proposed algorithm outperforms state-of-the-art heuristics in [1] when the input data distribution is known.

2 Solution Approach

With complete information on whether a job is early or tardy in a given instance, the $1|\tilde{d}_i| \sum w_i U_i$ problem can be solved in polynomial time. Indeed, it is sufficient to schedule the jobs in ascending order of D_j $(j \in N)$, which will be a due date $(D_j = d_j)$ for *early* job and a deadline $(D_j = \tilde{d}_j)$ for *tardy* job. More details can be found in [12]. Thus, the main challenge is to decide whether a given job is early or tardy. In this paper, we use supervised machine learning to make such a decision. A typical naive ML approach (sometimes denoted as an end-to-end approach in the literature) decides purely based on the job features. However, in our method, the decision is made differently. Consider the following theorem, presented in [1].

Theorem 1. (Dominance theorem) *Let π^* be an optimal schedule and for jobs i and j holds $w_j > w_i$, $p_j \leq p_i$, $d_j \geq d_i$, $\tilde{d}_j \leq \tilde{d}_i$. Then if the job i is early in π^*, the same holds for j; and if the job j is tardy in π^*, the same holds for i.*

We can see that if there is a certain relation between the parameters of two jobs, then a decision about one of them can be propagated to another. Drawing an analogy, we formulate this in terms of apriori and conditional probabilities. Our goal is to estimate the likelihood $\widetilde{Pr}(j)$ of job j being early, given that we know the probability of job i being early or tardy. Assume that job i has an apriori probability $Pr(i)$ of being early (i_E). Then, it is tardy (i_T) with a probability $1 - Pr(i)$ since earliness and tardiness are mutually exclusive. Let $Pr(j \mid i_E)$ and $Pr(j \mid i_T)$ denote the conditional probability of j being early if i happened to be early or tardy, respectively. We then express the desired probability $\widetilde{Pr}(j)$ as a marginal probability:

$$\widetilde{Pr}(j) = Pr(j \mid i_E)\, Pr(i) + Pr(j \mid i_T)\,(1 - Pr(i)) \tag{1}$$

We utilize two neural network oracles to predict the values on the right side of the equation. The first oracle estimates the apriori probability $Pr(i)$, and the second does the same for conditional probabilities $Pr(j \mid i_E)$ and $Pr(j \mid i_T)$. A rounded average of different marginal estimates $\widetilde{Pr}(j)$, computed with respect to different jobs i, represents the decision about job j.

The proposed machine learning approach has several advantages. First, it takes into account the combinatorial side of the problem by considering the context provided by other jobs rather than just relying on individual job parameters. Secondly, our approach is more balanced as it incorporates both apriori and conditional probability estimates made by two independent oracles. Our observations show that using both oracles positively impacts the final objective value $f(\pi)$, resulting in a 7–10% improvement compared to using only apriori probabilities. Lastly, our decision-making method can be easily combined with Theorem 1: when the theorem can be applied directly, the oracle does not need to be called to estimate conditional probabilities.

Classification procedure. We have introduced the concept of our oracle and discussed its features and benefits. Now, we will explain how our oracle aids decision-making in the problem instance by classifying jobs as early or tardy. We formalize this procedure in Algorithm 1. The first step is to compute apriori estimates $Pr(j)$ for all $j \in N$ using P_{apr} oracle. Next, we randomly select a subset $S \subseteq N$ of k jobs and compute the conditional probabilities for all pairs of jobs $j \in N$ and $i \in S$. Here we check the preconditions of the dominance theorem: if they hold for some jobs i and j (this fact is denoted in the algorithm's pseudocode with I_j^E and I_j^T), then either $Pr(j \mid i_E)$ or $Pr(j \mid i_T)$ are known with certainty; otherwise, both conditional probabilities are computed by P_{cond} oracle. Finally, we compute a sequence of $|S| = k$ marginal probabilities $\widetilde{Pr}(j)$ for each $j \in N$. The predicted class c_j is obtained by rounding off the average value of these marginal probabilities to the closest integer, where 1 represents early, and 0 represents tardy.

Algorithm 1 *Classify* function

Require: set of jobs $N = \{1; 2; ...; n\}$; oracles P_{apr}, P_{cond}; $k \in \mathbb{N}$
 1: $Pr(j) \leftarrow P_{apr}(j), \quad j \in N$ ▷ making apriori estimates
 2: $S \leftarrow Subset(N), |S| = k$ ▷ random subset of k jobs
 3: **for** $j \in N, i \in S$ **do**   ▷ making conditional estimates
 4:      $I_j^E \leftarrow (w_j > w_i) \ \& \ (p_j \leq p_i) \ \& \ (d_j \geq d_i) \ \& \ (\tilde{d}_j \leq \tilde{d}_i)$
 5:      $I_j^T \leftarrow (w_j < w_i) \ \& \ (p_j \geq p_i) \ \& \ (d_j \leq d_i) \ \& \ (\tilde{d}_j \geq \tilde{d}_i)$
 6:      $Pr(j \mid i_E) \leftarrow 1$ **if** $I_j^E = $ "true" **else** $P_{cond}(j, i_E)$ ▷ predict by oracle or DT
 7:      $Pr(j \mid i_T) \leftarrow 0$ **if** $I_j^T = $ "true" **else** $P_{cond}(j, i_T)$
 8: **end for**
 9: **for** $j \in N$ **do**
10:     $\widetilde{Pr}(j) \leftarrow \frac{1}{k} \sum_{i \in S} Pr(j \mid i_E) \, Pr(i) + Pr(j \mid i_T) \, (1 - Pr(i))$ ▷ marginal estimates
11:     $c_j \leftarrow $ "early" **if** $\widetilde{Pr}(j) \geq 0.5$ **else** "tardy"   ▷ final decision
12: **end for**
13: **return** $c_1, ..., c_n$; $\widetilde{Pr}(1), ..., \widetilde{Pr}(n)$ ▷ predicted classes and marginal estimates

---

Prediction by neural networks. In this section, we provide details about the implementation and training of our neural network oracle, complementing the general perspective presented in the previous sections. At first, we used the Autogluon framework [4], which provides various models for tabular predictions, including KNN, neural networks, LightGBM trees, random forests, and XGBoost. After fitting our data to these different models, we have settled on the neural network model as one of the most accurate. We employed a fully connected multi-layer perceptron with a *Tanh* activation function. This model consists of 8-8-2 neurons in the input-hidden-output layers for estimating apriori probabilities and 17-64-2 neurons for estimating conditional probabilities. We experimented with various configurations, including 3-5 layers with up to 64 neurons each, and tried both *Tanh* and *ReLU* activation functions before settling on this final configuration.

A job j is represented by an eight-dimensional vector of features $h(j)$, which includes its weight w, duration p, due date d, deadline $\tilde{d}$, and four derived features: $\frac{w}{p}$, $w - p$, $\frac{d}{\tilde{d}}$, $\tilde{d} - d$. All features are normalized to $[0; 1]$ interval. The network that estimates the apriori probability takes $h(j)$ as input for a given job j. The network that estimates the conditional probability takes the vector $h(i)$ concatenated with $h(j) - h(i)$, where the subtraction is performed component-wise. The idea is to determine whether we end in a point labeled "early" if we start in $h(i)$ and move along the vector $h(j)$ - $h(i)$. We avoid directly concatenating $h(i)$ and $h(j)$ to prevent the network from acting like an apriori NN. Finally, we concatenate $[h(i), h(j) - h(i)]$ with a boolean value 0 or 1 depending on which probability we are estimating: $P(j \mid i_E)$ or $P(j \mid i_T)$. The optimal solution's components serve as labels. A job is labeled as 1 if it's considered early in the optimal solution and 0 otherwise. While we experimented with more complex features, like histograms based on job weights, duration, due dates, and deadlines, we found that the assembly of the eight features described above generalizes better for larger instances.

We trained a neural network to estimate apriori probabilities using instances of 50 to 5000 jobs. Obtaining labels for most instances of this size was easy using an exact solver. The feature-label pairs were split into training and validation sets with a ratio of 80:20, resulting in approximately 1.7 million pairs. For the second neural network that estimates conditional probabilities, we focused on instances with 1000 jobs only. We used sampling to cover more instances and obtained 25 million feature-label pairs in total. Both models were trained for 20 epochs using the AdamW optimizer with a learning rate of 10^{-3}.

Solving subproblems with ILP. In the previous two subsections, we discussed how our oracle classifies jobs on early or tardy. Suppose we have executed Algorithm 1 on a given problem instance and obtained predicted classes c_j and probabilities $\widetilde{Pr}(j)$ for each $j \in N$. However, relying solely on these predictions for scheduling can be risky, as even a single incorrect prediction may lead to significant deviations from optimal value $f(\pi^*)$. Therefore, we aim to use the predictions differently, focusing on the reduction theorem described in [1]. Suppose a given job $j \in N$ is known to be early ($D_j = d_j$) or tardy ($D_j = \tilde{d}_j$) in an optimal solution. A *reduced* problem is formulated on the set of jobs $N' = N \setminus \{j\}$ with the data modified as follows:

$$w'_i = w_i, \quad p'_i = p_i \quad (i \in N') \tag{2}$$

$$d'_i = \begin{cases} \min(d_i, D_j - p_j), & if \ d_i \leq D_j \\ d_i - p_j, & otherwise \end{cases} \quad (i \in N') \tag{3}$$

$$\tilde{d}'_i = \begin{cases} \min(\tilde{d}_i, D_j - p_j), & if \ \tilde{d}_i \leq D_j \\ \tilde{d}_i - p_j, & otherwise \end{cases} \quad (i \in N') \tag{4}$$

Theorem 2. (Reduction theorem) *There exists a feasible schedule π with an early set of jobs E_π if and only if there exists a feasible schedule π' with early set of jobs $E'_\pi = E_\pi \setminus \{j\}$ for the reduced problem.*

We aim to leverage our oracle to reduce the problem to itself, but of a smaller size, removing the jobs with reliable predictions from the original instance. We can apply the reduction theorem to those jobs and solve the obtained subproblem to optimality with some general ILP solver (LINGO, Gurobi, etc.). Combining the reliable predictions of our neural network with an optimal solution to the reduced problem provides updated predictions for the original problem. We first analyze how reliable are the predictions from our neural network. To address this, we conducted an experiment using the training set, as shown in Figure 1.

Let's consider the left sub-figure first. The x-axis displays predicted probabilities of a job being early, with a bin size of a histogram equal to 0.01. The y-axis shows the empirical frequency of prediction errors for each probability, given by the fraction $(\frac{\nu}{r})_q$, where q is the predicted probability, r is the total number of samples with that probability, and ν is the number of incorrectly classified samples. We employed a total of 500,000 samples uniformly distributed with respect to q. The resulting graph shows that the neural network is the most reliable when predicting probabilities close to 0 or 1, and most of the errors occur when the predicted probabilities are close to 0.5. Additionally, the network's error distribution appears to be approximately normal.

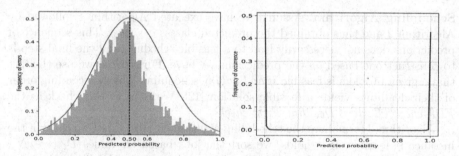

Fig. 1. Frequency of errors (left) and frequency of predicted probabilities (right)

The right-hand side of Fig. 1 shows how frequently our oracle predicts a random job with one or another probability given by the x-axis. We can see that the neural network almost always predicts the jobs having high confidence, e.g., most of $\widetilde{Pr}(j)$ probabilities are close to 0 or 1. Analyzing both graphs, we observe that the network achieves the lowest error rates for predictions with probabilities close to 0 or 1, which also comprise the majority of all predictions. This is a positive outcome, indicating that we can trust the network when it makes such predictions. However, the error rate increases as the predicted probability approaches 0.5, demonstrating that the network is more error-prone in this range.

Algorithm 2 *Update* function

Require: set of jobs $N = \{1; 2; ...; n\}$; $\gamma \in \mathbb{N}$ $(0 \leq \gamma \leq n)$
Require: jobs predicted classes $c_1, ..., c_n$; predicted probabilities $Pr(j), ..., Pr(j)$
1: $(j_1, ..., j_n) \leftarrow Sort(N, |Pr(j) - 0.5|)$, $j \in N$ ▷ order jobs by $|Pr(j) - 0.5|$ asc.
2: $N' = N \setminus \{j_{\gamma+1}, ..., j_n\}$ ▷ reduce the original instance
3: $(s_1, ..., s_\gamma) \leftarrow ILP(N', time \leq 60s)$ ▷ try to solve reduced problem by ILP
4: $(c_{j_1}, ..., c_{j_\gamma}) \leftarrow (s_1, ..., s_\gamma)$ **if** $\neq ILP$ *solution exists*
5: **return** $c_1, ..., c_n$ ▷ update predicted classes if a solution was found

---

The ideas outlined above are formalized in Algorithm 2, which we refer to as the *Update* function. At the start of the algorithm, we choose the number of jobs γ to be solved by a general ILP solver. This value can be arbitrarily chosen between 0 and n. Assuming that the neural network has just returned the predicted classes c_j and predicted probabilities $Pr(j)$ for each $j \in N$ (as described in Algorithm 1), we begin by sorting the jobs in ascending order of the criterion $|Pr(j) - 0.5|$, $j \in N$; this rearranges the jobs as $j_1, ..., j_n$ (line 1). Next, we apply the reduction theorem (line 2), removing jobs $j_{\gamma+1}, ..., j_n$ (which are predicted closer to 0 or 1) and keeping the remaining jobs to be solved by ILP. We then solve the reduced instance by ILP with a time limit of 60 seconds (line 3). If the solution $s_1, ..., s_\gamma$ was found, it replaces the corresponding predictions made by the neural network (line 4). Otherwise, we keep all the predictions made by the neural network unchanged.

Scheduling Algorithm. Assume we have executed Algorithm 1 followed by Algorithm 2 and thus obtained the predicted classes $c_1, ..., c_n$. This sequence of predictions does not necessarily lead to a feasible schedule, and the final step is to construct one based on the predictions we have. Further on, we use the fact that a given problem is feasible *if and only if* scheduling jobs in ascending order of their deadlines yields a feasible solution [12]. We refer to this check as the *EDF check* (*Earliest Deadline First check*).

Algorithm 3 formalizes the scheduling of classified jobs. First, we check if the instance is feasible. If it holds, we sort the jobs based on values D_i $(i \in N)$, which is a due date if a job is predicted as early and the deadline otherwise. This results in a permutation π, where the job with the smallest D value stands in the first (leftmost) position, and the job with the largest D value is in the last (rightmost) place. We introduce a cursor m and start with the first job j in permutation π. If j is predicted as tardy, we schedule it immediately and move to the next job (lines 8, 11, 14–16). If j is predicted as early, we perform an *EDF* check to determine if we can schedule the remaining unscheduled jobs (line 9). If the check passes, we schedule j and move to the next job (lines 14–16). If the check fails, we do not schedule j. Instead, we change the predicted class c_j to tardy, update the sorting key of j to deadline ($D_j = \tilde{d}_j$) and push j to a new position in π such that the permutation is sorted again (lines 17–19). We repeat the algorithm steps until all jobs are scheduled. In the end, the cursor stands to the right of the last job in π, which is the output schedule.

Algorithm 3 Scheduling algorithm

Require: set of jobs $N = \{1; 2; ...; n\}$; predicted classes $c_1, ..., c_n$
1: **return** $\emptyset$ **if** $EDF(N) =$ *"infeasible"*
2: $D_i \leftarrow d_i$ **if** $c_i =$ *"early"* **else** $\tilde{d}_i$ $(i \in N)$
3: $\pi \leftarrow Sort(N, D_j)$ ▷ jobs ordered by D_i $(i \in N)$ ascending
4: $S \leftarrow \emptyset$ ▷ a set of scheduled jobs S
5: $m \leftarrow 1$ ▷ a cursor m
6: **while** $m \leq n$ **do**
7:     $j \leftarrow \pi(m)$ ▷ consider the m-th job j from π
8:     **if** $c_j =$ *"early"* **then**   ▷ if it is predicted as early
9:         $\alpha = EDF(N \setminus (S \cup \{j\}))$ ▷ could we schedule the rest by EDF
10:        $schedNow \leftarrow true$ **if** $\alpha =$ *"feasible"* **else** $false$
11:    **else**
12:        $schedNow \leftarrow true$
13:    **end if**
14:    **if** $schedNow$ **then**   ▷ schedule if it's *early* and passes EDF or if it's *tardy*
15:        $S \leftarrow S \cup \{j\}$
16:        $m \leftarrow m + 1$
17:    **else**   ▷ otherwise, put j further in π
18:        $D_j \leftarrow \tilde{d}_j$
19:        $\pi \leftarrow Push(j, \pi)$ ▷ a new order of jobs where j is placed by $D_j = \tilde{d}_j$
20:    **end if**
21: **end while**
22: **return** π

Proposition 1. *Algorithm 3 halts and produces a feasible schedule if one exists.*

Proof. The algorithm terminates after at most $2n$ steps because on each step a job is either scheduled immediately or forced to become tardy and will be scheduled when the cursor reaches it the second time.

Assume that we are given a feasible instance. To prove that the algorithm always produces a feasible schedule, we need to show that scheduling a job j allows us to schedule the remaining unscheduled jobs without violating their deadlines. There are three mutually exclusive cases:

Case 1. A job j has an early predicted class and passes the EDF check. In this case, the EDF check confirms that scheduling the remaining jobs after j will not violate any deadlines. Thus, scheduling j preserves the ability to construct a feasible schedule.

Case 2. A job j has an early predicted class but fails the EDF check. In this case, j is not scheduled at this moment, and only the permutation π can change. So, if there was an opportunity to construct a feasible schedule, it would remain.

Case 3. A job j has a tardy predicted class. Here we make two observations. First, the jobs in π are always kept sorted during the algorithm, so the sorting key D_j of job j is always the smallest value of D among the remaining unscheduled jobs. Second, since j has a tardy predicted class, $D_j = \tilde{d}_j$. Therefore, scheduling j works as the very first step of scheduling all the remaining jobs by the EDF rule. It preserves the opportunity to construct a feasible schedule, as the remaining unscheduled jobs can still be scheduled by running the *EDF* until the end. This completes the proof.

3   Experimental Results

Table 1. Comparison of optimality gaps and the numbers of optimal solutions

(0.1–3)	Optimal solutions ($\cdot$/100)				Avg optimality gap, %			
n	Ours	Bapt.	Rand	Early	Ours	Bapt.	Rand	Early
500	**71**	22	0	0	0.0684	**0.0264**	66.888	73.037
1000	**74**	13	0	0	0.0199	**0.0127**	65.857	73.574
2000	**70**	27	0	0	0.0091	**0.0050**	66.775	73.462
3000	**60**	27	0	0	0.0064	**0.0037**	66.779	74.042
4000	**61**	32	0	0	0.0039	**0.0025**	66.625	73.808
5000	**56**	37	0	0	0.0041	**0.0011**	66.487	73.543
(0.1–7)	Optimal solutions ($\cdot$/100)				Avg optimality gap, %			
n	Ours	Bapt.	Rand	Early	Ours	Bapt.	Rand	Early
500	**86**	20	0	0	0.3472	**0.0167**	38.097	59.836
1000	**92**	19	0	0	**0.0026**	0.0077	38.048	60.528
2000	**99**	17	0	0	**0.0001**	0.0031	37.653	60.512
3000	**76**	20	0	0	**0.0005**	0.0020	37.790	60.316
4000	**57**	11	0	0	**0.0008**	0.0014	37.601	60.360
5000	**63**	26	0	0	**0.0008**	0.0009	37.602	60.146
(0.3–5)	Optimal solutions ($\cdot$/100)				Avg optimality gap, %			
n	Ours	Bapt.	Rand	Early	Ours	Bapt.	Rand	Early
500	**88**	30	0	0	0.3040	**0.0162**	40.957	49.378
1000	**94**	22	0	0	**0.0012**	0.0072	40.730	49.160
2000	**93**	35	0	0	**0.0005**	0.0027	40.861	49.212
3000	**92**	35	0	0	**0.0009**	0.0019	41.226	49.321
4000	**83**	50	0	0	**0.0003**	0.0013	40.884	49.460
5000	**82**	52	0	0	**0.0003**	0.0007	40.976	49.354
(0.3–7)	Optimal solutions ($\cdot$/100)				Avg optimality gap, %			
n	Ours	Bapt.	Rand	Early	Ours	Bapt.	Rand	Early
500	**93**	23	0	0	**0.0033**	0.0117	33.365	40.763
1000	**95**	27	0	0	**0.0011**	0.0055	33.756	41.085
2000	**94**	28	0	0	**0.0007**	0.0035	33.611	40.637
3000	**94**	42	0	0	**0.0007**	0.0016	33.643	40.353
4000	**85**	45	0	0	**0.0005**	0.0009	33.656	40.416
5000	**79**	44	0	0	**0.0003**	0.0007	33.670	40.526
(0.5–7)	Optimal solutions ($\cdot$/100)				Avg optimality gap, %			
n	Ours	Bapt.	Rand	Early	Ours	Bapt.	Rand	Early
500	**90**	21	0	0	**0.0018**	0.0133	31.994	30.422
1000	**99**	32	0	0	**0.0001**	0.0036	32.210	30.134
2000	**96**	42	0	0	**0.0010**	0.0018	32.240	30.339
3000	**88**	46	0	0	**0.0001**	0.0011	32.092	30.273
4000	**87**	59	0	0	**0.0001**	0.0006	32.255	30.338
5000	**85**	56	0	0	**0.0001**	0.0003	32.122	30.473

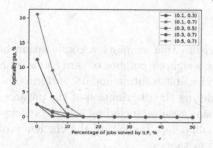 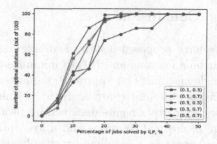

Fig. 2. Impact of γ on the optimality gap and number of optimal solutions

To ensure a fair comparison with [1], we use their instance generation method, where weights and durations are random natural numbers uniformly distributed on the interval $[1, 100]$. We also use the same distribution of due dates, which are random numbers between $u \sum_{i=1}^{n} p_i$ and $v \sum_{i=1}^{n} p_i$, where (u, v) are selected from the set $(0.1, 0.3), (0.1, 0.7), (0.3, 0.5), (0.3, 0.7), (0.5, 0.7)$. Our implementation of the proposed algorithm is in Python, and we tested it in Google Colab. Both the code and data are available at https://github.com/CTU-IIG/EPIA.

We compare the results of our approach with those of Baptiste et al.'s state-of-the-art heuristic and two other methods that are identical to ours but use different oracles: in the first method (Rand), jobs are predicted to be early or tardy randomly with 0.5 probability; in the second approach (Early), every job is predicted to be early with probability 1. We use two evaluation criteria: optimality gap and the number of optimal solutions achieved out of 100 instances. The optimality gap is the ratio $\frac{f(\pi^*) - f(\pi)}{f(\pi^*)} \cdot 100\%$, where π and π^* represent the constructed and optimal schedules, respectively. We first conduct an experiment on our algorithm alone to demonstrate how the optimality gap and the number of optimal solutions change when we increase the fraction of jobs solved by the ILP, i.e., the γ parameter in Algorithm 2. The results are presented in Fig. 2. The instance size is fixed to 1000 jobs, and the classification of each job in a given instance uses $k = 500$ jobs to estimate conditional probabilities.

Table 1 presents a comparison of our approach with the other heuristics. Our algorithm significantly outperforms them in terms of the number of optimal solutions, always achieving more than half, with a maximum of 99 out of 100. For most distributions and instance sizes, our approach also demonstrates the best optimality gap. However, we should note that Baptiste's heuristic is still superior in terms of running time: 1 second for 500–3000 jobs, 1.5 seconds for 4000 jobs, and 3 seconds for 5000 jobs. The respective running times of our algorithm are 2–15, 19, and 28 seconds; the same for Rand and Early approaches. Finally, we attempted to execute the simple rule-based heuristics *EDD*, *ATC*, and *EDF*. However, the first two did not produce feasible solutions for any instance, and the optimality gap of *EDF* is similar to the random oracle and equals 64–66%.

4 Conclusion

We have proposed a novel heuristic algorithm that employs a combination of machine learning and ILP to minimize the weighted number of tardy jobs on a single machine. Our approach guarantees a feasible solution and outperforms the current state-of-the-art heuristic by considering the distribution of the parameters. Our experiments demonstrate promising results, including a high percentage of optimal solutions and a low optimality gap, indicating the efficiency of our approach in handling practically-sized instances.

References

1. Baptiste, P., Croce, F.D., Grosso, A., T'kindt, V.: Sequencing a single machine with due dates and deadlines: an ILP-based approach to solve very large instances. J. Sched. **13**(1), 39–47 (2010)
2. Bengio, Y., Lodi, A., Prouvost, A.: Machine learning for combinatorial optimization: a methodological tour d'horizon. Eur. J. Oper. Res. **290**(2), 405–421 (2021)
3. Bouška, M., Šcha, P., Novák, A., Hanzálek, Z.: Deep learning-driven scheduling algorithm for a single machine problem minimizing the total tardiness. Eur. J. Oper. Res. (2022)
4. Erickson, N., Mueller, J., Shirkov, A., Zhang, H., Larroy, P., Li, M., Smola, A.J.: AutoGluon-tabular: robust and accurate AutoML for structured data. CoRR arXiv:abs/2003.06505 (2020)
5. Graham, R., Lawler, E., Lenstra, J., Kan, A.: Optimization and approximation in deterministic sequencing and scheduling: a survey. In: Hammer, P., Johnson, E., Korte, B. (eds.) Discrete Optimization II, Annals of Discrete Mathematics, vol. 5, pp. 287–326. Elsevier (1979)
6. Hariri, A.M.A., Potts, C.N.: Single machine scheduling with deadlines to minimize the weighted number of tardy jobs. Manage. Sci. **40**(12), 1712–1719 (1994)
7. Hejl, L., Šúcha, P., Novák, A., Hanzálek, Z.: Minimizing the weighted number of tardy jobs on a single machine: Strongly correlated instances. Eur. J. Oper. Res. **298**(2), 413–424 (2022)
8. Karimi-Mamaghan, M., Mohammadi, M., Meyer, P., Karimi-Mamaghan, A.M., Talbi, E.G.: Machine learning at the service of meta-heuristics for solving combinatorial optimization problems: a state-of-the-art. Eur. J. Oper. Res. **296**(2), 393–422 (2022)
9. Li, Y., Fadda, E., Manerba, D., Tadei, R., Terzo, O.: Reinforcement learning algorithms for online single-machine scheduling. In: 2020 15th Conference on Computer Science and Information Systems (FedCSIS), pp. 277–283 (2020)
10. Mazyavkina, N., Sviridov, S., Ivanov, S., Burnaev, E.: Reinforcement learning for combinatorial optimization: a survey. Comput. Oper. Res. **134** (2021)
11. Parmentier, A., T'Kindt, V.: Structured learning based heuristics to solve the single machine scheduling problem with release times and sum of completion times. Eur. J. Oper. Res. (2022)
12. Pinedo, M.L.: Scheduling. Theory, Algorithms, and Systems, p. 233. Springer, New York (2012)
13. Yuan, J.: Unary NP-hardness of minimizing the number of tardy jobs with deadlines. J. Sched. **20**(2), 211–218 (2017)

Heuristic Search Optimisation Using Planning and Curriculum Learning Techniques

Leah Chrestien[(✉)], Tomáš Pevný, Stefan Edelkamp, and Antonín Komenda

Czech Technical University in Prague, Jugoslávských partyzánů 3, 160 00 Praha,
Czech Republic
leah.chrestien@aic.fel.cvut.cz, {pevnytom,stefan.edelkamp}@fel.cvut.cz,
antonin.komenda@agents.fel.cvut.cz

Abstract. Learning a well-informed heuristic function for hard planning domains is an elusive problem. Although there are known neural network architectures to represent such heuristic knowledge, it is not obvious what concrete information is learned and whether techniques aimed at understanding the structure help in improving the quality of the heuristics. This paper presents a network model that learns a heuristic function capable of relating distant parts of the state space via optimal plan imitation using the attention mechanism which drastically improves the learning of a good heuristic function. The learning of this heuristic function is further improved by the use of curriculum learning, where newly solved problem instances are added to the training set, which, in turn, helps to solve problems of higher complexities and train from harder problem instances. The methodologies used in this paper far exceed the performances of all existing baselines including known deep learning approaches and classical planning heuristics. We demonstrate its effectiveness and success on grid-type PDDL domains, namely Sokoban, maze-with-teleports and sliding tile puzzles.

Keywords: Planning · Optimizing heuristic functions · Deep learning

1 Introduction

Classical Planning has always relied on strong heuristic functions to approximate distances to the nearest goal [3]. Its quality is measured by how well it performs when used inside a planner, i.e., it depends on the quality of the solution and the time taken to generate it. A major drawback of classical planning is the need to formulate problems by extensively capturing information from the environment. Recent years observe a progress in using visual representations to capture the specifics of a problem [2]. Yet, there is still a big gap between the length of optimal plans and the plans found by planners using learnt heuristic functions.

A significant amount of importance is given to developing deep networks that are able to learn strong heuristics [5] and policies [22]. In learning for planning,

© The Author(s), under exclusive license to Springer Nature Switzerland AG 2023
N. Moniz et al. (Eds.): EPIA 2023, LNAI 14115, pp. 495–507, 2023.
https://doi.org/10.1007/978-3-031-49008-8_39

the methods rely heavily on either hand-coded logical problem representations [26] or deep convolution neural networks [8] that learns to imitate an expert. While there exists successful approaches in training neural networks (NNs) to learn heuristic estimates of various problem domains [8,25], designing a meaningful NN architecture to extract the relevant information from the data set is still an open-ended problem.

This work extends the work by [8,16] by addressing limitations of convolutional neural network, which capture only local dependencies. We propose to use self-attention and position encoding [24], as we believe a strong heuristic function needs to relate "distant" parts of the state space.

In our default experimental settings, NNs realizing heuristic functions are trained on plans of small problem instances created by classical planners. While this allows us to generalize across more difficult instances such that we can measure distances to optimal plan lengths, they do not achieve the best results for two reasons. First, even though the generalization of A*-NN is surprisingly good as will be seen below, there is still a scope of large-scale improvement on previously unseen, larger and more complex environments. Second, classical domain independent planners can solve only small problem instances anyway, which means that obtaining plans from large ones is difficult. We demonstrate that this problem can be partially mitigated by curriculum learning [4], where the NN is retrained/fine-tuned using plans from problems it has previously solved.

The proposed approach is compared to state-of-the-art domain-independent planners, namely SymBA*[21], Lama [15], and Mercury [10] and to currently best combination of A* and CNNs [8] on three grid domains: (1) **Sokoban** where each maze consists of walls, empty spaces, boxes, targets and an agent; the goal is to push the boxes to target locations; the boxes can only be pushed and not pulled in the game; (2) **Maze-with-Teleports** where the goal for an agent is to reach the goal position via interconnected teleports; (3) **Sliding-Tile** where blocks are moved to achieve an end configuration.

The paper is organised as follows. We first discuss the prior art in deep learning for planning, especially on problems where state can be represented as a tensor. Next, we review formal basics of classical planning. Then, we highlight the shortcomings of a prior state of the art and propose a solution that addresses some of these shortcomings. Here, we introduce the basics of the attention mechanism from NLP and explain the role of positional encoding in learning distances. Finally, the proposed networks are compared to other state of the art methods. In the last section, we discuss a few possible extensions of our work.

2   Related Work

The application of learning algorithms to improve planning dates back to the original STRIPS planner [6], which learned triangle tables or macros that could later be exploited by the planner. This approach attracted more interest as machine learning algorithms and has gained a steady popularity since. Earlier uses of NN to learn policies and heuristics for deducing strategic positions and moves known to us considered chess boards [20] and backgammon [19]. Their use in Go [18] raised a considerable interest in public once it beat the top players in the game. Heuristic functions were also learnt for single agent games such as Sokoban [8,14] and Rubik's cube [1]. In 2011, a special learning track was introduced in the international planning competition (IPC), which concluded that the performance of NNs is promising in learning heuristic functions. A perpendicular approach to the above is to learn functions combining a portfolio of existing heuristic function [25] or to select a heuristic function from a portfolio [11]. A very interesting problem is to learn a transition operator as in [2] together with a visual execution of the plan, but this is outside the scope of our work.

Our work differs from the above as it focuses on (i) identifying *good building blocks* of the neural networks for grid domains and (ii) discusses the difficult and importance of a training set and shows that curriculum learning can be of a great help. The resulting networks are general and their performance exceeds that of prior art including SOTA classical planners.

3   Classical Planning

We construct our problem domains in a classical setting, i.e. fully observable and deterministic.

In classical planning, a STRIPS [6] planning task is defined by a tuple $\Pi = \langle F, A, I, G \rangle$. F denotes a set of facts which can hold in the environment (for instance, in Sokoban, a particular box at a particular position is a fact). A state s of the environment is defined as a set of facts holding in that particular s, i.e. $s \subseteq F$. The set of all states is, therefore, defined as all possible subsets of F as $S = 2^F$. $I \in S$ is the initial state of the problem and $G \subseteq F$ is a goal condition comprising facts which has to hold in a goal state. An action a, if applicable and applied, transforms a state s into a successor state s' denoted as $a(s) = s'$ (if the action is not applicable, we assume it returns a distinct failure value $a(s) = \bot$). All actions of the problem are contained in the action set A, i.e. $a \in A$. The sets S and A define the state-action transition system.

Let $\pi = (a_1, a_2, \ldots, a_l)$, we call π a plan of length l solving a planning task Π iff $a_l(\ldots a_2(a_1(I))\ldots) \supseteq G$. We assume a unit cost for all actions, therefore the plan length and plan cost are equal. Moreover, let π_s denote a plan from a state s, not I. An optimal solution (plan) is defined as a minimal length solution of a problem Π and is denoted as π^* together with its length $l^* = |\pi^*|$.

A heuristic function h is defined as $h : S \rightarrow R^{\geq 0}$ and provides an approximation of the optimal plan length from a state s to a goal state $s_g \supseteq G$, formally $h(s) \approx l^*$, where $l^* = |\pi_s^*|$.

In our experiments, we choose domains encoded in PDDL [7], where a planning problem is compactly represented in a lifted form based on predicates and operators. This representation is grounded into a STRIPS planning task Π, which is subsequently solved by the planner using a heuristic search navigating in the state-action transition system graph and resulting in a solution plan π.

4   Planner's Architecture

Given the initial state I, each partial plan $\pi = (a_1, a_2, \ldots, a_k)$, $k < l$ induces a sequence of states $(s_0 = I, s_1, s_2, \ldots, s_k)$ with $s_k = a_k(\ldots a_2(a_1(I)))$.

States are for the purpose of the the neural network encoded as a binary values of all prepositions, which are in case of grid domains arranged in the same grid. The input to a neural network encoding a state is therefore a binary tensor, which is very well suited for contemporary deep learning libraries and execution on GPU. The output of the network is the heuristic value provided by the *value head*, which is in some cases supplemented by the distribution on all possible next actions provided by the *policy head* (the rationale for policy head is that according to [8], it improves the quality of the learnt heuristic). The training sets for neural networks consists of optimal plans for selected problem instances, which were generated by the optimal planner SymBA* [21]. More precisely, given the plans in the training set, we generate pairs $(s_i, \delta(s_i))$, where δ is cost of an optimal plan from s_i to the goal. For the sake of simplicity, $\delta(s_i)$ is the distance $l - i$ of the state s_i to the goal s_l in the optimal plan $(s_0 = I, s_1, s_2, \ldots, s_i, \ldots, s_l)$. Evaluating the network for a given state, directly serves as an estimator in our heuristic search planner. In curriculum learning, the training set with the optimal plans is augmented by newly found plans on more difficult problem instances. These newly found plans do not have to be optimal but are typically very close to being so.

For some domains (e.g. Sokoban), where the policy head is useful, the plans also contain the action input (s_{i-1}, a_i) needed to train the policy head. Since our aim is finding (close-to-)optimal plans, we used A* [9] as the search algorithm for exploring the planning state space. The training used ADAM [12] variant of stochastic gradient descent with default settings and a batch-size of 500.

5   The Proposed Neural Network

The best architecture of NN implementing a heuristic function for Sokoban known to us was proposed by Groshev [8]. We believe its biggest drawback is that it relies solely on convolution (which is strictly a local operator) thus limiting the neural network in synthesizing information from two distant parts of the maze. To understand the aforementioned statement, let us introduce some formal notations.

Let the input to the neural network be denoted by $x \in R^{h,w,d_0}$, where h and w is the height and width of the maze respectively, and d_0 varies with the number of channels as explained above. Intermediate outputs are denoted by $z^i = L_i(z^{i-1})$, where L is some neural network layer (consisting of convolution C etc.) and for the sake of convenience, we set $z^0 = x$. All z are three dimensional tensors, i.e. $z^i \in R^{h,w,d_i}$. Notice that all intermediate outputs z^i have the same width and height as the maze (ensured by padding), while the third dimension which is the number of output filter(s) differs. Value $z^i_{u,v}$ denotes a vector created from z^i as $(z^i_{u,v,1}, z^i_{u,v,2}, \ldots, z^i_{u,v,d_i})$. Below, this vector will be called a *hidden vector* at position (u, v) and can be seen as a description of the properties of this position.

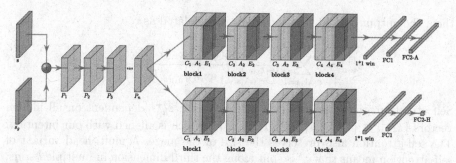

Fig. 1. The structure of our neural network. A current state s and a goal state s_g are fed into a variable number of pre-processing convolution (pre-conv) layers, $P_1..P_n$. In our case, we use 7 pre-conv layers. All convolution filters in the pre-conv layers are of the same shape 3×3 with 64 filters. Then the network splits into two branches and each branch has four blocks, each block containing a convolution layer (C) followed by a multi head attention operation with 2 heads (A) and a positional encoding layer (E). There are 180 filters in each of these convolution layers in the blocks. At all stages, the original dimension of the input is preserved through padding. The output from block 4 is flattened by applying a 1×1 window around the agent's location before being passed onto the fully connected layers (FC1) and the action prediction output (FC2-A) and a single output for heuristic prediction (FC2-H). For the sake of picture clarity, skip connections are not shown in the neural network.

In Groshev's architecture [8] consisting of only convolution layers, the hidden vector $z_{u,v,.}^{i+1}$ is calculated from hidden vectors $\{z_{u',v',.}^{i}|u' \in \{u-1, u, u+1\}, v' \in \{v-1, v, v+1\}\}$, where the convolution has dimensions 3×3 and therefore uses information from a close neighborhood. Yet, we believe that any good heuristic requires features that relay information from different parts of the maze since Sokoban, Sliding-Tile and Maze-with-Teleports are all non-local problems. To address this issue, our network (see Fig. 1) features two additional types of layers, namely, the attention and the positional encoding layer, described below.

Convolution, Attention, and Position Encoding: The self-attention mechanism, [24] first introduced in NLP, allows to relate distant parts of input together. The output of self-attention from z^i is calculated in the following manner. At first, the output from previous layer z^i is divided into three tensors of the same height, width, and depth, i.e.

$$\boldsymbol{k} = z_{\cdot,\cdot,j}^{i} \quad j \in \left\{1, \ldots, \frac{d_i}{3}\right\}$$

$$\boldsymbol{q} = z_{\cdot,\cdot,j}^{i} \quad j \in \left\{\frac{d_i}{3}+1, \ldots, \frac{2d_i}{3}\right\}$$

$$\boldsymbol{v} = z_{\cdot,\cdot,j}^{i} \quad j \in \left\{\frac{2d_i}{3}+1, \ldots, d_i\right\}$$

then, the output z^{i+1} at position (u, v) is calculated as

$$z_{u,v}^{i+1} = \sum_{r=1,s=1}^{h,w} \frac{\exp(\boldsymbol{q}_{u,v} \cdot \boldsymbol{k}_{r,s})}{\sum_{r'=1,s'=1}^{h,w} \exp(\boldsymbol{q}_{u,v} \cdot \boldsymbol{k}_{r',s'})} \cdot v_{r,s} \qquad (1)$$

Self attention, therefore, makes a hidden vector $z_{u,v}^{j+1}$ dependent on all hidden vectors $\{z_{r,s}^j | r \in \{1, \ldots, h\}, s \in \{1, \ldots, w\}\}$, which is aligned with our intention. The self-attention also preserves the size of the maze. A multi-head variant of self-attention means that z^i is split along the third dimension in multiple $\boldsymbol{k}$s, $\boldsymbol{q}$s, and $\boldsymbol{v}$s. The weighted sum is performed independent of each triple (k, q, z) and the resulting tensors are concatenated along the third dimension. We refer the reader for further details to [24].

While self-attention captures information from different parts of the maze, it does not have a sense of a distance. This implies that it cannot distinguish close and far neighborhoods. To address this issue, we add positional encoding, which augments the tensor $\mathbf{z}^i \in R^{h,w,d_i}$ with another tensor $\mathbf{e} \in R^{h,w,d_e}$ containing outputs of harmonic functions along the third dimension. Harmonic functions were chosen, because of their linear composability properties [24].[1] Because our mazes are two dimensional, the distances are split up into row and column distances where $p, q \in [0, d_i/4)$ assigns positions with sine values at even indexes and cosine values at odd indexes. The positional encoding tensor $\mathbf{e} \in R^{h,w,d_e}$ has elements equal to

$$e_{u,v,2p} = \sin(\theta(p)u) \qquad\qquad e_{u,v,2p+1} = \cos(\theta(p)u)$$
$$e_{u,v,2q+\frac{d_e}{2}} = \sin(\theta(q)v) \qquad\qquad e_{u,v,2q+1+\frac{d_e}{2}} = \cos(\theta(q)v),$$

where $\theta(p) = \dfrac{1}{10000^{\frac{4p}{d_e}}}$. On appending this tensor to the input z^i along the third dimension, we get

$$z_{u,v,\cdot}^{i+1} = [z_{u,v,\cdot}^i, e_{u,v,\cdot}].$$

With respect to the above, we propose using blocks combining Convolution, Attention, and Position encoding, in this order (we call them CoAt blocks), as a part of our NN architecture. The CoAt blocks can therefore relate hidden vectors from a local neighborhood through convolution, from a distant part of the maze through attention, and calculate distances between them through position encoding, as has been explained in [23]. Since CoAt blocks preserve the size of the maze,[2] they are "scale-free" in the sense that they can be used on a maze of any size.

The input to the network is the current state of the game and a goal state, s and s_g, respectively. Each state is represented by a tensor of dimensions equal to

---

[1] The composability of harmonic functions is based on the following property $\cos(\theta_1 + \theta_2) = \cos(\theta_1)\cos(\theta_2) - \sin(\theta_1)\sin(\theta_2) = (\cos(\theta_1), \sin(\theta_1)) \cdot (\sin(\theta_1), \sin(\theta_2))$, where $\cdot$ denotes the inner product of two vectors, which appears in Eq. (1) in inner product of $\mathbf{q}_{u,v}$ and $\mathbf{k}_{r,s}$.

[2] Convolution layers are appropriately padded to preserve sizes.

width and height (fixed to 10×10 for Sokoban, 15×15 for Maze-with-Teleports, and 5×5 for Sliding-Tile) of the maze $\times$ objects. The objects stand for one-hot encoding of the object states on a grid position (e.g., for Sokoban, we have wall, empty, box, agent and box target, for Maze-with-Teleport agent, wall, floor, goal and teleports 1–4, for sliding tile, we have a channel for each number, all of which can be derived automatically from the grounded representation.

6 Curriculum Learning

The second contribution of our work is to promote curriculum learning [4]. One of the drawbacks in learning the heuristic functions for planning is that when generating training set with existing planners, we quickly hit the limit of their capability in solving more complex problems. This can limit the learnt heuristic function in solving more complex problems. To further improve our heuristic function to scale to bigger problems, we re-train our network on an extended training set, which includes harder problem instances.

The protocol used in the experimental section of this paper is as follows. We first train the heuristic network on a training set containing problem instances that are quickly solvable by an optimal planner. Then we use this NN as a heuristic function inside A* search to solve more difficult problem instances. Their solutions are used to extend the training set on which the neural network is re-trained. By doing so, the NN is gradually trained on more difficult problem instances which improves its quality. As this procedure is fairly intuitive and yet computationally expensive, we demonstrate its effects on the Sokoban domain.

7 Experimental Results

This section first briefly describes the details of training the NN and then presents the experimental results on the selected benchmark domains: Sokoban, Sliding Tile and Maze-with-Teleports. For all the three domains, we use the output from the heuristic network inside A* to generate solutions. A* algorithms with learnt heuristic functions realized by the proposed convolution-attention-position networks (further denoted as A*-CoAt) are compared to A* with learned heuristic function realized by convolutional networks as proposed in [8] (denoted as A*-CNN), and to the state of the art planners LAMA [15], SymBA* [21], and Mercury [10]. We emphasize that A*-CNN and A*-CoAt uses vanilla A* search algorithm [9] without any additional tweaks. In case of Sokoban, we also compare our planner to a solution based on Reinforcement Learning [14].

On all the compared domains, we analyse the strength of our learnt heuristic and generalization property by solving grid mazes of increasing complexities, approximated by the number of boxes in Sokoban, grids of higher dimensions in Sliding-Tile and Maze-with-Teleports, and rotated mazes in Maze-with-Teleports.

7.1 Training

Sokoban: The training set for Sokoban was created by randomly generating 40000 Sokoban instances using gym-sokoban [17]. Each instance has dimension 10×10 and it always contains only 3 boxes (and an agent). In each plan trajectory, the distance from a current state to the goal state is learned as the heuristic value, $h(s_i)$. In line with [8], the neural network also uses the policy head during training.

Maze-with-Teleports: The training set contained 10000 maze problems of dimension 15×15, generated by using a maze creator.[3] Random walls were broken to create teleports. We added a total of 4 pairs of teleports that connect different parts of the maze inside each training sample. The mazes for training were generated such that the initial position of the agent was in the upper-left corner and the goal was in the lower-right corner. Later, in our evaluations, we rotate each maze to investigate whether the heuristic function is rotation independent.

Sliding puzzle: The training set contained 10000 puzzles of size 5×5. These puzzles were generated using.[4] During evaluation, we test our approach on puzzles of higher dimensions such as 6×6 and 7×7, all of which were generated with.[5] We ensured that all the puzzles in the test and train set are solvable.

7.2 Comparison to Prior State-of-the-Art

Sokoban: The evaluation set consists of 2000 mazes of dimensions 10×10 with 3, 4, 5, 6 or 7 boxes (recall that the training set contains mazes with only 3 boxes). Unless said otherwise, the quality of heuristics is measured by the relative number of solved mazes, which is also known as *coverage*. Table 1 shows the coverage of compared planners, where *all* planners were given 10 minutes to solve each Sokoban instance. We see that the classical planners solved all test mazes with 3 and 4 boxes but as the number of boxes increase, the A*-NN starts to have an edge. On problem instances with 6 and 7 boxes, A*-CoAt achieved the best performance, even though it was trained only on mazes with 3 boxes. Thus, the NNs have successfully managed to *extrapolate* to environments with more complex problems. The same table shows, that A*-CoAt offers better coverage than A*-CNN, and we can also observe that curriculum learning (see column captioned curr.) significantly improves the coverage.

We attribute SymBA*'s poor performance to its feature of always returning optimal plans while we are content with sub-optimal plans. LAMA had even lower success in solving more complicated mazes than SymBA*, despite having the option to output sub-optimal plans. To conclude, with an increase in the complexity of the mazes, the neural networks outshine the classical planners which makes them a useful alternative in the Sokoban domain.

---

[3] https://github.com/ravenkls/Maze-Generator-and-Solver.
[4] https://github.com/levilelis/h-levin/.
[5] https://github.com/YahyaAlaaMassoud/Sliding-Puzzle-A-Star-Solver.

Table 1. Fraction of solved Sokoban mazes (coverage, higher is better) of SymBA* (SBA*), Mercury (Mrcy), LAMA, A*-CNN (caption CNN) and the proposed A*-CoAt (caption CoAt). A*-CNN and A*-CoAt (with caption normal) use networks trained on mazes with three bozes; A*-CoAt (with caption curr.) used curriculum learning. The quality of plans (not shown here) generated by CoAt are very close to the optimal while in the case of CNN, it is not always so.

#b	SBA*	Mrcy	LAMA	Normal CNN	CoAt	curr. CoAt
3	1	1	1	0.92	0.94	0.95
4	1	1	1	0.87	0.91	0.93
5	**0.95**	0.75	0.89	0.83	0.89	0.91
6	0.69	0.60	0.65	0.69	**0.76**	**0.85**
7	0.45	0.24	0.32	0.58	**0.63**	**0.80**

CoAt network without curriculum learning is also on par with Deep Mind's implementation of Reinforcement Learning (DM-RL) in solving Sokoban [14]. Instead of re-implementing DM-RL by ourselves, we report the results on their test set[6] containing 10×10 Sokoban mazes with 4 boxes. While DM-RL had a coverage of 90%, our A*-CoAt (trained on mazes with three boxes) has a coverage 87%. A*-CoAt with curriculum learning has a coverage of 98.29%,[7] which greatly improves over the DM-RL. Taking into account that DM-RL's training set contained 10^{10} state-action pairs from mazes **with 4 boxes**, A*-CoAt achieves higher coverage using a training set which is several orders of magnitude smaller.

Maze-with-Teleports: The evaluation set contains a total of 2100 training samples of dimensions 15×15, 20×20, 30×30, 40×40, 50×50, 55×55 and 60×60. Each maze in the evaluation set contains 4 pairs of teleports that connect different parts of the maze. From Table 2, we see that the performance of A*-CNN and A*-CoAt (initially trained on 15×15 mazes) is the same as SymBA*[8] for dimensions up to 40×40 and is consistently better for problem instances of size 50×50, 55×55 and 60×60.

All "No Rotation" mazes were created such that the agents start in the top left corner and the goal is in the bottom right corner. This allows us to study to which extent the learnt heuristic is rotation-independent (domain independent planners are rotation invariant by default). The same Table therefore reports fraction of solved mazes that have been rotated by 90°, 180° and 270°. The results clearly show that the proposed heuristic function featuring CoAt blocks generalizes better than the one utilizing only convolutions, as the solved rotated

---

[6] Available at https://github.com/deepmind/boxoban-levels.

[7] https://github.com/deepmind/boxoban-levels/blob/master/unfiltered/test/000.txt.

[8] The planners and NNs were given 10 minutes to solve each maze instance.

Table 2. Fraction of solved mazes with teleports (coverage) of SymBA*, A* algorithm with convolution network [8] (denoted as CNN) and that with the proposed Convolution-Position-Attention (CoAt) network. Only non-rotated mazes (No Rotation) of size 15 × 15 were used to train the heuristic function. On mazes rotated by 90°, 180°, 270°, the heuristic function has to extrapolate outside its training set.

Size	SBA*	No Rotation		90° rotation		180° rotation		270° rotation	
		CNN	CoAt	CNN	CoAt	CNN	CoAt	CNN	CoAt
15 × 15	1	1	1	1	1	1	1	1	1
20 × 20	1	1	1	1	1	1	1	1	1
30 × 30	1	1	1	1	1	1	1	1	1
40 × 40	1	1	1	1	1	1	1	1	1
50 × 50	0.92	0.94	**1**	0.91	1	0.92	1	0.91	1
55 × 55	0.55	0.78	**0.89**	0.71	0.85	0.70	0.87	0.69	0.87
60 × 60	–	0.73	**0.76**	0.68	0.75	0.66	0.74	0.68	0.75

Table 3. Fraction of solved Sliding-tile mazes (coverage, higher is better) of SymBA* (SBA*), Mercury (Mrcy), LAMA, A*-CNN (caption CNN) and the proposed A*-CoAt (caption CoAt). A*-CNN and A*-CoAt (with caption normal) use networks trained on mazes with three different dimensions; A*-CoAt (with caption curr.) used curriculum learning.

Size	SBA*	Mrcy	LAMA	Normal		Curr.
				CNN	CoAt	CoAt
5 × 5	0.54	0.32	0.89	0.72	0.83	**0.92**
6 × 6	0.21	–	0.25	0.56	0.72	**0.81**
7 × 7	–	–	–	0.35	0.41	**0.62**

instances of A*-CoAt network are comparable to the non-rotated case. Rotating mazes have no effect on SymBA* (the complexity is solely dependent on the grid size) and the coverage rate stays unaffected.

From the results in Table 2, it can be concluded that the CoAt blocks (1) improve detection of non-local actions (teleports) compared to state-of-the-art planners such as SymBA*; (2) learn 'useful' information from the mazes which makes the network robust to rotations; (3) learn to approximate distances inside the mazes which results in a scale-free heuristic function.

Sliding-Tile: The evaluation set contains a total of 200 test samples of dimensions 5 × 5, 6 × 6 and 7 × 7. From Table 3, we see that the performance of A*-CNN and A*-CoAt (initially trained on 5 × 5 mazes) consistently outperforms the performance of planners.[9] SymBA* is the most reliable of all the planners but performs poorly when compared to the NNs. Of the NNs, the CoAt network

---

[9] The planners and NNs were given 10 minutes to solve each maze instance.

solves a larger number of instances as compared to the CNN network and records an even higher improvement in coverage after curriculum learning.

8   Conclusion and Future Work

We have proposed a building blocks of neural network able to learn strong heuristic function for PDDL domains with an underlying grid structure without the need for any specific domain knowledge. It is to be noted that even though we have generated training data from a classical planner on small problem sizes, our proposed architecture is able to generalize and successfully solve more difficult problem instances, where it surpasses classical domain-independent planners, while improving on previously known state-of-the-art.

Our experiments further suggest that the learnt heuristic can further improve, if it is retrained/fine-tuned on problem instances it has previously solved. This form of curriculum learning aids the heuristic function in solving mainly large and more complex problem instances that are otherwise not solvable by domain independent planners within 10 minutes.

As future work, our next goal would be to better understand if the learnt heuristic function is similar to something that is already known, or something so novel that it can further enrich the field; i.e., what kind of underlying problem structure we can learn by which network type, possibly in the form of studying generic types [13].

We believe that an improvement in the heuristic function is tied to the generation of problem instances that inherently possess the right level of difficulty, by which we mean that they have to be just on the edge of solvability, such that the plan can be created and added to the training set. We are fully aware that the problem instance generation itself is a hard problem, but we cannot imagine the above solution to be better than specialized domain-dependent Sokoban solvers without such a generator (unless the collection of all Sokoban mazes posses this property).

We also question the average estimation errors minimized during learning of the heuristic function. It might put too much emphasis on simple problem instances that are already abundant in the training set while neglecting the difficult ones. We wish to answer some of the above question in the future in an endeavour to generate strong, scale-free heuristics.

Acknowledgments. This work has been supported by project numbers 22-32620S and 22-30043S from Czech Science Foundation and OP VVV project CZ.02.1.01/0.0/0.0/16_019/0000765 "Research Center for Informatics".

References

1. Agostinelli, F., McAleer, S., Shmakov, A., Baldi, P.: Solving the rubik's cube with deep reinforcement learning and search. Nature Mach. Intell. **1**(8), 356–363 (2019)
2. Asai, M., Fukunaga, A.: Classical planning in deep latent space: Bridging the subsymbolic-symbolic boundary. arXiv preprint arXiv:1705.00154 (2017)
3. Bonet, B., Geffner, H.: Planning as heuristic search. Artif. Intell. **129**(1–2), 5–33 (2001)
4. Elman, J.L.: Learning and development in neural networks: the importance of starting small. Cognition **48**(1), 71–99 (1993)
5. Ernandes, M., Gori, M.: Likely-admissible and sub-symbolic heuristics. In: Proceedings of the 16th European Conference on Artificial Intelligence, pp. 613–617 (2004)
6. Fikes, R.E., Nilsson, N.J.: Strips: a new approach to the application of theorem proving to problem solving. Artif. Intell. **2**(3–4), 189–208 (1971)
7. Fox, M., Long, D.: Pddl2. 1: An extension to pddl for expressing temporal planning domains. J. Artif. Intell. Res. **20**, 61–124 (2003)
8. Groshev, E., Goldstein, M., Tamar, A., Srivastava, S., Abbeel, P.: Learning generalized reactive policies using deep neural networks. arXiv:1708.07280 (2017)
9. Hart, P.E., Nilsson, N.J., Raphael, B.: A formal basis for the heuristic determination of minimum cost paths. IEEE Trans. Syst. Sci. Cybern. **4**(2), 100–107 (1968)
10. Katz, M., Hoffmann, J.: Mercury planner: Pushing the limits of partial delete relaxation. In: IPC 2014 Planner Abstracts, pp. 43–47 (2014)
11. Katz, M., Sohrabi, S., Samulowitz, H., Sievers, S.: Delfi: Online planner selection for cost-optimal planning. In: IPC-9 Planner Abstracts, pp. 57–64 (2018)
12. Kingma, D.P., Ba, J.: Adam: A method for stochastic optimization. arXiv:1412.6980 (2014)
13. Long, D., Fox, M.: Automatic synthesis and use of generic types in planning. In: AAAI, pp. 196–205. AAAI Press (2000)
14. Racanière, S., Weber, T., Reichert, D., Buesing, L., Guez, A., Jimenez Rezende, D., Puigdomènech Badia, A., Vinyals, O., Heess, N., Li, Y., et al.: Imagination-augmented agents for deep reinforcement learning. Adv. Neural. Inf. Process. Syst. **30**, 5690–5701 (2017)
15. Richter, S., Westphal, M.: The lama planner: Guiding cost-based anytime planning with landmarks. J. Artif. Intell. Res. **39**, 127–177 (2010)
16. Schaal, S.: Is imitation learning the route to humanoid robots? Trends Cogn. Sci. **3**(6), 233–242 (1999)
17. Schrader, M.P.B.: gym-sokoban. github.com/mpSchrader/gym-sokoban (2018)
18. Silver, D., Schrittwieser, J., Simonyan, K., Antonoglou, I., Huang, A., Guez, A., Hubert, T., Baker, L., Lai, M., Bolton, A., et al.: Mastering the game of go without human knowledge. Nature **550**(7676), 354–359 (2017)
19. Tesauro, G.: Programming backgammon using self-teaching neural nets. Artif. Intell. **134**(1–2), 181–199 (2002)
20. Thrun, S.: Learning to play the game of chess. Adv. Neural. Inf. Process. Syst. **7**, 1069–1076 (1994)
21. Torralba, A., Alcázar, V., Borrajo, D., Kissmann, P., Edelkamp, S.: Symba*: A symbolic bidirectional a* planner. In: International Planning Competition, pp. 105–108 (2014)
22. Torrey, L., Shavlik, J., Walker, T., Maclin, R.: Skill acquisition via transfer learning and advice taking. In: European Conference on Machine Learning, pp. 425–436. Springer (2006)

23. Tsai, Y.H.H., Bai, S., Yamada, M., Morency, L.P., Salakhutdinov, R.: Transformer dissection: An unified understanding for transformer's attention via the lens of kernel. arXiv:1908.11775 (2019)
24. Vaswani, A., Shazeer, N., Parmar, N., Uszkoreit, J., Jones, L., Gomez, A.N., Kaiser, Ł, Polosukhin, I.: Attention is all you need. Adv. Neural. Inf. Process. Syst. **30**, 5998–6008 (2017)
25. Virseda, J., Borrajo, D., Alcázar, V.: Learning heuristic functions for cost-based planning. Plan. Learn. 6 (2013)
26. Yoon, S.W., Fern, A., Givan, R.: Inductive policy selection for first-order mdps. arXiv preprint arXiv:1301.0614 (2012)

Social Simulation and Modelling

Review of Agent-Based Evacuation Models in Python

Josef Janda and Kamila Štekerová[(✉)] [iD]

University of Hradec Králové, Rokitanského 62, 50003 Hradec Králové, Czech Republic
kamila.stekerova@uhk.cz

Abstract. The aim of this paper is to explore agent-based evacuation models in Python by conducting a systematic literature search using the PRISMA methodology. The principles of evacuation models are briefly described. Python packages and libraries for agent-based modelling frameworks are explained. Two research questions are defined. The first question aims to find out what typical current agent-based evacuation models look like in sense of application domain and location, number of agents, time and space scale etc.). The second question focuses on the details of the use of the Python programming language and libraries in implementations of agent-based evacuation models. The results of the PRISMA review are presented. Overall, Python is a suitable language for the development of agent-based evacuation models, as evidenced by the number of programming libraries and tools, as well as the growing number of scientific publications in last six years. However, most of the currently published models suffer from many shortcomings. A main surprise is the lack of adherence to standards in describing the agent-based computational model, providing source code and sharing documentation of experiments.

Keywords: Agent-based model · Evacuation · PRISMA · Python · Simulation

1 Introduction

Agent-based models and simulations allow us to study various complex processes and phenomena, to predict the future or to reconstruct past events. Evacuation modelling is an important interdisciplinary application area of agent-based models, where the response of large populations to disasters, extreme or crisis situations (such as tsunamis, floods, fires or terrorist attacks) can be captured. Python [1] is the most popular programming language [2]. In this paper, we explore the possibilities of creating evacuation agent-based models and simulations using Python libraries.

1.1 Evacuation

Evacuation can be indoor or outdoor, short-term or long-term, spontaneous or controlled. Spontaneous evacuation occurs as an arbitrary response by people to a hazard or crisis. It is generally assumed that people's behavior during spontaneous evacuation is rational

© The Author(s), under exclusive license to Springer Nature Switzerland AG 2023
N. Moniz et al. (Eds.): EPIA 2023, LNAI 14115, pp. 511–522, 2023.
https://doi.org/10.1007/978-3-031-49008-8_40

[3]. However, exceeding a certain number of people in one place can lead to panic. At the same time, research and interviews with people who have experienced such events show that people have a natural ability to move in the right direction and help others, especially children, women, and the elderly [3]. A controlled evacuation is a set of actions taken by authorities and policy makers, most often in response to an imminent or ongoing disaster such as a flash flood, hazardous substance spill, fire, tornado, terrorist or wartime activity, or another major emergency. When an evacuation is ordered, everyone is required to comply with the evacuation order.

Computational models of evacuation are classified as macroscopic, microscopic, or mesoscopic [4–7]. Macroscopic models are characterized by a top-down approach, they provide an aggregate view of the whole in which crowd motion is described by global variables such as flow, pressure, velocity, density. Microscopic models take the opposite, bottom-up approach. Each agent is modelled as a unique entity with assigned properties and attributes. A prominent feature for the microscopic view is the attempt to approximate real world conditions by the real world by creating realistic agents: the individual behavior has a large impact on evacuation rates and may be critical for evacuation models [8, 9]. Simulations can be computationally intensive, especially for large models with many agents and many iterations [4].

Mesoscopic models are a combination of macroscopic and microscopic approaches. The models include the movement of individual agents and follow the overall flow of the crowd, but no longer address communication at the level of the agents themselves. There is therefore a trade-off between the computational complexity of a complex model and its predictive value.

In the case of evacuation models, the similarity between fluid flow and crowd movement is exploited. The disadvantage of this approach is that emergent outcomes arising from the behavior of individuals cannot be observed. The advantage of is that it is less computationally intensive compared to microscopic models [4].

1.2   Agent-Based Modelling in Python

Python is a high-level general-purpose programming language [2]. A major advantage of Python is undoubtedly the readily available libraries that provide functions that facilitate the use of mathematical operations, further extending the language's applicability. The following Python frameworks are available for agent-based modelling [10]:

- **AgentPy** [11] is an open-source library written in Python 3. Agents are embedded in the environment (grid, contiguous space, combination of several elements). It is possible to run simulations, collect data and load stored data.
- **Mesa** was created as an alternative to NetLogo [12], one of the best-known agent-based modelling software. At the time of its creation, Mesa was the only one that could present interactive animation of a simulation in web browsers using JavaScript, HTML5, CSS3 and Bootstrap. Mesa has been released as open-source software, licensed under Apache 2.0, and its source code is available [13]. The Mesa application framework is divided into three basic packages [14]:

- Modelling package includes entities of agent classes, the model container, environment, agent action sequence planner, agent movement planner, scheduler, environment scheduler. It provides elements for controlling the setting of variables in the input data.
- The visualization package provides elements for displaying the simulation run in a web-based environment. It uses Apache, WebSocket, HTML 5 and JavaScript services. Computational models and graphs formed from the values obtained during the model run are animated directly in the web browser.
- An analysis package provides tools for storing and analyzing simulation data.

- **Repast4Py** [15] is a collection of Python-based open-source software. Repast4Py is focused on agent-based model development and provides tools for modeling and experimentation with agents. It provides features to exploit distributed execution and is thus suitable for use in computations with multiple cores. Although Repast4Py, when implementing distributed performance, these cores do not interfere with each other's compartments. Communication between cores is secured through messaging.
- **Slapp** [16] Swarm-Like Protocol in Python is an implementation of Swarm in Python, not using its libraries but only its protocols. Swarm supports a hierarchical structure, where groups of agents are nested within another group. Swarm models are models that are voluntarily self-organized, collective and decentralized. Swarm algorithms are used in complex systems with intelligent objects involving communication, decision making and mobility. Swarm has been very successful, as evidenced by its participation in projects such as NetLogo, Repast, Ascape. Slapp includes entities such as event scheduler, model, agent. When used, these entities are inherited from Python libraries.
- **Spade** [17] (Smart Python Multi-Agent Development Environment) is an agent-based platform based on the XMPP protocol. Agents communicate via XMPP servers. Spade uses the capabilities of Python 3.6. The agent consists of a collection of behavioral policies, a mechanism for connecting to the Swarm platform, and a component for dispatching messages between agents to access the communication server. A unique identifier and password are used to access the agent's communication server. When an agent is registered, an attempt is automatically made to connect to the communication server and this connection is maintained throughout the life of the agent. The behavior of the agent is given as a role, which the agent can invoke on the server using repetitive patterns. The behavior can be cyclical—regularly recurring, one-off, or stateful, which allows for more complex behavior templates.

In addition to the platforms described above, it is also possible to use other features of Python, including:

- **SimPy** [18], a Python-based discrete event process simulator. This simulator has been released under a license from MIT, with a promise of free use, both for redistribution and for sale and license extensions. The authors of the framework mention that maximum emphasis has been placed on ease of use. SimPy is then used to simulate processes using the Python generator functions. This framework is a suitable choice for the creation of vehicle or customer agents, as well as for the simulation of shared resources and their utilization. The performance of SimPy is also sufficient for real-time simulations. Although SimPy does not provide support for infinite functionality simulations, according to the authors it is possible to use this feature [18].

- **NL4Py** [19] is a Python library that provides functionality for parallel connection to simulations of models created for NetLogo [12]. Its main advantage is the ability to control simulations and extract data from them that can be further processed using Python. It is possible to use Python libraries such as NumPy [19], Mesa [14], SciPy [20], Pandas [21], Matplotlib [22] and others. NL4Py works by establishing client-server communication. It uses Python on the client side and Java Servlet on the server side. A two-way communication then takes place, with commands being sent for execution, including initial attributes to Netlogo, and then values returned from the simulation. These values can then be processed using Python. The disadvantage is the higher computational demand on the machine [23].

2 Systematic Review

A systematic search for agent-based evacuation models using Python was conducted using the PRISMA methodology [24]. The aim of the review is to answer two research questions. The first question aims to find out what a typical agent-based evacuation model looks like, and the second question focuses on the details of the use of the Python programming language.

Similar research has been carried out by [25–28]. The authors of [25] studied models of crowd movement and the emergence of crowd panic among participants in the pilgrimage to Mecca. The main interest of the authors is to analyze the situation under normal and extraordinary conditions, they were interested in the possibilities of preventing panic and crowd disasters. The authors noted that micro-level models do not involve emergence, the maximum number of agents in simulated models is 25,000 (while the real number of pilgrims is up to 2 million), and the models are of three types (agent-based model networks, models on cellular automata, social models). Another inspiring research study [26] focused on the agent-based simulation of the Covid-19 pandemic, the main objective of which was to investigate the ways in which agent-based models can be used in pandemic simulation and decision making on possible interventions. The PRISMA review of agent-based modelling for flood risk assessment was provided in [27]. They conclude by noting in particular the complexity and need to understand the system prior to modelling and the need to conceptualize it. They also point to the low (25%) use of the ODD design protocol [48] and the potential inadequacy of this in the design of individual works.

2.1 Research Questions

Two research questions were formulated, the main objective of which was to provide an overview of agent-based evacuation models in Python:

- **Question 1**: What does a typical evacuation agent-based model look like (i.e. the basic summary of the model). Thus, the following information was extracted from the papers:

- What is the purpose of the model?
- Who is the model intended for?
- Where was the model developed?
- What type of evacuation is addressed (indoor, outdoor)?
- What is the size or scale of the model?
- Is the standard Overview—Design—Details protocol (ODD) [48] available?
- Are the source codes available?
- To what extent is the model realistic (i.e. how is it connected to real world phenomena; is it an abstract model or location and time specific model)?
- Is it possible to monitor simulations with real data and in real time?

- **Question 2**: How Python is used for implementation, in particular:

  - Is Python used for the main application code?
  - What methods and tools are used to process the data?

The information from the articles was tabulated and statistically evaluated and the results are presented in the following section.

2.2 Results

Authors of the systematic review searched for up-to-date papers published between 2017 and 2023 in scientific journals and conference proceedings, written in English, with full text available. After an initial cross-search in four scientific databases (Web of Science, Springer, ScienceDirect and ACM Digital Library) a total of 301 records were found (Table 1).

Table 1. Databases, search queries and number of results

Database	Query	Results
Springer	'Agent-based AND Python AND evacuation'	156
ACM digital library	[All: agent-based] AND [All: python] AND [All: evacuation]	92
ScienceDirect	Agent-based AND Python AND evacuation	52
Web of science	Agent-based AND Python AND evacuation (All Fields)	1

A basic content analysis of these articles was done manually. After analyzing the retrieved records using the method of reading their abstracts and computerizing the content of the search terms, a total of 264 articles were excluded, leaving 36 texts for further study. After a detailed reading of their content, a further 18 papers were excluded because they did not meet the search criteria (4 were review studies, 5 were studies that only mentioned Python, 4 were studies that only dealt with parts of the problem, 1 paper analyzed posts about the flood response on the social networking site Twitter), 4 papers

Table 2. Papers included in the study

References	Paper	Theme	Environment	Size of model	Real time	Source code available
[29]	Belotti (2022)	Crowd evacuation	Indoor, outdoor	54 agents in corridor 3 × 38 m	No	Yes
[30]	Couasnon (2019)	Ship evacuation	Indoor	838 agents, 180 m long ship	No	No
[31]	Burger (2017)	Explosion	Outdoor	262 × 234 km, 22 000 000 agents	No	No
[32]	Datta (2018)	Crowd evacuation	Size of Indoor	1800 m^2 with 450, 1012 m^2 with 190 agents	No	No
[33]	Feng (2021)	Hurricane	Outdoor	4 million cars	Partially	No
[34]	Gao (2021)	Traffic flow	Outdoor	City with max. 43068 inhabitants	No	No
[35]	Garibay (2021)	Unspecified	Indoor, outdoor	Variable	Yes	No
[36]	Gerostathopoulos (2019)	Traffic flow	Outdoor	600 cars, 113 streets	No	Yes
[37]	Gödel. (2022)	Crowd evacuation	Indoor, outdoor	20, 40, 60 agents, corridor width 0.8−1.2 m	No	Yes
[38]	Gude (2020)	Traffic flow, water	Outdoor	Cellular automaton, 10 × 10 cells	No	No
[39]	Chu (2017)	Crowd evacuation	Indoor	0−500 agents, 1 floor 388 m^2 area	No	No
[40]	Krasuski (2019)	Fire	Indoor	Unspecified, 1 floor of the building	Yes	No

(continued)

Table 2. (*continued*)

References	Paper	Theme	Environment	Size of model	Real time	Source code available
[41]	Mayr (2021)	Improving evacuation guidelines	Indoor	Train station 21240 m^2, up to 2000 agents	Yes	Yes
[42]	Richardson (2022)	Fire	Indoor	1000 agents	No	No
[43]	Selvek 2020	Evacuation	Indoor	1 floor of the building, 811 agents	No	Yes
[44]	Schantz (2022)	Evacuation	Indoor	Conference building 3156 m^2, 1100 agents	No	No
[45]	Aalami (2021)	Evacuation	Outdoor	50×50 km^2, 50 locations, 30 000 agents	No	No
[46]	Tan (2019)	Evacuation guided by chatbot	Indoor, outdoor	Unspecified	No	No
[47]	Vandewalle (2019)	Dynamic changing evacuation routes	Outdoor	100 agents	Partially	No

were simply introductions to software that dealt with the problem. Finally, 19 papers remained for the detailed study (Fig. 1, Table 2).

In relation to research Question 1, the following information was obtained from papers:

- **What is the purpose of the model**? Most of the models are general models without considering the cause and its consequences (such as fire and heat, smoke and low visibility, etc.). General evacuation models are described in 11 papers (58%), with the second most common application being traffic management (4 papers, 22%) and the third being fire evacuation (2 papers, 11%). One paper is dedicated to ship evacuation and one to post-explosion evacuation (5%).
- **Who is the model intended for**? By improving some parts of existing models is devoted to 11 papers (58%), simulation in traffic management and evacuation decision making is 3 papers (16%) are devoted to the same topic. The design of buildings, roads and ships is the subject of 2 papers (11%).

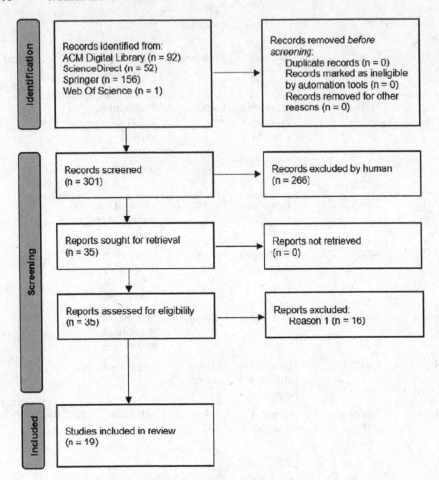

Fig. 1. PRISMA flow diagram of the review process.

- **Where was the model developed?** A typical application of the model is in a confined public space such as an airport departure corridor, a metro station, a concert hall or a conference building. In particular, the models are designed to identify critical locations (bottlenecks) where crowds are concentrated and can potentially cause panic. These areas are the focus of 10 papers (53%). Network models are typically used for transport systems and corridors (6 papers, 32%), 2 papers do not specify the embedding space (11%) and 1 paper mentions a cellular automaton (5%).
- **What type of evacuation is addressed (indoor, outdoor)?** This question refers to the deployment of the model in an indoor location (e.g. airport terminal, railway station or conference building) or an outdoor location (usually a part of the city). Indoor locations are the focus of 8 papers (42%), outdoor locations are the focus of 7 papers (37%), and both indoor and outdoor locations are the focus of 4 papers (21%).
- **What is the size or scale of the model?** The number of agents varied widely in the papers reviewed: unspecified in 4 papers (21%); up to 100 in 3 papers (16%); up

to 1000 in 6 papers (32%); over 1000 in 4 papers (21%); over 1000000 agents in 2 papers (11%). The size of the model is understood as the extent of the area covered (map). Small models cover indoor areas such as an airport terminal, bridge or ship deck. The category of medium models is defined for concert or commercial buildings or the city district, the category of large models is intended for cities and conurbations and models without specification of the size of the map are classified as other. Small models are the most common (9 papers, 47%), with only 3 papers describing large models. In 4 papers the size of the evacuation area was not specified.

- **Is the ODD protocol available**? The full version of the ODD protocol was not included in any of the papers. However, this does not exclude the relevance of the content of the protocol. Some papers include parts of the protocol in an unordered form.
- **Are the source codes available**? Surprisingly, in most cases, the source code of the model is not available (12 papers, 63%).
- **To what extent is the model realistic**? Model realism refers to the degree of similarity between the model and the real world and is assessed through model validation and verification. Most often (in 9 cases, i.e. 50%) this is not mentioned at all. In 8 cases (42%) both model validation and verification are used. In one paper validation is mentioned and in one paper verification is mentioned (5%).
- **Is it possible to monitor simulations with real data and in real time**? Unfortunately, in most cases (13 papers, 68%) it is not possible to use a model to follow a simulation in real time and with real data.

Question 2: Python implementation of models was analyzed with these results:

- **Is Python used for the main application code**? Python is most often used (14 papers, 74%) as the main application code. In addition, its capabilities are used in the context of data processing, both on the input and output side. This is, for example, the coupling of the program with Open Street Map data or the Global Information System. Very often they are used libraries described in the chapter Implementation options in Python, it is Pandas, Mat-plotlib, NetworkX, NumPy, SciPy and others.
- **What methods are used to process the data**? The most common methods for finding the shortest path for agents use knowledge from graph theory. A shared clipboard is used for interactions between agents, where agents store messages. These messages contain attributes of who the message is addressed to and who the message is from. Moore's neighbourhood property is used for orientation in the neighbourhood and the von Neumann neighbourhood. The environment in more detailed models for the outdoor simulations is obtained from Open Street Map datasets. The movement of the agents is controlled by a central step, with each agent taking one step towards the goal with each iteration of the cycle. The results are usually interpreted using clear graphs generated by the Python library Matplotlib. The data are usually presented in tables and compared with the results of previous studies. Reliability, i.e. the repeatability of the measurements, is also discussed in most papers.

3 Conclusion

Certainly, an important factor in deciding whether to use an agent-based model to simulate evacuation for decision support and scenario development in a real-world situation is to ensure the maximum predictive value of the model. The basic parameters are obviously validation, verification, and the use of good quality input data. However, this systematic review found that only 6 models of 19 are based on actual measurements. In 13 cases the data are generated by the model. Models often have no quality control system and, unfortunately, most do not appear to be based on validated input data. Only 50% of the cases use some form of validation or verification of the models. One would expect this feature, as well as adherence to a standard ODD protocol (which was not directly mentioned in any of the papers), to be much more widely used. To assess the quality of the model, it would be useful to look more closely at the origin of the input data on which the authors of the papers base their models. By using previous studies, the authors seem to assume the provision of good quality input data.

Acknowledgement. This work was supported by the internal specific research "Information and knowledge management and cognitive science in tourism 7", Faculty of Informatics and Management, University of Hradec Králové, Czech Republic.

References

1. TIOBE Index, https://www.tiobe.com/tiobe-index/. Accessed 15 Apr. 2023
2. Python.org, https://www.python.org/. Accessed 15 Apr. 2023
3. Cuesta, A., Abreu, O., Alvear, D. (eds.): Evacuation Modeling Trends. Springer, Cham (2016)
4. Kaur, N., Kaur, H.: A Multi-agent based evacuation planning for disaster management: a narrative review. Arch. Comput. Methods Eng. (2022)
5. Manley, M., Kim, Y.S., et al.: Modeling emergency evacuation of individuals with disabilities in a densely populated airport. Transp. Res. Record: J. Transp. Res. Board **2206**(1), 32–38 (2011)
6. Aljamal, M. A., Rakha, H. A. et al.: Comparison of microscopic and mesoscopic traffic modeling tools for evacuation analysis. In: 21st International Conference on Intelligent Transportation Systems (ITSC), pp. 321–2326 (2018)
7. Yuksel, M.E.: Agent-based evacuation modeling with multiple exits using NeuroEvolution of Augmenting Topologies. Adv. Eng. Inf. **35** (2018)
8. Levinson, D., Chen, W.: Paving New Ground. Working Papers 200509, University of Minnesota: Nexus Research Group (2004)
9. Sherman, M., Peyrot, M., et al.: Modeling pre-evacuation delay by evacuees in World Trade Center Towers 1 and 2 on Sept. 11, 2001: a revisit using regression analysis. Fire Saf. J. **46**(7), 414–424 (2011)
10. Pal, C., Leon, F. et al.: A Review of Platforms for the Development of Agent Systems (2020). arXiv:2007.08961
11. Foramitti, J.: AgentPy: a package for agent-based modeling in Python. J. Open Sour. Softw. **6** (62) (2021)
12. NetLogo homepage, https://ccl.northwestern.edu/netlogo/. Accessed 15 Apr. 2023
13. Kazil, J., Masad, D., Crooks, A.: Utilizing Python for agent-based modeling: the mesa framework. In: Social, Cultural, and Behavioral Modeling, pp. 308–317. Springer, Cham (2020)

14. Masad, D., Kazil, J.: MESA: an agent-based modeling framework. In: MESA an Agent Based Modeling, pp. 51–58 (2015)
15. Repast4Py, https://repast.github.io/repast4py.site/index.html. Accessed 15 Apr. 2023
16. Slapp, https://github.com/terna/SLAPP3/blob/. Accessed 15 Apr. 2023
17. SPADE 3.2.2 documentation, https://spade-mas.readthedocs.io/en/latest/model.html. Accessed 15 Apr. 2023
18. simpy: Event discrete, process-based simulation for Python, https://simpy.readthedocs.io. Accessed 15 Apr. 2023
19. Oliphant, T. E.: A guide to NumPy, volume 1. Trelgol Publishing (2006)
20. McKinney, W.: Data structures for statistical computing in Python. In: Proceedings of the 9th Python in Science Conference, pp. 56–61 (2010)
21. McKinney, W.: pandas: a foundational python library for data analysis and statistics. Python High Perform. Sci. Comput. (2011)
22. Matplotlib—Visualization with Python. https://matplotlib.org/. Accessed 15 Apr. 2023
23. Gunaratne, C.; Garibay, I.: NL4Py: agent-based modeling in Python with parallelizable NetLogo workspaces. SoftwareX, vol. 16 (2021)
24. PRISMA, http://prisma-statement.org/. Accessed 15 Apr. 2015
25. Owaidah, A., Olaru, D. et al.: Review of modelling and simulating crowds at mass gathering events: hajj as a case study. J. Artif. Soc. Soc. Simul. 22(2) (2019)
26. Lorig, F., Johansson, E., Davidsson, P.: Agent-Based social simulation of the covid-19 pandemic: a systematic review. J. Artif. Soc. Soc. Simul. 24 (2021)
27. Anshuka, A., van Ogtrop, F., et al.: A systematic review of agent-based model for flood risk management and assessment using the ODD protocol. Nat. Hazards 112(3), 2739–2771 (2022)
28. Mls, K.; Kořínek et al.: Agent-based models of human response to natural hazards: systematic review of tsunami evacuation. Natural Hazards, vol. 15, pp. 1887–1908 (2023)
29. Belotti, M., Martins, F.: Analysis and verification of the social forces model in pedestrian lane formation scenarios. J. Brazilian Soc. Mech. Sci. Eng. 43(6) (2021)
30. Couasnon, P., de Magnienville, Q. et al.: A multi-agent system for the simulation of ship evacuation. Web and Wireless Geographical, Information Systems, vol. 11474, pp. 63–74, Springer, Cham (2019)
31. Burger, A., Oz, T. et al.: Generation of realistic mega-city populations and social networks for agent-based modeling. In: Proceedings of the 2017 International Conference of The Computational Social Science Societyof the Americas, CSS 2017, Association for Computing Machinery, New York (2017)
32. Datta, S., Behzadan, A. H.: EVAQ: person-specific large crowd evacuation modeling. In: Proceedings of the Workshop on Human-Habitat for Health (H3): Human-Habitat Multimodal Interaction for Promoting Health and Well-Being in the Internet of Things Era, H3 '18, Association for Computing Machinery, New York (2018)
33. Feng, K., Lin, N.: Reconstructing and analyzing the traffic flow during evacuation in Hurricane Irma (2017). Transportation Research Part D:80 Transport and Environment, vol. 94 (2021)
34. Gao, R., Zha, A. et al.: Hybrid modeling and predictive control of large-scale crowd movement in road network. In: Proceedings of the 24th International Conference on Hybrid Systems: Computation and Control, HSCC, Association for Computing Machinery, New York (2021)
35. Gunaratne, C., Garibay, I.: NL4Py: agent-based modeling in Python with parallelizable NetLogo workspaces. SoftwareX, vol. 16 (2021)
36. Gerostathopoulos, I., Pournaras, E.: TRAPPed in traffic? A self-adaptive framework for decentralized traffic optimization. In: Proceedings of the 14th International Symposium on Software Engineering for Adaptive and Self-Managing Systems, SEAMS '19, pp. 32–38 IEEE Press (2019)

37. Gödel, M., Bode, N., Köster, G. et al.: Bayesian inference methods to calibrate crowd dynamics models for safety applications. Saf. Sci. **147** (2022)

38. Gude, V., Corns, S., Dagli, C., et al.: Agent based modeling for flood inundation mapping and rerouting. Procedia Comput. Sci. **168**, 170–176 (2020)

39. Chu, J.C., Chen, A.Y., Lin, Y.-F.: Variable guidance for pedestrian evacuation considering congestion, hazard, and compliance behaviour. Transp. Res. Part C: Emerg. Technol. **85**, 664–683 (2017)

40. Krasuski, A., Krenski, K.: A-Evac: the evacuation simulator for stochastic environment. Fire Technol. **55**(5), 1707–1732 (2019)

41. Mayr, C.M., Schuhbäck, S. et al.: Analysis of information dissemination through direct communication in a moving crowd. Saf. Sci. **142** (2021)

42. Richardson, O., Jalba, A., Muntean, A.: Effects of Environment knowledge in evacuation scenarios involving fire and smoke: a multiscale modelling and simulation approach. Fire Technol **55**(2), 415–436 (2019)

43. Selvek, R., Surynek, P.: Towards smart behavior of agents in evacuation planning based on local cooperative path finding. Knowledge Discovery, Knowledge Engineering and Knowledge Management, vol. 1297, pp. 302–321. Spinger, Cham (2020)

44. Schantz, A., Ehtamo, H.: Minimizing the evacuation time of a crowd from a complex building using rescue guides. Physica A: Stat. Mech. Appl. **594** (2022)

45. Aalami, S., Kattan, L.: Fair transit trip planning in emergency evacuations: a combinatorial approach. Transp. Res Part C: Emerg. Technol. **122** (2021)

46. Kim, H. W., Choi, C.: Interactive modeling environment based on the system entity structure and model base. In: Methods and Applications for Modeling and Simulation of Complex Systems, vol. 1094, pp. 54-64. Springer, Singapore (2019)

47. Vandewalle, R., Kang, J.-Y., Yin, D. et al.: Integrating CyberGIS-Jupyter and spatial agent-based modelling to evaluate emergency evacuation time. In: Proceedings of the 2nd ACM SIGSPATIAL International Workshop on GeoSpatial Simulation, GeoSim'19, pp. 28–31, Association for Computing Machinery, New York (2019)

48. Grimm, V., Berger, U., et al.: The ODD protocol: A review and first update. Ecol. Model. **221**(23), 2760–2768 (2010)

Author Index

Printed in the United States
by Baker & Taylor Publisher Services

Printed in the United States
by Baker & Taylor Publisher Services